TOM BARRY

IRA FREEDOM FIGHTER

D1621100

'When public opinion comes to measure the success of a man's life by his service to the State and to his fellows, rather than by the fortune he has amassed for selfish aims, then public opinion is worthy to control a great Nation and may hope to hold that Nation in the highest place in the councils of the world.'

An Cosantóir

'No guerilla leader had a chance unless he was able to think faster than the enemy. And because his belly was hungrier than theirs he did think fast.'

To Donncha Ó Dulaing, RTÉ Radio

'They had gone down into the mire to destroy us and our nation, and down after them we had to go.'

Guerilla Days in Ireland

'A good commander has to drive his men, to discipline them … discipline must be enforced.'

To Nollaig Ó Gadhra, RTÉ Radio

'There is nothing romantic about war. The only war I can justify to myself is a war of liberation.'

To Kenneth Griffith, RTÉ Radio

'I would hate to hurt a living relative of one who died for Ireland.'

Letter to Miah McGrath

'I hope it will be clear that I was not alone just to the dead but just and generous to the living also.'

Letter to Miah McGrath

'We have followed the technical training of major powers. British and American text books have been studied to the exclusion of all others and the minds of our senior officers have become saturated with the strategy and tactics of major powers … if war ever comes all their theories based on this type of education will be impracticable and [they] will be compelled to adapt themselves to the realities of a war situation here.'

To a group in Cork

TOM BARRY

IRA FREEDOM FIGHTER

'In war, it is not the men who count, it is the man'
NAPOLEON

MEDA RYAN

MERCIER PRESS

MERCIER PRESS
Douglas Village, Cork
www.mercierpress.ie

Trade enquiries to COLUMBA MERCIER DISTRIBUTION,
55a Spruce Avenue, Stillorgan Industrial Park, Blackrock, Dublin

1 85635 425 3

10 9 8 7 6 5 4 3 2 1

TO THE MEN AND WOMEN OF WEST CORK
who fought in their way, in their time, to give us the Ireland we have today

Printed in Ireland by Colour Books Ltd

CONTENTS

ACKNOWLEDGMENTS

I owe a debt of gratitude to David Willis who gave me Tom Barry's Papers, without which this book would be incomplete. I am also indebted to John Browne, Jean Crowley, Lieut Colonel Eamonn Moriarty and Dave O'Sullivan who gave me their unique personal recordings and videos of Tom Barry.

I am extremely grateful to Professor Gearóid Ó Tuathaigh of the National University of Ireland, Galway, for reading the manuscript, for his helpful suggestions and for his advice and his encouragement.

As I look through my notebook of names and addresses, I notice with sadness that many of those who willingly gave information are no longer with us. But without their generosity of spirit I could not have completed this worthwhile study. A sincere word of gratitude is due to those who went out of their way to help me in my research, people like Brendan O'Neill and the late Dan Joe O'Mahony who drove me around and organised appointments; Dómhnall Mac Giolla Phoil helped to locate people, and with his wife Mary, was a constant source of encouragement, he also read the manuscript and offered helpful suggestions. Eily Hales McCarthy and her husband Gus were always at the other end of a telephone to listen to my problems.

Jack Lane and Michael MacEvilly have been a constant source of assistance and with Séamus Lantry, Eileen Murphy and Manus O'Riordan, kept me posted on source material and publications, so that my mailbox was never dull. Brian Murphy in his unique way provided me with the necessary stimulus to continue.

Criostóir de Baróid was always willing to offer help and advice as was Pádraig Ó Cuanacháin and Bernie Whyte. Dr T. Ryle Dwyer, Professor Eunan O'Halpin and Rena Dardis, Anvil Press, kindly supplied me with private documents, and Dr Brian Hanley gave me some source references. Sheila Barry Irlam and Gerald Barry were most helpful in putting family events into context. Seán Kelleher, Louis Whyte, Con O'Callaghan and Johnny Hayes of the Kilmichael Commemoration Committee willingly responded to my probing queries.

As well as thanking Dan Collins, Kate O'Callaghan, Donncha Ó Dulaing, and Nollaig Ó Gadhra of RTÉ for the use of documentary material, I am also grateful to Majella Breen and Ian Lee in RTÉ Sound Archives who were courteous and generous with their time as was Barbara Durack and Pat Butler of the RTÉ TV Programme Archive Department.

The directors and staff at all the libraries were most helpful. I sincerely wish to thank Kieran Wyse, Cork County Library who responded to my every query and was more than generous with his time, he, like Tim Cadogan and the late Pádraig Ó Maidín of the Cork County Library speedily replied to my requests. Della Murphy, National Library of Ireland was extremely helpful during my research and also Dr Noel Kissane and his diligent staff in the National Library Manuscript Department. Seamus Helferty and Kerry Holland, of UCD Archives Department and the efficient staff there, deserve special mention, as does the late Comdt Peter Young, and Capt. Victor Laing, Comdt Pat Brennan and the staff at the Military Archives, Dublin. Thanks also to the staff in the National Archives and Trinity College Archives staff. The kindness and assistance rendered by Patricia McCarthy, by Brian McGee and staff at the Cork Archives Institute and by Stella Cherry and staff at the Cork Public Museum and by Mick O'Connell, Clonakilty Museum is very much appreciated.

Thanks to the late Raymond Smith and the library staff of the Irish Independent *who were generous with their time; the library staffs of the former offices of the* Irish Press, *the offices of the* Irish Times, *the (Cork)* Irish Examiner *and the* Southern Star, *especially the* Southern Star's *editor Liam O'Regan, who filled me in on incidents in relation to his father, Joe O'Regan; he also gave me his father's personal correspondence from Tom Barry. Thomas McCarthy and Eamonn Kirwin of the Cork City Library, Noel Crowley, Mary Moroney, Maureen Comber, Peter Beirne and all other staff of Clare County Library were always most helpful and courteous, as were the Library staff at Mary Immaculate College, Limerick, Mike McGuine, Limerick City*

Library, Iris Neeson of the Tralee County Library and Brian Looby and Eamonn Browne, Kerry County Library and Gerry White, Collins Barracks.

I am deeply grateful to the many who supplied me with personal documents and for being generous with their time: Gerald Ahern, Dan Cahalane, Michael Collins (Waterford), Liam Deasy, Jim Kearney, Liam Lynch family, Ned O'Sullivan, Bill Hales, Maura Murphy, Ann Hales, D. V. Horgan, Jim Hurley, John Pierce, John Young, Yvonee Purcell, Cormac O'Malley for permission to use his father's, Ernie O'Malley, papers and Leslie Bean de Barra. Paddy Connolly supplied me with photographs from his personal collection and for these I am most grateful. I am also indebted to the following family members who gave photographs: Nellie O'Donovan, Maura O'Donovan, John Young, Joan Dineen, Finbar Deasy, Brendan O'Neill, Charlotte Barrett, Bill Barrett, Gerard O'Brien, Eily Hales McCarthy, Seán Hales, Anna Hennigan, John Browne and Seán Kelleher.

There are so many who helped bring this work to fruition: Brendan Ashe, Paddy Casey, Nellie Casey, Eileen O'Brien, Christy Barrett, Joan Dineen, Margaret White, Pat Buttimer, John Whelton, Jim Kearney, Bill Powell, A. J. S. Brady, Nudge Callanan, M. J. Costello, Kathy Hayes, John L. O'Sullivan, Tom Kelleher, Paddy O'Sullivan, Jack O'Driscoll, James McCarthy, Tadgh Ó Cathasaigh, Patrick O'Sullivan, Ned Barrett (Kilbrittain), Dr Ned Barrett, Dan Canty, Charlie O'Keeffe, Annie O'Leary, Jack (Doheny) Lynch, Charlie O'Donoghue, Liam O'Donoghue, Minie Madden, Denis O'Mahony, Dan O'Callaghan, Brigid O'Mahony, Leo Meade, Kitty O'Leary, Cully Lawton, Denis O'Callaghan, Jerh Fehily, Mick McCarthy, Jerh Cronin, Den Carey, Liam French, Dan Collins, Jack O'Driscoll, Nancy Crowley, Mary Crowley, Michael Lyons, Eileen O'Mahony, Oliver O'Mahony, Lily O'Donovan Coughlan, Charlie Foley, Tom Foley, Liam O'Donoghue, Cormac MacCárthaigh, Riobárd Ó Longpuirt, Maggie Sheehan, Nora Foley Dineen, Josie Foley, Joe Walsh, Michael O' Sullivan, Mary Caverly, Nora O'Sullivan, Richard Coughlan, Liam Barrett, Bridie Crowley Manning, J. M. Feehan, Denis Lordan, Vivion de Valera, Mary Hough, Fr Donal O'Mahony, Fr John Chisholm, Kathleen Lane Lordan, Liz McEniry, Mary Leland, Cormac K. H. O'Mahony, John Fitzgerald, Dan Hourihane, May Twomey, Pat O'Donovan, Nelius Flynn, Denis Lordan, Paddy O'Brien (Girlough), Paddy O'Brien (Liscarrol), Seán Hyde, Tim O'Connell, Jim Doyle, Dan Collins, Brigid O'Mahony, Kathleen Lane, Ned Galvin, Jerh (Jerry) Cronin, Sonny O'Sullivan, Hannah O'Mahony, Billy Good, Snr, Billy Barry, Peg Barrett, John O'Donovan, Ned Young, Hannah Deasy, Molly O'Neill Walsh, Seán (John) O'Riordan, Dan Sandow O'Donovan, Miah Deasy, Bernie Whyte, Seamus O'Quigley, Seán MacBride, Frank Aiken, Ernest Blythe, Dave Neligan, Madge Hales Murphy, Denis O'Neill, James O'Mahony, Jack O'Sullivan, Brendan Vaughan, Donal McSweeney, Diarmuid Begley, Eileen Lynch O'Neill, Ruairí Ó Brádraigh, Fr T. J. (Tom) Hogan, Seán Spellissy, Maurice Healy, Colm Price, Maureen O'Sullivan, Ena O'Neill, Michael Bradley, Humphrey Lynch, Joe Cahill, and of course the late Tom Barry who was so helpful and courteous and therefore aided in the framing of this book.

Grateful thanks is also due to the staff at Brooklyn Central Library, and Mid Manhattan Library, New York, the Public Records Office, Surrey, the British Library Board Newspaper Library, also Bodleian Library, University of Oxford and the Imperial War Museum, Manuscript Department.

A sincere thank you to all at Mercier Press, who worked with me through the final draft of the manuscript. A special word of gratitude is due to members of my family and to my many relatives and friends for their patience throughout my years of research.

I want to thank in particular the people of Cork city and from there west to the shores of Bantry Bay who gave me cups of tea, full meals and even offered accommodation while I travelled throughout the area in the course of my research. Thanks is also due to the many who could not help directly but took the trouble to write or telephone explaining where information could be obtained.

If I have omitted anybody it has not been deliberate, as the contributions of all have been gratefully accepted.

PREFACE

In 1982, I wrote a book called *The Tom Barry Story*, commissioned by Mercier Press. Because, at the time I had to confine the book to a certain number of words, I didn't use a substantial amount of my accumulated material. Therefore, when a Kilmichael ambush controversy arose in 1998, together with the question by Peter Hart, in *The IRA & Its Enemies: Violence and Community in Cork 1916–1923*, regarding sectarianism in West Cork IRA during the 1920–22 period, I saw the need for a fuller biography of one of the great architects of modern guerrilla warfare in Ireland's fight for freedom. Because I had interviewed Tom Barry extensively and also the men who fought with him I believed that in the interest of historical accuracy certain issues required further investigation.

After *The Tom Barry Story* was published, David Willis approached me, saying he had acquired Tom Barry's letters and documents and asked if I was interested in consulting them. Having taken a cursory look I initially dismissed the idea of using them for research, as they were in a dreadful state. Some were torn, water marked, in black plastic bags, having been salvaged by a builder while demolishing and renovating Tom Barry's flat after his death. But, in 1998 I felt if I was to undertake writing a full biography of Tom Barry I would have to tackle this substantial body of papers. This existing collection has been extremely important in clarifying controversial aspects of his life. Furthermore, in my research I obtained a number of personal recordings of Tom Barry and a home video, together with a vast amount of material, much of it unedited and not transmitted, in the RTÉ Sound Archives and TV Archives – all recorded in my acknowledgments. Numerous records have survived in personal documents and in the various archives in Ireland and England, thus throwing new light on a man of action, who spent a lifetime, in his unique way, trying to unite Ireland under one flag.

Moreover, I had interviews with some of the men who fought with Tom Barry, in his flying column in the War of Independence, the Civil War, the IRA conflicts in the 1920s, 1930s, 1940s, 1950s and right up to his death. I had accumulated a sizeable number of tape recordings and notes from men and women who were willing, honest and open with their accounts of ambushes and events.

In a certain way I have worked on this all my life. Growing up near the town of Bandon in West Cork I was acutely aware that a group of Volunteers known as the Third West Cork Brigade had played a major part in the fight for the freedom of Ireland. Before I ever heard of De Valera or Michael Collins, Tom Barry, with his flying column, was a household name.

We knew the words of 'The Boys of Kilmichael', 'The Upton Ambush' and 'The Men of Barry's Column' because they were taught by nationally-minded teachers in schools and sung by local men and women doing their daily work or meeting at threshing or station parties. For me the songs had a special significance because my uncle, Pat O'Donovan was one of 'the boys of Kilmichael' and my mother's family was deeply involved in the Republican movement. But I was also influenced by the fact that the Hales family, who experienced so much trauma and who were the original organisers of the Volunteers in West Cork, were neighbours. Also, during those formative years, I became acquainted with many men, each of whom were known in the locality as 'one of the Old IRA'. My father took a great interest in history as told by these people. His family hadn't been involved in the Volunteer movement, but he was a descendant of an evicted family. On some Sunday afternoons he would visit one of these old IRA men, and invariably, while quite young, I would travel with him, so I got to know these men and women who were involved in Ireland's fight for freedom. I listened to their personal stories and I saw tears in many men's eyes. All this was an invaluable insight for later. Furthermore, my mother's 'inside' knowledge aided the discussions.

Later as I thought about writing a book on the Third West Cork Brigade, I interviewed a number of men and women during the 1970s and early 1980s. I spoke extensively to the man who trained and led the flying column – Commandant General Tom Barry. We discussed ambushes and incidents, and though I had not decided to write a biography of him at the time, he jokingly mentioned this possibility at our last meeting. Because there is overlapping in much of the nine interviews and in our many meetings and conversations, I have not dated each throughout this work, but have done so with other contributors.

I have covered the Kilmichael ambush in depth, as I knew it was vital for history that the record of what exactly occurred should be investigated in so far as this was possible. It was imperative, I felt, to explore the ambush details and subsequent records.

The necessity of being vigilant with interviewees struck me very forcibly early on. Having familiarised myself with locations, with people's background, I soon became alert to either unintentional or perhaps deliberate suggestions of an 'untrue' viewpoint. While I regard oral evidence as an important part of history, as many participants wouldn't take the trouble to consign their experience to paper, I am also aware of the importance of self-censorship, accuracy and a search for the truth. Tom Barry drew my attention to this early on when he spoke to me of the method used by Military History Bureau members. Their brief was to record without question, every word that contributors proffered. He suggested burning that segment of the collection. This is dealt with within this book.

Relatives of those who played important parts in many of the ambushes, raids or events mentioned and whose names are not quoted, will, I hope, understand that this work is about one man, Tom Barry, and the part he played in the important activities upon which his life touched. However, I would like to say that his greatness and success was helped by the men and women who worked and fought bravely with him.

I knew from my research that Tom Barry was the 'mighty' man, the legendary commander – ruthless, daring, cold-blooded, unselfish, benign, irritable, sometimes uncompromising or compromising, open-minded or single-minded, depending on the circumstances. Described by an ex-detective sergeant as 'the most principled man' he ever met, Barry, with his out-spoken opinions, made him constantly a controversial figure. Professor Gearóid Ó Tuathaigh in an RTÉ recording in 1980, described Barry and his flying column's 'contribution in the establishment of the twenty-six county state' as an integral part of a much more general attempt 'to subvert what was the constituted authority in the land' in order to 'implement the decisions' of the suppressed Dáil. Barry's brief term as chief-of-staff of the IRA, his constant battle with the State and the Church added colour to his activities. Having discovered this colourful character whom I had got to know, and whose faults and virtues presented themselves to me, I was aware that in order to be true to myself, to readers and to him, I would have to present the 'full' man.

After *The Tom Barry Story* was published, Cardinal Tomás Ó Fiaich, Primate of all Ireland, rang me. He believed that more than any other freedom fighter, Tom Barry deserved credit for what he had done for the Irish people. The cardinal had met Barry and said that Barry's first words were of freedom – 'freedom for the Irish people to be themselves and to be masters of their own country'.

In a broadcast tribute to him after his death, Donncha Ó Dulaing, who had interviewed him when he was in his early eighties, said he found him with 'his back as straight as his point of view'. In that transmission Denis Conroy described him as 'one of the greatest men this country every produced'. He was the man, Dave Neligan records, that Mick Collins 'thought the world of' and believed 'he truly helped' bring the British government 'to its knees'. He was a Republican activist who held no bitterness towards comrades who took the opposing side in the Civil War, and he tried, where possible, to heal 'wounds' left because of the conflict.

Being aware that Tom Barry's deeds, his strength of character and his controversies will be remembered not alone in the county of Cork which he loved, but throughout Ireland and amongst Irish people everywhere, it is my hope therefore, that in presenting the 'rounded' man with all his faults he will be seen as a human being, who was capable of distinguishing the ideal from the real situation, and emerging as a true patriot.

MEDA RYAN
March 2003

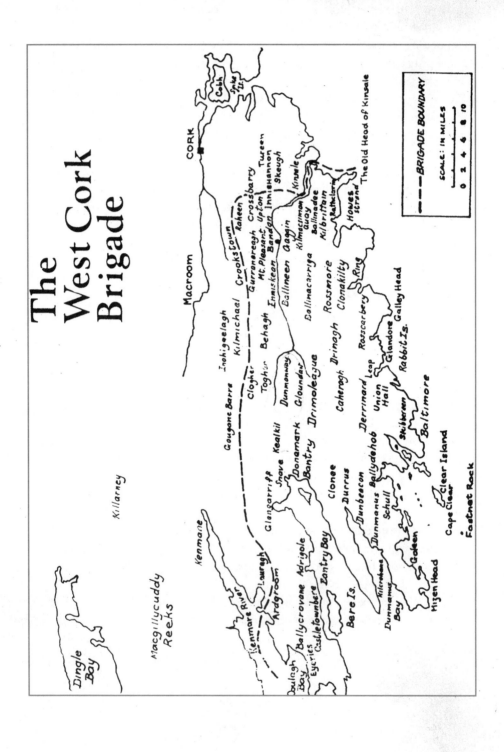

The
West Cork
Brigade

INTRODUCTION

When Tom Barry was appointed commander of the Third West Cork Brigade Flying Column he took a vow to dedicate himself to working to see Ireland as an independent nation. As the years progressed, he was mindful of a partitioned Ireland, and could quote by heart the 1916 Proclamation, which contained the declaration, 'of the people of Ireland to the ownership of Ireland'. He described the document as 'a brief history in itself' that noted that 'Ireland had suffered at the hands of the English for those seven centuries' and had resorted to arms 'six times' in the previous 'three hundred years'.

When he returned to Ireland, having fought in the Great War, he began to study Irish history and the attempts made by previous generations who tried to free Ireland from British domination. He found a dichotomy between his role fighting as a British soldier for the freedom of 'small nations' while his own country continued to be suppressed by British rule.[1]

There is no doubt that Tom Barry deserves a prominent place in Irish history; that his role as a freedom fighter has not been given a merited place in history is certain; that he is among the most important historical figures in obtaining independence for the twenty-six county Irish state is irrefutable.

Tom Barry spent his formative years in West Cork. This part of the country had a tradition of learning – from the hedge schools to the state schools; a tradition of sport, athletics and Gaelic games; a tradition of emigration dating back to the famine; a tradition of yearning for independence, especially since the formation of the Fenians. There had been tithes, rack rents, insecurity of tenure and evictions. Several families in the area were either connected to, or knew, evicted families. This, coupled with the Fenian movement, influenced many West Cork citizens, and permeated the region at a time when morale was low after famine had decimated the area, especially Skibbereen and its hinterland. Members of several West Cork families were involved in the Fenian movement, including the Hales, the Deasys, the many branches of the O'Donovans, the O'Briens, the O'Mahonys, etc. Prominent members included the executed William Philip Allen of Bandon – one of the Manchester martyrs – involved in the rescue of Timothy Kelly and of Timothy Deasy, Clonakilty. These men, like Clonakilty's Eugene Davis and Jeremiah O'Donovan Rossa (Rosscarbery), were steeped in the Fenian movement.

The Irish Volunteers were formed in southern Ireland in November 1913, in response to the formation of the Ulster Volunteers. In West Cork, Volunteers were engaged in drilling, parading and general discipline from 1915 onwards.

Before the 1916 Rising a group of West Cork Volunteers set out on foot for Tralee Bay to obtain arms and ammunition from the *Aud*. Outside Millstreet, they received word of the ill-fated cargo, and had to return. Some of these men were arrested and jailed for many months.

The participation of West Cork men in the Dublin Easter Rising, their sub-sequent term in internment camps, plus the execution of the Rising leaders had a profound effect on all Irish people, not least on Tom Barry who was far from his native shores at the time.

By 1917, when all political prisoners were released and conscription for the Great War was looming, Volunteers in West Cork were aware that parading, drilling and public meetings were in preparation for further military action, if the need arose.

In West Cork poverty was widespread. The livelihood of a large segment of the population was dependent on manual labour. Small farm-holders some-times used a barter type system, where eggs, fowl, grain, potatoes and vege-tables were given to shops in return for groceries. This poverty ran side by side with the comfortable living style of the ascendancy class. Many people be-lieved that if Ireland had their own elected government, justice, together with the necessities of life would be more evenly distributed.

Liam Deasy records that news of the success in 1917 of Sinn Féin candi-dates, Joe McGuinness, Count Plunkett, Eamon de Valera and W. T. Cosgrave, 'caused great excitement' in West Cork. This was followed by De Valera's elec-tion as president of both Sinn Féin and of the Volunteers. Soon afterwards De Valera was welcomed to Bandon 'by massive crowds, marching men, cyclist groups, and most striking of all, many horsemen from rural areas paraded for the event'. This 'helped to create a strong sense of confidence in the Nationalist movement.' In 1918 the threat of conscription sent large numbers flocking to the Volunteers. There were arrests in West Cork, as elsewhere, of men like Neilus Connolly, Skibbereen who spent some time in Strangeways jail before escaping with five others, blooded from the barbed wire. The Royal Irish Constabulary (RIC) was continually harassing the Volunteers and their difficulties were added to when the *Skibbereen Eagle* used its column to denigrate the organisation.[2]

Home Rule, which looked imminent before the Great War, was suspended for its duration, but was not honoured when the war ended. The overwhelm-ing success of Sinn Féin in the 1918 election meant that the Irish people placed their trust in their own representatives. Nationalist Ireland, though disillu-sioned, found common hope as Sinn Féin was united with the Volunteers against the Military Service Act. The meeting of the First Dáil, on 21 January 1919, laid the constitutional basis of the new Irish state, 34 of the elected representatives were 'absent' in jail.[3] The Dáil had been declared an illegal assembly; prohi-bition by the British parliament necessitated its members holding meetings in secret. As the RIC scoured the country and arrested Volunteers and Sinn Féin members, it was obvious that the British government wanted these new-found 'troublemakers' in custody.

Instead of trying to curb the disquiet by communication, the British ad-ministration, in banning Dáil Éireann, only fuelled the Volunteers' effort to obtain arms and ammunition by raids and attacks on RIC barracks and other military premises. British acquiescence in incidents like the RIC's killing of Cork's lord mayor, Tomás MacCurtain in March 1920 and the introduction of the Auxiliaries and the Black and Tans by mid-1920 gave priority to militarism rather than political diplomacy and persuasion. The oath of allegiance to the Dáil of the Irish Republic by Volunteers established them as an army for that parliament.

According to Lionel Curtis, imperial activist, writer and drafter of policies for Lloyd George, 'Sir Edward Carson threatened to revive the Ulster Volunteers' in response to Sir Horace Plunkett's (Irish Dominion League) manifesto demand for Irish Home Rule. Lloyd George denied the application of President Wilson's principles of a Paris Peace hearing for Ireland in July 1920. And on 23 July *The Times* 'published its plan for settlement of the Irish question on the lines of partition, and thereafter definitely transferred its support from the cause of Unionism to that of Home Rule'.[4]

The partition-framing mould had been publicly set in motion by mid-1920. As Professor Joe Lee noted, if Sinn Féin 'were out-witted on the north, it was not in December 1921, but already in December 1920 when they proved powerless to prevent the imposition of the Government of Ireland Act'.[5]

Lionel Curtis found that by 1 January 1920 it was difficult for the police to obtain recruits in Ireland so 'a recruiting office was opened in London. Men who had served in the war as NCOs were selected, and as they were sent to Ireland faster than police uniforms could be made for them' relationships did not 'improve'.[6] 'Even Loyalists were resorting to Republican Courts'. Curtis found Sinn Féin 'a movement' which, 'throughout seems free from a sordid taint ...' therefore 'the criminal courts of Sinn Féin were a direct challenge. To ignore it would have meant the most practical admission that Sinn Féin was ruling the country. Government decided to accept the challenge. Col Byrne, the chief inspector of police, was displaced and Sir Hamar Greenwood became Irish secretary and appointed General Tudor as police adviser to himself', and General Macready was appointed commander-in-chief. The decision to recruit Auxiliaries and the Black and Tans meant that as 1920 progressed a state of military action became pervasive in Ireland.[7]

Tom Barry, in a wide-ranging talk to a select group in Cork in the early 1970s, prefaced his talk by outlining a brief history of Ireland's fight against British domination: 'when we went into this revolution, we had to feel that we were doing it for a purpose, we had been slaves for 700 years. 'Twas time that that was ended!' He spoke of the election and formation of 'Dáil Éireann as a government set up by the people of the country', at the same time, he said, 'there was also the British government – the *de facto* government who had the power and arms ... They proclaimed the Irish government that was set up. They proclaimed anything that was Nationalistic – the GAA, Cumann na mBan, the IRA and Sinn Féin. The logical conclusion was that men and women were arrested – they resisted arrest and that resistance led to shooting. Perhaps it wasn't started in the best possible way, but it had to work out that way, because it was the British who set the pace. It would have been better if the Volunteers were more ready. They could have taken barracks – but it didn't work out like that because the British were setting the pace all the time and so this led to guerrilla warfare.'[8]

Cork county was divided into three brigades and a state of war existed by the time the flying columns were formed in late 1920 and early 1921. In September 1920, with the formation of the Third West Cork Brigade Flying Column, the appointment of Tom Barry as training officer and then as commander, guerrilla fighting began to reach a more intense level.

The Irish people who committed themselves to fight for their country were idealists but it was idealism rooted in the reality of the ultimate goal of independence. It took steel-like determination, willpower and self-sacrifice to continue day after day and night after night, often wet, cold and hungry, against all the odds. But as Jack Hennessy, a flying column veteran, put it: 'All we wanted was to get rid of the enemy in our midst – to get our freedom.' (Jack Hennessy was caught, severely beaten by the RIC on 10 July 1920, and his house was burned.) To gain this freedom the fighting men needed unselfish support. 'People who weren't alive then will never understand the spirit of the people,' Tom Barry said.[9] Life was harrowing for these fighters and also for the civilian population. 'It is difficult for those who have never known decision-making in war to think themselves into the minds of those operating in wartime – any wartime, but especially into the minds of those fighting against overwhelming odds, for whom any miscalculation could mean disaster for oneself, for one's comrades, and one's cause,' J. J. Lee wrote.[10]

Tom Barry always described the people of West Cork as 'a grand people'. The people knew they had a reason to fight. 'There were families who were very poor. When we went into some of these houses, it was painful to see these people, without shoes, with scanty clothing in the freezing cold, with little to eat.'[11] But these people were unselfish, according to flying column participant, Tim O'Donoghue: they backed 'the column and the fighting men to the last man; the mixed civilian population who were good could not have been much better. They were the best this country or any other country ever produced; old and young of them gave their all to the army of the Republic. Night and day saw them standing to and behind the men of the column. Enough credit can never be given to the old folk who sat up at night to give their beds and accommodation to "the lads", who scouted and acted as sentries often all night as the column rested. The true history of their unselfish and marvellous support could never be told in a short article. Ireland has reason to remember them, and leaders who today (December 1937) say they move towards the National goal as fast as the people want them, libel those of our race who proved in 1920–1921 and later, that they will always move as fast as honest leadership will take them'.[12]

Arguments persist as to whether military intervention was necessary to obtain Irish Independence because of the possibility that the British administration would eventually grant Home Rule. Tom Barry had no doubt but that persuasion and coaxing would never have worked. The British 'had no intention of conceding without a fight. They proved that!' As Ronan Fanning noted, 'Lloyd George's Tory-dominated government would not have moved from the 1914-style niggardliness of the Government of Ireland Act of 1920 ... if they had not been impelled to do so ...'[13]

Tom Barry came towards me. Although almost eighty years of age he walked erect. Every move and gesture was exact; each came with ease, yet as if calculated, carved and sharpened. He straightened his shoulders and thrust his hand into his pocket and pulled out a page severed from a newspaper. 'Look,' he said, 'the bloody fellow in his interview kept calling me an old man!' Commandant-General Tom Barry, the man who became a legend in his own lifetime declared, 'I never like interviews, simply because I don't know how what I say will be twisted.' He chuckled when I produced a copy of his book *Guerilla Days in Ireland*. 'He had one too. Bloody fellow. Do you know it became a world bestseller? There must be a copy of it in every military academy in the world.' He paused. 'Guerrilla warfare! I'd like the opportunity to do it all again, having learned from my mistakes. I'd like to see Ireland united.' He sang softly:

> *And Ireland long a Province be*
> *A Nation once again.*

The softness crept into those laughing eyes. Eyes that remembered experiences of gun-fire, Mills bombs and explosives, of sleet, snow and rain falling on him and his men; of sleeping rough while evading enemy capture; of long hours continuously marching through fields, bogs and rivers; of the blood of battle and the killing of enemies and spies.

Practically every adjective that could be applied to describe a human being had been used to portray the man beside me.

'Yes. They said I was ruthless, daring, savage, bloodthirsty, even heartless.' He laughed, thumped his chest. 'That pounder gave me a smattering of trouble, but it has served me well. Yerra what matter! Some of our own men – the clergy called me and my comrades "murderers".'

His father Thomas Barry, born into a small farm at Bohonagh, outside the town of Rosscarbery, went to the local National School and worked on the farm before joining the Royal Irish Constabulary (RIC) in 1893. Following his initial training and short assignments in a few Irish towns he was sent to Liscarrol (East Riding) in Co. Cork. While there he met and fell in love with Margaret O'Donovan, an attractive-looking girl and daughter of a respectable businessman.

From the outset her family was against this relationship, especially her father who believed his daughter could do better. However, the young pair were not be separated so when Thomas was transferred to a post in Killorglin, Co. Kerry, Margaret eloped with her young lover. She and Thomas were married, disowned by her family, and settled in their home at Chubs Corner in Killorglin. A year later their eldest son, Eddie, the first of fourteen children, was born.[1] On 1 July 1897 their second child was born. Baptised in the local Catholic church and christened Thomas Bernardine, he was affectionately known as Bernie, but was later known to the world as Commandant-General Tom Barry. He was a child who as an adult would in no small way be responsible for changing the course of Irish history and securing freedom for his people who were subject to British rule. He would one day destroy barracks like the one where his father worked and be responsible for the deaths of RIC men like his father.

On 29 December 1907, disillusioned with the RIC, Thomas resigned and returned to his native Rosscarbery where he operated a business, with his Aunt Hannah (Barry) Collins and Uncle Jerh Collins, known as The Arcade. This shop, with a bar at the back, sold groceries, meat and hardware and later, in an upstairs department, a line of ladies and gents suits and hats. The younger members of the family were sent to the convent school from where the boys transferred to Ardagh boys' school. When young Tom (Bernie) attended the Boys' National School, his master John McCarthy discovered that he was a bright pupil so he encouraged him by giving him books to read and inviting him to his house to give him further tuition in the evenings.

John McCarthy, a teacher who was known to turn the history book upside down on his desk and give his own version, instilled the spirit of nationalism into many a lad in that school. He encouraged the playing of Gaelic games after school hours and Tom, who was on the local football team, was a quick runner, agile and light on his feet. Many an evening was spent with the local lads who would competitively race each other in their bare feet around Jeff Wycherley's field beside the church. He learned to swim in 'Sweeney's Hole'. His first introduction was 'a push off the hill by older boys into a twelve foot drop – I had to sink or swim!'[2]

Schoolmaster McCarthy was also a great sportsman and had a sporting rifle. As he roamed the fields shooting rabbits, pigeons and woodcock, his companion was often the young Tom Barry.

'The old master told me,' Jerh Fehily recalls, 'that he was in a way responsible for the victories of West Cork. "Because," he said, 'not alone did I give Tom Barry his formal education, but I took him one day when he was quite young and showed him how to hold, carry, load and fire the gun".'[3]

Young Tom was up to all the pranks of high-spirited boys of his age. To cut the cost of milk for their large family the Barry's rented a field at the other end of the town where they kept a cow. Tom's task each evening was to bring home the cow. One evening his pal bet him a penny that he wouldn't ride the cow through the town. 'No sooner said than done,' said Kathy Hayes. 'He jumped on the cow's back and headed for the town. The dogs went mad, barking, jumping and pulling the cow's tail. Naturally people came to the doors to see what was causing the racket. Through the town, round the corner, hell for leather! Bernie clung on. At the stall door he threw himself on a heap of manure just in time to save his head.'[4] Afterwards he wondered which was the most serious crime, the disgrace of the family in front of the neighbours or that the cow was in calf, as he got 'a tongue lashing' when he arrived home.[5] Wild, adventurous and a leader, 'he was always into tricks,' Kathy Hayes recalls. 'People from the surrounding countryside would travel to Mass in a pony and trap. They'd tie the horses in a yard at the top of the town.' With other lads he'd untie the horses. They would race them up and down the hill and around the fields. 'When the owners would come out from Mass the horses would be in a lather of sweat. He was a terror!'[6]

Tom's aunts, his mother's sisters, kept in touch with her and were aware that Tom was extremely intelligent. The Barrys couldn't afford to send him for further education, so the aunts decided to pay for his education at Mungret College, near Limerick.[7] In boarding-school his studies progressed and during holidays he also kept up his game-shooting with his former schoolmaster. As the years went by young Tom Barry would move away from Rosscarbery, but his love for this town, situated on a hill overlooking an inlet of the Atlantic Ocean and set in the rugged countryside of West Cork, and for its people would never diminish. He wanted to be forever known as a West Cork man.

Business for the Barry family at The Arcade was not great and with such a large family their money dwindled, so they decided to sell their property and move to a house in Upper Convent Hill, Bandon. His father then worked in various shops in Bandon.

Bandon was a Loyalist town. In the early part of the fifteenth century when the town was founded, hundreds of families were moved from England to Bandon. Following the plantation of the fertile lands around the area the town drew up its charter in 1613. One of its first acts was to pass a by-law, 'That no Roman Catholic be permitted to reside in the town'. A notice outside one of the nine-foot-thick walls read:

A Turk, A Jew or an Atheist,
May live in this town, but no Papist.

Somebody came at night and wrote under it:

He that wrote these lines did write them well,
As the same is written on the gates of hell.[8]

The Bandon Militia was formed and 'became part of the English forces of occupation in Ireland, ready at all times to march against their Irish neighbours and to help in crushing any effort to get rid of English rule.'[9] By the early part of the twentieth century the walls had become only a historical memory and catholic families were living in the town, but it was a garrison town where the sentiments of many of its inhabitants were pro-British. The elder Thomas Barry was a Redmondite believing in Home Rule. He expressed such sentiments at home, though his wife Margaret believed in a more Nationalist tradition.

In 1914, Tom, at 17, got a job as a clerk in Emerson's, protestant merchants in MacSwiney's Quay, Bandon. The firm dealt in machinery, coal, manure, oil, timber and general provisions. Here this bright young lad had his first taste of employment and remained for nine months. During this time he would cycle the twenty odd miles to Rosscarbery on Sunday's to meet his girl friend Kathy Hayes as well as his other friends.

But young Tom was anxious for adventure. In 1915 Britain, at war with Germany, was looking for army recruits in Ireland. So on 30 June, Tom, with a friend Frank McMurrough enlisted in the RFA at Cork and became a soldier in the British army. He is described as: 'Height, 5' 10". Brown hair. Clean-shaven. Smart appearance. Large mole on left thigh'.[10]

'I went to war for no other reason than that I wanted to see what war was like, to get a gun, to see new countries and to feel a grown man. That was my primary motive at the time'.[11] So he bade goodbye to Kathy, to rugged Rosscarbery's hills, bog lands and surrounding sea which he loved, the dear friends of his youth in that district, his acquaintances in Bandon and most of all, his parents, brothers and sisters and set out for his initial training in the British army.[12] First he went to Athlone and then to Woolwich. When the army was about to embark for France, news of their requirement in Mesopotamia (now Iraq) meant they had to head in that direction. He was offered a commission in the Munsters, but refused it.'[13] So in January 1916 Tom set foot in Basra. Here he was gassed and was taken back to Bologna and then to the Royal Hospital in Woolwich. Soon he returned to his regiment.[14]

Tom was content with the lot of a soldier and enjoyed the excitement, though with hindsight, he became immensely critical of the handling of the campaign in Mesopotamia.[15] After futile attempts, costing many lives, in trying to break the Turkish-German ring, the Mesopotamian Expeditionary Force under General Townsend withdrew from Kut el Amara to rest. The 30,000 beleaguered troops camped twelve miles away – a safe distance from view and from fire range. Tom, with some more of the boys, was strolling towards the orderly tent where war communiqués were generally displayed. 'We usually scanned these things,' he said, 'and paid little heed to war news, but this particular evening a heading caught my eye. It was under the heading of: SPECIAL – REBELLION IN DUBLIN. I read it and re-read it three or four times. It concerned Dublin and my people, the Irish.' He maintained that this was the turning point in his life. 'It put me thinking. What the hell am I doing with the British army? It's with the Irish I should be!'[16] The notice told of the 1916 Rising in Dublin where a group of 'rebels' who took over the GPO, Liberty Hall and other places, were shelled and overcome by the crown forces and many of the 'rebels' killed. The communiqué covered several weeks and told of arrests, the execution of the leaders and the jailing of hundreds of 'rebels'.

The Great War dragged on; he was Bombardier Barry of the British army.

In 1917 he was among those who returned from the borders of Asiatic Russia, where he had been wounded. However, his injury wasn't serious and he was back in action in a short time. December of that year found him in Egypt with the field regiment in which he was serving, supporting General Allenby's army in his advance on Jaffa and Jerusalem. Like all the other soldiers he took the hardships in his stride. From there he served in Italy, then France and back to England in 1919.

Ireland was only across the water, so after demobilisation he returned to Cork in February 1919, and made his way back to his parents' home in Bandon.

CAUGHT UP IN THE MOVEMENT

The people of the United Kingdom of Great Britain and Ireland went to the polls in a general election in December 1918. Tom Barry was outside Le Harve. The Great War had ended – a war in which approximately 50,000 men of Irish birth and many more of Irish blood had given their lives.

Two men whose lives entwined with Tom Barry's life were Eamon de Valera and Michael Collins. American born De Valera defended Boland's Mills during the 1916 Easter Rising. After capture he escaped death but was sentenced to a term of penal servitude. In the summer of 1917 he was released, but was again imprisoned in May 1918. During his release in November 1917 he was elected president of Sinn Féin and of the Irish Volunteers, the military wing of the Sinn Féin movement which later became known as the Irish Republican army (IRA).

In November 1913 at the foundation meeting of the Irish Volunteers Eoin MacNeill stated that 'British politics are controlled by British interests, and complicated by problems of great importance to the people of Great Britain.' The Volunteers, he said, 'will form a prominent element in the national life under a national government.'[1] On election day 1918, De Valera and other candidates were in jail; nevertheless Sinn Féin fought every seat in Ireland except two and won 73 out of the 103 seats they contested. On Tuesday, 21 January 1919, those elected Sinn Féin Members not in jail met in Dublin to form the First Dáil Éireann, thereby setting up the government of the Irish Republic. Of the 73 Sinn Féin MPs elected to Westminster 36 were in prison and the rest refused to take their seats in Westminster when the new parliament assembled on 4 February 1919.

A neighbour of Tom Barry's, Michael Collins, a 1916 Rising participant, became minister of finance and minister of home affairs in the First Dáil, later, president of the supreme council of the Irish Republican Brotherhood (IRB), and director of intelligence. The IRB wanted total separation from Britain and complete autonomy for Ireland, but was prepared in the interim to co-operate with Home Rulers. However, in 1913 events superseded compromise – the formation in January of the Ulster Volunteer Force (UVF) to resist Home Rule implementation, and in November the formation of the Irish Volunteers to meet Nationalist demands. The Home Rule Bill (Third) for Ireland was signed on 18 September 1914, but by agreement with the Ulster Unionists and the Irish Parliamentary Party it was suspended for the duration of the First World War and the question of a legislative parliament for Ireland, in British government discussions since 1866, remained unresolved.

Meanwhile in West Cork local Volunteers were secretly meeting, drilling and recruiting new members.[2] Tom Barry, the ex-British soldier, was back in Bandon. Immediately he began to study more Irish history to discover why the

Irish nation had to rise up against England in 1916. When he had read the communiqué about the execution of the 1916 leaders while in Mesopotamia he found it 'a rude awakening, guns being fired at the people of my own race by soldiers of the same army with which I was serving.'[3] Yet back in Ireland since February 1919, he was constantly seen in the company of the British army personnel stationed at Bandon and fraternised with ex-British soldiers in an Oliver Plunkett Street premises. Actions such as this were held against him when he tried to join the IRA and indeed his critics condemned him for such deeds, but he maintained that he went with the spirit of those who had fought with him. (He was not officially discharged from the British army until 31 March 1920.)[4]

As the months (1919)passed Tom moved cautiously into a different circle of friends in Bandon, though throughout this period members of the British forces kept in close contact with him and invited him to meetings in the Young Men's Hall, a type of club for the Royal Irish Constabulary (RIC) and ex-soldiers.[5] Soon afterwards Tom enrolled in Skerry's College, Cork, where he studied Law, English and Business Affairs. During the first months at Skerry's College, this smart young man was often seen in the early morning, the collar of his coat turned up, as he rushed down Convent Hill making his way to the station for the train to Cork. In the evenings he would often meet his girlfriend Annie O'Leary. The pair would sometimes be seen dancing in the town hall. His relationship with Kathy Hayes had faded, though he remained 'a good friend' throughout his life. During the War of Independence she became involved with him in the movement, and later in life whenever he was in the area, he visited her public house where she lived with her husband and family in Rosscarbery.[6]

As winter set in, he stayed in the Camden Hotel near Patrick's Bridge, Cork, returning home at weekends. While attending Skerry's College he met a young man named Bill Hales. Bill belonged to one of the greatest Nationalist families in West Cork, members of whom were among the founders of the Volunteer movement in the area. This changed Tom's life forever. Tom Hales was brigade commander of the Third West Cork Brigade that had been formed in late 1918. Bill, Seán, Bob and sister Madge were all involved in the movement. As the father Robert Hales, a Fenian, sat with his family and neighbours, around the fireside in Knocknacurra at night, he'd tell stories of the 1798 Rebellion, the famine in Ireland and the Fenian movement. Bill invited Tom to come to his home one evening. Here the first seeds of Republicanism were sown, as Tom became a regular visitor to the Hales' family home. (Even though after the Treaty that family was split, and brother fought against brother, Tom Barry held them all in high esteem.)

'The condition of the people was very depressed at that time.' The older members of Tom's family had already left for secure employment in Liverpool. Tom's father, unable to earn sufficient to support the younger members of the family, would soon leave for Liverpool. With the aid of a first cousin he got 'a good job' as a store manager, and later joined the Liverpool police. Then the entire family moved, and Tom was alone. 'Emigration to other lands was many a person's story at the time. I missed my family, but I had great friends … I was anxious to complete my studies in Skerry's College and get a job.' However, his life shortly changed utterly.[7]

On 21 January 1919 Séamus Robinson, Dan Breen and other Volunteers in Tipperary ambushed police who were escorting council-men as they were taking gelignite to a quarry. The cargo was secured, but two policemen were killed. Similar incidents to secure firearms took place later throughout the country. There were raids and arrests by the military. The British government declared Dáil Éireann and other Nationalist organisations illegal. Soon it became evident that force would be used to secure the British hold on Ireland. Volunteers kept secretly drilling and re-organising in tandem with raids and arrests by the police. In 1920 large reinforcements of Auxiliary military and Black and Tan forces were poured into Ireland to suppress the elected parliament of the people and to reinforce the military police.[8]

Under the leadership of men such as Liam Deasy, Seán Buckley, Charlie Hurley, Seán and Tom Hales, a Volunteer force had been building up in West Cork since before 1916. In fact, a group under the leadership of Tom Hales had set out from the Bandon, Ballinadee and Kilbrittain area to aid in the landing of arms from the *Aud* – the 'Casement' ship – at Tralee bay in April 1916. They had gone past Millstreet in north Cork and were heading for the border of Kerry when a scout arrived to tell them to return home.

After the 1916 Rising, Volunteers in West Cork periodically assembled, and towards the end of 1918 and early 1919 a large force existed. Secret drilling continued, but the absence of arms meant that means of obtaining them had to be devised. Though there were incidents, one of the first recorded group actions took place on 10 June 1919 when a party of Volunteers held up Constable Bolger and five soldiers outside Kilbrittain, and confiscated their rifles and equipment. In many areas in West Cork raids on police barracks and coastguard stations to obtain arms and ammunition became more frequent.

In November 1919 Maurice Donegan led an assault on a British motor torpedo boat in Bantry Bay, and secured a good quantity of arms and ammunition; this as well as raids around Kilbrittain, Bandon, and other West Cork areas formed the basis of armaments for the Cork No. 3 Brigade.

By now the police were using a heavy hand. On 5 June 1920, in Westminster an MP, W. Long, stated that 'the police have not only shot, but they have shot with extremely good effect citizens … engaged in disloyal conduct and … hoped that they do it again.'[9]

The British Essex Regiment with 40 officers and 971 other ranks arrived in Co. Cork with Companies A, B, C, D. In March 1920 two platoons of D Company (The Essex) under the command of Major A. E. Percival arrived in Bandon. Major Percival became one of Tom Barry's deadly enemies. With the men of his force he used the strongest methods to terrorise the people of West Cork.

According to Kathleen Keyes McDonnell, 'Long before we knew his name, he had struck terror into the whole countryside, swinging two guns at once with dash and swagger, glorying in his power and ingenuity; he had no match at all in this part of the country ... Fortunately for this country there was then living in Bandon a young man, recently demobilised from the British army, who was destined to become one of the greatest guerrilla leaders in the War of Independence. Percival had now met his match ... this man was Tom Barry.'[10]

One day Tom and a companion were stopped by British forces in the Laurel Walk, Bandon, and Tom was taken off to the barracks. Apparently, 'he got a bit of a hiding'. This, it seems, was to obtain information about the IRA that he would have been expected to have acquired from the Hales family. Whether it was also meant as a warning, it certainly had that effect on Tom. The result was, that a 'changed' Tom Barry emerged. He admitted he was held up 'several times and questioned about people by pups who had seen no war. The arrogance of the conqueror, the invader made me realise some day if there was a fight coming I would be on the side of Ireland'.[11]

Shortly after this incident he approached Seán Buckley, brigade intelligence officer, and asked if he would be accepted in the IRA. Naturally, because of Tom's past history, the West Cork IRA officers were reluctant to consent without first having him 'checked'. Seán Buckley told him to complete his studies in Skerry's College until the end of the summer term, and meanwhile perhaps he could do some intelligence work for them, particularly in the Bandon area. On 2 July 1919 Seán Buckley enlisted Tom to assist him in intelligence work. From August 'onwards (outside his other activities)' Tom gave 'extremely valuable information about the British Military and Police forces and their moves,' Seán Buckley wrote. 'His work helped us in a great measure to maintain the IRA without losses during a very difficult period ... He took as grave risks' during this period 'as he did in later times when he commanded the men of West Cork in action.'

One evening towards the end of November 1919, Tom with Mick O'Herlihy and a few Bandon Volunteers went to the 'Kilbrittain district' to secure men so that the Bandon police 'who were beating the people with trench tool handles' could be dislodged. Tom and Mick O'Herlihy asked Con Crowley, Cork No. 3 brigade staff captain for 'the loan of two revolvers which I gave them,' Con wrote. Barry, Herlihy, Con Crowley and Tom Hales entered Bandon on several nights 'armed with revolvers'. Barry, from his intelligence work with Seán Buckley knew the men to target. 'Their forthright actions halted, at least temporarily, the frightening activities,' according to Tom Hales. Soon Barry became engaged in the securing of arms and 'was always one of the men carrying a revolver' while engaged 'in his important Intelligence work'.[12]

On Wednesday, 3 May 1920, the first batch of prisoners, 15 men from Tipperary, arrived at Cork jail. On the same night Terence MacSwiney, the lord mayor of Cork, following a meeting in the Hales house in Knocknacurra, escaped arrest by jumping through the back window as the military approached the house. MacSwiney had previously dismissed the warning given by Tom Hales not to sleep in the house; Tom himself and Seán went to a hide-out for the night.

But in August Terence MacSwiney was arrested in Cork City Hall. He went on hunger-strike in Brixton Prison, thus focusing world attention on the Irish cause. He died in October 1920 on the seventy-fifth day of his hunger-strike.

In July Barry's friend Tom Hales with Pat Harte, brigade quartermaster, were arrested. Having failed to get information from them the police handed them over to Percival and the Essex torture squad from whom they received one of the worst torture treatments in the War of Independence. They were stripped, dragged for miles after a lorry, their hair was pulled out and their nails were pulled off with pincers. Finally Pat Harte was transferred to a mental hospital and remained insane until his death a few years later. Tom Hales, who kept his sanity but suffered severely, was sentenced to penal servitude and held in Pentonville Jail, where he was kept until after the Treaty was signed. In the British account Ewan Butler notes that there is no mention of the torture, only that 'reliable information was a matter of extreme difficulty' that 'scanty details pieced together from captured documents had to suffice.'[13]

As an explanation for Tom Barry's change of attitude Charlie O'Keeffe recalls, 'I know that the torture of Hales and Harte had a profound effect on Barry. At the time it was easy to turn a person. I remember in my own case I was in Newcestown at the sports. It was the same Sunday that young Galvin was shot during an ambush at Lissarda near Crookstown. When I heard that, coming back, it annoyed me so much that I decided there and then to join the movement.'[14]

Tom Barry didn't know then, nor was he ever to know, that the first reaction of Seán Buckley and other brigade officers was one of mistrust. Why was the son of an RIC man, who had spent four years in the British army and upheld their policy upon his return to Ireland, seeking membership of the IRA? 'Naturally we had to be cautious. Questions were asked: Could he be a spy? Was he genuine? They set traps for him. He was well tested before being accepted,' Tom Kelleher commented.[15]

Once he joined, he got caught up in the movement. He himself says that he had never read the programme of Sinn Féin. Nor was he concerned that three-fourths of the people of all Ireland had at the end of 1918 'declared in a British general election for a Sovereign Independent Irish Republic, nor that Dáil Éireann had accepted responsibility for the IRA'.

'These things seemed to be of little matter then. But what did matter was that one had to decide whether to aid the occupying forces and be a traitor, sit on the ditch and be a cynic or join your own people and do the right thing.' However, as the struggle developed and many young men died by the bullet, 'one soon learned that programmes that included political, social and economic contexts were important,' he maintained. 'Being the army of a democratically elected government, defending its people and its embryonic institutions changed the world-wide image of the IRA and enhanced the morale of its Volunteers.'[16] Tom felt 'the outlawing – the banning of Dáil Éireann, the elected parliament of the people' should be challenged.[17] In August Seán Buckley, Charlie Hurley, Liam Deasy and other officers knew that in the rapidly changing pattern of action by the 'ruthlessness' of enemy 'extremists in Bandon and Bantry,' morale had reached a low ebb. To counteract this a trained brigade column was required; consequently a suitable officer to train and lead the new force was considered. The name of Tom Barry was once more brought to the fore. Seán Buckley sent for him; he was no longer staying at home as he anticipated another swoop by the British forces.

The meeting between Tom Barry and the officers took place in Barrett's, Killeady, where the urgency of training men to fight and to defend themselves was discussed. Barry says he was reluctant to get involved at first as he wanted 'to complete' his education in 'college in Cork and get a job'.[18] A week later Tom, invited to attend a staff meeting at brigade headquarters in O'Mahony's of Belrose, was questioned by Charlie Hurley and Ted O'Sullivan while other officers listened. Liam Deasy said, 'I observed his reactions closely. His answers were direct and clear. He was smart and military in his appearance and gave the impression of being sharp, quick and dynamic. He presented himself to me as a very likeable person and won my complete confidence … we felt that he would have much to offer as a professional soldier who had seen active military service in the Middle East. His subsequent distinguished service in the national cause became an inspiration, and as a guerrilla fighter his name became a household word throughout the country.'[19] Initially Tom Barry was reluctant to allow his name to go forward. However he consented, and having been proposed and seconded, his name was entered on the register and he was appointed officer in charge of training. 'I told them I knew damn all about it, but I'd do my best'.[20] 'Once he was told he was accepted he got going right away,' Danny Canty recalled. 'He stood up and spoke. He talked of past history and our obligation towards Ireland and why we should fight for this country of ours. He filled us with fire, telling us we needed to train. Any of us who liked could go home, but he'd prefer we'd stay, as he wanted to begin right away. That was a Saturday evening. He took us up the hills and we worked together that evening and all day Sunday. We didn't go to Mass or meeting. I will always remember this good-looking young fellow, full of life and ambition, his hair blowing in the summer breeze.'[21]

That Sunday afternoon was forever etched in Seán MacCárthaigh's mind. Tom's vitality impressed him as he pushed young lads like himself to act with soldiery precision. 'On a few occasions subsequently on your way to Skerry's College, we travelled together … on the morning train'. Seán approached Charlie Hurley on his intention to abandon his studies and join the fighting column. However, Charlie 'ordered' him back to the city to continue his work as the intelligence gatherer and co-ordinator of dispatches between the Cork brigades. It was 'more important from their view point at this juncture as they could not arm all the men available locally.'[22]

Personnel at this intense Belrose meeting outlined a system of training the brigade. Tom Kelleher observed that 'Barry was bursting with constructive ideas that were debated fully. He was mature beyond his years – a genius.'[23]

A few weeks later Tom gave another preliminary talk at Coakley's near Begley's forge. Tom Kelleher was present. 'I can almost memorise it to this day. It was all about Ireland, and how it was once a nation and will be again, that we were entitled to our freedom, but we'll have to fight for it he said, and we'll have to get it. It was powerful stuff. We were filled with enthusiasm. Then he said, "Training is important. We'll have to get going right away".'[24]

Brigid O'Mahony recognised him arriving at her aunt's house one day, sporting a beard and wearing a hat. 'Be careful of him, he's a British spy,' she said to her uncle. 'I know him; he was in the British army; his sisters are in our school.' Her uncle passed on the word, which was met with the rebuke, 'Tell her [Brigid] to keep her mouth shut; we know he's Tom Barry, he's with us now,' was the reply.[25]

The Third West Cork Brigade was one of the three Cork brigades formed on 5 January 1919. Its eastern boundary extended west of the Old Head of Kinsale, north to a point two miles south of Waterfall, west to one mile south of Cookstown skirting Kilmichael, to the southern end of the Pass of Keimineigh on the Kerry border, then west of Glengarriff to the sea enclosing all of the Castletownbere peninsula. The drawbacks of the brigade were many: shortage of arms, machine-guns, bombs, explosives and engineering material; lack of transport, no barracks to retire to; and the hardship of obtaining food and clothing as they went from one area to another. Also, unlike the enemy, the British troops, who had battle experience gained during the 1914– 1918 War and were accustomed to fighting and bloodshed, the West Cork IRA had no experience of war. Most of the members were untrained in the use of arms, tactical manoeuvring and foot-drill, but under Tom Barry's leadership, armed with the willingness to learn, the brigade became highly efficient.

According to Barry, 'This was the force which was to attempt to break by armed action the British domination of seven centuries' duration. Behind it was a tradition of failure … And sadly it must be recorded that when West Cork women and children died in 1846 and 1847 of hunger, and the British ascendancy seized their food, not a West Cork man drove a pike through any of the murderers of his family.'[26]

In the brigade there were seven battalions, organised around the chief towns. Each battalion was divided into companies and these in turn were divided into sections. Unlike a regular army, numbers were flexible, depending on population and activity in a locality.

Battalion staff and company officers were to be trained first. These in turn were to act as training officers to their home units. Barry suggested the setting up of five separate training camps so that the brigade would be able to call upon the services of a large body of men as the need arose. The locations chosen were in Kilbrittain, Ballymurphy, Dunmanway, Schull and Bantry. The camp houses were chosen for their isolation and for having a good range of outside buildings for the Volunteers to sleep in while scouts and sentries kept watch.

The first training camp commenced at the end of September in O'Brien's, Clounbuig, Kilbrittain – a house where the males and the females were all involved in the movement. All the men slept in the one barn. Training continued for about ten hours a day, generally extended to a week to inculcate military discipline and to teach elementary tactics. 'The men were told to act as if they were expecting an attack at any hour of the day or night … They practised occupying their defence positions, aiming and trigger pressing and moving in extended order as directed. It was an unorthodox approach to training, but the circumstances necessitated this departure,' he recalled. All that mattered he felt was that the men would obey orders, shoot straight and move in proper formation. 'Their ability to salute or to form fours smartly wasn't in the circumstances, considered.'

The full military practice together with the lectures, written work and map-reading meant, according to Barry, 'that the men's minds held nothing but thoughts of war.'

'I stressed to the men that they would be called upon to undertake long marches, they would often go hungry and sleep rough – in a field or in a barn. "You may leave home one day and never return," I told them.'[27] Charlie Hurley, brigade OC arrived one day; he observed for a short while, had a few words with Barry, fell in with a section, joined the sharp, swift manoeuvring of side arms. John Fitzgerald said 'it was a moment I will not forget when Charlie announced that from now on Tom Barry was brigade column commander. Without doubt he was as sharp and as fit a man as ever wore shoe leather!'[28] Barry embarked on organising a guerrilla force that would be one of the strongest in Ireland. His keen observation, strict discipline, good organisation and fearless, dynamic personality gave confidence and inspiration to those that fought and planned with him. 'There is such a thing as a born soldier, and Tom Barry was one,' said Danny Canty. 'Once he was in the movement he threw his heart into it. He was in it in spirit and in body. The soldier in him wanted to push the men forward.'[29] This lightly built twenty-three year old was winning the respect of the men he was to lead: he had to prove his worth more than any of his men. 'You have to make sure that your troops are more afraid of you than they are of the enemy. I did that.' [30]

'The men had the courage, they had idealism in their souls, all they needed was the spark to ignite, and Barry provided that spark.'[31]

TRAINING, AMBUSHES, ACTION, AUXILIARY CONFRONTATION

Recruiting for the Black and Tans opened in England on 1 January 1920. Ten shillings a day was offered to men willing to join the British forces in Ireland 'to get rid of a gangster fighting element' and 'make it a hell for rebels to live in'. They were joined in August by the Auxiliary division, all ex-officers of commissioned rank who had seen active service during the 1914–1918 War. The 'Auxies' were paid £1 per day and wore dark blue uniforms and dark Balmoral bonnets. Throughout the year hundreds of troops poured into West Cork.

In the summer of 1920 enemy pressure increased with the landing of a further 2,000 troops in Bantry. Bandon, Innishannon, Dunmanway, Rosscarbery and other towns in the area were heavily re-inforced with British troops. It was this contingent that the Third West Cork Brigade, which never numbered in strength more than 110 armed active service Volunteers, had to fight and even overcome by guerrilla tactics.

Reports reached the column that the Essex regiment was continually looting, burning houses and harassing Irish citizens. John Connolly, an unarmed Volunteer, was arrested by the Essex, and was found dead some weeks later in a park, near Bandon. Seán Buckley's home was burned, as was that of the Hales family in Knocknacurra. Tom Barry was incensed; he placed the blame particularly on Major Percival and decided he would have to deal with him. (He was the same Major Percival who, in 1941, surrendered Singapore to lesser forces.)[1] 'This officer was easily the most viciously anti-Irish of all serving British officers', Tom Barry remarked.[2]

Tom was in a training camp in Ballymurphy, near Upton. Acting on their intelligence reports he and another Volunteer went to Bandon and waited in a doorway for Percival to pass by at 7.45 p.m. on his nightly visit to the home of a local bank manager, prior to his town raids. Percival never appeared and they had to retire disappointed. News reached them next day that Percival had in fact left the barracks at 6 p.m. but in another direction. While Barry and his companion lay in wait for him, Percival and his men were raiding local houses.

Following each camp, training engagements were sought, but invariably the military failed to respond. After the first training camp Barry organised an ambush on the Dunmanway-Ballineen road at Farranlobus where British soldiers travelled daily in a particular formation. This well-organised ambush with men in strategic positions had a good field of fire. Though they waited until nightfall, the enemy failed to travel that day. This confirmed the column officers' suspicions that informers were active. Tom kept pressing for action, as informing would wreck their hard work.[3]

On the night of 21 October 1920, 31 rifle-men were mobilised at Dan

Delaney's to prepare for the Toureen (Tureen) ambush.[4] Tom leaned against a door-frame and watched four men in a small room putting the finishing touches to a mine. Paddy Crowley was helping Charlie Hurley and Seán Hales and Dick Barrett were chatting. The ambush, which was to engage two or three lorries of the Essex Regiment en route from Bandon to Cork at Toureen, outside brigade boundaries, was well planned. Tom's motto was, 'Fight and win. Don't look for a retreat'.

At 4 a.m. on 22 October 1920 the flying column moved off to occupy positions at Toureen. The men were divided into three sections: Liam Deasy with nine rifle-men inside the ditch at the eastern end; Charlie Hurley at the centre with two rifle-men to explode the mine, with the remainder of his party further east; and Tom Barry with his section of ten men, five kneeling and five standing at the western side behind a loosely tied gate. According to Barry's plan the explosion of the mine was to bring the leading lorry to a halt, forcing the second vehicle to stop. The spot where this was expected to occur was in front of the farm gate; the men under Barry's section waited here. Each action was rehearsed several times. Before the men took their places Tom performed a small ceremony. From the British War Office, he had just received three medals 'in a neat cardboard box' won 'in service to the crown'. He distributed one to each of his section commanders 'with orders to put them up'.[5] With his concern for civilians, Barry had already seen to the evacuation of the Roberts family from the nearby farm to the house of some neighbours. Two rifle-men escorted them, with orders to ensure that no one left the house.

Shortly after nine o'clock the scouts signalled the approach of the first lorry. As it passed over the mine Charlie Hurley depressed the plunger of his exploder; nothing happened. Deasy's section fired, but the lorry sped off towards Cork.

Tom Barry flung open the gate and jumped on the road as the second lorry approached. He threw a bomb, which didn't explode but the lorry lurched and got stuck in a dyke. The men jumped out, some were mortally wounded as they left the lorry. A sharp fight followed with some of the IRA facing the Essex men directly, some with little cover. After some intense fighting Lieut Dixon and four soldiers were dead. The Essex men offered to surrender and raised their hands.

Barry, in command, blew his whistle for cease-fire. In military style he ordered his men to collect the guns and ammunition. None of his men were injured. He asked the column to make the wounded Essex comfortable. They were supplied with bandages, as their first-aid equipment was in the first lorry, which had escaped. The dead men were pulled from the vicinity and the lorry, sprinkled with petrol, was burned. Barry then called the unwounded to attention and addressed them. He told them that their ruffianism, the beatings of helpless prisoners and their terrorism of the civilian population had been noted. 'Torturing of prisoners like Tom Hales and Pat Harte weren't forgotten.

The murder of John Connolly, Bandon, having been held for a week was a foul deed,' he said. 'You have been treated like soldiers on this occasion,' he told their senior surviving sergeant. 'Tell Major Percival, if you continue to torture and murder, expect to be treated only as murderers.' The senior sergeant thanked the IRA for their fair treatment and said he would convey the message.[6]

He knew he made two mistakes in the Toureen ambush. He should have warned the advance section of the possibility of failure with the exploder; in that event they should have been ready to attack the first lorry. Also his throwing of the bomb into the lorry could have caused harm to his own men as well as to the enemy at such close range.[7] Speed was essential Barry knew as reinforcements from Cork or Bandon could be on the scene shortly. The column marched cross country towards Kilmacsimon Quay, procured a large boat from the Deasy brothers, divided into sections and rowed across.

At Chambers Cross Charlie Hurley had presented Tom with Lieut Dixon's revolver and field equipment while ceremoniously speaking a few words on behalf of the column. His first ambush was a success.

British propaganda went into overdrive. It reported the ambush as 'one of the first operations carried out by a flying column against the crown forces ... Probably about 150 rebels took part ... the rebels charged them with fixed bayonets ... Regardless of the agonies, which the troops were suffering, they dragged off their equipment' ... The 'rebels' are described as savage. They 'kicked Dickenson's dead body,' and 'rendered no assistance' to the wounded.[8] Ewan Butler points to 'the British account of the affair' lacking credibility with their version 'that the mine was wired to the ignition-coil of a Ford car' when there was no car.[9]

That night, as the column billeted in Kilbrittain, up to 400 Essex Regiment and the Black and Tans, led by the surviving sergeant of the Toureen ambush, went on the rampage in Bandon. They smashed property and terrorised anyone remotely connected with the Nationalist movement. However, Loyalists in the town also suffered, as the military did not discriminate in their victims. Bandon Hosiery factory was burned to the ground, as was M & C Healy Malting & Corn Stores. 'Shops were attacked wholesale; every plate glass window in the South Main Street and Bridge Street was smashed to smithereens. Many houses were set on fire and some burnt out. Premises were broken into and wrecked.' Thirty-four known premises in town were 'damaged or wrecked'.[10] It was the first major devastation and burning of a town in the county. After the Loyalists complained to the British divisional headquarters in Cork, their commanding officer had the regiment and Tans confined to barracks next day.[11]

Meanwhile, Barry and his column, now with extra men, equipped with the captured arms, moved towards Bandon and waited in ambush positions to engage the enemy. They did not succeed so the column was then disbanded.

While Tom waited for the transfer of rifles for another training camp he decided to target a judge who, despite a warning, was particularly harsh in passing sentences on IRA prisoners. Charlie Hurley and Tom, both in stocking-feet, pushed themselves along the overhead railway close to Lee's Hotel, Bandon (now the Munster Arms), to within close range of the room where Judge Sealy slept. Each night the judge entered the room at approximately 11 o'clock, go to the window and breathe in the night air. On this particular night the room remained dark until 11.10 and it was some time before a figure appeared at the window. Charlie Hurley had taken the first pressure on the trigger and was waiting for Tom's 'Now!' to signal their simultaneous fire.

'I took aim and gently touched the trigger of a Peter the Painter automatic with a stock attached. The blind sprang up revealing a woman, and I have never fathomed yet why it did not cause the very, very light pressure required on the trigger to fire the bullet. We lay motionless,' Tom recalled, 'while the woman peered out into the darkness. Speechless we crawled away about 70 yards'.[12] Tom said they walked away 'happy at not having killed the woman, that we forgot our failure to shoot the judge.' (Apparently, Judge Sealy had asked that day to be moved to a larger room.)

The deaths of Sealy and Percival would, according to Tom, have been more useful than the deaths of many private soldiers. 'Percival was a leading instrument in the plan for our destruction, while the judge was an important prop to British power. This judge, technically a civilian, had large armed forces at his disposal. British law administrations and British military forces were complementary.'[13] At a brigade council meeting in Coppeen on 31 October Tom had asked for and had been given absolute command of the flying column. His decisions would be his and his alone without interference. He would take full responsibility, would be subject to no authority and would have to take the blame for any failure or disaster.[14]

Tom Barry was appointed official commander of the flying column. Charlie Hurley expressed his gratitude for the 'outstanding service which Barry had already rendered.'[15] By this time many battalion OC's had reported assaults by the Auxiliaries in their districts. Though it was felt by all that they should be challenged, no definite decision was reached.[16] Tom moved on to the Bantry area, trained 55 officers from the Bantry, Schull and Castletownbere battalions, then had some of the rifles sent to Dunmanway to train that battalion in the fifth and final training camp. One night in Bantry the men were soaked to the skin. At nightfall Barry made sure they had a change of clothing and whatever comfort was available before he considered his own welfare.[17]

On Sunday 20 November at a brigade council meeting in Gloun the incursion of the Macroom Auxiliaries into the Third West Cork Brigade area was discussed at length. Charlie Hurley said that 'they should be tackled. We knew they were well trained in fighting and drill.'[18] The men were unaware that as their meeting progressed this force held 'the Bantry Line road to Cork in the village of Coppeen, three miles east of Gloun.' Some men left the meeting and were held up at Coppeen by Col Craik and his Auxiliary force; the men gave a believable alibi and had a 'providential escape'.[19] Deasy maintained that the incursion and cruel treatment meted out by the Macroom Auxiliaries helped to make 'Tom determined to attack this force. He had a remarkable grasp of military psychology, which enabled him to anticipate the actions of his enemy. That is why he believed they would continue to travel the same road on the following Sunday … Like all of us he kept his council and did not allow for the slightest suspicion.'[20]

On the same day in Dublin, in simultaneous predawn raids in Dublin, Michael Collins' men killed 11 British intelligence agents. In retaliation the Black and Tans invaded a football match at Croke Park that afternoon and fired indiscriminately at the teams and at an estimated 7,000 spectators, killing 12 civilians including one player, Michael Hogan, and wounding 60. This day became known as Bloody Sunday.

Barry returned from the meeting to Farrell's training camp at Clogher, northwest of Dunmanway. At this time, 150 'C' Company Auxiliaries were stationed at Macroom Castle. They were recruited to break the IRA's force and squash Ireland's resistance to British rule. Harassing people in Ballingeary after Sunday Mass was a game for 'the Castle Auxies. Every neighbour in the district had been raided. They broke furniture, pulled men, women and children from their beds at all hours of the night, made wrecks of houses and brought misery … A bad lot!'[21]

'They had a special technique', Tom Barry wrote. 'Fast lorries of them would come roaring into a village, the occupants would jump out, firing shots and ordering all the inhabitants out of doors'.[22] After house raids, people were beaten up, men stripped and beaten in front of women – their deeds of terrorism were numerous. At certain times they concentrated on raiding south into the West Cork brigade area.[23]

One of their 'great games' was to drive through the country, stop the lorry, take 'pot shots' to scatter up earth beside a man working in the field. This would be followed by great laughter as the man ran for cover. This happened to Richard Coughlan on a few occasions and he was 'lucky' to escape. 'Their bullets injured many innocent people'.[24] Two soldiers at a gate took 'pot shots' at William Hawkes who worked in a field with his father. He ran, jumped over the fence. After the third shot he fell. 'The young man was maimed for life; his leg had to be amputated at the hip.'[25] Micheál Ó Súilleabháin knew that the 'marauding' Auxiliaries in Macroom Castle 'were a tough crowd … I had plenty of experience of their physical fitness when I had to run from them on several occasions.' While working in a haggard one day he feared for his life. 'If a man ran and was seen running, he was shot down. He could possibly be shot too for standing still. That was the order of the day. Nobody doubted it.'[26] Mick Sullivan recalled 'a clear frosty' morning around 'a quarter to eight' when 'four hostages' were made run in front of a lorry of Macroom Auxies. Major Graw and his officers fired shots as if 'looking for a direct line of fire and missing the lads ... I never heard anything like the screams for the air was all clear ... the Auxiliaries were terrorising the countryside.'[27] Lieut Col S. F. Smyth, divisional commander RIC Munster, issued an order on 17 June 1920 that 'a policeman is perfectly justified in shooting any man who he has good reason to believe is carrying arms and who does not immediately throw up his hands when ordered'.[28] On 1 November 1920 one of the Macroom Castle Auxiliaries entered a house in Ballyvourney village 'called out a married man named Jim Lehane, a man who would not hurt a fly'. He took this 'innocent civilian' across the road and 'shot him dead.' The Auxiliary was Cadet Cecil Guthrie. That night as he drank in a local pub he boasted that he 'got the bastard' and that it was 'one way of teaching' them manners. The local intelligence unit was informed.

Nine days later Christy Lucey a Volunteer from Cork City, staying with friends in Ballingeary, was unarmed when the Macroom Auxies shot him dead. The Auxies met the local curate Fr Donncha Ó Donnchú and 'gleefully roared, "There's work for you back there!"'[29]

Back in August 1920 Liam Deasy had been one of the officers from country areas to attend a GHQ meeting in Dublin where Richard Mulcahy C/S and Michael Collins D/I were present. The 'two main items for decision' were (a) 'the principle of ambushing ...' (b) 'How to deal with the new problem created by the introduction of the Auxiliaries into the country, a strong force of whom had taken up quarters in the town of Macroom ...'[30]

Col Buxton Smyth, commander 'C' Company Auxiliaries in Macroom Castle found it hard to hold and control his men. 'Within the first few months 25 men left this company,' he told Katherine Everett. 'They had no room for exercise. They can't walk a yard or go into a shop without danger, and they are savage for revenge'.[31]

General Crozier who commanded the 'Auxies' in Ireland struggled to maintain some sort of discipline in the force and wrote in his book *Ireland Forever:*

> Up to November 1, 1920, I had 'dismissed' or 'dispensed' with the services of over fifty Auxiliary policemen (ex-officers) for various acts of indiscipline, but after that date a heavy and hidden hand came down. My powers of dismissal and dispersal were taken from me. Why? I had to wait a few months to find out. 'They' feared a kick-back from England caused by 'talk' on the part of the 'kicked-out'. Later 'they' got the 'kick' in return.[32]

In mid-November the British government 'decided to arrest and intern all rebels known to be IRA officers, or to be engaged in the perpetration of serious outrages. Very large numbers were secured at the first onslaught ... a considerable part of the work of intelligence officers from this time onwards consisted in collecting evidence.'[33]

The raids had a serious effect on the morale of the people; also they dampened the spirits of IRA members. Tom Barry decided that he and his 36 trained rifle-men at Clogher camp, who 'appeared to be splendid natural fighters', would take on the most dreaded enemy force in their area. This unit was new to military training – apart from three men who had previously attended a training camp and one had fought in Toureen – and was about to fight as a team.

Military raiding parties interrupted the training on three occasions. Twice the men were almost forced to take on the enemy. However, Barry had a definite objective for the following Sunday and would not be diverted. He and his men were going to take on the enemy on their own terms, choose their own battleground and avoid confrontation if unprepared for ambush. From the outset, he decided that military discipline of this guerrilla army was paramount. He divided them into three sections and appointed a commander to each.[34]

Liam Deasy and Charlie Hurley having visited the training camp were aware that 'Tom Barry was planning to ambush the Macroom Auxiliaries who were making incursions' into Cork No. 3 Brigade area.[35]

On Friday of that week, accompanied by Michael McCarthy, Tom went on horseback to select an ambush position. The spot was carefully chosen and mapped out – a desolate hill, bog and heather covered area south of Kilmichael. Two or three Crossley tenders, each carrying about 10 Auxiliaries from Macroom, travelled down this road daily as they went on their rampage in various directions throughout the Third West Cork Brigade area. The area chosen for the ambush was outside the brigade boundary. Barry said 'we were no respecters of borders, and had crossed out on many occasions. Toureen and Kilmichael fights were fought ... inside the boundaries of Cork No. 1 Brigade'. Liam Deasy records the value of 'the co-operation we received at all times' from Cork No. 1 Brigade.[36] Co-ordination between brigades was essential for harmony 'as enemy pressure became more and more insistent during the course of 1920 – in the south and south-west more particularly – adjoining brigades made tentative efforts at liaison with one another.' Crossbarry and Kilmurry Company 'co-operated closely with the Third Brigade throughout 1920–21.'[37] Seán Mac-Cárthaigh, as intelligence officer and area 'IRB centre' brought 'written and verbal dispatches from Cork No. 1 to Cork No. 3 H. Qrs' each Friday evening. Josephine Marchmount – confidential secretary to staff officer Captain Webb who was chief officer to Major Strickland – was an invaluable intelligence agent. Josephine and Nora Wallace worked in tandem. Nora in her shop in St Augustine Street became the keeper of a police cipher key and with their contacts in Cork city post office 'Wire messages' were regularly decoded and kept Florrie O'Donoghue and his intelligence team 'a step ahead' of their enemies. Intelligence work done by both Josephine and Nora went undetected throughout the war and was regarded by O'Donoghue as of equivalent value 'to a strong column of men'.[38]

Barry and Michael McCarthy travelled on horseback to the Kilmichael/ Shanacashel area on Friday evening, 26 November, and decided on an ambush site. 'We were the only two people who knew, up to late Saturday night, where we hoped to fight on Sunday.' Conscious of the terrain Barry decided that the Auxiliaries had to be apprehended in the stretch of road between Kilmichael and Gleann crossroads. He felt they could not engage the enemy nearer to Macroom, as reinforcements would arrive quickly from base. Beyond Gleann crossroads the Auxiliaries had previously diverged in different directions, so 'they had to be got before they reached that cross.'[39]

An idea for slowing down the travelling lorries came to him when he saw Paddy O'Brien in an IRA officer's tunic. The Auxies wouldn't have seen this uniform before and if Barry wore it and stood in view they might slow down to investigate. He exchanged his civilian coat for O'Brien's uniform for the forthcoming engagement.

At 2 a.m. on the morning of 28 November 1920, the column met in a farmyard at Ahilane, Enniskeane. Each of the 36 men was armed with a rifle and 36 rounds of ammunition per man, a few had revolvers and Barry also carried two Mills bombs, captured at Toureen. At 3 a.m the men were told that the attack would be on the Macroom Auxiliaries. Fr O'Connell came on horse-back from Enniskeane to hear the men's confessions. There was every possibility that all these men, including Barry, would be dead within twenty-four hours. Beside a ditch, 'silently, one by one, their rifles slung, the IRA men went to him and returned to the ranks.'

Then the priest said, 'Are the boys going to attack the Sassanach, Tom?'

'Yes, Father, we hope so.'

The priest raised his voice, 'Good luck, boys! I know you will win. God keep ye all! Now I will give you my blessing.'

The men all knelt for the blessing. Then the priest mounted his horse and rode into the darkness.[40]

The men set out for the long cross-country march against the lashing rain. Soon every man was drenched, but silently continued to march. It was a cold, black, miserable November night.

Pat Deasy, a young Volunteer, who had been ill for a few days previously followed the column at a distance. A few miles before they reached Kilmichael during a rest halt he made his presence known. Flyer Nyhan brought him to Barry. He pleaded that he be allowed fight and was difficult to resist, so Barry relented. Due to shortage of guns his substitute was sent home.

Around 8.15 a.m. the flying column reached the ambush position. The men had trudged through the bitter night against the lashing rain. They were cold, hungry and drenched wet. Military tactics were needed. 'In true Barry fashion he told us it would be a fight until the end; either we wiped them out or they wiped us out. But he said, "We'll wipe them out. We'll smash the bloody fellows. Today will be an important day, not only for you, for West Cork but for Ireland".'[41]

Barry knew that most of these men had a story to tell. Jack Hennessy's parents' home was raided by the RIC on 10 July 1920. Jack was beaten and their home was burned to the ground. Ned Young's parents were active in politics, his father though an elderly man was arrested and was regularly exhibited as a hostage in the Auxiliary lorries while out on raids, to prevent being fired upon.[42] In October the Black and Tans had come to John Lordan's home to arrest his father and uncle – 'wanted' for their support of the Republican cause. They were not there so the enemy burned their house.[43] When John heard that the column was seeking action, he tossed a coin with Dan Canty and won the toss for the one rifle they had between them. Barry gladly placed him in No. 2 section.[44]

Much precision went into Barry's plan. 'He was quick to size things up! So quick, sharp, a soldier to his fingertips!'[45] During training he had learned of each man's ability and thought about where individuals should be posted. Sections were rehearsed so that each man knew where his comrades were positioned. Barry's military experience, discipline and training taught him the value of a positive approach. His instructions on the plan of attack and the positions the men were to occupy allowed for no retreat. In this bleak, desolate spot of stone, bog land and heather Barry and his men would be so close to their enemy that they could not easily miss their target. At the eastern end of the ambuscade he would be in position at a command post from where he would direct the fight, supported by three picked marksmen: John (Flyer) Nyhan, Jim (Spud) Murphy and Mick O'Herihy.[46]

Approximately ten yards from this position beyond a large heather-covered rock with a good field of fire lay ten rifle-men of No. 1 section. At the western end of the ambuscade on the northern side of the road the rifle-men of No. 2 section waited. They would cover the curve and the stretch of road by which the Auxies would approach the ambush area.

As an insurance against the arrival of a third lorry, No. 3 section was divided. Six rifle-men were posted to the north of the ambuscade about twenty yards from the path of the enemy, with a good field of fire on the approach road. In a shrewd tactic Barry had the remaining rifle-men of that section under Stephen O'Neill, section commander posted about 50 yards south of the road on a chain of rocks, mainly to prevent the Auxiliaries from jumping over the low ditch and establishing fighting positions there. Unarmed scouts were, as was usual, posted at both ends of the ambush area. Major Percival of the Essex Regiment noted that 'the IRA were no fools in the conduct of guerrilla warfare … they even laid down certain principles of war … one of these principles was the principle of security.'[47]

Clothes, wet from the night of sleet and rain, clung to the men's bodies as they lay on soggy soil. The hours passed slowly. The men had had no food since six o'clock the previous evening and no sleep. 'The cold was intense'. It had begun to freeze as the men lay, so that their clothes grew stiff on their bodies. 'It was a test of endurance and toughness,' Barry recalled. Around mid-day the Kelly's in an isolated house sent down a basin, a few iron buckets of tea and a bastable cake 'probably all these honest people had'.[48] But this did not go far among the column of men. 'It was a hard wait. We were waiting all day, all day!' Pat O'Donovan recalled.[49] The men were warned to lie there. 'They were told not to move.' Local people on their way to Mass were asked to go home and to keep silent. The men had to lie all day, practically without moving, in the freezing cold.[50]

As time dragged towards evening, the men were at a low ebb. Nervous, cold, wet, hungry, all they could do was wait, hope and sometimes interrupt their thoughts with a prayer. Barry was standing in open view in his borrowed Volunteer uniform. 'All the time he fingered carefully the all-important Mills bomb, and for the thousandth time he went over his strategy.'[51] There was 'a fifty-fifty chance that he would be shot on sight'.[52]

It was just past 4 p.m. when the scouts to the north of the position signalled that the enemy was in sight. Barry's men lay prone and rigid, awaiting his order to open fire. To Barry's horror a side-car bearing five armed IRA Volunteers came around the bend. These men who should have reached the training camp the previous Sunday did not receive the mobilisation order in time. Now, not alone were they endangering their own lives, but they almost upset the operation of the entire column. Instantly Barry reacted. 'Gallop up the lane; the Auxies are here! Gallop! Gallop!' he shouted. The grey horse galloped and the men disappeared from sight and did not re-appear until the fight was over.

Seconds later, at 4.05 p.m. the first lorry came around the bend into the ambush position. The driver, apparently observing the uniformed figure, began to slow down.

'I was afraid they were going to stop altogether,' said Barry. 'I had the Mills bomb in my hand and the pin out, ready to throw.'[53] When the lorry was within yards, having driven unsuspectingly past No. 3 and No. 2 sections, Barry hurled the bomb, blew his whistle and fired his automatic.

The grenade landed on the driver's seat of the open top lorry. It exploded. It killed the driver and his companion. Rifle-shots rang out from Barry and his men. The lorry lurched forward. Auxiliaries, who were not severely wounded by the blast, jumped out and responded to the IRA's shots. Soon Barry and the men beside him were on the road in the fight. Revolvers were at times used at point blank range on the somewhat dazed enemy. The fight was intense, even hand-to-hand action. Rifle-butts replaced rifle-shots. 'So close were the combatants that in one instance the pumping blood from an Auxiliary's severed artery struck one attacker full in the mouth before the Auxiliary hit the ground. The Auxiliaries were cursing and yelling as they fought, but the IRA were tight-lipped, as ruthlessly and coldly they out-fought them.'[54]

This encounter was short, sharp and bloody. All of the nine Auxiliaries spread on the road seemed to be either dead or dying. Barry passed one whom he thought was dead, but he rose and took aim at him. Flyer Nyhan's quick action with his bayonet halted the gunner. Barry got a side glimpse of this action. Brisk movement was vital. Waiting only to pick up a rifle and some of the Auxies' clips of ammunition Barry commanded the three men from the command post to follow him. The second lorry was being engaged by No. 2 section.

This second group of Auxies was crouched on the road having taken what little cover they could as No. 2 section was 'engaging strongly' from their higher vantage position. Barry with the three rifle-men jogged in single file along the dyke with rifles at the ready. When they were about half ways between the two lorries, 'I heard these fellows shouting, "We surrender! We surrender!" … We saw them, some of them threw their rifles away,' Barry recalled. Firing stopped. Silence from the first lorry verified it had been wiped out.

No. 2 section Volunteers, who were only about 15 to 20 yards away from the enemy, thought the fight was over. Some stood up. 'Immediately the Auxies opened on them' with revolvers. Bullets hit Volunteers who stood up and accepted the surrender.

Barry, Spud Murphy, Flyer Nyhan and Mick O'Herlihy observed what had happened and jogged closer. They were now about 25 yards behind (moving towards) the enemy who spotted them. In their sandwiched position, the Auxies again shouted a surrender.

Realising that the Auxies had again opened fire with their revolvers. Barry shouted: 'Rapid fire, and do not stop until I tell ye!' Barry and the three men dropped down and 'let them have it from behind'. No. 2 section also responded to Barry's 'Rapid fire'. The Auxies realising that they were jammed, kept firing. Barry shouted to his men to keep firing. At this stage the Auxies were shown no mercy, regardless of whether some had thrown away their arms or not.

'We advanced into them still firing, making sure they were all dead. Now for that I take full responsibility. The only blame I have to myself is that I didn't warn these young lads about the old war trick of a false surrender,' said Barry. He never forgave himself for this. 'They stood up because they were green and I didn't warn them.'[55]

Scattered on the road all the Auxiliaries appeared dead. Barry gave the 'cease-fire' command and an eerie silence followed as the sounds of the last shots died away.

Barry climbed the short distance to where he had seen his men fall. Two Volunteers were dead – Michael McCarthy, who originally came with Barry to mark out the site of the ambush, and Jim O'Sullivan shot through the jaw. Pat Deasy, Liam Deasy's young brother who had followed the column and implored Barry to allow him to fight was bleeding profusely from bullet wounds.

Barry sent a scout to summon a doctor, another to get a priest, he detailed four men to get a door as a stretcher for Pat Deasy. When Barry spoke to him, Pat smiled. Barry records that he himself turned away and had to refuse his dying wish for a drink of water. This lad, not yet sixteen, died later in a neighbouring house.[56]

Eighteen Volunteers were told to collect the arms and documents of the dead Auxiliaries and to pull the bodies away from the lorries and the remainder of the column were ordered to soak the tenders in petrol and prepare them for burning.[57] A flask of brandy was found in each of the Auxiliaries pockets.[58]

Some Volunteers were in a state of shock. Unlike Barry, they had never seen so many dead men with severe body wounds. Barry, conscious of this and of the necessity of jerking them back to reality, gave the command, 'Fall in at the double!' The men from each section closed upon their leader, got the 'attention' command, were numbered off and ordered to re-load. Their commander ordered them to slope arms; then he inspected them. He felt the only medicine available to counteract strain and shock was foot drill among the dying and the dead. If they encountered more British troops during retirement, inefficiency would show. 'If they didn't keep discipline, we might lose everything. Discipline was all we had.' Barry marched and counter-marched his column, their faces lit in the winter twilight by the flickering light from the burning vehicles, their boots slipping in pools of blood. 'His iron will as much as anything else was the stuff of survival, of victory'.[59]

Before they left Kilmichael some of the men were physically sick. The shock of the fight and the drill beside the bodies and the blood were too much for one man whom John Whelton knew. 'He came home shortly after, and was a physical wreck. He shouldn't have been there in the first place, as he couldn't take that type of thing. Within six months his hair was snow white. After that Barry decided he would emphasise stronger than ever what they were facing, and if they couldn't take it, they were out.'[60]

The column was halted before the rock where the bodies of the two dead Volunteers lay and was ordered to 'Present Arms', as a final tribute to their comrades. The men were again formed into sections; then the order to march was given. Some Volunteers from the local company as well as those who had come earlier in a grey horse and side-car helped with the care of the dead men. Taking the bodies cross-country through bogs, burying them by day, re-digging and moving by night, it took over a week to reach Castletown-Kenneigh graveyard for burial.[61]

Critics have said that Barry should have accepted the second surrender call. In Liam Deasy's *Towards Ireland Free* published in 1973, there is no mention of a false surrender.[62] The absence of this detail angered Barry. In a booklet *The Reality of the Anglo-Irish War 1920–1921 in West Cork* that Tom Barry wrote, afterwards, he cited commander of Section No. 3, Stephen O'Neill's version in *The Kerryman*, 12 December 1937: 'after the false surrender, fire was again opened by the Auxiliaries with fatal results to two of our comrades who exposed themselves, believing the surrender to be genuine. We renewed the attack vigorously and never desisted until the enemy were annihilated.'[63] Responding to criticism Barry wrote, 'perhaps, I should have taken a second false surrender and let a few more Volunteers be killed treacherously.'[64]

General Crozier, commander at the time of the Auxiliaries in Ireland, in his book *Ireland Forever* accepted that there was a false surrender. 'It was perfectly true that the wounded had been put to death after the ambush, but the reason for this barbarous inhumanity became understandable, although inexcusable,' he wrote. Because, 'arms were supposed to have been surrendered, but a wounded Auxiliary whipped out a revolver while lying on the ground and shot a "Shinner" with the result that all his comrades were put to death with him.'[65]

Initially I investigated the false surrender for *The Tom Barry Story*.[66] After a brief surrender call, fire was re-opened. Was this the time the Volunteers were killed? It appears as if Pat Deasy jumped up during the fight to have a good shot and was wounded before the surrender call. However he had two wounds, one was a grazed side-stomach wound and the other higher up, internal nearer his heart, believed to be the fatal wound. Pat O'Donovan and Tim O'Connell at either side of him, both knew of the side graze wound before the surrender call.[67] He got up during the surrender, as firing began again. The shot which hit Jim O'Sullivan had first struck the bolt of his own rifle and then hit him in the head, killing him instantly. This, it seems, was after the surrender call. Barry was certain that two men fell from shots fired after the surrender call. 'We saw three of our comrades on No. 2 section stand up, one crouched and two upright. Suddenly the Auxiliaries were firing again with revolvers', Barry wrote.[68]

Certainly in the second stage of the fight when Barry and the three men from the command post advanced, there were surrender cries. There was a lull. Tim O'Connell, Pat O'Donovan and James O'Mahony all in No. 2 section, in the direct line of fire (where the three men who were fatally wounded were positioned), were certain that the ambush was over. Then shots from Auxies guns rang out once more.[69] Barry's response was decisive. He commanded his men to return fire. Whether or not some of the 'Auxies' had dropped arms, they were shot – some at point blank range.

One Volunteer, Jack O'Sullivan told me that he had come behind a man and ordered him to drop his gun, which he did. He was walking him up the road as a prisoner when a shot dropped him at his feet.[70] At this stage Barry didn't want prisoners – especially men who used deceptive tactics. Most of the Volunteers present to whom I spoke said, 'It was either them or us.' Barry said he accepted full responsibility for shooting them outright. 'Soldiers who had cheated in war deserved to die'.

'We had to; if three or four more of our lads stood up, they'd have got it too. I couldn't take the chance that they wouldn't grab a gun.'[71] In the Liam Deasy book the account of the ambush differs in vital parts from other written accounts.[72] Paddy O'Brien's account begins: 'We paraded at 5.00 a.m. on Sunday morning, and after a breakfast of tea, bread and butter we set out on the five mile march to Kilmichael ... Tom Barry divided the column into two sections, taking charge of one section himself.'[73] The facts are: they had a late evening meal, had their confessions heard and set out from there shortly after 3 a.m. for their 18-mile cross-county journey against the lashing rain. Because O'Brien (as per Deasy) states: 'I was given orders to maintain contact with different units', Barry in his booklet *The Reality of the Anglo Irish* – asks, 'by whom and for what purpose?' He also asks why the Deasy account has O'Brien 'practically taking over' the ambush as well as the training camp prior to it though 'he never held any rank'.[74] Rev. John Chisholm edited Liam Deasy's book *Towards Ireland Free*, and said: 'I endeavoured to preserve the style found in the manuscripts supplied to me, but I am conscious that all too often it is my own style which prevails.'[75] Flor Crowley, a West Cork teacher with an intimate knowledge of West Cork brigade events 'gleaned' that the book 'was ghost written from incidents supplied by Liam Deasy.'[76]

In Paddy O'Brien's account of the ambush, there are passages such as: 'Time seemed to move slowly. Yet in spite of the tense air of expectancy spirits were still high, though here and there a pale face glimpsed through the shifting mist reflected the inner fears of a youth facing the ordeal of battle for the first time, and possibility of death ... The enemy was coming. All weariness vanished, the quiet talk ceased, safety catches were released, rifle-bolts were drawn and a bullet filled the breach ... ' In dealing with the horse and side-car crisis and Barry's order, the O'Brien report calls it 'a pony and trap' and states: 'Never on the dramatic stage was a transformation scene carried out with such dispatch nor indeed with such efficiency.'[77] When I questioned Fr Chisholm if Paddy O'Brien wrote or spoke in this manner, he admitted that he himself had 'a free hand' in the composition.[78]

In his *Refutations, Corrections and Comments* on Liam Deasy's *Towards Ireland Free*, Barry said that of all the inaccurate accounts, in *Towards Ireland Free* that of Kilmichael, 'angered me the most'. In particular he was angry with the 'presentation of the engagement at Kilmichael and the training camp immediately prior to it ... would appear to be like a scene from "Dad's Army" whilst the fight could be summed up as a galaxy of names and "we waited; Auxies came, we shooted and all dead".'[79]

As Barry implies, it was an extremely abbreviated description of the ambush, containing numerous errors and omissions. He took up the point in the Deasy book that the men knew of the forthcoming attack, whereas for security purposes only Michael McCarthy and himself knew the exact location.[80] Most significant was the account in the book that the column was divided into only two sections, rather than the three, with No. 3 section sub-divided, plus a command post. The *Towards Ireland Free* accounts of several incidents at Kilmichael vary from other written accounts.[81] Barry said that the absence in the Deasy book of any mention of the false surrender of the Auxiliaries was questioned by 'reviewers in national daily newspapers ... without getting any answer from Deasy' regarding 'its omission ... the account of the false surrender, which brought about the extermination of the surviving terrorists, had never been challenged until Deasy's book by its omission, almost fifty-three years afterwards.'[82] Barry was angry as he felt it depicted him as 'a bloodythirsty' commander. 'I challenge Deasy and his editor, Reverend Professor Chisholm, to state publicly why they omitted from such a voluminous and presumptuous account of history the salient historical fact of the false surrender of the Auxiliaries at one of the major military victories of its kind in 1920–1921, not alone in County Cork, but in all Ireland.'[83]

There are errors and omissions in the O'Brien account of Kilmichael such as: (a) the omission of No. 3 section and the sub-section; (b) four men listed beside Barry rather than three; (c) Barry's actions are incorrect: the Mills bomb did not kill 'all' in the first lorry instantly; (d) three Volunteers did not die during the ambush, two died, one died later of wounds; (e) most important of all, this account does not mention any surrender, it just describes a fight to the finish.[84] Neither does this account 'describe an accepted surrender and a subsequent execution of all prisoners.'[85]

Unknown to Barry, Liam Deasy had been ill for some time before the publication of *Towards Ireland Free*. Barry's *Reality of the Anglo-Irish War ... Refutations and Corrections* ... was in the hands of the publishers when Deasy died on 20 August 1974.[86]

After publication of Tom Barry's booklet, some former members of the West Cork Brigade disassociated themselves from the contents of Barry's booklet. Only one of the men, Paddy O'Brien fought in Kilmichael. He was ill when he signed the form, and told me afterwards that he was not aware of what he was signing. He believed that his signature was 'to help with the book' and confirm that 'Liam Deasy was a great officer who knew all about the Third West Cork Brigade'. He was unaware that there were errors in the account of Kilmichael 'in the book', as he hadn't analysed it.[87] Paddy's son Liam said 'I grew up with the knowledge of the false surrender. From my meeting with these men, they always said that Tom made men of them.'[88] The other 11 Kilmichael survivors did not sign – not all were asked. Those who were, and knew of the omission and the controversy, refused. (As many of the signatories regretted signing, the facts of this controversy will be dealt with later – in chronological order). Liam Deasy died in August 1974, and the original letter with signatures 'in the possession' of Flor Begley was published in December 1974.[89]

(Paddy O'Brien was among the many participants in the Kilmichael ambush who mentioned the false surrender to me: ' ... Well sure, it was that false surrender, that's how our boys were killed. The Auxies paid for their tricks. Those boyos did a lot of havoc [in] ... the country.)[90] Paddy O'Brien did not see the men fall as he was in the sub-section of No. 3 section (across the road), but he did hear the surrender call, the lull and the resumption of Auxiliary firing. 'They were not far away from us.'[91]

Den Carey remembers Tom, in his latter years, after he had had a few drinks, 'he'd talk about Kilmichael and tears would fill his eyes. "It's the one thing I'll never forget till the day I die. It pierces my heart to think of the lads being shot down by an enemy," he'd say, "while they held the white flag." He'd always ask, "why didn't I warn them? I'll regret it forever. 'Twas an old trick of the British

– the false surrender!" He'd go mad over it.'[92] In an interview with Nollaig Ó Gadhra in 1969, Barry spoke of the Auxiliaries' deceptive methods of the false surrender. 'I have a vivid recollection of that … if they hadn't done the false surrender … No! I wouldn't have killed a prisoner.'[93]

(On Sunday 28 November 1982, after a ceremony in Castletown-Kenneigh graveyard where the men killed in Kilmichael are buried, a discussion, which began in Mrs Peggy O'Callaghan's kitchen and ended in Creedon's Hotel, Inchageela, centred on the Kilmichael ambush. Two survivors, Ned Young and Jack O'Sullivan could recall exactly where they were and how they felt. Because of the occasion, 'the false surrender' and its consequences for their comrades was discussed. I can recall *The Tom Barry Story* had been published. The discussion was wide-ranging and the two survivors regretted the wedge that had been driven between Tom Barry and Liam Deasy. I took no notes. Many of those present are still alive.)

Tom Barry's *Guerilla Days in Ireland* was first serialised in *The Irish Press* in 1948 and published in book form in 1949. Before this Barry wrote a full account of the Kilmichael ambush in *An Cosantóir*, 1941, and in *Rebel Cork's Fighting Story*, March 1947. Barry stated, in 1973, that the false surrender account was never challenged until its omission from *Towards Ireland Free* 'fifty-three years afterwards' caused reviewers to question the omission. Neither Deasy nor any of the men who had participated in the Kilmichael ambush made any correction on Barry's published accounts at that time.[94] Furthermore, in November 1969 a television programme *Seven Days* invited veterans from the Kilmichael and Crossbarry ambushes to the studio. The false surrender aspect was not refuted by any of the men. When asked if he had any regrets Ned Young replied, 'No. None!' Jack Hennessy said, 'all we wanted to do was to get rid of the enemy in our midst'. Nudge Callanan who signed the statement (was not at Kilmichael but at Crossbarry) told Brian Farrell of the need to tackle the Auxiliaries as 'they were terrorising the country'. In answer to the presenter's question to the group if any of them had regrets, there was a chorus: 'None. No. No. None.' Barry said, 'People who weren't born then will never appreciate the spirit of those who fought.'[95]

In a side issue to the Kilmichael ambush, Barry queried Liam Deasy's kind words about Lieut Col Crake (Craik) commander of the Auxiliary garrison who was killed that day at Kilmichael. In *Towards Ireland Free* there is an account that Deasy was held up twice previously by Crake and allowed to go free.[96] Barry asks: 'I wonder how Deasy got to know his name, and if he is sure it was Crake who was present, as the men in charge of such raiding parties never introduced themselves. Deasy states that when ever he thinks of Kilmichael he thinks of four men, the three IRA freedom fighters who died and Crake … because of "the soldierly humanity which he showed" 'to Deasy when arrested.[97] When I questioned Rev. Fr Chisholm on this, he said that it was only natural that Deasy would also think kindly of this man who did not arrest him.[98] However, Deasy was unarmed and gave a false name, purporting to be a private citizen without military connections.[99] Major Percival found that 'hostile leaders were seldom known by sight and often gave false names. A number of them thus slipped through our hands after being actually captured.'[100]

Flor Crowley remembers a very different Craik (Crake), who came to his home some days before the Kilmichael ambush and questioned his father on the whereabouts of a Danny Crowley who had participated in the Mountpleasant ambush in February 1920. The Danny he was seeking was not Flor's brother, but a neighbour. In a raid on houses, by Craik and his men, one morning other lads escaped but Danny 'was cut to pieces by close range bullets ... a savagely mutilated corpse, with almost twenty-five bullet wounds. I know because I saw the corpse with part of its jaw shot away', he wrote. 'The two men who laid him out described in gruesome detail what his broken body looked like.'[101]

When the ambush was over Barry thought all the Auxiliaries were dead, but some of his men informed him one man had escaped. According to the British casualties list at Kilmichael, Cadet C. J. Guthrie, late Royal Air Force, 'is missing' and Cadet H. F. Forde, MC, late Royal Air Force, 'is wounded'.[102]

Guthrie, driver of the second lorry, slipped over the ditch, off through the fields in the direction of Macroom barracks. When he reached the River Lee at Dromcarra he couldn't cross and was forced to take to the road. He went to Stephen Twohig's house and asked to be taken in his pony and trap to Macroom. Twohig refused. Two Volunteers in the house at the time recognised the uniform so they followed him. 'Realising the danger of letting him into town with the certainty of immediate reprisals on the surrounding country ... they held him up by using a pipe disguised as a gun, and shot him with his own weapon.' This was not the only reason why they shot him and buried him in Anahala bog. From intelligence reports it was known that Guthrie had killed Jim Lehane, 'an innocent civilian' and boasted of the deed some days before. He gave them his name, not realising they knew what he had done.[103] On 26 November 1926, Guthrie's body was removed to Inchageela old graveyard – a tombstone now marks the spot.[104]

When the doctor went out, the following day, to Kilmichael he found Lieut H. F. Forde's pulse still beating. He was removed to Shanakiel Hospital, Cork, and contrary to all opinions, lived for many years afterwards. A bullet scraped his brain and he was partially paralysed and had a bad limp throughout his life. 'Forde was awarded £10,000 compensation'.[105]

According to Bill Munroe, 'after "the first shock" of the ambush "had passed" the Macroom Castle Auxiliaries' 'immediate reaction was to hunt down as many of the ambushers as we could and exterminate them'. But their commander Col Buxton Smyth 'counselled patience'. Getting 'participants' was 'a difficult task as potential informers were much too scared to come forward and the raids carried out were based on previous information.' This regiment was recalled to Dublin and replaced by another company.[106]

Col Buxton Smyth hadn't ordered his men to take grenades in the tenders that day. Afterwards he regretted it. He was unhappy at his men's lawlessness in burning so many houses. Furthermore, knowing that men under his command broke a military rule by falsifying their surrender call they brought ignominy on him; he was recalled to England, so like Brigadier Crozier, he resigned his position. A year later he was found in a toilet, shot through the head by his own bullet. He died 'on Wandsworth Common, having been let down by the government and having become destitute'.[107]

KILMICHAEL – THE FALSE SURRENDER QUESTION

During the Kilmichael Ambush, was there a false surrender or not?

Peter Hart published a book in 1998, *The IRA & Its Enemies,* and concluded that, 'British information seems to have been remarkably accurate. Barry's "history" of Kilmichael, on the other hand, is riddled with lies and evasions. There was no false surrender as he described it. The surviving Auxiliaries were simply "exterminated".'[1] Peter Hart, as part of his evidence, uses a 'Rebel Commandant's report' from Sir Peter Strickland's papers. This report purports to have been written by Tom Barry after the ambush. It is contained in typescript with other typed documents and also in booklet form compiled by 'General Staff of the 6th Divisional Area'. There is no mention of a false surrender in this report.[2] Peter Hart further cites the omission of the false surrender in an article by Tom Barry in the *Irish Press,* 26 November 1932, as being 'a direct contradiction, in substance and tone, of what he wrote in 1949'.[3] In a television documentary Hart draws attention to the non-mention of a false surrender and questions Barry's 'lies and evasions'.[4]

In Barry's later writings and broadcasts he did not fail to mention the false surrender and stressed that the order to kill the enemy, for their deceptive tactics in this military engagement, was his and his alone. He never evaded responsibility for the final actions of the ambush.[5]

He told Kenneth Griffith that 'having seen the false surrender I told the men to keep firing and we did until the last of them was dead. I blame myself of course for our own losses, because I should have seen through the false surrender trick. It is as old as war itself. It was in the Boer War in South Africa'.[6] In an RTÉ/TV interview in 1966 at the Kilmichael ambush site Barry gave details of the ambush. Having spoken of the false surrender and his order to continue firing, he said, 'I want here and now publicly to take full responsibility that we wouldn't take prisoners after their false surrender and after killing two of our men'.[7] Furthermore, in a lecture to history students in University College, Galway, he outlined the ambushes, describing his own position as 'The Commander'. He mentioned the false surrender, and said that three of the men stood up. 'They were green and weren't properly advised by their commander'.[8]

But, if there was no false surrender, 'if there was no trick, the Auxiliaries were gunned down "for no reason",' and Barry's account is 'riddled with lies and evasions', then according to Kevin Myers in an *Irish Times* piece on Peter Hart's book, 'Tom Barry systematically slaughtered disarmed RIC Auxiliaries after they had surrendered. Barry's story that they had resumed firing under a false flag of surrender is a fiction concocted by Barry himself.'[9]

On 2 December 1920, *The Times* published 'an official report' issued by 'a senior officer of police in the Cork neighbourhood':

District Inspector Crake took out a patrol ... in search of a man ... When dusk was falling about 5 p.m. ... It is surmised from an examination of the site and from inquiries that the attackers, who were all clad in khaki and trench coats, and wore steel helmets, had drawn their motor lorry across the road and were mistaken by the first car of cadets for military ... Something had aroused the suspicion of the cadets who had got out of the first car. Shooting began and three were killed instantaneously ... The cadets in the second car ran along the road to the help of their comrades. Then from a depression in the hillside behind the second car came a devastating fire at close range. The cadets were shot down by concealed men from the stone walls, and all around a direct fire from the ambushers' lorry also swept down the road. After firing had continued for some time, and many men were wounded, overwhelming forces of the ambushers came out and forcibly disarmed the survivors.

There followed a brutal massacre, the policy of the murder gang ... The dead and wounded were hacked about the head with axes, shot guns were fired into their bodies, and they were savagely mutilated. The one survivor, who was wounded, was hit about the head and left for dead ... The ambushing party departed in lorries ... Cadet C. J. Guthrie ... is missing.'[10]

The foregoing 'official report' written just after the ambush differs from an official typewritten report later compiled by the general staff of the 6th Division under General Sir Peter Strickland. The typewritten report states:

As the Auxiliaries approached, they were confronted by a man in British soldier's uniform, and wearing a steel helmet. He stated he was a soldier that his lorry had broken down ... the alleged troops, many of whom were dressed as British soldiers and wore steel helmets. A fierce fire was at once opened on them [Auxiliaries] ... the overwhelming forces of the assassins came out of hiding and disarmed the survivors, and the most brutal massacre of the whole rebellion followed ... they were indiscriminately hacked with axes and bayonets.[11]

In the initial report the lorry 'drawn' across the road brought the patrol to a halt. In the second, 'the soldier' spoke to them because he was in trouble. But, in neither of the military reports is there a mention of a surrender. Nor is there a mention of it in the report by British propagandist, Major C. J. C. Street (intelligence officer).[12] In each case it is an outright fight until all are dead, or appeared dead!

It is difficult to agree with Peter Hart that much of the British 'information' has been 'remarkably accurate'.[13] He says, 'some of them [Volunteers] were wearing steel helmets.'[14] I have failed to find any reliable evidence to support the British reports. They did not have any lorry transport to barricade the road, to carry axes or to depart. Nor is there any other evidence that the Auxiliaries 'unsuspecting' got 'out' of their own transport to 'approach the motor lorry'.[15] Barry, having thrown a Mills bomb, made sure they would stop.

When the second lorry came round the bend into No. 2 section's firing range, the driver halted, jumped out and escaped. No. 2 section opened fire.

They were stretched behind rocks, close above their targets.[16]

Peter Hart stated that 'Jim O'Sullivan and Michael McCarthy, were hit in the head and killed where they lay.' In a footnote he wrote: 'All of the men interviewed agree on this point: McCarthy and O'Sullivan did not stand up and did not die because of a fake surrender. Two of these veterans considered Barry's account to be an insult to the memory of these men.'[17]

Dan Hourihane, who was beside Jim O'Sullivan told me, 'I'll never forget it – same as 'twas only yesterday. After they shouted that surrender, it was silence! Jim lifted himself. Thought it was over. God rest his soul!' He paused for a silent memory. (Dan was captured afterwards while 'on the run'. He was imprisoned in Spike Island, and was severely beaten several times. His fingernails and toenails were pulled out, part of the index finger of his left hand was snapped off.)[18]

Michael McCarthy was beside Jack Hennessy. Hennessy claimed he 'almost' got up around the same time as McCarthy when 'the Auxies shouted'. He thought 'it was all over' but ducked, and was wounded in the scalp. Hennessy and Hourihane went over this many times, and often wondered if there was something they could have done. 'McCarthy had got a bullet through the head and lay dead. I continued to load and fire, but the blood dripped from my forehead and blocked the breach of my rifle. I dropped the rifle and took up McCarthy's.'[19]

Peter Hart gives an account of an interview conducted with AF, a scout:

One I.R.A. man came upon a wounded Auxiliary 'crying after me', and told Barry. He said, 'finish him', placed his revolver to the man's head and pulled the trigger [footnote inserted here]. 'Barry made us', said another. 'He shot one, then we shot one.' Eventually each man was shot in the head. Some of the Volunteers apparently refused to take part and several 'were getting hysterical' from the shock of so much death on both sides.

In a footnote he wrote that the 'quotations are from the interview with AF'. A previous footnote states:

One witness (AF – a scout [19 November, 1989] rather than a rifleman, and therefore further away from the ambush site than the other interviewees) saw several Auxiliaries surrender *after* the three Volunteers were hit, but then heard further firing, some of which he believed came from the Englishmen. Because of this, he says there was a sort of false surrender, but that no I.R.A. men died as a result.[20]

Scouts were not 'small fry' as described by Peter Hart.[21] A scout's job during an ambush was onerous – mainly to alert the men to the arrival of any enemy help. Tom O'Neill (referring to scouts in another context) wrote, 'it was often even harder and more dangerous for them than the men who had to go into action.' Barry wrote that 'no one worried if he fought as a rifle-man, a section commander, or in any other rank during an action with the enemy … to them nothing mattered but the pursuit of the movement for freedom.'[22] The three

51

scouts and two dispatch scouts *[unarmed]* at Kilmichael were too far away from the ambuscade to know if, or when, a Volunteer stood up, was injured or killed during the ambush. One scout at the north-eastern side was over a quarter of a mile away, signalling to the second scout. The third scout was west of the command post – at the other side of the ambuscade. Furthermore, the scouts had to remain in their positions until the ambush was over – until the 'cease-fire'. Dispatch scouts moved from the ambuscade once action began. Peter Hart mentions 'ten scouts' at Kilmichael. Just three scouts were on ambush location. After-ambush helpers assisted with the wounded and the dead, but did not participate in the ambush and were not engaged in scouting duty or any other related tasks during the ambush.[23]

Furthermore, according to autobiographical details all the scouts and after-ambush helpers, who were in Kilmichael that day, were dead by the late 1970s. All rifle-men at Kilmichael were dead by 19 November 1989.[24]

Peter Hart wrote that 'interviewees were extremely nervous about discussing Kilmichael in detail.' Therefore, he wrote, 'Names have been withheld to protect confidentiality'.[25] Arising out of interviews, he states that: 'As a large number of these interviewees requested that part or all of their testimony be quoted anonymously, I refer to them using initials only. The republican activists' initials begin with "A"' (i.e., AA, 3 April & 25 June 1988; AB, 2 April 1988; AC, 6 April 1990; AD, 2 April 1988 & 28 April 1989; AE, 28 April 1989 & 19 Nov. 1989; AF a scout, 19 November 1989).[26]

In a radio programme when queried on the names of interviewees, Peter Hart responded: 'Actually, I'd prefer not to say because I did it under condition of anonymity and certainly the two men I talked to who were there were rather concerned and actually their children were rather concerned about what they were saying.'[27] Furthermore, Peter Hart has written: 'I was also fortunate enough to be given a tour of the ambush site by one of my interviewees.'[28]

If, including scouts and helpers, records show the last Kilmichael ambush survivor Ned Young (whose faculties were impaired during his final years) died on 13 November 1989 aged ninety-seven; the second last, Jack O'Sullivan in 1986; Tim O'Connell 1983, Patrick (Pat) O'Donovan 1981 (all rifle-men) then who are these people who could not stand over their names and the information that they gave regarding the Kilmichael ambush when Peter Hart interviewed them in 1988, 1989? Who were, 'all of the men interviewed [who] agree on this point: McCarthy and O'Sullivan did not stand up and did not die because of a fake surrender'? Who were the, 'Two of these veterans' who 'considered Barry's account to be an insult to the memory of these men' who were killed?[29]

Scouts were John Kelly (d. 1959), Tim O'Sullivan (d. 1965), Dan O'Driscoll (d. 1967) and dispatch scouts Neilus Cotter (d. 1952) and Seán Falvey (d. 1971).[30]

(For my research, I consulted the published (1938) list plus previous and subsequent records of those involved in the Kilmichael ambush. But, Peter Hart wrote that he interviewed two people – 'AA, 3 Apr., 25 June 1988; AF, 19 Nov. 1989'. Perhaps if Peter Hart revealed their names, the credibility of these two witnesses who claim to give a first-hand account could be examined. Their version of events to Peter Hart contradicts so many others, and while they remain anonymous, the story of the Kilmichael ambush will remain clouded in controversy.)

Who was Scout AF who gave Peter Hart, on 19 November 1989, the graphic account of Tom Barry placing the revolver to the 'crying' man's head to 'finish him' then 'pulled the trigger' and of Barry's 'procedure' after 'the surrendered Englishmen had been executed'?[31]

Jack Lane wrote: 'Apart from anything else the very idea of a participant in the Kilmichael ambush wanting to remain anonymous nearly 70 years after the event beggars belief.'[32]

(Participants of that period were willing to discuss the awfulness of the ambush and to stand over anything they said when I interviewed them in the 1970s and early 1980s. In fact all interviewees were proud to have taken such an active part in the fight for freedom and considered Kilmichael ambush a landmark. Many of the survivors attended an annual reunion at the anniversary commemoration.)[33]

The interviews conducted by Fr Chisholm in the late 1960s with Kilmichael ambush participants give horrific accounts of the ambush.[34] None of the participants publicly contradicted Tom Barry's, Stephen O'Neill's or other published accounts that recorded the false surrender story by saying 'there was no false surrender'.

(I grew up in the area and I listened to people get very angry that 'The Auxies' picked up their guns after their surrender cries. My uncle, Pat O'Donovan, was in No. 2 section, where the three Volunteers who were fatally shot were positioned. He, like others interviewed, said that he heard 'the surrender' call.)

Jim O'Sullivan's nieces, Joan and Margaret, grew up with the story from participants that 'he heard the surrender' got up and was fatally wounded. 'We never heard anything, ever, only that they were tricked by the false surrender,' Joan recalls. (In 1956, Jim's brother, Con, while on a visit home from Chicago, put the iron cross at the No. 2 section spot.)[35]

Louis Whyte who has been involved in the Kilmichael commemoration committee said, 'we listened to the men over the years as they talked about Kilmichael and they always talked about the false surrender. In fact some of them blamed themselves because those other lads were killed … they talked after funerals, at functions, gatherings, after Mass. We listened to them in groups, when they were off their guard as it were, and they never talked down the false surrender. It was a fact. I stand over that.'[36]

Dómhnall MacGiolla Phoil who was involved with Tom Barry and other survivors in the formation of the Kilmichael commemoration committee 'never, never heard any of them disputing the fact that there was a false surrender. All over the years, since I knew these men in the early 1960s, it was in their story of the Kilmichael ambush. There was no need to doubt them. In fact I grew up knowing it.'[37]

Seán Kelleher, also involved with Barry and participants in organising the Kilmichael commemoration events over the years, was adamant 'that those lads were wronged by that deceitful false surrender. We went over this so many times!'[38]

Pádraig Long as 'a schoolboy in December 1920s recalled the teacher who described 'the incident' of the 'Auxies' who 'threw down their rifles' shouted 'we surrender' and the subsequent Volunteers' acceptance – and the resumption of 'firing'. Twelve-year-old-Johanna Hallahan can vividly recall the local anger at the deception of the Auxies with their false surrender tactics.[39]

There is no doubt but the Kilmichael ambush was, as Barry said, 'a vicious battle, a bloody battle ... it was probably the bloodiest fight in Ireland.' He accepted full responsibility for his order to resume the fight after the surrender was falsified.[40] Standing on the Kilmichael site in the 1960s for a television programme he said, 'It was a bloody fight. It was a bitter fight. It was a savage fight.'[41] For as long as they lived, those who fought in the Kilmichael ambush, while left with a vivid memory, could and did recall its awfulness. Faced with imminent death in such a horrific fashion 'all senses are in a pretty sharp state' and 'memory is likely to be least faulty' due to such an indelible print created by the circumstances.[42] Because of the death of comrades, Barry's lifetime regret of not having warned his men of 'the false surrender' trick was mitigated slightly in the knowledge that because of their lack of fighting experience he had placed them in the best military positions. 'There are no good or bad shots at ten yards range!' he wrote.[43]

In 1938 when the *Irish Press* photographer asked Tom Barry to assemble the survivors of Kilmichael, many came who had not participated in that ambush. 'Barry wasn't long putting the run on them'.[44]

In a television interview, 1969, Barry sat in the studio with the survivors of the Kilmichael ambush and other men of the flying column. Speaking of 'the bloodiest fight in Ireland' he said, 'I for one would have been satisfied to lose 10 men ... These men [the Volunteers] did not relish close fighting. It was hardly a fair battle to put men who had no real experience in battle against men who were commissioned ... It was a test of endurance. In guerrilla warfare the element of surprise and mobility are all important.'[45]

'The fight was planned and carried out on the basis that the IRA would be well satisfied to lose man for man in smashing the Auxiliaries, for the nation's morale could not for long be maintained were its citizens to be killed off without an armed challenge', Barry wrote in 1941.[46]

Speaking on a television interview from the ambush site at Kilmichael in the 1960s he was emphatic about the false surrender and his responsibility for the subsequent action of the column.[47] 'I blame myself for our losses, because I should have seen through the false surrender trick', he told Kenneth Griffith.[48]

In an RTÉ Radio interview with Nollaig Ó Gadhra, in 1969 about various aspects of his life, he talked about Kilmichael and when the interviewer was moving on to something else Barry drew him back: 'Only for the false surrender, I would never forgive them for that!'[49]

Dave O'Sullivan in a home video off-the-cuff discussion on Kilmichael asked, 'were you ruthless?'

'I wasn't ruthless then. They killed two of my men with a false surrender and we wiped them out then. Afterwards we knew what to expect'.[50]

In December 1974, responding to the implication that men were attacked when dead, Barry called it a 'despicable suggestion that I attacked a dead man'.[51]

The RTÉ drama department intended making a film on the Kilmichael ambush, so in 1979 Mr Haines 'travelled' the Kilmichael ambush area with Tom Barry. Though Barry was favourable to the presentation he had great reservations and sent a hand-written letter to Dan Nolan, his publisher at Anvil Press:

> You will recollect the British propaganda machine announced to the world that we had not alone massacred Cadets but we had mutilated their dead bodies with axes and hatchets. This dam (sic) lie was even partially contradicted by their own communiqué when they had to give the names of their dead Cadets with their ranks from Captains to Lieutenant-Colonel and their World War 1 decorations. They were of course, killed as I wrote in *Guerilla Days,* after killing two I.R.A. men after a false surrender.
>
> Now on reading the Mr Haines script I was shocked to read that the script supports the British accusation of mutilation after death except that instead of using hatchets and axes the I.R.A. used bayonets to mutilate the corpses. This is as false as the British accusation. Also the statement that the men of No. 2 section had to be physically restrained by me is is (sic) entirely contrary to fact as when I reached them they were stunned and shocked as men behind that rock were dead. Indeed it was because of the stunned condition of this that the Column was drilled on the road.
>
> Again, there were only two bayonets in the whole Column and they were held by Nyhan and Herlihy both of which were close to me at the Command post and on the road throughout the whole action.
>
> Now Dan, there are many more incorrect statements, but I am not prepared to discuss a single one of them until this part is rectified. It is untrue and a libel on my dead comrades.
>
> Finally I am aware that this presentation is an R.T.E. drama and a certain amount of licence is unavoidable, but most certainly not this.[52]

The drama never came to fruition.

From the British perspective there are three 'official' reports – each different in parts.[53]

Peter Hart suggests that there was no false surrender based to some extent on an 'after action report' in the Strickland Papers that allegedly Tom Barry 'The Rebel Commandant' wrote and that was captured later.[54] Peter Hart chooses the absence of the mention of a false surrender in this report to say that there was no false surrender, yet he accepts that there was *a surrender*, despite this omission also in the report.[55]

On the Sunday night (past midnight/early morning) Charlie Hurley, brigade commandant, heard of the day's events from Tom Barry as they talked into the night.[56] It was Tuesday when Charlie Hurley got to brigade headquarters and told Liam Deasy all that had happened at Kilmichael – including the news of his brother's death (Pat) and that of two more Volunteers.[57]

Following the ambush, word soon circulated in the area that the Auxiliaries had participated in a false surrender. Imperial activist and writer, Lionel Curtis in early 1921 wrote:

> Last autumn a party of police was ambushed at Kilmichael, near Cork. Every member of the party but one was killed, and the bodies were shamefully mutilated. It is alleged by Sinn Féin that a white flag was put up by the police, and that when the attacking party approached to accept the surrender, fire was opened upon them.

Curtis wasn't sure of 'the truth' of this 'notorious episode' but said it 'was obtained from a trustworthy source in the district.' He was critical of 'the absence of strict discipline' in the Auxiliary force and stated that after the 'next provocation' came the burning of Cork – 'started by men in the crown forces'.[58]

Piaras Béaslaí wrote in 1926: 'what really happened on the occasion was that after the fight had continued for some time, some of the Auxiliaries offered to surrender. When Volunteers advanced to take the surrender they were fired on.' Béaslaí notes that among the party of Auxiliaries 'of whom one, left for dead ... survived to tell the tale ... the tale the survivor told was full of falsehoods and gross misrepresentations. For instance, he asserted that all of the Auxiliaries took them for a party of English soldiers – a ridiculous fable – and he [Forde] absurdly exaggerated the numbers of the attackers.'

Ernie O'Malley, a recorder of events of the time, wrote that 'the cadets' had 'killed some of the men who went out to take their surrender, and the column men wiped out the rest of them'.[59]

In the British record, the 'Rebel Commandant's report on the affair' is undated and typed with quotation marks into an official record. Furthermore, it was typed after the Truce because the military's own follow-up report, in the same document, mentions Barry as being 'afterwards appointed Liaison Officer'. Basic elements point to a forgery. Most of the sentences contain elements that are at variance with written versions and also with that of participants' information.[60]

Here is what they call 'the Rebel Commandant's report on the affair':

> The column paraded at 3.15 a.m. on Sunday morning. It comprised 32 men armed with rifles, bayonets, five revolvers, and 100 rounds of ammunition per man. We marched for four hours, and reached a position on the Macroom-Dunmanway road in the townland of Shanacashel. We camped in that position until 4.15 p.m., and then decided that as the enemy searches were completed, that it would be safe to return to our camp. Accordingly, we started the return journey. About five min-

utes after the start we sighted two enemy lorries moving along the Macroom-Dunmanway road at a distance of about 1,900 yards from us. The country in that particular district is of a hilly and rocky nature, and, although suitable to fighting, it is not at all suitable to retiring without being seen. I decided to attack the lorries. The action was carried out in the following manner:

I divided the column into three sections, viz: one to attack the first lorry. This section was in a position to have ample cover, and at the same time to bring a frontal and flank fire to bear on the enemy. The second section was in a position about 120 yards from the first section, and at the same side of the road. Its duty was to let the first lorry pass to No. 1 section and to attack the second lorry. The third section was occupying sniping positions along the other side of the road, and also guarding both flanks. The action was carried out successfully. Sixteen of the enemy who were belonging to the Auxiliary Police from Macroom Castle being killed, one wounded and escaped, and is now missing.

The captures were as follows … [it lists them] and two lorries, which were subsequently burnt.

Our casualties were:

One killed, and two who have subsequently died of wounds.

O.C. Flying Column,

3rd Cork Brigade.

P.S.: I attribute our casualties to the fact that those three men (who were part of No. 2 Section) were too anxious to get into close quarters with the enemy. They were our best men, and did not know danger in this or any previous actions. They discarded their cover, and it was not until the finish of the action that P. Deasy was killed by a revolver bullet from one of the enemy whom he thought dead.

Typed after this report is: 'The true facts are as follows …' then the official version is given (see above p. 50).[61]

Peter Hart in his book states: 'That this is an authentic captured document seems unquestionable.' In correspondence to the *Irish Times* in 1998 a number of people sought to tease out the contents of 'the Rebel Commandant's report', whether it was authentic and whether or not there was a false surrender at Kilmichael.[62]

Dr Brian Murphy put the alleged report into a time frame. After the ambush (28 November 1920) Barry with the column was at the camp at Granure, south of Kilmichael when Charlie Hurley got 'a verbal report' from Barry in the early morning hours. The next few days found the column trying to evade the enemy. Barry was in hospital from 3 to 28 December 1920. 'In this context questions arise as to the need to make a report, and the opportunity to do so … One cannot but feel that far more evidence is required before Barry's account [in his articles, book and broadcasts] may be dismissed as "lies and evasions".'[63]

(In a lecture to UCG history students when mentioning the late arrival to the ambush site of the horse and side car, Tom Barry said, 'there was a mistake in transmission. No orders or anything else were written at that time – in our brigade anyway.')[64]

'IRA column men were well aware of the dangers of correspondence being captured: Tom Barry and Seán Moylan had a deep contempt for what they regarded as "pen pushers" in the command structure. Their emphasis was on action, not paperwork and with that went the conviction that they were fighting the war where it mattered.'[65]

If Tom Barry wrote this report for his superiors, he would surely have the number of men under his command correct. The first sentence in this report has the time of arrival at the ambush site incorrect (important to Barry, always a stickler for time); the second sentence has '32 men' instead of the correct 36 men. That sentence also mentions '100 rounds of ammunition per man'. With that amount Barry could have stormed Macroom Castle! In the early 1970s speaking to an audience in Cork he said, 'We had only 30 to 36 rounds per man throughout the period, and this would last only one to one and half hours no matter how you would conserve it.'[66]

They travelled for five and a quarter hours not 'four hours' as given in the third sentence.

The report (allegedly Barry's) states that the column 'camped in that position until 4.15 p.m.' and 'we started the return journey. About five minutes after the start we sighted two enemy lorries ... I decided to attack the lorries ... I divided the column into three sections ...' (a) The facts are that the column remained in position. If the column had moved off, how could any commander get his men into the sections and a sub-section and be so well positioned to instantly take on the enemy? Why would Barry write that he had moved off when he hadn't, as in doing so, he would have been condemning himself by engaging the enemy from an unprepared position? Why suggest that 'the ambush was an accident' so that he 'could stay in charge', as Peter Hart has stated.[67] If Barry meant to impress fellow officers, then from a guerrilla tactical viewpoint of preparedness, they would be foolish to leave him in charge. Furthermore, he couldn't have pretended that the ambush was fought in any way other than as it happened, because on the morning after the ambush, Charlie Hurley, brigade OC spoke to the men 'with praise of the military spirit in which the whole operation was carried out ... He went round to each individual member of the column, and in his own humble, quiet way encouraged him, thanked him for the honour he had brought to the brigade.'[68]

Moreover, all other accounts of the ambush throughout the years, regardless of the teller, state that the men were in *situ* and followed Barry's action orders. Despite this, Peter Hart in a letter to the *Irish Times* has endeavoured to justify why Barry 'would lie about whether or not the ambush was planned ... I believe Barry's omission and lies form a coherent pattern in that they eliminate the controversial aspects of the event. He didn't have authority to launch a risky ambush outside brigade boundaries, and he hadn't told his superiors, so he claimed it was an accident.'[69] However, Liam Deasy and Charlie Hurley had visited the training camp. According to Liam Deasy, they were aware that 'Tom Barry's scheme to ambush the Auxiliaries who were making incursions into our Brigade area from Macroom had been maturing.'[70] Though Cork No. 1 Brigade was planning 'a big scheme' attack on the Macroom Auxiliaries, they were 'happy' with Barry's coup.[71]

(b) There is no mention in the 'Rebel Commandant's report' of the subsection nor the manned command post, each an important device by Barry. Why would Barry omit this important tactic, which was far more important than describing the terrain?

(c) The ambush lasted approximately twenty minutes. This alleged report has the ambush starting around the time the engagement was over. Barry would have got the time correct. ('One of Barry's mannerisms was that he constantly kept his eye on the time'.)[72]

Some of the terminology in this report (allegedly Barry's) has all the aspects of one written from the Auxiliary barrack viewpoint:

(a) 'We camped in that position.' They didn't camp. They got into ambush positions, which is what Barry would have said.

(b) ' ... and then decided that as the enemy searches were completed.' Barry would have used the words 'raids' or 'rampages.' The barrack would have used 'searches'. In one British report they were going 'in search of a wanted man'. Barry was aware from previous experience that there was no completion to their 'raids'. He later told Nollaig Ó Gadhra, 'about 4 o'clock I had my mind made up they weren't coming, and I decided I would give them another ten minutes. Surely at five past four they sailed into us!'[73]

(c) 'One wounded and escaped and is now missing.' Barry's men told him that one escaped, how did he know whether or not he was 'now missing'? In Macroom Castle they knew he was 'now missing'! In their official report they listed Cadet Guthrie as 'missing'.

(d) 'Sixteen of the enemy ... being killed', this report states. If Barry counted properly there were seventeen on the road – all, he believed, dead. In the British report which follows Barry's alleged report (in this typewritten document) it states that 'of the party of eighteen, sixteen were found lying dead on the spot one had disappeared' and 'one left for dead'.[74] The first official report has sixteen dead, 'one wounded', and 'one missing'. Two subsequent official reports contain 'sixteen members of the Macroom Auxiliary Police ... only one of the sixteen escaped ... missing.'[75]

(e) In a short report on an ambush, would Barry write, 'the action was carried out successfully' against 'the Auxiliary Police from Macroom Castle' (giving them their full title)?

(f) This report lists 'the captures'. There is a discrepancy between this list and what Barry in later years wrote that they captured. The obvious explanation being that the Castle Auxiliaries knew what went out in the tenders and did not return – hence accuracy from their viewpoint when compiling the 'Commandant's report'. However, the Mills bomb thrown by Barry must have destroyed some arms and ammunition, also Barry and command post men, used captured ammunition in the conclusion of the fight, as he has stated. Furthermore, listed among 'the captures' on the 'Rebel Commandant's report' are 'two lorries, which were subsequently burnt.' It is unlikely that Barry would list the lorries as 'captures' when, elsewhere he has stated, 'we burned the lorries', rather than 'were subsequently burnt'. Moreover, the Castle Auxiliaries saw fit not to mention the loss of important documentation. In all the records of the Kilmichael 'captures' Barry mentions 'most important of all' was the sandbag full of Auxies' papers and notebooks' among the 'captured' items. '

(g) The last sentence of this report says: 'our casualties were: One killed, and two who have subsequently died of wounds.' It was the other way round. Two were killed and one died of wounds. This, and the P.S. are the most telling sentences in the report and it demonstrates that Tom Barry was not the author.

(h) The 'Rebel Commandant's' P. S. blames the 'casualties to the fact that these three men (who were part of No. 2 section) were too anxious to get into close quarters with the enemy … they discarded their cover, and … P. Deasy was killed [*note the word 'killed'*] by a revolver bullet from one of the enemy whom he thought dead.' This conveys the impression that Deasy got 'into close quarters' on the road. None of No. 2 section went on the road during the ambush. These men did not move closer to the enemy, they remained in their positions, but the few stood up during the 'surrender' call when firing ceased.[76]

(i) If Barry wrote that report for Liam Deasy and Charlie Hurley would he say 'They were our best men …' Barry would have to command the remaining men in the continuing conflict. But most important, would he single out P. Deasy (he has called him Pat Deasy elsewhere) and say he was killed in the ambush when he wasn't? Barry knew he was gravely injured. Would Barry not mention the names of the two men (section commander – Michael McCarthy and Jim O'Sullivan), who were killed outright and to whom he had asked the column to 'present arms'? Why would he deliberately write that these were the 'two who have subsequently died of wounds'? Pat Deasy fatally wounded, died around 10 p.m. in Buttimer's, some distance away. Seán Falvey, a dispatch scout, took the news to Barry in Granure that night. (Note: the official British report also mentions P. Deasy not Pat Deasy.)

Of particular note is the omission from the report of Barry standing on the road to confront the lorries. Barry was unlikely to forget it, so if he wrote this report he would surely have mentioned the daring ploy that marked the opening of the attack.

Peter Hart states that this 'authentic captured document seems unquestionable', because it 'contains details such as the division of the column into three sections and their deployment, the length of the march to Kilmichael, the time the ambush took place, and the fact that two of the three IRA casualties died of wounds.'[77]

Yet, as has been analysed, the sub-sections, the opening time, and in particular the incorrect statement on deaths, in the 'Commandant's report' contrast greatly from the available evidence. Therefore, a definite question mark must be placed over the authenticity of the document.[78]

It is significant that this 'Rebel Commandant's report' does not tally with the British official version which has a 'telling' sentence. The official British report describes the hacking of bodies with axes and brutal massacre, then states: 'The Commandant of the Brigade Flying Column omitted all mention of these incidents from his report.' Logic dictates he would omit it in a report for his superiors. If, as seems likely, they forged the 'Rebel Commandant's report', then the omission of the savagery from it adds credibility to the document. Furthermore, it aids their official version. Significant also is the statement in the alleged Barry's Report that the column had 'started their return journey' when they 'sighted two enemy lorries', then 'divided the column into three sections' and attacked the enemy.

Caught unawares, they came at the patrol with what they describe in their own propaganda introduction as the 'cold-blooded brutality' of a 'Murder Gang' without discipline. Moreover, one official military report of the event states: 'This atrocity emphasised the lawless state of Co. Cork and the surrounding counties, and the inadequacy of the existing powers to deal with the situation there.'[79]

'It was as a bloodthirsty commander that the British propagandists depicted me in the aftermath of Kilmichael,' Tom Barry wrote, 'and it was as monsters that my men of the Column and I, who had fought at Kilmichael, were presented. The British, of course, did not make the slightest reference to the false surrender of the Auxiliaries.'[80]

The British cabinet accepted the ambush as 'a military operation'. Lloyd George sent over Sir Hamar Greenwood, chief secretary for Ireland. It 'seemed to him', to Bonar Law and to Tom Jones that this ambush was 'of a different character from the preceding operations. The others were assassinations. This last was a military operation,' Tom Jones records, 'and there was a good deal to be said for declaring a state of siege or promulgating martial law in that corner of Ireland.'[81]

Of significant importance is the testimony of Brigadier General Crozier, commander of the Auxiliaries from 1919 to 1920. He came to Ireland (having resigned) 'as a civilian, at the request of Sir Hamar Greenwood to give evidence' on the Kilmichael ambush. In his 'Unpublished Memoirs' he wrote, 'I took particular care to enquire into this story of mutilation, as it appeared to me to be quite unlike the normal or abnormal act of Irishmen. The correct story I found to be as follows: The lorries were held up by land mines and the leading lorry was partly destroyed. The men were called upon to surrender and did so throwing up their hands and grounding their rifles. Each policeman carried a revolver in addition to a rifle. One policeman shot a Sinn Féiner at close quarters with his revolver after he had grounded his rifle and put his hands up. A hand-to-hand combat of the fiercest kind ensued, the butts of rifles, revolvers, crowbars being used, hence the battered condition of the police. When it is intended to kill a man with a butt-end there is no hitting him in the legs.'[82] This account clarifies that the 'false surrender' story was in circulation in the area shortly after the ambush, and was not fabricated by Tom Barry or anybody else later.

Crozier said that 'the Auxiliary police were soldiers in disguise under no army and no R.I.C. code.' His endorsement is weighty. He resigned from his position 'because the combat was being carried out on foul lines, by selected and foul men, for a grossly foul purpose, based on the most satanic of all rules that "the end justifies the means".'[83]

Out of the Kilmichael ambush was there an end to be justified, was a forged report a means to do so? Who wrote the 'Rebel Commandant's report' that Peter Hart describes as Barry's 'after-action report' and why the need?[84]

Barry wrote in his memoirs:

> The foulest of all British weapons has ever been 'atrocity' propaganda. No axe was in possession of the I.R.A. and no corpse was interfered with. This mutilation allegation was a vicious and calumnious lie. Well may one ask where Lord French got his information ... To clinch this exposure of lying British propaganda, it is as well to state here that after the Truce with the British in July 1921, Sir Alfred Cope, then Assistant British Under-Secretary for Ireland, called on me in Cork for a written statement that the I.R.A. had killed the Auxiliaries in Kilmichael, since this was essential before the British Government could pay compensation to the dependents. He informed me that the British Government had no evidence as to how these men had met their deaths, as there were no survivors to testify in court and the dying Auxiliary had never recovered consciousness. Incidentally, he was refused any statement.[85]

'It was a vicious fight. There was no mutilation'. He told history students in UCG he wanted 'to nail that propaganda. There was hand to hand fighting, butts of rifles were used.'[86]

It was incorrect to tell Tom Barry in 1921 that the survivor did not recover consciousness. Not conscious enough, perhaps, to swear to tell the truth about the false surrender. Was it in the hope of getting a statement from Barry that Cope did not give Barry the full facts? If the British establishment had already got 'The Rebel Commandant's report' why were they still looking for one from 'The Rebel Commandant'? Barry's refusal of Cope's request meant the invention of 'an alternative', according to Stephen Brady.[87] 'It was right to say,' the Cork Examiner reported in January 1921, that 'as there was no living [British Military] witness to tell exactly what happened, it could only be conjectured.'[88]

A. J. S. (Stephen) Brady was an assistant in T. P. Grainger's solicitor's office – the firm that represented and processed the claims for the relatives of the Auxiliaries killed at Kilmichael. Mr Brady confirmed that Lieut H. F. Forde received £10,000, after the Truce had been called. The Freeman's Journal had a photograph of Forde in the Military Hospital, Cork on 17 January 1921. 'He was confined to a wheelchair for some time, later he walked with a pronounced limp and lived until a few years ago', Mr Brady recalled in November 1980.[89]

Stephen Brady was aware that 'the statement' of the castle men was 'exaggerated'. The 'more harrowing it [the ambush] was, the hacking of bodies and the cruelty of the engagement, the better the compensation.' Mr Brady was aware that Cope had called to Tom Barry 'and he had refused to co-operate'. In the solicitor's office 'Cope discussed the position with the chief [his boss] and then left for the castle. They wanted a statement – a report saying there was an ambush or attack and that they killed the Auxiliaries outright ... Barry was liaison officer around that time.' Contact between the solicitors' office and the castle was 'intense' after which the 'reports from the two sides' were presented. 'I won't say how that came about, but it helped the families to get good compensation,' said Mr Brady. Wondering what he meant by 'reports from the two sides', I queried it.

'I'm not saying. It's just that the families needed good evidence for their compensation case. Naturally their comrades helped', Mr Brady said. (I was unaware at that time of the existence of the *alleged* 'Commandant's' (Barry's) report and did not therefore pursue the issue.)[90] Bill Munroe, an Auxiliary in the castle gives his exaggerated account of 'the ambushers' in lorries and khaki uniforms. The official reports have echoes of this account. There is no mention of a false surrender. 'Out of 21 men, 20 lay on the road dead' where 'at least 3 took a long time to die', according to Munroe.

Auxiliary Munroe recorded that, 'after the first shock had passed our immediate reaction was to hunt down as many of the ambushers as we could and exterminate them.'[91]

Percival found that, 'Owing to the constant searches carried out by crown forces it was exceedingly difficult for the IRA to issue anything in the way of written orders, but they did succeed ... largely by verbal instructions.'[92]

Referring to the 'Rebel Commandant's report' Peter Hart has asked, 'If it was a forgery, why was it kept secret? Why wasn't it written to support the British version?'[93]

It seems to have fulfilled the requirements for the establishment's purpose to propound the report as Barry's. This 'Rebel Commandant's report' should have eliminated the necessity for secrecy, would have made great newspaper headlines, would have aided British propaganda, would have militated against Tom Barry, the IRA and GHQ, if it was a genuine document.

Dr Jeremiah Kelleher, Macroom coroner examined the bodies of the dead Auxiliaries. Since the Restoration of Order in Ireland Act became law on 9 August 1920, Secret Military Courts of Enquiry conducted coroners' inquests. Dr Kelleher had always been anti-Republican. Moreover, when the IRA shot his son, an RIC man in Longford, he became even more extreme in his views. However, 'his code of honour has to be referred to, because when ever he treated IRA men it is believed that he kept it confidential.'[94]

On Tuesday 30 November, the day after the bodies were brought in, 'A Military Inquiry in lieu of inquest was opened at Macroom Castle ... into the cause of death of the victims of the ambush.' The injuries of sixteen Auxiliaries who were killed are listed. There is no mention of an axe or brutal beating. A. F. Poole died from 'bullet wounds in chest and shoulder; fracture of bones of face, caused by heavy instrument'. He was in the first lorry, which was hit by the Mills bomb. Men had bullet wounds, lacerations, skull wounds and other severe injuries. Two, already dead of wounds, received a further wound as the fighting continued. It lists two of the men who had 'explosive bullet' wounds.[95]

'A "Mills bomb" (No. 36 Mk. 1 Grenade) exploded in the cab of the first lorry. The casing of the "Mills bomb" was made of cast iron and was deeply scored to facilitate fragmentation. When the grenade exploded in the confined space of the cab, those shrapnel fragments would have inflicted horrific jagged wounds on the driver and front seat passenger, and also on some of the furtherest forward of the Auxiliaries, who were in the rear of the open-top lorry, whether killed outright or not', according to Lieut Col Eamonn Moriarty. Furthermore, as Barry wrote, 'a few [Volunteers] had revolvers'. These were captured from British sources. 'The British Welbey revolver of the period fired a ·455 inch round-nosed, soft lead bullet ... weighing 17 gram. It was a low velocity round ... and did not have great penetrative power. On impact it would flatten and its cross-section area would increase significantly, thus causing gaping wounds with great internal damage'. In addition there were the captured, what the medical report called 'explosive bullets'. These were 'expanding bullets', Lieut Col Eamonn Moriarty explained, as, 'at that time, there was no such thing as an explosive bullet'. Service bullets with the point cut (scored) and doctored to open on impact were used by the Auxiliaries. These bullets would expand on impact thus causing considerable damage, bone fragmentation and nasty wounds. When this type of bullet is discharged, 'its destructive effect on bone and tissue is greater than that caused by an internal charge'.[96]

It is not known whether the bullets that Barry and his men picked up on that day or previously in the Toureen ambush or elsewhere were expanding bullets. What is known is that most of the arms and ammunition that the Volunteers used were captured from the British military. Moreover, there was close fighting as Barry described, with 'rifle-butts replacing rifle-shots' with pressure, and 'point blank' shots. On contact all would have created considerable body disfigurement. Barry wrote that the fight between the Volunteers and the Auxiliaries after the Mills bomb had been thrown was intense and even became 'a hand-to-hand one. Revolvers were used at point blank range.'[97]

Bill Munroe, one of the Auxiliaries who came to collect the bodies next day, said: 'They [the Auxiliaries] had put up a tremendous fight as there were literally hundreds of empty [cartridge] cases beside them ... They must have kept the enemy under cover for a comparatively long time.'[98]

On 11 January 1921, at Macroom Courthouse, County Court Judge Hynes 'took up the hearing of malicious injury applications'. 'Huge' sums were sought. Concluding the compensation plea, counsel said that because of the severity of injuries 'which these undoubtedly were' awards were sought 'for compensation tempered with generosity rather than with justice.'[99]

On Saturday 15 January at Macroom Quarter Sessions Judge Hynes delivered his judgement in connection with claims made by relatives of the '15 killed and one dangerously wounded.' (Some reports state 15 killed, with other reports state 16, but the judge here mentions 15.) 'The wounded survivor was incapable of giving any evidence, so not one of the unhappy party was alive to give one any description of the ambush,' according to the report. But 'there could be no doubt but that fifteen of the party were murdered. So the claim for compensation came within the Provisions of the Criminal Injuries Act 1919 as amended by the Criminal Injuries Act 1920.'

The families were awarded varying amounts. F. H. Forde's father sought compensation of £15,000. However, the judge withheld judgement for a sitting in Bandon at some further date, stating that compensation should be about £9,000, but he 'would not say until he further considered the matter whether it should be £8,000 or £10,000.' It took some months before 'the huge sums' were given to the victims.[100]

There was a tendency towards exaggeration – Professor John A. Murphy, in a television documentary on the Kilmichael ambush said that 'under the Malicious Injuries Act ... the more horrific the account, the greater the compensation.'[101]

On Monday 29 November in the House of Commons Sir Hamar Greenwood said he had received a telegram that fifteen 'Auxiliary officers' under District Inspector Craik were killed and 'one is missing and one was wounded'. They had been 'ambushed by eighty to a hundred men'. The head of the police force sent him a further telegram that the ambushers were all dressed 'in khaki, with steel helmets' fired 'from both sides of the road ... poor fellows were disarmed, and brutally murdered. The bodies were rifled ...' Sir Hamar Greenwood said, 'I do not think the House would care to pursue questions about some odd patrol in Ulster, or the burning of some farm, in the face of this challenge to the authority of this house and of civilisation (cheers).'[102]

Propaganda aided the British military actions. In Dublin just a week previous to the Kilmichael ambush Volunteers Dick McKee, Peadar Clancy and Conor Clune (innocent civilian) were arrested in Dublin. Their bodies, recovered by relatives, contained 'a mass of bruises and bayonet wounds'. McKee had 'broken ribs' and all had bullet wounds. According to General Crozier, the Dublin Castle propaganda organ composed a story of 'the men's ruse' to leave the room from 'their kind hearted officers' and were then 'killed while trying to escape'.[103]

The *Irish Press*, 26 November 1932, published a piece on the Kilmichael ambush. It accompanied 'a list of the men of the Cork No. 3 Brigade who gave their lives for liberty, in the West Cork area.' The piece is presented as a summary. Tom Barry was extremely unhappy that his article was not published as written. In a letter to the editor he wrote:

> ... I know you mentioned that you have to omit any details that you feel would be libellous and also that space on your paper was a consideration, however important facts should not have been omitted. While you left other details in you crammed the ambush into one small paragraph. One of the most important facts of the Kilmichael ambush was the false surrender by the Auxies. Three of our lads thought it was all over and stood up. The Auxies began to shoot again after shouting 'we surrender'. That is why I shouted, 'Rapid Fire and do not stop until I tell you'.
>
> It is important for the good men of West Cork who fought there, and those lads who were fatally shot there, that you print the story in full. I would like this done. If you felt you had to omit some part which you thought had to be omitted, you should have sent me the altered copy in advance. Because so much of it was cut out and altered there are other errors in the publication. But it is the omission of the false surrender that concerns me most.
>
> You should print the full article, and give an explanation regarding that one on 26th. Would you kindly let me know what you are going to do about the matter.[104]

So the omission of the false surrender in the *Irish Press* article was not the work of Tom Barry. When Tom Barry's *Guerilla Days* was being serialised in the *Irish Press* in 1948, he had further publication problems. Correspondence shows Barry's considerable annoyance with the editor for altering his instalments. He maintained the least he (Tom) could expect was the editor's agreement with the author. 'People,' he wrote, 'will not understand the pressure of space and all the other valid considerations.' It is obvious from his 1948 correspondence that he feared a repetition of the synopsising of his 1932 Kilmichael ambush article. This seemed to give him much heartache and shows that he was a stickler for facts. (The 1948 correspondence will be dealt with later in chronological order.)[105]

In 1941 when Barry's articles under 'Eyewitness' in *An Cosantóir* were published, some sentences were altered, and some paragraphs were omitted 'owing to the international [war] situation' at the time. However, the false surrender is published as Barry wrote it.[106]

Peter Hart wrote in his book: 'At least two Auxiliaries stood with their hands up and surrendered'.[107] In a letter to the *Irish Times* concluding the debate on the false surrender, he wrote: 'it is possible that one or more Auxiliaries surrendered while others kept firing. Or that a wounded policeman ignored the surrender and shot an IRA man when he approached. And it is certainly possible that some of the column did believe that they had been tricked. However, what is clear is that there was no "false surrender" as Barry depicted it. There was no trick being played, and at most only one guerrilla died after the surrenders began.'[108]

These Auxiliaries were commissioned officers with war experience on one or more fronts. Most had been decorated. Three had received Military Crosses, and one the Distinguished Flying Cross.[109] General Tudor wished 'to utilise the war experience and military knowledge of these capable officers with a view to frustrating the raiding and ambush tactics of the Sinn Féin murder clubs'.[110]

Sir Hamar Greenwood in the House of Commons on 29 November said that 'the Auxiliary division was composed entirely of ex-officers, selected for conspicuous merit in the war'.[111]

The Macroom Auxiliaries left their barracks on 28 November, fully armed and prepared for any military conflict that might arise. In the combat that arose at Kilmichael, a distinction should be drawn between the resumption of the fight following a surrender and the continuation of the fight without a stop. Trained, these officers knew the rules of war. Either an Auxiliary/Auxiliaries shouted 'we surrender' or they didn't. If they didn't, then it was a fight to the finish. If they did, as has been accepted, and a firearm was once more used then the surrender call was falsified, thereby resuming an open fight.

According to Jack Lane 'soldiers act under command, whether fighting or surrendering. And in a concentrated engagement like Kilmichael it was certainly not open to some Auxiliaries to surrender while others kept on fighting. By conceding that "one guerrilla" may have been shot after a surrender, Hart gives away the substance of his case'[112] – his theory is that 'Barry's "history" of Kilmichael … is riddled with lies and evasions.'[113]

From Lashing November Rain to Hospital Bed

Darkness fell on the bleak, open countryside of Kilmichael as Barry, conscious of his responsibility to his men, decided the column should stay together in case of an attack. Again it began to rain heavily. The wind-driven sleet battered against the men's faces as he drove the tired column southwards. Soaked to the skin, burdened by heavy weapons – their own and those of the enemy – the men, who had hardly eaten anything for over 36 hours, continued on their weary journey. They trudged southwards and crossed the Bandon river and reached Granure, eleven miles south of Kilmichael, by 11 p.m.

With little food and without sleep, the column covered 36 miles in rough conditions, lay cramped for seven hours and 'half-frozen on the damp ground without being able to risk enough movement to warm themselves', and fought a desperate ambush all within twenty-four hours.[1]

It was still lashing rain as they entered the unoccupied Granure cottage, off-loaded their arms, ammunition and sat, wet, on the stone floor. The local Ballinacarriga Company provided tea, bread, butter and candles. Before they ate, with heads bowed in reflection, they crossed themselves and in sadness offered a silent prayer for their dead comrades. 'I remember every move. Yes. Every move,' Pat O'Donovan measured each word. He paused as if living the sad memory. 'Every. Single. Move.' Their link was broken, but yet forever tied.[2]

Having placed straw on the floor, the column lay down in the same sodden clothes to rest for the night. 'I looked on them and a thrill of pride ran through me as I thought no army in the world could ever have more uncomplaining men ... Their discipline was the finest. Compulsion or punishment was not required for this Volunteer army; they risked their lives and uncomplainingly suffered.'[3]

Barry went outside, spoke to the scouts and the sentries. He returned and looked at the men who were all asleep. Then he settled on the straw in a corner. But his mind was so active he couldn't sleep. The November cold or wet didn't bother him. As he looked at the ceiling of the dimly lit kitchen he thought of his dead comrades and the mistake he had made. 'Our dead! Two of them might be alive now had I warned them of the bogus surrender trick which is as old as war itself.'[4]

'Why did I not warn them?' He thought of the families who would have to be told![5]

Finally, he fell asleep only to be awakened a half-an-hour later when Charlie Hurley pressed his shoulder. Charlie had been in Clonakilty and heard extraordinary stories of Kilmichael. He walked the fifteen miles to get the real story. The pair tip-toed out, had a smoke and chatted for about an hour. Tom went over in detail the events of the previous days and nights. He had a few tasks for Charlie the following day, including the difficult one of visiting Liam Deasy to inform him of the death of his brother, Pat.[6] He discussed with Charlie the possibility of the capture and destruction of two military posts in Bandon. He told Charlie that there was a prospect of carrying out the barracks' raid, by bribing two Essex Regiment men, who had been arrested by a local company officer. They were dressed as civilians and said they wanted help to get back to England. The company officer discovered that they were spies. One of the men had a brother who was a sergeant in the barracks and Tom hoped to buy him because he felt he would have more inside knowledge. Tom had spoken to the two men separately on the Thursday night before the Kilmichael ambush. He made a proposition to the man who 'was anxious to get out' his brother, the Essex sergeant. He would get him £3,000 and a safe passage from the country if he agreed with a plan.[7]

An appointment was made with the sergeant to meet a senior IRA official (Tom) at 8.30 p.m. on 3 December outside of Bandon. Under supervision the spy wrote a letter and had it posted. Before being taken away, Tom warned him of the consequences of treachery, and 'he undertook to keep the arrangement secret from the other deserter'. Both were kept under guard as prisoners.[8]

Tom's discussion with Charlie helped. Now, he could rest while Charlie took command of the night watch with the local company. Back on the bed of straw, still in wet clothes, he lay, but a sharp pain in his chest made him uncomfortable. The thought of getting an inside track to Bandon military barracks, to supplies of Mills bombs, explosives, engineering equipment, thousands of rifles and ammunition to the formation of a formidable IRA striking force, kept his mind racing and his spirits buoyant. He slept uneasily.

The success of Kilmichael, the first major victory against the British forces, boosted the morale of the Volunteer movement, not alone in the West Cork Flying Column, but throughout the whole of Ireland, as it came at a time when the IRA was beginning to lose heart. 'He inspired the struggle. Then they got going in other parts of the country.'[9]

Its significance went 'far beyond the capture of arms. It demolished permanently the then growing and carefully fostered fiction that the Auxiliaries were invincible. It was timely. The struggle had entered a grim and decisive phase. At the time there were 51 battalions of British troops in Ireland.' There was 'a shifting of weight of occupation forces'. Munster 'held 20,000 troops, 1,800 RIC 340 Auxiliaries and 370 Marines … The IRA appeared to have been driven underground and its activities reduced to minor, sporadic outbursts.'[10]

Flor Crowley remembers that 'for everybody living in West Cork, Kilmichael and the shooting of Canon Magner [see p. 75] were watersheds in their political lives. What little pro-British sympathies the 'pension' and the Land Acts had been able to buy were shattered by the realisation that our own boys, our neighbours' sons and grandsons, had been able to wipe out the cream of the

British army, had been able to conquer the men who had just conquered the Germans and the Turks.'[11]

Michael Collins' success in breaking the British intelligence network on Bloody Sunday followed 'by the success of Tom Barry in wiping out a unit of the "invincible" Auxiliaries at Kilmichael, convinced the British that they could not win at a cost they could afford to pay', according to Todd Andrews. He 'had organised the most spectacularly successful flying column. His exploits became legendary. He became a folk hero in his life-time.'[12]

The day's events became remembered not only in story but also in song. John F. Hourihane of the West Cork Brigade composed *The Boys of Kilmichael* shortly afterwards.

> *Forget not the Boys of Kilmichael,*
> *Those gallant lads stalwart and true,*
> *Who fought 'neath the green flag of Erin*
> *And conquered the red, white and blue . . .*
> *The sun to the west was sinking*
> *'Twas the eve of a cold winter's day*
> *The Tans whom we wearily waited,*
> *Drove into the spot where we lay.*
> *Then over the hills went the echo,*
> *The sound of the rifle and gun.*
> *And the flame of their lorries gave tidings*
> *That the Boys of Kilmichael had won.*

John Hourihane, whose brother, Dan, was one of 'the boys of Kilmichael', was one of the 'picked men ordered to stand duty at the cottage in Granure' the night of the ambush. He composed the verses shortly afterwards 'in order to perpetuate and preserve the event. It got out of my hands before I could finish it, and it was only in later years that I completed it,' he wrote later to Tom Barry from Boston. 'One night I was escorting Charlie Hurley along the Phale road when suddenly I thought of the pencilled verses in my pocket. I at once decided that I should get rid of them and so I placed them underneath a wooden gate leading to a friendly neighbour's house. Apparently, one of the households found them and before I could memorise them they were being sung throughout the neighbourhood. I often since thought that had we been surprised by the enemy with these lines in my pocket, and while my apprehension meant nothing, what would the arrest of Charlie at that time mean to the Third Cork Brigade!' John, who took a very active part in Barry's flying column, emigrated to Boston after 'the troubles.'[13] (The author of this song has for all these years remained unknown.)

On the Monday when the Auxiliaries were on their way to Kilmichael to collect the bodies, they forced elderly postmaster Jim Coughlan to walk 'behind the lorries'. They shot at Jim O'Mahony and Jer Hogan 'who had a narrow escape' and later confined Jim Coughlan to Cork jail for three months. On Tuesday when troops returned 'to comb the area' they shot dead Denny Sullivan, an innocent civilian, who had come to Cronin's Kilmichael Bar, for pro-visions.[14]

The British establishment ordered that henceforth 'Known Rebels' be 'car-ried as hostages for the safe conduct of the occupants in all motor vehicles.'[15]

The coffins of the Auxiliaries were solemnly paraded through Cork city on 2 December, on their way to England for burial. Brigadier-General Higginson's Seventeenth Infantry Brigade 'issued a request that all business premises and shops be closed between the hours of 11 a.m. and 2 p.m. as a mark of respect for the officers, Cadets and Constables of the Auxiliary division, RIC, killed in ambush near Kilmichael, 28 November 1920.' A large body of troops, RIC and Tans enforced the 'request'.[16]

On 10 December the British prime minister 'told the House of Commons that his government was ready to meet certain specified members of Dáil Éire-ann, illegal organisation though it was, for negotiations, and would give them safe conduct to London. Meanwhile, however, Mr Lloyd George added, the Bri-tish government would intensify its campaign against Sinn Féin by proclaim-ing martial law over large parts of Ireland.'[17]

Lord French's proclamation, which has been regarded as a propaganda edict, read in part:

> Because of attacks on crown forces culminating in an ambush, massacre and muti-lation with axes of sixteen cadets by a large body of men wearing trench-helmets and disguised in the uniform of British soldiers, and who are still at large, now I do declare Martial Law proclaimed in the County of Cork, East and West Riding, the City of Cork, Tipperary, North and South Riding, the City and County of Lime-rick.[18]

Ewan Butler says that the most probable explanation for the falsified report on Kilmichael 'is that the Auxiliaries, having suffered their first serious reverse at Irish hands, falsified ... partly in order to excuse their defeat and partly in order to ensure that the most condign measures were taken against their assailants.'[19]

Further to this proclamation, General Sir Neville Macready, the command-er-in-chief, issued his own proclamation stating that persons caught with ille-gal arms or explosives were liable to sentence of death. Public meetings were forbidden and every householder was required to affix to the inside of the front door a list of the occupants by age, sex and occupation.[20]

The following proclamation was posted up in Macroom and printed in all the daily papers:

NEW POLICE ORDER IN MACROOM
December 1st, 1920

Whereas foul murders of servants of the crown have been carried out by dis-affected persons, and whereas such persons immediately before the murders ap-peared to be peaceful and loyal people, but have produced pistols from their poc-kets, therefore it is ordered that all males passing through Macroom shall not appear in public with their hands in their pockets. Any male infringing this order is liable to be shot at sight.

By order.

AUXILIARY DIVISION, R.I.C.
Macroom Castle[21]

The declaration of regional Martial Law meant that the British establishment 'now recognised the IRA as an army and not, as they had previously suggested, rebel murderers'.[22]

Meanwhile the fight of Barry and his men had to continue; it was a fight for survival, a fight for success. For three days he manoeuvred his men in zig-zag fashion across the countryside. Often they narrowly avoided a clash with the British. Troops scoured the country, from Dunmanway, Ballineen, Bandon, Crookstown and Macroom. The Volunteers had to be prepared to live rough, remain 'on the run' and try to avoid capture.

Reprisals by burning, looting, pot-shots at civilians and beating were carried out in all the surrounding areas of Kilmichael and Macroom. Shops, homes, hay barns, outhouses were destroyed at Kilmichael, Johnstown and Inchageela. Several farmhouses for miles around Kilmichael were burned. In the Corn Mills and home of McDonnell's, Castlelack, a distance away, the Essex Regiment 'made a shambles of the place' – furniture 'smashed and set alight; business records and valuable books feeding the flames. Bathroom flooding had brought down the dining-room ceiling, ruining the room and its contents. In every direction damage was evident.'[23] Most of the local houses around Kilmichael and Shanacashel were burned, including O'Donoghue's, Kelly's and O'Mahony's – houses close to the ambush site.[24] According to Charlie Browne: 'The force created some thorough scoundrels who used unsparingly the power handed out to them by an unscrupulous government.' Charlie's house was burned. Dan Corkery's house and business were bombed to the ground also Cornelius Kelleher's home as well as several others in Cork No. 1 Brigade area. Peter Hart wrote that, 'Only a few half-hearted reprisals against houses and hay-sheds were carried out around Macroom, belying their [the Auxiliaries] reputation as terrorists'. However, many accounts show that the reprisals led to large-scale looting and burnings of dwellings and outhouses. It spread over Cork No. 1 and Cork No. 2 brigade areas. The local school was closed for two weeks. 'Many of the locals left home and went to stay with friends and relations as they knew the Auxiliaries would be back'.[25]

Over the weeks that followed, the homes of many of those who had participated in the ambush were raided. The forces from Dunmanway raided Pat O'Donovan's Drominidy home 'wrecked the house, broke ware, furniture and even tore up sheets.' They told his mother and sister to have the coffin ready. Two weeks later they got word to send a shirt and stockings. 'At least we knew he was alive', his sister recalled.[26]

72

On the night of 3 December a car was to pick up Tom Barry and three rifle-men, then collect the sergeant's brother who would be taken with a gun trained on him to the rendezvous with the Essex Sergeant. Barry, whose chest pains had been intermittent, got a sudden spasm and collapsed. When he regained cons-ciousness he was in McCarthy's, Kilmoylerane, being anointed by a priest while Dr Fehilly stood by. For four days and nights he lay almost motionless, while Cumann na mBan girls, a nurse and Pat O'Mahony watched and waited. The doctor said that his heart had been displaced, and under no circumstances could he be moved. He was 'extremely ill'. On the fifth day wrapped in blankets he was lifted into a car and taken to the Mercy Hospital Cork.[27] Here he remained, in secret, with a displaced heart condition for all of December. Seán MacCárth-aig, IO, who had 'jumped' on his bike to make 'provision for a wounded volun-teer' was 'amazed to see the patient' in the bed as Tom's identity was known to only a few while his progress was carefully monitored.[28]

Lieut Jim O'Donoghue and section-commander Joe Begley were accom-panying Capt. John Galvin to where Galvin was to meet Tom Barry outside Bandon. O'Donoghue and Begley, unaware Barry was ill and could not turn up, were about to turn back, when Essex Regiment men sprung on them. The following morning the three maltreated bodies were found on the roadside. The savage killing of these men reverberated throughout the county and beyond. 'It is perhaps just as well that there are no details of treatment meted out …' Barry wrote.[29] When this episode in Barry's serialisation appeared in the *Irish Press* John Galvin's brother, Miah, wrote to Tom Barry. He believed his brother was armed, that Tom had misrepresented him. In response, Tom wrote that 'two brigade officers and John were to be only those who were aware of the proposal for above all the Essex sergeant had to be assured of the secrecy of the move.' They were 'certainly unarmed on that night and got no chance what-ever to fight for their lives by the savages who butchered them. The note I sent John was to "come alone and come unarmed"… I would burn the book if I thought I had belittled any man who died for Ireland. Indeed, the book would never have been written except that I wanted to record for all time the sacri-fices of the men of that generation … I did not want it serialised atal (*sic*) but the *Irish Press* got after me and pressed me very hard, in addition to offering me a good sum of money. I still refused until it dawned on me that if I agreed to serialisation, it would enable anyone to write me and point out any omissions I had unwittingly made of any man's sacrifice … I am more than glad you wrote me.' He explained the episode in detail to Miah. On 23 February 1921 when 'two naval wireless men stationed with the Essex in Bandon' were cap-tured 'they were allowed to live because they proved that they did not take up station in Bandon until a week after the lads were killed. They stated, however that they knew the three were unarmed when captured and that Percival him-self did the shooting . I will re write the account of their deaths … I will not say they were unarmed but neither will I say they were armed unless I get proof

... You see I DO KNOW that John (R.I.P.) was told to come unarmed and alone'. The Volunteers each had a revolver bullet in the forehead, and their bodies showed marks of severe 'ill-treatment'.[30]

In response to the question as to whether or not Joe Galvin had participated in the Toureen ambush, Barry would make further enquiries he said as he 'would hate to hurt a living relative of one who died for Ireland.'[31] Correspondence shows that Barry went to considerable trouble to establish the truth. (His treatment of this episode should be borne in mind when analysing the Kilmichael ambush. Correctness was important!)

The two pseudo-deserter spies had been held under guard in a few 'British Loyalist homes'. Despite IRA vigilance, the men slipped a note for the Bandon Essex. Strickland noted afterwards that the 'soldier who tried to pose as a local Irishman was found out immediately.'[32] Some time after the event the IRA executed the men. Then in April 1922 their Loyalist hosts met a similar fate when it was discovered that they had done a considerable amount of informing and had caused the arrests and deaths of IRA members.[33]

On the night of 11 December 1920 Volunteers from Cork No. 1 Brigade set up an ambush at Dillon's Cross, Cork. One Auxiliary was killed and eleven wounded. 'Soon after the ambush three civilians, Cornelius Delaney, Jeremiah Delaney and their uncle were taken out of their houses and shot on the roadside'. Afterwards Cork experienced 'a weekend of terror,' according to *The Times*, when the city was 'set in flames' by Auxiliaries and Black and Tans who went on a rampage.[34] It was horrific. 'The streets were crowded and the shops were full of people'. Innocent civilians were 'flogged', stones were thrown in windows and firemen were fired upon. Captain Myers, Superintendent of the Dublin Fire brigade found 'that the destruction of Cork is much worse than that caused in Dublin in the Easter week rebellion ... he considers high explosives were employed, for by no other means could such an amount of solid masonry be hurled across the thoroughfares.'[35]

An Auxiliary from K Company, Dunmanway, called Charlie, in a letter to his mother, wrote that 'during the burning and looting of Cork' he 'took perforce a reluctant part'. With 'murder, arson and looting, we did it all night never mind how much the well-intentioned Hammer [Hamar] Greenwood would excuse us ... it baffles description.'[36] Another Auxiliary was 'very actively employed to boot until the dawn on Sunday ... we took sweet revenge', because of the Dillon's Cross ambush.[37]

Afterwards General Crozier criticised 'the manner in which the government lied to cover up the guilt of their agents.' Lloyd George promised to publish 'the Strickland Report' on the burnings, 'but having seen it he broke his word. He did not dare to allow the public to read of the disgraceful doings of their "law" enforcing officers', Crozier wrote.[38] The British government was embarrassed. There were only two copies of the report and Macready kept one in his safe. Greenwood said, 'If we publish it now we shall only be giving ourselves away to our enemies. We must base ourselves on the ground that it is disclosing confidential communications.' It was decided to keep the report's outcome, on the burning of Cork, under wraps. Greenwood disclosed that the 'company had been disbanded' and all were 'dispersed into other units ... [we should] Say – "Acts of indiscipline". They came from the slums to loot'.[39]

Tom Barry, slowly recovering in hospital, heard of burning of Cork from Sr Mary who feared that the hospital would be burned.

A few days later he was told of 'the Dunmanway horror'. Seventy-three years old Canon Magner of Dunmanway never made any secret of his Sinn Féin sympathies. On 15 December, 20-year old, Tadgh Crowley was helping the canon push his motor-car to get it started. Two Crossley tenders of 'K Company' Auxiliaries passed by on their way to Cork. In one of the tenders Cadet Sergeant Hart asked the driver to stop. Cadet Hart went back and 'spoke to the civilian'. The driver (witness in the 'General Court-Martial Trial') saw Hart 'fire one revolver shot at the civilian, who dropped on the pavement. Immediately afterwards the accused [Hart] spoke to the priest, and a couple of minutes afterwards witness heard another shot and saw the priest fall to the ground.'[40] The captain of 'K Company' stood 'one foot on the road, the other on the running-board of the tender, one hand in his pocket, the other leaning on the door frame as the shooting was done'. Mr Brady, a government magistrate, who came on the scene, reported it. Hart was summoned to a trial.[41] Initially, his plea of being 'unfit' for the trial troubled the British cabinet. They found it 'peculiarly unfortunate in view of the fact that the murderer of Mr Sheehy-Skeffington has also been declared insane'.[42] An angry Lloyd George wanted Hart 'tried and hanged', but Macready insisted on an official trial. A furious Mark Sturgis wrote that 'those who let him loose on the world in charge of a party armed to the teeth should take his place in the dock.'[43]

The government magistrate, who later resigned, insisted on a trial.[44] Then the British cabinet ordered a further medical examination to 'put the matter beyond doubt' and so opened the way for a trial to proceed.[45] The 'Trial Report' states that Hart was angry, as his comrade had died from wounds received in an ambush on 11 December. The Auxiliary witness reported that Hart said, 'I should like to see Ireland swept with fire, and I should like to lead the boys'.[46]

James Reader, BL, defending Cadet Hart responded to a question from the bench that 'in his opinion the accused was at the present moment capable of following the evidence and fit to understand the details ...' When the trial concluded, the court found 'that the accused was guilty of the offences with which he had been charged, but was insane at the time of their commission. The finding has been confirmed and promulgated.' The newspaper account states, 'It is believed that Cadet Hart will be confined in a Criminal Lunatic Asylum during the pleasure of the Lord Lieutenant'.[47]

In the British parliament Major Archer-Shee, a government backbencher asked if 'this cadet was made insane by a massacre [Dillon's Cross] which had taken place a few days before?'

Sir Hamar Greenwood, secretary of state replied that Cadet Hart's 'chum' was 'massacred' in the Dillon's Cross ambush and 'undoubtedly that had an effect on his mind.' Greenwood then named the medical men who decided on his 'insanity'. Whereupon Mr Lawson, Labour asked 'whether it had yet been decided by the medical authorities how long this cadet was going to remain insane?'[48]

In the 'captured letter' an Auxiliary, from this K Company, wrote to his mother:

> In all my life and in all the tales of fiction I have read I have never experienced such orgies of murder, arson and looting as I have witnessed during the past 16 days with the RIC Auxiliaries. It baffles description and we are supposed to be officers and gentlemen. There are quite a number of decent fellows – likewise a lot of ruffians ... one of our heroes held up a car with a priest and a civilian in it and shot them both through the head without cause or provocation. We were very kindly received by the people, but the worst ... of the cold-blooded murder is that no one will come within a mile of us now and all the shops are closed.
>
> The brute who did it has been sodden with drink for some time and has been sent to ... [*difficult to decipher*] under arrest for examination by reports in lunacy. If certified sane he will be court-martialled and shot. The poor old priest was 65 and everybody's friend.[49]

F. P. Crozier, commander of the Auxiliaries in Ireland at the time, called it 'the most cowardly and meanest crime'. The 'police-murderer' charged with 'insanity' was inexcusable as he 'was sane enough to be fully armed on a public road but not sufficiently sober to be able to control himself'.[50]

Many of those in West Cork, who had up to now felt little sympathy for Barry and the IRA, supported them because of the callous murders and burnings being committed on behalf of the British crown.

On 18 December, Dr Daniel Coholan, Bishop of Cork, and a native of Kilmichael parish, in a pastoral letter stated that any Roman Catholic who took part in an ambush was a murderer and would be excommunicated.[51] When Barry, still lying in bed, heard this from Sr Mary, he was worried because the vast majority of his men were staunch Catholics, and he wondered whether this might have dealt a mortal blow to the flying column. His fears were lessened when Charlie Hurley came to visit that night. Charlie brought ammunition for his Colt automatic. Charlie did not want to worry him – 'the men would continue to fight', he said. He also told Tom about an ambush attack near Gaggin under his command on 8 December that had failed, resulting in the death of Michael McLean, one of the column. McLean in Volunteer uniform was 'cut off from the column during the fight', captured by Essex members and tortured to death. Sixteen-year-old Timothy Sullivan was also taken prisoner and witnessed Essex men twisting McLean's arms 'up behind his back, prodding him with bayonets and revolvers, at the same time shouting at him to tell the names of the men in the column'. They then 'tied him to a lorry and dragged him into

Bandon.' (He was 18, 'only son of a widowed mother'.)[52] Seán MacCárthaig remembers that night in hospital, Charlie 'despondent', wanted Barry to take over from him, as brigade OC. 'Things seemed to be going against him. He would serve wherever you wanted him as a fighter,' MacCárthaig reminded Tom.[53] The following Saturday night when Liam Deasy called to see Tom, he was happy to see him so improved and Liam agreed to stay the night with him. 'But the Reverend Mother came in on us,' said Liam, 'and though Barry pleaded, she refused. We both had lots to discuss.'[54]

In the serialisation of his book Barry decried the bishop and was taken to task by the *Irish Press* editor. But Barry responded that 'it is a very mild exposition of a very serious act aimed to destroy the armed independence movement … it should have been dealt with in a stronger manner.'

Barry understood the difficulty of the *Irish Press*, but he told Liam Mac-Gowan 'not to touch it'. If it was necessary to do so then he wanted put 'in italics in brackets some such sentence … that the author writes strongly of the Excommunication Order'. And he asked that the corrections and 'deletions' be sent on to him.[55]

Strickland, commander of the 6th Division, wrote in his diary, Sunday 12 December 1920: 'Bishop came in afternoon to ask [if] I have question for some of his people'.[56] Barry, in his notes stated: 'Everyone knew that if the IRA laid down their arms as requested by the Bishop at least 200 members in Cork City and county would be killed off within a week by the British forces. Yet Dr Coholan did not even extract a promise from the British commanding officer that there would be no executions or murders if the fight for independence stopped.'[57]

Tom's health was improving. He was allowed to take short walks around the room. Towards the end of the month his doctors told him that he would be discharged in a few days and would have to avoid exertion for some months, perhaps take a long sea trip. But Tom had other ideas. He grew impatient. On the night of 28 December he slipped out, headed towards brigade head-quarters; once outside the city he took to the fields. Suddenly a thought struck him: if he dropped dead as the doctors' said could happen, his body could remain in the field for months being eaten by rats. The vision of such a predicament horrified him, so he got out on the road. It was 2 a.m. when he reached O'Mahony's at Belrose. He went in by the sitting-room window, which was always left unclasped.[58]

'I removed my boots and tip-toed upstairs to the large bedroom reserved for us. When I lit a match Charlie jumped up. "Mother of God! How did you get here?"

'I walked the whole twelve miles, so I must be cured. Shove over there, and give me the warm place.'[59]

Lord Tom, Burgatia, Rosscarbery, Michael Collins

Since early December 1920 the British government had engaged in 'indirect negotiations with the leaders of Sinn Féin' and was according to *The Times* 'exploring avenues' to peace. Archbishop Clune of Australia had met and acted as intermediary between Lloyd George and the Irish leaders, especially Michael Collins.[1]

Meanwhile the terror of the Auxiliaries and the Black and Tans continued. Scores of unarmed Volunteers and their supporters were arrested, and many were tortured. In West Cork civilians were beaten, many homes, factories and creameries were burned. Since the bishop's decree, Auxiliaries, Black and Tans and military were daily raiding homes in the countryside. The Essex regiment killed two unarmed Volunteers, Pat O'Donovan and Denis Hegarty in mid January.[2]

As 1921 began Tom Barry and Charlie Hurley talked. Charlie had disbanded the flying column after the 8 December Gaggin ambush, and was upset. He felt he had handled it badly. Tom assured him he had done his best. Together they'd make it.

When the Irish problem came up in the British House of Commons, Cork was again the county to be dreaded, so troops were poured into Bantry, Bere Island, Bandon, Ballincollig, Cork city and Cobh. At headquarters in O'Mahony's of Belrose, Tom, Charlie, Seán Buckley, Liam Deasy and other officers of the Third West Cork Brigade discussed the future. Their decision: Get going again.[3]

In the early days of January Tom and some leading officers had to find out if Bishop Coholan's excommunication threat would have an effect on the men, so they made a tour of the companies. The men were told that anyone who felt, because of religious scruples, unable to carry on in the IRA was free to leave. 'Not one man in any company did so,' said Jim Kearney.

'We were convinced that Tom was one of the greatest leaders of all time. Any man who went out in the road to stop the lorries as he did in Kilmichael, wouldn't we do anything for him? Men would even die for him.'[4]

Policy and strategy were outlined. Each battalion was instructed 'to send rifle-men to re-form the Brigade Flying Column which was to mobilise on 18 January 1921. Meanwhile, the Bandon battalion section was to assemble immediately to carry out the first attack of the New Year.' Barry in a letter to Mr Dempsey, *Irish Press* later wrote: 'since Bishop's Excommunication … Cork 1 Brigade was also inactive for all that period, the fact of the resumption of the attacks was all important – far more so than the curfew.'[5]

Shortage of arms was their biggest problem, so attacks were made on Kilbrittain, Innishannon and Bandon Barracks. Two well-planned attacks on Kilbrittain Barracks failed because explosives did not work. A raid on Innishannon Barracks in a fortified village was their next target. If this 'inconvenient' building could be destroyed and the arms captured, Charlie Hurley and Barry decided, the difficulties that the Bandon battalion now experienced would be removed. To find out the feasibility of a raid, Barry and Hurley crept quietly down the village at 1 a.m. on 17 January 1921. Even if they had been innocent unarmed civilians this action would have rendered them liable to arrest and punishment since the curfew was now strictly enforced. Crouching beneath the shadows of the houses, the two men came within twenty yards of the police barracks, fired six rounds at its shutters from their automatics and then ran back to watch.

Immediately, from the barracks gun-fire started, and a moment later the flare of rockets lit the winter sky. The two men had proof that this barracks was prepared; troops from Bandon, Dunmanway and other areas would be on the way shortly. Barry and Hurley made their way to high ground and waited. Below, the defenders of the police barracks continued to fire at nothing. The two smiled with satisfaction at this venture, and also at how easily they had acquired their information. Fifty minutes after their foray lorries were seen approaching Innishannon from the Brinny direction on the northern road. Satisfied, the two men returned to headquarters.[6]

At headquarters they received a welcome cargo from Michael Collins. Leslie Price (Charlie Hurley's girl friend) with Moya Llewelyn Davies, intelligence officer, had motored from Dublin with wrapped guns and ammunition hidden in cases of ladies clothes and underwear and sometimes hidden in bags of flour. Leslie, as chief organiser for Cumann na mBan, had been travelling on her bicycle throughout West Cork as well as countrywide setting up membership groups. Periodically, on visits to GHQ she'd return with guns in her luggage. She did quite a few 'missions' with Moya in her 'motor car' transporting guns from Michael Collins to the Cork brigades. Michael Collins (know to them as Mick) often sent notes to Leslie. The notes began with 'Leslie dearest' or 'Dearest Leslie' or some endearment, signed 'Love M'. This would would give the appearance of love note if intercepted. Strickland in an interview believed that 'in many cases arms would be brought out, for use at the scene of an ambush or other attack, by women who concealed them in their skirts.' Their method of 'getting at' women was to raid houses, he said.[7]

Two days of intensive training of 70 rifle-men followed. This was the strongest number in the flying column to date. Equipped with arms and ammunition, Barry divided his men into seven sections and moved to take up positions at Mawbeg, five miles outside Bandon on the Ballineen road. Most days of the week a convoy of five lorries of the First Essex travelled from Bandon on this road, the plan was to ambush them. Before the ambush an informer was arrested and brought before a court-martial. Details of his activities were known for some time. Found guilty, the man was shot. His body, bearing a boldly lettered placard 'Shot by the IRA! Spies and Informers Beware!' was positioned on the roadside in a conspicuous place while the column lay in wait. Barry calculated that even if the Essex were not inclined to come out, passers-by might report the body and a party would be sent out to investigate. The men lay in wait from early morning on 22 January, but after seven hours of anti-cipation with no sign of British troops Barry reluctantly decided to withdraw his column.

Next day Barry and his men again took up positions a little closer to Bandon. The body of another self-confessed informer was labelled and laid on the roadside. Barry made sure the news would reach the barracks by having word passed to a military sympathiser who would spread the tidings. Another long fruitless wait followed. Through their intelligence section word reached Barry that the barracks had been aware of the column beside the corpse on each occasion. With the largest column yet mustered, he decided they should not be mobilised in vain. In sections he marched the men across the Bandon River to a pre-arranged meal in a number of houses and billets. He had tried to get the Bandon forces one way, now he would try another!

Curfew in Bandon was between 10 p.m. and 6 a.m. and an Essex patrol con-sisting of an officer and 45 men marched out of the barracks on the North Main Street each night at 10.30 p.m. Barry decided to attack this patrol. The timing of the whole operation was a matter of precise calculation. Barry divided his men into sections. As a masking device two sections were positioned to attack Black and Tan posts in the northern side of the town with a third under Liam Deasy to attack the barracks at the western end. The main body of the flying column at Shannon Street (now Oliver Plunkett Street) – the point furthest from the barracks where the military curfew party generally made their about-turn. A barricade against armoured cars was set up in a lane through which the IRA was to withdraw. All Barry's sections were to reach positions at precisely 11.05 p.m. Simultaneous attacks were to last on posts for seven minutes. The men were 'well schooled as to their actions'.

Midnight passed and no patrol appeared. By 2.55 a.m. it looked as if the enemy was in possession of information. Barry asked himself if he were com-mander of the opposing forces what would he do? Instantly he visualised troops from all surrounding barracks encircling them. However Barry felt some form of attack was necessary if only from the point of view of morale for his own men. He brought the detached sections into action. They opened fire on the barracks, but nobody came out. Immediately he fired his signal shots for his men to withdraw. Soon incoming enemy fire began to crackle.

Barry knew informers had sold his plan but discovered that they could penetrate the heart of the most dreaded enemy garrison in the area and the enemy failed to tackle them, eventhough there was some fighting close to the military barracks and Vol Dan O'Reilly was killed. At this point the morale of the men, which had risen after Kilmichael, continued to rise, with Barry at the helm, to a new peak of confidence. It wasn't for the want of trying that there were no major engagements. 'Where the IRA were active it affected the British troops more … We entered Bandon, a garrison town at least 40 to 50 times. It was necessary to keep on the offensive and to be aggressive.'[8]

No time was to be lost. Barry and Hurley prepared to put what they had learned from the dummy attack on Innishannon into operation.[9]

On the night following the Bandon affair, Barry posted 18 rifle-men at Brinny on a byroad in the Innishannon direction. Ten men took up positions on the direct road between Bandon and Innishannon and 10 more covered the Innishannon-Cork road. Commandant Barry and 32 rifle-men were positioned for the actual attack on Innishannon Barracks. Three parties of four men were placed to open fire on the back and side windows and doors of the barracks to prevent any inmates from bursting out. The remaining 20 men were equally divided into sections.

They laid a mine and Barry himself was prepared to rush the front door when the explosion went off. The plunger was depressed but no explosion followed. The rifle-men opened fired, the defenders sent out rockets, and after much shooting and wasting of ammunition nothing happened; no re-inforcements appeared. Barry cursed himself for his dummy attack. He also cursed the useless explosive; they must try to find an explosives expert! 'Rifle and revolver bullets were about as useful as snowballs against those strong enemy posts.'[10]

He left four men behind to keep the garrison busy, and marched the rest of his column north-westward to Brinny and on to Newcestown, which they reached on the morning of 28 January 1921. Barry was aware of the courage of his men, prepared to walk into towns and villages and openly attack fortified barracks. He sent two small sections to harass the Bandon enemy posts and prevent them from resting, while the flying column moved off to Ahiohill to billet. Now, he set sights on the well-fortified Rosscarbery Barracks. Tom Kingston, a British Loyalist known as Lord Tom, was the owner of Burgatia House, a large mansion a mile outside Rosscarbery. Through the IRA civil courts he was charged with espionage. As well as constantly conveying information on IRA activities, he secretly carried all 'Military mail' between Rosscarbery and Clonakilty enemy garrisons. Expecting a long and arduous battle at Rosscarbery, Tom Barry decided to take the family hostage and billet his men for a day's rest. It was a daring idea with the house so close to Rosscarbery and retreat cut off by the sea, but Barry had a plan made and scouts well placed.

Barry found that 'a continual worry' for him were the 'nests of British Loyalists' when he was preparing for an engagement. There was 'a possibility that an informer would see the flying column pass, and slip in to report to the forces that the IRA were preparing for ambush.' It required constant vigilance.[11]

At 3 a.m. the column moved in and took Lord Tom and his household hostage. The house was well stocked, so Tadgh Sullivan and a few more men prepared a great feed of bacon, eggs, bread, butter and tea for all. John L. O'Sullivan and Paul Leary were to meet Lar Cunningham and go into Clonakilty to bring out a suspected spy for trial at Rosscarbery. John L. recalls: 'we set out walking from Castlefreke to meet Cunningham. When we met at Clonakilty he told us that the order was countermanded; we were to go to Ballyvackey and pick up our rifles there and go to Sam's Cross where orders would be left for us. We went on, picked up our rifles and then on to Maurice Collins' house (Michael Collins' brother). It was four o'clock in the morning. Maurice came down the stairs to tell us Barry left instructions that we were not to go to the column at that hour, as he was afraid that dogs barking or any other noise would draw attention to where the column was; we were to go back and be with the column at half-nine in the morning.

'We both went home as we felt, being on the run, we may not have a chance of being home for a long time again. When I think of the irony of it ... I was just coming down the stairs at half-eight in the morning when British military who had come on cycle patrol were inside in the hall before me.'

John L. was then arrested, questioned and knocked about. He was certain that only for Fr. Hurley arriving on a sick call, he would have been severely beaten that morning. Blood was already flowing from his mouth. He was sent to Spike Island where he got a 'woeful doing' and then to Maryborough until after the Truce was signed.[12]

Lord Tom was put on trial at Burgatia House. Barry led the questioning which continued for over an hour. Since the beginning of the year Barry had become very conscious of 'the menace of spies'. Lord Tom admitted that he had been secretly engaged in carrying dispatches between Rosscarbery, Dunmanway and Clonakilty garrisons. During their intelligence mail raids, Barry said, 'We wondered why there was no mail going to Rosscarbery'. Lord Tom confessed he constantly took the mail in his motor-car. 'He was only trying to organise an anti-Sinn Féin Party in the interests of peace', he explained. In summing up Barry told Kingston that he deserved to die. The evidence of spying against the army of the elected government of his own country was strong against him, but not conclusive. He would spare his life, as he had not caused the death of any member of the IRA. 'Once this siege is over', he told Kingston, he would have 24 hours to leave the country. His house would be burned; his property would be forfeited to the Irish Republic to be distributed to the brigade men in the area who were without means of subsistence, as it had originally been taken from the Irish people during the Plantation. Kingston appeared 'surprised and relieved that he was not to be shot'.[13]

Lord Tom had only gone to his room when Jack Corkery rushed in to announce the arrival of the postman. A former regular soldier in the British army, this man might, if left complete his rounds, report the IRA presence. His not returning, however, might also cause trouble. When brought to Barry and questioned, he said he was in sympathy with the IRA and swore on Lord Tom's bible that he would quietly go on his rounds and say nothing. He was released at 12.30 p.m.

Three and a half hours later sentries noted a movement of Black and Tans in the woods, and further reports indicated that army lorries had been sighted. The postman had sold the day. Barry had sent a man, as a civilian on horseback to monitor movements. Mick Deasy, 'column sentry with revolver' located in the 'adjoining avenue' was one of the men covering the rider. 'Shots were fired at the horse' from military 'in concealed positions'. Barry had, of course, foreseen this possibility. Immediately he ordered the Volunteers into their positions. Their backs were to the sea and ammunition was, as always, scarce. The only way open to them was to fight their way out. But with only 40 rounds for each rifle Barry had the haunting fear of encirclement. He ordered his men into their strategic positions; some sections would have to move swiftly outside, but not yet. He told them not to fire until he blew the whistle. The enemy opened fire from a distance, smashing windows. They dropped down and continued to advance firing, but got no response. They were knocking sparks off the stones of the house. Puzzled, they moved closer as Barry had hoped. He blew the whistle. A burst of IRA fire rang out. The enemy scattered off in disorder. Barry dispatched further sections to follow up until eventually all was quiet.[14]

This incident shows the discipline of Barry's men. Had only one of them panicked and disobeyed orders, the outcome would most likely have been disastrous for the column, as encirclement and reinforcements would soon follow. According to Jim Kearney, 'There was one amazing feature about Barry. When he set up an ambush, he never looked for a line of retreat. He went out to fight and to win. He always thought positively. If you look at many of the ambushes, take Kilmichael and Burgatia, if the tables were turned, if it went the other way, they would be wiped out! In open countryside, or at the water's edge, there was no means of retreat. But he went out to win, and win he did.'[15]

Burgatia House had to be burned that night; to wait would add to the possibility that the house would be heavily guarded later, Barry sent his men off to billets. Then with Jim Hurley and Con O'Leary he returned, piled the furniture, sprinkled the place with paraffin and set the house ablaze. In anticipation he waited in hiding with his two companions for an hour, but the Tans did not come out. At 10 p.m. the three men moved off, circling Rosscarbery until they got behind the barracks. In a sheltered position, crouched behind a wall overlooking the barracks, they opened fire on the soldiers who were moving around. Soon the enemy retaliated heavily and accurately. The men escaped through the hills and went off to join the column at Kilbree.

Some critics would say that the Burgatia ambush was a futile exercise, a waste of valuable ammunition. Putting this question to some of the men who took part, brought the response that it was 'another example of Barry's tactics'. The chance was worth taking so that the men would be well rested and ready 'to take on Rosscarbery Barracks'. But the postman who informed the military foiled that attack. The success of the escape boosted their morale, and it also 'showed the British forces that the IRA was a strong army'.[16]

According to Barry the attack on the enemy in Rosscarbery on the night of the Burgatia ambush was imperative as a matter of prestige. This was typical of his tactics. After the Bandon raid he remained behind with nine men to use some fire; after Kilbrittain he was one of four; in Innishannon he remained with three and now with two others in Rosscarbery. He decided on this demonstration as proof that the IRA was always prepared for more.

British propaganda reporting went into action. *The Daily Sketch* reported that Michael Collins (whose elusiveness and dare-devil deeds in Dublin were great at the time) led an ambush on a white horse in Burgatia near his West Cork home place: '20 constables were attacked by 400 rebels …'

Michael Collins in a letter to his sister wrote: '… oh lovely! The white horse story was an exaggeration. I have not ridden a white horse since I rode Gipsy and used her mane as a bridle.'[17] The propaganda publicity department stated that 'the rebels lost six dead', but the constables suffered no casualties. But no casualties meant no compensation! Yet claims were heard by the county court and reported in the press 25 April. According to *An t-Óglach*, 'The constabulary who claimed compensation showed a fine sense of loyalty in repeating on oath the fictions of Dublin Castle adding the romantic detail that the rebel cohorts had seven camp fires. Their numbers by the time the claims came to be heard had risen to 500.' Head Constable Downs 'swore that during the fight a bullet grazed his nose and went through his moustache, and he had suffered defective memory.' He was awarded £1,000. Sergeant Twomey who fell and hurt his knee was awarded £35. A few of them 'felt nervous' and received £25 each. Others were awarded £25 for incidents such as a wrist watch being hit and a bullet went through a sleeve.[18]

The anticipated roundup that began the following day had Barry with his column trailing the forces for two days as they scoured the countryside. This method was risky. He had to venture as if out on a frozen lake, 'stepping cautiously.' Barry found this tactic worked well.[19]

On 5 February he went to John O'Mahony's, Kilmeen, to attend a brigade council meeting that lasted twelve hours. Decisions were taken to fine-tune their method of 'cracking the ring of spies and informers'. Mail was to be intercepted and opened only by a responsible battalion officer, and there was to be closer liaison between the three Cork brigades. The trenching of roads was to be undertaken, but consideration had also to be given that while such directive could paralyse the enemy it could also affect the movements of ordinary citizens. Therefore a detailed, responsible plan was drafted for each battalion.

At this time Volunteers Joe O'Regan and Barney O'Driscoll 'duped' a prominent Protestant with 'Loyalist affiliations, to travel to Wales, on a boat, with a cargo of butter from Aughadown Creameries, operated by the O'Regan family. When in Cardiff they ensured that the Loyalist became indisposed through drink while the butter was unloaded' and the ship's cargo reloaded. 'It was customary for the O'Regans to bring back coal when they travelled over with butter.'

On this occasion 'a consignment of 170 rifles and 10,000 rounds of ammunition was placed in the hold' before the coal was loaded.

'On arrival at the customs in Queenstown, the two IRA men paraded the Loyalist up to the customs officer, who, on recognising him, invited the three to tea. The boat then proceeded to the banks of the River Ilen near Aughadown, where the arms were transferred to butter boxes for dispatch, later', to Tom Barry's flying column.[20]

Barry discovered apathy among the people in Skibbereen towards the cause of nationalism in the early days of 1921, and it was his intention to enliven the town. The town was garrisoned by a strong detachment of the King's Regiment, commanded by Col Hudson (a likeable character, according to Barry), which had maintained quite a degree of inactivity. On 9 February at about 8 p.m. Barry, with a column of 55, approached the town. Forty-three were left in ambush position outside the town, and Barry led 12 into the town to engage the enemy. Although they advanced within a short distance of the troops no move was made to oppose them, and when the Volunteers opened fire the sentries were withdrawn. Having shot out the street lamps the IRA took up positions at street corners.

A short while after this, a group of unarmed soldiers came out and were detained by the Volunteers. They were sent off in a commandeered side-car to a near-by farmhouse with orders from Barry that their escorts were to see that they were well fed and supplied with drink. A cheerful party developed apparently. In the early hours of the morning the soldiers, having been brought back to the town in the side-car in a merry mood, sauntered back to the barracks singing rebel songs. If these soldiers had belonged to the Bandon Essex, Barry's treatment of them would have been totally different; the man who could shoot a spy or kill a soldier was capable of kindness to the enemy who did his work without showing cruelty. They were well treated they were told 'because of their fair attitude to IRA prisoners'.[21]

Barry and his party retired. They could hold the town but they couldn't lure the forces from the army garrison; nor did the barracks send out a search party next day. Day was dawning when the column reached billets north of Drimoleague.

With a few men Barry went in the Rosscarbery direction to size up the barracks and town situation for a forthcoming attack. He had just sent a section with Spud Murphy to billets and was moving in the direction of Rosscarbery when a small group of military opened fire on him and his two companions. Kathy Hayes and two other Cumann na mBan members who had been out delivering a dispatch had passed the military. Crossing a field they saw Murphy's section and informed them; soon they heard gunfire. Spud Murphy guessed Barry was in trouble. He crossed the road, opened fire to confuse the enemy and give them the impression that they were trapped. This allowed Barry and his two companions to escape. Instantly the military retreated to barracks.[22]

Barry then set his sights on Drimoleague Barracks, eight miles north of Skibbereen. He borrowed a respectable coat. Accompanied by a Cumann na mBan member he drove through the village in a pony and trap to view barracks and surroundings.

On the 12 February 1921, having first moved the civilians from the local houses to safety, he and 30 rifle-men launched their attack. Again the explosive failed to go off. Following this Barry decided that unless they could get somebody to make proper explosives, shooting up barracks should be abandoned. He admitted he said more curses than prayers at this juncture. 'We couldn't even blow in a bloody door'.[23]

On the morning of 16 February a dispatch with bad news reached Tom about a train ambush at Upton Station led by his friend Charlie Hurley on the previous day. Three IRA men were killed, and one fatally wounded. Charlie was wounded in the face. Six civilians including a woman were killed during the fight in which six soldiers were wounded. Tom got a horse, 'rode through the night to Charlie' and arrived at Forde's, Ballymurphy, next morning.[24] In a letter to Joe O'Regan, flying column veteran and *Southern Star*, editor, Tom later wrote: 'I felt far more the deaths of those men in Upton – a military failure – than I did for men who died in military successes … The poor devils [fighters that day] were subject to a lot of criticism at that time so I think I put them [critics] back in their proper place.'[25]

During the ten days previous to 15 February, except Sunday, 20 soldiers of the First Essex had travelled each day in one carriage on the evening train from Cork to Bandon. Charlie decided to attack this target with 13 IRA Volunteers. On that particular day the soldiers left Cork in one compartment as usual, but at Kinsale Junction about 36 other heavily armed soldiers joined them and mingled with the civilian passengers.

Two scouts were detailed to travel on the train to indicate the carriage position of the troops. Through a misadventure the men did not get on the train; when it stopped at Upton Station a few IRA men opened the attack on a group of soldiers in the carriage ahead of the troop carriage. The British military replied, killing three. Tom Kelleher, Jim Kearney and Flor Begley somehow managed to bring Charlie and Dan O'Mahony to safety, though O'Mahony died a few years later as a result of his wounds.[26]

Tom Barry knew that Charlie, who had led the ambush, was not alone physically but also emotionally wounded. However, he assured Charlie that had the scouts travelled and no extra troops got on the 'attack in all probability would have been a success ... It could be any commander's story.' However, he later discovered that the ambush had been sold, hence the extra soldiers.[27]

More bad news awaited Tom when he returned to the flying column on that evening of 17 February 1921. Forces had killed four Volunteers in the Kilbrittain company area. While trenching a road at Crois na Leanbh, members of the Essex Regiment surprised them. Their bodies were found on the morning of 16 February stretched together near the unfinished cutting, each with a bullet wound through the head.[28]

Having returned from a brigade council meeting Tom went to bed, but being worried about the safety of the flying column; he rose shortly afterwards to check the sentries and have a general look around. In addition to sentries, he had always taken the precaution of protecting the flying column against surprise attacks by having an outer ring of scouts drawn from the local company. Those scouts were armed with revolvers borrowed from the flying column to fire warning shots in the event of being unable to slip back to the billets to report approaching enemies.

On this particular night Tom, having visited the sentries, went to inspect this outer ring of scouts. Pat O'Driscoll was relieving another man as Tom approached. To ensure that Pat knew his full responsibilities he asked the man to detail his duties for the relief scout. Tom was close to both as they stood about a foot apart facing each other and the scout described his duties. About halfway through his description a shot rang out and Pat swayed. Tom grabbed him and lowered him gently to the ground. He was dead.

Tom turned to the man who dropped his Webley revolver, horrified at having shot his best friend. When Tom spoke he didn't answer but gave a moan and collapsed. Apparently, as Tom was speaking, he had been unconsciously fingering the trigger of his revolver and had unknowingly pressed the very light spring-trigger. This was an incident Tom was to remember all his life with sadness as he felt it was the man's nervousness in his presence that had caused the accident.[29]

There were only two other fatal accidents with firearms in the West Cork flying column. Captain Jeremiah O'Mahony, who had fought at Kilmichael, was one night cleaning his rifle in December 1920 at home when it went off and shot him. Timothy Whooley died under similar circumstances and Johnny O'Brien of Clounbuig escaped with a grazed head in an earlier incident.

By early March 1921, enemy intimidation presented a problem for the flying column. Tom, accompanied by Mick Crowley and two other rifle-men, went to Castletown-Kenneigh on brigade business. At Nyhan's they were informed that on that morning a Dunmanway Auxiliary Company had occupied the village of Ballineen in force, rounded up all the men and formed them into what they called 'Civil Guard'. They instructed them to report on IRA movements and fill in IRA-made road-trenches. With an Auxiliary escort and under threat of death they were forced to work.

Instantly, Barry decided that this move of using civilians against Irishmen had to be cracked. With a few men he went to a small hill about 400 yards from the road; down below they saw about two dozen civilians with shovels filling in a deep trench. Their escort lay in positions behind the adjoining fence and all that could be seen were their berets and the barrels of their rifles. Barry instructed his companions to spatter the ground with shots but not to kill anyone. The Auxiliaries replied and the new 'Civil Guard' scattered. When a few days later the Auxiliaries tried to round up more men for their operation, they were told they would prefer to be killed by the Auxiliaries than by the IRA. So that trick by the forces wasn't tried again.

In all cases civilians were not to be inconvenienced Barry decided. Alternative roads suitable for the horse and cart, transport for the ordinary people, but not suitable for army lorries were to be mapped out.

At a special council meeting of the Anti Sinn Féin Society held in Cork on 5 December 1920, 'it was proposed and passed' that in Bandon where 'crown forces may be molested' that Sinn Féin and IRA 'whether leaders or not three persons will be taken and shot', immediately 'after which the chapel bell will toll'.

Further 'it was decided that the houses and property of these people should be burned and their families taken and detained'. To this end notices were posted in Bandon. 'Remember Irishmen ... internment camps are ready for all suspicious persons ... the safest thing for you to do is to take your hands out of your pockets if you have them in, or you are liable to be shot on sight.' The notice ended, 'God Save the King. God Save Ireland – Members of the crown forces'.[30]

Barry, in *Guerilla Days*, describes the 2–4 February 1921 as 'The Twelve Dark Days' because during that period 11 officers and IRA men were killed. Some, like the two Coffey brothers, were killed in their beds. Two masked civilians, one of them a woman known as 'Foxy Bess', had led the killers directly to the room where the young men slept. The killers were members of the British Action espionage circle, known also as The Protestant Action Group.

Paddy Crowley, a battalion commandant, was ill in bed at O'Neill's, Maryborough. Essex men raided the house. Unable to hide, he ran, was wounded, then fell and they shot him where he lay. Barry said that not one of their enemy had been killed during that period. 'The morale of our units was bound to suffer if fatal casualties continued, with none being inflicted on the enemy'. Hundreds of young men, within a radius of twenty miles around Bandon were arrested. All reported being beaten and tortured, some were hoisted as 'stool pigeons' in military lorries that travelled the countryside on raids. Many men not involved in the IRA were jailed.[31]

'Drumhead court-martials for dealing with rebels caught with arms in their hands' were set up, according to General Percival'. Penalties for harbouring rebels, or for failing to report ambushes, etc., or for giving the wrong name' were enforced.[32]

'Under propaganda auspices a weekly incentive to "murder" indiscriminately was issued to the police in the form of a weekly summary printed and published by the government', General Crozier records, 'while instructions to "murder and ask questions after" were issued secretly to selected police officers from Dublin Castle.' The district county inspector's 'weekly summary' contained statistics, details of spies, casualties, burnings, killing – from a propaganda viewpoint. The 'stamping out of terrorism by murder' was instituted.[33]

For the future Barry decided he would not show mercy to the Bandon Essex Regiment under Percival as they continued to torture, wound and kill defenceless IRA prisoners. They lacked mercy to the sick, the unarmed, and created havoc when raiding homes and burned many. 'They had killed in us too the virtue for mercy … Orders issued by me in 1921 were to shoot every member of the Essex at sight, armed or unarmed, and not to accept their surrender under any circumstances. We had tried to play the game of war by the rules accepted by the civilised world', but now immunity had come to an end. In other areas the rules of war were to be observed, mercy would be shown, but not in Bandon.[34]

Barry quotes Napoleon as having allegedly said, 'There are two levers for moving men: interest and fear'; but he himself added a third, counter-terror. 'The Essex, the Auxiliaries and all British terrorist forces would be destroyed as far as our strength was capable of killing them', he wrote.[35]

Barry decided to have another go at the Bandon stronghold. A 44 strong column was mustered on 23 February for another attack on a curfew patrol. The men carried rifles and pistols and wore their new uniforms – a khaki-type coat with a cape at the back. As usual Barry had them detailed and divided into sections for their approach to the town. At 8.20 p.m. they reached their chosen place of attack. 'Accurate timing was essential'. Barry, as column commander believed it was imperative that the decision when to attack rested with him. He went forward alone, clearly visible under a full moon, clad in uniform, leggings and full field equipment. Mick Crowley followed a distance behind with a section, they crossed the bridge at the end of the town where the section stopped. Barry went up South Main Street and met an IRA sympathiser who told him that the patrol was coming. Barry hastened back towards the scout to signal the column to advance.

But as he made his way back, the sound of marching feet and English voices brought him to an abrupt halt. His first reaction was to run. He said it is amazing how quickly things run through your head when confronted with a situation, how quickly you think and dismiss thoughts. He was sure that it was the end. There was no escape. Should he make a run for it? 'No. My reason flashed the warning that if I turned and ran I would be shot in the back. I stood my ground as five military rounded the North Main Street corner and advanced across the bridge towards me.'

The gunfight commenced. Facing the enemy Barry opened fire with revolver in one hand and an automatic in the other. Mick Crowley, whom he had posted at the north end of the bridge, joined in. The Tan swinging his revolver as he came into view was the first to fall. A second staggered across the road and then fell. Barry missed the third as he sprang to the other side of the road, but Crowley got him. The fourth man had bolted back to the barracks at the sound of the first shot and the fifth had dropped to the ground, as a trained soldier will when under fire. Now he leaped up, sprang round the corner escaping the first shot aimed at him. Barry in a fury ran after him brandishing his guns but didn't fire, because, as he says, 'I was mad. I just wanted to get my hands on him'. Confronting, in a close range situation, Constable Perrier, a known spy in the dreaded Essex Regiment whom they had been watching, made him lose his temper. Perrier had made attempts to join the IRA under the guise of a deserter. 'I was guilty of the most senseless act of my life, for I ran after him,' Barry admitted. (A man who was so disciplined and so insistent on discipline could view this action as a reckless act. On reflection later, he was self critical of this action, as he said it was an irrational act and he recorded that Perrier could have turned around and shot him.)

Still running, Barry slipped his revolver into his pocket to free his left hand: he retained the colt automatic in his right hand. The panic-stricken soldier ran into an open doorway. As he cleared the small counter Barry vaulted after him, grabbing him by the shoulder. He shook him and shot him twice at point-blank range.[36]

'Are you all right in there,' shouted Tom Kelleher, who had followed him. Kelleher remained at the door in case more British military should come along.

'I got the bloody fellow,' Barry said, as he emerged.

'Why didn't you fire on him going in?'

'I wanted to shake the bastard first.'

Unperturbed Barry began to check his gun and reload it.

'You would think the British were a hundred miles away,' Tom Kelleher recalled.

Barry shook himself, straightened his shoulders: 'a spy. Bastard! Pretending he was in sympathy with us.'[37]

He bolted down the street to meet the remainder of the column who were dealing with the other patrol. As Kelleher and Barry ran, bullets were knocking sparks off the flagstones behind them. But as Jim Kearney says, 'There was never a bullet made to shoot Barry.'[38]

Reaching the rendezvous outside Bandon, Barry found the two other sections waiting. John Lordan captured two naval officers and following interrogation, Barry allowed them to go free 'as they were not guilty of any murder of unarmed Irishmen'. But he gave them a note for Percival. He named unarmed IRA men who were tortured to death and warned him of dire consequences. 'Henceforth your unit, in common with other terrorists, will be subject to reprisals for every outrage committed by it ... The Essex Regiment has burned and destroyed nearly 50 West Cork homes, long before such burnings had become the official policy of the British military government in Ireland.'[1]

Major C. J. Street, British intelligence officer downplayed the lawlessness of the Auxiliaries as 'a few bad apples' within the force. However, Lloyd George and his cabinet acknowledged their ruthlessness in December 1920 when Archbishop Clune was negotiating a settlement between both countries. In a three-point plan that included the surrender of arms, etc., government knowledge of a vendetta was exposed. Point No. 3 recorded:

> Sinn Féin to order the cessation of all violence in return for which the government to stop reprisals of shop looting, raids, burnings, floggings, execution without court-martial (not admitted) and people only to be executed after due court-martial.[2]

Lord Russell acknowledged that some of the Auxiliaries 'exploits were shameful and the army's reputation suffered through them.'[3]

Fire-raising gangs accompanied raiding parties and roved over West Cork. Farmhouses, labourers' cottages and shops went up in flames leaving desolation and misery in their wake. Over 50 years later the harrowing scenes of 'mothers with young families out under a tarpaulin tent or in a hen house on a bitter winter's night' after their home and belongings were gutted was etched in Barry's memory. This was 'mostly always done with glee'. Dan Cahalane recalled many families who 'suffered this terrible torture. It had to be stopped.'[4]

To counter this terror, GHQ sanctioned the burning of British Loyalist homes in retaliation. 'The West Cork Brigade was slow to commence a campaign of counter-burnings', said Barry. 'They [British military] started the burning, as they did with the Boers in South Africa. We found it necessary to react'.[5] When the threat was ignored, the IRA burned two Loyalist houses for each Nationalist house burned. This created an outcry from the British Loyalists in West Cork. Now caught-up in terrorism they demanded that British forces should cease destroying Republican homes. Members in the House of Commons pleaded on behalf of their constituents, stating that two small farmhouses were worth less than £1,000, whereas four large British Loyalists houses were worth over £20,000. Bill Hales, whose home was burned to the ground, said 'the counter-terror worked'. Though many Republican homes had been destroyed, many were now saved 'from destruction'.[6]

Michael Collins wrote: 'for myself my conscience is clear. There is no crime in detecting and destroying, in war time, the spy and the informer'.[7] So orders went out from GHQ to the brigades of the IRA. In the Third West Cork Brigade orders were transmitted in a memorandum by the brigade intelligence officer to battalion commanders to procure evidence of suspected spies and to intensify raids on mail carriers and post offices, thus obtaining further evidence. Women helped in this process.

Barry with Liam Deasy, Charlie Hurley, Seán Buckley and other officers in the brigade area turned their attention to spies. It was evident that the British forces had an extensive espionage service in the West Cork area and it was felt that the IRA and their activities would be short-lived unless this was broken. May Twomey, who worked in Bandon post office with Anna Mulqueen intercepted correspondence which was passed on to Seán Buckley, intelligence officer and his team. 'We knew that men were being sold; we knew that there were several types of spies and informers.' Between 17 January and 16 February 1921, Barry said that 'as a result of information given to the enemy, nine IRA within a 12 mile radius of Bandon were captured and murdered'.[8]

Barry regretted the turn events were taking but spies had to be dealt with 'coldly and ruthlessly to ensure the survival of the IRA'. He said that every national movement in Ireland had failed because of spies and informers – 'the only source of enemy intelligence … we had hesitated too long to strike ... we, the brigade officers, must always bear a certain responsibility for the needless deaths of many of our own Volunteers'. There were 'spies who took blood money' and 'unpaid informers from the wealthier land-owning class who hated the Republican movement – were the worst'.[9]

Major Percival noted that in some districts all civilians were treated as hostile. It was the IO's duty to find out 'the political sympathies of every civilian … if friendly whether they are prepared to give information and if so what is their information worth.' He kept a largescale map on the wall where every farm and house was marked and there was a note on the sympathies of the occupier, therefore 'before any officer went on a raid,' he wrote, 'we had all available information'.[10] Lieut Gen. Hugh Jeudwine, GOC Fifth Division, said that 'in intelligence … every raid, every search, every encounter, successful or unsuccessful provided information.'[11]

Percival ordered that the IO 'must keep in close touch with the Loyalist especially those who were are not afraid to tell him what they know … if the IRA suspected a Loyalist of giving information or being too friendly with the crown forces, it meant certain death to him,' Percival noted. Usually, visitation to these houses 'took place after dark'. Percival tells how he blackmailed a local company officer into giving information in return for immunity. The officer was 'convicted of some small offence and sentenced to six months' imprisonment'.

Percival wrote that 'he proved very useful'.[12]

There is no indication that Barry or any of the senior officers were aware of this man's activities at this time. However, when a man was either 'captured or surrendered voluntary whilst armed with a rifle' at the Upton train ambush, their suspicions were roused. Flor Begley notes that 'the column could have been wiped out as a result of this man's betrayal of many vital facts relating to Brigade H. Qrs. and the movements of senior Brigade officers'. Though with the IRA, he did not participate in any engagement for some time before Upton, but 'turned up that day with a rifle'. Afterwards Charlie Hurley investigated his actions, discovered 'he hid in a house, never fired a shot but remained there to be arrested, waiting!' Within a week of this arrest the IRA were 'tipped off by a friendly RIC sergeant to be careful as he had given the game away, meaning he had talked a lot.' Upon general release this 'Coy. Captain volunteered a statement' said 'that he gave information whilst under the influence of drugs, etc.' He was court-martialled, sentenced to death which was 'commuted to exile for life'. Neither Tom Barry nor any of the Cork No. 3 Brigade men were aware at the time that it was due to his information that Charlie Hurley was killed and 'several other captures were effected in this neighbourhood'.[13]

'Every civilian should be looked on as a potential enemy,' Percival emphasised to his regiment. 'It would have been impossible to carry out any operations without having a reasonably good intelligence service,' he wrote. With this in mind he used 'Loyalist sympathisers' to the fullest extent.[14] Strickland's division found that 'information obtained from civilian agents' helped the 6th Division track down 'arms dumps' and 'rebels'.[15]

'Some were ready to tell what they knew, frequently without asking for payment … small presents were more acceptable … Most informants, preferred to tell verbally what they knew … A method frequently employed was to carry out a raid on and search the house of an informer, and during the course of it an opportunity could be found to speak to him or her.' Occasionally, 'an informant' would be 'arrested' during 'curfew hours', and in the security of barracks impart with 'valuable' information.[16] Some 'loyal inhabitants' who 'have incurred the displeasure of the IRA and are therefore unable to reside in their homes' were 'recompensed out of a special intelligence fund and transferred to England,' according to Strickland's records. It was considered 'the duty of the government, to help loyal citizens of the United Kingdom.'[17]

Barry and the officers of the Third West Cork Brigade knew they had a difficult task, and they knew some though not all of their enemy's methods of seeking information, such as putting 'stool pigeons' into jail to mingle with IRA prisoners. 'Stool pigeons' pretended to be in sympathy with the IRA and tried to obtain information.[18]

IRA officers implemented various forms of interrogation. But 'a tight rein was kept on all battalions, no spy was executed without the sanction of a brigade officer,' according to Liam Deasy.[19] Barry dressed in leggings and trench coat and sporting a captured Auxiliary's tasselled beret visited houses of suspected informers. Speaking with a British accent, he questioned them about the IRA. Information was given freely as they believed they were speaking to a member of the British forces.

He told of one occasion, wearing the captured Auxiliary's tasselled beret, when he was readily admitted into the home of a 'a Loyalist informer'. Three armed IRA officers waited outside. The man was not on their list until they were freely given his name when on another 'visitation'. This 'visitor' was ushered into the drawing-room where the man drinking whiskey asked him to join him in a drink. Barry refused. He never drank spirits until after dinner! The man grumbled because the authorities took so long to respond to his call. In explaining the reason for his message, he named two IRA men he had tracked to a barn, gave their names and how best to trap them. He produced a notebook, and again complained about delays in acting on his previous messages. 'If you people were quicker to act on information the IRA would be finished in the locality long ago.' He poured out details of IRA movements and activities in the area. As he warmed to his subject he also poured himself another glass of whiskey, asked his 'visitor' was he sure he wouldn't have one. 'No thanks!' Barry politely declined. He correctly named the local IRA officers, and the names of senior officers whom he called 'The Big Shots'. He went on to name 'reliable men' who like him were helping the authorities.

'In vivid detail he boasted about information which led to the murder of two of my men,' said Barry. 'This was proof. My blood began to stir as the maid brought more water for the whiskey, and he poured himself another. Again I refused. "He'll have tea," he said. I said, "No." She brought it anyway and left. My pulse beat faster, I knew I was going to kill him.'

'"Don't move," I said. "Keep your hands on the table." I drew my companion from my pocket, blew the whistle, told him who I was – one of "the Big Shots" he named. The whiskey glass fell from his hand ...' Hearing the sound of the whistle, Barry's fellow officers came in. The man was court-martialled. He admitted making the statements and his incriminating activities. A few hours later he was shot.[20]

One informer in Innishannon, according to Barry 'was not only an important organiser of espionage against the IRA, but guided in person raiding parties of the Essex Regiment.' It was well known from inside information that he wore a mask. But one night in a victim's house, his mask slipped. From that December night in 1920, he was guarded by four Black and Tans. On the night he was shot the Tans failed in their aim on the IRA raiding party.[21]

'We cleared thirteen spies out in one month ... Spies got no mercy. The spy is the paid man; he's the blood-money scoundrel, but he's not as dangerous as the informer. The spy takes his chance ...'[22] The 'unpleasant duty of dealing with spies and informers' Liam Deasy believed was 'necessary' as 'British gold and Irish greed' would outstrip the Volunteer efforts to secure 'freedom'. 'Incidents convinced us beyond all possible doubt that information was being supplied to the enemy'.[23]

On the rare occasion when a man tried to take advantage of the situation for his own reasons, Tom was unbending; his capacity for sizing up facts and motives was said to be extremely accurate. When he decided that a spy deserved to be shot following a court-martial, if circumstances permitted he either ordered the execution to be done or performed it himself. Occasionally the spy was asked to leave the country.

There was the odd occasion when a member tried to take advantage of the situation. One man in an effort to have his neighbour shot because of some disagreement told Barry more than once that he was a spy. Having put some preliminary questions to the Volunteer, Barry decided that his motives were other than honourable. Barry was writing at a table when the Volunteer again approached him. 'Look,' said Barry, placing his own gun on the table, 'go away and shoot him.'

The man knew that Barry didn't believe him. He looked at Barry, then at the gun, and walked away.'[24]

As Barry was writing his book he had the names of those involved in espionage and the details of their activities. 'At first I listed the names and addresses of those sixteen British agents who were shot by the West Cork Brigade of the IRA Then the thought came of the pain such a listing would bring to those traitors' descendants and relatives … Innocent men and women should not suffer for the sins of their fathers,' he wrote. The daily press 'of the first six months of 1921 will supply all particulars' of those 'executed including the official British announcements of the deaths of their agents,' he wrote to the editor of the *Irish Press*. Mr Sweetnam was happy with Barry's omission of names, but he also wanted Lord Tom Kingston's name omitted, as 'it might be embarrassing to other Kingstons'. Barry disagreed with that one, as Burgatia House would identify it in any case.[25]

Barry and his column knew that one man dressed in a woman's hood cloak was a constant caller to Bandon barracks. 'He sold Brinny ambush'. Several attempts 'to get him', failed. The British government sent 'the informer and his family' to England. 'A member of GHQ squad followed, but failed to find him.'[26]

Major B. L. Montgomery of the Seventeenth Brigade, told Percival that he 'regarded all civilians as "shinners".' His 'whole attention was given to defeating the rebels and it never bothered me a bit,' he wrote, 'how many houses were burned.' In his 'general remarks' he suggested, 'that to win a war of that sort you must be ruthless; Oliver Cromwell, or the Germans, would have settled it in a very short time. Now-a-days public opinion precludes such methods; the nation would never allow it; and the politicians would lose their jobs if they sanctioned it.'[27]

The British, Barry said, were met with their own weapons. 'They had gone down in the mire to destroy us and our nation, and down after them we had to go to stop them.'[28] As a result of this drastic action IRA casualties were greatly reduced. 'There can be no doubt as to why the death roll of the West Cork IRA dropped so amazingly; it was solely because British terror was met by a not less effective IRA counter-terror.'

Even after 'a lapse of years' he believed he had nothing 'to apologise for', in fact he felt 'the decision should have been taken earlier' when more of his men would have been saved. The step these officers believed they had to take was 'not an easy one' Barry said, 'for one's mind was darkened and one's outlook made bleak by the decisions which had to be taken.'[29]

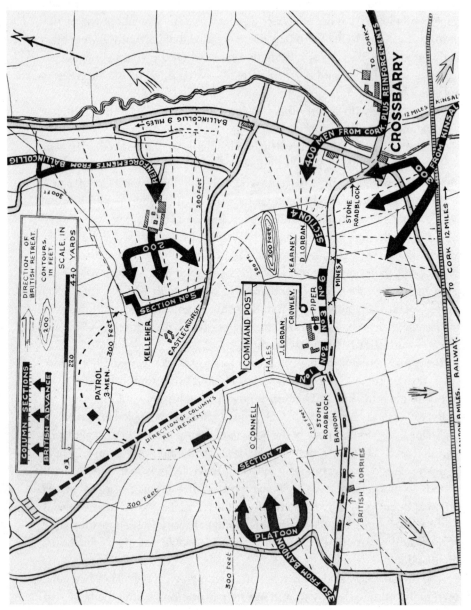

Map of Crossbarry ambush, p. 98

Wedding of Tom Barry's aunt, Elizabeth O'Donovan to Edward O'Sullivan

Front: Edward O'Donovan (Tom's uncle), Edward's girl friend (name unknown)
Seated L. to R.: Con O'Donovan (poet, Aunt Katie's husband); Hannah (Tom's aunt),
Edward O'Sullivan (groom), Elizabeth (bride, Tom's aunt), May (Tom's aunt), Mary
O'Donovan (Tom's grandmother)
Standing L. to R.: Tom's grandaunt (name unknown), Katie (Tom's aunt), two priests (family
friends, names unknown), Margaret (Tom's mother)

The young Tom Barry

Tom's younger sisters and brother,
Gertrude, Maureen and Jack Barry

Group taken after release from Wormwood Scrubs prison, May/June 1920. They had been interned in early 1920 and went on hunger strike. From left: J. Ahearne, Castlemartyr; M. Sweeney, Limerick; Stephen O'Neill, Clonakilty; John 'Flyer' Nyhan, Clonakilty; Pat Harte, Clonakilty; Joe Flynn, Clonakilty; S. O'Connor, Clare; J. Brazil, Waterford
(Clonakilty Museum)

Having left Wormwood Scrubs, May/June 1920 – after a period on hunger strike
Front row L. to R.: *Felix Cronin, Tipperary (later married Kitty Kiernan, Michael Collins' girl friend), Miss Egan, Cumann na mBan, Pat O'Leary (Kilmurry Company), Flor Begley (Bandon Battalion, Barry's Flying Column – Piper Crossbarry)*
Back row L. to R.: *Paddy Crowley (Barry's Flying Column, Kilbrittain Company), Dan Canty (Barry's Flying Column, Newcestown Company)*

Front row left to right: *Denis Galvin (Barry's Flying Column, Bandon Company), Jerry Fitzgerald (Barry's Flying Column, Kilbrittain Company)*
Back row left to right: *Seán Lehane (Barry's Flying Column), Charlie Daly (Kerry), Jack Fitzgerald (Barry's Flying Column, Kilbrittain Company)*

Tom Hales, OC (Ballinadee Coy). A founder of West Cork Volunteers, arrested, tortured 1920, in Pentonville jail until Treaty signing

Paddy O'Brien (Barry's Flying Column – Ballinacarriga Company – fought in Kilmichael and other engagements)

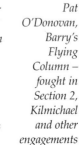

Tom Kelleher (Crosspound Coy), Section Commander, fought in Crossbarry, Rosscarbery and other engagements

Pat O'Donovan, Barry's Flying Column – fought in Section 2, Kilmichael and other engagements

Liam Deasy, Third Cork Brigade O/C, later adjutant First Southern Division

Major A. E. Percival, Essex Regiment (Kinsale and Bandon). The most dreaded commander of enemy forces in the Third Cork Brigade. (In 1941, he surrendered in Singapore to inferior forces)

Tom Barry's revolver in Cork Public Museum (Cork Public Museum)

Described as 'a little leisure from hunting assassins' in a captured officer's album

*Jim 'Spud' Murphy, Barry's Flying Column –
fought at Command Post during Kilmichael
ambush*
(Clonakilty Museum)

*Ned (Edward) Young, Barry's Flying
Column (last survivor of the Kilmichael
ambush)*

*Jim O'Sullivan, Barry's Flying Column –
shot dead by Auxiliaries at Kilmichael*

*Michael MacCarthy, Barry's Flying Column
– shot dead by Auxiliaries at Kilmichael*

Pat Deasy, Barry's Flying Column –
fatally wounded at Kilmichael

Picture of Michael Collins, Commander-in-
Chief, taken (for his fiancee, Kitty Kiernan) in
Portobello Barracks shortly before he was killed

Leslie Price, Chief Organiser of Cumann na mBan, married Tom Barry, 22 August 1921, later
known as Leslie Bean de Barra, Chairman of The Red Cross
(Courtesy of her niece Máire)

At the wedding in Dublin of Tom Barry to Leslie Price, 22 August 1921

L. to R., seated on ground: Dick Cotter, Eamonn Price, Eva Price, Phyllis Ryan, Gearóid Ó Súilleabháin

Front row, seated: Máirín McCarvock, Harry Boland, Jennie Wyse Power, Archdeacon O'Callaghan, PP, Mrs Price, Liam Deasy, Leslie Price, President Eamon de Valera, Tom Barry, Dr Nancy Wyse Power, Mr Price, Mary McSwiney, Countess Markievicz

First row standing: Seán Lehane, Kathleen Kerrigan, Jack Price, Pete Kearney, Jim Hurley, Ted Sullivan, Mick Collins, Seán McCarthy, Mick Crowley, Dick Mulcahy, Mrs O'Donovan, Eoin O'Duffy, Mrs Tom Cullen, Kathleen Phelan, Liam Tobin, Emmet Dalton, Marie O'Reilly, Tom Cullen Aoife Taafe, Rory O'Connor, Susan Colum, Seán McSwiney, Fr Tom Duggan, Fiona Plunkett, Treasa Ní Mhodhráin, Tadhg Sullivan, Seán Buckley, Eileen Colum, Agnes Sharpe

Second row standing: Hotel Proprietor, Seán Hales, Liam Devlin, Vincent Gogan, Paddy Dalton, Mick Price, Joe O'Reilly

(Cork City Museum)

The Glasshouse
24th April 1935
12-30 PM

My Leslie: This is a small note which I hope to be able to slip to you at your visit today despite the Military Police. I have just got your letter and I am waiting waiting for you. I told you not to come but still if you had not, I should have had an awful disappointment.

The first batch of twelve have gone since 9.30. and we will arrive at Collins Barracks about 10.45 tomorrow. So be there at that time. I read all about your Limerick lecture. It was very good and I felt so proud of you. Still when I get out you will have something else to do and that will be to love me all the time.

I have no idea how long our sentences will be. However long, please remember that I shall go through in flying colours and be back to you strong, fit and unchanged. Through all the time I will be in, I shall think always of you and love you all the time. Not love you more than I do now because that would be impossible.

I have written Joe McGrath yesterday. It is no compliment. Today I heard from Seán C., Jer & Jim O'B. Jim's was a scream. I will send you McGrath's letter as soon as I get it.

Au revoir my sweetheart. I shall love you while I live and afterwards if it is possible for humans to do so. I shall be longing to get back to you and then we shall be so happy again. I send you all my kisses and all of my love.

Your sweetheart
Tom

Tom's love letter from prison to Leslie – 12.30 p.m. 24 April 1935

Hotel-Pension Elite

Inhaberin: Ida Lasar
WIEN I, WIPPLINGERSTRASSE 32
Ecke Börseplatz
Tel. 63 25 18, 63 51 13

Im Stadtzentrum gelegen.
In allen Zimmern Fließwasser,
Zentralheizung, Telephon.
Zimmer mit Privatbad.

Vienna, Tuesday Aug. 28th
Wien, am

5-30 p.

Darling – This is only a short note being written with one eye
with [Bhanna?] (and listening to nothing) as we sit in session.
The Hotel is quite comfortable – except that the bed is the
complete Hair mattress which we knew years ago without
internal springs and is very restful – I woke at
3 a.m. and then at 5-30 a.m. – Alas, no Tos & no Tea.
We went to 8 a.m. Mass at a Redemptorist Church
about 10 minutes walk from hotel. Then we had our coffee
+ buns and came to the Hofburg – President's residence –
to enrol for the Conference. We had our lunch here at
Cafe – 16/- each – not bad stuff. Then we came into
this meeting – and at 6 pm we go to a Reception by
the Governor of Lower Austria – in the Vienna
woods – only it is raining.

I think so much of you, my love. I love only
you. M. [Mutta?] says she sends her greetings &
that here she has not met anyone nicer than you –
[Somehow?] so.

All all my love
your own
Lottie

Leslie wrote to Tom from Vienna, and signed it 'Lottie' which was Tom's pet name for her
(Courtesy of Sighle Humphreys Papers, UCDA)

At Castletown-Kenneigh graveyard, crowd assembled for the unveiling of monument over the graves of the three Volunteers fatally wounded during the Kilmichael Ambush

At Blueshirt Congress, August 1934, General Eoin O'Duffy takes the organisation's salute (Tom Barry, OC, 'New' IRA, Cork, challenged sections of this group)

Tom Barry (centre) *and his friend Jack Doheny Lynch [on Tom's left] and other prisoners upon release from Arbour Hill on 24 July 1934*

Tom Barry heads the survivors of the Kilmichael ambush, 1966

Tom Barry chatting with Archdeacon Tom Duggan (who had been involved in peace negotiations during Civil War) and Chief Supt Philip Chambers

Tom Barry and his friend Detective Sergeant John Browne in the Mardyke, Cork

Tom Barry signing his book in the United States

Tom Barry speaking, 1930s, beside Section 2, Kilmichael ambush site, where the three Volunteers were fatally wounded

Parade in Bandon to unveiling of monument to West Cork's Heroic Dead by President Seán T. O'Kelly, 2 August 1953

Front L to R.: *Comdt Ted O'Sullivan, Gen Liam Deasy, President O'Kelly, Comdt Gen. Tom Barry.*

Second Row: *QM Dan Holland, QM Tadhg O'Sullivan, Col Brennan ADC, Seán McCarthy*
Third row: *Con Crowley, Pat Walsh*

Parade passing British Military Barracks' ruin where once Percival and his Essex garrison had tortured and murdered some the men being honoured
(Courtesy of Paddy Connolly)

Tom Barry unveiling monument to Michael Collins at Sam's Cross, Easter Sunday, April 1966
(Cork Public Museum)

Tom Barry addressing troops of the Irish army and an estimated 15,000 people at the Michael Collins monument unveiling, April 1966
(Cork Public Museum)

Tom Barry in 1949

Tom Barry in the Mardyke, Cork

Tom and Leslie's mortuary card

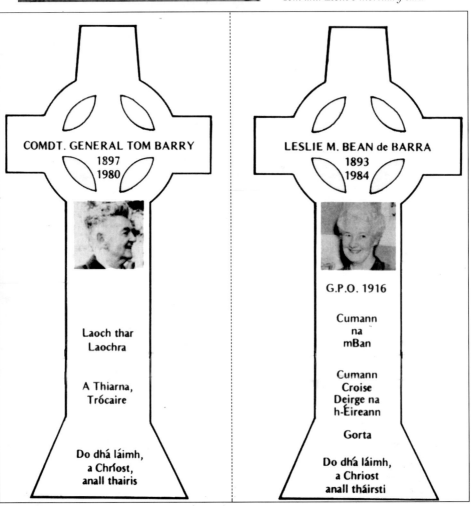

COMDT. GENERAL TOM BARRY
1897
1980

Laoch thar
Laochra

A Thiarna,
Trócaire

Do dhá láimh,
a Chríost,
anall thairis

LESLIE M. BEAN de BARRA
1893
1984

G.P.O. 1916

Cumann
na
mBan

Cumann
Croise
Deirge na
h-Éireann

Gorta

Do dhá láimh,
a Chriost
anall tháirsti

CROSSBARRY'S LANDMARK SUCCESS

By March 1921, the Third West Cork Brigade was an army, well trained and experienced in guerrilla warfare. This style of fighting required a commander able to make split-second decisions and the men under him able to act immediately on his commands to out-wit and out-fight an army trained in regular warfare. Their intelligence section was now much better equipped with binoculars, telescopes and other field equipment, and they had mastered Morse code signalling. Tom had learned message-sending and decoding in the British army and passed on these invaluable skills. 'Smoke, mirror and light signals could be sent from Kinsale to the top of Ballyhandle, on to Belrose and into Lovell's Hill and from there to Bantry. It only took seven minutes to send a signal from Kinsale to Bantry – 50 miles approximately cross-country. (Tom's friend Dick Barrett, a teacher at Gurranes National School was an expert. Later he took the anti-Treaty side, was arrested and executed while in custody, during the Civil War.)[1] Meanwhile, the flying column was mobilised to the strength of 104 officers and men and had, to Barry's relief, obtained an explosives expert, Capt McCarthy, a former officer of the Royal Engineers with strong Republican sympathies. Another asset to the column was Flor Begley, intelligence officer, who would use his well-known talent as a player of the bagpipes. 'I had formed an opinion that the best soldiers will fight even better to the strains of their traditional war songs,' said Barry. 'You know, we Irish love this rousing music; it puts life into our blood.'[2] Word reached the flying column that the British garrison in the area, was being strengthened by 300 troops who had arrived in Kinsale and were to travel to Bandon on 17 March. Barry mobilised his column and moved into ambush position on the main Bandon-Kinsale road. He had 'made arrangements to have the pipes collected' so that St Patrick's Day could be celebrated 'by ambushing some lorries to the accompaniment' of Flor Begley on the pipes.[3] 'We had been marching all night.' Dr Nudge Callanan recalls, 'and when dawn came I remember looking out over a wall and I saw reeds waving. I said to Dan Holland, "Come here, Dan. Would you tell me where we are?"

'"This is a place called Shippool; it's an estuary of the Bandon River."

'We had three mines down and I remember damn well we were very hungry. We called one of the local fellows who was scouting and asked him to bring us down a bucket of tea from the house above. He brought us down a bucket of cocoa without milk or sugar, and it was the grandest cocoa I ever drank.'[4]

The column remained all St Patrick's Day in seven sections of 14 rifle-men in each, including their section commander, and officers.[5] It was a miserable, biting wind-hard March day's wait and each man was poised for the unexpected. Barry had them positioned for a major battle. Towards evening two

Cumann na mBan girls arrived on bicycles to tell them that the Kinsale military knew they were there. The British had set out but returned because of information received. 'We knew then we were sold', said Barry who never traced the informant. Immediately he began to move his column on. Barry's leadership was tested as he grappled to get so many men to act in an orderly disciplined manner.[6] They had withdrawn about a mile from the ambushscade when Barry shouted to his men to halt, flatten, face downwards. 'A British reconnaissance plane zoomed low over the ambush position and then started searching as we lay flat and still in extended order hidden in the dykes ... I worried through the night as to how to get the column out of an attempted encirclement which would surely come.' Barry was certain that the people in the plane had spotted them and would be able to estimate the general direction of the IRA march as being towards the Upton-Crossbarry-Crosspound area.

Barry manoeuvred his men to Skeugh. They remained beside the ditches throughout the biting frosty night and then spent an 'uneasy day' after Seán Mac-Cárthaig brought ominous word that all garrisons were exceptionally quite. Strict security measures were adopted as they moved on to Ballyhandle where the column of 104 men billeted in several houses on the night of 18 March. Barry doubled the usual ring of scouts. He had not slept, and had eaten very little over the last two days and nights. In John O'Leary's, filled with apprehension, he refused a bed and instead lay fully dressed on the sofa. It was not long before Tom Kelleher and Mick Crowley rushed in. They had seen lights and heard lorries some miles to the west. It was almost 2.30 a.m. Further sounds came from the south. 'And our great friends, the dogs were barking'. Instantly, Barry ordered that his men be alerted. When they assembled, he told them they were surrounded and no doubt out-numbered. 'I had to decide without delay whether to fight or to retire and attempt to evade action.'

This wasn't an easy decision, because any section could be caught while retiring, possibly with heavy casualties. Furthermore, the shortage of ammunition, only 36–40 rounds per man, called for a swift and intensive fight at close quarters.

He did not know then that starting at 1 a.m. on the morning of 19 March, 400 troops had left Cork, 200 Ballincollig, 300 Kinsale and 350 Bandon. Later 120 Auxiliaries left Macroom. Later still more troops left Clonakilty and Cork.

Neither did he know until later that the local officer who had been 'arrested' at Upton by Percival's men had 'sold' their whereabouts. Seán Mac-Cárthaigh met Fr Ned Fitzgerald in the city who told him that prison officers had entered this man's cell on the 'eve of Crossbarry' and 'that things did not look too good from the information side'. MacCárthaigh took the train, headed for headquarters to warn Seán Buckley and Charlie Hurley. But they did not heed his warning. By the time word of the 'sell out' got to Barry he had given his ambush orders.[7] Once it was certain that the sounds of lorries could be heard from different areas, Tom Barry 'Column Commander, having ordered all ranks to fall in, delivered a spirited talk. He pointed out that it was the duty of every man to give his best that day and to obey the orders of his superior officers.'[8] He said 'that we would first smash one side of the encirclement on the Cross-barry road, and then deal with the others; above all no man or section was to retire from positions, and all were assured that they would be reinforced speedily if and when attacked. Then and only then was the decision taken to fight at Crossbarry.'[9] They were an encircled body, so Barry decision was precise. They would smash one side and fight their way out.

It was only at this stage that sections were allotted their positions, so Barry had to plan and plan quickly. His plan had to be decisive and they had to attack in such a way as to break the encirclement. He mobilised his men into seven sections, each with a section commander, and there were three officers with Barry as commanding officer. 'If not exactly pale with fear, I was a worried man,' Barry wrote.[10] Had he known what the 6th Division had in mind he would have been more worried. Their 'informant' who had given himself up at Upton, was in jail and 'hoping to save his life, asked to see the Bde. I.O', and then gave them 'a great deal of information', Percival recorded. He told them that 'HD. Qrs. of the Third Cork Bde. IRA were located in a group of farms in the Bally-murphy townland and that there was a dug-out in the same locality'. He also told them that 'John Hales and his column often made use of the area about two miles to the north of Cross Barry, and that this place was headquarters.' Accurate information on 'the actual houses used by the rebels' was in their possession. At 'a conference with the commanders of each party [Essex; Second Hants, First Manchs. & Aux. Divs] held at brigade headquarters on 18 March', a decision was taken 'to surround the area with troops'. They would 'drive in-wards meeting on the road which divided the two areas' at Crossbarry. Trans-port from each district would get to a certain point and the military would then 'proceed on foot' to 'a rendezvous' and be 'in position at 0600 hours'. However, some of the lorries took wrong turns, and though 'the officers had maps' they 'did not like to show a light … for fear of disclosing their presence.'[11] It appears that 'the informant' gave the name John Hales (this is Seán Hales) as column commander instead of Tom Barry of whom there is no mention.[12] Flor Begley was in no doubt but that the information 'obtained by the British' led to the selling of the Upton ambush, led to the subsequent 'round up', led to the near entrapment of the flying column at Crossbarry, led to the arrest and torture of many men.[13]

The well-laid plans of several regiments were in disarray when they reached the crossroads, because Barry had his men waiting, prepared to attack. At 3.30 a.m. with his column in prepared sections, he moved towards Crossbarry. An hour later they were in position, mainly on high ground west of the double cross-roads twelve miles from Cork city and eight miles from Bandon. The distant sounds of barking dogs, and humming vehicles could be heard while the IRA men crouched with the hard March wind on their faces as they awaited Barry's order to commence. He spoke. 'The column must stand and fight to the last man and the last round.'[14] The 104 men were divided into six sections and stretched inside the ditch, in the form of a triangle, with No. 7 section at the other side of the road (later moving into position to form a square). Barry had two small stone walls built to block a boreen at the western side and a road at the eastern flank of the ambuscade, thus preventing armoured cars from entering and flanking the column. Two mines were embedded in the road. It was extremely well planned. 'The column leader stressed to me the responsibility which my section would have in the fight', Tom Kelleher wrote. Kelleher's section was at the rear 'to protect the main body'. Communication between Barry as column commander and the other officers and the various sections was to be maintained by runners. The command post (Barry) was movable between the centre sections. 'Even though sections saw no enemy they were not to move to the aid of other sections, as the enemy were operating on various sides.'[15] Throughout the night Cumann na mBan members ran through fields, some in relays to convey directions of the slow-moving British vehicles to Barry and his men.

At 6.30 a.m. shots were heard in the distance. Tom's great friend, Charlie Hurley, who had been wounded at the Upton ambush, was in Fordes, a 'safe house' a few miles away when Major Halahan and officers of the First Essex burst in. Hurley, dressed only in his shirt and trousers, came down the stairs a revolver in each hand. The military stood in the kitchen at the foot of the stairs. Charlie kept firing 'as he rushed them'. He left one dead, two wounded and 'he made for the back door'. He was shot and fell dead in the back yard. The sound of the firing from Fordes made the men at the ambush site tenser, although they did not learn until late that night of Charlie's death. Tom had sent two men to warn Charlie to get out, but the Ballincollig military who were on the way to Crossbarry captured them.[16]

At 8 a.m., the long convoy of army lorries began to creep slowly abreast of the centre of the IRA position, moving towards the mine. The explosion blocked the road and announced the opening of the assault. Liam Deasy and Tom Barry flattened against the ditch as the leading lorry approached. Suddenly it slowed. Soldiers began to shout. Disregarding his stringent orders, a Volunteer from No. 3 section moved from his barn door to look out. He was spotted. The lorry halted immediately and its shouting occupants opened fire. He had messed up Barry's plan.

The British troops tumbled from their lorries which were by now strung out along the ambush position. 'The crackling of the rifle-fire and bursting of the bombs rent the quiet morning air … Above all other sounds could be heard the crack of the Peter the Painter, held in the hand of the column leader [Tom Barry]. This sound encouraged the men and gave them renewed energy.' No. 3 section opened fire and No. 1 and No. 2 sections did likewise, while No. 7 section took on the rear. The sound of gun-fire mingled with 'the old war songs' and 'rousing marches and tunes' on Flor Begley's bagpipes stimulated the column as bullets whizzed all round.[17] The Volunteers firing was often at point blank range because their positions were so close to the road. The enemy was confused and demoralised. Many ran panic-stricken as volley after volley was fired. As some scrambled across the fields, Barry ordered three sections to follow them. They chased the enemy (who became completely disorganised) through fields using rapid fire and killed many of them. This first phase of the action was over. The British encircling lines were smashed.[18]

Barry's policy was to 'hit without delay, hit hard, and hit as many separate points on the cordon as is possible.' In this way 'the forces surrounded by the cordon' were able to punch 'a hole in a weak part of the cordon'.[19] An order was given to collect the arms and equipment from the dead. These were a welcome bonus, and included in the haul was a brand-new Lewis gun and eight drums of ammunition. The dead were dragged to the side of the road while the lorries were drenched with petrol and set alight. Barry, having broken the encirclement, could now have withdrawn toward the south, but he decided they would stand their ground and wait for the next flood of attackers. Edward White, a prisoner in one enemy lorry though not an IRA man, had been arrested that morning and escaped during the firing, now helped to carry the captured machine-gun. The British forces had introduced 'a measure' of 'carrying "hostages" with all road convoys' to prevent attacks, according to Strickland. But it didn't work on this occasion.[20] The first three lorries were burning when rifle-fire was heard from Denis Lordan's section and Barry moved up to support them. Heavy fighting was exchanged for some time. Protected only by a small ditch, they fought 'like lions' – again the enemy ran in confusion, leaving their dead.

Newcomers to the scene brought No. 7 section into action. The British here had been on house raids and apparently were surprised by the sudden attack. When they found themselves in the midst of an ambush they fought for some time but then scattered. Forces had come from Kinsale, Cork, Dunmanway, Bandon and Macroom. Capt. Bill Powell, Crookstown Company, Cork No. 1 Brigade, had been arrested the previous week and was under guard and peeling potatoes in Macroom Castle kitchen, when panic hit the military. He heard shouts, 'Ambush at Upton, retreating to Crookstown woods!' Within 'ten minutes he heard lorries starting up and taking off'.[21]

During a short lull Barry went around encouraging his men, because he knew there was more to come. Ten minutes later another 200 British arrived, bringing Tom Kelleher's section in the rear under attack. The British crept close to the ditch and expected to catch the rear of the column off guard. But Kelleher's men were waiting. They allowed the British military to come within 50 yards before opening fire and hitting a number of them. Hurriedly the remainder retired to cover from where they continued to fire. Immediately Barry sent Spud Murphy (arm in sling from previous injury) with 11 rifle-men to reinforce Kelleher' section. There were now 26 officers and men facing this large

101

British column. Barry, anticipating that the military contingent might try to out-flank the position, extended his men northwards. The enemy met with such heavy fire that they were forced to retreat once more.

As other sections were not now in action, Barry moved the whole flying column (except O'Connell's section) to the left flank towards Kelleher's posi-tion to strike with full strength at this British unit now reinforced with the Essex men who had fled earlier. 'The column commander ordered: "Fall in! Get ready! Target: Enemy concentration on your immediate front! Range 300. Three rounds fire!" Three times in succession a 100 rifles barked.' The enemy 'broke in all directions'.[22] Kelleher's section had to fight 'the most prolonged and dan-gerous part of the whole engagement', Barry said.

British dead and wounded were strewn on the Crossbarry road, in the fields south of it, in front of Denis Lordan's section, near Christy O'Connell's section, and as Barry moved up to Tom Kelleher when the shots had died down he looked at a number of dead British soldiers.

'He tapped me on the shoulder. "I thought you were dead," he laughed. "Great job! Great work!" he says. Then he turned to John Lordan. "Excellent!" he said. "You did great bloody fighting down on the road."

'"'Tisn't everybody would get excellent at school," says John.

'"I know," says Barry. "That's the reason I gave you excellent."

'Then he turned to me. "We've a great day's work done here." And he swung around and walked back to inspect his column.'[23]

The column lost three men – Jeremiah O'Leary, Con Daly and Peter Mona-han. Peter Monahan was not his correct name. He was a British soldier with parents from Fermoy who deserted to join the IRA. Though a headstone is erected in the name of Peter Monahan in Bandon graveyard, he will remain forever the 'unknown soldier'. Dan Corcoran and Jim Crowley were seriously wounded, others were slightly wounded.

Two hours had elapsed since the opening of the fight, and Barry said, 'We were in possession of the countryside; no British military were visible, and our task was completed.' Yet he could never be sure; more troops could be en-countered as they retired to billets.

Undoubtedly Barry's genius as a commander was proved on this occa-sion. He had learned from past mistakes. He adopted the only 'sound policy' by deciding 'to attack one side of the encircling troops, before the other British forces closed in.'[24] Moreover, he knew that while the British military were not good at close fighting, his own men were; they had tenacity and courage. He told Seán Feehan years later, 'I put them close so that they'd fight or die, and I knew bloody well they'd fight!'[25] Pax O'Faolain said that Barry was a soldier in every way. 'He could take a dozen lads and make soldiers of them. He was a tradesman, and that was his trade. As well as that he had a damned good head.'[26]

According to the British version: 'The rebels – more by good luck than good guidance – managed to get into a position from which they were able to defend themselves, and from this point they put up a spirited resistance to the military attack.'[27] But as Barry said, 'Nobody can tell any guerrilla leader how he should fight with his force but himself.'[28] Strickland said 'if the outcome had been successful' from the British viewpoint it 'might easily have had decisive results as regards rebel activity in West Cork.'[29] Barry afterwards wrote for the Irish army magazine that the 'British handling of motorised infantry was defective and slipshod, the officer 'sent at least 16 lorries of troops towards or in to the ambush area before a single foot soldier reached it ... Whatever the reason the British paid dearly for it.'[30] Fifty years later Barry said Crossbarry 'may have been a decisive factor in getting the British establishment to think of a Truce. I am not claiming that it was, as there were other fights all over the country, but it is quite possible that it was very important for this nation, for the army, and for the Republic.[31] Tom Barry's fight at Crossbarry was 'a major turning point' for the British establishment', Nudge Callanan, participant, believed.[32]

Addressing Irish army officers 40 years later, Lieut Col Eamonn Moriarty spoke on location of how Tom Barry took the advantage of fighting 'when in fact the man was practically surrounded, and the timing which is everything ... I can see that Tom had very strong discipline, and it was what kept his unit together.'[33]

Like Kilmichael, it was one of the great victories for the Third West Cork Brigade and, indeed, for Ireland. Though Kilmichael was the most decisive ambush for the country and the Volunteer movement, Crossbarry was the greatest battle that was fought during the Irish fight for freedom.

According to the account in the *Daily Mail*, London, the British casualties numbered 35, though another report says 39 dead and 47 wounded.

As with Kilmichael the balladmaker was to pen the epic ambush for posterity:

> *They sought to wipe the column out,*
> *From east to west, from north to south,*
> *'Till at Crossbarry's bloody rout,*
> *They woke from their day-dreaming.*
> *Though ten to one they were that day,*
> *Our boys were victors in the fray,*
> *An' over the hills we marched away*
> *With bagpipes merrily screaming.*[34]

Ahead of Barry and his men was the long circuitous march, up to 20 miles, to billets – carrying the seriously wounded and the bodies of three dead comrades. Before walking on at an easy pace, under strict discipline Barry drew up the column in line of sections. He told them they had done well. He decided 'the get away' should 'be rapid'.[35]

The men hadn't slept or eaten for over 24 hours. 'They had marched, waited and fought all night.' They had to walk many miles before getting tea and bread and butter. Barry ordered scout guards to travel 300 yards ahead of the main body. First he ordered the men out on the road, and told them to walk 300 to 400 yards backwards, 'to step backwards'. If 'the military came along they would spot the footprints. Our commander was so wise, he thought of everything.' He sent other Volunteers to secure three horses and carts. Others were to organise food along the way. Flankers went at an easy pace – all would have to be prepared to fight again at any stage. Through his field glasses Barry observed some British forces as the column retired, they appeared leaderless 'arguing as to what to do next'. Barry helped them make up their minds. He ordered, ' Fall in! Fire!' His men responded. The enemy scattered.[36]

'I remember well getting up on a cart carrying ammunition. I was so tired I fell into a dead sleep,' says Nudge Callanan, 'and I didn't care if the whole damn thing blew up.'[37]

Along the way they had further minor encounters with distant British military; they returned fire, but neither side pursued the action.

Having put some distance between them and the enemy Barry and his men took a slower pace. As they marched along, his mind went back over the events of the night and the morning. He has said that a long chapter could be written about each of the 104 men – many of whom will remain unmentioned in history – and 'whose behaviour surpassed even my high expectation of such a smashing body of West Cork fighters. It was a composite victory of 104 officers and men banded together as disciplined comrades. No genius of leadership or no prowess of any officer or man was responsible, for all shared in the effort that shocked the confidence of the British authorities in the power of their armed forces … The greatness of those men of the flying column had a double-edged effect on me. One knew they could be relied on to the last, but on the other hand, I grew to have such an affectionate regard for them that I worried continually in case I failed them through negligence or inefficiency. I dreaded to lose a single one of them through some fault of mine. Their confidence in me was even disturbing.'[38]

In fact he bore this great love for the men he fought with until the day he died. Although he lost some friends through some petty disagreement, nevertheless if they were ever in trouble or needed anything, he would come to their assistance. Indeed, no matter which side of the Civil War the men who had fought with him took, he respected them and still called them 'my men'.[39]

Writing on the Crossbarry ambush, Liam Deasy noted that Tom Barry 'proved himself an ideal column commander. At the camps organised by him he had trained the officers well, and in the many engagements in which he fought he had won the confidence and respect of everyone who served under him. He was a strict disciplinarian and a good strategist, but he was something greater still: he was a leader of unsurpassed bravery, who was in the thick of every fight, and so oblivious of personal risk that his men felt it an honour to be able to follow him.'[40]

Travelling across ditches, fields and roads they reached Kilbornane by evening. Here they would eat. Barry stood on a ditch and watched the flying column pass. Though without food or rest, unshaven, caps with peaks turned back or in their pockets, with trench coats hung open and muddy leggings, they walked past with a spring in their step, rifles at the trail, or slung across their backs. 'As they came in to pass where I stood, their shoulders jerked back so that no one would assume they were tiring', Barry wrote. He knew these 'tough men' also as 'light-hearted youths' caught up in the fight 'for freedom from the chains of oppression and British aggression' would 'normally have been happy working' on their farms, shops or at school. Barry was proud that they never doubted his decisions. 'I shall always cherish the fact that never once during all the Anglo-Irish struggle did any officer or man question any of my decisions or show to me anything but the greatest loyalty and comradeship.'[41]

'Every one of us trusted Tom, we didn't want anything to happen to him as we fought together in our goal for freedom,' Denis Lordan recalled. Tom had no parents, brothers or sisters living in West Cork, and unlike most of the men, never had a shirt or a sock 'sent from home'. But the men gave him theirs. On parade he was 'Commandant' but in billets he was 'Tom' one of 'the boys'.[42] 'After I had been hurt and when long marches with the column was an effort', Tom wrote, 'during a halt some of the men would come with a saddled horse "Commandant, this horse is idle and you might as well ride him the rest of the way"'. Because of their kindness and loyalty he would examine his conscience to see if he 'had ordered some movement which might have been better left unexecuted'.[43] These 'God-fearing men believed in one thing – the freedom of Ireland, and were prepared to follow Barry to the death … and were prepared to give their all with him.'[44]

Darkness had already set in as the column reached O'Sullivan's of Gurranreagh, in the parish of Kilmichael, outside the Third West Cork Brigade area. They 'were not respecters of borders and had crossed on many occasions', and had fought Toureen and Kilmichael in Cork No. 1 area.

As the weary men moved into billets, news reached them that the shots they had heard from Crossbarry in the morning were those that killed Tom's friend, Charlie Hurley. Tom says Charlie foretold his own death. 'One day, as I was chaffing him, he turned to me and said quite gravely, "When I am killed by them I shall be alone. I shall die fighting them, but none of you will be with me." And so it was.'[45]

A few days before the Crossbarry ambush Charlie had given 'a silver ring' to Flor Begley and asked him to get a wedding ring of the same size 'with three stones in it'. At the billet the night before they left for the march to Crossbarry, Flor said to Charlie, 'I hadn't a chance to get that ring for you yet – you'd never know what would happen to me tomorrow, so here you'd better take it!' The ring that Charlie wanted was for his bride-to-be Leslie Price, Cumann na mBan organiser. Flor thought about getting the silver ring again to return it to Leslie at the funeral and to then tell her the story, but he decided against it.[46]

The evening after Crossbarry ambush, Tom, Liam Deasy and a column of men set out for Clogagh. 'We marched and marched all Saturday and Sunday nights, although already weary and tired after the long fight at Crossbarry on Saturday morning until 2 a.m. on Monday when we arrived at Clogagh village.' Cumann na mBan members had smuggled Charlie Hurley's body from the Bandon Workhouse morgue, where British soldiers had taken it. Leslie Price, Charlie's fiancée and Bridie Crowley with colleagues drove with it through the night in a pony and trap. Seán MacCárthaigh drove Brigid O'Mahony 'with some of his brain matter [from the fatal scene] to be buried with his remains.' The two scouts whom Barry sent to the local priest, returned.

'He won't come, it doesn't suit him to come out,' they said.

'It doesn't suit him to come out,' said Barry exasperated. 'I'll get him down.'

Barry raced across the boreen to the presbytery, heaved in the door and rushed up the stairs. In the bedroom he told the startled priest 'in blue pyjamas' to 'Get down to the graveyard and say the prayers over Charlie Hurley.'

Up to a 100 rifle-men formed a guard of honour as the priest performed the ceremony. From the church the men with rifles reversed 'slow-marched to the graveyard, with Charlie's body in their midst. I have seen many pathetic scenes in a not uneventful life, but the memory of that night's burial remains foremost. Perhaps it may be that because Charlie was my great comrade and I loved him greatly, the scene was seared into my memory. It is still fresh and clear – the dirge of the war pipes played by Flor Begley, the slow march of the brigade flying column, the small group of only six other mourners, the rain-soaked sky and earth and the wintry moon that shone as we followed him to his grave.' Begley's war-pipes caoined a lament. The priest spoke the prayers. Barry ordered his men to 'Present arms'. They fired three volleys and the *Last Post* cut the air. Then Tom Barry spoke a final tribute to his friend, comrade-in-arms and gallant hero. Those who were present have called this 'a sad memorable occasion' – the laying to rest of their brigade commandant.

Tom Barry crossed the graveyard and spoke to Leslie Price, the girl Charlie had asked him 'to take care of'. A strip cut from the end-length of the tricolour, which draped the coffin, was rolled up ribbon-like and in a touching gesture, Tom ceremoniously handed it to Leslie.[47]

Almost 60 years later in a hospital bed she recalled Tom's kindness as they both shed some tears at the graveside that night – both had lost a true friend.

Weighed down with their thoughts the column set out again at 3.30 a.m. and marched to cross the dangerous Clonakilty-Bandon main road before dawn broke. Around 7.30 a.m. they reached Ahiohill eight miles away, having had an almost continuous march of 32 miles without food or sleep. The column retired to billets, exhausted.

FORMATION OF THE FIRST SOUTHERN DIVISION

The success at Crossbarry brought new hope to the IRA all over Ireland. Other areas looked towards the Rebel County for inspiration to continue. Barry, though only 23 years of age, was by now 'one of the big generals of the struggle against the British.'[1] The morale of the Third West Cork Brigade was particularly high. Although one-third of the British forces in Ireland were concentrated in the Cork area, the British still found that it was not enough. Garrisons in West Cork were again strengthened. The papers of the following day carried conflicting reports but all admitted heavy losses for the British forces and that three lorries had been destroyed (according to the *Cork Examiner*), three more retreated to Innishannon and Crossbarry and reinforcements had met with similar misadventures from the attackers.[2]

Several houses in the region were raided and ransacked. Four Republican farmhouses in the Crossbarry vicinity were burned, including O'Mahony's of Belrose, brigade headquarters and Jerh Delaney's and Tom Kelleher's. A few weeks later two more Republican houses were burned. IRA reprisal resulted in the burning of eight Loyalists' homes. This action put a stop to burnings for the time being, Barry recalls.[3]

In a propaganda piece General Strickland reversed the story when he stated that his men had burned houses as 'a reprisal for the burning of Loyalist houses at Crossbarry', and would continue with this policy. 'If two Loyalists houses are burned three Sinn Féin Houses will be burned officially and if that does not stop, six Sinn Féin houses will probably be burned.'[4]

British newspapers reacted strongly to the 'Rebel forces' and their 'effrontery in playing the bagpipes'.[5] The *Cork Examiner* tells of the British forces retreating at three points and that after the ambush the road was 'strewn with dead and wounded'.[6] British garrisons in West Cork reacted by lengthening the curfew period in many towns. It was now fixed at 7 p.m. in Bandon. This did not hinder Tom Barry and his men. A few days after the announcement of the 7 p.m. curfew order, Barry entered Bandon at 10 p.m. with a few men to shoot a spy. Through their intelligence network they were aware of his movements and he was shot as he walked down the street. Indeed so respected was this agent that a compulsory order to close all business houses in Bandon on the day of the funeral was issued.[7]

Now that Charlie Hurley was dead, it meant that the brigade officers had to choose a commandant to look after matters at headquarters. Liam Deasy, the adjutant, knew every company in the unit, had experience in reports and communications between brigade and GHQ, and was the obvious choice. He travelled to Dublin with Dick Barrett to have the appointment sanctioned.

Tom Barry now set his sights on Rosscarbery Barracks. Michael Collins had said, 'The most difficult barracks in Ireland to take is Rosscarbery'. He doubted if it would ever be captured as the enemy had boasted that it was well fortified and could not be penetrated. So Tom decided he would let his former neighbour see that nothing was impossible for the men of the Third West Cork Flying Column.

Tom Kelleher had been detailed to bring 60 pounds of gun cotton and 40 pounds of tonnite from a store in Bandon. In what can only be described as a daring venture, his sister Ellen, dressed in old clothes, took a horse and cart into the town to bring out the materials. At Murphy's Hardware she collected the material, covered it over with loaves of bread and other groceries and drove off down South Main Street past the soldiers. At Sutton's Corner she was stopped. While a soldier was searching the cart she gave the horse a little pick, and off he went leaving the soldier standing.[8]

Other material for the mine and bombs was collected from Berehaven. Barry was delighted when the ingredients arrived safely and he instructed Charles McCarthy, their newly acquired bomb-making expert, to make sure that this one wouldn't fail, as Rosscarbery Barracks had to be taken. Tim O'Donoghue and the men 'worked' at John O'Mahony's house. 'Anyone listening to the banter and joking as we worked would never have realised we were going into action in such a short time.' The camaraderie kept up their morale and for Tom Barry there was personal pride and integrity involved, as GHQ in Dublin would be viewing the situation.[9]

Four days after Crossbarry, 22 March 1921, Barry was in Ahiohill outside Clonakilty where he had mobilised 70 rifle-men, some of whom had taken part in Crossbarry, but most of whom were newly-trained or who had been involved in other actions in the West Cork area. With Jim Hurley, who had been hurt destroying a bridge in Clonakilty earlier in the month, Barry and his column set out on Wednesday morning, 23 March, and arrived in position at a railway line five miles outside Clonakilty and prepared to attack a train of British troops scheduled to travel from Clonakilty to Skibbereen. It was, however, an enemy trick. They had booked carriages, knowing the IRA would hear of it, but instead travelled by road. Barry said that when this news reached them, 'We grinned, conceded them a point for being able to fool us, and immediately withdrew.'

That night the column moved again. The British forces knew there was activity in the area and started a rounding-up process. For five days Barry and his column zigzagged through the country, avoiding capture or confrontation. It was bitterly cold and began to snow heavily, and despite sleeping only in sheds and with little food, it did not deter Barry and his men. They reached Benduff, three miles outside Rosscarbery on 30 March. In the evening Tim O'Donoghue, Tom Kelleher and a few more men arrived with some of the well-made mines and explosives.

The column were paraded at 9 p.m. and told for the first time that the actual target was Rosscarbery Barracks, and that they were to move off at midnight. Barry outlined the plan. So that there would be no misunderstanding he repeated the detailed duties of each section several times. He had learned from the error of the man who allowed himself to be seen by the enemy at Crossbarry. Three groups of five rifle-men were detailed to cut telegraph wires and block roads, mainly by felling trees on all the roads into Rosscarbery from the garrison towns of Skibbereen, Dunmanway and Clonakilty. Those groups moved off at 11 p.m. The cutting of the wires was to commence at 1 a.m. precisely, ten minutes before the opening of the attack.

The main body, 55 strong, was to be led by an assault force of 10 officers and men, each armed with rifle and two pistols. This detachment would lay the mine against the barracks' door and storm into the building after it exploded. Ten more men would follow them carrying torches of paraffin-soaked sacking, which were to be thrown into the barracks to expose the targets. The third group of 12 would cover the back and sides of the building to prevent the garrison from emerging. A fourth detachment of 12 rifle-men was sub-divided into three groups of four to hold the roads in the immediate town vicinity in case of surprise enemy reinforcement, and also to prevent any informer from leaving the town. The fifth group of the remaining 11 rifle-men was to act as a reserve party. Immediately the attack commenced, they ordered all the shops that sold petrol and paraffin to open and put the fuel into a dozen buckets and bottles. Tom Moloney and James Hayes of the local company were given revolvers and were to act as guides.

Barry had prepared for every possibility and provided the explosives worked, the night should be theirs. The barracks was strongly fortified with barbed wire and steel shutters and stood apart from other houses. The defenders numbered 22 war-service experienced men who had been seen, during exercise periods, bringing a machine-gun onto the roof. The Volunteers were prepared for this.

Barry says he was prepared to lose several men if necessary to destroy this base because if this barracks was destroyed, it would mean the IRA would have an area of roughly 270 square miles free of the enemy and could use it as a base because the majority of the people in the area were behind them. As was usual before a major attack, Barry remained alone with his thoughts to plan for any eventuality, but he knew, as with all guerrilla warfare, chances must be taken. He knew Rosscarbery well, the place of his childhood, and his mind returned to these events 'to ease the strain of waiting' until it was time to move.[10]

The column moved off at midnight. A mile outside Rosscarbery they were halted, ordered to remove their boots and tie them on to their back equipment. The mine and bombs were taken from a farm cart and the explosive put on to a churn stand. Tom Kelleher remembers the problem they had when Volunteers were called to take the explosive on the first leg of the journey. It was to be shouldered like a coffin, but one Volunteer was too tall and tilted the sensitive explosive at a dangerous angle, so Barry decided to pick even-sized men. It was a hard decision because he could be sending men to their death, rather than their volunteering to take the front line.[11]

All bootless the flying column padded into Rosscarbery. In fact so successful was their movement that not one inhabitant in the town knew they had moved in. By this time the snow had stopped, but as they were very wet, the cold and the hunger didn't bother them. They took up their allotted positions at 1.10 a.m. precisely.

The first task was to ascertain if there was any sign of enemy awareness of a forthcoming attack. Then they had to find out if the little gate to the entrance of the pathway to the barracks was locked. Barry removed his equipment and wriggled on his stomach to investigate. The gate was not locked but the latch was down. He retraced his snail-like movements. Jack Corkery, Peter Kearney, Christy O'Connell and Tom Kelleher moved gingerly with the 80-pound bomb carried coffin-like; each held a revolver in his free hand.

Denis Lordan applied a lighted candle to both fuses simultaneously.

'As far I can remember the explosive was timed for seven minutes. It was spurting fire into the air. Barry ran in front of us, snapped the latch, opened the gate and bolted ahead. The path had barbed wire at both sides. It was so narrow our stockinged-feet were in, and our free shoulder out. I put my hand against the barracks' door. We had been warned to leave it down very, very slowly, as it was extremely sensitive. Sparks were flying as we put it against the door. Barry and Mick Crowley had a flat stone; they pushed it under, to tilt it forward', Tom Kelleher recalled.

'Of all the tests of men's courage in guerrilla warfare, that of carrying a mine across an open space on a bright night and properly placing it against an enemy post is, in my opinion, the greatest', Barry wrote.

'The men had been warned to come back in single file; if they rushed they might get stuck in the barbed wire. As the last man left the path, they threw themselves down and blocked their ears. The roar of the explosion vibrated the vicinity in a matter of seconds.

'I never saw anything like it. The windows and doors stood in mid-air and fell to the ground. Some of us had been picked to rush the barracks, but we hadn't a hope. It was full of smoke.'[12]

The men of the column were instructed to put their alternative plan into action, though their surroundings cramped them slightly, as getting into firing position was difficult.

The explosion had blown the roof off an evacuated house across the road. Barry ordered four rifle-men back to this house to fire at the upper windows of the barracks. (Four of the column had invaded the post office and destroyed the telephone and telegraphic system.) The volume of enemy fire was great. Barry lobbed his Mills bomb, which exploded in the hallway, but soon this only brought a strong reply from the garrison.

Though it was not a dark night, still, they had to keep some of their sacking burning so that the target would be visible. The enemy began to lob bombs, but according to Barry they forgot to follow the usual practice of counting two before throwing a Mills bomb at a near-by target. As the attackers were within yards of the building, they were able to lie flat to protect their heads until each explosion went off. Barry and his men counted the seconds, lit their homemade canister bombs by candle, and lobbed them forward. And so a bombing duel commenced, with each side using rifle, revolvers and bombs.

Tim O'Donoghue feared for Barry's life, as he was 'for hours dodging bombs, throwing in bombs, paraffin,' shooting, without a break and often exposed in the open from the glare of the flames.

'We'll soon be without a commander', O'Donoghue shouted to Jim Hurley. 'Not at all; he has a charmed life', Hurley shouted back. The intensity of the fighting continued.

It was two hours before the garrison abandoned the ground floor, but they continued to fight from the upper storey. Some of the column, by this time, had entered the barracks and tried to bring down the ceiling by exploding sevenpound charges, but the stone building was a solid structure. Heavy rifle-fire came down the stairs. Barry then set fire to the stairs. Soon it was wrapped in flames, but the garrison still held out.

After an action that lasted almost five hours, the garrison surrendered. To prevent the future use of their arms and ammunition by the IRA they threw them into the flames on the lower floor. Having lowered their wounded from a back window, the rest followed them into the back garden to await their fate at the hands of their captors. Two constables lost their lives and were burned in the flames, and nine were wounded. Tom Barry praised these British military as throughout the conflict 'this garrison had not killed or wounded a single citizen, nor had they burned houses, or effected any arrests. They were unique in this respect.' He said they fought exceptionally well and defended their barrack to the end.

Barry ordered some column men to take them to neighbouring houses where they received medical treatment. He sent an escort with more to the nearby Convent of Mercy. All Barry wanted in this attack was to destroy the barracks so that they would have a hide-out area for the Volunteers. He didn't want to kill any of this force, whom, he said, 'never ran amok'.

It was the longest and toughest fight fought in West Cork. The men of the flying column excelled. They took great risks, put their own lives in danger many times during the long night hours. The IRA suffered no casualties and now had a free area that was never again occupied by the enemy.[13]

Again the balladeer put the event to words and music:

When Barry saw the Tans efface,
The spirit of his fighting race,

Right through his soul did madly chase
His blood went boiling over.
He marched his men to Rossa's town
And burned that famous fortress down,
And never again will Britain's crown
Her foothold there recover.

Day dawned. After the night's echoes of resounding weapons, Rosscarbery seemed sedated. Barry ordered his men to fall into sections, thanked them and faced them for the town square. They paraded through the square and being in such high spirits began to sing some rebel songs, the harmony of their voices echoing notes of triumph through the frosty morning air. Just in case informers might shortly be at work, Barry marched his column first to the west, then north for a few miles and then turned eastwards for the 11-mile journey to Rossmore.

By midday reports reached the column that lorries of British forces were moving from Bandon, Clonakilty and Dunmanway, but because of the 'felled' trees and road trenches, it was late afternoon before they reached the smouldering ruin of the barracks. Barry's deception worked because the forces continued to comb out the western area.

The flying column marched a further 22 miles to the east; they waded through the water in a shallow part of the Bandon River and cold and wet reached Newcestown before dawn. Barry got a dispatch to meet Liam Deasy and other officers at Foley's near Béal na mBláth. Here Tom and brigade officers held a meeting; he gave them an up-to-date report on the Rosscarbery events. Later that night Tom was in the kitchen chatting when he collapsed. The two Foley girls, Nora and Josie, went across the fields for a local doctor. With the aid of a scout they brought a slightly intoxicated doctor to examine Tom. Fr Coakley came and administered the last rites to him.

The strain of all the previous months, and especially the nerve-racking Rosscarbery engagement, had once again put a strain on Tom's heart. After some days he was again taken in secret to the Mercy Hospital. This time his stay was shorter. He had no intention of remaining indoors once he knew he was all right. His ailment was described again as 'heart misplacement', which settled back after a short rest and medication.

The British propaganda went into full swing stating that 'the attackers numbered 200'. Sergeant Shea and Constable Bowles were killed, having 'put up a most sturdy defence. The 'attackers carried away their dead and wounded'.[14]

Encouragement came in the form of a letter from Michael Collins in GHQ:

To: The Brigade Adjutant,
Cork 3 Brigade.

I have just received report of the Rosscarbery fight. It was a splendid performance and, as I know the position of the place so well, I appreciate it all the more. I hope some time shortly to make the acquaintance of the officer who arranged this encounter and carried it out with such gallantry and efficiency.

D/I.[15]

Michael Collins and the GHQ men were now appreciating Tom Barry's worth, which had been recognised by the men of the flying column.

Revenge for Rosscarbery was taken by burning Michael Collins' former homestead, then owned by his brother, Seán. If the intention was to divide the opinion of Collins and Barry, and cause anguish, on the contrary it bonded their association.

Throughout Ireland the IRA was almost entirely dependent upon captured arms, and GHQ was constantly being petitioned to try to import arms by some means.

Michael Collins, a close friend of the Hales family of Bandon, was frequently in touch with Donal Hales who was in Italy and writing sympathetically in Italian newspapers about the Irish cause. Through him arrangements were made to send a shipment of arms to the seaside village of Squince, near Union Hall. The earlier part of April was taken up with brigade and battalion council meetings in connection with the proposed largescale landing. Barry would have preferred to use a port in another part of the county because he felt that this part of West Cork was the section of the country most 'steamrolled' by the British forces.

GHQ had invited the County Cork brigades to nominate an officer with seagoing experience to travel to Italy and return with the consignment. Michael Leahy, second-in-command of Cork No. 1 Brigade, was chosen for the mission. Now, in mid-April, GHQ informed No. 3 Brigade that Leahy's return on an Italian ship carrying 20,000 rifles, 500 machine-guns and 5,000,000 rounds of ammunition could be expected shortly. [16]

Tom, Liam Deasy and other officers had been working on plans for mobilising the column to ensure the safety of the arms. They organised dumps in Cork and Kerry, drew up transport maps and arranged for the commandeering of lorries and other motor transport. During the last week, using only trusted local men for security reasons, they worked to perfect a plan that would leave little or nothing to chance. They examined charts to be sure how far the Italian ship could sail into Union Hall harbour. Trawlers and small boats onto which the cargo would be transferred were listed, drivers chosen and routes worked out. They arranged for the destruction of the other roads and bridges and for parties of IRA rifle-men to delay any enemy moving in any potentially obstructive direction. Barry said, 'we had given much thought during the early months of the year to this landing of arms, and the responsibility weighed heavily on the few of us who knew of it. We had many headaches, and because of the absolute necessity for complete secrecy, we could not delegate inquiries or any part of the work to any but a few specially selected officers.'[17]

The IRA's movements were being slightly hindered by British military involved in a round up in the Union Hall district. One April night Barry and four officers, after a local battalion and brigade council meeting had been held, were sleeping in a house near Union Hall when scouts woke them at 4 a.m. with the news that British troops were approaching. Pausing only to pull on trousers, grab guns and equipment, they fled. But Seán Buckley, IO, had the post that had been stolen the previous morning. It was in a heap on the table. He jumped, bundled them up, grabbed his coat, ran and hid it in a good spot in the yard and followed the others into the haggard. Soon they heard soldiers hammering at the front door with the butts of their rifles. In the pitch darkness, they held on to each other's guns so that they could stay together. Carefully edging each step they reached a small field some distance up the hill. Buckley was unarmed, but Barry had two revolvers and a rifle. He gave Buckley a revolver and some ammunition. The five freezing cold officers took up positions, one at each ditch with Barry ready to make for wherever the attack came from. The sounds of enemy were all around. Barry had left his socks, pullover, cap, trench coat and leggings behind. In the April night coldness they could only wait, hope and shiver. Buckley had been at a meeting in Baltimore the previous day, on instructions from Michael Collins, to check up on the position of Baltimore Co-op Fishery, which had been set up with the help of a Republican government loan. He had been respectably dressed and took his detachable white collar and tie from his pocket and began to put them on, believing if caught, respectability would win. 'I always had more faith in wits than weapons'. When Barry vaulted towards him and saw a soldier dressed like he was, in the face of an enemy, he left fly at Seán in language that was 'hot enough to set the heather ablaze.'

Believing they were surrounded, they remained silent in the cold for some hours until eventually the dogs were silent. Before leaving the troops arrested the owner of the house when they found the beds warm and the men's clothing strewn of the floor. After the owner pleaded with them, saying the IRA had guns and so he had no alternative, he was released. But the patrol carried away two trench coats belonging to Seán and Tom.

Col Hudson and men from the Skibbereen garrison had conducted the raid. Later, Barry wrote a letter to Col Hudson demanding the return of the trench coats, pointing out that they were 'not contraband of war'. He put it in an invoice from the raided mail, and apologised 'for the unavoidable interference with his private correspondence, regretting that he was unable to wait to receive his men when they called and hoped to be better prepared next time and promising them a warm welcome.'

Some days later the colonel called on the editor and manager of the *Southern Star*, Dick Connolly, informing him of the letter he had received from Tom Barry. He said he agreed with the sentiments expressed and handed him the coats, requesting that they be returned to Tom Barry. Barry described Col Hudson as a kindly gentleman who didn't indulge in the torture of captured IRA. It was this man's garrison they had failed to draw into conflict in February and whose men had been given a good time. If Hudson had caught up with Barry on this occasion there is, of course, no doubt but that he would have done his duty. Barry admired a man whether enemy or friend for doing his job well, as long as he kept to civilised rules.

Years later, Barry with a wry smile, spoke of this man of principle, with whom he had dinner during the Truce. He became a brigadier later, went to India and wrote 'several letters' to 'General Tom Barry, Cork'. Barry was 'in prison at the time'.[18]

Barry found that generally the RIC 'were a different type' to the Auxiliaries and the Tans. 'You'd get a bad RIC man just as you'd get a bad saint in heaven. Sure you had a fellow called Lucifer up there, and he created hell, I believe! Many RIC resigned in mid 1920s as they didn't like what their "helpers" were doing and weren't prepared to stand for it!'[19]

After Tom Barry and Liam Deasy were satisfied that they had attended to all arrangements for the importation of the arms, they cycled through the night. There were some hair-raising episodes when they heard the sound of military vehicles and had to hide in boreens. On two occasions they had to heave the bicycles over a wall and vault after them. They arrived by morning at O'Mahony's of Belrose, Upton. Because the house had been burned the family now lived in the barn.

Despite all the effort, their hard work and weeks of planning, the ship never arrived. Eventually (much later) Madge Hales returned from her visit to her brother, Donal, in Italy and went straight to Michael Collins with the details of the difficulties encountered in trying to secure the shipment. Their brother Seán Hales was also aware of the situation, but Barry never knew the facts regarding the shipment.[20] Apparently, he drew his own conclusions. In an interview with Raymond Smith he said that the British were helped by the refusal of other nations 'to sell Ireland one rifle or a bandolier of ammunition. Ireland was refused a hearing at the Peace Conference. And tens of thousands of American veterans on demobilisation passed through Ireland on army leave, but not one offered to stay and lend a hand in Ireland's fight for freedom.'[21]

With only a few hours sleep, Barry and Deasy left Belrose, for a meeting at Kippagh in the North Cork No. 2 Brigade area. It took them two days to walk cross-country. This, they felt was the safest method of travelling. On the first night they met up with Seán O'Hegarty and Florrie O'Donoghue of Cork No. 1 Brigade. They billeted in a friendly house and compared notes on activities. 'I already knew those Cork 1 officers and liked them well', Barry wrote. He regarded Hegarty as a man of 'fine character, keen brain and personality' who worked 'tirelessly and efficiently' as commander, and O'Donoghue as 'shrewd, calm and capable, an all round officer whose speciality was intelligence bracketed justly with Michael Collins.'[22]

GHQ had issued an order to hold a meeting on 24 April 1921 at Lynch's farmhouse in Kippagh, near Millstreet. Delegates from nine brigades were to attend to establish the First Southern division in accordance with the Dublin directive. Because only five of the nine brigades were represented, Barry expressed disappointment.

'Liam Deasy, Brigadier of West Cork, came over the mountains,' Ernie O'Malley a staff captain from Dublin wrote. 'With him was Tom Barry who commanded the Brigade column. His light bushy hair stood straight up like a windblown hedge. There were two guns in his belt; they touched almost when he stuck both hands in his trousers' pockets … he was fearless and very much admired by West Cork.'[23]

The meeting opened, chaired and addressed by Ernie O'Malley who brought orders for the formation of the division. These he read aloud to the delegates with, according to Barry, 'military terminology rolling off his tongue'. It certainly didn't appear to be the way to win the attention of men who had been through so much and who had practical experience of fighting. The men O'Malley was dealing with were shrewd and mentally alert. There were men like Liam Lynch, Deasy, Moylan, Cork No. 2 Brigade; Humphrey Murphy, Andy Cooney, Dan Breen, John Joe Rice, Kerry, and other well known IRA men. O'Malley continued to speak and the more he used words like 'terrain' and 'topography' the more he angered his listeners.

Seán O'Hegarty, commanding Cork No. 1 Brigade, began to shuffle. At the next mention of 'terrain and topography' he jumped to his feet and told him to shut up. He voiced the bitter feelings that many of the IRA fighting officers now entertained towards GHQ. He asked why didn't a senior staff officer like Michael Collins or Richard Mulcahy come, or for that matter why didn't any of these ever think it worth their while to visit any of the active fighting units in the south?

When a break for food was announced Seán, went and located a bucket, soap and a towel. He asked Tom to go down to the stream with him. He scooped up buckets of water and 'judging by the violent manner with which he splashed them over my soaped head and body he was still thinking of "terrain and topography",' Barry wrote.[24]

After the meal Tom listened to O'Malley again. He had begun to dislike him. He could take it no longer and was on his feet. In *On Another Man's Wound* O'Malley describes Barry's contribution as being 'assertive, aggressive, almost spitting out his words directly'. He told the meeting that the orders from GHQ bore no relation whatever to the realities of the situation in the south. There was no point he said in using 'ornate language and meaningless military phrases' to impress hard-bitten officers who were daily fighting forces against all odds. GHQ didn't understand what was required to make split-second decisions when a group of men were in danger of being surrounded, or the quick action needed when an ambush or barracks' attack didn't go according to plan. It just wouldn't work having brigades moving around in a large body when, he said, 'the three Cork brigades could hardly muster 300 rifles between them, were without automatic weapons, artillery or transport, had no proper signalling equipment and no proper staff arrangements.'[25]

Barry in *Guerilla Days in Ireland* says, 'Not one of us was opposed to the setting up of the unit of a division as such, but we were at a loss to understand how its establishment on paper would help the brigades at the most critical period of their existence.' They were all in an angry mood. Seán Moylan of Cork jumped up: 'We started this war with hurleys, but, by heavens, it seems to me we will all finish it off with fountain pens.'[26]

Barry said, 'My own opinion remains that in guerrilla warfare no unit larger than a brigade could ever be effective as a striking force, and it could not be directed in its activities by a higher authority from outside the brigade area.'[27]

Nevertheless, the First Southern Division was set up. The divisional commandant elected was the daring Liam Lynch. He had commanded the party that had attacked the first British troops in the Anglo-Irish war at Fermoy in 1919 and he had been an active IRA officer in the Cork No. 2 Brigade area.[28]

Before the meeting closed Barry suggested that something should be done to try to stop the executions and torturing of IRA prisoners. He told of the harassment of civilians in West Cork. Funerals of men 'killed in action or murdered were broken up by soldiers'. People were searched, held for long hours with their hands held up 'sometimes they had to kneel or to sing *God Save the King* … People had been flogged with whips, belt-buckles and canes.' Of immediate concern was the 'torture of prisoners by some of the intelligence staff of their 6th Division.' O'Malley heard these men speak with passion and concern. Major General Sir E. P. Strickland, the British GOC in the martial law area should be threatened with reprisals. It shouldn't end by being a threat, Barry said; they would carry out the reprisals. O'Hegarty supported him forcibly. This proposal met with enthusiasm and a lively discussion followed.

Four of O'Hegarty's Volunteers of Cork No. 1 Brigade and one from the Tipperary area were to be executed before a firing squad in Cork, towards the end of April. The meeting agreed on a definite action plan. Liam Lynch undertook to write to General Strickland informing him of their decision. A plan of reprisals was drawn up in case Strickland ignored the warning and each officer returned home to his own area, and prepared for a 'shoot-up day' on 14 May throughout the divisional area. O'Malley undertook to inform the Limerick,

Tipperary and Kilkenny brigades to carry out similar raids on the day.[29]

Back in West Cork they found that when the forces raided houses they seized bicycles. If this continued the officers of Cork No. 3 felt they would be deprived of their fastest mode of transport. The brigade council issued an order that all bicycles, except those that were needed and whose owners could be depended on, should be secured from enemy hands. On the 8 May 1921, in every parish in the brigade area, at least 3,000 of the 5,000 Volunteers on the roll swept through the countryside in twos or threes and efficiently carried out the task.

The column had another set back as the Essex began a round-up. Three Volunteers were killed. Frank Hurley was captured; he was armed and told to walk towards a field. A friend hidden behind the ditch found his maltreated body on the roadside a half a mile from the barracks. Geoffrey Canty was with others and was unarmed, he was shot at as he saw a patrol approaching, the shot injured his ankle. The others got away. His body was found later. Con Murphy was also shot dead. Propaganda stated it was 'while trying to escape'.[30]

Meanwhile the executions of the four Cork Volunteers had taken place on 28 April. Immediately Barry set up his action plan. Between 1 February and 4 May 11 prisoners from Cork No. 1 and Cork No. 2 Brigades had been shot before a British firing squad in Cork jail. Barry says that in the Bandon area 'none of our Volunteers were ever to be judicially executed, since the British officers in our brigade area invariably acted as judge, jury and executioner, without bothering about the formality of a trial for suspected IRA men.'[31] K Company Auxiliaries in Dunmanway captured Tim O'Connell, who had taken part in the Kilmichael ambush. In the Dunmanway Workhouse they beat him unconscious, they stripped, kicked and tortured him, he lost his hearing and had nose problems for the rest of his life. There was blood everywhere. This Auxiliary Company tortured Tadhg Ó Séaghdha and Jerh Fehilly in a most inhuman way.

Ten British garrisons, scattered over the West Cork area between Innishannon and Castletownbere (about 80 miles), were to be attacked simultaneously by the IRA on Saturday 14 May at 3 p.m. Barry decided he would engage the First Essex in Bandon. The intention was to have a short, sharp shoot-up in each area, and all IRA arms were to be at the disposal of the 12 officers and the men detailed for the attacks.

A month previously an old Ford Model T car had been captured from the Essex and hidden in a field under a haystack. Barry decided it was time to bring it out. For two days prior to the action, Seán Lehane practised driving it to orders: 'Slow! Fast! Turn! Ditch!' At the order to ditch, he would jam the brakes, and they would 'clear' the ditch for cover. The hood of the car was removed, the windscreen stripped and the Lewis gun, captured at Crossbarry, was mounted on it.

Anna Hurley, leader of the Cumann na mBan in Bandon, and sister of Frank who had been killed the previous week by the Essex Regiment, agreed to go to Bandon to observe enemy movements. She reported, on returning, that the military were busily sand-bagging their posts in North Main Street. Obviously, The garrison had been warned, but the attack had to be executed.

The seven selected men were too many for the car, so two men were dropped off outside the town. All were armed with pistols, rifles and two Mills bombs. Barry, dressed in his IRA uniform, sat on the back-rest of the front seat with his feet at each side of Seán Lehane the driver.

Only a few hundred yards from the army barracks, but just outside the town, a sentry was sighted. Barry calmly calculated the situation. To shoot would be fatal. It was better to drive slowly past. The sentry was standing on the road-side ditch looking towards them with his rifle and bayonet at the 'At Ease' position. 'Take no notice,' Barry whispered.

When they were quite close the sentry jerked his rifle to the 'On Guard' position, but possibly seeing the uniform and assuming that the IRA did not drive around openly, he brought his rifle to 'Slope'. As they drove past he saluted smartly. Barry casually returned his salute. They drove on.

The plan of attack was not an elaborate one. They were to enter Bandon, drive down slowly through North Main Street past the barracks and the police post and fire at anybody in a British uniform. Then they would drive across the bridge along South Main Street and out on the Kilbrittain Road, where the members of the Bandon Company were waiting, ready to block any enemy pursuit.

However, as frequently happened, the plan was abruptly changed; shortly after passing the sentry they noticed a large party of troops in a field. Some of the soldiers were in full battle-order with steel helmets and others were kicking a football. Immediately Barry ordered, 'Halt! Open Fire!' The Lewis gun and the rifles went into action. Then there was a 'Forward! Turn!' for the driver as some shots were fired back. Continuing to fire they drove back towards the road from which they had come. The car raced past where the sentry had stood. Fortunately for him he had now vanished. They drove four miles before stopping up a byroad to throw petrol on the car and set it alight.

The silence was broken when Seán Lehane, a good singer, put his voice into action as the flames soared:

We will pay them back woe for woe,
Give them back blow for blow,
Out and make way for the Bold Fenian men.

Their task completed they set off cross-country in the direction of Newcestown. In the Bandon attack, according to the reports in the papers the following day, an Essex soldier had been killed and seven Black and Tans injured. Apparently, the foray, after Barry and his men sped out from Bandon, turned into a major episode of machine-gun and rifle-fire. This, according to the *Cork Exami-*

ner, 16 May 1921, lasted for about an hour as the British 'shelled the enemy'. Two civilians were wounded. Throughout West Cork, attacks on all ten locations took place on target at around three o'clock. The official British losses in the area were seven men killed and thirteen wounded; the IRA had no casualties.[32]

Tom saw 'no conclusion' to the conflict 'except victory'.[33]

To Michael Collins and GHQ

The Government of Ireland Act was to commence operation on 19 May 1921. As a gesture of conciliation to those of the majority faith in southern Ireland, Lord Fitzalan succeeded Lord French as lord-lieutenant. When nominations for a general election in southern and northern Ireland closed on 13 May, De Valera as President of Sinn Féin declared that the 'election is nothing less than the legitimacy of the Republic.' In southern Ireland Republican candidates were returned unopposed in 124 of the 128 constituencies.

However, the IRA war continued. In West Cork alone British forces facing the guerrilla fighters numbered 12,600 men including 11 infantry battalions, 1,150 police, 540 Auxiliaries, two brigades of field artillery and a machine-gun battalion', according to the British war records.

Winston Churchill, as chairman of the cabinet committee on Irish affairs, said that in order to crush the IRA, 'A hundred thousand new special troops must be raised, thousands of motor cars must be armoured and equipped; the three southern provinces of Ireland must be closely laced with cordons of block-houses and barbed-wire; a systematic rummaging and questioning of every individual must be put in force.'[1]

Despite all this, Barry and his flying column were determined to continue. A massive ambush using over 100 men was being planned for Gloundaw on the Dunmanway-Drimoleague road; but before the ambush was scheduled to take place, Barry had to take a trip to Dublin.

Over the previous months GHQ had decided that they would like to see the man who was so capable, daring and brave in training and leading the men of the Third West Cork Brigade Flying Column. He was also the man who never hesitated to disagree with orders or recommendations from GHQ, and would send a swift message of his disagreement. De Valera fixed 19 May as the day for the meeting with Barry.

Getting to Dublin was a problem for a man whom the British wanted to get their hands on. He was, at this time in the British Gazette, *Hue & Cry* 'one of the most wanted men' in Ireland. By car would be unsafe, so train was the chosen mode of transport. Tom, who was a little nervous about his forthcoming journey, decided he would travel as a medical student. He was coached in medical terminology by a number of medical students on active service. This preparation had to be thorough because, as he was aware, should he be captured and recognised, 'The British had more than ample evidence against me to enable one of their drumhead court-martials to rapidly arrange my exit at the end of a rope or before their firing squads'.[2] Consequently, he was provided with notes on medicine, textbooks, forceps and other paraphernalia usually found in the possession of a second-year medical student. He borrowed a name from Ted Ryder, near Crookstown, who lent him used envelopes and letters.

O'Mahonys of Belrose bought him a hat, shoes, shirt, socks and pyjamas. Kathleen O'Connell of the Ballydehob Cumann na mBan, who had been keeping his only suit in storage, was to have it delivered to Caheragh, Skibbereen headquarters, on 16 May.

Barry travelled all night on horseback and arrived at headquarters on the morning of 16 May. He was tired, and rolled up in a few army blankets; he fell asleep immediately in a makeshift bivouac erected in a nearby field, camouflaged by a thick growth of briars. After a few hours he was 'rudely pulled out' of his blankets when news that a large column of British military on foot had halted a few miles down the road, and was enquiring for him by name.

The scout bringing the suit, who was travelling with the parcel labelled with Tom's name and rank, was waylaid by a British officer, but refused to give details. The British officer, equipped with the parcel and dressed in the scout's clothes, made enquiries and was almost to Barry's destination when one householder suspected something and crossed the fields ahead of the officer thus giving Barry enough time to get out before British soldiers came and surrounded the place.

Tom Barry was upset at losing his only real suit of clothes so close to the day of travelling. A tailor in Crookstown was summoned. He promised to work all through the night and have another suit ready in the morning. Tom went back cross-country to Belrose and stayed there that night before setting out for Dublin. Suits of clothes obviously weren't in his favour. A member of the Cumann na mBan who brought the speedily made suit to Belrose was followed. Tom grabbed the suit, changed and just leaped through the opened side window before soldiers arrived to raid the premises.

Later that evening undaunted the O'Mahony girls, whose home had been burned a few weeks previously and were staying in a barn, drove him in a pony and trap to Cork railway station, handed him his first-class return ticket and a number of pro-British newspapers and periodicals. With a new name, a new suit, a new hat and other alien attachments he walked nervously past the Black and Tans and other military personnel.[3]

Deciding that he would be less noticeable amongst others he entered a carriage where three men were already seated. Two looked like businessmen and one like a British military officer, so he decided he would sit opposite him. Within a short space of time they were engaged in a friendly conversation. The soldier was 'going on a spot of leave and not sorry to leave this damned country'. Of course Tom didn't blame him with all the trouble going on, and in exchange for the officer's confidence he gave him all the data about the problems of being a medical student. He had been studying so hard he had suspected lung trouble and was going to Dublin to be examined by a specialist.

At the first military check at Mallow Station, Tom's companion produced his identity card and informed the sergeant of the search party that Tom was a medical student and everything was all right. This process was repeated at two further checks during the journey. The two parted company at Kingsbridge and wished each other luck, the officer to return to the British military barracks, Tom to the IRA headquarters. In later years Tom said, 'I wish I met him afterwards, because he was a damn nice fellow.'[4]

Tom met Gearóid O'Sullivan and Michael Collins on arrival at Liam Devlin's and was taken in their company to O'Donovan's house in the suburbs where he was to stay during his six nights in Dublin. Each morning he would leave the house with one of these men who conducted their business under the guise of businessmen. He met all the officers at GHQ as well as 'The Squad'. He couldn't help contrasting their lives – posing as businessmen with attaché cases, putting in regular hours, coming and going to an office – with those of the hunted, insecure men of the West Cork Brigade.

One night Michael Collins, Gearóid O'Sullivan, Seán Ó Muirthile and Tom – four of Ireland's most wanted men – were returning in a jaunting car when a large party of Auxiliaries stopped them.

'Act drunk,' Collins whispered as the Auxies ordered them out. He proceeded to give a masterly performance, joking and blasting in turn while being searched. In no time he had the search party laughing, and Barry trying to put on his act couldn't help but wonder how callously the Essex would treat such a performance in the fields down south.

Treating them as a few merry men, the Auxiliaries allowed them to go on their way. Tom was alarmed, and afterwards asked Collins why they didn't send a scout on in front. 'You're a windy beggar from West Cork', said Collins. Tom was furious and lashed out. 'You're a member of the Dáil and might be slightly immune. It may not be easy to sustain murder charges against GHQ officers but they'd have no problem in finding a charge of murder against me. You handle them your way, but I like to face these bloody fellows with a revolver.' They continued to argue out the point. Eventually Tom was convinced that the methods GHQ adopted were the best for them in a Dublin situation, but they wouldn't do in West Cork.[5]

Tom, who was always fascinated by military matters, enjoyed his conversations with the chief-of-staff, Richard Mulcahy, whom he found meticulous as he probed him on training and tactics, and asked how he was able to take a flying column into action, with so little backing. However his meeting with Cathal Brugha was unsatisfactory. Collins introduced the pair and left immediately. 'Cathal, with a minimum of words, asked me some questions and used only monosyllables to comment on my replies.' Tom 'completely failed to elicit a single one of his views on the policy and tactics of the IRA or on defence of which he was the responsible minister.' Later he discovered that 'a coolness' existed between Collins and Brugha, perhaps in relation to the IRB connection. Tom 'came to the conclusion' that his 'extreme reserve' was 'due to his natural suspicions' that Tom 'was one of the Collins party'.[6] Tom himself never joined the IRB. Robert Barton in response to Tom's query on IRB membership, said that he [Barton] 'was never an enthusiastic member of the IRB' and that 'Dev and Cathal Brugha left after 1916, probably on account of the then spirit … About Dev's membership I can vouch for as MacDonagh mentioned [it to] me in Holy Week 1916. Collins asked me in 1917 to speak to Dev on the matter, but Dev refused to rejoin'. So too did Cathal Brugha.[7]

Barry found that the men in GHQ 'were very interested in the different engagements we'd had in Cork because up to then all they'd had was press reports. I also saw a worse thing, and that was the beginning of political cliques in Dublin. It didn't break out until after the Treaty, but you could see it developing before that'.[8]

Tom found Michael Collins 'outstanding' as director of intelligence, 'the driving force and the backbone' of GHQ. 'A tireless, ruthless, dominating man of great capacity, he worked like a trojan in innumerable capacities to defeat the enemy.' He entered every branch of headquarters. From conversations with him, Tom got an insight into how, with his 'many helpers Mick was continually cracking their intelligence code messages'.

Tom found Mick full of life and energy; he would come bouncing into Liam Devlin's or Vaughan's and challenge someone to wrestle him. Tom himself, being rather light, had no intention of accepting the challenge; but one night Mick decided he wouldn't take 'no' for an answer. He bounced forward and the two men swayed as they jostled round and round the room, and shortly they fell together. 'Then we were really fighting!' The two aggressive men had to be pulled apart by Gearóid O'Sullivan, Seán Ó Muirthile and others. On their feet once more, the two were angry and said they wanted to fight it out; they were not finished. A few minutes later Collins laughed, bent forward, shook Tom's hand, and then clinched his fist in front of the smiling Tom, whereupon the others all joined in.

Barry, with Collins most of this time, was present during his interviews with different departments and found that Collins delved deeply into the work of units before speaking to country officers. One man who, Barry recounts, commanded a unit outstanding for inefficiency and lack of energy, was asking Collins for arms. Collins got up, thrust his hands into his pockets, shot back at the petitioner, 'what the hell does a lot of lousers like you want arms for? You have rifles and revolvers galore but you have never yet used them.' He tackled the man about a Black and Tan who was allowed to roam the area unhindered, terrorising and shooting people, and he finished up by telling him to, 'Get to hell out of this office and don't come back until you've done some fighting!'

Collins drove Barry into the suburbs of Dublin on 23 May to meet Eamon de Valera. Some people warned him that Dev was a cold, austere, aloof and unsmiling man. Others said he was anxious to appease the British and wished to repudiate the County Cork brigades. But Dev soon put him at ease. Barry found him extremely likeable and spent two and a half hours discussing the West Cork Brigade and the ambushes. Dev seemed to be very well informed of their activities and wanted full details of each action. He asked about Kilmichael, Crossbarry, Rosscarbery, Toureen and other engagements, and listened carefully while Barry answered the questions.

Barry talked about the difficulties the West Cork Brigade would face now that the summer season had arrived with the shorter nights and longer days. Military raids would be easier and cover would be more difficult for the IRA. He spoke about the ammunition shortage, and Dev was hopeful that 'Mick would get some through in time'.

Several times he seemed to ask about the opinions of the people, and how well they supported the IRA. Towards the close of their talk Dev asked, 'How long can the West Cork flying column keep the field against the British?'

'It depends on the British reinforcements, and the amount of arms we are able to obtain,' said Barry. After a pause he told him they could last another five years.

Dev bolted upright. 'A bit too optimistic', came his reply. Barry knew he exaggerated, but says he never regretted this overly optimistic view.[9]

Barry had arranged to leave Dublin on 24 May but Michael Collins asked him to stay for another day to see a demonstration of a new sub-machine-gun, the Thompson. An Irish-American ex-army officer had smuggled two of the guns into the country. Following the demonstration, Collins asked Barry to take the first shot. At first Barry declined, fearing he would be off target and would consequently be letting himself and the West Cork Brigade down. They insisted. He took aim and smashed all the distant bricks to pieces.[10]

Before they went to sleep that night Collins talked with Barry into the early hours about 'the many abortive peace feelers sent out by the British government since the commencement of hostilities. He had a great distrust of the motives behind those enemy moves, and considered them, in the main, as attempts to seduce the support of the people from the Irish Republican army.'

Michael gave Tom great encouragement and told him he was very proud of the men of his native West Cork. He was glad that Lloyd George had singled out the ambushes of Kilmichael and Crossbarry in communiqués leading to a truce. There were times when Collins teased. Barry argued. The two debated and laughed at their differences. They parted on the morning of 25 May. Collins said goodbye to the 'medical student', advising him to keep up the good work and to keep the West Cork flag flying![11]

Apart from the casual inspection and routine check of the train by the military Tom's trip from Dublin was uneventful. Three men of the Cork No. 1 Brigade met him at the station. All four walked briskly across the road to a waiting horse and trap. Dick Casey, a 14-year-old Fianna boy, sat inside. Tom took the reins, thanked the Volunteers and set off with Dick for what he hoped would be a problem-free journey to headquarters.

They chatted as the horse ambled along. Almost two hours later they were just on the incline near home (headquarters) and had almost reached the entrance gate to O'Mahony's Belrose, when approximately 40 steel-helmeted heads rose from inside the ditches on both sides of the road. Barry pulled back the horse, because if he turned in at the gate nothing would save them.

Soldiers crowded around as they ordered them to step down. Responding to the 'Hands Up' Barry's heart sank. As his hands reached skywards he caught a glimpse of the merciless Essex Regiment identification. He suddenly realised that Dick hadn't been coached for such an eventuality and in answer to the officer's question he called out loudly for his companion's benefit that he was Ted Ryder, a medical student from Cork College. 'I'm going home to my mother's farm near Crookstown, and this is Dick Casey the son of one of our farm labourers. He brought the horse and trap to Cork to bring me home.'

Tom was searched. They emptied out every scrap on his person. His medical paraphernalia was tumbled out and examined. They checked *The Times* and *The Daily Mail* to see if he had anything marked. They questioned him about his Republican views and as to why he was returning home in the middle of a term. He used his doctor's excuse. After a further lapse of time, the questioning officer told him to 'Go in there' where a group of local men had been taken prisoners and were just inside O'Mahony's gate. Walking down the road he saw these men. They all knew him and could give him away. 'I had to think hard,' he said. Immediately he assumed a snobbish attitude, asking the officer if he would expect him to associate with those Republicans. The officer grinned and said, 'Wait on the road!' While he waited, other groups of the regiment began to converge on the road; troops seemed to be everywhere. Barry didn't know then that the Essex were involved in a massive round-up. There were over 200 British soldiers in the area. The officer brought him a map and told him to point out his home. Awkwardly Barry fumbled, 'I've never seen one of these before. I don't think I can find it.'

'Wait for the major,' the officer said.

After an interval that seemed like hours, the major came up the road. Barry felt weak at the knees as Major Percival walked towards him carrying a colt automatic in his hand. 'The fear of death itself was overshadowed by the great fear of torture and a lingering exit'. He prayed as he was brought face to face with Percival, and he hoped he could stand up to the ordeal.

'And then, mercifully, for no explainable reason, I was no longer afraid. For whatever reason, after the first fifteen minutes, I was calm and detached.'

Percival questioned him, his hard eyes staring, piercing, 'his buck teeth' showing. He walked away, came back, removed Barry's hat, stared again and went away. After some time Barry heard the wonderful words, 'Release him'. Percival turned and strode briskly down the road.

Tempted to put the horse into a gallop but allowing better sense to prevail Tom guided the animal at an easy pace, headed for Tom Kelleher's, gave a well-earned thanks to young Dick Casey, got a fresh horse and collected his guns from the dump. 'Then a vow was taken that never again while hostilities were on would those guns be separated from me!'

Almost 60 years later he said, 'It was the one time I really wished I had a gun. Then I'd face death bravely if I got the bastard, Percival, first.'[12]

As Tom mounted the horse Mrs Kelleher came running out, a jug of milk in one hand and a bottle of holy water in the other. He drank the milk as the woman prayed out loud that 'God would protect us all from the Sassanach', while she sprinkled about half the contents of the bottle on Tom and his horse. This widowed woman and her family were using an outhouse as a dwelling as her home had been burned after the Crossbarry ambush.

It was an all-night ride of about 40 miles to Gloundaw where the major ambush, which he had planned with Deasy before his Dublin trip, was to take place. He changed horses twice and reached his destination without further confrontation with the enemy.

Gloundaw was a bleak open country area between Dunmanway and Drimoleague with high ground on both sides of the road which, like Kilmichael, did not allow for a retreat. When Barry arrived after his long journey the column was already moving into position. Liam Deasy handed over the column to Tom and left for headquarters. The men had billeted in the Drominidy area at 2 a.m., risen at 4 a.m. on 28 May 1921 and moved for Gloundaw after a bread and butter breakfast in the neighbouring houses. A full strength brigade flying column of 100 rifle-men, supported by 20 armed men from the local companies were organised for the attack. Many of the men who had taken part in Kilmichael, Crossbarry and other ambushes and barrack attacks were there.

The plan necessitated the local Drimoleague Company shooting-up the barracks or a Tan company. This, it was felt, would lure the military who would be summoned from Dunmanway. The men at Gloundaw lay in wait in sections, stretched inside the ditches along the road between the two centres – all other roads had been blocked by trenches and felled trees, so that they would have to travel this road. Tom Ward and Liam Deasy had arranged for a party of five men under the command of Dan O'Driscoll to take up position to the left of the barracks behind a fence running parallel to the railway line for the attack on Drimoleague barracks.

The men were in position at Gloundaw by 6.30 a.m. At each end of the ambuscade, Barry placed a section to break through any encirclement which might occur. He had other sections strategically placed. Willie O'Sullivan, a machine-gunner with British army experience, manned the captured Crossbarry Lewis gun. Mines were placed at both entrances, a number of men carried hand grenades and home-made bombs, and a large explosive was mounted on a horse-cart which was, at a given command, to be pushed by a few men, down the lane-way across the road at the commander's signal. The column were prepared to meet a convoy of forces which could bring into action anything from six to ten lorries. This was to be a major battle, and Barry having taken all precautions, was hopeful of a major success.

By 8.30 a.m. action commenced when a Black and Tan was shot outside Drimoleague Barracks. Immediately Patrick O'Mahony set out on his bicycle to deliver word to the waiting column.

Now it was certain that the Auxiliaries would come. Barry, walking along the rough ground immediately overlooking the road where over 100 fighting men were stretched out motionless, sensed the increasing tension, for a tough fight was anticipated. As the day passed and hours ticked away slowly, the men waited, but the enemy never showed. After the shooting of the Black and Tan the Auxiliaries in Dunmanway were in lorries ready for their journey to Drimoleague when a man was seen approaching the first of six lorries and subsequently the forces were ordered to return to their quarters.

The men who lay in wait that day have said, had the ambush taken place, it would certainly have been a slaughter for some side. Barry was prepared to win, but it is almost certain that men would have been lost. It was nightfall when he withdrew the column to billets in the Drominidy area.[1]

The following evening word reached the column that there was a large movement of troops in several regions: Clonakilty, Bandon, Dunmanway, Skibbereen and Bantry. It was obvious that a massive round-up was under way. Fear of being encircled again entered Tom Barry's mind and this time he knew the enemy would be more prepared.

All men had to be alerted immediately. Word was sent round to the various houses where the column was billeted, or to those who knew where the dug-outs were. A battery of people criss-crossed the area with the verbal dispatch. Two young girls, Lily and Mary O'Donovan, set out across the fields shortly after 2 a.m.

'It was a very dark night, and every once-in-a-while we would have to stop and listen in case of any military movement. But the most difficult part was when we had to cross the road.' Frightened but determined as 'men's lives were at stake' they roused several men in field dug-outs, and when they came near Mrs Young's yard the dogs began to bark so they clung to each other.

'The lads had a dug-out in her back kitchen, but that night they weren't there so we had to go across the fields to Andrew Timsy [McCarthy's] house. James, who was in bed, stuck his head out of the window.' They told him word had to be got to the lads immediately as there was a massive round-up. He knew the field dug-outs where they might be and said he'd take care of it, told them to go home quickly as they could be in danger.[2]

All the men headed, as instructed, to a field behind Pat O'Donovan's. Barry got them into quick formation, gave them a few snap instructions, and began to weave eastwards to get to the rear of the enemy. Soon he discovered that the only way open was to move forward (westwards) and try to avoid confrontation. With little food and snatches of sleep the men edged on.

On the third day after Gloundaw, news came that thousands of enemy were sweeping north Cork. They had formed a line right across the county in a thorough combing action. British navy troops and marines patrolled the Atlantic Ocean. Meanwhile, 'the column had commenced to weave its way, by day and night, avoiding the largest and most threatening round-up in its history.'[3]

Barry was leading his column towards the Bantry direction when word reached him of a largescale troop movement towards the Kerry-Cork border from Kerry. It seemed as if they were walking on the edge of a precipice. The enemy advanced from all directions. Barry did not know then that troops from as far away as Templemore and the Curragh had been drafted in to capture him and his flying column. Now one of the most wanted men in Ireland, Barry was more concerned for his men than he was for himself. The IRA were being driven from east to west into a wall of British troops on the border between the two counties. By the fourth evening they wove in front of the on-coming British forces, driven on relentlessly, their corner getting narrower while the enemy lines contracted as they closed in. This whole episode was the most frightening of all the events which had taken place over the previous months. There was the constant dread for Barry and his men of being totally destroyed; each dispatch received, brought added gloom and a feeling of being trapped without hope of escape. It became a fight for survival.

That night the flying column moved noiselessly along the grassy fields, their rifles at the ready with a bullet in each breech. At midnight they arrived at the Valley of Coomhola near the shores of Bantry Bay. Here they were billeted in a number of houses, outhouses, dug-outs and were fed by the hospitable people after their long weary journey.

'Gone were the merry quips, the laughter and the songs one usually heard in other days when approaching a billet. The men now sat round, their rifles between their knees, silent and thoughtful.' Barry observed that each man was freshly shaven, their boots shone with 'extra polish' and their rifles gleamed, and they did not appear nervous. Salutes were 'more formal' it was as if they were making a special effort to exude an air of military confidence.[4]

For the night, sentries and scouts were doubled with the aid of local companies, and the men rested without removing clothes or boots and with rifles at the ready. Tom tried to relax and had a smoke with the other officers in Marcella Hurley's drawing-room. Marcella, a famed Feiseanna singer, entertained them with traditional and national songs as she played the piano.

News that navy sloops were landing marines and soldiers in Bantry Bay and that the slopes of Shehey mountain were being shelled, in what must have been an effort to get the IRA to emerge, had Barry consulting local men as to the feasibility of bringing the flying column during darkness across the treacherous boggy slopes between Gougane Barra and Kerry, thus emerging outside the circle of troops. Barry got his men to stand to arms while scouts were sent in each direction to seek information of enemy approach. He told his men that they might have to stand and fight at a moment's notice. But his intention was to avoid the enemy if possible.

Fifteen minutes later the column was moving up the old hilly road to the Kerry border. Having travelled some distance they halted to await darkness. Then the march was resumed. Though tired, they did not show it.

With the aid of a number of ropes tied together, a local man warned each man to keep on the path following the man in front as he led the full column through a nightmare march in heavy darkness. Sometimes the men sank knee-deep in boggy ground; often one walked on the heels of the man in front. Periodically one stumbled, but each clung to the rope or the equipment of the man in front. In the long night hours they trailed, avoiding a slip down an embankment to certain death. Before daybreak, they arrived at the top of Deep Valley Desmond.

Now began the descent. Aided by stretched out rifles and ropes, hours passed as the men swung and slithered down the rugged passage from the mountaintop to level ground at Gougane Barra. Some were bruised and hurt but none were badly injured. At last Barry felt they were outside the ring of roads likely to be used by the enemy.

With mountains all around, rocks and hills well covered with bracken, Barry found a fortified position, so that if the forces came they would fight, and pray that their ammunition would last the pace. As the rumblings of enemy transport could be heard in the distance they remained in their stronghold until nightfall. Rumours of enemy movement kept the column the on alert. Silently 'each man prayed'. All night they waited. Barry decided to remain in this secluded spot, sheltered in the valley from the activities beyond.

Word came in the morning that the forces had returned to barracks having spent seven days raking the countryside, sleeping in bivouacs and fed by Service Army Service Corps.

In Cronin's Hotel the column was fed. Now that the enemy had withdrawn to their barracks, Barry organised his flying column and gave them a spirited talk: if possible they would avoid the enemy but they would be ready to out-fight any British barrage. Once back in their own brigade area he felt it would be important, now more than ever, to show friend and foe that the flying column could not be destroyed or intimidated.[5]

Fifty years later Barry was to take a sanguine look back at this type of British operation: 'I was to read one operations' order signed by General Strickland which detailed the use of over 5,500 troops, some of whom came from as far away as the midlands and the Curragh to sweep through the three Cork Brigade areas. Although we at first feared these massive formations, we found that it was not very difficult to evade battle with them. They had no success in any of the Cork Brigade areas, as some hundreds of the surviving veterans can testify.'[6]

On 2 June 1921 Sir Hamar Greenwood, British chief secretary for Ireland, stated in the British House of Commons that the total enlisted strength of the Auxiliary Division in Ireland was 1,498 officers and men – one-third were in the Cork area. This does not take into account the RIC, the naval forces, armed coastguard stations or even the 23 Black and Tan garrisons in Co. Cork. In a document captured by the IRA dated 17 May 1921 and signed by Major General Strickland, general officer commanding the 6th Division, a list of British forces operating in Co. Cork was given in detail – an approximate total of 8,800 first-time infantry troops. Added to this there was the Machine-Gun Corps, 580 officers and men; Royal Field Artillery, 727 officers and men; Royal Garrison Artillery, 440 officers and men; Royal Engineers, 240 officers and men; divisional and brigade headquarters' staff, 200 officers and men; Auxiliary division, 540 officers and men.[7] Against this field force were the Irish Republican army and the Irish people.

The small force of IRA could not be mobilised 'for a major operation likely to continue for a day,' Barry admitted, 'as its ammunition did not exceed 50 rounds a rifle, two fills for revolvers and automatics, and a few full drums for each machine-gun.' But they were prepared to take on this force (at odds of almost 40-to-1) because as they fought, as in each of the major ambushes, they captured arms and ammunition which allowed them to continue; as at Kilmichael and Crossbarry they used the captured booty against the enemy, on the spot.

In the 23 battalion areas of Cork city and county 10,000 enrolled Volunteers backed the flying column. Those who hadn't experience in field fighting, Barry said, lacked only the arms to enable them to face any enemy. But these Volunteers carried out intelligence work, dug trenches, scouted, guarded and arranged billets, maintained communications, collected money for the army fund – they were in fact the wall that supported Barry's flying column.

Added to this were the activities of Cumann na mBan who worked tirelessly. They did intelligence work, carried dispatches, mended and washed clothes and cooked meals at all hours of the day or night. They helped arrange funerals of their dead comrades, often risking their lives in doing so. (A group of Cumann na mBan girls stole Charlie Hurley's body from the Bandon Hospital morgue at the peril of their lives.) Leslie Price, Hurley's girlfriend, had worked long and hard. She had travelled throughout the whole of West Cork mainly on her bicycle, and encouraged the women in their work with the men so that together they would win freedom for the Irish people.

Propping up this wall were the people of West Cork, who gave their beds, their food and their loyalty to the men of the column. The support of the people convinced Tom Barry that the cause they were working for was a righteous one. Children going to school, a woman driving to the market in a horse and cart, a publican or shopkeeper in the course of his/her daily task, employees in post offices and railways – everybody had an ear tuned, and eyes trained for the unexpected, prepared to report to the column, to do anything to help protect the lives of the men 'on the run'. Help was often given at a price. Military reprisals in the form of houses being looted, furniture smashed, women insulted, old men prodded with rifle-butts, and houses and property burned.

As an example of what the people were prepared to do, Tom tells of a night when, with two men, he called at a thatched house near Dunmanway where a family with young children were eking out an existence on a few acres: 'It was five o'clock on a winter's morning. Tired and weary, we knocked at their door. The woman of the house greeted the three of us. Having raked the fire, put on the kettle, she asked us to tend to it, as she had to go out. Putting on her working boots she went away, and we sat silent as we guessed the reason for her early morning journey.

'She returned having gone half a mile to a luckier neighbour to borrow butter and eggs for her visitors. Her family could not afford these luxuries very often, but she never failed to have them when "The Boys" called. I know she would have to skimp, scrape and save to repay the borrowed luxuries later. Although acutely uncomfortable at the trouble we were causing, we dared not attempt to stop her or to refuse the eggs or the butter, as had we done so we would have hurt that fine pride so pronounced amongst the grand people who enrich West Cork.'[8]

Dr Dorothy Stophard, who described herself as an Irish Protestant Nationalist spent some time helping the wounded IRA in the Kilbrittain/Bandon area, recalled seeing 'families living in lofts, cattle sheds, or other makeshift dwellings whilst they scrabbled in the ruins of their burnt houses for belongings. Big houses also went up in flames, but to these Dorothy had not the entrée, being only called there on a red ticket to attend to the domestic staff.'[9]

People risked their lives by allowing their houses to be used. O'Mahony's home at Belrose (headquarters), where Tom, Charlie Hurley, Liam Deasy, Dick Barrett, Seán Hales, Tom Hales and many of the men of the column laughed, joked, sang and planned ambushes, was burned to the ground by Percival and his men. The night before burning this large house, they locked the five women upstairs in a room and used the rest of the house for billeting and eating. The following morning they set it alight and the flames were already soaring when Percival allowed the women to jump to safety. He showed his one touch of humanity to the horses; he had them brought out of the stables and tied to trees while he burned the outhouses. 'A bullet would be too good for him', commented Barry.[10]

When Percival discovered through his 'intelligence' spy source that the 'medical student' whom he had released from his grasp was Tom Barry, he and his men went on a rampage of raiding and harassing. Several houses were burned. After the Crossbarry fight helpless civilians in the area were told to get out of their homes; they grabbed a few belongings, their small children, and stood outside as they watched their hard-earned possessions go up in flames. Now upon his return from Gougane Barra following the raking operations and further burning orgies by the British forces, Barry was incensed. He ordered reprisals by burning property of 'active British supporters'. These included the Allin Institute – a meeting place for British Loyalists, which was situated at a strategic entrance to Bandon. The IRA broke into Bandon Brewery, stole the whiskey to set the institute ablaze in a fire which illuminated the town on a dark June night.[11] Barry wanted to teach them a lesson to 'once and for all end their fire terror'. His ruse worked, as the enemy did not reply to those counter burnings.[12] The military recorded that their 'policy of authorised punishments' in burning the houses of 'prominent members or officers of the IRA' had found a backlash.[13] On the night the IRA burned Bandon workhouse, Barry took a small column, divided in sections, into town. Barry felt some of his men were over-confident as they casually stood on the bridge and watched another 'symbol of British conquest' being destroyed. After a shoot-up he moved them out, as their 'over-confidence might easily lead to disaster'.[14]

During the June hostilities the West Cork IRA kidnapped a number of British Loyalists, both from the armed forces and the civilian administration. 'The action was taken to prevent the continuous shooting of prisoners by the British troops.' Three coastguards at Howe's Strand, three Royal Marines at Castletownsend, a British major at Bantry and four justices of the peace at Bandon and Clonakilty were all taken as hostages. The British administration was informed that should they shoot or hang any IRA, the hostages would receive similar treatment.'[1]

In Bandon, as well as the justices of the peace, a party under the direction of Seán 'Buckshot' Hales and Jim O'Mahony kidnapped Lord Bandon under Tom Barry's instructions. Lord Bandon, Earl of Cork and Lord Lieutenant was held in high esteem by the British government. He was a descendant of Col Bernard, a British adventurer, who for his military service 'in destroying the Irish, had been granted the lands of the dispossessed O'Mahonys'. His first cousin, the Earl of Midleton was 'head of the southern Unionists'.

'We wrote to General Strickland and to the British Prime Minister' to inform them 'that if there was one execution of one of our men held prisoners that Lord Bandon would swing from the nearest telegraph pole'.[2]

Denis Lordan got in through the conservatory and let his comrades in through the main hall door. They looked through some rooms, but failed to find the occupants. Hales looked at Lordan, 'As the bird has flown we will burn the nest', he said. No preparations had been made to burn Bandon castle, so they piled some furniture and curtains and set it alight. In another detached quarter they located Lord Bandon. Seán Hales, Jim O'Mahony and Charlie O'Keeffe kidnapped him and brought him 'out in a side car to a farmhouse near Clogagh' where he was 'guarded by the Clogagh Coy ... He got the best food and brandy, and whiskey daily.'[3] In his presence, Barry instructed the guard to shoot him should the British appear likely to try a recapture. He knew the threat would be implemented and so became a model prisoner. As he played cards with the men he often told 'his guard not to make so much noise as a British rounding up party might hear'. One evening as the Essex moved towards a house in Barryroe where he was being held, the woman of the house 'had a nightdress pulled over her clothes and she was popped into the double bed with the Earl in the hope that he might be mistaken for her husband by the soldiers. The lads hid outside.' The Essex passed by 'little thinking how near they were to their object'. Dorothy Stopford reflected that 'he probably discovered more about his neighbours in Co. Cork than he had learned in seventy-odd years living amongst them in his castle.'[4]

Tom, with Seán Hales, dictated letters to Lord Bandon which he signed. They were sent to Lloyd George and General Strickland 'giving particulars of the fate that awaited him and appealing to them to ensure that no IRA prisoner would be killed. He [Lord Bandon] wanted the IRA taken seriously. There was also the appeal for a worthwhile truce.' These 'Lord Bandon' letters were intended to put pressure on the British administration.[5]

In June the Essex killed three Volunteers – Daniel Crowley killed near his home, Matthew Donovan was taken some distance and killed on the roadside, John Murphy, a farm labourer, was bayoneted to death in the field where he had been working. Barry said 'when the news came of this brutal outrage, Lord Bandon's life hung on a very slender thread'. Luckily for him 'although three of our patriot soldiers were brutally killed by the army of occupation' the IRA's 'ultimatum could not possibly have reached' the authorities at the time.[6]

In West Cork the chronic problem of the lack of ammunition became increasingly acute. Tom Barry, bitterly disappointed at the failure of the Italian ship to arrive, decided to resort to new tactics that he felt would have a more penetrating effect on the British government.

Tom, with some of the column intended to attack a passing troop train at Kinsale Junction, on the Crossbarry line, went to the home of Barrett's in Killeady. Willie, an active IRA Volunteer was away, and Tom apologetically told Mrs Barrett, who had four young children, that they would have to use her home as one of the firing positions to cover the railway station close-by. He felt guilty asking a woman for such a favour. Angrily she asked, 'Do you think the Barretts will worry if their home is burned afterwards?'

She simply asked for permission to take the children to the safety of a neighbour's house. When she returned she made tea for the men before the fight. As happened many times the troops were not on the train. Later it became known that an informer had tipped them off.[7]

The column was now involved mainly in shoot-ups. During these few weeks Barry and his men entered Bandon no less than eight times – an Essex soldier, a Black and Tan and an enemy agent were shot. Under local officers, every enemy post 'was sniped several times'. The British forces were pestered in many areas; soldiers were fired at entering railway stations and Barry was involved in five sniping attacks on Innishannon and other barracks. It was his intention to annoy them to the extreme. They tried to bring them from their barracks but were unsuccessful in luring them to a confrontation.[8]

The officers of Cork No. 3 Brigade were aware that the British army maintenance engineers had viewed several large buildings in West Cork that they intended to take over as temporary barracks. Field-Marshal Sir Henry Wilson noted that Marquess Curzon and the prime minister had decided to send five battalions to Silesia. Wilson said, 'directly England was safe, every available man should go to Ireland, that even four battalions now on the Rhine ought also to go to Ireland ... unless we crushed out the murder-gang this summer we should lose Ireland to the empire.' Two days later Wilson noted that 'Macready absolutely backs up my contention that we must knock out or at least knock under, the Sinn Féiners this summer or we shall lose Ireland … we must make our effort now, or else, tacitly and in fact, agree that we were beaten.'[9]

One night in June Tom, Liam Deasy and other officers attended a Bandon battalion council meeting near Ballinadee and afterwards they set out for Rossmore, 17 miles away. The men were walking past Balwin's Bridge and along the Currivreeda Road about a mile outside Bandon, when Liam Deasy said jokingly, 'Tough on you, Tom, to be so near Bandon and yet so far from it!'

Tom stopped, faced him with a never-let-it-be-said attitude. 'Why shouldn't we go in now that we are so near and have a go at the curfew patrol?'

Liam said his challenge was a rash one, but he accepted, and immediately they changed direction. 'He had terrier courage. He'd go in and bark and bite'. The four men went in, took up their position at Warner's Lane, where they expected the curfew patrol to pass. They waited some time but the enemy did not come. Eventually they left the town and headed for Rossmore.

According to Liam Deasy, 'our visit became the talk of the town next day. The fact that four armed Volunteers, two of them well known to the townspeople, could dare to enter Bandon would soon be known to the enemy … but it had its morale value.'[10]

Orders came from GHQ that Commandant Barry was posted to the staff of the First Southern Division, so on 26 June he led his flying column into action for the last time. He was near Rosscarbery saying goodbye to some of his comrades when word reached them that the Auxiliaries had entered the town. He wasn't sure if it was a raid or if they were about to repossess the town. He regretted that he had only 33 men with him. Within 20 minutes he had them regrouped in three sections and they were on the march. One section was sent to enter the town from the high ground. With the stronger IRA group he would open the attack from the east. They advanced to engage what was believed to be a body of 150 Auxiliaries.

A burst of fire was heard when the western section encountered a few of the enemy. After a skirmish the enemy rapidly retired. Barry and his two sections engaged the enemy wounding some. After about 15 minutes 'of wild and erratic fire' Barry with his small party knew it would be foolhardy to continue when the odds were too heavily against them. He withdrew his men eastwards and was not pursued by the Auxiliaries. Later he heard that the Auxies had withdrawn around the same time.[11]

Tom headed back to headquarters to meet Liam Deasy and others.

On 29 June, Tom and Liam set out for North Cork near the Kerry border where a divisional training camp was to open on 1 July for a fortnight. Liam Lynch had appointed Tom as operations' officer and IRA deputy divisional commander of the First Southern Division. He was to conduct this training camp which was to be attended by the commandants and three senior officers from each of the nine brigade areas.[12] Barry was now the first IRA deputy divisional O/C in Ireland. He was in control of co-ordinating all flying columns in Cork, Kerry, Waterford and West Limerick. Gearóid O'Sullivan, adjutant general, told him that Michael Collins and GHQ 'had decided on the appointment before Liam Lynch had suggested it'. When Barry questioned the adjutant on 'the grave responsibility of this position' especially if an occasion arose when Barry himself disagreed with Lynch 'on strategy or major tactics about the use of those armed men.' The adjutant assured Barry that Lynch had agreed to give him full divisional O/C responsibility. This divisional area 'was both numerically and in fighting power as strong as the three next divisions in Ireland combined'. (Barry was again given this title within the army executive council during the Civil War.)

Tom wasn't in agreement with the idea of a divisional training camp then, nor was he with the hindsight of almost 60 years. His first objection had to do with security. By bringing together so many senior officers, he felt that the IRA was running the risk of putting the entire armed effort in the south-west of Ireland in jeopardy. If the officers were to be captured or wiped out in a confrontation it would cripple the decision-making of the remaining Volunteers, as well as being a devastating blow to morale.

His other objection was based upon his opinion that guerrilla warfare can only be learned in the field and cannot be taught. He said that the amount to be learned in the proposed camp could be circulated to all brigades on half a sheet of notepaper. In July 1971, he told Raymond Smith that the circular could have read: 'Select as your active service leaders men who are dedicated, will lead from the front are not afraid to die. Men who will judge a situation, attack or refuse battle, who realise that they and their Volunteers are alone: men who must above all be security minded, make instant decisions and ensure that they are carried out.'[13]

Barry said that is was useless to try to train men 'who had already proved that they neither could not, nor would not fight'. Instead of forming divisions, he felt that by the opening of 1921, GHQ should have weeded out useless commanders and staffs who hindered other brigade areas.

Barry wanted men with initiative and aggression. Such men could have come to the active areas from the inactive ones. Such a system would be superior to any camp training, he insisted, because they would see and participate in action. He knew that there were men in other areas just as capable of guerrilla fighting as those in the West Cork area if they were properly trained and commanded. 'Any kind of war is a serious responsibility, but this was particularly true of that in which our small guerrilla force was pitted against the then mighty Britain.'[14]

In spite of his disagreement, Barry respected Liam Lynch's decision on the divisional training camp and continued on his way towards the Cork-Kerry border where the proposed camp was to be conducted. However, at the end of their day's journey Tom and Liam Deasy were stopped by a dispatch from Lynch informing them that the area of the proposed camp was infested with the enemy and that it would be advisable to wait until the enemy withdrew. Next day they returned to West Cork.

Back in West Cork Tom Barry provisionally disbanded the flying column and with his comrades continued to follow the bulletins in the daily papers. On 4 July it was announced that the Truce between the Irish and British forces had been agreed upon. Though the morale and confidence of the Third Cork Brigade was high Tom and his men welcomed the Truce. For those on the run and for the ordinary citizens it was a rest from the hardships and killing of war. He was also glad that the enemy had been forced to offer terms that were, in his opinion, a signal of victory for the IRA.

Strickland obviously disillusioned wrote: 'and so this is the end of 2-years toil. A year on we had a perfect "organisation" and had "them" beat – a short time more would have completed it thoroughly. All our labours and energy occupying have been thrown in the gutter'.[15]

Weighing up the activities of the war, Tom said, 'I made my brigade flying column fight aggressively, and I placed it in many difficult and dangerous situations, but those were risks well calculated by me. On the other hand, I never had any hesitation in avoiding battle with the British and retiring the column if we had not a reasonable hope of victory.' In his opinion military men throughout the world judge the success of a battle by the number of casualties inflicted on the enemy 'and West Cork had done fairly well in this respect'. In the precarious situation of guerrilla warfare, however, Tom also judged results on how few men were lost in action in achieving victory. He considered his men as part of his family and hated to lose any, so he felt happy at the end of this period because, he said, 'The flying column under my command lost only seven with seven or eight wounded in all its many actions.' British acknowledged casualties during the same period were over 100 dead and 93 wounded.[16]

Fifty years later as he looked back on those days he was convinced that if the British government had felt that they could out-fight the IRA, then they would have further increased their strength in Ireland as they had in past history.

'I am one of those who believe' that the Volunteers were never 'fully stretched from 1919–1921. Had the British succeeded in bringing in another 70,000 troops, the real test of the people and of the IRA could have begun.'[17] Barry and different IRA men entered 'Bandon which was a garrison town between 40 and 50 times altogether, we tried to bring them out, especially over the last three to four months, but they didn't come out.'[18]

He never doubted that the column could continue harassing during the summer months and would survive the British summer offensive. Neither did he under-rate the potential of the immensely increased forces with which they were threatened and which would undoubtedly push against them if the negotiations did not succeed. Field Marshal Sir Henry Wilson was prepared to pour 'every available man' into Ireland.[19] Montgomery believed 'that Lloyd George was really right in what he did; if we had gone on we could probably have squashed the rebellion as a temporary measure, but it would have broken out again like an ulcer the moment we had removed the troops; I think the rebels would have refused battle, and hidden away their arms, etc., until we had gone'.[20]

If the British government came to recognise the IRA, which was a startling upheaval of British policy, it was, according to Barry, 'due only to the British recognition that they had not defeated and could not reasonably hope to defeat in the measurable future, the armed forces of the Irish nation.'[21]

In the daily papers Tom Barry and the officers read of Lloyd George's invitation to President de Valera and such colleagues as he might select to come to London to explore the possibility of a settlement. Negotiations regarding a Truce had begun. During this process Lloyd George requested information about Lord Bandon. On Tuesday 6 July, Mick Collins, Diarmuid Hegarty and Gearóid O'Sullivan sent for the Cumann na mBan director of organisation, Leslie Price. They 'instructed' her to visit Tom Barry in West Cork to obtain 'full details of the health and condition of the Earl of Bandon … a very highly placed member of the British House of Lords'. De Valera was 'to discuss terms of the Truce with Lord Midleton' on Friday 8 July. 'Midleton had stated that he would not discuss terms until he knew that Bandon was safe and sound. Midleton and Bandon were cousins.'

Leslie left Dublin on the first train on Wednesday morning 7 July; she had to be back by mid-day Friday. Having arrived at the train station in Cork she set out on a borrowed bicycle for Dunmanway. Having cycled thirty miles, she met Paddy Walsh at Coppeen. He drove her in a pony trap to Caheragh and then to Skibbereen. Here they got a fresh pony and drove to Schull, only to be told that Tom Barry and the men had gone to Kealkil, outside Bantry. At Kealkil they were told Tom was back in Caheragh where they had left. It was after midnight on Thursday night when Leslie located Tom in a field, asleep in a bunker. She got 'a withering look' from him. 'Tell Dublin headquarters to come down and see how my men are!' Then he softened: 'Lord Bandon is getting better dinners than the boys!' He had been with him the night before, and 'had seen the old man playing cards with his guards and urging them not to talk or laugh too loudly in case the British forces would come and attack them'. Tom assured her that he was being properly treated, and in a whisper expressed the hope that his plan would be fruitful. Having obtained the information and assurances, Leslie, with a change of ponies again, set out for Cork to catch the first train. She was back to meet De Valera in Dublin by 11.30 a.m. Friday. 'Exhausted! I slept for twelve hours', she wrote.[22]

According to Percival, in kidnapping Lord Bandon, the IRA's 'object [was] to conclude a Truce'. Percival wrote that 'a well-known lady, who had become an ardent Sinn Féiner, came down to Castle Bernard and said to Lady Bandon, "I have been sent down by our people to warn you that, unless the government conclude a Truce, Lord Bandon will be killed." The reply [Lady Bandon's] was "If that is all you have to say, you had better go home." It would have been impossible to carry out any operations', Percival wrote, 'without having a reasonably good intelligence service'.[23] Barry would smile had he known of Percival's intelligence service on this occasion!

The justices were released when the peace talks made it obvious that a Truce was imminent. However, Lord Bandon was held, being moved periodically to different houses to avoid a British swoop.

Lord Bandon's deputy lieutenant, R. Bence Jones of Clonakilty escaped being kidnapped – as he was absent from home, meeting General Strickland. Some days later Bill Daly and other captured IRA men were informed that their death sentence would be postponed.[24]

Could the IRA have carried on if there had been no Truce? 'No participant can speak with accuracy on the overall position of the IRA throughout Ireland on that date ... My own views are based only on the intimate knowledge of one area, a general association with several others and what fellow officers told me afterwards of their brigades.

'The IRA in July 1921 were stronger in number – in spite of several thousands arrested – than they were in July 1920. In addition there were ten times more experienced, tough fighters.'[25]

Tom Barry had always maintained, according to Denis O'Callaghan, that 'one Volunteer was worth 100 paid soldiers, and this certainly has been proved. He also proved that the IRA could destroy the British civilian intelligence machinery.' A drop in the number of IRA casualties occurred as spying and informing became dangerous. 'Our army was a war army. It was made up of all types, all kinds, all classes. I can say without any fear of contradiction with 100 of these West Cork men, half armed with neither rations, supplies, telephone equipment, or any kind of decent accommodation, if I was offered 1,000 of the British army of that period in Ireland, with all the advantages, with all their barracks to retire into, by choice, I'd take the 100 of West Cork men, especially men who believed in what they were doing.'[26]

Barry admitted that in a defensive action against British artillery, planes, armoured-cars and fire-power, the IRA would not have stood a chance. However, in the event of a troop build-up, he said, 'Every wanted man in his area would be gathered into a flying column which would be through the blockade lines before the enemy had got set to commence their sweeps. Once outside the perimeter, the commander would have a choice of moving into a lightly held area or watching for a chance to harass the British from their rear.'[27]

The harassment could be continued for years, but by then the cost in lives and energy would have been great. However, according to Barry the cost would not have been on the Irish side alone and with hindsight he asked, 'Would the losses have been any greater than they were for the Irish who suffered two years of a bitter Civil War?' He was convinced that if the leaders had foreseen the consequences of the Truce, none of them would have agreed to it, certainly not on the British terms of negotiations.

At the time though, Barry was acutely aware of what a further build-up of British troops in his area during the summer of 1921 could mean. Michael Collins was in constant touch with the brigade leaders in all areas and also with outside sources regarding the securing of arms and ammunition, and so had a complete picture of the over-all situation. Florrie O'Donoghue, IO, says that 'for 9 months every day practically before the end of Tan War, Collins and I had communication'. There was 'closer contacts between brigades for communication was [part] of intelligence'. O'Donoghue had 'a distinct view that closer cooperation between places in the south was necessary'. He had found many holes in the British intelligence system and their use of 'Loyalists' informers. 'The British really thought they could organise an intelligence system. They had not learned their difficulties or they certainly did not know their own inherent weakness'.[28]

Though national resistance against British rule and administration was general, 'GHQ was in no position to control the fighting in the different brigade areas ... Each unit fought its own battles, won its own victories or stood up to its own defeats'. Consequently, 'the British High Command quite logically concentrated on wiping out the fighting men of the active districts'.[29]

The invitation by the British prime minister to the Irish leaders to attend a conference and to list the terms of the Truce were the best indication to Barry as to the success of guerrilla warfare. 'The only language they [the British] listened to or could understand was that of the rifle, the revolver, the bomb and the crackling of the flames which cost them so dearly in blood and treasure.'[30]

'The general election of 1918 had given the people an opportunity, under an election that was held under the British authority at the time, to declare their wish about the men of 1916, and the declaration of the Republic. The people opted for a Republic,' Barry said. 'But the British had no respect for the people at the polls even though they boasted about democracy.' Professor John A. Murphy spoke of 'Barry and his West Cork column's contribution' which 'helped bring about a state of affairs where the British were anxious to make a truce. In 1919 and 1920 all the British wanted was to give a very limited form of Home Rule. If, in the summer of 1921 they were anxious to offer Dominion Status, there was an enormous difference.'

By July 1921 the Government of Ireland Act of December 1920 imposed a six county border. The May 1921 six county elections led to a parliament for the area in June. Professor John A. Murphy put it into a framework: 'The War of Independence took place within the mandate' of the 1918 victory within 'the Dáil which spoke for Nationalist Ireland. The physical struggle was, as it were, mandated by that parliament ... Crossbarry, Kilmichael and so on must be fitted into the pattern.'[31]

Now a time had arrived when the fighting could stop. The British parliament was ready to negotiate. Since he became column commander shortly after joining the IRA Tom Barry had had moments of great hope and of great glory, moments of joy, of sorrow, of hate, of aggression, of deep sadness and a hundred thousand other moments as he tried to steer his men towards success. During all this time he doesn't appear to have entertained any thoughts of despair – for him the sun would eventually come out and shine. And the spirit of the people in spite of their sorrow had a buoyancy which could not be quelled.

As an example of why he thought British aggression had failed, he told of a touching memory when one day in February he left the column to visit the parents of Lieut Patrick Crowley of Kilbrittain after he had been killed by the Essex Regiment.

With another officer Tom came out through the woods. Mrs Crowley, a frail, ageing woman dressed in black, was sitting on a stool in the yard gazing at the ruins of their burned-out-home. Her husband, a grey-bearded, thin man, was moving some rubble to strengthen a hen house which alone escaped the orgy of destruction. Towards the end of their days, their son Paddy was killed the previous week; Denis lay badly hurt in a British jail after a merciless beating by his captors; Con was also in prison under the name of Paddy Murphy with a shadow of death hanging over him should his identity be discovered. The fourth remaining son Mick had been seriously wounded early in the struggle, and his chance of survival was not great. Their two daughters, in Cumann na mBan, Ciss and Bridie were away on IRA business and would not be back until late that night. 'The sorrows and sufferings of this ageing couple must have weighed heavily upon them, but there was no sign of weakness or complaining as they listened to our words of sympathy at the death of their son. British money could not buy them, nor could British guile and duplicity wean from them their support of the Irish Republican army. People with spirit like this were as truly soldiers of the resistance movement as any Volunteer of the Flying Column.'

Tom had a high regard for his men and though there were dissensions in other brigade areas he was 'happy to record that in the West Cork Brigade no such bickerings or dissensions ever existed. The brigade staff set an example of good comradeship that could not be surpassed. We were a happy family, bound together by close ties.' All that mattered to them was 'the pursuit of the movement for freedom.'[32]

Peter Hart wrote that men in Tom Barry's Column 'contained only those who were loyal to him personally, who went anti-Treaty "to a man", stuck with him afterwards … and who agreed with his version of history.' He cites Barry's comment regarding Paddy O'Brien's Kilmichael ambush account in the Deasy book. Hart wrote that men 'who were not part of this group, like Paddy O'Brien, were not part of the column, according to Barry himself'.[33] Other accounts show that Barry, O'Brien and flying column men, were at the period under review, comrades in arms, 'fighting for the one objective'. (Later, men such as Seán Hales, John L. O'Sullivan, some Kilmichael and other flying column men became pro-Treaty).[34]

Flor Begley, told Ernie O'Malley that 'Tom Barry was a hard man, very strict but very good to his column men, and they loved him. "Did you have a good billet?" he would say to them next day, "and how were you fed?" And if they had not been, he would do his best for them.'[35]

'It has to be remembered,' Comdt Christy O'Sullivan told Irish army officers, that Tom Barry trained several different columns over a period. The men were changed from time to time, but the commander was never changed which shows that the brigade had the utmost confidence in him.' Comdt O'Sullivan met many men who had 'participated in engagements' under 'General Tom Barry ' and 'one thing all agree, is the sheer confidence which they had in their column commander at all times, even in the worst of positions.' Whenever he was absent 'there was always a feeling of tension and uncertainty', when he was present they were 'relaxed and confident'.[36]

Barry himself was alert, always. Being a keen bridge card player, and like Liam Lynch, a good draughts player, Barry constantly tried to anticipate the moves of his opponents. 'A good leader is one who attempts something that is possible, not what is impossible,' he pointed out almost fifty years later. He had his men prepared for any eventuality, to think ahead, to react quickly, ready to vault over a ditch or wall as they marched. To get to brigade meetings and return quickly to his column he travelled on horseback. He had a horse that would jump ditches, walls, everything – 'a winner of the Ballsbridge show owned by a great-great nephew of Daniel O'Connell.'[37]

Col M. J. Costello summed up the success of Barry's flying column with 'good leadership'. And he quotes Napoleon: 'In war, it is not men who count, it is the man'.

With particular reference to Crossbarry, Col Costello wrote, 'If the men of Crossbarry had not been led with skill and determination, there would have been no fight to write about. They would simply have been mopped up ... If even one step had been neglected, if the leader had been content, as so many of us are prone to be, with something less than absolute thoroughness and attention to every detail in providing for the security of his command,' it would have been disastrous. Furthermore, 'in the superior morale qualities of Barry's column, is to be found another reason for the result of the action and an object lesson in the truth and importance of Napoleon's remark: "the morale is to the physical as three is to one".' Barry's success Col Costello said was the men's 'confidence in their commander, a confidence learned in other fights, and an intense patriotism were foundations of this high morale and discipline.'[38] The Third West Cork Brigade Flying Column carried the name of their commander and became known as 'Barry's Flying Column'. The ballad maker penned the song:

When British Terror failed to win
Allegiance from our people then,
The Black and Tans they were brought in,
They thought they'd teach us manners ...
The grander tune of all is played
By the fighting squad of the Third Brigade,
Whose glorious deeds will never fade,
The men of Barry's Column.[39]

When the Truce came into force the fighting men of West Cork were dazed by the speed of events, and their first reaction was one of disbelief. They felt it couldn't last beyond the month. 'Whatever decisions were made at GHQ before the Truce and however these decisions were influenced by the military situation, they were certainly made without consultation with one of the areas which had borne the brunt of the fighting,' Barry wrote in an unpublished document. 'Lynch was at division headquarters when the official notification of the Truce was received … no previous indication of such a possibility had come from an *official* source, and little notice was taken of the newspaper rumours which preceded it. He issued the necessary orders for the cessation of hostilities but it was clear to him that if the Truce was prolonged … the effect on morale and efficiency was bound to be detrimental.'[40]

Although the flying column was provisionally disbanded, nevertheless its members were ordered to remain on call in case hostilities were resumed. They were to dump their guns, put them aside – but, as it happened, not put them away forever.

Lord Bandon was released.

On the day the Truce was announced a dispatch arrived for Tom from the adjutant-general stating that the president had appointed him chief liaison officer of the martial law area, covering eight southern counties. He did not welcome the president's appointment. However, he took up this position on Monday 11 July 1921, the day the Truce came into force.

As noon approached on 11 July he hid his colt automatic, bade a temporary goodbye to his friends, and set out for Cork city. It was the end of a phase, but not the end of his guerrilla days.

TRUCE AND MARRIAGE TO LESLIE MARY PRICE

It was Easter Monday morning 1916. Ireland was part of the British empire, its seat of government in Ireland controlled from Dublin Castle with a British army.

At ten o'clock on this sunny morning a group of armed men wearing unfamiliar green uniforms and slouched hats marched determinedly, taking up positions at various points in Dublin city. One group marched with their leader Pádraig Pearse through Sackville Street (later O'Connell Street), swung into the General Post Office and ordered the staff out a gunpoint. Windows were barricaded and the tricolour – the green, white and orange symbol of the Republic, which was to be proclaimed – was raised on top of the building. The Proclamation was then read. Although the Rising was to fail in its aim of achieving independence for the Irish Republic, without this rising there might have been no subsequent success.

On the north side of Dublin on that Easter Monday morning a group of women Volunteers mobilised. Shortly after assembly they were disbanded and told to go home, as there would be no rebellion. Among this group of women was nineteen-year-old Dublin-born Leslie Price. A national teacher trained in the Dominican Convent, Belfast, she was a member of Cumann na mBan and had acquired knowledge of first aid through this organisation.

Between the great strike and lock-out of 1913 and the 1916 Rising she acted as secret courier for men like Pearse, Seán Mac Diarmada and Tom Clarke. Tom Clarke's tobacconist shop was used as a 'post office depot' for the organisation. Present at the funeral in Glasnevin of the Fenian, O'Donovan Rossa in 1915, Leslie said that the graveside oration delivered by Pádraig Pearse left an indelible mark on her: 'The fools, the fools! – They have left us our Fenian dead. And while Ireland holds these graves, Ireland unfree shall never be at peace'. Soon she decided to join Cumann na mBan.

Leslie Price helped those Volunteers who were trying to free Ireland from British domination. She knew that her brothers Seán and Eamonn had already marched with Pearse, so she and her friend Brid Dixon decided that they would go to the GPO instead of going home. It was about 1 p.m. when they arrived there and reported to Tom Clarke.

Initially they cooked meals and helped the men in the Hibernian Bank. On Tuesday forenoon the building came under attack from British troops. Leslie was standing beside Capt. Tom Weafer, OC of the Hibernian Garrison, when a bullet whizzed past her and into his stomach. As she was about to attend to him another bullet lodged in the chest of man who had gone to Capt. Weafer's aid. She had just time to say a prayer in Weafer's ear when he died.

146

The small garrison was ordered to evacuate to the GPO However, Tom Clarke asked Leslie to stand by. With the other women she acted as courier between the GPO and Fr Matthew Hall, carrying messages backwards and forwards to the background of gunfire, blood and death. On Wednesday, field guns opened a strong bombardment which set many of the buildings in Sackville Street on fire. The upper storey of the GPO was wrecked. The defenders fired incessantly, and with the aid of the women the wounded were evacuated. On Thursday there was continuous bombardment by the British forces as they gradually closed in on the GPO when barricades went up at the top of Moore Street. Up to this, she was not scared. But when Tom Clarke sent her to cross Sackville Street into Marlborough Street to get a priest to come to the GPO, she felt 'really frightened'. With 'bullets whizzing everywhere' she hugged the walls, intermittently darting into the shadows. At 'any moment' she felt a bullet could get her in the back. During a gripping few minutes she hid beneath Parnell's statue where British troops had blocked the way with a manned barricade. Eventually she 'skirted' it.

With her 'heart pounding' she arrived at the presbytery (opposite the Department of Education) which was occupied by British troops. A few minutes later she had to face the return journey. This time she was not alone. A priest went with her. Safely back, her horror mission accomplished, her normal state of mind returned. That night as the shelling bombarded the GPO and timber and concrete scattered everywhere, Leslie darted around to help the wounded. The shelling, the shouting, the terror and the burning continued.

Pearse, whom Leslie remembers as a quiet, gentle type of man, called all the women (about 25 of them) together on Friday morning around 10 o'clock. He told them they would have to leave. It was a sad occasion. Some of the Cumann na mBan protested, saying they would like to stay and help to the end. 'But really we knew we'd have been a handicap, it was better for us to go.'

As Leslie was about to leave she passed Tom Clarke (who would later die before a firing squad). He caught her hand and said, 'Tell my wife the men were wonderful to the –' he didn't finish the sentence, but she knew the missing word was 'the end'. About three of the young women remained behind, and Leslie with the others filed out of the side door into the smoke, ruins and dead bodies on Henry Street. With Louise Gavan Duffy who was in charge, under the protection of the white flag, these young women carried some wounded men on stretchers and took them to Jervis Street Hospital.

Knowing that they might be arrested on the way home – as they were – they concocted a story. They said that they were pupils at the Dominican Convent who had been out walking with their teacher, Miss Louise Gavan Duffy (who was in fact a teacher at that school), and that while they were passing the GPO the men had called on them to come and help. Eventually, following some further questioning, they were released and went as arranged (because they knew they might be followed) to the Dominican Convent where the nuns kept them until it was safe to go home.

Following these events Leslie spent her time visiting prisoners and talking to their dependents. Her brother Seán had been one of the stretcher-bearers who took the wounded James Connolly from the GPO. Years later she recalled those 'sad days' when they listened 'for tidings' as the men 'were shot one by one'. Like the many Volunteers of that time, both Seán and Eamonn Price were arrested and interned in Frongoch for some months.

Her period as a schoolteacher wasn't a very happy or satisfactory one, as the authorities kept checking to establish if she was actually taking class or whether she was influencing her pupils in some way. Eventually she gave up teaching and became an organiser for Cumann na mBan. Elected director of organisation she mustered women in the four provinces, and got to know the headquarters of every brigade in the country. Her bicycle was her constant train companion. When she got to a destination it speeded her movement and helped her execute her task more efficiently.

It was on one such visit to Cork that she met Charlie Hurley. As the months progressed their friendship deepened. However, fate intervened and Charlie was killed. Since that sad night in the Clogagh graveyard she had met Tom Barry on a few occasions – briefly at meetings and when she brought guns and ammunition. When she was sent to Cork to check on the welfare of the hostage Lord Bandon for De Valera, she had a long talk with Tom.

With the implementation of a Truce in July 1921 Tom decided he would like to meet Leslie again, so with the consent of the O'Mahony family of Belrose she was invited for a holiday. Following a whirlwind romance the couple decided to get married. The wedding took place in St Joseph's church, Berkeley Road, with the reception in Vaughan's Hotel in Dublin on 22 August 1921.

Leslie, wearing a white frilly blouse, navy suit and picture hat upon which was set a cluster of varied-coloured flowers, looked radiant. Her mother, father and her four brothers attended, as well as her only sister, Eva, who was her bridesmaid.

The Dáil was adjourned for a day to allow invited members to attend the wedding. Many of the great names in modern Irish history were present: Eamon de Valera, Michael Collins, Richard Mulcahy, Countess Markievicz, Liam Tobin, Seán Hales, Liam Lynch, Liam Deasy and the best man, Dick Barrett, and many more – friends and working companions of Leslie and Tom. The only known photograph in existence has De Valera, President of Sinn Féin, seated between Leslie and Tom. Whether this is because the photographer was paid for by the Dáil or because of De Valera's importance at the time is unknown. But it is a historic record of unity some months before many would fight each other.

This marriage, born out of war, blossomed and matured into a deep love and understanding as the years progressed. The honeymoon was spent in West Cork, and during the early days of their marriage, they stayed in O'Mahony's converted house in Belrose and in Barrett's, Killeady. They had no home.[1] For many of their earlier years together, Tom told his friend John Browne of hardships when they 'had to count the cream crackers, and measure the butter!'[2]

For their twenty-fifth anniversary Tom gave Leslie a gold Claddagh ring. 'This,' she said, proudly fingering it in a hospital bed 60 years after their wedding, 'this is the heart enclapsed by hands and crowned with love.' She then drew attention to the gold disc broach, which pinned the top of her bed jacket together. 'He gave me this for our fiftieth anniversary. "Twas hand-made and engraved in Egans. Isn't it nice!'. Encircled within a Celtic design was the following:

22-8–1921
To Leslie Mary
With Love
Tom
22-8–1971

From the early days of marriage Tom had to keep on the move. In his new role as chief liaison officer for the martial law area, he was said to have been very strict. His instructions were to report to the OC Seventeenth Infantry Brigade at 3 o'clock on 11 July 1921. He travelled in uniform to Cork city and notified 'the enemy' also 'in uniform' of his presence. Brigadier-General Higginson telephoned him at HQ Cork Brigade and asked if he was in uniform. Barry said, 'Yes!' Higginson would see him, but not in uniform. Barry said, 'I don't intend entering Victoria Barracks in uniform. But I've worn it for the past 12 months and will continue to wear it when and where I please'.

He entered the barracks dressed in civilian clothes, and was escorted by two officers to General Strickland's office.

'You are the representative of De Valera here?' one officer asked.

'I am not! I want you to understand that I am an officer appointed by GHQ IRA to meet you and co-operate in carrying out Truce terms'. The officer went in and then returned.

'I'm afraid the general can't receive you. He's been in touch with headquarters and he can't receive you except as Mr de Valera's representative.'

'That's fine with me. I didn't want to see him in the first place. It was he who requested the meeting.'

Barry believed it was deliberate on the part of the British administration not to recognise the IRA as an army. 'I was a soldier fighting in a war, and when the Truce came I was appointed by the government of the Republic to represent its army, and I wasn't about to be looked on as henchman for De Valera or anybody else.'

He made a statement to the officer. Then he told the officer to repeat his words: 'General Barry will be glad to meet you if you are meeting him as an officer of the Irish Republican army, and not as De Valera's representative, Mr Collins' representative or Mr X's representative.'

He waited for some time. Strickland's message stated that he did not re-cognise the IRA, nor would he do so. But, Barry was adamant, he would only deal with him in his capacity as an IRA officer, and if Strickland was unwilling to deal with him as an IRA officer, he would leave immediately. He was deter-mined he wouldn't be side-tracked on this issue. When asked if he would speak with Higginson, Barry adopted the same attitude and received a similar response. He returned to his office.

As other officers in the martial law area had similar problems with Higgin-son and enemy police, Barry convened a meeting of all liaison officers in Mal-low. He told them that they should deal with the enemy only as IRA officers. He 'instructed them' to cease all co-operation with the enemy until he heard from GHQ because the 'enemy police were continually breaking the truce'. Fully armed, the police paraded up and down in front of his office (HQ Cork) in Turner's Hotel and they seized two of his motor-cars. Barry sent his com-plaints on the IRA official notepaper, but the enemy 'refused to deal with any complaint registered on that notepaper'. Barry then sent his complaints to Comdt Duggan, chief liaison officer, Dublin Castle who referred him to Divi-sional Commissioner Dunlop, RIC. Dunlop asked that the breach of 'the truce terms by the police' should be referred to him.

'Not until two IRA cars are returned', Barry said.

Dunlop said one was a stolen car and he would 'not recommend its return; however if a permit was procured for the other, it would be given back'.

'I've driven cars without permits and will continue to do so'. Barry was em-phatic.

Dunlop said he would await instructions from Dublin. By mid August the matter remained unchanged.[3]

'I rang Mick [Collins] after. He was quite silent about it.' On a visit to Cork and to his home place, he met Barry. 'There's trouble over that!' he said, but told him not to worry. A few days later Barry got a message to report to Dublin to meet General Macready.

In Vaughan's Hotel he slept in the bed Collins used, had a bath and shave in the morning and got into his best suit. He was 'having a smoke' after break-fast when Collins came in with Ned Duggan, chief liaison officer, dressed 'in a black coat, waxed moustache, black hat, striped pants and spats.' Barry didn't take to his 'aping of the British'. He told Collins he wasn't the best man to meet Macready; however he relented after some persuasion. The two went off in a 'posh car'.

On being escorted into the room Macready stood up, shook hands with Duggan, whom he had met previously, and ignored Barry. Then he stated, 'Well Mr Duggan this black-guardism by you Irish chaps, it'll have to stop – assaulting troops …' As he continued with the 'diatribe' Duggan replied, 'Yes, General, it will be done.' The more he said 'yes general', the more Barry began to fume. Then Macready spoke of an incident in Tipperary where he said some

British soldiers had been beaten up. Barry was aware of the incident and knew that the soldiers were drunk and provocative. 'Our own fellows weren't always blameless … sometimes we had to take action we'd fire them out of the IRA, tell them to get out of the country, tell them they were a disgrace … But I'd say four out of five cases were started by the British … Anyway Duggan continued with, "Yes, General!" – Christ, I was starting to boil.'

After about 15 minutes, Macready turned, 'Now, Barry, you've heard what's to be done'.

Barry laughed and said, 'I'm listening, Macready! And I'm listening to Mr "Yes General, it will be done" Duggan. Well you know Macready and Duggan it won't be done! None of these things will take place and I'll see that they won't, even if we make bits of the Truce. From your behaviour here, the sooner we get to grips again and fight it out the better!'

He was furious that 'troops of the elected government' were being referred to 'as if we were the army of occupation'. As Barry watched Macready turn 'blue' he thought of a speech Lord French, who 'despised' Macready, made on leaving Ireland. He went to the door, turned and said, 'After all your crude and insulting behaviour, Macready, I can well understand what Lord French meant when he said at his farewell dinner, when the wine was flowing, that the one big regret he had was leaving behind his decent staff to a flat-footed bastard of a London policeman.'

Barry told the driver to take him back to Collins. He told Mick the story – 'every bit' including his repetition of what Lord French had said.

'You didn't!'

'I did.'

'Where's Duggan?'

'I don't know. I hope to Christ he's gone into the bloody Liffey! I left him behind with Macready.'[4]

Among the terms of the Truce were, 'No provocative display of forces, armed or unarmed ... To discountenance and prevent any action likely to cause disturbance of the peace which might necessitate military interference.' Therefore, on one occasion Tom was annoyed when he found a group of IRA men openly drilling. His honesty would not allow him deviate from the rules. The men maintained that it was merely a practice – judging by the reports in the newspapers, and the manner in which negotiations were progressing between London and Dublin delegates, they might have to take up arms again against the British. Never for a moment did they envisage a call to arms against their own people.

Tom Barry was impatient. He was torn. Progression towards normalisation and stability was too slow. He threatened to resign. Mulcahy did not take too kindly to this, but the ill discipline of the IRA and that of the enemy disturbed him more. 'We have either truce or war, and whoever by any want of discipline reopens the war prematurely, will have to be held accountable for it,' Tom wrote.[5]

Over in London one night on the way home after a fiery session with the British delegation, Michael Collins broke his stride, turned to Emmet Dalton and said, 'I wish I had Tom Barry here. We need a man like him to face Lloyd George!'[6] On Collins' next visit to Dublin he sent word to Barry to go to London. In Hans Place, Collins questioned him 'about strengths and about reasons why, if the British wanted' more garrisons that they couldn't get them. 'They had several garrisons here [in Ireland] already and they wanted more'. Collins and the negotiators wanted to have Barry's opinion on various military aspects, and 'when these things would come up in Hans Place at night' Barry would give his viewpoint.[7] 'Collins valued Barry's opinion. He had great respect for that man. He said one night in Hans Place that we wouldn't be here at all [negotiating] only for Tom Barry', Emmet Dalton recalled. 'He wished he had him at the negotiating table, and told him so, too. There's no doubt but Barry wouldn't have taken any of Lloyd George's bluff. Whether his forceful approach would have worked it's hard to know.'[8]

One day Tom set out for Downing Street where he was to have a word with Mick prior to a negotiating session. He wore a long trench coat. It was a very wild day and his coat blew up. Photographers hovered around. In taking a picture of Mick Collins they got a view of Barry from the back with 'his two skits' (guns) exposed. Next day a photo with the caption, 'Gunmen in Downing Street!' landed on Lloyd George's desk. A fuming Lloyd George accosted Collins, 'Is this true?'

Collins opened his coat. 'If you want to know I'm armed myself!'[9]

While in Britain, Barry took the opportunity of visiting his friend Tom Hales, who was still in Pentonville Jail. On 15 November, Jenny (Jennie) Wyse Power in a letter to Sighle Humphreys, wrote that 'Leslie tells us that in two months time her new companion [Tom Barry] expects the only work he is good at, to be going again'.[10] In a further letter on 21 November Jenny wrote, 'I am certain things are critical. House [Michael Collins] told Sara [Jenny Wyse Power] that he expected things going again any day now … Leslie has definitely gone and was very lonely in the finish. It is difficult to explain why her spouse's [Tom Barry] work has changed; but I will try find out all.' She believed he disliked being liaison officer, 'his power and capabilities lay one way only and you understand what that way was. This got tangled up all over Munster where he was the chief … a crux came when it became necessary to take orders from civil as well as military people'.[11]

Tom Barry, Liam Lynch, Liam Deasy and other officers in the Southern Division, who welcomed a Truce, only wanted a short one. A short Truce followed by a renewal of the armed conflict when talks were not proving meaningful, would, they felt, with hindsight, have forced the British government into a more meaningful Treaty.[12] In any case the Truce period was too long, because the Irish people were uncertain and the IRA had not really put their guns away. 'The Truce lasted for a year and it ended in Civil War. It was a heart-breaking period for those who had built up the IRA. When the first flush of over-hopeful expectation had passed, serious problems emerged, more difficult to deal with than any which the leaders had previously encountered. 'A nation's destiny had passed for the moment from the hands of the soldiers into the field of diplomacy and the army was in large part a helpless spectator of a course of events which contained all the elements of disaster.'[13]

On the night of 6 December Articles of Agreement for the Treaty signed by a delegation in London created the circumstances for those guns to be used later by friend against friend and brother against brother.

When the Treaty was signed the first reaction of the Irish people was one of rejoicing. Barry said it took him 24 hours to understand it. 'Once I absorbed it, I knew it wasn't freedom – so did the people who signed, let's be fair to them! There was the continuation of partition, there was the oath of allegiance, the governor general and there were the bases. I'm not opening an attack on those who signed ...'[14]

When Barry analysed it, he found that 'we would continue to be a subject race, subject to an oath of allegiance'. With 'the press of the country' and 'supporters of the establishment backing it' he decided something should be done, so he 'drafted half a page notice pointing out the disadvantages of the Treaty', gave it to the *Cork Examiner*, but they refused 'to take' it. 'I visited them a few hours later with a half a dozen armed men, and I said, "Publish this or you can pay for it!"' Though he accepted it wasn't right, he maintained that 'somebody had to let these facts be known.'[15]

When the Dáil reconvened on 3 January 1922, the Treaty debate continued; on 7 January the Treaty was accepted by 64 votes to 57. De Valera resigned as president of the Dáil and Arthur Griffith was elected in his place. De Valera left the house in protest followed by his supporters.

So now in Ireland there were two groups – pro-Treaty and anti-Treaty. News travelled quickly and immediately people began to take sides. Tom and his companions met and debated long and hard the terms of the Treaty and the reasons for De Valera's opposition to it. Tom felt that they had fought too hard to relinquish and accept less than a 32-county Republic or pay allegiance to the British crown. He agreed with Liam Lynch who explained, 'my attitude is now as always to fight on for the recognition of the Republic.'[16] Tom won the confidence of the majority of his men who decided to stick together. 'From the day on which Dáil Éireann took its decision for acceptance of the Treaty, the wedge of division was driven into the ranks of the IRA,' Tom wrote. 'Liam Lynch devoted all his energies to an effort directed towards keeping the army united in loyalty to its original allegiance. So far as his division was concerned he was largely successful, but he realised that unless the whole army could evolve a policy of agreement on fundamental principles where the political leaders had failed, civil war was inevitable.'[17]

The Treaty was already signed when Tom Hales was released from Pentonville Jail, and because of Michael Collins' close connection with the Hales family Collins expected Tom would back the Treaty. His brother, Seán, agreed with Collins' point of view and was later a member of the Free State Dáil. When Tom Hales took the anti-Treaty side, Collins said, 'More than any man, I would have valued his support'.[18]

Since the handing over of Dublin Castle to the Provisional Government in Dublin, local IRA units around the country had been taking over British evacuated positions. Ammunition, which the Republicans would use at a future date, was also collected.

Throughout the country there were pro-Treaty and anti-Treaty divisions of opinion. In places like Limerick there were open clashes of opinion. The Volunteer army was split, but very often the attitude of a group was determined by the decision of its commanding officer. There are those in West Cork who maintain that if Tom Barry had taken a different course, it is possible that history would have been different. Having known both De Valera and Michael Collins, he believed in the sincerity of both, so when he saw another war looming, he tried to keep the people of West Cork together.

He attended the Mansion House convention on 26 March 1922, which was prohibited by the Dáil, and was only attended by anti-Treaty men. They appointed an executive, which was to be the army's supreme authority. Barry was one of five men from the executive elected to the army council on 28 March.[19]

Afterwards Tom went to Cork, got some men together and went to Limerick where trouble was brewing. William Street Barracks, evacuated by the Auxiliaries, was occupied by anti-Treatyites who also occupied hotels and a wing of the mental hospital. Barry and members of the army council 'agreed to support the views of the Second Southern Division'. Barry wanted 'an issue to be made' of 'the occupation' of Limerick 'as a most strategic point'. Travelling with Rory O'Connor he met Ernie O'Malley, Tipperary officers, and Tom Hales with his West Cork Brigade. The collective anti-Treaty officers nominated Barry 'to command the different Divisional Units'. The situation was explosive as pro-Treatyites occupied the castle and a number of other evacuated British posts. Already the anti-Treatyites had begun to organise into a separate force, repudiating its nominal allegiance to the Dáil. At Mulcahy's suggestion, Liam Lynch and Oscar Traynor travelled from Dublin to Limerick to help avert a clash. Traynor found Michael Brennan, pro-Treatyite, prepared 'to fight and he was puffed out in his uniform like a peacock'. On the other side the mediators 'had an awful job with Barry'. Eventually they succeeded in an agreement as the men 'marched off singing and carrying their guns. We had to try and impress on Barry that there would be fighting at some time,' Traynor wrote.[20] The Limerick agreement was considered 'a climbdown by the Provisional Government'.[21]

When the convention met again on 9 April 1922, feeling was strong against the Treatyites. Therefore, on the night of 13 April, Rory O'Connor, Tom Barry, Liam Lynch, Ernie O'Malley, Seán Moylan, Seán MacBride and others set up headquarters in the Four Courts.

During this period Tom and Leslie were spending most of their time in Dublin, staying in Leslie's original home with the Price family. Leslie was involved with the White Cross – an American charitable relief organisation that helped alleviate hardships for families, and disbursed $5,000,000,000 dollars that the American Relief organisation had collected. They arranged the distribution of boatloads of clothes and food shipped from America. [22]

Back in West Cork the British military had evacuated all premises held during the war. When 'K Company' of the Auxiliaries vacated Dunmanway workhouse they left behind a diary and confidential documents, which were found by the IRA. The documentation was sensational – especially the list of informers' names. The meticulously kept record 'showed that the writer of this diary not only knew a great deal about the men of whom he wrote but that he was also expert in judging the details that mattered'. The information was so accurate that 'only a very well informed spy system could account for some of the entries in the book, and many of the facts laid down could only have been supplied by people who knew not only the countryside but everybody who lived in it as only natives can know these things', according to Flor Crowley who analysed the diary. 'It was the work of a man who had many useful "contacts" not merely in one part of the area but all over it, a statement that is not a happy one to write or to believe no matter how strong the evidence'.

Entries of men were in alphabetical order. Minute detail is given of the Kilmichael men, and all 'on the run'. As an example: 'Brien Pat, Girlough, Captain IRA has sometimes slept at home. Height 5'6" inclined to be stout, short, square not bad-looking. Very thick dark brown hair, round face, long lines around eyes, blue eyes, wears a cap, twice in raids, his house said to be burned by "unknown men" 6/2/1921'. The "unknown men" is in quotes and heavily underlined – not unknown, of course, to the Auxiliary recorder. A further entry has details of 'O'Brien' who 'always wears breeches, dark hair brushed back, wears brown coat and black hat. Goes to Mass at Ballincarriga, ten o'clock'.

The informer who knew the colour and details of O'Brien's eyes, hair, clothing and the Mass he attended knew him well. Thirty-two year old Michael O'Dwyer is described: '5'10" clean-shaven, bullet head, flat chin grey eyes, darkish fair hair, broad shoulders, tapering body, wears narrow trousers, cap, bandy legs, rather jerky in speech'. Flor Crowley asks: 'How many of us could describe even our best friends as accurately and in as much detail as that?'[1] Flor Crowley (a teenager in 1920, afterwards a teacher) says the details 'has had some shocks for me and must have shocks for anybody who lived through and can still remember the 1920–1921 period in West Cork'. The IRA gathered 'quite a lot of paper' in this haul, dispatched it to brigade headquarters and Seán Buckley IO and staff at Bandon; later some of it made its way to Seán MacCárthaigh, IO, Cork 'I'm afraid', Flor Crowley wrote, 'that the period under review had more than its quota of informers.'[2]

In the 6th Divisional headquarters Cork, covering the martial law area 'the various intelligence officers' compiled 'the Black Lists'. By 'gaining confidence of the rank and file' these intelligence men secured 'useful information and hints regarding the best method of obtaining it themselves from the more friendly disposed civilians. By degrees a certain number of civilians were selected for intelligence purposes' according to the Strickland Report. Their 'Black Lists contained details of the career of about 2,000 rebel leaders, all of whom were fit cases for deportation'. Tom Barry's name would have been in the Bandon Essex headquarters list. (I am not aware if any other regiment left records behind, as happened in Dunmanway.)[3]

'Local Centres were empowered to employ any local agents they could collect' and once the intelligence officer was 'posted' and 'Local Centres' established they 'worked in collaboration in their respective areas', intelligence police officer, Ormonde Winter noted.[4] Intelligence obtained by 'the crown forces improved steadily … more information was forthcoming and tactical methods were getting better.'[5]

General Strickland in a newspaper interview in January 1921 suggested setting-up a 'Vigilance Committee' to 'assist in intelligence work – the collection of information'; he believed that 'under martial law … there was a chance for well-disposed people to play' that part.[6]

The Dunmanway 'find' confirmed the existence of a British Loyalist vigilante type organisation called, 'The Loyalist Action Group', known locally as 'The Protestant Action Group'. But it had nothing to do with religious practice. This espionage underground organisation was affiliated to the 'County Anti-Sinn Féin Society' ('League')', 'Unionist Anti-Partition League' and to 'The Grand Orange Lodge of Ireland'. During the first week of January 1921, a 'Loyalist civil wing' initiated a rally near Enniskeane at Murragh, Protestant church 'on a dark night, during curfew'. When brothers James and Timothy Coffey, near Enniskeane were killed in their beds in February 1921, one of the men, recognised in the tussle when his mask fell, was a neighbour and 'member of the Loyalist Action Group'.[7] When men with blackened faces burned the Hales' Knocknacurra home 'one of the men was recognised'. Before this episode the Volunteers believed he was an informer, 'now they knew!' He and his family like many others in similar circumstances, 'got safe passage and protection' in England.[8]

Loyal Protestants 'whose houses had been burned and whose property had been destroyed by rebel forces' were compensated, according to a debate in the House of Commons in May 1922 when Sir Hamar Greenwood spoke of the Compensation Commission.[9]

On 26 April 1922, Michael O'Neill and his comrades called on Thomas Hornibrook, as they required a car, for what they called, 'IRA business'.[10] 'The major immobilised the car each evening by removing the magneto'; the men 'entered the house looking for the magneto.'[11] Thomas and Samuel Hornibrook and Capt. Herbert Woods were committed Loyalists. Woods was an ex-British officer with the DS, MC and MM decorations. Matilda Woods, Thomas Hornibrook's daughter and Herbert's wife, stated that her father 'was a magistrate for Cork County – my husband [Herbert Woods] and I were always staunch Loyalists'. These men were extremely anti-Republican and in regular contact and supplying information to the Bandon Essex. Demanding a car from them was seen, in IRA terms, as legitimate.[12]

Over a three-day period, from 26 to 28 April 1922, a spate of killing took place in West Cork. The outrages were 'sparked' when Capt. Woods shot IRA man Michael O'Neill in the hallway of Thomas Hornibrook's house at Ballygroman, near Ballincollig on Wednesday 26 April. Despite knocking several times, O'Neill and comrades failed to be admitted to Hornibrooks. They then entered by an unfastened window. After O'Neill was fatally injured his comrades took him 'down the avenue' and got a priest, who pronounced him dead. Next morning Charlie O'Donoghue 'motored' to Bandon and reported the incident. O'Donoghue confirmed that 'four military men' returned with him, and were met by Thomas Hornibrook, Sam Hornibrook and Capt. Herbert Woods, Hornibrook's son-in-law. Woods admitted to them that he had shot O'Neill.

At the inquest, the jury returned a verdict 'that Michael O'Neill was brutally murdered in the house of Thomas Hornibrook while in execution of his duty as an officer of the IRA … by a man named Woods in company with two Hornibrooks, Thomas and Samuel'. County Inspector O'Mahony stated that 'Woods was an ex military officer'.[13] Some days later (though it is not reported in the Irish daily newspapers) Capt. Woods, Thomas Hornibrook and his son Samuel went missing, unaccounted for, and in time presumed killed. Although an exaggerated account is given in the *Morning Post*, of 'about 100' IRA who 'surrounded the house and smashed in the door', definite records are not available to confirm their deaths. Their house was burned sometime after the incident.[14]

Over the next two days more men of the same religion and outlook – loyal Protestants in the Dunmanway-Ballineen-Murragh area, were shot dead. Three were from Dunmanway, seven including the 'principal victim' Revd Ralph Harbord (son of Revd Richard C. M. Harbord), Murragh Rectory, were from the Ballineen area. All of these named were associated with the Murragh 'Loyalist Action Group'. On that same night 27 April, a post office official, son of process server, sheriff's officer and caretaker of the masonic lodge, was shot dead.[15]

Because the men killed at this period were Protestants and as the majority of the IRA were Catholic, an insinuation has arisen in recent years, that the motive for killing the men was driven by sectarianism. Despite his admission in *The IRA and Its Enemies* that those killed or threatened 'had been marked out as enemies' some of whom '"went out drinking with Black and Tans",' Peter Hart concludes the motives were 'sectarian' rather than disloyalty to the Republican cause by informing on their fight for freedom activities.[16]

According to Peter Hart, when 'the men of the Cork IRA' used 'the term "informer" [it] meant simply "enemy" and enemies were defined by their religion, class, connections, respectability ... Traitors, by definition, had to be outsiders and monsters, the obverse of the Volunteers' embodiment of communal virtues'.[17]

Yet all of the surnames (in the Dunmanway/Ballineen/Enniskeane district) of those shot in the closing days of April 1922, were listed as 'helpful citizens' in the Dunmanway 'find'. But the first names of two of those fatally shot are not on the list – only last names are there. In one case a son was shot when his father was not at home. An elderly man was shot instead of his brother who had been 'wanted' by the IRA, and he had been 'one of the men' who 'fingered' IRA men resulting in their arrests, torture and the deaths. Those who saw the documents knew the names of the 'helpful citizens' – some of whom 'escaped'. (Only one Loyalist was listed in the diary, the others were in separate dossiers.)[18]

In Dunmanway three were shot dead on 27 April. Francis Fitzmaurice, solicitor and land agent had an inside track on the IRA and their activities during the 1919–921 period. He was a friend of James Buttimer, retired draper and of David Grey, chemist. 'It was not until afterwards, it was firmly established that they were informers, and it was learned that they had done untold damage to the IRA with all the information that they gave,' Eileen Lynch recalled. Eileen was a ten-year old girl at that period. She remembers when 'Dr Grey was killed'. Though not a doctor, this chemist was called 'Doctor' because 'he'd put a bandage on' if the children had a cut finger, skinned heel or such. 'As far as we could see he was very kind.' Children were warned and chastised against giving chat or information to 'Dr Grey'. But he prised information from some children, in their innocence. 'Our house was a safe house. Neither my father nor uncles, though they were drilled and could use a gun, were in the flying column; but there were always men on the run in our house.' Leslie Price, a constant caller, like Tom Barry and other brigade officers, would meet there, and were lucky to escape being caught during raids, and especially on the night that the trigger-happy Auxiliary shot their cat in the kitchen. Dr Grey would query the Lynch children whose older brother was a dispatch carrier. 'We learned to remain secretive. We knew he [Grey] was an informer.' The adults warned them against those others suspected of giving information to K Company Auxiliaries. Mr Fitzmaurice 'also known' lived and had his office in Carbery House. 'It is totally untrue to say that they were killed because they were Protestants. If that was so, why were so many Protestants not interfered with?' Eileen Lynch asks. 'There were the O'Meara's in the square, who had a butcher shop – lovely people, who were never interfered with. Never! There were Wilsons across from us, who had a shop. Atkins were marvellous; they even helped people on the run. There was Henry Smyth who was most helpful; the Coxes – that family gave land for the Catholic Church to be built on.' Eileen went on to list a number of Protestant families who, like their Catholic neighbours in West Cork, were not involved in the movement – some helped, including Sam Maguire's family, some didn't, but there was no intimidation of them.[19] Brendan O'Neill whose family hailed from Ballineen and were 'strong Republicans', could list many Protestant families who remained undisturbed and unharmed in that area, during the conflict.[20]

Dunmanway Rector, Rev. Canon Wilson, found it necessary to write to the *Irish Times* to correct the 'erroneous' report that 'the Church of Ireland minister and the Methodist minister' were attacked. Though their houses were 'situated close to the houses attacked, no insult or attack of any kind were made on us or on our families personally. Immediately after the first outrage I was called upon to attend the first victim', he wrote.[21]

Understandably, at the time 'a storm of protest against the killing of Protestant was raised, *inter alia*, by such Republican groups as the Belfast brigade of the IRA and the Republican controlled council of Cork.'[22]

Bishop Coholan, the Catholic bishop of Cork, sent a telegram to the parish priest in Enniskeane postponing the administration of confirmation due to 'the sorrow and mourning in the homes of Protestant neighbours'. Canon Coholan, Bandon, the bishop's brother, 'strongly condemned the awful happenings'. The canon said, 'We may have been disappointed by the action of some people in the past who did not stand up for the nation's interest, but it was not Irish to trample on a fallen foe'. He appealed to the people 'to uphold the national authority'. Whatever their actions were in the past, it was now past and should not be resurrected.[23]

In the Dáil, Griffith stated that Dáil Éireann 'does not know and cannot know, as a National government, any distinction of class or creed. In its name, I express the horror of the Irish nation at the Dunmanway murders.' Seán T. O'Kelly wished to associate 'the anti-Treaty side' with these sentiments of Griffith'.[24]

The General Synod Members of the Church of Ireland issued 'a call of goodwill on men of all religious persuasions to unite …'[25] A convention of Irish Protestant Churches in Dublin placed 'on record' that apart from this incident 'hostility to Protestants by reason of their religion has been almost, if not wholly, unknown in the twenty-six counties in which Protestants are in the minority.' A similar 'statement emanated from a convention of Protestants Churches in Schull, in the heart of West Cork Brigade area, on 1 May 1922.' Arising out of Peter Hart's suggestion of an IRA vendetta against Protestants, Criostóir de Baróid notes that 'no responsible political commentator or newspaper of the time ever made the allegation that the IRA military campaign was sectarian.'[26]

The suggestion of non-action at this period by the Bandon/Dunmanway IRA cannot be substantiated.[27] Officers, including Tom Barry, Liam Deasy and Dick Barrett, were in Dublin at this time of Provisional Government administration, when efforts were being made to consolidate the army and ward off a

Civil War in an atmosphere of country-wide disturbances. Some Protestants left the area: those who had been involved in informing felt in imminent danger. Barry returned briefly to West Cork and with Tom Hales, Flor Begley, Seán Buckley and other local IRA officers set up 'guards' in districts throughout the brigade area. He wanted to avoid recrimination or 'grudges' held. 'One very important fact', Jim Kearney wrote, 'the Third Brigade had a guard on the [loyalist] Protestant houses at that time to protect them. I was one of the guards so I should know.' Denis Lordan, Charlie O'Keeffe and a substantial number of men were appointed 'guards' in round-the-clock protection in case other citizens, some known to have informed during 'the troubles', would become victims.[28] 'Barry didn't want revenge. "We will all have to live as neighbours. We are trying to make peace now and settle our differences".' This was a few months prior to the outbreak of Civil War.[29] Tom Barry heard that because of a neighbouring feud, some men were going 'to set upon' Billy Good, Calatrim, Bandon, a Protestant and First World War British army officer. Tom with a few officers hid in the lane-way. Billy was housing the dog for the night and became fearful when he heard the voice "'… Get out of here! This is your last warning! You'll get no more!'" Tom Barry 'intercepted' the men, told them to get out of the locality and 'not to come back' as 'the Good family were decent people'; they had not done any harm.[30]

Months earlier, during 'Truce times', Barry had 'commuted to exile for life' the sentence on 'the informer' who was 'found guilty' of selling both the Crossbarry and Upton ambushes, causing the death of his close friend Charlie Hurley and the arrest of several IRA. 'Because of this man's betrayal of many vital facts', Flor Begley wrote, 'the column could have been wiped out.'[31]

In Bantry, brigade officer, Ted O'Sullivan and close friend of Tom Barry publicly stated that 'ample provision was made and steps taken to see that the wave of human destruction didn't enter' that area. 'Protestants and Catholics will, as they hitherto have, dwell together here in peace, harmony and good relations.'[32]

Comdt Con Connolly and Stephen O'Neill (section commander at Kilmichael and no relation to Michael O'Neill who was shot) condemned 'the recent shootings'. At a Bandon district council meeting Seán Buckley, chairman (former Third Cork Brigade intelligence officer, and Tom Barry's friend and comrade), said he wished 'to tender to the relatives of the victims our sincere sympathy'. Timothy Murphy supporting the motion, said that many Protestants 'during the recent troubles … had sheltered our brave men and had sympathy with us in our trouble … these cruel shootings are contrary to every conception of justice and liberty, contrary to every sentiment of religious and moral obligation to one another. In Easter week the men that proclaimed the Republic did so with a fervent prayer that no one would dishonour it by cowardice or inhumanity.' Seán Buckley in concluding the debate drew attention to some of 'the greatest patriots' of the past who were of Protestant faith. He could and would personally 'bear testimony' to 'the willingness' of his 'Protestant neighbours who sheltered the men who were hunted by the British forces.' Many of the men who were 'most wanted by the enemy were sheltered', he said, 'and supported' by them. He had it 'from the lips of leading Protestants in this district that they were willing to live and give allegiance to the government of the Republic.'[33]

On 28 April Comdt Tom Hales, on behalf of the Third Brigade issued a 'Definite Military Order to all Battalion Commandants' in his brigade that any 'soldier in the area was neither to interfere with or insult any person … Even capital punishment will be meted out' to those 'not upholding the rigid discipline of a military force.' In his statement he promised 'to give all citizens in this area, every protection within' his 'power'. Comdt Con Connolly, Skibbereen, in a *Public Notice* stated that the IRA would do all in their 'power to protect the lives and property of all citizens irrespective of creed' and would 'faithfully observe the amnesty proclaimed by Mr M. Collins.'[34] Sinn Féin-led Cork county council condemned the killing and asked the 'the authorities charged with peace and order to afford protection to all classes'. This 'resolution' was forwarded to 'the Protestant bishop of Cork.'[35] Tom Barry, Liam Deasy, Tom Hales and Seán Buckley travelled to Skibbereen and helped Con Connolly and the Skibbereen IRA with 'house-guard' protection rota administration, to back up the Bandon-Clonakilty-Dunmanway-Ballineen protection teams.[36]

Tom Kelleher and another IRA comrade caught up with thieves, unconnected with the IRA, who, taking advantage of the climate at the time, had stolen cattle from Mr Wilson, a Protestant farmer near Bandon and were en route with them to Kinsale fair. Kelleher ordered the men to return the animals. The order was 'promptly' obeyed. Tom Barry's first cousin, Paddy O'Brien, 'appointed permanent guards to protect John Winters, a Protestant landlord' who was in dispute with local farmers. Rather than going to the Establishment courts, Winters went to the Sinn Féin courts at the time to seek 'redress', and got it.[37]

During the War of Independence Macready stated that he had covered the country with spies from end to end.'[38] Florrie O'Donoghue found: 'There were no hostile people, as far as we knew except Loyalists all of whom we knew.'[39] Much useful information was obtained for the three Cork brigades from Josephine Marchmount, a confidential secretary to Captain Webb, chief officer to Major Strickland, Cork Military Barracks.[40]

In a captured British document Strickland wrote: 'I want … the troops and police' to seek out people for intelligence purposes, to get 'in touch with the people in a friendly way, so as to enlist the waverers on our side … Remember we have two moral objectives, i.e., to hearten the morale of the Loyalist and waverer and to dishearten the morale of the gunmen.' Money 'is' available 'to pay for intelligence'. Also 'if protection and repatriation to England are required by individuals who have given VALUABLE information' this should be done. The document states 'the following is a list of the flying columns of the IRA and the localities in which they are thought to be harbouring ...' ('Valuable' is written in bold caps.)[41] It is difficult to agree with Peter Hart's suggestion that the IRA's targeting of spies and informers during the war 'had little or nothing to do with the victims' actual behaviour' but their religion, and that as the 'war continued to escalate right up to the July 1921 truce ... anti-Protestant violence rose along with it'.[42] Hart states that the 'IRA had begun to seize Protestants to use as hostages.' As has been demonstrated, these individuals such as Lord Bandon were kidnapped (later released) under Tom Barry's direction, because of their status and power in society and as a bargaining ploy and had nothing to do with their religion. (It is unlikely that Tom Barry or other IRA members thought of religion.) Hart has suggested that, 'The revolution made Protestants "fair game" to any of their neighbours, whether angry or covetous.' (In the course of my extensive interviews over the years with ex-IRA participants of the period I did not hear of 'ethnic cleansing' and 'ethnic conflict'.[43] There is no evidence that this scenario entered the equation for Tom Barry and his comrades in the Third West Cork Brigade.)

Throughout the period of conflict up to the Truce, Seán Buckley IO successfully organised Republican courts and Republican police in West Cork so that spies or informers were not killed without a court-martial or Republican court appearance. These Sinn Féin or Republican courts also investigated 'robberies, assaults, recovered stolen property and administered swift punishment of wrong doers.'

Tom Barry and officers in West Cork, who allowed proceedings to be dealt with within this system, drew a distinction between Protestantism and Loyalism, when it became known to them that persons who were loyal (Loyalist) to the British monarch betrayed fellow countrymen, and formed a 'League'. When the IRA's intelligence department in Cork county found proof of informants at work, they dealt with the situation within the confines of the war as set out by GHQ. Religion was not a distinguishing factor. 'Rigorous and stern action was for us a necessary duty in dealing with spies and informers', Liam Deasy recorded. 'This unpleasant duty was necessary when seen against the light of many noble efforts made down the ages to secure our freedom' which 'was defeated by English gold and Irish greed'.[44]

Tom Barry in *Guerilla Days* wrote that 'British Imperialists' used a 'technique of "Divide and Conquer". They have consistently urged class against class, district against district, creed against creed ... In 1920 and 1921 they fanned the flame of religious intolerance between Catholics and Protestants. Whenever one of their agents not of the faith of the majority was shot, they announced his death as Mr X, a Protestant. But, although the West Cork Brigade [during the war, in 1921] shot five Catholics who were British agents in quick succession, never once did the term Catholic appear after those men's names in the British announcements of their deaths.' This was, he stated, their propaganda method of making (succeeding in cases) 'the Protestants of Ireland' believe they would be 'victimised' under 'a Republican government of Ireland'. Barry tells a story of 'an informer' who spoke with warped logic of the Protestant religion being under threat and felt duty bound to betray the IRA. Barry didn't bother correcting him as he was 'going to die' anyway.[45] Barry, speaking of informers and spies, told Nollaig Ó Gadhra that they 'executed 15. Incidentally, for those who are bigots – 9 Catholics and 6 Protestants! British propaganda announced him [in each case] as a Protestant landowner. But if it was a Catholic who was executed for spying – "blood money", he was only mentioned by name, never that he was a Catholic.'[46]

'They were all as guilty as hell. The Loyalists informers weren't doing it for money ... and were far more dangerous' than the spy. 'We had our information'.[47]

Peter Hart also states that 'the conspiracy theories and the terminology of hatred' and 'sectarianism was embedded in the Irish revolution, north and south.'[48] However, Barry told Donncha Ó Dulaing in the early 1970s: 'We never killed a man or interfered with a man because of his religion, we didn't give three straws, they were human beings to us and they were treated as that and there was never a breath of sectarianism, but we had to face facts ... We lost men who were sold or given away – sleeping in barns and outhouses ... The informer was far more dangerous because he had intelligence and was used by the British who were clever at propaganda publicity. They used the divide and conquer principle ... in the newspapers ... They were no more shot because they were Protestant or Jew or Atheists or anything else. They were shot because we had in their own confessions they were doing the job, and they had caused loss of Irish Republican army men's lives.'[49]

When Tom Barry initially wrote *Guerilla Days*, he named the spies and informers who were shot during the war, but because the *Irish Press* in the serialisation of the book before publication felt this would create problems for relatives, the editor asked him to omit names and to tone down the language. Finally he agreed for the sake of the families. He said, 'Two resided in (naming the district)' and 'two more resided in' – and so on. 'This does not add to the identification of any particular spy, but if the IP so desires this sentence could read (four came from the First Battalion, two from Fourth Battalion, etc.) ... I take it there is no objection to the general references', he wrote.[50]

To argue in the case of Protestant informers who were shot, that it was not the fact of their being informers that determined their fate, or to go further and claim that, 'The gunmen, it may be inferred, did not seek merely to punish Protestants but to drive them out altogether', is difficult to agree with, in the light of the evidence now available.[51]

Despite identifying a British Loyalist connection in the dramatic events of April 1922, 'the fact of the victim's religion is inescapable', Hart wrote. 'These men were shot because they were Protestants. No Catholic Free Staters, landlords, or "spies" were shot or even shot at. The sectarian antagonism which drove this massacre was interwoven with political hysteria and local vendettas, but it was sectarian none the less. "Our fellas took it out on the Protestants".[52]

However, Brian Murphy points out that Peter Hart took that latter quotation out of context as it 'refers to a completely different incident in the Civil War'. Denis Lordan of Barry's flying column told Dorothy Stopford, a Protestant, that 'the boys' went to a Protestant house to seize a motor car, were fired on, and one was killed. Then '"our fellas took it out on the Protestants". The descriptive word "Protestant" is used, but both the original motive for the raid (the stealing of a car), and the subsequent reprisal, on account of the killing of a comrade, was not occasioned by sectarian motive. Indeed, it was not even recorded if anyone was killed as part of the reprisal.'[53]

Dr Murphy asserts that, 'to link Lordan's comments with the Dunmanway massacres [of April 1922] is misleading, a misrepresentation which is compounded by calling the chapter [in his book] "Taking it out on the Protestants". Moreover, in adopting this sectarian interpretation of events, Hart rejects the opinion of one of his sources, an IRA veteran, who maintained that the massacre was the product of anarchy, and that "we had nothing against" the Protestants.'[54]

Peter Hart speculates on a 'plausible explanation' of 'at least two and possibly as many as five, separate groups involved' in the killings, 'probably including members of ... Volunteers.' He further writes that, 'All of the men identified as participants were committed republicans – veterans of the Tan War who went on to fight in the Civil War ... These men probably acted on their own initiative – but with the connivance or acquiescence of local units. This is demonstrated by the non-intervention of the I.R.A. garrisons in Dunmanway and elsewhere.'[55] The facts do not bear out local units 'acquiescence' nor 'the non-intervention' theory as already discussed, nor does the IRA's veteran's comment that he quotes, back up the theory, nor is it known who committed the killings.

'These were revenge killings on many levels' Hart records, and list reasons of *probabilities* of 'the desire for vengeance', because the 'minority population of West Cork were seen not only as past enemies and current undesirables but also as a future fifth column in the struggle which many I.R.A. men saw coming'.[56] In a sweeping statement he writes that the 'atmosphere of fear and polarization provided the communal context for the massacre. One could not have taken place without the other. Protestants ... were seen as outsiders and enemies, not just by the I.R.A. but by a large segment of the Catholic population as well.'[57]

Furthermore he noted that: 'Within this rhetoric of ethnic intolerance can be detected the quasi-millenarian idea of a final reckoning of the ancient conflict between settlers and natives. To some republicans, revolution meant righting old wrongs, no matter how old, and establishing the republic entailed the reversal of the old order.'[58] However, the action Tom Barry and other officers took to quell the disturbances together with the statements of Tom Hales, Seán

Buckley, Con Connolly, Ted O'Sullivan (all Third Cork Brigade officers) demonstrate that these suggestions misrepresent the position. To consign to the pages of history an account of magnified vendetta by the IRA and by some Irish citizens as blanket intolerance against fellow citizens, in early 1922 and during the previous war does not appear to be justified, from the evidence now available. (Peter Hart has used interviews with people whom he has acknowledged in his sources with initials (e.g., CR, RG, GD, etc.). It is unknown whether these initials are exact or fictitious. Some are certainly fictitious as he has written: 'Protestant men and women begin with a "B"' (e.g., BB, BF, BG, BO, etc.). In any case all are anonymous. (Tom Barry was to hammer home vigilance regarding the recording of history, and insisted, as will be later demonstrated, that historiography should be above reproach.)[59]

Dan Cahalane, IRA veteran, of Barry's flying column said that 'religious beliefs had nothing to do with Republican beliefs. Some Protestants were most helpful' during the struggle. 'Others who wanted to hold on to Imperialism were only loyal to that master'. The killing 'of those men at that particular time was unhelpful to our [Republican] cause'. Dan pointed to where one shooting took place in April 1922. He had purchased the house later and had no idea who was responsible for 'the awful' killing, though he admitted to knowing 'the names' of informers from the Dunmanway 'haul'. He was 'shocked'.[60]

Jack Fitzgerald recalled for Ernie O'Malley that in the 'Kilbrittain district Protestants were not shot as spies, [because] they knew that the men were fighting for a principle, they said that the others – other districts around Ballineen and areas were different.' Jack, who was in Donegal during the Civil War, found 'the best crowd were the Presbyterians for they knew that we were fighting for a principle.'[61] This is very different from the scenario that Peter Hart paints: 'All the nightmare images of ethnic conflict in the twentieth century are here', and uses a sweeping statement of, 'the transformation of life-long neighbours into enemies, the conspiracy theories and the terminology of hatred' where 'sectarianism was embedded in the Irish revolution, north and south. Any accounting of its violence and consequences must encompass the dreary steeples of Bandon ...'[62]

But beneath the 'steeples of Bandon' many men 'on the run' were harboured by people with limited resources. Some of these sympathetic citizens 'ran up' sizeable bills with Protestant merchants like Jeffers', Goods' and other shops in Bandon and never a word leaked out. Indeed the merchants did not put undue pressure on the individuals for payment. Many other members of the Protestant community in the area risked everything, including alienation from fellow religious, because 'they had this desire' to have 'our own government', and be 'an independent country'. 'Being Protestant' did 'not necessarily' mean 'being loyal to the crown'.[63] Flor Begley through his IRA intelligence work, had the names of many spies and informers. He quotes a man who worked for 'a Protestant farmer' being surrounded one day. Percival and his

men were doing the rounds and informed the man that 'he knew his movements' and the rifles he had hidden in the shed. 'I have my own intelligence
service here and I know everything'. He was being transported in a tender
with two other prisoners, but managed to escape. 'Right enough', Flor Begley
wrote, 'the information was deadly accurate.'[64]

In questioning Peter Hart's interpretation that there was an IRA campaign
of hostility towards Protestants 'because of their religion', Brian Murphy asserts that 'Erskine Childers, a Protestant, was in no doubt that there was no element of sectarianism in the Nationalist struggle for independence'. Childers
found that 'at no time' had civilians – 'Protestant Unionists living scattered and
isolated in the south and west, been victimised by the Republicans on account
of their religion or religious opinion or religion' (sic).[65]

Because Peter Hart is selective both in his representation of facts and only
partially quotes from the chosen paragraph in the official British *Record of the
Rebellion in Ireland*, Jack Lane affirms that 'Hart engages in trickery to try to prove
his theory that the Bandon Protestants were killed because they were Protestants' and concludes, 'he fails'. Brian Murphy asserts that Peter Hart 'heightens
the suspicion' that Protestants 'were killed for religious motives', because Hart
wrote: 'The truth was that, as British intelligence officers recognised, "in the
south the Protestants and those who supported the government rarely gave
much information because, except by chance, they had not got it to give".' However, Peter Hart omitted (as Brian Murphy notes) the paragraph's conclusion:

> An exception to this rule was in the Bandon area where there were many Protes-
> tant farmers who gave information. Although the intelligence officer of this area
> was exceptionally experienced and although the troops were most active it proved
> almost impossible to protect these brave men, many of whom were murdered
> while almost all the remainder suffered grave material loss.[66]

Peter Hart compounds this further in a footnote that he gives in editing *British
Intelligence in Ireland, 1920–21*. Despite the recording in Sir Jeudwine Papers confirming that there was 'an exception' to the 'rule' in the giving of information
by 'Protestant farmers' in 'the Bandon area', Peter Hart writes in a footnote: 'Some
condemned West Cork Protestants did give, or try to give, information but
there is no evidence that they acted *en masse* despite this statement.' Though
dismissing this 'evidence' he has in his 'introduction' written: 'Rarely has the
secret life of the British state been so exposed to inquiry as is now possible with
these confidential histories.'[67]

Jack Lane questions the 'moral difference between giving and trying to
give information in the circumstance of the time'. Is there a 'distinction enough
to dismiss one and not the other as a deliberate act of assisting the government's war effort to defeat the IRA?' The report clearly states, that 'in the Bandon area ... many Protestant farmers evidence' was supplied. To state that they
didn't give it 'en masse' (all together) in a war situation pushes the limits of
credulity.[68]

This evidence indicates that the IRA killing of spies and informers and the part played by Tom Barry was not sectarian, but based on their intelligence of the 'many ... who gave information', as noted by Montgomery, who 'often found that the best intelligence was received by us in Cork'. Smith's diary notes: '"One T" is shrieking for help, but we can't guard *everyone*' ('T' = Tout?).[69] Sir Jeudwine records that in Cork, 'There were numerous informers, however, and most of them were procured by and gave their information to military intelligence.'[70]

Brian Murphy in his analysis, names Protestants (including West Cork resident doctor Dorothy Stopford, Denis Lordan's friend) who were prominently involved in the Republican movement, and asks, 'Could these Protestants have acted in such a manner, if their fellow religionists were the calculated targets of sectarian attacks?' Dr Murphy concludes, 'Hart's findings on this important issue of sectarianism are open to question'.[71]

In 1949 after the publication of his book, Barry received letters some mentioning his 'well-handled' account of Protestants. One correspondent, Risteárd Ó Glaisne from Bandon referred to the April 1922 killing. As an 'Irish Protestant' he used 'the Irish form' of his name as 'an affirmation' of his 'belief' in Ireland 'and as a vote of confidence in the attempt to cultivate that sadly withered tree assiduously'. He was 'delighted' that Barry 'should go to the trouble of correcting ... the stupid misunderstandings of a small group'. Ó Glaisne was only 'acquainted with the record of the Irish "over-ground",' so he appreciated getting 'the whole truth' because he was confident he said that Barry's 'would be a version' which he 'could quote with some confidence'. Ó Glaisne gave Barry the details he obtained from 'the narrow' perspective:

> I always loathe having bitter prejudices paraded as mature judgements, and that is what one has almost always to endure when Irish Protestants of a now-elderly generation speak of 1918-21 – what continually amazes me, as a matter of fact, is that men with these prejudices seared across an area of their minds can now live happily in the twenty-six county state thinking and acting constructively, as they do; I think the explanation is that, having been treated decently for years as they have been, they have resigned themselves to the *status quo*, and only recall with bitterness now the memories they have of those years as one occasionally draws down an old dust-covered box from an attic.

John Chinnery had been 'wanted' by the IRA, and was shot while harnessing a horse in April 1922. Risteárd Ó Glaisne met Chinnery's brother some time afterwards and 'was surprised and delighted by his outlook. As a Protestant he is, I would say, typical of the best of his generation, a man of deep, direct piety. But he was also very happily progressive. He evinced the keenest interest in Irish and spoke in conversation of "our own governments" – that phrase can always be regarded as strikingly significant from an Irish Protestant ... We must eradicate traditional prejudices ... because I think Protestantism as a spiritual force will have to be more vigorous if ever in the history of Protestantism it is to justify itself in Ireland.' Writing on one of the cases, Ó Glaisne understood that the IRA had called to Chinnery's house 'on a number of occasions' and failed to get him. He 'was suspected of giving the military police information on the whereabouts of the IRA'. He was caught 'open-handed' one day, when 'he dropped a letter' as he 'was passing some police', Ó Glaisne wrote.[72]

Ó Glaisne pulled no punches as he told of those who were shot, and he would not want any 'prejudices' continued. 'Don't forget,' he wrote 'that when these ordinarily quiet, humorous, positive philosophic people think about "The Troubles", "The Bad Times", all their ordinary attitudes forsake them … A brushful of incidents and ignorant rumours smeared this part of their minds at that time with a tar which is undefaceable. Quite undefaceable! I have often thought to right wrong impressions, have after much mutual invitation succeeded in reducing bigots to silence, only to find the same old prejudices come out again six months later.' When speaking to the 'older Irish Protestants' regarding the past he says he finds 'a barren chagrin' but 'younger Irish Protestants have minds which cannot receive old bitternesses'.[73]

Risteárd Ó Glaisne was writing for publication, material in relation to Protestants: 'It gives me opportunities of telling them all sorts of home truths quite frankly and blankly which might be considered disloyal if I were speaking to a wider audience,' he wrote. He asked Tom's advice on a publisher: 'I am not only stimulating Irish Protestants to be Irish but also to be Protestant'.[74]

In 1963, when Desmond Fennell wrote an article, *The Failure of the Irish Revolution and its Success* he stated that 'the revolution' was 'an attempt on the part of the Irish Catholic people to gain material and spiritual conditions of life more favourable to their fulfilment as human beings.' Barry took issue with these sentiments after Fr. Henry asked him to write a 'comment' on the essay for the *Capuchin Annual*. Barry wrote the article, but decided 'after consideration' that he would prefer not to have it published 'because of the danger of misinterpretation by Catholic readers, especially the young.'

Desmond Fennell's 'contention that the fight for Freedom was a Catholic one is something I could not agree with, and I could not deal with honestly', Barry wrote in a letter to the editor, Fr Henry, 'unless I dealt with' other points among them – 'Leadership down through the ages since the Penal Days, i.e., 1798, 1867, even land fights [which] were essentially by Protestants.' Furthermore, 'in all fairness to the British empire, in 1916 there were no disabilities for Catholics in Ireland, instead they were perfectly free to practice their faith.' He mentioned Bishop Coholan's excommunication order (1920) against the IRA – 'we had to look at Volunteers dying without the benefit of Confession,' which they held dear. In his 'Comment' he wrote, 'I wish I could write truthfully … that the IRA were fighting for spiritual conditions and for "a pure land" … There could be men within the movement imbued with those high motives but I never met one of them.' The main motive was 'to drive the British occupation forces from the land; to establish a Republic and to undo the conquest … the armed struggle was only one phase of the revolution.' He told Fr Henry, 'I would never feel happy about dealing in public with such a delicate issue' as any religious aspect to 'the revolution'.[75]

Tom Barry enunciated 'a vast difference between British Loyalism and Protestantism' where the first is 'politically motivated' and in the second the '1916 Proclamation guarantees religious and civil liberties to all citizens'. Religious 'bigotry was not confined to the Protestants for the ignorant and petty-minded Catholics had their fair share of this ancient curse'.[76]

Monica Sullivan 'an Irish Republican Protestant' set forth for Barry 'the reason why the Irish are Catholics is the black record of the Protestant settlers. If they had not given a bad reputation to the religion they professed it is probable that the Irish would have been interested in the Reformation and accepted it, as did the Gaels of Scotland, descendants of the Ancient Irish.'[77]

The strongest evidence that the war was not sectarian comes from Lionel Curtis, political adviser to Lloyd George and influential Imperial activist and writer with an interest in Irish Affairs. He wrote in early 1921 that when 'a brave prelate,' spoke out in Cork his 'flock have turned their back on him' and evoked the rejoinder: 'We take our religion, not our politics, from Rome'. Therefore, 'to conceive the struggle as religious in character is in any case misleading', he wrote. 'Protestants in the south do not complain of persecution on sectarian grounds. If Protestant farmers are murdered, it is not by reason of their religion, but rather because they are under suspicion as Loyalist. The distinction is fine, but a real one.'[78]

Barry related that the 'majority of West Cork Protestants lived at peace throughout the whole struggle and were not interfered with by the IRA'. All the IRA wanted was that they 'would not stand with our enemy' and not succumb to British propaganda. The 'majority' he said, 'accepted this position, and let it be said that we found them men of honour whose word was their bond.'[79]

In enunciating his conviction on the war and its accompanying horror, Barry did not believe 'that war is a glorious thing. I think it is bestial, and the First World War taught me that. There's nothing romantic about war. The only war that I can justify to myself is a war of liberation.' Those engaged in the fight dislike it because 'they know the hardships and they know the suffering, not alone of the soldiers but of their kith and kin. It often struck my mind when we killed Britishers that there were women and children maybe left without a husband, without a father. I want to make that very, very clear.'[80]

Meanwhile in Dublin, throughout April and May 1922, negotiations (some secretly) between the Beggar's Bush army section (pro-Treaty) and the Four Courts executive (anti-Treaty) continued in the hope of healing the army split. Ultimately, it became apparent that no army settlement could be arrived at without a corresponding political settlement and vice versa. The political conferences broke down twice – the last time irrevocably. Then came the 'De Valera- Collins pact.' This 'pact' hammered out on 18 and 19 May 1922, as a compromise to prevent civil war, provided for a general election to form a coalition government in which pro-and anti-Treaty elements had representation proportionate to their strength in the Dáil.[1]

In the Four Courts, Tom Barry, Rory O'Connor, Ernie O'Malley, Dick Barrett and other IRA men discussed further strategy. Some felt that attacking the British in the north should be the next step towards gaining a full Republic. They also felt that this might unite the anti-Treaty and pro-Treaty groups once more. Meanwhile they believed it was imperative to secure more arms. Under the command of the Provisional Government army, a new police force was being trained in a camp in Kildare. The Four Courts executive discovered that two lorries containing men, arms and ammunition would be travelling towards Dublin on a certain night. These should be waylaid.

A Crossley tender, an armoured car and other vehicles commandeered by the Four Courts men set out at intervals for Kildare, then stopped outside the Curragh so that all the cars would travel in convoy. Tom Barry, Rory O'Connor and Ernie O'Malley halted a lorry, explaining that they wanted to have another go at the British. Many of the men on the lorry agreed and handed over their arms without question. Most of the convoy, which was now led by Tom Barry and Rory O'Connor, proceeded towards the police camp in Kildare while Ernie O'Malley with a few men remained to cut the telegraph wires.

The lights of the cars were seen in the darkness. Barry and O'Connor went ahead and succeeded in getting all the rifles and ammunition. 'They even gave us tenders to remove the stuff. Some of them are coming back to the [Four] Courts,' said Rory O'Connor.[2]

With Barry and O'Connor in command the convoy started back for Dublin hoping not to be halted. 'I sat in a tender on a pile of rifles. The men whistled and sang. We were in good spirits and reached the Four Courts before dawn with our treasure trove,' Ernie O'Malley recalled.[3]

Tom Barry was in the thick of it now, and with a quantity of arms, ammunition and men who had fought the guerrilla war during the previous years he was ready to take on the cause of the Republic.

Liam Lynch, chief-of-staff, decided with the executive to call another convention in the Mansion House on 18 June 1922. Tom Barry, Liam Deasy, Tom

Hales, Rory O'Connor and delegates from other parts of the country were present. On 12 June the minister for defence had written to the army executive setting out proposals for re-unification. These proposals were not acceptable to all the members of the executive and indeed did not receive enthusiastic support. Seán O'Hegarty, Tom Hales and Florrie O'Donoghue resigned on an issue concerning a general election and were replaced on the executive by Tom Barry, Tom Derrig and Pax Whelan.[4]

There were many who wanted action and not appeasement: they stated that Griffith and Collins appeared to be trimming the Republic by their action of continuing contact with Britain. The formation of a new Dáil, a new army and a new police force had all been established by the Treatyites and the strong voices of the meeting were not in favour of these developments. Lynch was criticised for failing to take stronger action, and in the absence of his coming to a definite decision, 'Tom Barry moved a resolution that the IRA at once attack the British and renew the war.'[5] Only posts in Dublin and the six counties were then still occupied by foreign troops. The resolution put forward proposed to declare war on the British, giving 72 hours notice prior to hostilities. Some confusion arose as to when the 72 hours should become operative.

Lynch, disagreeing with Barry's point of view and feeling that such action would be irresponsible, urged moderation. Both Barry and Lynch were strong-minded Republicans and spent some time arguing tactics instead of principles. Barry and his supporters believed that direct action would bring the pro-Treaty soldiers in Beggar's Bush and throughout the country back into a united front when they could take on Britain – the common enemy – in the north. 'Barry and Seán O'Hegarty had the same sentiments. Don't talk, but act.'[6]

'To my mind, it was very foolish of Barry to have put forward such a re-solution at the convention. It was neither the time nor the place for it', according to Seán MacBride. 'In fact it meant putting the onus of declaring war on Great Britain on a body of men who had been selected by various units of the army to select an executive which was to appoint a chief-of-staff and to direct the policy of the army until a Republican government was formed. I understand that Barry proposed that motion to counter-balance Liam Lynch's proposals and to avoid the repetition of such incidents. As a policy the substance of his motion was quite right, but by putting it forward at a convention without consulting anybody, as he did, was putting those who supported that policy in a very awkward position'.[7] Florence O'Donoghue 'committed to record that Cathal Brugha approved this resolution.'[8]

Tom Barry's motion was passed by a couple of votes. 'This was challenged on the grounds that there was a brigade present which wasn't represented at the last convention; after a long discussion the objection was upheld and a fresh vote was taken, and the motion was lost.'[9] After some heated discussion on his compromise proposals Liam Lynch said he would no longer go on as chief-of-staff. Twelve members of the executive who had voted with Tom Barry chose Joseph McKelvey as their new chief-of-staff.

'Though Rory O'Connor and Liam Mellows saw Barry's mistake in bringing forward this motion as a proposal to the convention, without any previous discussion, they understood that this was the only policy that could be consistently followed by the anti-Treatyites. Barry and Rory O'Connor would not accept the continued delay; they stood up, left the room followed by their supporters and announced they were returning to the Four Courts. It fell on Seán MacBride to announce to the convention that a further convention would be held in the Four Courts the next morning. 'There was an absolute silence and I could hear my steps like shots from the top of the room to the door. A few more delegates came out'. The split was deepening.[10]

The convention meeting continued. Cathal Brugha, Seán Lehane, Liam Mellows, Florrie O'Donoghue and others, though they had voted in favour of 'the War declaration', remained in the room. 'The temper of the convention, and of the majority wishes of the executive, was such that all hope of army unification was dead.' Afterwards Lynch moved his headquarters to the Clarence Hotel. Ernie O'Malley waited until the end of the meeting. When he returned to the men in the Four Courts he had difficulty in gaining entrance, as the guard had been strengthened.[11]

What was started by De Valera and his supporters by voting against the Treaty and walking out might have been resolved by peaceful means, but there were those who believed that the only method of obtaining freedom for all Ireland against Britain was through physical force. Amongst such advocates was Tom Barry. He was convinced that it was the guerrilla tactics that had brought Lloyd George and his government 'to accept that the Irish must be listened to', according to Seán MacBride, who also left for the Four Courts.[12]

Deep bitterness was now being felt about the north of Ireland because Catholics continued to be killed and property burned. Collins accepted the Treaty as a step towards a united Ireland, but the anti-Treaty section had no intention of paying allegiance to a British king. They also felt that the Treaty only copperfastened the 1920 Government of Ireland Act and its acceptance of a divided Ireland. The recognised IRA headquarters was now the Four Courts where Tom Barry, Joe McKelvey, Rory O'Connor, Liam Mellows, Dick Barrett and the others met to decide on their next move. However, for both the Provisional Government and the men in the Four Courts events were moving swiftly and inevitably to a climax.

Following the unveiling on 22 June 1922 of a memorial to railway men killed in the First World War, Field Marshal Sir Henry Wilson, Military Adviser to the 'new State of Northern Ireland', was assassinated in London. Commandant Dunne and Volunteer O'Sullivan of the IRA's London battalion were arrested, and there was no doubt in the minds of the British ministers at that time that the Four Courts' garrison was to blame for the killing. All the indications are that this was not so. Rory O'Connor made a public statement that he had nothing to do with the killing. 'If we had, we would admit it'. Whether or not an earlier order given by Michael Collins was never cancelled is still unclear.[13]

Despite Collins' allegiance to his colleagues in the Provisional Government and honouring the Treaty signature, he was, up to this period, engaged in a dualist approach in relation to exchanging guns and aiding the Four Courts' executive to send them to the north. By this action he was engaged in placating both of the divisions that resulted from the army split. The Four Courts' garrison continued to commandeer vehicles and even arms held by the remaining British troops. With some other men Barry, accustomed to this type of operation, easily secured a number of these. Meanwhile, Churchill and the British government criticised the Provisional Government for making no move against these attacks.[14]

The result of the election, which was preceded by an unsuccessful pact between De Valera and Collins, was not announced until 24 June and showed that out of 128 seats 58 were pro-Treaty and 35 anti-Treaty.

Lloyd George wrote to Michael Collins stating that he was no longer prepared to permit 'the ambiguous position of Rory O'Connor ... and his followers and his arsenal in open rebellion in the heart of Dublin', so he asked Michael Collins to 'formally' bring it 'to an end forthwith'. He offered 'the necessary pieces of artillery' to aid the process.[15]

Matters were brought swiftly to a head by news that J. J. (Ginger) O'Connell, pro-Treaty deputy chief-of-staff, was taken hostage by Four Courts' executive forces. Before this, Leo Henderson had been arrested by pro-Treaty (Provisional Government) troops as he had commandeered transport for removal of supplies to the north – supplies that Michael Collins in his dual role had sanctioned. The Four Courts' executive held O'Connell in order to bargain the release of Henderson. 'We in the Army Council who held the view that the "Treaty" people were simply playing for time until the split in the Anti-Treaty forces widened and until they had built up an army of Staters to attack us,' decided on a certain strategy.[16]

On Wednesday 28 June, an ultimatum delivered to the Four Courts' garrison to surrender by 4 a.m. yielded no response. Field guns acquired from the British forces and supervised by British personnel opened fire on the Four Courts. The Civil War officially began.[17]

Liam Lynch, awakened in the Clarence Hotel by the sound of firing, set out with Liam Deasy and Seán Moylan for Cork. 'The tragedy which he [Lynch] had tried so hard to avoid had happened.'[18] Tom Barry's great friend Dick Barrett – who in earlier months had been in the Four Courts – had returned from his few days in West Cork. He was passing through Dublin on his way to London to attempt a rescue of Dunne and O'Sullivan when he saw the guns lining up outside the Four Courts. He went to join his comrades. Barry was in the south side of the city having come up from Cork, where he had been under the care of Dr Blake 'one of the doctors then treating him' for the recurring problem since the Kilmichael ambush, of 'a strained heart and side'.

De Valera had not yet agreed to the course Rory O'Connor and his men were pursuing and was amazed when he heard that the Four Courts was being shelled. Rory O'Connor and Mellows later told Barry that an early meeting on the 28 June between Liam Lynch and the Four Courts garrison, 'regarding unity had come to no conclusion.' After the ultimatum 'Lynch said he was with them and would leave immediately for the country. No chief-of-staff was actually appointed … but Liam Lynch subsequently and rightly in the confusion took over the command.'

By Thursday, as shelling continued, an appeal was made to the commander of a section of pro-Treaty troops to allow a nurse and a woman companion into the Four Courts. The pro-Treaty officer was suspicious, and rightly so. The 'nurse' was Tom Barry. Tom felt that his fighting power would add strength to the garrison and had secured the nurse's uniform through his wife Leslie. Earlier Moss Twomey said to Barry and Dick Barrett. 'You would do better to get the fellows inside out', and he had tried to persuade them both to go back down the country.[19] Tom was arrested and became the first prisoner of the Civil War.

The big guns roared; the Four Courts was set on fire; and amidst thunderous noise and clouds of black smoke the garrison surrendered.

Barry was among 180 prisoners taken to Mountjoy Jail. Dave Neligan was given the specific job of taking Barry in. 'Listen, Barry,' he said, 'don't try any tricks with me. It's not the Duke of Wellington's regiment you're dealing with now. You'll get your head blown off!'

'Don't worry, I won't!'[20]

As Peadar O'Donnell and his comrades, having been refused entrance to the Four Courts, were being arrested, they saw Barry being taken away, so they shouted words of encouragement to him and his escort. Later, as the prisoners stood at their windows in Mountjoy, overlooking the roadway, they were faced by soldiers who 'lined up' and fired 'volleys'. Though initially the targets were off, the men decided they had better obey the order of the governor and stand clear of the window because 'the State soldiers were only too willing to take a pot shot.'[21]

Leslie got a note stating that her 'husband was still in Mountjoy Military Prison' and the writer was 'glad to say very well'. He would be 'allowed parcels'. His cheque book, with apologies for 'delay', would be returned forthwith.[22]

Tom, with the others, was placed in 'D' wing. Soon they planned their escape. 'We put the cell doors out of action by the simple expedient of wedging the Bible between the hinged door and the frame,' Peadar O'Donnell recalled. 'Rory O'Connor, Liam Mellows, Joe McKelvey, Tom Barry and I, all members of the IRA executive, came together a good deal as a sort of camp council. Barry's only thought all the time was to escape. Perhaps he had a premonition of what could happen to him if he remained. Actually we all had the notion to escape, and had now begun to dig a tunnel'. However, due to structural problems, they encountered 'technical difficulties' with water seeping in, so they had to abandon the tunnel-digging. Barry was extremely restless and insisted on fixing a date of escape, then he urged, 'Let us get down to the plans.'[23]

On 1 July Barry wrote a letter to the OC Dublin Brigade, and had it smuggled out:

> About 80 of us are here including McKelvey, Rory, Mellows. We are having a tough time enough. O'Duffy's instructions are that we be treated as common criminals and have no preferential or political statement. The boys had to be shifted in and some fainted at the treatment they received. They were also wounded boys here. They were dragged along the corridors and flung into cells. It is hell to see our fellows treated like that for the sake of satisfying Collins' and O'Duffy's spite. They have refused to even let us move out to the lavatory and we are to receive criminal diet, etc.
>
> We started smashing up last night as a protest and this show is in ruins nearly. Rumour has it that the executive are to be plugged after court-martial (the usual English style) but the sooner it comes the better.
>
> If we could get some guns in here we may have a sporting chance of shooting our way out. Have you any ideas on the matter?
>
> I was caught very badly, but I could not help it. However, what we want now is to get out.
>
> Best of luck.
>
> In haste.
>
> Tom Barry
>
> No exercise yet – 4.55.
>
> One of our men Hussy has just been shot by Free Staters. They fired a volley through prisoners corridors. We are getting desperate.
>
> Tom Barry.

(Note the mention of, 'McKelvey, Rory and Mellows'; Barry's name was linked in the prison authorities' eyes, with these three, to be 'plugged') This letter was captured in Blessington. Shortly, these selected men were moved to C wing.[24]

Despite Barry's belief that Collins was being satisfied, Neligan admitted that 'Collins thought the world' of Barry who was 'a column leader of genius. By Christ he was!'[25]

One Saturday evening Tom spoke to prison officer, Ignatius O'Rourke 'through C wing circle railings' (over 47 years later, O'Rourke recalled the details for Tom):

> You made me an offer of £5,000 if I took the chance of letting yourself and four other C wing prisoners escape. You told me you'd give me the cheque and I could cash it ... I remember how I felt at the offer and what I said to you in retort. Had I known some weeks later, when I seen the four you mentioned being executed I might have thought better, without the acceptance of £5,000 for my assistance in their release.[26]

It is ironic that it was the four men in C wing – Joe McKelvey, Rory O'Connor,

Liam Mellows and Dick Barrett (best man at Tom Barry's wedding) – who were executed on 8 December. (Barry most likely would have been executed if he was still in custody at that time.) [27]

'Barry could not wait, and finally made a bid for freedom in a Free State army coat' and leggings. [28]

Rory O'Connor gave Barry £5 'he had kept hidden somehow'. Clad in the uniform with the former owner's pass, all covered by a 'dust coat' with cap under his arm Barry walked behind Rory O'Connor. Elsewhere Dick Barrett and a few lads started 'a mock fight' as they played football. They had been 'preparing the stage effects for a few weeks.' Unseen, Barry slipped out of the 'dust coat' crawled under the barbed wire, put on his uniform cap and stood up. He walked quickly towards the sentry. 'Do you see that wire sentry?' Barry said, as he pointed to the opening through which he had crawled. 'Take my tip and report that when you go off: take a tip from an old soldier!' Then he noticed that the sentry held 'his rifle by the muzzle with the butt end trailing'. It was a major offence for a sentry, according to Barry. 'Shoulder your rifle', Barry shouted. 'The governor and his staff are coming out – and shout at those fellows to stop fighting!' Barry walked slowly towards the wicket-gate, knocked, 'Open up, I'm going out for a drink,' he called to the man who opened the window slot. The man opened the gate bolt, then immediately slammed it back, and re-opened the slot. 'You're not a soldier,' he said excitedly, 'You're the prisoner Barry.' Barry discreetly stole away for the main entrance and joined a queue of soldiers at the first of two iron-barred gates where their passes were being glanced over prior to being allowed through. A soldier in line invited Barry to a 'hooly'. He 'readily accepted'. He was third from the gate when an officer dashed out of the gatehouse, 'Close the gate', he shouted. 'Nobody leave. A prisoner is loose in uniform!' Police officer Ignatius O'Rourke 'was walking down by the big wall' and noticed a 'badly dressed' soldier; 'nothing seemed to fit'. He recalled that Barry 'had stooped to fix his left leggings' as O'Rourke passed and 'for some reason became suspicious'. He went to the main gate and waited. 'I stopped you and asked your name.' Barry responded, 'Tommy O'Brien'.

Barry answered all the questions smartly and produced his pass. 'You are Tom Barry', said O'Rourke.

Barry pointed to the pass-out – 7 p.m. to 11.30 p.m. 'Do you not believe this?'

O'Rourke immediately put a guard on Barry and went for the military governor who would know Tom Barry. The soldiers were lined up for inspection. Tom says, 'we came smartly to attention'. Seán O'Connell whom Tom had met with Michael Collins the previous year, walked straight up, removed the cap, stuck it back again, and said, 'Hard luck Tom!' [29]

The military governor rushed out, 'Where is he, where is he?' Tom never a man to miss a trick said, 'He's gone, gone twenty minutes ago!' Instantly the governor recognised his man. He shook hands and said, 'That was a narrow thing, Tom!' Peadar O'Donnell and his comrades looked on in dismay. 'He was within an ace of success.'[30]

Inside in his office O'Hegarty 'produced £1 from his pocket and sent for a bottle of whiskey to celebrate the great capture.' In the office joining Tom Barry in a drink were Ginger O'Connell, Joe Dolan, Bob Martin and a few others. 'After all the excitement had died down Dermot O'Hegarty instructed me to take you down to B Basement,' Ignatius O'Rourke recalled. 'I'll never forget the state of the cell you were put into.' When O'Rourke reported the conditions, O'Hegarty said that there was no option. O'Rourke, on leave from 8 p.m. until 4 a.m. discovered that nobody had visited Tom in the cell during all this time. 'I was disgusted and went down myself … You complained of lack of air saying you were near suffocated and asked to knock out a few panes of glass'.

'Use your shoe', said O'Rourke. Barry asked O'Rourke to give him his revolver. 'I'll break them with the butt'. O'Rourke hesitated. He knew Tom's reputation in the IRA and recalled for Tom:

> I wasn't inclined to hand you my gun without first breaking it and extracting the six-pound. You asked me not to break it, and gave me your word of Honour that you'd hand it back to me loaded as it was. I handed you my revolver loaded and you stood on the heating pipe in the cell, and broke five little window pains. I stood over very close to you expecting anything to happen. And true to your word of honour you handed me back the revolver. What a relief I got when you did, is only known to myself. Never in my life did I feel fear until I handed you my gun. No one would believe what I am relating only those who acted the part. Had you decided to knock me out, you could have walked out a free man because I had all the keys of the respective gates on my person. We were also about the same height and age. Had you walked up to the circle and out through the circle door it's hardly likely you'd have been questioned because the three fellows there were half asleep when I walked up. It was also me who was given the job of taking you out for recreation forenoon and afternoon during your basement confinement. And be it said to your credit not once did you pass an uncomplimentary remark to me either about myself or the state I was serving, so much so that I always think of you with the kindness of feeling… I am an honest believer in historical truth, and would like to expose the self-invested interested group, who availed of every opportunity during our unfortunate split to further their own ends.

For three weeks Barry was held in solitary confinement in this punishment cell. He didn't know what his fate would be or how long he would be held in confinement, and during this time he says he kept convincing himself that he would escape. In the early hours of his twenty-first morning – shortly after 1 a.m. five or six soldiers came to his cell, threw in his boots, told him to dress at once as he was going to another prison. He dressed, but said he would not go. 'I've done my time in this hell-hole!' They threw him on the ground, caught his legs and dragged him up the iron steps. His head banged and bumped on each step up to ground level. Almost unconscious, he was pushed into an armoured car, and taken to Kilmainham Jail. The governor, Seán Ó Murthuile, whom Tom described as 'a decent man and humane prison governor', had waited up, though it was after 2 o'clock. When he saw Tom's condition he was angry and immediately got him medical attention. After some days, once he was well, he was again allowed to mix with the prisoners.[31]

Here Tom made another unsuccessful attempt to escape. This time he had a full Free State uniform, but again his uniform was such a misfit, so baggy around the knees and the coat was so huge that he was halted in his bid for freedom. This time the governor, Seán Ó Muirthile had known Tom and didn't prescribe any punishment.[32]

On the night of 23 August 1922 he was talking with some other prisoners in the corridor outside the top tier of cells when somebody came with the news that Michael Collins had been shot dead in West Cork the previous night – Tom's first wedding anniversary. One year on, these men who were united at his wedding, were now fighting and killing one another. Word spread around quickly so that everybody knew. A questioning silence spread throughout the jail.

Tom recalled looking down shortly afterwards from the corridor above 'on the extraordinary picture of about a thousand kneeling Republican prisoners spontaneously reciting the Rosary aloud for the repose of the soul of the dead Michael Collins, commander-in-chief of the Free State forces.' He felt there was little logic in such an action, but it was a wonderful tribute to the part played by a man who had worked tirelessly in the struggle to gain independence for Ireland. Even through all the bitterness of Civil War 'those Republican prisoners remembered that the dead leader, latterly their enemy, was once the driving force and the inspiration in their struggle against the British forces of occupation.'[33]

Tom was unaware at that time of the value Michael Collins had placed on his integrity. The previous week when Collins visited Maryborough prison while on his army inspection tour, he specifically asked for, and spoke to, Republican prisoner, Tomás Ó Maoileóin. He asked him if he would 'attend a meeting of senior officers *to try to put an end to this damned thing*'. Collins 'slapped one fist into a palm in characteristic fashion: *That's fine, the three Toms' will fix it.*' The three Toms were Tom Barry, Tom Hales and Tomás Ó Maoileóin – all strong Republican activists and friends of Collins. Collins, who 'appeared to be acting on his own' did not mention 'any political aspects' but suggested they meet with some of his own senior officers 'to arrange for a cessation of hostilities'.[34] (When Barry got out of jail, later, he 'interviewed' men who had participated in the ambush and spoke to the man 'who fired the long range shot' that killed Collins.)[35]

On the 30 August, just eight days after Collins' death, Monsignor O'Hagan, rector of the Irish College in Rome who was in Ireland, was contacted by Seán T. O'Kelly who wrote to Richard Mulcahy requesting him to hold a meeting with Tom Barry, Liam Mellows, Rory O'Connor, Oscar Traynor – all in jail. Mulcahy agreed. O'Connor and Mellows jointly welcomed 'any efforts promising to end this new and unnatural attack on the independence of the country.' However, when Liam Lynch was informed he was unhappy and wondered why 'not direct negotiations?' Lynch himself was still free. Mulcahy sent Liam Tobin into Kilmainham, where 'hot words on both sides' ended in stalemate, as Tobin tried 'to bully Barry and place obstacles in the way of the talks', according to O'Kelly, who believed the Provisional Government was only copper-fastening the continuance 'of the war until the very last bit of ammunition of the Republicans has been expended and the last of their men imprisoned or shot.'[36]

A little over a week after the Kilmainham incident, early in September, Barry was removed to Gormanstown Camp, which was still being wired up. This internment camp was intended to be secure, so that Barry and his equals would have no hope of escape. The military were determined not to let Barry from their grip.[37]

On his way in, a Free State officer remarked, 'We have you now, Barry, and by God you won't get away from us!' Willing to accept any challenge Barry said, 'I'll bet you ten bob I'll be out within 24 hours.'

'I'll take you on because, by hell, you won't!'

Inside the compound, which wasn't yet fully organised, officers and soldiers were busy taking in prisoners. Soon Barry noticed workmen putting up some posts and barbed wire on a fence. He walked across the enclosure, pretended he was doing some fixing, and took up a plank on his shoulder. Nobody noticed. He looked like one of the workmen. Shortly he went to the 'blind' side. 'It was a chance to be taken in a flash, and Barry in such cases is lightning.'[38]

(It was almost 40 years later when he collected the bet – at a protest meeting in Cork city concerning the sale and division of the De Vesci Estate. The once 'enemy' officer and Barry chatted freely on that day, united in the cause of the small farmer. Barry laughed when he recalled the event. That day he showed Brendan O'Neill the ten-shilling note – collected without interest.)[39]

Tom Barry was free – lucky to be free!

He was lucky because on 7 December 1922. Dáil Deputy Seán Hales was shot dead in Dublin and his companion Pádraic Ó Maille was seriously wounded. Acting ruthlessly and swiftly the Free State government decided to execute four prisoners, one from each province – four important Republican men who had been in prison since the surrender of the Four Courts.

Dick Barrett, of Barry's flying column, was the man chosen for Munster. (Dick, a teacher, had been imprisoned on Spike Island in 1921 and with Tom Crofts and Bill Quirke had escaped in a row boat.). Ernest Blythe, the then minister for local government, told me that if Tom Barry had still been in jail he would have been the man executed for Munster. Blythe had no hesitation in saying they would have been glad 'to get' Barry.[40]

It is ironic that Seán Hales, Tom Barry and Dick Barrett, who had often slept in 'the big bed' together in O'Mahony's of Belrose while 'on the run' during the War of Independence, had their lives balanced against each other.

As the fight in Dublin, which marked the beginning of the Civil War, continued, many uncaptured Republicans retreated to the south hoping to defend a line from Waterford to Limerick. They were as yet reluctant to take offensive action against their own 'brothers' in the army of the Provisional Government. However, the war was on and Provisional Government forces (pro-Treatyites) advanced towards the south. Since the opening of recruitment they outnumbered the anti-Treatyites and had the additional advantage of British supplied armoured cars and artillery.

In a series of attacks Provisional Government forces took Waterford and Limerick. Because of sea-borne landing attacks, the anti-Treatyites had to evacuate Cork city on 11 August. That same day Liam Lynch evacuated and burned Fermoy Barracks. The anti-Treaty forces (later known as Republicans) were forced to take to the hills once more, but this time it was different. A large proportion of the people who had been sympathetic to the IRA during the war against the British was now hostile.

It was early September and Tom Barry, having escaped from Gormanstown Camp, made his way as quickly and as secretly as possible across the fields. Although he was very tired and twilight had set in he kept going until darkness fell, as he was afraid to approach any house in case he would end up in 'the wrong hands'. He found a comfortable corner of a field, settled down for the night on a grassy patch and fell into a deep sleep.

When he awoke in the morning he discovered there was a river – he never found out the name of it – flowing somewhere nearby. He made his way towards the river where he found a boat moored. Seeing a cottage in the far distance and feeling that the inhabitants might be friendly, he untied the boat and used the oars to paddle across to the other bank.

As he moved across the fields and drew near to the cottage he noticed smoke rising from the chimney into the early morning air. 'They're poor people,' he thought to himself. 'They can't be too bad.'

He went in the unlocked door. The woman of the house told him her husband had gone to work. When he told her he had been out all night and was hungry she gave him tea. As they talked he discovered that they hadn't ever got involved in the movement; she knew about the Civil War, but didn't know which side was winning or which side was right. Sure that he was on safe ground he told her that he had escaped from the prison camp. She knew somebody who was in the Republican movement – on De Valera's side, she said – and directed him to that house. From there he was directed to a group who were attached to an IRA fighting section, and they helped him on towards Cork.[1]

In Lorrha, Co. Tipperary, he collected 'a Thompson machine-gun, the only one we had and brought it on to Cork with him'.[2] With a hand-held sub-machine-gun he could travel almost as a one-man army. He made his way across country to West Cork, having acquired names of 'sympathetic' houses along the way where he could expect food and rest. Eventually he reached the Woods' home, situated between Crookstown and Newcestown, north of Bandon, where the Republican press section had set up their printing equipment. Under the direction of Erskine Childers, aided by Robert Lankford and Seán Hyde, they turned out anti-Treaty propaganda with single-minded zeal.

Tom was brought up-to-date on developments. He and Liam Deasy decided to get the men fully into action. After they drew up a plan, with dispatch messages prepared for different companies, Tom and Liam moved further west, where they met Pat Buttimer.

'Word reached me to meet them in Kealkil. I didn't question how they came, but they told me they had important documents.' Buttimer, who knew the area well, guided them for over four miles cross-country, avoiding the main roads. 'The Free State army was scattered everywhere'. When the two men reached Buttimer's home place they wouldn't come in 'not even for a cup of tea – it was too dangerous'.[3]

Documents later captured by pro-Treaty (government) troops outlined the ideal column which 'was to consist of 35 men, including engineers, signallers and machine-gunners, sub-divided into squads of five men and a leader, who would keep in close contact, and the war was to be carried on by all the methods used against the British. The difficulty and importance of communications was stressed in these documents.'[4] The captured documents had apparently been drawn up by Barry and Deasy, although it is uncertain if these were the same documents they had on this occasion.

Outside Dunmanway, Deasy and Barry met others of the Dunmanway Company, and Barry went to work right away. 'Once he was back it made a terrible difference,' Dan Cahalane recalls. 'He was a superb commander. The column was stronger now during this period than at any time during the Tan War. If that man had enough arms and ammunition for his men nothing would stop him.'[5]

It was agreed that he should take over a brigade column 'whose principal objectives will be the development of town attacks' using up to 200 men.[6]

On 26 September, a pro-Treaty officer reported that there are 'rumours today of Dunmanway being taken and that Tommie Barry is leading his men on towards Clon. Buckshot [Seán Hales] said they [government forces] would be safe here except that Barry came along'. This report tells of prisoners taken out by government forces to remove trees off the Dunmanway road, some tried to escape and were fired on, one was shot dead.[7]

De Valera, who had never much heart for the fight, was anxious for more cohesion between the military and political leaders. He urged abandonment of the military struggle, but found Liam Lynch unco-operative.

A blow to the morale of the Republican forces came in October when the

Catholic hierarchy condemned the IRA Volunteers for resisting and withdrew the right of the sacraments. Tom Barry and his men were once again censured for their actions. 'That really didn't bother me. During my lifetime I was excommunicated five times'.[8]

Through intermediaries, Major General Emmet Dalton, pro-Treaty, sent proposals to Deasy and Barry suggesting an unconditional surrender. Upon discovering that this would be unacceptable to Republican forces, Dalton dropped out and Tom Ennis, who had been acting with him, took over negotiations. Tom Ennis and Charlie Russell met Liam Deasy and Tom Barry near Crookstown on 13 October 1922. 'The proposals put forward by the Free State officers were reported to the executive meeting at Ballybacon three days later, but they were not of such a nature as to merit any serious consideration, and they achieved nothing.'[9]

Despite considerable risk, Tom Barry was among the 16-man army executive who attended a meeting on 28 October, presided over by Liam Lynch. The members pledged 'an allegiance ... in reasserting our ancient right to be a free people and a free nation, owing allegiance to no foreign authority'.[10] Afterwards Liam Lynch wrote to all divisions on the views of the executive.[11] At this meeting Barry was appointed operations officer in the southern division. Later Lynch appointed him as director of operations, in charge of all anti-Treaty divisional O/Cs. In this role Lynch recognised him as *ipso facto*, deputy chief-of-staff. By early November with the aid of several districts officers in the southern division he had organised a massive 580 riflemen where they 'rung in' Cork city, held all roads to Macroom, Bandon, Kinsale, Cobh. In this forceful operation Barry's strategic plan secured many Cork towns for the Republicans.[12]

He got some men together, sprung on Bandon and took it. The West Cork twin-towns of Ballineen and Enniskeane were in the hands of the pro-Treaty forces, so Barry decided to capture them. Bill Powell, First Brigade area, received word to go to Kenneigh where Barry was mobilising a column to take Ballineen and Enniskeane.

'I arrived on the morning of 4 November at 4 o'clock. Barry told me to pick out seven men. "Go down and take Ballineen," he said. Then he turned to Spud Murphy, "Get seven more and go down and give Bill a hand!"' So he put the men into sections, detailed them and rehearsed tactics. On command they fell into formation and advanced on Ballineen moving towards the barracks. Barry had hoped to get the armoured car, which was in the barracks, but just as the attack began, instead of using it, a soldier drove it out the road in the opposite direction.

It was a hard fight, but shortly the pro-Treaty soldiers ran out across the road and jumped over a wall. Barry and his men entered the barracks and continued to fire. They tunnelled through the houses, making their way toward the end of the town. Eventually the soldiers put up their hands in surrender. Barry and his men had captured Ballineen.

'What could we do with these prisoners? We couldn't hold them, as we had no place to put them, so all we could do, was relieve them of their arms and let them go. It was a ridiculous situation,' said Bill Powell.

Barry and his men then entered Enniskeane, fought and captured it. Both towns were now in Republican hands.[13]

By now Republicans were acutely aware of their inability to beat the superior opposition, but they could conduct guerrilla activities indefinitely. So circumstances reached stalemate for the government.

Under the Emergency Powers, unauthorised possession of a fire arm was now punishable by death, as it had been in the martial law areas under the British. Erskine Childers, who had produced the last issue of his not very impartial paper in the Coole mountain district between Dunmanway and Macroom, went to the Wicklow area where he was arrested on 10 November. Found in the possession of a small revolver given to him as a gesture of friendship by Michael Collins, he was tried by court-martial and executed by a firing squad.

On 16 November 'a meeting of the executive of the IRA was held'. Ten of the 12 members available were present, including Tom Barry. A decision was taken 'to proclaim a Provisional Republican government in consultation with the Republican members of Dáil Éireann' with all departments as 'before July 1921'. The report stated that 'the Republic is now in direct communication with Gr. Britain, and USA and has several representatives overseas'. They discussed the military situation in detail, and concluded that there should be 'more effective co-operation between the different areas' as it was 'anticipated that big results' would follow 'from future co-ordination of activities'. Liam Lynch in his follow-up report stated: 'It is now clear that there is to be no compromise of the Republic on our side and this must urge us to further perfect our organisation and to exercise redoubled energy and effort in prosecution of the war.'[14]

The day after Childers was shot (17 November), Barry moved with his column towards Glengariff and after a swift attack took the town.

The possession of an armoured car would, Barry felt, be a great asset to the Republicans. A feasible chance of getting one presented itself when John (Jock) McPeak, who had been a gunner in the *Slieve na mBan* armoured car used during the Béal na mBláth ambush when Michael Collins was killed, indicated that he wished to desert from the forces of the Provisional Government and join the Republicans.

Barry asked two Cumann na mBan members, Anna Mulqueen and May Twomey, to give McPeak 'the once over'. They were instructed that one of the conditions of his acceptance would be to bring with him the *Slieve na mBan* armoured car stationed in the Devonshire Arms barracks in Bandon. On 2 December Billy Barry, dressed in 'a Free State uniform', and John McPeak stole the armoured car and drove it from the barracks out on the Laragh road towards Tinkers Cross.[15]

At Crookstown Mrs Galvin insisted in getting into the *Slieve na mBan*. When

Jimmy Lordan pointed out its' advantages, she exclaimed, 'God Jimmy, ye'll have the Republic in a week!'

'Yerra mam, I think we'll give them a month!' Jimmy responded optimistically, with 'his roguish smile'.[16]

Equipped with the armoured car, a driver, a gunner and men, Barry marched on Inchageela, put up a strong fight, and took it, securing further ammunition. They went on to Ballyvourney and after a short fight, took the village. Barry led his men on to Ballymakeera where another armoured car was secured. It was then on to Kealkil where a hard fight led to success. 'He was fighting fit and slept little', Bill Powell recalled, and remembers him as 'a brilliant organiser, a brilliant soldier. He was, I would say, one of *the* greatest Irishmen. He thought both militarily and politically'.[17] Liam Deasy noted 'a marked improvement in organisation' in the West Cork Brigade now that Barry was in command.[18] Lynch complimented Barry's 'splendid' operation where 20 'troops were able to keep 400 of the enemy engaged in this out of the way, and troublesome country.'[19] According to Jerh Cronin he was 'a man capable of conquering fear. He had the speed and dash that would take him through dangerous places. He'd face a lion.'[20]

Matters were becoming worse nationally, and often atrocities far more severe that those experienced during the 'Tan War' were taking place. In Dublin on 8 November for instance, a group of men were parading when machine-gun fire, from government forces, was opened up on them from across the Grand Canal resulting in 20 deaths. Four soldiers, dragged James Spain from a house and shot him five times. The following night anti-Treatyites retaliated by attacking Portobello Barracks and other places. In country areas similar atrocities were being committed. Bitterness and hatred had set in. In Kerry some of the most vicious attacks were committed against prisoners during the Civil War period.[21]

On 30 November Liam Lynch issued an order, which the government captured, stating that all members of the government or members of the Dáil who had voted for the emergency powers were to be shot on sight. Following this, Dáil Deputy Seán Hales, though absent from the Dáil during the vote on the emergency powers bill, was shot in Dublin on 7 December. Controversy has surrounded his death, and there are those who have stated that the fatal bullet was meant for his travelling companion Deputy Pádraic Ó Maille. But in later years Bill O'Donoghue saw Tom Barry extremely angry one night saying, 'I'd like to know who issued the order for the murder of Seán Hales'.[22]

Barry never agreed with shooting for the sake of shooting, believing that the only way to fight a war was in a warlike fashion. In the early part of the War of Independence he ordered his men not to shoot any of the British forces while off duty. However, he revised his opinion in the early part of 1921, for the Essex Regiment only, because of Percival's callous and inhumane treatment of prisoners. Due to the low tactics to which Percival and his men had stooped, he ordered that they (Essex) should be shot at sight following written and verbal warnings, which went unheeded. He stressed it didn't apply to any other regiment.

Now, during the Civil War he asked his men not to shoot an unarmed soldier. 'We'll get them in a fight,' he said. He also disagreed with Liam Lynch's policy of burning barracks. If left intact, buildings could, he argued, be used to hold prisoners and perhaps hostages since the people were no longer willing to give their houses as they had done during the War of Independence.[23]

In Dublin at a Cumann na mBan meeting Tom's wife, Leslie who was 'violently Anti T [Treaty]' was convinced that unless the organisers 'withdrew' and 'stopped discussion the organisation [Cumann na mBan] was gone'. She agreed with her husband that the fight had to continue.[24]

Chief-of-staff, Liam Lynch and Tom Barry, operations officer, organised a selection of men to prepare for a northern offensive. Jack Fitzgerald, Seán Lehane, Charlie Daly and Stephen O'Neill left from Bandon and picked up 'stuff' in Moore Park outside Fermoy. To accompany Tom Lane, 'Dick Willis was picked as a Thompson gunman'. They were up in Donegal as a part of a division preparing to attack Derry. Tom Barry hoped at the time that this would bring the Free State government into the decision to join in a united attack against Britain.[25] He believed that his part in the Civil War was to help Republicans win control, so that the army then united could fight for the common cause of Ireland.

Meanwhile, Brigadier Lacy and a group from Tipperary sent word to Tom to come to their area and to bring some of his best men with him, as most of this area was in the hands of the pro-Treaty forces. Following the deaths of his friends on 7 and 8 December, Barry, with Brigadier Lacy, Bill Quirke, Michael Sheehan, Michael Sadlier and Sparkey Breen, organised about a 100 men for an attack on Carrick-on-Suir.[26]

Barry familiarised himself with the surroundings and then spent over a week training the men under his command. He prepared a detailed plan with sections, section commanders and positions. It was a bitterly cold, frosty night as they prepared for the attack. As in former engagements he led the attack and was the first man to stand out, with a Mills bomb in one hand and a revolver in the other.

It has been described as a 'spectacular attack' when they took the town having lured the Free State troops into action. They captured 115 rifles, two machine-guns and a large quantity of stores and clothing. They took Captain Balfe, OC of the pro-Treaty forces prisoner, but freed him after two days. All other 110 prisoners, 'officers and soldiers' were released 'unharmed after a few hours' despite the execution of seven more Republicans on the same day. The situation was farcical: Republicans continued to release prisoners while the state continued to execute Republicans in custody.[27]

On 13 December Barry and his men marched on Thomastown, put up a hard fight and took it. Within four days Barry' column had forced the surrender of Callan, Mullinavat, as well as Thomastown.

In Callan the commanding officer of the pro-Treaty forces, Ned Sommers, felt disillusioned, believed he had been lured into the Free State army under false pretences, and so switched sides. The move cost him his life some months later when he tried to shoot his way out to avoid being captured.

On the way back from Kilkenny to Tipperary, the Republicans had to cross a marsh; Jack Hennessy remembered the bitter rain beating through them as they marched across north Tipperary. They were cold, wet and hungry yet Barry was determined, he planned to strike in the northern direction through Tipperary to Templemore, then eastwards to the Curragh, from where Dublin, the capital would be within sight. However, he had to lie low for a few days because of 'enemy activity'.[28]

By 19 December Barry believed that if he could muster the strength of all Republicans, victory would be theirs. Now as director of operations he had secured, for the first time ever, a typist. From field headquarters he set out his views in a long document for all OCs. He wanted to know the 'strength of activities' in each area, the 'number of arms and ammunition dumped' and 'a survey of towns' that could be attacked. He wrote, that with 'a properly organised scheme of attacks on enemy's communication lines we can make his position hopeless in towns, but this cannot be done effectively until a study of the area is made'. He was determined that this war should be on a more organised footing as 'opportunities' were 'not being availed of owing to lack of direction and control of our armed forces. This must cease and officers in charge of divisional operations will be responsible that the activities and energies of our forces will be directed and controlled in an efficient manner in their areas. '[29]

The winter and the war dragged on. During these frosty nights they huddled at the side of a ditch or in a hay barn, a stall or a shed being warmed by the breath of the cows. Barry, with some other leaders, led the men on to Templemore where there was an amount of ammunition worth capturing. 'We had to fight all day,' Jack Hennessy, who was wounded and brought to safety, said, 'Two rifles and captured Free State topcoats were used as a stretcher.'[30]

Could the men sustain this brilliant sweep? Men who were by now in the days of December and January at a low ebb due to lack of sleep, insufficient food and hard slogging through the frost and the rain? Yet the word of Tom Barry and his men's arrival was enough; he marched through villages and towns where Free State forces hardly stood to fight. 'They practically handed the places over to him.'[31] His reputation as the daring, elusive commander, the man who could neither be caught nor killed, had made him a legendary figure and a man to be feared. He led and drove his men depending on the circumstances. 'Single minded and authoritative. He was quick to pick things up and quick to size things up!'[32]

With troops he marched on Limerick, took over hotels, surrounded pro-Treaty forces on a Sunday morning as they were on parade. He told them he was Tom Barry, then said, 'Drop your guns!' And they did.

He marched on to the Curragh and took 800 rifles from the civic guard. It began to look as if they were on 'the comeback militarily'. De Valera said to him, 'It's a pity you weren't out earlier, Tom. You'd have made a better job of the line fighting.'

'Hang it all, if I had my way there would be no line fighting. It would be fought out in Dublin in three days and we'd have shifted them.'

Barry maintained that when the Four Courts was attacked, anti-Treaty troops should have been brought in from the south and west and taken them [pro-Treaty forces] on in Dublin city. 'Dublin might have been left in a shambles, but at least it would have been over.'[33]

Meanwhile, the increasing strength of the Free State government forces in some areas accelerated the daily capture of Republicans. There was also the added threat of execution for those caught carrying arms. By the end of January 55 executions of prisoners had been carried out. In all, the total number of executions was to rise to 77 in the course of the war, as the policy of the Free State government was the ultimate destruction of Republicans.[34]

Ernest Blythe said that for his part they would have gone on executing anti-Treatyites, 'until we had got the last man, if they didn't give in'.[35]

Undaunted, Barry wrote to the adjutant general as he wanted the overall position to be assessed 'from a proper angle and not from paper reports'. With this in mind he intended sending 'a special messenger to CS requesting him to come down' from GHQ. Aided by 'six officers' he wanted to front a further column 'over the Third Southern area.'[36]

The futility of the fight had taken a heavy toll on the enthusiasm of the guerrilla fighters. Ruthless tactics of the Free State on the prison population were found to influence the Republicans on the ground. Liam Deasy, another officer of the executive, commanding Lynch's Southern Command and formerly of the Third West Cork Brigade, was captured in Clonmel on 18 January 1923, tried by court-martial and sentenced to death. Deasy was ready for death when at 4 a.m. a message came through from Mulcahy to send him to Dublin. De Valera described this as 'the biggest blow'.[37]

Deasy maintained that he had been endeavouring to try to end the war without actually surrendering the Republic. Now in prison he was in a difficult position. How much pressure was forced on him is unknown. In any case he signed a document which urged 'unconditional surrender of arms and men as required by General Mulcahy. In pursuance of this undertaking I am asked to appeal for a similar undertaking of acceptance from the following …'A total of fifteen names are listed, including Eamon de Valera, Tom Barry, Liam Lynch and Frank Aiken. He maintained that his 'execution would not be suspended' unless he signed the prepared statement. He was given time to consider and 'in the best interests of the country' he said, he agreed to sign.[38]

Lynch answered the communiqué with a brusque refusal; he sent a message to all ranks urging them not to 'surrender the strong position you have so dearly won. The war will go on until the independence or our country is recognised by enemies, foreign and domestic.'[39] In a letter to Fr Tom Duggan, Cork, Lynch 'painfully noted' Liam Deasy's 'communication'. He found 'the enemy' proposals were 'that of mad men … Unless the enemy has completely lost his Irish outlook he would not ask such terms … Even if our last leader or Volunteer is to be wiped out we will not accept being British subjects'. The 'enemy in his non-Irish methods seems to forget that it was practically our forces alone who drove the common enemy to discuss peace terms with us,' Lynch wrote. He was angry at the 'savage' war and 'unchecked policy' of daily executions, with the 'energies' of neutral people concentrated on the anti-Treaty 'forces'.[40]

Though the Liam Deasy document was sent out on 29 January 1923, it was not published until 9 February. Barry maintained that Deasy's 'Manifesto crippled' the Republicans, it 'put the tin hat on us' as 'we were at our very highest level of success'. Ernie O'Malley, who was totally against any compromise, was with Deasy in Mountjoy Jail; he found it difficult 'to contain' himself.[41] To clarify his position Deasy wrote a six-page letter to Liam Lynch stating that his views were 'not altered as a result of imprisonment' as 'previous to my arrest I had decided to advocate a termination of the present hostilities'. When Barry was handed a copy of 'Deasy's apologia' by 'a senior brigade officer's widow' in the 1970s, he believed that 'it probably never reached Lynch.'

Barry wrote:

For the record I must state: (1) I met Liam Deasy in the Glen of Aherlow a few days before his arrest and he never uttered one word that hostilities should cease. (2) At the first meeting of the executive after his arrest … the question was raised as to whether any of the members had heard Deasy mention or knew of any officer to whom Deasy suggested hostilities should be ended. The answer was, No.[42]

The holding of an executive meeting now became a priority for Tom Barry. On 9 February accompanied by Tom Crofts, he went to Dublin to impress on Liam Lynch the gravity of the situation. Lynch was reluctant to hold a meeting. Back in Ballyvourney next day Barry and Crofts drafted a strong request to Lynch for an executive meeting.[43]

As far as Barry was concerned he would like to get the views of other members; also for him timing was important – there was a time to fight and a time to stop. Fight from a position of strength. When there was a hope of winning – then fight. He had never wanted the Civil War. It was too painful, more painful then he had ever thought possible. Deasy's 'procedure had a bad effect', Charlie Browne recalled. 'We got a letter from Barry repudiating Deasy, and a letter from Liam Lynch, which was an order to be read to all ranks.' The men 'looked forward to an honourable settlement.'[44]

After Seán Lehane had seen Liam Deasy in jail he told Jack Fitzgerald of Deasy's position. 'Why didn't he die as well as the rest?' Jack asked.

'Dead men are no use to us now,' Seán responded.[45]

Republicans 'Dump Arms and Cease Fire'

By February 1923 Barry realised that 'the war of brothers' was only bleeding the Irish people; the British were no longer in the war; an observation period was necessary; the iron hand of the Free State government needed some melting; that perhaps by some form of negotiations Republicanism might again be cemented, thus affording the opportunity of bringing about a united Ireland.

Meanwhile Fr Tom Duggan who had been a British army chaplain with Republican sympathies was anxious to heal divisions caused by the Civil War. He met Liam Lynch but found him totally unco-operative and un-compromising. He then got in touch with Tom Barry and found him much more understanding and flexible. Despite the fact that Lynch wrote to Fr Duggan demanding that he discontinue with peace feelers, Duggan felt that Barry was one man who could differentiate between an ideal situation and a real one. Barry went to endless trouble endeavouring to effectuate an executive meeting.

A meeting of the First Southern Division, to which Lynch was invited but didn't attend, was held in Cronin's of Gougane Barra, West Cork. Barry suggested, and it was again agreed, to send Lynch a further request to attend a meeting of the executive because he was the only member who was strongly opposed to negotiations. Todd Andrews believed that Lynch's reasoning was that De Valera could easily be manipulated into 'a compromise peace' situation, and this was one of the reasons Lynch 'opposed the holding of a meeting of the executive.'[1]

Some weeks later when Barry heard of the 'Free State atrocities' in Ballyseedy, Co. Kerry, he was shocked. Nine prisoners were taken from jail, tied to a mine and blown to pieces, one, Stephen Fuller miraculously escaped by being hurled onto a tree. Five prisoners in Killarney were similarly treated. Four were killed. At Caherciveen a few days later five more met a similar fate. The incidents were sparked when Republicans who had placed a mine, off the main road near Knocknagoshal, killed four of the Free State forces and badly injured another. The turn events were taking saddened him very much. Was this what he had fought so hard for – Irishmen murdering Irishmen? Things seemed to have lost proportion; it just could not go on.[2]

At this time, Flor O'Donoghue with Fr Duggan and other neutral men were endeavouring to have a truce called. On 13 February, before Barry's request letter reached Lynch, Lynch had already left Dublin for his journey south. By mid-February he arrived in the Ballingeary district where he met Todd Andrews. On 25 February, Flor O'Donoghue and a few (neutral) men went to meet Tom Barry and 'put the Truce idea to him and he approved'; it was worthy of consideration, though he had conditions, such as that 'all men join an association.'[3]

Then on 26 February 18 officers attended the first Southern Division council meeting in Ballingeary which lasted three days. Seán O'Hegarty arrived in disguise; he asked Mick Murphy what he thought. Through 'the dark and dismal' passages there was 'the inevitable beam of humour. Mick looked him over, 'saw the scraggy beard, the battered, weather-worn hat, the old coat and the hob-nailed boots. He stepped back from Seán and said, "you look like the fellow in the thirteenth Station of the Cross handing up the nails".'[4]

At the council meeting, Barry was among those who again put forward a demand on Lynch to call an executive meeting saying that Lynch 'alone was responsible for not calling it'. Lynch's argument was that they had no power to make peace or war because the imprisoned members would have to be released to produce a comprehensive decision.[5]

Lynch listened to the men who had the pulse of the situation, and got a more realistic view of the position than he could have visualised from headquarters in Dublin. 'The majority, while believing that military victory was no longer a possibility expressed a willingness to continue the struggle.'[6] Barry emphasised strongly that in the entire country their strength did not exceed 8,000. As Lynch heard the outspoken opinion of Barry and his comrades he became more convinced that they were in a crisis situation. But he was determined that the fight should go on.[7]

Eventually Barry, using persuasive language with aggressive power, commanded that a meeting of the executive should be held – just as he would command that an ambush be carried out. He failed to understand why Lynch was so single-minded in his attitude and why Lynch failed to respond to requests from De Valera to see him.

Barry said that if he believed that by continuing the struggle, success would be achieved, he wouldn't hesitate for one moment. However, the strength of their forces was reduced, their armament supplies were diminishing and the general conditions as regards prisoners and the lack of people-support, all pointed to the fact that the continuation of hostilities was futile.

Each of the 18 officers present expressed his opinion, and as Lynch listened to their outspoken views, he realised that a crisis had come and that a meeting of the executive could no longer be deferred. Finally, with full agreement from the group, a decision to call an executive meeting was taken. Throughout this period a number of churchmen and other dignitaries had made approaches to Barry to use his influence and persuasive powers to bring an end to hostilities; they were also in touch with Cosgrave and Mulcahy. Florrie O'Donoghue of the neutral executive (intermediaries negotiating peace) also found De Valera difficult. 'No truce for him. Wish he were doing some of the fighting,' he wrote.[8]

While arrangements were being made for the executive meeting a proposal for the cessation of hostilities was addressed by the archbishop of Cashel, Dr Harty. A number of priests and laymen came to Barry with 'a request that it should be circulated to IRA leaders … in the interests of the future of Ireland'.[9] Tom in a letter to the bishop and also to the press agreed to the 'request' as he felt it was his 'bounden duty' not to influence but to pass on the request. However, the army executive 'unanimously rejected' the proposals.[10]

Lynch finally sent De Valera an invitation to attend an executive meeting in the Monavullagh Mountains in Co. Waterford. Sporting a beard he travelled with Frank Aiken and Austin Stack in a large car, posing as an American.

Meanwhile, Tom Barry, Tom Crofts and some other officers joined Todd Andrews and Liam Lynch as they headed for the executive meeting. Andrews and Lynch were in bed one night when they were awakened abruptly as the door of their bedroom was kicked open. 'A figure appeared with a lighted candle in one hand and in the other a sheet of paper. I was terrified by this sudden and violent intrusion,' Todd Andrew wrote. 'My first reaction was that the end had come at last, that we were at the mercy of the Staters. Liam recognised, more quickly than I, that the visitor was Tom Barry. He waved the piece of paper about shouting angrily "Lynch! Did you write this?" The paper in Barry's hand was Liam's order to withdraw from peace feelers. Liam merely replied, "Yes".

'A tirade of abuse followed from Barry, mainly directed at asserting the superiority of his fighting record. Barry's peroration was dramatic: "I fought more in a week than you did in your life." Liam said nothing. Having emptied himself of indignation, Barry withdrew slamming the door ... Barry's dramatic entrance holding the candle-stick with the lighted candle struck me as having something of the character of an Abbey Theatre farce.'[11]

Tom Barry, Crofts, Lynch, Andrews and other officers reached Carriganimma near Macroom for the first part of their journey to the executive meeting. A lorry had been provided to take them towards Araglin outside Fermoy. Todd Andrews says that everybody was in a good humour and there was 'sly nudging' when Tom Barry automatically took command.

'We drove into the night and it was easy to see why Barry was probably the best field commander in the IRA. Before approaching any crossroads he dismounted, covering the passage of the lorry with the bodyguard. The operation he was commanding wasn't complicated, but his air of confident authority impressed me. One felt safe with Barry in charge.'[12]

Around midnight they arrived outside Kilworth where they previously decided to abandon the lorry and continue on foot towards Araglin. Feeling thirsty, they decided to call to a pub. Before they knocked up the proprietor, Barry placed a guard around the premises.

They had one drink each and moved off in three pony-traps provided by the local company to pre-arranged billets organised by these North Corkmen. 'The boys' had some days previously commandeered a lorry-load of bacon from Sir John Keane's factory at Cappoquin. They distributed it among the people of the area, so Barry, Lynch, Andrews and all the others had a wholesome meal in the morning before trudging 20 miles over the Knockmealdowns to Ballinamult, Co. Waterford. 'It was a welcome addition to their monotonous diet which consisted almost entirely of bread, butter, eggs and tea'.[13]

The available members of the executive assembled on 23 March 1923 at James Cullinane's, Bliantas, Co. Waterford.[14] Anxious to stop the war, De Valera stated that Irish sovereignty and the abolition of the oath were pre-requisite. Tom Barry proposed that the executive recognise that continued resistance would not further the cause of independence. This meeting, with deep discussion, took three days. Three significant aspects of the situation were considered. First, the heavy losses by death or capture of officers and men; second, the policy of executions which had been suspended by the Free State authorities in February, but resumed again in March; and third, the lack of weapons which might enable attacks on posts to be made successfully.

At this time the total strength of the Republican army was about 8,000. Jails and internment camps held an estimated 13,000 prisoners. Against the 8,000 still in the field the Free State government could muster 38,000 combat troops. There was no effective answer to the executions' policy, short of retaliation, equally lawless and cruel, and Lynch had forbidden any such action. At the time Michael Cremin was negotiating the purchase of mountain artillery on the continent, but there was no indication that he would be successful.[15]

On 25 March the members had to move into the Nire valley because of reports of raiding forces in the area. Here the session continued at John Wall's, Glenanore, until 26 March. A motion which had clauses to be put before the next executive meeting, with terms for the Republican government to enter into negotiations, resulted in five for and five against. Lynch did not vote. Then Tom Barry proposed: 'That in the opinion of the executive further armed resistance and operation against F. S. government will not further the cause of independence of the country.'

De Valera spoke in favour of the motion, but was not allowed to vote. The motion, which Lynch voted against, was defeated by one vote. It proved impossible to reconcile the divergent views held by the executive members. Lynch still believed in possible victory. Finally, a decision was taken to adjourn the meeting and re-assemble three weeks later on 10 April.[16]

Barry, Crofts and McSwiney returned to the Ballyvourney area. A few days later Fr Duggan approached Barry saying he hoped that some form of c ompromise could be achieved.

The reconvened executive meeting was to be held near Goatenbridge at the foot of the Knockmealdown mountains. Before dawn on Tuesday 10 April, the scouts at Croagh schoolhouse reported a party of Free State troops moving in two files along the grass margins at each side of the road.

Barry, Liam Lynch and all the men were alerted. They assembled around 5 a.m. at Bill Houlihans, the house nearest the mountains and were having cups of tea and chatting while they awaited further reports. A scout rushed in about 8 a.m. saying that another column of Free State troops was approaching over the mountains to their left. Their line of escape was being threatened. They were about to be encircled. Lynch 'turned to Barry, "You take charge Tom", which he did and succeeded in getting the members of the government and those of the executive council away in safety.' Leaving the house they dashed up a glen towards the mountains. Soon some Free State troops appeared over a rise, and the first shots were exchanged. Barry and all the officers carried only revolvers or automatics . None had rifles, so their fire was quite ineffective at the range. The party continued up the mountain, over a hundred yards. Again they came into the view of approximately 50 Free State troops. Heavy fire opened up.

Liam Lynch, chief-of-staff and Seán Hyde were in the rear. There was another lull, 'then one single shot rang out. Liam fell'. He died later that night in Clonmel Hospital.[17]

Four of the eleven officers were captured while trying to make their getaway. Barry, with his creative imagination, foiled capture by pretending he was a farmer driving home his cows for milking as Free State troops combed the fields close by. Eventually he got to a dug-out in South Tipperary where he remained for a few days.

Owing to Liam Lynch's death, the executive, with Frank Aiken succeeding as chief-of-staff, did not meet until 20 April 1923. Aiken, Barry and Liam Pilkington were appointed as an army council. At this meeting the executive decided to call on De Valera, as head of the Republican government and the army council, to make peace under certain terms, with the Free State authorities. Barry had quite a controversial exchange with Frank Aiken. Aiken accused Barry 'of running around making peace,' while Barry accused Aiken 'of dodging the fighting' and conveying 'utterances' to 'executive meetings' that he (Barry) would be 'responsible for a Republican defeat'.[18]

With his army council comrades Barry attended a meeting on 26 and 27 April. De Valera presided. The main discussion centred round a cease-fire. Finally, a decision was taken that they would issue a proclamation announcing their readiness to negotiate an immediate cease-fire. Coupled with this was the order issued by Frank Aiken under the 'Special Army Order' for suspension of all operations from 30 April.[19]

Shortly after the implementation of the cease-fire derogatory rumours circulated regarding Barry's part in 'peace feelers'. Tom wrote to Mary MacSwiney on 9 May saying he was annoyed regarding the rumours that he was personally negotiating with 'the Free State people. I have not troubled to refute those falsehoods to any except a few who matter and I number you amongst those.' He wanted to meet her to discuss the position.

> Personally my position is that I have given as my view that we cannot beat the Free State people. If we can force them to accept a negotiated peace on the basis of 1,2,3 of the published proclamation (see Appendix III) we have saved the Independence of the country, established what we have been fighting for – Independence as a

right – and preserved its continuity. We remain in the position of custodians of those agreed principles even though a Republican government be not in power and we shall be bound always to ensure that those principles are being acted on by any means in our power. Our moral right to do so is contained in those principles and they are agreed to by our present enemy. I should say that if we have to resort within a few days or years our position will from every point of view be much better.

He would only agree to 'a negotiated peace' on the sovereign rights of the nation being derived from the people of Ireland. 'I at any rate will not agree to any other basis.'

> When beaten to the ropes – and we are not beaten that bad yet – and then when I could fight no longer, say, you have beaten me in arms but you will never make me accept that "Treaty" on your conditions. I will never agree to a living lie. I would still say to them that they killed, tortured and destroyed our people, to uphold foreign domination and that the only thing that prevents my destroying that rotten immoral government is that I have not strength enough left to do so.
>
> If those negotiations are turned down by the Free State I favour going ahead with the war. That briefly is my position and I will ask you to believe that whilst the struggle for the Republic is going on that I will not be one of those who will drop out, although perhaps I have felt tired and depressed at such times as LD's [Liam Deasy's] action and prisoners, documents, etc.[20]

Barry was correct in his observation of 'the disturbing rumours' because Florrie O'Donoghue in his diary believed that 'the Barry business ended any chance of success by our arm', by being in touch with 'both sides'. (In later life Barry and O'Donoghue became close friends. The diary was written at the time when emotions ran high.)[21]

The 'peace feeler' rumours angered Barry because he said he only acted 'as courier' to circulate to army executive members 'the Archbishop Harty Proposals' given to him by Fr Duggan.[22]

It does appear that Barry was incorrectly blamed for informing the Free State government that the army executive was contemplating 'A General Laying Down of Arms' and wanted a peace settlement. Since 16 April they were aware of the position, because a notebook found on the captured Austin Stack contained 'a draft of a memorandum, prepared for signature by all available members, which called' on De Valera 'for a general laying down of arms'. Stack's hand written memorandum mentioned 'the gravity of the situation of the army of the Republic'; the futility 'of further military efforts' necessitated 'an immediate cessation of hostilities'. It concludes with the Volunteers' requirement to hand in their arms 'pending the election of a government, the free choice of the people.'[23]

Barry said, 'any Civil War is bad. Like within a family – daggers drawn! I believe the Civil War would have been over in three days [initially] if the IRA had acted properly.' The Republicans 'could have won it in Dublin' he hadn't the slightest doubt 'anytime up to June – especially around March, when we

were at conventions and discussions, appointing executive and issuing statements. We had about 30,000 men, and we had arms. If 10,000 were put into
Dublin, we could take over … banks, the railway station, Beggars Bush and the
rest … I have no doubt in the world but the British would come in, and we'd
be forced back into hostilities,' resulting in a lasting final outcome. Those were
his views, he said, 'as a military man'.[24]

Now in May, with Senators Jameson and Douglas acting as intermediaries
between the Free State government and the army council the negotiations
went through stormy passages. The oath was the kernel of the problem. Finally
the decision by the army council (Barry, Aiken, Pilkington) to 'dump arms' and
'cease-fire' which had been given, came into effect on 24 May 1923.[25] An intelligence report with the names of prominent leaders, states 'T Barry is presently
supposed to be in Liverpool'.[26] This information was incorrect.

The ceasefire solved none of the problems brought about by the Treaty. It
only induced a stronger hand by the pro-Treaty party and created more bitterness. Not alone were prisoners not released, but Republican combatants continued to be rounded up to add to the 15,000 by this time already interned. Fearing that they might return to their hidden arsenals, the leaders of the Free State
knew what was already occupying prisoners' minds, and how easy their companions outside could be induced to renew the struggle, so they resorted to a
firm stance.

A Public Safety Act passed by the Dáil in June allowed anti-Treatyites to be
arrested without trial. As this was a body blow to Republicans, there were those
who tried to save 'the fighting men'. Tom Barry sent an appeal 'as a matter of
extreme urgency' to the IRB Supreme Council 'to intervene' and use 'its influence to stop the now unnecessary and therefore vindictive pursuit' of IRA members countrywide 'by the Free State troops'. The members 'had dumped their arms
for the most part', he wrote. 'Irrespective' of allegiance to 'one side or the other'
he wanted men saved 'for future work for the Republic'. A few weeks later he
sent a document signed by Tom Crofts, Thomas O'Sullivan and himself to Frank
Aiken C/S (20 June) stating that they, as executive members, would have to 'appeal directly to men if something was not done immediately to secure immunity from arrest.' This 'document' Aiken maintained, was 'a threat' and an
'accusation' of 'government [Republican] and army neglect of duty'. Consequently, he issued an order (No. 20, 24 June) 'pointing out that any man who attempted to usurp the powers of the proper authorities of the army would be
severely dealt with.'[27]

This order was read and discussed at a 'government and army council'
meeting on 30 June. Barry said 'he had no intention of accusing government
and army council of neglect of duty, and read a letter, which he was sending to
army officers who had seen a copy of his letter to C/S'. In the letter he explained
that though he often disagreed with 'the government and army council' policy
he believed that they 'had always done their best for the country and the army.'

Discussion also centred on a memo Barry had sent to the president of the Republican government (De Valera) on the destruction of arms. All, 'with the exception' of Barry were 'strongly against destruction of arms'. Barry believed that this gesture could help ease the plight of prisoners awaiting execution as the execution of prisoners went against all his beliefs of the code of war.[28] Barry had made 'The Leinster House Proposals' – an army council confidential document.

During the June exchange, when Barry 'realised that militarily' they were sending a signal of defeat, he asserted that a way could found to turn it into 'victory'. Being against the Treaty from its initiation, he proposed 'that a picked force of Volunteers should rush and capture Leinster House and all its occupants' thus putting 'an end to the Free State government'. De Valera and Aiken questioned him 'as to the feasibility' of the operation. In Barry's 'considered opinion' it was 'quite feasible'. He 'offered to take personal charge of the attacking party'. If agreed, it would bring 'a successful conclusion' to the war 'from a Republican point of view.'[29] To 'occupy Dublin for an honourable exit for our defeated force … would not have altered the result, but would have redeemed our defeat and thus hastened the Republican resurgence,' Barry wrote. As Barry generally thought actions through, it is unlikely that this was an impulsive decision. Aiken C/S opposed these 'Leinster House Proposals'.[30] Barry wrote later:

> At this time [April – July 1923] military resistance to a vastly greater Free State army had spent itself. We were faced with the fact that there were 20,000 Republicans in jails, whilst only a few hundred men were left in arms throughout the country. Added to this seventy-eight of our soldiers had already been executed and further batches were awaiting their legal murder, having already been notified. This slaughter would have continued whilst the Free State Government had the slightest pretence of armed resistance to justify it. To implement the Cease Fire and Dump Arms orders Mr De Valera proposed the setting up of a Government and Army Council. This was agreed to … The duty of the Council was to stop the war in the most advantageous way possible for the Republican Movement; to save the lives of our men awaiting execution; to preserve Republican morale and to control and co-ordinate all efforts by Republican and military bodies towards a Republican resurgence.[31]

Barry's document of 'immunity from arrest' came to a head at an army executive meeting, held on 11 and 12 July 1923 when Aiken 'pointed out that those officers [including Barry] had threatened to take action' without army approval. Unusual for Barry, he was late for the meeting. Apparently, he wanted the discussion to proceed before his arrival. However, the meeting 'decided to defer further discussion in order to ascertain if Comdt Gen. Barry would attend.' During a lengthy discussion Aiken put it to Barry that unless he obeyed Order No. 20 he would have to ask him to resign. Barry said he would resign from the army executive council and tendered his resignation in writing. Obviously he had anticipated this, as he had his letter prepared:

1. Accept my resignation from the Army Executive Council, Army Council and as an Officer of the I.R.A.
2. Lest my resignation may be interpreted (sic) as a result of my wanting to compromise, I wish to make it clear in this as in former communications, that any policy I suggested was suggested only if the majority of the Executive decided that such policy did not (a) compromise any National Principle. (b) Deny the right of any future party to prevent by force of arms if necessary the functioning of any Government not based on the complete independence of Ireland.
3. I also wish to state that the rumours propagated in some cases by Republicans as to my negotiating for peace with the Free State, are absolutely false. Lies, suspicion and distrust are broadcasted, and I have no option but to remove myself from a position wherein I can be suspected of compromising the position. I have never entered into negotiations for peace by compromise with the Free State.
4. I cannot withdraw my responsibility in sending you the signed communication with the three Div. O/C's. I believed then and now, that we are bound to arrange for the safety of our men by every means in our powers, once a/b of Par. 2 are not infringed on. I admit a technical breach of discipline, but I do not withdraw my act.
5. When arms are taken up again in a fight for the complete independence of Ireland, I will again be available for service. Should it be decided at any future date that the Executive should have to bear any responsibility for any acts of our Army committed in the war, I should like to be included.[32]

Chief-of-staff, Aiken asked him to reconsider his decision and 'withdraw his resignation'. But Barry was not for turning. So the meeting 'unanimously agreed to accept it'.[33] Before the meeting closed Comdt P. O'Brien was elected to fill the vacancy due to Tom Barry's resignation.[34]

A decision to hold a general election on 27 August made the Republican position difficult, as they hadn't accepted the terms of the Free State.[35]

De Valera and his party contested the election under the banner of Sinn Féin. But, while in Ennis on 15 August addressing his constituents, shots rang out, one got him in the leg, another, aimed at him, hit and wounded Cumann na mBan member Peg Barrett, who had jumped on the platform to shield him when gunfire erupted. He was arrested and spent eleven months in prison.[36]

Winning 63 of the 153 seats, Cosgrave (Free State) was returned to power. But it was a shock to his party to discover that he had only a majority because De Valera's party of 44 were either in prison or refused to take the oath.

The government was faced with a problem when prisoners in Tintown, Dundalk internment camp had gone on hunger-strike. Many of Barry's former Volunteer comrades had already fasted 40 days – including Jim Kearney and Timmy Sullivan. (Both were participants in the Beál na mBláth ambush during the Civil War when Michael Collins was fatally shot – they were among the last prisoners to be released in 1924.) The situation was serious. Republican chief-of-staff, Aiken reported to his executive: 'After the elections the enemy offensive to treat our prisoners as individuals and as criminals began. The Mountjoy prisoners suffered the worst as they were subjected to very brutal treatment.' Aiken ordered that all Volunteers should do their best 'to arouse indignation among the people' and 'demand their release'. Kilmainham prisoners like the others who were interned continued their hunger-strike for over 30 days.[37]

The prisoners had asked the army executive for permission to hunger-strike. But during discussion at 11 and 12 July meeting, it was unanimously decided that hunger-striking was a matter for individuals.[38]

In October, Barry who had previously resigned from IRA/GHQ army council and executive, but still remained an IRA member, wrote to Frank Aiken CS. 'I feel it is my duty to offer my help in any way I can … Men's lives are again in danger and whatever past opinions may be as to tactics and policy, I believe it is the duty of every Volunteer to co-operate and help in every way he possibly can. The fight in the jails looks as if it will be the most important yet fought and surely if the men inside are to fight until the end, we outside should also be in it.' He offered his assistance in 'some way other than being simply "on the run".'[39]

Frank Aiken responded with 'delight' to Tom's offer of help. 'I knew you would be coming along once there was something doing'. He believed that the men intended 'to stick it. The Staters are finding themselves between two stools at the present time, because if they release the men, we win, and if they keep them on till some of them die, we win'.[40]

Already Eoin O'Duffy, garda commissioner, was concerned that the country was in 'a disturbed' state. In listing the countrywide areas that were creating problems he named Tom Barry among those in West Cork as a 'prominent' leader 'of the forces of disorder' and suggested that the Free State army establish 'military posts' linked with 'mobile columns' and 'a system of night patrols'.[41]

Barry told Aiken that 'matters were getting fairly warm' down in West Cork where 'several battalions of Staters are trying to get us'. With other officers he was 'arranging resolutions of protest' and 'putting pressure' on 'certain individuals (such as sec. and chairman of ITGWU) … to bring pressure to bear on the Staters for the release of the men.' With 300 men on hunger-strike, Barry said, 'the majority will stick it and that will mean the deaths of most of our very best in jail'. In a long letter to Aiken, Barry said if men 'died, our fighting men' will continue with 'greater determination' against 'a tyranny whose objective is to wipe out all Republicans'. If the hunger-strike is not responded to 'it is the beginning of the end but before the end comes we will have to fight again' and 'next time the gloves will be off. At least mine will be. I had not them off in the last campaign'. Meanwhile 'as to what our work will be it is for you to say what you want done'.[42] When two prisoners, Dinny Barry and Andy O'Sullivan, died, the hunger-strike was called off. Some men were very weak and had already been fasting for up to forty days.[43]

In November 1923, Barry turned down Frank Aiken's (C/S) offer of deputy chief-of-staff of the IRA. 'Considering that the experience gained by a majority of all units in our organisation for the past five years is equal if not more so to that of mine,' he wrote. 'I think it only fair to state that I would be doing an injustice to the organisation in general by taking on work I don't feel equal to. However, I shall be only too pleased to give any assistance in local

Batt. or Division.'[44] Frank Aiken was disappointed because he 'considered he was' suitable and that the O/C First Southern Division should 'definitely have him attached to Cork No. 2 Brigade.'[45]

On 20 December 1923, 'acting on information received that Tom Barry would not be pursued further he and another officer decided to make a test case of themselves and accordingly appeared at a Cork County Council meeting.'

Barry with Tom Hales ascended the staircase; both were walking along the corridor towards the public gallery when they were 'accosted'. Tom Barry was taken into 'one of the military offices' and held. Tom Hales remained in the corridor. During his detention Barry stated that he had been 'a member of the Executive Council during the war against the Free State and that he accepted the responsibilities that his participation and his post involved. Furthermore, that he neither apologised for nor regretted any of his actions during that period.'

Despite rumours to the contrary, he did not, according to Tom Crofts, 'directly or indirectly' use any influence to procure immunity from arrest.' After four hours he was released.[46]

A number of prisoners were released due to pressure on the Free State government from 'neutral' sources. However, once the hunger-strike was over, the rounding-up – 'internment without trial' – continued well into 1924 (the bulk of Republicans were finally released when De Valera was released in July). Barry now remained 'on the run' until stability reigned once more. During this period he was sometimes in Dublin. When in West Cork he periodically stayed in the Kealkil area near Bantry, billeting in houses where his wife Leslie was also accommodated.

Always on the move, he travelled countrywide on IRA activities. In January 1925 when he was in Clonmel he was 'informed that there was a girl lying wounded' in hospital from a bullet wound 'hit by the Staters' on the night Carrick-on-Suir was captured, (9 Dec. 1922). She had been delivering a dispatch 'was called on to halt by Staters but refused'. Barry wrote to Frank Aiken, 'I feel rather responsible, being the officer in charge of the attack on the town... she is now under notice to leave the hospital as she is unable to pay.' He spoke to the doctor and matron and agreed to take responsibility for her expenses and suggested to Aiken that 'the army' would advance her '£30 or £40' and then 'the question of compensation' with the White Cross should be arranged.[47]

Liam Deasy was released with all other prisoners in 1924. Because it appeared to the IRA men that his document calling for 'unconditional surrender of arms and men' issued from jail during his captivity had indicated weakness in the Republican ranks to the Free State government, he was, upon release, subjected to a court-martial for treachery. Before going on trial he was allowed to pick somebody to defend him. His choice was Tom Barry. In Dublin in January 1925 he was charged with 'cowardice and treason'. He 'made no defence to the charges'. Barry spoke very forcibly for Deasy.

Deasy was found guilty and sentenced to death. Barry made a 'plea for mitigation'. He stated that the man 'who touched a hair on Deasy's head' would have 'to reckon' with himself. He stressed that 'enough blood had been lost for wrong reasons' and that the Irish people had enough unjust deaths on their hands. 'The death sentence' was 'commuted to "Dismissal with ignominy from the Irish Republican army".' He 'was expelled from the IRA for ever'.[48]

Deasy's reprieve somehow caused resentment among colleagues. For whatever reason, this resentment built over the years. But it was only in the latter days of their lives that Barry and Deasy, two friends, became embroiled in a public controversy.

Tom, like all his comrades regretted the Civil War, because of the legacy of bitterness it left in some areas. He said that though there were not too many casualties during the Civil War, yet 'we all lost dear friends and we'll never forget them, and we won't forget the Civil War … In Cork we did not keep up that bitterness … The average fellow who was in the Free State army and who went in for a motive that wasn't savage, I understood and became friends with these men within fifteen years.'[49]

For Tom Barry the war was over. The warrior with all the heroic attributes could get rid of his guns, but he would only bury them where he knew they could be retrieved because Ireland was not yet united under one flag.

'GOAL FOR THE DECLARATION OF A REPUBLIC'

Order was restored in the Free State by the end of 1924. The ideals of many Republicans were shattered. Released from jail to face unemployment, their best option was the emigrant ship, mainly to America or Canada. Large numbers of those who had fought, especially on the anti-Treaty side in the Civil War, without counting the cost, decided to make a new life, in what had been known to their forefathers as, 'the land of opportunity'.

Tom Barry had been married since the autumn of 1921 but had not seen his wife Leslie more than a few dozen times as he had been 'on the run'. At last peace reigned, but not for too long because Tom Barry, the soldier, had begun a job for his country which was not completed to his satisfaction. However, his next task was to get work to support his wife who was living on private means – staying mainly with the Barrett family at Killeady near Crossbarry. Up to now his only job had been soldiering, and he admitted he would have left with all the others on an emigrant ship for the USA and taken his wife with him if he had had the money. He obtained a job with Cleeves Milk Company, based in Limerick. He spent some time there and also at a branch in Clonmel. Leslie had considered 'buying a pub and general shop in Bandon' in 1922. At the time her friend Jennie Wyse Power 'was very sorry' for Leslie. 'Talk about marrying in haste'.[1] However, it does appear that neither Leslie nor Tom had any regrets, they were prepared to live this turbulent way of life.

During 1925, because of insufficient American funds, there was a cutback in all Republican activities. Though some of the IRA executive (men like De Valera, Aiken and Lemass) had been placing their sights on a political arena, a large number of men including Tom Barry, Seán MacBride, Maurice Twomey and others remained apolitical.

On 14 November a general army convention opened in Dalkey. A new constitution and a new direction, mainly the work of Aiken, was drawn up. The soldier in Barry again began to stir. There was a strong condemnation of the failure of the army council to continue to train; he suggested that 'A definite time be laid down within which a revolution shall be attempted, say five years.'[2]

Peadar O'Donnell in a resolution demanded that 'the army of the Republic sever its connection with the Dáil, and act under an independent Executive, such Executive be given the power to declare war when in its opinion, a suitable opportunity arises to rid the Republic of its enemies and maintain it in accordance with the proclamation of 1916.'[3]

A stampede almost broke out when Mick Noel Murphy, CO Cork No. 1 Brigade urged a positive vote on Peadar O'Donnell's motion to save the IRA from the jaws of Leinster House. Barry supported him and the motion was carried. A new army council was elected with Andy Cooney as chief-of-staff getting an implicit mandate to lead the IRA back from the steps of Leinster House to the field of battle.

After the convention many important IRA men were arrested and in jail, and so the new executive (following a plan by George Gilmore) carried out a dramatic rescue in November, freeing 19 prisoners from Mountjoy. An extraordinary Árd Fheis of the Sinn Féin executive, held on 9–11 March 1926, brought about a split and a new departure from the Republican movement. Both factions had the same objectives, but could not agree on the means of achieving them. A majority of Sinn Féin did not want a split. De Valera resigned as president, withdrew from Sinn Féin and set about organising his followers into a new party, later to be known as Fianna Fáil, in preparation for entering the Dáil – once the problem of the oath to the British crown had been removed.

The army council, of which Barry was again a member, suggested proposals for co-operation between the army council, Sinn Féin and Fianna Fáil hoping to halt the split in view of the forthcoming election in June 1927.[4] Barry was in touch with Dr P. McCartan regarding the IRA and co-operation with other Republican bodies for the achievement of 'unity in Ireland for the cause of Ireland' for which he had fought.[5] Peadar O'Donnell also made efforts to salvage something from the 1927 political split. The Fianna Fáil executive found the proposals 'unacceptable'. Nevertheless the army council pursued the issue and wrote specifically to De Valera in the belief that co-ordination between Fianna Fáil, Sinn Féin and Óglaigh na h-Éireann would present 'a favourable opportunity of defeating the Free State parties at the election'.[6] Efforts to weld together the Republican parties were unsuccessful at this juncture.[7]

A significant change took place when De Valera led the Fianna Fáil members (having won 44 seats) to Leinster House on 12 August. He pushed the Bible aside, signed his name and passed through the portals towards power.

However, the IRA, since the dumping of arms in the previous years, reorganised, maintained the structure and kept contact with Clan na Gael in America. Due to its organisational ability the IRA was now a strong underground revolutionary force. Army council meetings and GHQ conferences continued, with talented men like Tom Barry, Moss Twomey, Mick Price, Seán MacBride and several others, promoting ideas and all agreeing that the achievements of the past must hold the key to the future.

Barry, with Seán Buckley, decided that the past should be remembered and set about organising a parade through Bandon, but the chief superintendent of the gardaí warned them that he wouldn't be responsible for the number of men killed as parades were officially banned. Deciding the time was not yet right, the men abandoned their idea.[8]

When members of the general army convention met in January 1929, they found themselves confronted with problems similar to those they had faced at the previous convention. New men like Frank Ryan were admitted; but the inner circle still contained strong militaristic men like Barry. Out of this old group many strands of opinion developed and new groups were formed.

Down in West Cork as the early 1930s dawned, Barry was no longer content to leave the arms in the dumps, so he intensified his secret drilling. Events were taking a turn for the worse. In Dublin, in January 1931, P. J. Carroll was shot and in Tipperary Superintendent Curtin was shot.

An old IRA comrade, Flyer Nyhan, was being buried in Clonakilty and Barry organised a 'firing party', though the use of firearms was prohibited. Following the funeral those in the firing squad were arrested and tried some days later in court. Barry, who was in command but not in the (visible) possession of a gun, was not arrested, but sat in the gallery listening to the trials. Upon hearing the judge passing a sarcastic remark about Barry and his flying column, the incensed Barry, overflowing with aggression, shouted 'You shoneen bastard!' leaped from the gallery and landed on the judge's back, thus earning a few months in prison for himself.[9]

He was out in time for the big rally held on 21 June to commemorate Wolfe Tone at Bodenstown – an opportunity to display the extent of the IRA strength.

In October 1931 the Cumann na nGaedheal government declared the IRA and several other organisations to be unlawful, and followed this by setting up the 'Special Powers Tribunal' consisting of five military officers. This, with an election looming, strengthened Barry's hand and those in the military IRA wing, to focus on getting De Valera and his party into power.

In late 1931 and in the early days of 1932 Barry had many men in secret military training; these were young boys during the War of Independence. John O'Donovan, whose brother Pat had been one of the men at Kilmichael, was only nine years old in 1921 when he was taking a message for the IRA and was almost caught in cross-fire between them and the Tans. Ten years later he remembers Barry telling them where the 'dumps' were and instructing them to secure the arms.

'We were out in the fields training and our target practice was a poster of Cosgrave – his electioneering poster. His nose was the bull's eye. The weeks before the 1932 election we were under intensive training' under Barry.[10]

This was a crucial general election, as it meant the installation of Eamon de Valera whom the Republicans – the anti-Treaty element – recognised as their leader. They firmly believed that not alone would it mean a change of government, but also that the army, the police force and the civil service would all be under Republican control.

During his electioneering, De Valera promised the IRA that if elected political prisoners would be released within hours of his announcing his cabinet. Also there was pride, born out of the bitterness of Civil War, involved in the fighting through the ballot box of this election. If that did not succeed, as far as Barry was concerned, they would again resort to arms – they would make it quick and decisive. They were ready. Cork was ready.

Dan Cahalane says West Cork was well organised by Barry, though the matter has been kept relatively secret over the years. 'I remember well,' he says, 'on the night that the results of the election were being announced. Donovans in Drominidy was one of the few houses who had a wireless, and we were all there ... People were hanging from the ceiling. When the ten o'clock news came, a cheering wave of relief gushed through the house and the yard. However, we waited for the late news before we went home happily to our beds.'[11]

With De Valera back in power the military tribunal was suspended and the declaration orders, that made the IRA, Saor Éire and other organisations unlawful, were revoked. Barry and Seán Russell 'believed De Valera would re-declare the Republic and resume the *national advance.*'[12]

On all fronts De Valera moved rapidly. He introduced legislation to remove 'the hated' oath of allegiance and informed the British that his government would no longer pay the Land Annuities. The British government reacted by putting higher taxes on Irish products exported to Britain, and so the 'Economic War' began.

Against this background an association comprising ex-members of the National Army – the Army Comrades Association – came quietly into being. This organisation was strongly pro-Cumann na nGaedheal and moved toward the formation of the militant Blueshirts.[13]

The IRA continued to drill. They felt that now was the time to push forward for a 32-county Republic, and amongst its strong advocates were men like Tom Barry and Peadar O'Donnell.

Again the men in West Cork drew Tom into military matters. Seán Buckley approached him and told him that 'a chap' named Tadhg Lynch was 'anxious to get in touch' with him 'with a view to re-organising the Old Cork 3 Area of the IRA'. After Barry met some young men he told CS Moss Twomey, 'in short, some of them wanted me to go out and get the organisation restarted in that area.' He suggested that Twomey should send somebody from GHQ, so that an organiser and staff be appointed 'as a first attempt' at 're-organisation'. Tadhg Lynch was ready to take over the mantle, and Barry suggested that Lynch be appointed 'official organiser'. Seán Buckley and Barry agreed to meet a group some evening. 'It is not my mission to do anything to prevent the extension of the organisation', but to continue 'with the maintenance of the army until freedom is achieved', Barry wrote.

However he would not accept 'a social programme' at present being mooted, as the IRA's aim. They had 'no moral right to make war' on this issue. (Peadar O'Donnell had advocated this view.) 'I am ready again to take up arms against any government which is not based on a suffrage of a free people, I am not prepared to do so if the objective is a government by any section to enforce any particular social code,' Barry wrote. War for 'complete independence of the country' was justified but he could not accept the right of any organisation 'to make war' to obtain a 'social programme against the wishes of the majority of the people'.

Barry felt obliged to let Moss Twomey 'know' his views, otherwise, he said, 'I should not feel quite honest.[14] A series of communications between Moss Twomey, Mick Price and Barry were pursued to establish the appointment of Tadhg Lynch as an IRA organiser in Cork.[15]

In early July, at De Valera's request, Barry had 'one and a half hours conversation' with him in Cork regarding 'National Defence' – the organisation of 'a volunteer force by the Free State'. Barry, favourable to the suggestion, maintained that this could bring Fianna Fáil 'up against the British government', leading to a positive outcome regarding the north of Ireland. However, Barry 'would not rule out the possibility of armed conflict developing'. He suggested that 'the IRA executive should consider the question of forming part of the new force.' Though not a member of the IRA executive at the time (until later in the year), he 'promised Mr de Valera that he would meet the IRA executive and [then] let him know their views'.[16]

On 15 July, 1932, Barry went to Dublin, put forward his views on the De Valera meeting to the army council, and suggested 'the development of close co-operation between Fianna Fáil, IRA and Labour bodies to meet the crisis' as 'the situation must be met by political action'. Members would not agree to 'the abolition of the IRA' or its' fusion with Free State forces because they were 'bound to maintain the separate existence and independence of the army'. Moss Twomey, CS, found it difficult to convince Barry of the feasibility of any other action except 'a united military organisation'. Barry explained that his wish was for 'a new force', taking in the existing IRA, for full control 'to be used politically to force any government to declare the Republic.'[17]

Barry met Aiken, but De Valera was unable to keep a further appointment. On the night of 16 July 1932, Tom Barry, Frank Aiken, Seán MacBride and army council members met. Barry instantly suggested 'the forming of a military organisation under the Free State ministry of defence, to meet the crisis with the British'. He 'pleaded' that should 'a military clash' arise the best 'gesture to steady the country' would be 'a force which the IRA would join'. The army council suggested that 'the situation could best be met by political agreement' as 'a military force if formed is not enough'. They found Aiken, who spoke on behalf of the government, 'cautious'. He 'offered very little information' but 'hoped the IRA would see their way to join'. Next day, Sunday, Barry again met the army council; he said he was not 'advocating' the dissolution of the IRA nor of the body 'joining the Free State army'. The force he contemplated 'would not be a Free State army', but 'the force should recognise the Free State government and submit to the authority of the ministry of defence'. Barry's optimism was high. The present government he felt 'was travelling as fast as could be expected to the stage when the Republic could be again proclaimed and function.'[18]

Arising out of these exchanges, Fianna Fáil stated 'that they should retain control and responsibility … they could not accept any other organisations or bodies interfering.'[19] Barry was disappointed that the 'advances were not received in a better spirit'. He proposed the setting up of 'an anti-British committee comprising two representatives from each of the following in all districts – IRA, Sinn Féin, Fianna Fáil, Labour and ex-IRA. It could be called an anti-imperialist committee.' Their tasks 'would be to arrange meetings, propaganda, boycotting, picqueting (sic) of British papers, shops selling British goods and more direct action when suitable and required,' he wrote. 'If you think that my suggestion would lead to the formation throughout the country of a strong body … to be used as a lever towards the restoration of the Republic' then he would 'gladly' help. Most important was that 'Republican policy will be the dominating influence'.[20]

Barry was extremely angry with an article by Patrick Murphy in the *Sunday Express* the gist of which proffered the view that though De Valera 'corrects' the dissidents 'quietly he and his government pretend not to notice'. It was, he wrote 'the real IRA … who accepted the Treaty'.[21] The next day Barry wrote to Moss Twomey and told him that Patrick Murphy should 'be taken for a drive and given a dam (sic) good hiding … put on board' at Dun Laoghaire as his only chance – 'deportation' and 'burning of his paper'. The editor should be informed of his 'scurrilous production' and boycotted henceforth.[22]

By August 1932 Barry was happy with Fianna Fáil and believed that the party's views would concur with his own. He now wanted 'a final effort' to 're-unite … all Republicans – all struggling for the same goal'.[23] Tom worked for the Cork Harbour Board by day, but in all his spare time he was devoting his energies towards IRA activities.[24]

In a letter to *An Phoblacht*, Barry set out to correct a report that he 'asked young men present' at a commemoration in Dunmanway and 'who were not volunteers to join the Irish Republican army'. Controversy arose between the reporter and others as to what Barry actually said.[25] Barry further clarified for Moss Twomey the comments he had made, wherein he had asked that people should get their TDs 'to clearly understand that the people wanted the Republic restored now – not in ten or twenty years'. He wanted all 'women and the heads of families' to boycott British goods'. The IRA 'could only help by organising, arming, training and disciplining themselves, because in the last analysis of any situation arising out of a struggle between Ireland and England, it was the armed men who counted.'[26]

A period of unrest, the result of a combination of the bitterness left by the Civil War and the uncertainty of the political situation, prompted De Valera to get a clear mandate from the people by suddenly calling a general election for 24 January 1933. Barry again supported De Valera and held intensive drilling operations throughout Co. Cork. With IRA support De Valera's strategy worked.

Concern that the Free State Volunteer force being established, would 'sweep unattached youths into its ranks' had Barry proposing a motion at the March 1933 general army convention, that the IRA should notify all Fianna Fáil TDs of their objection to such a body. However, this motion was replaced by a decision to increase IRA recruitment efforts.[27]

At this time (March 1933) Barry was concerned that banks were putting 'pressure' on farmers. Four farms 'in the Upton district' outside Bandon were to be seized and offered for sale. Two of the farmers were 'ex-IRA'. The United Farmers Protection Association under the chairmanship of Tom Hales was helping them. But because of influences by others who were outside this association, Tom Barry felt the IRA should 'take a hand in the matter'. Already he had 'interviewed the solicitor to the bank at the request of and in the presence of the farmers concerned. I told him [solicitor] that neither sales nor seizures would be allowed and I also pointed out that he had already grabbed three farms himself, whilst acting as agent for the bank.' At a meeting of the Farmers Protection Association to be held in Cork, Barry with IRA members Tadhg Lynch and Tom Kelleher wished to attend. He informed Moss Twomey, CS, that they should 'take the lead ... as we are the only organisation who can crystallise and develop opposition to evictions', he wrote. The meeting could also be used to get 'people to stand again behind the IRA'. Due to Tom Hales' involvement in politics, he would prefer to get Tom Kelleher elected instead of Hales as chairman of the association.[28]

Moss Twomey told Barry, 'we need to be extremely careful in enquiring into every separate case of trouble with the bank'.[29] Barry and Kelleher with other volunteers attended the meeting to 'urge popular resistance'.[30] At a further meeting in Bandon where Barry was not in attendance, he heard reports that Tom Hales, TD, 'spoke disparagingly of the IRA' and stated that the 'present executive' was 'a harebrained lot'. Barry wasn't sure if the events were correctly reported to him. But he wrote to Tom Hales spelling out the position – 'if you cannot refer to the volunteers in a fair manner, omit all reference to the Irish Republican army'. Tom Hales did not attend the next meeting.[31]

A few days later Barry wrote to Moss Twomey: 'the banks are making offers of settlement in most cases at half the original debt. We have taken no further action ... but we are watching how matters will develop.' Barry was out most week-nights and all Saturdays in IRA 're-organisation' in West Cork villages. He compiled a *Programme for Training Camps*. 'One thing I am certain of is that we must now set out to show up the Fianna Fáil party for what they are'. He was organising 'boycott' meetings after Mass, holding parades on Sunday afternoons and arranging for 'Easter Lily sales'. (Organisation in places such as Innishannon, Ballineen, Bantry, Castletownbere, Myross, Ardfield, Rathbarry with 'speakers' at each venue kept him working non-stop.)[32]

Barry observed that there was 'great disillusionment taking place in the minds of the more sincere members of Fianna Fáil.' The army council should 'take advantage of it'.[33] Later in the year Moss Twomey told Joe McGarrity that the Fianna Fáil leadership suffocated the United Farmer's Association proposal to organise a conference of Republicans which led to Tom Hales resigning his Dáil seat.[34]

All of Barry's spare time was spent in IRA activity. With other Volunteers he was in Catletownbere, Bantry, Kealkil establishing training units which led to '40 officers and all the arms' available, assembling for a training camp. In correspondence to 'All Units' in West Cork, Barry advised them that the training would commence on Saturday and Sunday 27 and 28 May, and he wanted arms cleaned, and assembled. 'If any man is victimised owing to his being called up for training, notify me at once and the army will take up his case immediately'.[35] Moss Twomey told him he 'should act very cautiously in this business'.[36] Other areas wanted instructions, including Sligo. Barry told Twomey that he was 'sure' Twomey would 'agree that five minutes demonstration and verbal instruction is, as far as the usual batt. TO [training officer] is concerned, worth any one week's reading of text books'.[37] He wrote:

> We should get twenty hours training at this camp on foot drill, extended order drill, rifle drill, machine-gun drill, revolver practice, rifle-practice (each man will fire one round at a target in our last hour of camp) lectures in organisation, duties of officers, discipline and control of men, movements of troops, etc. In particular each officer will have to take his turn at drilling and moving the remainder of the squads, so as to be qualified to drill and command his own company.

He elucidated the 'great drawback' in 'assembling all our arms and officers without sufficient effective ammunition'. While appealing to the chief-of-staff for arms and ammunition, he wanted to know by return if he had 'any hopes of getting this stuff within a week'.[38]

Barry, with sights on the bigger picture of a United Ireland, first had to uproot the 'disturbing' element to secure a strong army. Inequality in the north of Ireland led him to 'believe there will be no real peace in Ireland until the crime of partition is ended, and until Ireland is again a united nation under one government of the Republic', he wrote.[39]

Meanwhile, the formation of the Blueshirts gave the militant wing of the IRA something to fight about. Barry believed that, as they represented fascism and had sprung out of Free State aspirations, they should be suppressed. Now, he had a cause and an opportunity to enlist young men into the IRA; within his forthcoming training camps he intended to cement the combination of youth with men who had practical experience. He intended changing methods to suit the time. This group soon became known as the 'New' IRA.[40]

At the March 1933 army convention Tom Barry stated that he had a major problem with the Army Comrades Association (ACA) – The Blue Shirts – in West Cork. In outlining how they were molesting IRA, shooting, burning, creating 'a menace' by making daily life difficult, he could find 'no way of handling these fellows but to dump them'. He wanted the convention to instruct the army council to act. While Andy Cooney sympathised with Barry's predicament, he believed that the situation was not as bad in any area as it was in West Cork. Without doubt it was 'very humiliating' to Barry 'to feel that his men are being kicked about,' Cooney said. 'If I were in charge of West Cork, I might be putting forward a proposition such as this.' Cooney opposed a blanket army council declaration 'to dump them' as Barry had suggested but added that in doing so he was aware that 'the prime schemers' in Dublin were allowed 'get off scot-free'.[41]

Disquiet had surfaced in the IRA because of the Catholic bishops' Lenten pastorals denunciation of the organisation. This was brought to the fore at the convention. Though condemnation by the Church was not new to Barry, he expressed disquiet that the Church suggested a link with the organisation and Communism, and argued that it could have an effect on IRA recruitment. Other delegates teased out the subject. But it was found that a socialist policy being pursued by some IRA members was unhelpful.[42] Later in the year in Bodenstown, Moss Twomey publicly denied IRA alliance with Communism.

A march to Government Buildings, as a first major effort of the Blueshirts National Guard, was arranged for Sunday, 13 August 1933. The army council of the IRA decided to attack O'Duffy's marchers, so the Cork IRA men travelled to Dublin. On the eve of the march the government revived Cosgrave's stringent measures of the military tribunal and banned the parade. O'Duffy called off the parade, but Barry and his men paraded. In the heightened atmosphere of tension, police baton charged the crowd who refused to disperse, and Barry was taken away by his comrades with a deep gash in his head and blood flowing down his face.

Under the leadership of men like Eoin O'Duffy and Ned Cronin the Blueshirt movement began to gain momentum. The ensuing result was that Barry and the rank and file of the IRA, especially in Cork under his leadership, 'threw itself enthusiastically into the struggle.'[43]

Leading a precarious life, Barry with some of his comrades decided to take on a Blueshirt element in West Cork. He challenged a fringe group in Clonakilty one evening. He thought he had 'shut them up', and that when word would reach their leaders their activities would be stalled. Barry, Tom Kelleher and the boys then hopped into the car to set out for Bandon. Instantly men piled into another car, followed, and began to shoot. As Barry's car tore past Ahiohill, and Ballinscarthy, through the winding roads of West Cork, Barry and Tom Kelleher with guns out the side-back windows, began to return fire. The driver kept his head. 'It was like prairie driving' as they knocked sparks off the bumpy road, the ditches and the black car behind. They swung around bends in the road, past Manch Bridge and in the straight. Suddenly their followers hit a ditch at Manch. Barry and his comrades shouted to nobody in particular and drove through Bandon without a policeman in sight.

Jerh Cronin remembers Barry's sense of humour in the midst of the tension of this Blueshirt activity. He was explaining why he had expelled somebody: 'Just imagine,' he said, 'a soldier of the Irish Republican army came home half drunk and decided when he saw some old woman with a blue shirt that he'd attack her. And that wasn't bad enough but didn't the old woman beat him. A member of the Irish Republican army to be such a loser!'[44]

Eoin O'Duffy was to address a meeting on the South Mall, Cork, on 1 October 1933 so Barry decided to have a counter-meeting. With several of the old IRA and those of a younger generation from throughout Cork city and county, he organised a gathering of hundreds, and assembled them to march towards O'Duffy's group. Fearing trouble, the gardaí stood six deep.

Jim Kearney was there. 'Barry went up on the platform in the Grand Parade; loud and clear he spoke, "I have broken through cordons before and I'll break through cordons again … battalion! Attention! Left turn!" And he faced us right for the guards. As we marched forward, they turned white. And just as we got to them – real close – he gave us the "Left turn!"' Quick, sharp and decisive – Barry's intention was to let the guards, O'Duffy and the government know that the IRA was still a redoubtable force.[45]

Barry went 'on the run' again. Kathy Hayes recalls a night in Rosscarbery, during this period, when she hid him in a cupboard covered with clothes during a raid. He wore, she remembers, a bulletproof vest at that time.[46]

Jack (Doheny) Lynch recalled being 'on the run' with Barry in 1933. 'We were all members of headquarters staff, and were inside in this house in Morehampton Road. We had no money, nothing much, and Barry always loved to have a bet on a horse. He loved horse racing; if he had money even in later years he'd go to the Curragh. Anyway he said to us, "There are two horses going here today and I think they should win." I don't think I had two shillings. Eventually we made up ten shillings between us. He wrote the docket and gave it to me. I had to steal out.

'The *Echo* came in. The two horses had won, and we got something like £30. That time you'd nearly buy a public house for £30. We hadn't had a drink for months, and never thought of it. So Barry rubbed his hands and said, "We'll go out tonight!"

'We got ready, put our guns inside our pockets, put on our coats and went off. We were in this pub, a swanky pub. Barry never asked us what we'd have. He sat down and called for a drink – brandies all round. We got the brandies and the lad was all, "Yes, sir! No, sir!" Must have thought that anyone calling brandies was very well off! And as he was going away from the table, Barry called, "Give me a packet of Woodbines now please".

'"Jasus," says I. "You made a right mess of it, brandy and Woodbines!" Well he got a fit of laughing.

'Shortly before he died he reminded me of this incident, and the tears of laughter rolled down his cheeks, "Me and my tupenny packet of Woodbines. Jack, didn't I always like my Woodbines!"'

Invariably, Barry talked with an air of confidence about his native county of Cork. 'When we were up in Dublin and we'd hear about something which had happened, he'd give me a slap on the back; "Jasus, they wouldn't do that down below with us, Jack!" He thought Cork was the greatest. He had this

211

type of individual pride and collective pride, and I feel it was this coupled with honour that pushed him forward in such a way as not to let down his own county and in fact gain for them a certain prestige.'[47]

When De Valera gave Col Eamonn Broy the task of recruiting men for an armed auxiliary force (Broy Harriers) to support the garda siochána, there was disquiet among Republicans. Because many were former IRA men with 'good records', Barry declared them as 'the greatest menace'. Conscious of a gradual acceptance of partition, Barry wanted action. 'We should rely on what we can do, not what we can say', he told a March 1934 IRA convention.[48]

On 2 May Barry, now described as 'one of the most famed and colourful guerrilla fighters of the Anglo-Irish war' was arrested and sentenced to jail for a year for possession of arms. He refused to recognise the court and attacked Fianna Fáil for its attitude to the Republic and its betrayal of the IRA.

He was released at Christmas. Deciding you couldn't put a good man down he struck off for Tralee on 6 January 1935, full of fighting spirit. To an assembled audience he lacerated the government, advocating military action.

In September 1934 Frank Edwards had been warned not to go to the Republican congress. Then in January Bishop Kinnane issued a rescript condemning him. He was sacked from his teaching post in Mount Sion, Waterford in January 1935. The IRA issued a statement saying that he wasn't a member. Barry organised a protest group from Cork and with Moss Twomey and Pádraig Mac-Logan held a protest meeting. 'Despite a statement read in all the churches forbidding attendance, over 5,000 attended.' But as the Catholic clergy continued to denounce Barry from the altar, he continued in turn to ignore their utterances.[49]

In March 1935 at a general army convention Seán MacBride introduced the issue of the formation of a political party, but it received no enthusiasm. Instead Tom Barry called on the members to support action within the six counties, within six months. Though consensus prevailed, the proposal was put on hold, when Moss Twomey alluded to the lack of resources.

A tram strike in Dublin, which paralysed the city, presented an opportunity for action. When the government enlisted the army to fulfil the tram workers duties, the IRA stepped in to assist the workers. As tyres were sniped and police were fired upon, the police in a swoop on 26 March detained 43.

That evening when Barry returned home to his wife Leslie in Dublin the gardaí came to the door and arrested him. He was charged for the 'seditious utterances' that he had made in January in Tralee.

Prior to Leslie's visit to 'The Glasshouse' on 24 April he wrote a note while he was 'waiting waiting'. He hoped to slip the note to her 'despite the military police', because his trial was due next day and he wanted her to be there. He complimented her on her Limerick lecture – a report of which he read in the newspaper:

> It was very good and I felt proud of you. Still when I get out you will have something else to do and that will be to love me all the time.

I have no idea how long our sentences will be. However long, please re-member that I shall go through in flying colours and be back to you strong, fit and unchanged. Through all the time I will be in, I shall think always of you and love you all the time. Not love you more than I do now because that would be im-possible ... Au revoir my sweetheart. I shall love you while I live and afterwards if it is possible for humans to do so. I shall be longing to get back to you and there we shall be so happy again. I send you all my kisses and all my love ... My Leslie
Your sweetheart,
Tom.[50]

Next day 25 April he was tried by a military tribunal at Collins' Barracks on the charge of 'sedition, unlawful association, refusal to answer questions and contempt'; he received an eighteen months jail sentence.[51] But he was out on parole by early June.[52]

However, while still in 'the Glasshouse' Frank Aiken, minister for defence accompanied by Vivion de Valera, was at a ceilidh in Dundalk on 13 May. Be-cause of government policy against the IRA, the audience was in a militant mood. When Aiken got on the stage, shouts of, 'Remember the 77' and, 'Up Tom Barry' burst forth. When he began to speak he was again interrupted with cries for Tom Barry. He said 'he did not wish to refer to Tom Barry'. But as the cheers of interruption continued the minister said, 'to those interrupters if they knew the part Tom Barry had taken in the Civil War they would not say very much about him.' After further interruptions Mr Aiken said, 'when the IRA were fight-ing and men were being executed, Tom Barry was running around the country trying to make peace.' The shout from the gallery of 'We must fight' ended Mr Aiken's appearance on stage.[53]

Barry's anger is evident in his response. In early June (out on parole) he sent a letter to all the Irish newspapers. In it he described Mr Aiken's remarks as of 'the meanest kind as he merely suggests to his audience, without defi-nitely stating so, that I was guilty of some dishonourable conduct during the "Civil" War. I demand that Mr Aiken should give details or else publicly with-draw his malicious innuendo.

'Clearly, he attempts to convey to the public that (a) I did not fight in the Civil War ... I leave judgement on that issue as to whether I fought or not to the Volunteers who were on active service with me in Cork, Tipperary and other parts of Ireland during the "Civil War". "The Old IRA" of Cork city and county, many of them supporters of Mr Aiken's party have already refuted Mr Aiken's allegations ... I challenge Mr Aiken to give the name of the person or persons with whom I negotiated or attempted to negotiate [peace]. Should he fail to do so, I demand the public withdrawal of his statement.' Barry elabo-rates his involvement 'as courier' for intermediary Fr Duggan in February 1923 'of copies of certain proposals addressed to individual members of the Army Executive, including Mr Aiken and myself,' which were ultimately rejected. Then 'further proposals' of March led to the 'Cease Fire and Dump Arms Orders'. Barry elucidates in detail the plight of men in jails at that time 'awaiting murder having already been notified.' Furthermore, 'I must stress here the fact that my election' to the Executive and Army Council 'in the "last" week of the Civil War was unanimous and that Mr Aiken actually supported it.

'I deeply regret I am forced into a public controversy over matters which have hitherto been regarded as confidential. I have no intention of emulating Mr Aiken's descent to false innuendoes.' The records of the period should help establish 'our respective opinions', he wrote. 'I resigned from the army executive owing to the adoption by the majority of that body of a policy which permitted the general hunger-strike … Mr Aiken was strongest in the appeals to me to reconsider my decision. Mr Aiken's attack now (12 years afterwards) does not arise out of the Civil War period, but out of present day circumstances.'[54] In his statement Barry stresses that he 'has publicly told younger volunteers that 'two phases' of the war have been fought; 'they will experience defeat' again but they should not give up until 'the connection' with England is broken. (This latter part was only, it appears, published in the *Cork Examiner*.)[55]

Frank Aiken said he had 'no intention of referring to Mr Barry in Dundalk. The remark I made was only drawn from me after long provocation.' In referring again to Barry's 'personal peace offer' and his 'unauthorised activities' Aiken said that Barry 'was not satisfied' with the Cease Fire and Dump Arms because he also wanted the arms 'destroyed'. He turned Barry's words and actions around, saying that it was he who 'forced' Barry to resign as Barry 'would not give an undertaking not to decide for himself when to make war and peace.' While he 'never disputed the fact that he fought courageously in the Black and Tan and Civil Wars' he was asking 'why he postponed resumption of military activities until Fianna Fáil became the government.'[56]

Whether it was to appease Tom Barry or to dampen the military enthusiasm of the young IRA men, his parole from the Curragh was extended for a further week.[57]

Barry in a letter to all the Irish dailies (7 June) wrote, 'I wish to protest at the fact that you did not publish my reply to Mr Aiken in full … I must ask that in ordinary fairness this letter will not be censored by you for publication.' In the letter he states that Mr Aiken 'has extended his attack on me … I emphatically deny the charges which Mr Aiken makes against me in his letter today. There is but one satisfactory way of dealing with Mr Aiken's charges … that is, that a committee of inquiry be set up to investigate all allegations, to receive evidence and publish their findings together with the evidence. I now propose this procedure to Mr Aiken and I am willing to submit to the judgement of the inquiry. There will be no difficulty in getting three or five impartial men who served as officers in the army at that period.'

He sets out a list with which 'the committee' should deal. Among them the fact that 'Mr Aiken joined the Provisional F/S forces in 1922,' drew his pay from the army, up to the Four Courts' attack, returned to Dundalk, became 'neutral' was arrested, escaped and avoided 'the scene' of 'fighting' during the Civil War 'except on one occasion'. That 'he travelled to executive meetings unarmed and thus helped to demoralise the Volunteers who expected a leader to be armed … his wobbling attitudes, indecisions and refusal to take part in armed operations, was mainly responsible for Republican defeat at that time.'[58]

Frank Aiken responded and gave his own record of his actions and again challenged Tom Barry on his record. He asks if Barry, who wanted the destruction of arms in 1923, waited to renew 'his military activities after Fianna Fáil became Government, now advocates re-arming and preparation for another civil war.' Aiken wrote that he, himself, was against the army convention in March 1922, and 'stood against the destruction of arms while the oath remained.'[59] 'I will have no further dealings with Tom Barry', Aiken declared.[60]

Barry in his response expressed his disappointment with Aiken for refusing his offer of 'an impartial committee' to referee charges that he refuses 'to substantiate'. Barry mentions Col David Reynolds, 'Free State GOC of Cork on February 1923' and other officers who could prove that 'at no time' did he 'make an offer of peace to the Free State forces.' He castigates Aiken for incorrectly and 'indecently' using 'the honoured name' of Liam Lynch to 'bolster up his attack on me.' Barry writes that, 'he was conscious of saving the remnants of the army' and 'saving the lives of the men awaiting execution', as this dictated his priority and the stance he had taken at the time. But now, because 'Mr Aiken so vilely attacked me', he wrote, 'I had no option but to take up the charges', and he asked him either to withdraw 'or prove his charges'.[61]

Tom Crofts, army executive officer, in a letter to the Irish dailies stated that in February 1923, 36 men 'in Cork gaol were sentenced to death and awaiting execution.' A number of Cork and Kerry officers including Tom Barry and himself met a deputation sent out by 'fellow prisoners'. Fr Duggan 'interviewed the GOC Cork command, with a view to preventing these executions, but he (Fr Duggan) assures me he was not authorised by either Tom Barry or any other officers to make a peace offer on their behalf.'[62]

Three IRA – James Donovan, Seán Coughlan, Seán MacSwiney – wrote to the daily newspapers contradicting Aiken's statement of Barry's military inactivity 'until the advent' of the Fianna Fáil government:

> We the undersigned, who were officers on the Staff of Cork 1 Brigade, Irish Republican Army, during that period, record the fact that Mr Barry was attached to this Brigade from the time of his return to Cork in 1927, and further that he carried out all duties assigned to him during that time.[63]

Nobody appears to have come to Mr Aiken's rescue. The correspondence closed when a New York Club sent a 'unanimously adopted' resolution 'with regard to Frank Aiken's comment of Tom Barry's record.'

> We the Liam Lynch IRA, Club of New York City, representing the exiled members of the Five Cork Brigades, challenge Frank Aiken or any of his followers to match records with Tom Barry during the fight for Irish Freedom.[64]

In June 1935, when Barry was fighting to keep IRA men out of jail and trying to defend his name, there were serious incursions upon working class Nationalist areas in Belfast, and July became an 'orgy of murder, arson, looting, assaults and sniping in which 13 died.'[65] Throughout July, riots continued, with mainly Catholics being killed, many severely wounded; 'over 2,000 were driven from their homes' and large numbers 'were forced from their workplaces'. Though 12 IRA were arrested there 'was ample opportunity' for its members 'to wage a sectarian war' and as previously 'it refused to do so. Protestants were not shot at or bombed after the rioting had ceased, while Catholics were.'[66] When Nationalist party candidates were contesting seats in November in Northern Ireland British election, Tom Barry spoke in Belfast to 'an estimated 10,000 strong' and warned of 'an approaching war' when the British administration would conscript Nationalists. In such a scenario of being 'tramped down by armed force, the only way to defeat that slavery is with a gun in your hand', he warned.[67]

Barry set out for England to see his friend Jack Doheny Lynch who was OC of the Republican forces in Britain. 'He stayed with me for a week, and it was a great week. We went to Manchester, our headquarters, doing all our travelling at night because it was cheaper and safer. Other places visited were Scotland, Birmingham, Liverpool, London and all over Coventry. Barry had a great sense of humour; we had a few good laughs. I can tell you he took a few chances.'

Barry took Jack Doheny with him to visit his parents in Liverpool. They got a 'grand tea – lamb chops and brown bread, and a grand welcome'. Sitting around the table afterwards, they were having a wide-ranging chat with Tom's mother and father when a family member rushed in shouting, 'There's a police car outside!' The two dived for the back door, cleared the wall and made their escape. That night they moved quickly to the country where they stayed for a few days. Then Barry, well used to slipping through loopholes, hid in a cargo boat and returned to Ireland.[68]

Barry wanted Ireland for the Irish; at least he wanted to see them getting a share in the work that was available. To this end his next target was the Freemasons in Cork, owners of large businesses known to employ only those of their own persuasion, despite consistent requests by influential people to broaden their employee personnel. 'You could never get one step up the ladder while they were at the foot of it,' he said.

On the night of 25 January 1936 the Masons were having a party in the Masonic Hall in Tuckey Street, all happily sitting around their tables, when Barry with a select group of men burst in, smashing the plates, cups and furniture and gave them an ultimatum. 'The incident had the desired effect; they became friendly and employed Catholics after that. Barry was a dangerous man to have on their backs', Jerh Cronin recalled.[69]

Barry lived at this time in Belgrave Place, Cork and on several occasions the house was raided, but the police failed to find him. Den Carey tells of a night when Barry was staying out in College Road and decided he'd like to go to

Counihan's pub as he was to go to Dublin the next morning for an operation for a stomach ulcer. He then insisted on going home. Seán Mitchel and Den Carey were with him.

'Leslie wasn't home. We knew where the key was, so we went in, and as I was about to close the door, two detectives stood in front of us. They looked at us, hesitated and walked away. I'm sure they were afraid when they saw the three of us.'

Instantly the three made their getaway. Den Carey took Barry to Jim Grey in Cobh who was to drive him to Dublin. But before he left Tom insisted on buying a bottle of whiskey, and apparently he drank so much of it that he didn't need the anaesthetic while being operated on! Though he seldom drank during a period of action and was prepared to face any enemy, he had an utter dread of hospitals and operations. However, his recovery didn't take too long – he joked that the whiskey before the operation aided the healing process.[70]

FROM IRA CHIEF-OF-STAFF TO IRA PENSION HUMILIATION

An IRA action squad arrived at Castletownsend-Skibbereen, the home of Vice-Admiral Henry Boyle Somerville, on 24 March 1936 at 9.30 p.m. The 72 year old admiral was well known in the area for giving references to any of the local lads who wanted to enlist in the British navy – an activity the IRA disliked.

Barry, the OC of Cork, annoyed with De Valera's policy of 'filling the jails with committed Republicans', had given the order 'to get' him. Barry, who could be ruthless enough to have given the order to kill him, told me his intention was a kidnapping to be used in a type of deal with the government; he did not elaborate. If Barry had intended having Somerville shot, as happened, he would have admitted it. It is almost certain that Barry anticipated that if pressure was forced, Dev would relent on his steel-type policy-grip, which he had secured on the IRA. However, the plan backfired and Barry had to go 'on the run' again.[1]

A month later another killing, this time sanctioned by GHQ, was carried out in Waterford. The country was shocked when John Egan 'dubbed a police spy' was shot. Fianna Fáil patience was sapped and the ties, which existed, snapped. Plans were prepared to end the IRA's repeated disruptions of normal life, so on 18 June it was declared an unlawful organisation.[2]

Moss Twomey CS was arrested on the 21 May and Seán MacBride was co-opted by the army council as CS. Meanwhile, conflict arose between Seán Russell and Seán MacBride as the routine of politics played second fiddle to Russell's desire to set off bombs in Britain. Barry, who totally disagreed with Russell's suggestion from the outset, was annoyed over 'the loss of two Thompson machine-guns' and wanted 'Russell court-martialled' over the incident.[3]

Though meticulous in other ways, Russell was careless in his account keeping. MacBride, as chief-of-staff, insisted on proper records. Backed by Barry he held a court-martial in the early summer of 1936. The case for misappropriation of funds was proved against Russell 'although everybody knew Russell had never kept a penny for himself but spent it on the IRA.'[4] This incident helped to create further divisions between Russell and the Barry/MacBride faction.

In July the Irish newspapers were reporting disturbances in Spain. By August, Frank Ryan had begun organising Republican Congress people and anybody else interested to fight on the Republican, or 'left' side in Spain. The Blueshirt movement, already split over leadership, found Eoin O'Duffy, looking on the Spanish Civil War as a crusade against Communism, deciding to organise men to fight for the Spanish Nationalists.

Seán Russell, had since 1929, been in touch with Joseph McGarrity in New York, and both were now, 1936, all set for a military action. The Russell plan involved the use of 'explosives with high destructive content (which) if let off in busy English cities would be the best method of freeing "occupied Ireland".'[5]

When the army convention met in Dublin the IRA had two action calls: Russell's British campaign, and Ryan's volunteers for the Spanish Republic.

After a few brief words from a speaker, Tom Barry jumped up on the rostrum and in a fiery speech insisted that the army leadership must act, and act soon. He had a plan of action: move in on a northern town and seize it, occupying buildings as had been done in 1916; move on and take another town. 'Barry, always kept that ultimate goal of a free united Ireland in view'. It could be done, he charged. Russell insisted that they would be destroying Irish property; far better to destroy England and get them on their knees. No. Barry would have none of this. 'That would be like what the Black and Tans did to us here. Why should we kill and maim English citizens? We'll fight them on our own ground. We'll take back our country.'[6]

To appease the fiery men the new army council offered the post of chief-of-staff to Tom Barry, who had been 'on the run' since the spring; if Barry wanted to invade the north, then let him shoulder the responsibility.

'Barry was a good choice. He was well-known and popular in the IRA and outside of it, one of the outstanding soldiers of the Black and Tan War and, as the Army Executive knew, far shrewder than his simple soldier image and far too practical to involve the IRA in any wild northern campaign of the scope proposed for England by Russell's advocates.'[7]

As for Frank Ryan's aid for the Spanish Republic, Barry would not agree. There would be no wild geese. The Volunteers were wanted for action at home, he insisted. Despite this decision, many Volunteers resigned and signed on for Spain. Eventually 400 Irishmen, most of them old IRA, went to Spain: 42 were killed, 12 captured (including Frank Ryan) and 114 were wounded – 'valuable men who could have been deployed in a more lasting, far-reaching service here at home' was how Barry viewed the situation, as he looked back over the space of forty years.[8]

Meanwhile in Ireland, the IRA had turned its attention to Tom Barry's northern campaign. In the north the movement was enthusiastic that at last the discussions and a form of action now centred on the prime enemy, Britain, rather than on antagonising De Valera and his government.

Barry outlined his policy to Joe McGarrity, the Clan na Gael leader in America. He hoped that internal IRA squabbling would be eliminated. 'When that new situation [northern campaign] is created there will be no room in our ranks for disunity or intrigues. With regard to Russell's proposed visit to you, the Army Council has decided that no speaker will be sent to the United States.' Reports by a messenger who returned with news of American help is 'not very encouraging … We can and intend to start without awaiting arrival from your side, but please remember there can be no sustained effort unless you succeed,' Barry wrote. He considered 'the Twenty-Six County people' (Government) as 'the first obstacle to the restoration of the Republic', and wanted McGarrity to tell his Clan members that the 'developments here' regarding the Russell plan, envisage no 'Swan Song'. In this letter Barry makes it quite clear that he would act as a soldier and would not involve the IRA in a bombing campaign in Britain.[9]

In the north of Ireland 'Loyalist extremism had re-emerged in the shape of the Ulster Protestant League' from 1931 onwards. Peadar O'Donnell in an address to the Orange Order in 1934, had appealed to Protestant workers and small farmers to co-operate with Catholics in the struggle for 'the transfer of power over production, distribution and exchange to the mass of the people'.[10] During the July 1935 disturbances, 'more than 2,000 driven from their homes', were Catholics. Sectarian outbreaks developed, and serious clashes erupted. 'While the violence ebbed in intensity after about a week, large numbers of Catholics were forced from their workplaces over the next fortnight.'[11]

Tom Barry and his IRA comrades believed that something should be done to eleviate the plight of their northern counterparts, and that if a 32 county Ireland was established, there would be greater harmony and equality. Back in Cork, 'on the run' and avoiding capture by staying in selected houses, Barry continued to train his men. Having advocated for years that IRA activists should 'engage' the British establishment in the north, Barry, now as chief-of-staff set out to do this. He was picking Cork men for the first round of this northern campaign. Mick McCarthy, Jerh Cronin, Jack (Doheny) Lynch, Den Carey, Jim O'Neill and others remember the intensity with which Barry trained his men. He was training a few hundred in all, coming from a wide radius. Sometimes outside Dunmanway, or on the grassy slopes of Belrose, or out in the Kerrypike, camps were in progress.

The Barry plan incorporated a raid on Armagh Military Barracks with an initial 26 man active service unit with Tadhg Lynch as his adjutant general. Take Gough barracks first and move on to the next 'earmarked' barracks. 'He had us drilled, thoroughly drilled. We had guns. We had ammunition. We'd fight!' Den Carey insisted.[12]

Jack Doheny Lynch, OC, Britain, was brought back from England on Barry's instructions, and sent up north to get the barracks' location, distance from houses and so on. He also had to carry out some military training, and with a nucleus of northern IRA supporters, had secured billets and depots. Barry went north to visit Jack Doheny and he met some local IRA units, visited locations, and sized-up positions for attack. Upon returning, the two, with other officers, discussed the plan.

The Cork men had imported over 500 Thompson guns, so a second group of men were armed, drilled and had full instructions to follow on.[13]

'There were about 100 of us out in Ballinscarthy training in preparation to attack the north which would begin with the taking of Armagh Barracks. We would have been the follow-up group,' said Dr Ned Barrett. 'We were under an intensive course and were told that 10% of us would be casualties; at least 10% of us would not return. We were never called; the raid never came off. I was prepared to die, actually. I didn't want to die, but when Barry told us to be ready, we had to be prepared.'[14]

'With Barry you had great courage, you had no fear. He'd build up your enthusiasm so that you'd feel brave and you'd follow him to the death.'[15]

The Cork Active Service men of the first group were mobilised. They had been to confession, were dressed as civilians and were ready to move on the initial leg of their journey to Dundalk and would be 'ferried northwards from there'. Barry had already organised that 'a large consignment of guns would go ahead of them. Russell was to secure that end of the plan.' For 'security reasons northerners were not involved' in this initial attack.

As the men in Cork waited for starting orders, a message arrived from GHQ to cancel the entire operation. A representative from Cumann na mBan brought the order. GHQ had assumed that outside of headquarters, only an intimate group in Cork and in the north knew of the forthcoming attack. However, they discovered that word had seeped through, and that it was been openly debated in the Belfast headquarters and among Cumann na mBan in Dublin.[16]

Instantly the Armagh raid was cancelled. The great northern campaign was over without a gun having been drawn or a shot having been fired. 'By God, we'd have pushed the British bastards out for good!' said Barry aggressively. 'We'd have taken it if things hadn't gone wrong', Den Carey was adamant.[17]

Jim O'Neill was critical, later, and believed that they should have gone ahead with the plans, regardless.

'It was to be a southern job. This was an effort on Barry's part to show that the south was not forgetting the north. He wanted it done as a spectacular well-timed effort, a psychological blow of strength for the northerners.' This was 'to set a flame throughout the six counties' based on the 1916 GPO strategy, but with better planning.[18]

In the north over the months ahead, spies, informers and others were 'eliminated'. There were an estimated 18 unsolved murders in Belfast between the Black and Tan war and the end of 1936, 'although the IRA' was not 'responsible for all of them.' In addition, disturbances along the border, the burning of Custom Houses on the 'occasion of King George V1's coronation visit to Belfast in July 1937', went ahead.[19]

A sizeable urban base of radical Republicanism in pockets of Derry, Belfast and South Armagh were ready to fight whenever the southern IRA would begin an offensive. These northern activists feared after this 'Armagh fiasco' that the Dublin GHQ 'was willing to leave the north to the mercies of the RUC.'[20] They 'were furious' with the 'calling off ' and it swung 'them firmly behind' the Russell plan.[21]

Jack Doheny Lynch and Barry were in the MacCurtain Hall, Cork, one evening discussing IRA duties. Suddenly someone shouted 'A raid!' Men 'skirted' into a room and were trapped. But Lynch and Barry climbed out the back window, swung on to the roof edge and then up, as the special branch scoured the building. Leading a precarious life at this time, ducking in and out of places, around corners, avoiding arrest, Barry, at times escaped almost by the tips of his fingers.[22]

Russell, feeling bitterness towards MacBride and Barry, left for America and in August 1936 he issued a strong propaganda statement containing forcible language about bombing England, using planes, explosives and other ammunition. Moreover, he wanted to whip up American support for his campaign. Meanwhile, Barry ran into trouble with the Russell followers at GHQ. In the hope of achieving harmony, as IRA chief-of-staff, he had made what he hoped were wise appointments. Peadar O'Flaherty (Dublin quartermaster general) did not get on with MacBride (intelligence officer) and refused to obey orders from the army council. Barry had to get O'Flaherty out, and rely on Tadhg Lynch and Tomás MacCurtain of Cork. But O'Flaherty went down the country seeking support for Russell. Unknown to Barry, Russell had reached an agreement with McGarrity in New York in 1936 on the bombing campaign.[23] Barry was 'shocked' by 'the depths of hatreds which existed between various members of GHQ.'[24] When Russell left for America without army council approval, he failed to tell Barry 'where the army's equipment was dumped'. Barry only knew of 'the Kildare dump' of '12 Thompsons still in US packing cases' when 'the police seized it'. With no resources Barry 'had to borrow £5 from Peadar O'Donnell to send a GHQ officer to Galway' to view dumps there.[25] This added to Barry's frustration.

With Frank Ryan, who returned to Dublin in May 1937, Barry organised a public meeting, though illegal because of the government anti-IRA sanction. 'Historic Liberty Hall was the land mark.' Despite Barry's disagreement with Ryan on the Spanish issue, he backed his Republican spirit and 'the protest against the government's message [of welcome] to King George'. Barry, Ryan and Tadhg Lynch marched with Cumann na mBan members. Scuffles broke out between the police and the organisers – 'the fiercest since 1913'. The police baton-charged the crowded Parnell Square. Sighle Humphreys, Cumann na mBan, 'walking directly behind the IRA', recalled 'the savage way police batoned Tom Barry. I really thought he was finished. He showed the most extraordinary courage that night; he just walked on straight ahead into a solid mass of police with batons drawn'.[26] Barry's 'skull was smashed by a rifle-butt' and he was brought to the crowded nearby flat where many of the blood-covered, baton-charged injured were brought. He does not remember what happened next. Later he ended up in a hospital bed with wounded and bandaged people all around him. 'It was a miracle he survived'.[27]

Meanwhile, Frank Ryan and Tadhg Lynch 'delivered a short address'. Lynch's 'coat and shirt were a mess of blood, but his voice, mind and body were vibrant with the passion of a great work well done.' The police charged again and Lynch, beaten unconscious, ended up in a hospital bed next to Barry.[28] When

Barry woke up, he told Tadhg Lynch 'who was not too bad, to slip out of the hospital and mobilise the Dublin Brigade for the following night with three armed sections.'[29]

Next evening, the various organisations again mobilised their members. Barry slipped out of hospital. The banned meeting was to be held a second time. Paddy Rigney and Donal O'Donoghue spoke. 'When Tom Barry, his head swathed in bandages', mounted the platform, a number of police moved in 'but angry shouts and the pressure of determined men against them made them retreat'. Before a gathering of over 5,000 extending through Cathal Brugha Street, and across O'Connell Street, the applause and cheering was so great that 'for several minutes' he was unable to speak. There were shouts of, 'Up Kilmichael! Up the Republic!'[30]

'Tonight' s meeting is a repeat one,' Barry began, 'to show that the Irish Republican army would march through the streets of Dublin when and how they liked.' He called for the restoration of the Republic and finished with a request 'for the furthering of the unity drive that brought them together until their common goal' of an Irish Republic 'was reached'. Frank Ryan spoke of the pleasure it gave him to be once again on a platform, and especially to be beside Tom Barry. Like Barry, he said he wanted 'Ireland free and united!'[31]

Some weeks later when the draft of the new constitution was released, Barry and his Republican followers disliked the copper-fastening of 'partition' which did not allow for 'equal rights and equal opportunities' which 'make up a free, united and independent nation.' He wrote of his hope that this 'new charter' meant that 'at last the people who had stood for freedom against the British and had stood in arms against their successors – the first Free State government – would now in an ordered national effort be welded into one unbeatable weapon which would break the connection with England, undo the conquest of Ireland and lay the foundations of a free and independent people, recognised by the world as a nation of free men and not British subjects.' The right of Republicans to express their views without a fear of being jailed 'was a right', he wrote. 'I know that the conquest cannot be undone by words or waving the tricolour.' No Republican could 'accept or vote' for the constitution because:

(1) It maintains our status as members of the British commonwealth of Nations, and therefore, purports to legislate for us as British subjects only.'

(2) This Constitution can only be voted on by the people of the Twenty-Six counties. Not alone does it not end partition but it perpetuates it by openly stating that it will only legislate for the people of the area known as Saorstat Éireann: that is the Twenty-Six Counties … It brazenly allows not alone the *de facto* Government of the Six Counties to continue in operation but it seeks to give a moral right to that British statelet to continue.

(3) It does not even express the Irish people's wishes that the British armies of occupation ... should be withdrawn ... If adopted by the Irish people [it] will ensure their remaining here until a strengthened and determined race which will first have to abrogate this document will order them to leave our shores, failing which they will attack them.[32]

All Republican groups were united – Cumann na mBan, Sinn Féin, the Fianna, the IRA, with Tom Barry as one of the principal speakers to unite the group. This 1937 Constitution, Barry said, 'would not give us our freedom' in a United Ireland. 'My name wasn't going to this constitution. We issued a statement saying that all Republicans were to abstain. Actually if we had come out and voted against it, we would have defeated it. If we did, we would have been voting in effect for the imposed British constitution of 1922.'[33] The vote for the constitution was carried and 'enacted by the people 1 July, 1937'. Barry disliked the situation because, he said, 'we were still in the British empire. So my fight was to pursue my goal for the declaration of a Republic.'[34]

At the graveside of Wolfe Tone in June 1937, where Tom Barry was the principal speaker, his words 'spoken not read' had, as always, the total attention of the crowd. Barry could speak for a considerable time without notes and was able to captivate any audience. In Bodenstown he told the assembled crowds that they 'should draw inspiration from the life and death' of Wolfe Tone – 'namely the establishment and maintenance of the sovereign Republic of Ireland.' He asked his listeners 'not to look backwards into history alone' but to take note also of 'the current struggle'.

From all corners of Ireland thousands formed the 'chain of marching separatists' who had come to listen and see the man they had heard so much about, *An Phoblacht* recorded. 'Ten men cycled from Sligo. A contingent cycled from Clonmel. From Dundalk they came by lorry ... Cumann na mBan, Mna na Poblachta, Fianna and Cumann na gCailiní were a colourful space ... again and again the ranks were swept with applause,' the reporter wrote. When the oration finished the reporter passed a group and over-heard 'one [who] asked what about tea! They hadn't the price of it ... This section of the population, the men of no property.'[35]

Some weeks later his friend, Tom Kelleher, was getting married. Barry was best man at his wedding. That afternoon Dr Ned Barrett was walking along Oliver Plunkett Street, Cork, with Jerry Crowley and Tom Barry, who was 'on the run'. Two detectives walked up behind them. One put his hand on Barry's shoulder and said his few words of arrest. Immediately Ned (describing himself as a violent young Republican at the time) made for the detective's throat. Barry shouted, 'Stand back!' Ned took the command, and Barry was taken away to Union Quay Barracks.

'It was suggested in Cork that day that we should rescue Barry. My father owned quarries and had gelignite, and though my father was not a violent man, I said to him that they're thinking about rescuing Barry.

'"Don't be a fool," he said.

'"Will you give me the stuff anyway?" I asked.

'"I appeal to you, don't do anything foolish," he said.

'"I won't, but give me the stuff," I said. Anyway he agreed.'

A meeting was held that night in Jim Counihan's, Pembroke Street, Cork, and according to some men who attended, feelings were very high. Once they had discovered that Dr Ned had obtained the gelignite they wanted to go to Union Quay and blast the barracks to release Barry.

In the midst of delegating people to do the job, Dr Ned jumped up: 'Does Tom Barry want to be rescued?' Nobody could answer the question so it was agreed that they would ask Leslie, Tom's wife, to find out his wishes.

No, he answered. He did not want to be rescued. It was lucky he said so, because it was almost certain a number of lives would have been lost in the attempt. Four days later Tom Barry was released.[36]

Den Carey, Tom's aide de camp, drove him around in an Austin mini. One night returning from a meeting in Kinsale, Barry was seated in the back of the crammed mini. At a sharp bend Carey drove straight into a wall. The car 'folded up like a concertina', but the men who were 'on the run' at the time, got out, stood on the road and thumbed back to Cork.

Another night eight men were packed into the mini. They were 'flying' down St Luke's hill. Carey footed the brakes. Suddenly he shouted, 'Tom the brakes aren't too good!'

Deep from the back seat Barry yelled, 'Jasus Den! I didn't ask you to drive me to heaven!'[37]

Though 'on the run' Barry, CS, went to Germany 'primarily to find out and if at all, the Nazis had penetrated the I.R.A.' because he was convinced that 'the bombing plan' of Britain was 'of course German inspired and financed.'[38] It was not until 'very late in the decade' that Britain through their intelligence agencies, learned of 'the IRA's sporadic contacts with Nazi Germany' initiated in 1935 which made them scrutinise such activities for their own security during the Second World War.[39]

Barry could by now see that the Russell plan was gaining support. He made another effort to counter it. At a convention with McGarrity present (but not Russell) Barry proposed that the Dublin Brigade of the IRA 'should march on the north that night'. The meeting, which lasted throughout the night, ended when the Russell scheme was carried by his supporters – beaten 'by one vote'.[40]

Hand-picked 'delegates from Britain supported the proposal' on the bombing of Britain.[41] It was 'a sour pill for many of the delegates to run counter to Barry whom they looked up to, and who always spoke with an air of authority and common sense.'[42]

Barry had said if the 'bombing' resolution was carried, he would leave his post. So at an army council meeting in Banba Hall, Dublin, he offered his resignation as chief-of-staff, but would remain on the army council executive. He disagreed with the bombing campaign, planned for England; furthermore, as a Cork man he wanted to return to Cork, and didn't really want to remain in Dublin, even 'on the run'. Accordingly, Mick Fitzpatrick took over the position of chief-of-staff.[43]

By April 1938, at a general army convention, which met in Abbey Street, Dublin, Russell and his advocates had ploughed much ground for their cause. Delegates from country areas expressed their impatience at the in-action of the inner circle of the GHQ army council. Barry, MacBride and Mick Fitzpatrick all came in for criticism.

The London bombing campaign was again brought to the fore, opposition to it centred around Barry who had totally condemned it as a foolish idea, 'doomed to failure as the dynamiters of the 1880s'. He wouldn't agree to it 'ethically, morally or physically'. There were, he said, enough British military in the six counties for the IRA to bomb, and that was the place out of which they should be bombed, not civilians in England – such would be similar to what the Black and Tans did in Ireland. In a flurry of bombastic language he asked what the hell's good was going to be gained from bombing cities. 'Leave a bomb in a cloak room, leave a bomb in a hotel, and be 40 or 60 miles away with a time bomb, and you blow to pieces somebody who is working for £3.10 or £3.30 a week!' If they wanted action, he insisted, he would be prepared to take a squad into the House of Commons or House of Lords and get the real culprits – the legislators.[44]

At this April 1938 IRA convention, Russell's supporters won control of the IRA. Russell, who had been court-martialled and suspended in January 1937, was now reinstated and appointed chief-of-staff. Five of the 12 executive members resigned – Tom Barry, Tomás MacCurtain, John Joe Sheehy, Seán Keating and Johnny O'Connor, stating that the army council was unrepresentative of the IRA, and in appointing a 'dismissed Volunteer' as chief-of-staff, had behaved unconstitutionally'.[45] After the formation of a new executive which had a majority committed to Russell, Barry 'publicly walked out' of this convention 'over the passing' of the 'resolution to start a bombing campaign', he told Sighle Humphreys as it was 'inspired and financed by the Nazi German Band of the USA'.[46] He 'could not be party to it as it was unethical and immoral'.[47] Moreover, he had no confidence in the new leadership and their scheme was 'unworthy of consideration by the IRA.'[48]

Back in Cork in May, Barry held meetings in the Thomas Ashe Hall, with Cork One (Cork City), Cork North-East, and Cork North Brigades, suggesting they refuse to give backing to the GHQ campaign. He felt they were being led down a road that would only lead to disaster.

By this time an Anglo-Irish agreement gave Ireland possession of the 'Treaty ports' and the Economic War ended.[49]

Barry, tired of being 'on the run' with no means of livelihood and depending on the goodness of his friends, returned to work and was not worried about recapture. During all this period of being in and out of jail, illegal drilling and continuance in the IRA, Tom Barry, though often with long leaves of absence, tried to hold down an executive position with the Cork Harbour Board, whose management was extremely tolerant. Always willing to take a chance and not miss an opportunity, he told Tim Pat Coogan that 'he had taken in arms at Cork Harbour.'[50]

Again he was arrested, but let go after a few days, as there was no specific charge, which could be pinned on him. De Valera may have aided the process as he knew 'how easily Barry could stir emotions in his favour. There were still those who would die for Barry.'[51]

This man, with rock-hard determination, was constantly concerned for the welfare of 'his men', all of whom were like brothers to him. He was annoyed at the 'continued victimisation of those sentenced by the military tribunal' to terms of imprisonment 'chiefly in connection with the national opposition to the Blue Shirt campaign'. The 70 to 80 men who had been employed 'under public bodies were no longer eligible for employment under those bodies' when they returned having 'served their sentences.'

Accordingly, he wrote to Seán T. [O'Kelly] in October 1938 and asked him, as a member of the government, 'to immediately take the necessary steps to remove all the disabilities at present operative' against those men. 'The clause that makes victimisation operative is the most damnable in a most damnable act. Men according to even all criminal law who serve their sentences have again equal rights as citizens, but here under this act, their punishment follows on and they are barred from certain employment.

'Another feature is that a number of men who served in the IRA during both periods of the fight for independence are barred under this act from receiving the pensions for service to which they are entitled.'[52] He quotes the specific case of Tom Kelleher an IRA man who was asked to write for 'pardon' to Mr Aiken, 'and then it might be all right.' This, he found unacceptable. It was Barry who initially insisted that the pension board should be set-up.

On 12 January 1939 the bombing campaign began in Britain with an ultimatum to the British government. The campaign itself was ill-conceived. With technical difficulties and several hitches, it was spread over a 15-month period with high civilian casualties. The final result added up to failure.

'I wouldn't have done the Birmingham job [bombing] if it was going to set Ireland free and flowing with milk and honey,' Barry said in an interview in the *Sunday Independent*, March 1976.[53] It was a tragic failure 'for about 100 decent young Irishmen who were misled completely', Barry wrote to Dr T. Ryle Dwyer.[54]

On 11 December 1939, the trial opened in Birmingham of five IRA men for an explosion in Coventry on 25 August. All five pleaded not guilty. Barry 'tried to force the De Valera government to act', but failed. Though he had drifted from the movement and disagreed with the bombing campaign, yet when he knew that neither Peter Barnes nor James McCormack was guilty of the crime and that they were to be executed, he addressed a massive meeting in Cork, proclaiming their innocence of the Coventry bombing.

He had called the meeting, he said, to explain to the people that the British government did not give a damn and were prepared to hang any two men without a fair trial.

His voice rang through the Grand Parade and the South Mall to 'the largest assembly ever held there' as he told his listeners he had informed the British government that he himself would go to England and would go to prison in their place while a proper trial was being conducted.

Jerh Cronin says, 'The British government wouldn't have it. They had heard enough of Barry in years gone by.'

The two men were hanged on Ash Wednesday morning 1940. According to British Records, 'Barnes and McCormack, for our purposes must be judged as common murderers'.[55]

In 1939 Tom went before the Service Pensions Board to obtain his pension under the Military Service Pensions Act 1934. He had great difficulty and received 'the scandalous award' of $5^3/4$ years approx. Rank B. 'He appealed and submitted statements in support of Rank and Service' from 12 senior officers, including 'An Taoiseach' De Valera and Florrie O'Donoghue. These men in turn were examined 'on oath'; moreover, 'other men testified on oath in Tom's case', and Tom himself testified 'on oath'. Barry's 'Rank and Service' were again being questioned in April 1940 at which time Tom Crofts asked Oscar Traynor, minister of defence, 'Why has Barry been treated like this? That is the question that every officer who is aware of Barry's humiliation is asking. There is the further humiliation to all of us senior officers who testified in writing and on oath as to Barry's rank and service.' Crofts wondered if 'there is any truth in the suggestion that because Frank Aiken and Tom Barry are and have been bad friends in the recent past, certain members of the Board have taken up a hostile and unfair attitude in Barry's case … He has had a rotten deal and his claim is open and above board if there ever was one.' In all the cases that Tom Crofts 'verified' he was 'never once put on oath' except in Barry's case.[56] (See Appendix IV.)

It was not until August 1943 that Barry got a handwritten letter from a Mrs O'Driscoll on behalf of Cornelius O'Driscoll of Woodside New York, who was in Ireland at that time, stating that he [Tom] would receive £15 p.a. payable from 1934 but subject to restrictions of receipts of 'Public Moneys' and further 'deductions'.[57] As his entitlement to a pension was not given with a good will it is understood among his friends that he never availed of a Military Service Pension. His case was 'handled in a totally different manner to that of any other prominent officer,' Tom Crofts wrote.[58]

In a countrywide swoop in the autumn of 1939 and the spring of 1940 a number of IRA were arrested. Active dissidents were imprisoned and detained for the duration of the war.

During this precarious period, Barry got news that his mother had died on 5 March 1940. Though his sister Gert rang a friend of Tom's who had a 'phone and advised for his own safety that he should not 'dream' of attending the funeral, nevertheless, he took a chance, 'a big chance!' Looking, 'the real business man – suitably dressed' he took the boat to Liverpool, then to Allerton cemetery for the funeral. He was 'cautious', left shortly afterwards and 'was sad that he couldn't spend more time with his father and other family members'. Leslie daren't travel with him because as a couple they would be easily identified. Tom was torn at this time and 'wished the situation' between the two countries was different.[59]

Having had a rough passage through the forty-odd years of his life Tom Barry felt the time had come for him to bow out of turbulent activity and settle into married life. However, he was to retain his fighting spirit for years to come.

SECOND WORLD WAR

Winston Churchill replaced Neville Chamberlain as prime minister in Britain on the day that Germany invaded Belgium and Holland. De Valera did not feel that Churchill's attitude would be favourable to Irish neutrality; certainly a speech which he made in 1922 in the House of Commons was looked upon as the ultimatum which helped kick-start the Civil War. In 1938 'he had vigorously opposed the handing over of the occupied ports in Ireland … his general attitude was common knowledge. From the beginning of the war he had chaffed at Irish neutrality.'[1]

De Valera had, in 1939, arranged for the Irish Red Cross to be established in Dublin. A month after its inception a meeting was held in Cork City Hall where the Lord Mayor Alderman James Hickey presided. On this occasion Leslie Bean de Barra, wife of General Tom Barry, became its honorary secretary.

She admitted that enthusiasm was high for the society because there was the anticipation that Ireland would be involved in the Second World War and their services would be necessary. With other voluntary members she studied and took examinations in first aid, hygiene and child welfare. Extremely dedicated and much in demand, she travelled throughout the country giving lectures and organising the Red Cross. In 1941 she was elected as Cork's representative to the Dublin Central Council.

Though De Valera took a firm stand on the question of Irish neutrality he nevertheless was preparing an army which could at least put up some resistance if the country was invaded.

Many of the IRA from the War of Independence years had later taken opposing sides during the Civil War. Now there came a 'bury the hatchet' plea. De Valera asked many of his former Republican friends like Tom Barry, Liam Deasy, Tom Crofts and others to join the army. They wouldn't have to go through the ordinary ranks, and would subsequently be posted to various places to command training camps. Barry willingly 'went alone' to Blackrock Garda Station several days 'before the mass enrolments'. After he had worked in the Cork Barracks with Col M. J. Costello for almost three weeks he was notified of a five week training course 'as a potential officer' to be conducted in the military college in the Curragh. He protested. He did not want 'either commission or course'. Nevertheless, he agreed and set out for the Curragh, but 'made it perfectly clear' that he had 'no intention of staying for the full course' but had come because he 'did not want to disobey an order.'[2]

Drilling up and down the square and the military discipline being doled out by young officers did not find favour with Barry. During a lecture one day an officer explained tactics of surrounding an enemy, drawing a diagram and describing on the blackboard with his chalk that moving the troops in a certain formation would result in breaking through the enemy line.

'Nonsense,' shouted Barry, jumping to his feet. 'You don't know what you're talking about,' and he sat down.

Theory and book information was very different from reality, as Barry knew.

Some days later, Col Costello sent him from Cork Barracks to inspect a squadron under Pat Buttimer (ex-IRA and veteran of Barry's flying column), officer-in-charge at Bantry House.

'I got a phone call saying that it was Tom Barry who was coming to inspect. The troops were all lined up – all "heelable" when he was brought from the gate by the guard. As soon as he showed his face the bugler began, and we all stood to attention. Tom stood by the guard while the bugler's salute was being blown. I went towards him, saluted him and told him the troops were ready for inspection.' After inspection, Buttimer dismissed the troops and the pair went in and had a drink. 'But the one thing that struck me was that he was wearing civilian clothes, and I needn't really have handed over my troops for inspection to anybody in "civvies". But I knew Barry so well I was delighted to be able to do it. I never heard anything about this breach of regulations afterwards.'[3]

Upon Barry's return to Cork and then to the Curragh he was told by Major Egan that the adjutant general had 'instructed him' that he 'was to be discharged from the army'. The official reason was 'services no longer required'.

In a letter to the commandant of the military college he listed four main reasons for returning to Cork Barracks. He would be 'happier serving in the Ranks' (Rank A) rather than as an officer, and did not wish to spend time away from where he 'expected to fight, if war comes', he wrote. Furthermore, it would be of no military value being grouped among 'young service men' with 'only a few days service in the army.' All his comrades (T. Crofts, F. O'Donoghue, M. Leahy, *et al*) 'were posted to different duties' and 'excused' from the course. 'I was the only one sent from this group,' he wrote to An Taoiseach, De Valera.

Dismissal from the army was 'a drastic punishment' without being given a reason, he wrote. 'I am not conscious that I have done anything wrong and I fail to understand why GHQ ordered my discharge without reason … I have been working in Cork city and county and I now ask that the officer commanding, Southern Command, be asked to report on my work and my conduct from the date of my attestation.'

Col Costello put him 'into operations' where he 'authenticated amongst others two important operation orders' headed *Defence and Plans for Action*. He wished he did not have to bother An Taoiseach in 'a time of national crisis' and had 'hesitated before writing'. Nor did he 'want any investigations now if such would divert officers from pressing duties … I will ask when this crisis is past or eased that the whole matter be gone fully into.'

Having apologised in writing to the commandant of the military college for 'any inconvenience', Barry assured him that he was 'not aware of any irregularity [in] refusing the course and returning to Cork.'[4]

Army records show that Private Tom Barry, number E410364, was enlisted on 1 July 1940 and discharged on 9 August 1940. The reason given for his discharge was 'services no longer required'.[5]

Tom Barry could not see a future for himself as a soldier of the Irish army as he did not want to concede to their wishes to be a commissioned officer. He returned to the Cork Harbour commissioners, was appointed general superintendent where with other duties he organised security, fire drill, attention to property – all the necessary precautions that had to be undertaken at a harbour during this 'difficult period', Liam French, the general manager, recalls. 'Trade had stopped, and the defence of our ports became an important factor, and Tom was an extremely shrewd and capable official.'[6]

Barry was a firm believer in neutrality. 'I had no connection with the IRA at the time, my thoughts were with staying out of war.'[7]

On 25 August De Valera told Barry, that 'the conditions which we are likely to face in the case of invasion would be very different from those of 1920–21 … our aim must be to go for the enemy at once wherever he appears, rather than to wait for him to advance against us. I would be surprised to learn that any contrary view is held in any responsible quarter'.[8]

Tom Barry, on the other hand, believed that 'this country' would only be invaded if 'another power' dropped 'all moral scruples' and decided that the cost in money and 'thousands of casualties' would be worth 'the gain'. Rather than inviting action, the army should take a 'defensive' role to 'nullify the invader's superiority… in the shortest possible time' if an attack came. The use of 'Irish forces to counter attack at night', the prevention of 'encirclement' with the use of 'controlled guerilla movement' should be part of the national policy and strategy. But most important, there should be 'leadership, first class staff work necessary for effective functioning' with officers taking full responsibility.[9]

Barry made himself available to the army's Southern Command for advice, became a great friend and was 'most helpful' to Col M. J. Costello, who found 'that Tom Barry's vision and capacity to size up situations' could not be surpassed. 'His role at the Harbour Board was vital at this juncture'. Furthermore, he embarked in training the local defence forces (LDF), thus making a worthwhile contribution to Cork's Civil Defence. These two men fought in the War of Independence. Unlike Barry, Costello supported the Treaty, yet it made no difference to their friendship.[10]

When Col Costello wrote memos or guidelines for the army he would often send them to Barry for an opinion. One such is in relation to 'sniping'. Barry disagreed 'with the tactical handling of snipers [in a platoon] as outlined in it [the memo] for in real war a unit Commander dare not allow a unit (of snipers) within his unit to "act more or less on its own". That is contrary to the principles of command and the responsibility, which such command implies.'

He believed that no section should be 'allowed act' on its own. He went on to explain the danger of the liberty 'to open an attack' without orders.[11]

Though Barry was a strong advocate of neutrality he had a fear that at some stage Ireland could be invaded and discussed this possibility with M. J. Costello. 'A very obvious and ideal place for occupation in Cork was the City Hall, no matter whether it was Germans or British came in. It was a strategic building in the city, on the water's edge. So with this senior officer, the pair went one night and planted 400 pounds of gelignite in the basement.'[12]

After the United States entered the war in December 1941, President Roosevelt and Winston Churchill agreed to allow American troops to complete their training in Northern Ireland. This began in January 1942. David Gray, American ambassador to Ireland, was extremely anxious to maintain a good relationship with De Valera and he in turn endeavoured to see that any allied airmen would be released without undue delay. However, Gray sent 'alarmist report to Washington' regarding 'stories' of German activists Edouard Hempel and Henning Thomsen's visits to Ireland. The men had come to Ireland, Grey informed Roosevelt, and met with former IRA men, Dan Breen and Tom Barry. In May 1942 Grey anticipated a German move on Ireland within a month. Grey wrote that Thomsen had 'been entertaining' Dan Breen in the Gresham Hotel, and that he (Grey) 'suspected' Breen 'of being on the German payroll'. Also Thomsen had 'twice' met Tom Barry.

T. Ryle Dwyer suggests that the German men's 'actions' may 'have been designed merely as a veiled threat to keep the Irish government from making too many concessions to the allies'.[13]

One morning the German minister, Hempel 'accompanied by a carload of detectives' called on Barry. The two men spoke 'for about an hour and a half.' Hempel 'made it clear immediately that he did not want any information from me except my reaction to any invasion of Ireland by either Germany or Britain,' Barry wrote to Dr T. Ryle Dwyer. 'At no time did he suggest that I should get IRA help for Germany.' Barry told Hempel 'early on' that he would inform De Valera of the conversation; he knew the detectives 'would' undoubtedly 'report' the meeting. Barry left 'Dr Hempel in no doubt,' he wrote 'that I backed our government's neutrality stand 100%, and I told [him] that Irishmen could not see any difference between the German imperialism which had ruthlessly destroyed small nations and British imperialism.' Consequently 'the first invaders would be our enemy'.

Barry, who regarded Hempel as 'a real friend of Ireland', had a second meeting that night and he with his wife, Leslie, were dinner guests at his hotel. Hempel said that the Irish 'should thank God for Sir John Maffey who undoubtedly is a restraining force on bellicose Churchill'. It is obvious from this letter that Barry disliked 'that scoundrel Gray' and was 'thankful' to have given him 'a few unhappy moments' as he believed 'the greatest danger of invasion came from USA.'[14]

Churchill was also concerned that the IRA might pose a threat. He had received a report through Major Desmond Morton that the 'War Office states categorically that the IRA is well armed and well organised, whereas the Eire defence forces are little short of derisory. There is information that a number of Germans have landed surreptitiously in Eire since the outbreak of the war' with regular communication between both countries. It meant on-going surveillance of IRA activities by British intelligence throughout the war.[15]

Hard work and dedication found Barry compiling articles well into the night hours. He set out military problems for army personnel – many were printed in *An Cosantóir – A Review for Army and L.D.F.* De Valera consulted him on several occasions 'and took his views on board. Barry was very strong on neutrality. Avoid antagonism was his motto at this period.'[16]

Between January and June 1941 he wrote accounts of the Kilmichael and the Crossbarry ambushes under the pseudonym 'Eyewitness' with the addition of 'Commentary and Conclusions'. Editorial deletions 'because of the [war] climate' meant that the details of the brandy flasks that the Auxiliaries carried and other incidentals in relation to them were omitted. However, 'the false surrender' of the Auxiliaries at Kilmichael was not censored.[17]

In a prepared paper Barry 'clarified' from his viewpoint, 'our defence policy' tied in with the 'dignity of man, the love of relatives, friends and neighbours and the love of the motherland.' As a 'small nation' we should not waste money in the air force, or naval service as 'we would be shot out of existence within twelve hours of the opening of hostilities.' Instead, we should concentrate on 'building up our ground forces,' and money should be spent on 'light artillery, anti-tank guns, machine-guns, mines and automatic rifles.' In the future rather than 'slavishly' having officers trained in the army schools of 'world powers' such as the US and Great Britain, we should send officers for training in countries similar to ours, such as Switzerland, Denmark, and Norway.'[18]

Tom visited his family in Liverpool before the war. His mother died on 5 March 1940; his father died on 28 July 1943; his sister Eileen 'who kept her illness to herself' died in September 1943. His sister Marjorie had already died. His sister Kitty (Kit) had malaria, and sister Gert was not well, nor was his brother John. Correspondence between Tom and his sister Gert shows that the family did not want to trouble Tom and Leslie in case entering Britain during these war years, would, as was likely, create problems for them. Gert wrote that 'I will be glad when this year is over – it's been wicked'. Only thirty-six, she died a month later, on 27 December. 1943. Though he wished he could be with them at this sad period of so many deaths within a short space of time, his precarious position dictated that he postpone any visit. When conditions had stabilised, shortly after the war, he went to see the remaining members of the family.[19]

From 1932 to 1937 Leslie was occupied with the establishment of the Cork branch of the Women's Industrial Development Association. Since she had joined the Red Cross and her election to the central council she had been intensely active and had earned a medal to add to her 1916–1922 medal. In 1945 after the war she was involved in the development of a peacetime programme. Accompanied by Maureen O'Sullivan she travelled all over Ireland setting up branches in towns and villages. As the Red Cross was founded at the start of the war, people associated it with war, 'so we decided to initiate ideas which we felt were necessary and hoped in time they would prove their worth and perhaps be taken over by the government'. 'We initiated the Blood Transfusion Service and the anti-Tuberculosis Scheme. In Cork we took a very big step in having every school child tested for Tuberculosis in its preliminary stages.' Leslie initiated a project of Water Safety and Life-saving and worked tirelessly for the society. New ideas were discussed between Tom and herself: he would give his opinion on views she wished to put to a meeting, perhaps even offer an alternative.

In 1949, 250 refugees came to Cork 'from war-torn countries including Poland, Czechoslovakia and Finland. They were accommodated in Rockgrove Camp site near Little Island'. Leslie organised a rotary staff with women to work on morning, afternoon and evening shifts; this continued over a two-year period, until their passage from Cobh to America was arranged. Throughout the following decades Leslie was deeply involved in the care of the aged and deprived in the community. She became the first woman to obtain the position as chairman of the Irish Red Cross.

Accompanied by Mollie Murphy, general secretary Irish Red Cross, she represented Ireland at international conferences in Toronto, Oslo, Monaco, New Delhi, Geneva, Vienna, The Hague, Athens, Istanbul, Czechoslovakia. She was a government nominee on the national health council. Much of the work was voluntary. Her concern for citizens led her to aid in the establishment of the Voluntary Health Insurance. Her idea was taken up by T. F. O'Higgins, who worked enthusiastically with her and others on this worthwhile project.

From every country she wrote to Tom. While in Vienna at a conference she told him of the gist of the conference, then added a personal note:

> Darling ... I think so much of you, my love, I love only you ...
> All all my love, your own, Lottie.[20] *[pet name]*

Being extremely capable and a wonderful organiser, her talents were in demand in many spheres. In many countries she represented Ireland in the food and health field, and was chairman of the Erinville Maternity Hospital, Cork. For her organisational ability and for her dedicated contribution to society and to the Red Cross, De Valera presented her with an honorary degree from University College, Cork, in 1966. In the early 1970s she helped with the northern refugees who came to Cork.[21]

Tom, as general superintendent and later as dredging superintendent manager with the Cork Harbour commissioners, was involved in a large project. The harbour had to be dredged so that the channel could be opened up to larger ships, and the site around Tivoli had to be reclaimed.

'There was another side to Barry; as well as being a soldier he had shrewd business acumen and contributed in no small way to the development of the port of Cork. He could be stern when the occasion called for it. He had the military background, which meant discipline, and he was always very fair. His concern was for people, seeing that they were happy in their jobs and had obtained such items as protective clothing for the workers. His relationship with the men, the union and the management was always just and fair. And when he was off duty he could sit down and have a drink with you and tell a yarn or a story as good as any man,' Mick McCarthy recalled.[22]

Now that the war had ended, Tom and Leslie decided to spend some days with relatives in Liverpool. They had a wonderful relaxed visit and were able to calmly go over events of the past number of years. It also gave Tom an opportunity to talk with family members, from whom he had been separated for so long. His parents had accepted Tom's decision to do what he did, and 'they were in their own way, proud of his achievements.'[23] 'In certain ways we were closer than many families who were together always.'[24]

In 1946 a vacancy occurred in Cork borough constituency. On the insistence of some colleagues Barry agreed to stand as an independent candidate. Initially he was reluctant, but then he relented. The following is a summary of his election manifesto:

> *Rights of Citizens*: The individual politician is 'free to support or oppose any measure on its merits and consequences'.
> *Political*: He was very strong on partition and wanted 'the restoration of the lost counties' neglected by successive governments.
> *Economics*: Among other challenges, legislation was required, he maintained, for 'the abolition of ground rent scandal' being given to 'foreigners'.
> *Social Justice*: Distribution of wealth; he set out a long document on how this should be done.

He crossed swords with Seán McEntee mainly over the Partition issue and with Michael O'Riordan over social issues.[25] Derogatory remarks made by other candidates on the controversy with Frank Aiken and also his definite stance within the IRA were unhelpful to his candidature. He did very little campaigning for this by-election. Accept the outcome – was his motto! The election was held on 15 June with the following results:

McGrath, Patrick (Fianna Fáil)	14,230
O'Driscoll, Michael (Fine Gael)	9,707
O'Riordan, Michael (Socialist)	3,184
Barry, Tom (Independent)	2,574

'The figures were those on the first preference, and after redistribution of sur-plus votes and the elimination of Mr O'Riordan and Mr Barry (both forfeited their deposits) Mr McGrath with strong Fianna Fáil backing was declared elected by a majority of 4,667 over Mr O'Driscoll.'[26]

Friends say Tom was a little disappointed but not badly hurt by the results. They felt that as a politician he would have been too outspoken, too individu-alistic to make a success of the job. He 'brushed it all aside very quickly', never became a member of a political party, as party politics didn't find favour with him; he always praised a member of a party who took a stand on any issue of principle. In later years he confessed his delight that he had remained 'outside politics' because people and issues were, he felt, manoeuvred to suit indivi-duals.[27]

Often 'the bitterness and hates' of the Civil War 'were kept up between political parties, and when issues of social progress and economic progress' were being discussed 'politicians approached each problem from the point of view of whether the man proposing was anti-Treaty or pro-Treaty,' he said. This was a stance, he disliked.[28] 'I'm not built for a public life', he told history students, 'I might make a good minister, but I'd make a very bad TD. I was in jail six times altogether.'[29]

A circular distributed by the department of local government in 1945 directed that the 'undesirable' practice of local authority officers 'making representa-tions through public representatives concerning remuneration and duties' should be discontinued, as it 'may render the officer liable to disciplinary action.' In bold capitals in the margin of the typewritten document Tom wrote: 'WHAT ARE REPS FOR!'[30]

In July 1948 when the Bureau of Military History was structured, its director, M. McDumphy asked Barry for any material 'within the terms of reference'. Later he acknowledged Barry's offer of 'documents' on loan 'not included' in his book, and his willingness to co-operate with the bureau.[1] However, Barry soon changed his view of the bureau because of the scope and method and instructions of acquiring data. Concerning the secrecy of holding 'under seal for whatever period' material given to the bureau, Barry, in a letter to the director, noted, that if statements could remain unopened until after the 'death of an individual' and 'would not be made amenable for libel or false assertions, calculated to injure other parties', then this would be a most harmful 'procedure'.[2] He wrote:

> The IRA like every other organisation had malicious members or men who developed a mental kink about other men and matters which had no foundation in fact. Past histories have been confused by the unearthing of such documents and I submit that the Bureau of Military History should have as its paramount duty the destruction of all records not authenticated or confirmed by immediate investigation. Nobody should have the right to submit any matter under seal for future examination. There should be an immediate investigation of every important statement made and the subject matter should only be filed after such an examination.

As an example Barry pointed out how he had dealt in his book with 'two reverses suffered by the West Cork IRA' under Charlie Hurley's leadership:

> You will admit that were I an enemy or even a lukewarm friend of Charlie's, I could have written quite differently and conveyed the opinion that Charlie was either inefficient or negligent on those occasions. I could have done this either by innuendo or omission and it would be very difficult to pin me down to having made a false statement about one of the greatest Irish soldiers of our time. Therefore, I contend that the collectors and recorders of the Bureau will influence the history of our period far more than the actual historians who will write it.[3]

Barry wanted the director to understand that his letter was 'not written in a carping spirit but only with a view to helping in the work of compiling an accurate and complete history.' He suggested that 'senior officers of divisions and brigades could best help by reading over and commenting on any important statement made by other officers.'[4]

It became well known that the 'compilers of this history' posed leading questions often to help backup certain stories. Genuine IRA men who had given time, effort and often their health and 'had been cold, wet, miserable and hungry' on occasions were maligned by a jealous neighbour who sometimes took credit for events in which he was a non participant'.

Barry expressed his 'great disappointment at the removal of Major Florrie O'Donoghue from the panel of recording officers', because 'O'Donoghue's knowledge of the south's contribution to the War of Independence is unrivalled', he wrote to the bureau director. 'All of us down here felt that he had the all important knowledge of the characters and records' that other bureau officers lacked. Moreover, 'he had the merit of being neutral in our Civil War.'[5] Tom 'appealed' to Dr T. O'Higgins, minister of defence 'to reconsider the decision not to continue Major F. O'Donoghue's services': while he accepted 'unreservedly' the minister's decision, as he had 'a post to return to', and 'regular army' officers were available to undertake this work. 'O'Donoghue knows nothing of my approach to you,' he wrote. 'I am only taking this action because of O'Donoghue's exceptional qualifications … I will go so far as to state that no one in the south of Ireland has his knowledge of the pre-Truce period.'[6] The decision was not reversed and the bureau accumulated their information as planned.

In 1969 as Tom finished a lecture to history students in University College, Galway, he told them he had *one thing* to say regarding the officers' accumulation of history for the Military History Bureau:

> You are historians, so it is important that you are aware of the facts. These officers went into districts, they met men singularly and everything a man told them they had to write it down in longhand. They couldn't ask a very simple question. [He banged the rostrum and repeated his remark] *They had to write everything down!* Years later as some of them told me after they retired from the army, they knew in many cases the man *wasn't there at all!'* [He emphasised *wasn't there at all*! Again he banged the rostrum.] They got the most extraordinary statements from fellows – and all these statements were put away. And fifty years afterwards they were to be handed over to a bunch of professional historians and so write a history from all that mix-um-gatherum. Well, if that is history!
>
> No other man could see what he wrote. I could be here in one company and could say John Browne ran away and he stole the firearms. It had to be taken down unquestionably … and nobody was entitled to see what was to be hidden away for all those years. Those of you who know history or who know something about history would be able to walk into a barracks and believe that!
>
> All, what these people collected should be taken out of their offices or whatever department it is in; there should be a match put to the whole lot of them, because if not, those who write these things will be able to justify what has been said so often lately – that the number of men who said they were in the GPO in 1916 Rising, wouldn't fit into Croke Park.
>
> The problem I have with these officers is that their instructions were to write down everything. This will be written and it will be what will be called 'the history of Ireland'. I'm very cynical always about this history … What I am saying to you as historians, that these stories that were collected are *not history*. [He emphasised this, and banged the rostrum again.] However, the material that was collected for the military pensions had to be verified. Most of those who verified them were honest. I got many [pension applications] for verification and if a man did not take part in an action, I could not, and would not, allow him to get a pension. [There was force, almost anger in his voice as he delivered this impromptu piece, prior to a questioning session, which ensued.][7]

Both in University College, Cork and in Maynooth College shortly after this occasion he repeated with similar force, this 'distortion of history' and wanted history students to be vigilant and only to use these sources with an open mind in their compilation of history. 'Fire would almost light in his eyes when he'd talk about this, because he knew there were those who told whoppers!'[8]

In 1974, after the publication of the Deasy book when Barry dealt with material that was at variance with written sources, he wrote of meeting with Lieut Col Halpin, recording officer for the bureau who told him of his obligation 'to record every single word from anyone … who claimed service with the I.R.A. It did not matter whether the deponent was obviously, mentally disturbed, intoxicated or a phoney, his statement had to be recorded.' Lack of policing the material, plus lack of redress 'by a maligned person' annoyed him.

'My interest now is how much of Deasy's or Fr Chisholm's alleged history came from this source, which must have included some very tall tales …

'God help Irish history!' was his cryptic remark. 'I would ask that a bonfire should be made of the lot in the Garden of Remembrance.' Here was 'the Barry fire' to which historian Pádraig Ó Maidín alluded.[9] (As there are missing pages in Barry's letters to the director of the Military History Bureau it is unknown what they contained, but judging by the existing parts, it must have been forceful.)

In the Mansion House, Dublin in 1948, Tom addressed a large audience for the one hundred and fiftieth anniversary of the 1798 Rising. He concentrated on the Wexford Rising. His portrayal of John Kelly, the boy from Killan was 'electrifying'. Barry 'captured the audience. He had charisma and the ability of being a descriptive speaker', Criostóir de Baróid recalled. 'You could listen to him forever!' The audience 'rewarded him with an emotional standing ovation.'[10]

In early 1949, Barry, with members of the West Cork Brigade memorial committee, undertook a project to erect a suitable monument 'to the memory of the Volunteers of the West Cork Brigade, Irish Republican Army, who died for Ireland from 1916 onwards.' Barry arranged with Seamus Murphy, sculptor, to carve on granite 'a suitable facing'. Money collected from veterans and from friends of the brigade in America took some years of dedication and organisation. On 8 August 1953, President Seán T. O'Kelly performed the official unveiling on the outskirts of Bandon.[11]

That evening Tom, trim, fit and full of energy sat with Tom Kelleher, Nudge Callanan, Mick McCarthy and other comrades 'over a pint' in the Kilmichael Bar, Bandon. The discussion centred around the Crossbarry ambush. 'Kelleher turned to Nudge Callanan. "Only for that drop of whiskey you gave me that day after the ambush, I don't think I'd survive. 'Twas the saving of me!"

'Barry turned around and banged his fist on the table. "Jasus! Didn't I tell you 'twas only to be used for medicinal purposes!" Thirty-two years had gone by and Barry was annoyed that his command wasn't carried to the letter!'[12]

Invitations to speak at commemoration ceremonies were extended to Barry – at unveilings such as the memorial to the memory of Willie McCarthy, Tralee, 'an ecclesiastical student' arrested while delivering dispatches, 'taken to RIC Barracks and later that night two Black and Tans took him to the Green … and murdered him.' There were places where they only wanted his presence. 'We will guarantee that we will not ask him to open his lips, come stand on the platform and unveil the monument'.[13] In Thurles IRA veterans who had organised a benevolent fund for a man who had not been well since internment in Wormwood Scrubs in 1920, wanted Tom Barry to come to their Easter Week commemoration. 'We are anxious to avoid a political speaker and while Barry may have taken sides, he is still regarded as an outstanding man here, and more or less aloof from politics'.[14]

Having contributed articles to *An Cosantóir, Rebel Cork's Fighting Story* and the *Irish Press* in the 1930s and early 1940s, Barry decided to write a book. Since 1937 he had written extended accounts of the major ambushes of Kilmichael and Crossbarry; now he would write on other ambushes and events of the Third West Cork Brigade in the War of Independence. Ted O'Sullivan, TD, believed 'it was a great idea to write up the history of the war, while there are so many alive to give first hand information.' O'Sullivan felt sure that brigade committees could 'verify detailed lists of all activities'.[15]

In questionnaires for his comrades, he allowed spaces for their responses, and went to tremendous trouble to check facts. Key people such as Jack Young and Florrie O'Donoghue collected statements from brigade members. Jack Young organised statements from authoritative sources, including his brother Ned and Paddy O'Brien (both Kilmichael ambush participants) and Liam Deasy. Barry acquired two large 1947 Browne and Nolan diaries, and wrote in alternative pages – using one side, and allowing the opposite for corrections and alterations.[16]

Tom presented Leslie, who had learned to type, with a typewriter one evening as she had agreed to type the book. 'He was extremely particular,' she said. 'At first I might change a word which I would think would be more suitable; he'd recognise it and insist that I type the whole page again. And if I made a mistake I'd have to type the page again; it just had to be correct. He wrote it, and it had to appear exactly as he wrote it. But that was the kind of person Tom was – extremely thorough.'[17]

Having worked on the manuscript throughout 1947, he had it ready for publication by March 1948. William Sweetnam, editor of the *Irish Press* contacted Tom and suggested that the paper would serialise the work. Initially Tom was reluctant to allow it be published in this manner, but decided that if there were any errors or dissenting voices the material could be corrected prior to book publication.[18]

'Truth to tell, the financial aspect of it is not to me the greatest', he told his friend, Connie Neenan, in June 1948. 'I wrote it primarily because of my pride in the men of my race and because I hope when I am dead that it will be the medium of some stabs at those British whom an Irishman should not forgive

– even when he is in the grave.'[19] Con responded, 'It is obvious that you are not interested in the financial angle of things but rather in the historic and national values. There is little financial compensation in writing – at least from the author's viewpoint.'[20]

Barry had already selected the title *Guerilla Days in Ireland* for the book. The *Irish Press* wrote an introduction on 1 May 1948 of 'the saga' of 'the West Cork Brigade Flying Column, the most aggressive striking force of the whole Republican army, written by the man who led it' in 'Ireland's fight for freedom'. The first instalment began in the *Irish Press* on 10 May, and the series ended on 3 July 1948.

Before this, correspondence flowed between Barry and the editor of the *Irish Press* regarding the alteration or omission of certain material. He acknowledged 'the right of the *Irish Press* to decide what should be omitted to avoid liability, for libel actions the words it considers likely to give offence to living people ... I will in a further letter make some suggestions on this, which will meet the views of the *Irish Press*.' He noted that the least he could expect was a statement accompanying each instalment that alterations had been made by agreement with the author.[21] Furthermore, he wanted it clarified that it was a book that was being serialised and not a series of articles, and that the *Irish Press* had obtained 'first serial rights of a book'.[22] After the first two instalments, Tom had problems and wrote to the editor, William Sweetnam, who responded: 'I accept, of course, your point that we should acknowledge that we have made deletions and propose to do so in all instalments which are not printed in full ... You will understand that an extract from a book in a daily paper can appear in a very different light to the publication of the same passage in the book itself.'[23]

Shortly after, some further deletions and editorial 'interference' disturbed Barry again. He informed the editor that such 'interference' would 'have to be' accompanied by an 'acknowledgement'. However, without his approval, he did not want any alterations involving 'omitting important facts' such as had been done with his article on Kilmichael (1932). He wanted reassurance of their promise 'to publish without the alteration of a single word.'[24]

A few weeks later Barry again expressed his anxiety. 'Adverse comment mounts,' he wrote on 4 June, 'that the instalments are being cut too drastically. Those people will not understand the pressure of space and all the other valid reasons.'[25] He told his friend Connie Neenan, 'The *Irish Press* is no friend of mine but I could not refuse to give it to them' because, he said, he wished to 'counter' the 'subtle British propaganda' in the *Independent*. His reference was to Winston Churchill's memoirs being highlighted in the *Irish Independent* at the time.[26]

He disagreed with Liam Mac Gowan, *Irish Press*, that his reference to Bishop Coholan's excommunication decree should be toned down. 'I consider it a very mild exposition of a treacherous act aimed to destroy the armed Independence movement by a man who should have been dealt with in a stronger manner ... do not touch it at all', he wrote, and he wanted inserted 'in italics, in brackets' a line of the 'strong language' used by the author which has been omitted.[27] He wrote the paragraph that he wanted inserted. Finally with the help of M. J. Costello he succeeded in getting the paper to publish the toned-down paragraph.[28]

On 25 June, Mr Sweetnam again responded to another letter from him.

'I would like to assure you at once that we have no intention of altering your Mss, or allowing any member of the staff to alter the Mss, except for those necessary deletions of the kind I have already notified you.

'I have looked into your complaint and find that certain mistakes were made at the "stone" where some matter in the galleys was transposed ... I have taken steps to see that they are prevented in future as far as possible.

'You will understand, however, that in the rush to produce a newspaper some mistakes are inevitable.'[29] It is obvious from the foregoing that Barry was a stickler for accuracy.

After a photo of Barry appeared with the second instalment he asked the editor, 'Where, oh where did the *Irish Press* get today's photograph of me? I suspect it must have been when, at some meeting, I was attacking the Fianna Fáil Govt!'

The editor responded, 'It was taken at a meeting when you were attacking, not the Fianna Fáil Government, but the *Irish Press*. That is what you get for not sending us an authorised photograph.'[30] Later when his book was being published the *Irish Press* were again seeking a photo. But Barry had 'a feeling against it', and rarely 'had a photograph taken deliberately'. He did not want to feel 'a presumptuous ass.' However, he finally consented.[31]

There were only a few dissenting voices during serialisation. Some were from those who claimed to be at venues or held titles, which clearly were un-true and one such was the claim by an alleged brigade OC in a certain area. (This correspondence is marked, 'not for publication'.) Barry had checked the details with Florence O'Donoghue, who in the 'course of his investigations for the Military Bureau' when he was assigned to it, claimed that the same man 'is not quite sound on top without being actually a mental case'.[32]

Meanwhile, Tom told Liam Mac Gowan, *Irish Press*, that he was taking a day off for the Phoenix Park races 'provided I am not dam (*sic*) well broke be-fore it, backing donkeys. Joe McGrath wrote me ten days ago that *Solar Slipper* is very well fancied to win the Derby tomorrow. Let's hope so, because if he does not, I will have to doff my hat and genuflect every time I pass my bank for the next few months.'[33]

The serialisation of Barry's manuscript in the *Irish Press* brought him hundreds of letters from readers countrywide including Third West Cork Brigade comrades, and veterans countrywide and abroad who had participated in both the War of Independence and in the Civil War.

Pat O'Mahony wrote, 'From the day I first met you, to this moment, I am convinced that without you it would be easy to write the history of our brigade.' Pat, later a policeman in Dungarvan, found that 'no other area could produce such a combination as yourself, Charlie Hurley, Liam Deasy, Jim Hurley, etc. ... But without you??? ... You are far too modest where your own part is concerned.'[1] Pat Callaghan believed that there would be 'no 26 County Republic only for Tom Barry.' Another correspondent Canon O'Connell, who heard the men's confession before the Kilmichael ambush (afterwards took the pro-Treaty side), described Barry as 'a second Napoleon'.[2]

People sent the *Irish Press* daily to friends in America, New Zealand, Australia and 'to good Irishmen everywhere'. Words of praise from young and old came in floods of letters. So many believed that 'you cannot read your tombstone when you're dead!' One letter finishes with, 'Thank you for "Guerilla Days" and your service to Ireland.'[3] Another wrote, 'You wield a pen as well as you wielded a gun in West Cork.'[4] Several of his former comrades wrote complimentary letters, including Pete Kearney, who was 'very pleased' and glad of the special mention of 'the medical group' from UCC. Tom's great friend, Seán Moylan, complimented him on 'the very great labour entailed in the digging up and co-relating of the facts.'[5] A few weeks later Pete Kearney wrote again to Tom of 'an eighty year old man in Clare who never read a paper had to have the *Press* delivered specially from Corofin every morning. Another old man from North Cork, on a visit to Co. Meath, made a great nuisance of himself to his rancher friend by producing copies of the paper.' Dan Breen looked forward to the book, because he wanted 'a full mouthfull at one go', and Jim Hurley of UCC forwarded a letter he had received from the chairman of the General Council of County Councils to Tom: 'Id like you to tell him [Tom] how proud I was to read of his epic courage and quality and of his epic telling of his services and those of his fellow soldiers. His is a proud chapter in our story and for us who have no story – there is the pride of a common blood to fill us full ... it makes me very proud of Cork blood and Irish blood. Thank him from one half Cork man and one whole Irishman.'[6] A man without Cork connections wrote how glad he was that Tom was reminding 'the present breed of young Irish men of what those who went before them suffered for Ireland.'[7]

In a letter to the *Irish Press* two Kerry writers jointly questioned Tom Barry's statement that in 1921 members of the inner cabinet were not members of the I.R.B. Barry in his response wrote: 'none of those mentioned attended a meeting of the I.R.B. from 1919 to the date of their death ... Both Brugha and Stack believed with President de Valera that once the elected parliament of the Republic was set up, the need for the I.R.B. lapsed and that all activities of militant young Ireland should be handled and controlled through the Irish Republican army ... No one who has read my views on De Valera and Brugha can have any doubt of my opinion that membership of the I.R.B. was not an essential for a believer of a fighting policy.'[8] Barry wrote to Robert Barton who clarified the issue for him. 'I can safely state that Dev. and Cathal Brugha left after 1916, probably on account of the then spirit.' Barton believed that Stack remained a member 'until after the general election of 1918 when his position as minister clashed. About Dev's membership I can vouch for as MacDonagh [executed 1916] mentioned it to me in Holy Week 1916. Collins approached me in 1917 to speak to Dev on the matter but Dev refused to rejoin.'[9]

Brugha had discussed the position with Eamonn Dore (friend of Seán MacDermott executed 1916) and Eamon Price (Leslie's brother) 'late in 1917' or the 'beginning of 1918.' So Dore knew that there was 'more to his [Brugha's] bitter campaign against the organisation' than 'the secret movement' policy. Believing the IRB 'had got into wrong hands and was moving that way', Brugha told Dore he would engage in a 'crusade' against it. Despite Dore's appeal he did not relent. Dore was 'convinced from the whole discussion that the rift between himself and Collins had started almost from their first meeting and that the "crusade" was a natural outcome.'[10]

Laurence McVerry wrote to the *Irish Press*, of 'the stirring episodes of immortal value. Ireland will long remember the Commandant General, firstly for the noble part he played in this epic struggle, secondly for the meticulous care he took in compiling the true facts about Ireland's gallant sons and daughters in their dealings with the enemy, and lastly for revealing to the world the shameful and cowardly action of the British government on this blessed land of ours ... May the memory of the "Guerilla Days in Ireland" never grow old, and may God grant that the "Boys that licked the Black and Tans" will not have died in vain.'[11]

In June 1948, the Corrigan Park Reconstruction committee in Belfast invited Barry to perform the opening ceremony of 'Outdoor Week'.[12] Barry, 'proud to accept the invitation' pointed out that his 'position in the six counties under British Rule' was 'not very secure'. He could be: (a) Stopped at the border and 'served with an Exclusion Order'; (b) 'Arrested for some previous speech within British held counties'; (c) 'Arrested immediately after performing ceremony', consequently he made suggestions as to how he would travel. He would not stay 'in a public hotel' but in a private residence and leave immediately afterwards. He said there were those who tried many times 'to get' him and 'may now wish to finish the job.'[13] Before travelling he asked if the committee had 'any objection to my dealing with Partition', and 'any objection to my speaking as strongly as I feel on this matter.' He suggested that if he was 'arrested before the ceremony' his address could be 'read by somebody else.'[14]

Later in the month Tom, on behalf of the divisional staff of 'the twenty-three Battalions which existed in Cork City and County on the date of the Truce with the British', invited President of Ireland, Seán T. O'Kelly to attend a dinner to be organised in his honour.[15]

The president replied that 'he would be disposed to give the most sympathetic consideration to the proposal if he could be assured' that the invitation had 'full knowledge of all the former Officers of the units mentioned'. Neither should the occasion be 'of a party or sectional character' due to the obligation of the 'President's position'.[16] In his response Barry wrote that 'of the 40 persons who might participate, 35 fought with the Republican forces in the Civil War, three against while two remained neutral ... Because of this it is now felt that the inviting body might be considered as one with a very definite political tinge although indeed no such gathering was ever intended.' Barry appreciated 'the special position of the President' and decided that the invitation should be postponed 'to some later date'. He assured him that the intention was only to honour him 'in his official capacity and to express our regard ... for his life long services to our Nation.'[17]

On 3 September 1948 Tom and Leslie were invited as guests to the 'Conferring of Freedom of Cork City on President Seán T. O'Kelly'. It was a formal occasion with a military guard of honour. 'Mr & Mrs Barry' were 'distinguished guests with reserved places' in the Lord Mayor's room. The ceremony began in the City Hall and 'about 12.50 p.m. cars took the party' to the Victoria Hotel for a sherry reception in the drawing-room. Then, on to lunch and a civic reception in the dining-room at 1.30 p.m. Tom sat beside the president's ADC and near Dr O'Rahilly, president of UCC. Leslie was at the top table side-seat, beside Dr Coholan, Catholic bishop of Cork. Following the after-lunch party and the president's speech, the Lord Mayor thanked the guests 'for attendance and the party dissolved'. Later that afternoon the President officially opened, St Raphael's, the children's preventorium, where Leslie Bean de Barra, Red Cross, played a 'welcoming role'.[18]

Tom Barry did not leave any note about how he felt in such prestigious company, or whether he doffed his hat – one of his favourite phrases – to the Lord Bishop! It is not known what conversation Leslie had with Bishop Coholan, the man who had issued an Excommunication Order against her husband after the Kilmichael Ambush, 1920![19]

Though Fianna Fáil had 'some fifteen months to run' in its majority government, De Valera called a surprise general election on 4 February 1948. Clann na Poblachta founded in 1946 by Seán Mac Bride promoted the Irish partition issue. This election brought a coalition of 'no less than six parties with some independents' into power. They elected John A. Costello as Taoiseach. Despite De Valera's loss of office he went ahead in March 1948 with his already planned tour of American cities to drum up support for the Northern Ireland cause, and appealed for the 'Reunification of Ireland'.[20] These activities were followed closely by Tom Barry.

John A. Costello of the Fine Gael-led government, was a guest of the Canadian Bar Association in Montreal on 1 September 1948, when he delivered an address on 'Ireland and International Affairs' with the text approved by the cabinet before his departure.

On 5 September the *Sunday Independent* carried the headline EXTERNAL RELATIONS ACT TO GO. Two days later the Taoiseach gave a press conference in Ottawa confirming that this was the government's intention, and in November the Republic of Ireland Bill was introduced in the Dáil.

An Anti-Partition Association had been in existence since April 1948. They had written to Barry to ask his assistance.[21] Barry had been invited by the lord mayor of Dublin to deliver 'an address on the 1798 Rising' in the Mansion House. Peadar O'Donnell with whom Tom had been working, suggested how Tom could use the occasion in his drive for a 'United Ireland'.[22] He believed Tom should 'set forth' his views for the lord mayor of Dublin and 'ask him' to call 'a conference' as a move towards a 'National Convention which would readily' give people a 'voice on freedom'. This could entail 'a live ceremony and the re-dedication of Independence.' Barry, of course, did not miss the opportunity to use the occasion to further the cause of full independence.[23]

After an announcement of a general election in Northern Ireland, the Taoiseach J. A. Costello invited the leaders of all political parties to a debate, on 25 January 1949, on how their 'assistance can be given to anti-Partition candidates contesting.' At an all-party meeting two days later it was decided that a public subscription should be set in motion for an anti-partition fund. The Mansion House committee and its offspring the Anti-Partition League provided a flood of propaganda about partition and published a tide of pamphlets describing discrimination and gerrymandering. Over £50,000 was collected which was to be used in supporting anti-partition candidates in the north in the general election and in sending 'anti-Partition speakers like Tom Barry and Denis Ireland on a tour of America and Britain to inveigh against the border (De Valera, too, went on a world tour to highlight the partition issue).'[24]

Arising out of this, the Unionists pointed out that their sectarian fears were justified – they would be over-run by IRA and Roman Catholic policy, therefore the border should remain. On the other hand, this issue helped the young members of the IRA to consolidate their opinion that the border should go.

The Republic of Ireland Bill came into force on Easter Monday 1949. At one minute to the hour of midnight on 17 April 1949 a group stood on the steps of the City Hall, Cork, including Tom Barry, Col J. O'Hanrahan, OC Southern command and Col J. Hannon, OC First Brigade. Beyond the steps and over the bridge and all along the Mall stood a throng estimated to be well over 20,000. Long before midnight crowds began to converge on City Hall. According to the *Cork Examiner*, 'they counted out the minutes of the old regime; they presented to the close observer a cross-section of the most eventful period of modern Irish history.

'In that gathering were grey beards who had watched at the deathbed of the constitutional movement, and who, in their own way, had effectively advanced the cause of Irish freedom. There were the middle-aged, who in the enthusiasm of their youth had snatched the torch from older hands, and whose readiness to sacrifice for the cause gave substance to the dream of insurrection. Deprived as the great majority were through no fault of their own of the honour of fighting in 1916, they seized the later opportunity with both hands and helped to write a glorious page of Irish history in 1920–1921. The generation which has grown up since then was also fully represented there to witness the transition from partial to full independence.'[25]

The last chime of the City Hall clock died away, military buglers sounded a fanfare and then all eyes turned to the steps of the building.

The naval corvette *L. E. Maev* under Lieut-Comd. J. Whyte, INS, was berthed nearby and ready for the occasion; her search-lights plus the flood-lights at the foot of the steps focused on Tom Barry reading the 1916 Proclamation:

> Irishmen and Irishwomen ... We declare the right of the people of Ireland to the ownership of Ireland, and to the unfettered control of Irish destinies, to be sovereign and indefeasible ...

Here was a precious moment for which the guerilla commander had fought.

In *Guerilla Days in Ireland* he wrote: 'The beauty of those words enthralled me. Lincoln at Gettysburg does not surpass it nor does any other recorded proclamation of history.'[26]

Following the reading of the proclamation, Tom Barry and the central group left the City Hall steps and reappeared a few moments later on the roof of the building where 'Mr Barry hoisted the tricolour to the top of the flagstaff. As the flag fluttered bravely a guard of honour drawn from the Fourth Infantry Brigade presented arms and buglers sounded the general salute and the reveille.'[27]

Then came the 21-gun salute fired at ten-second intervals from the quayside, followed by a party from the Fourth Battalion located on the roof of the City Hall who fired a final salute. The playing of the national anthem by the No. 2 Army Band bridged the formal part of the night's ceremonies towards a new dawn.[28]

Next day, Easter Monday, Barry was one of the 'special guests' invited to 'a luncheon at Collins' Barracks on' the occasion of the inauguration of the Republic of Ireland Act.'[29]

Being the central figure in the performance of this ceremony was a great honour for General Tom Barry. Why he was the man chosen by a Fine Gael-led government, nobody knows. 'It was believed that Costello felt that the Tom Barry element should not be ruffled, as trouble could erupt at any time, just as Dev did not want to antagonise that same man, or else they felt he was the most worthy of that honour!'[30]

Barry, in any case, had always affirmed his non-party stance, had been close friends of many who participated in the opposing side in the Civil War, and had tried on numerous occasions to secure an all-party consensus on an all-Ireland policy.

Having been actively seeking a publisher for his book, and reluctant to go for a British Publisher he wondered if anybody in Ireland would take on the challenge. He had great difficulty and had a substantial amount of correspondence with publishers. Putnams of New York & London were 'keenly interested', with their 'European manager' calling on M. J. Costello who gave them his own copy of the manuscript. Peadar O'Donnell suggested that George Bernard Shaw would write an introduction. 'I imagine your first reaction will be not to have anything to do with him, but I think in this you would be wrong' as it could be 'a decisive factor in getting the publishers to take up the matter with urgency and pay a decent factor.'[31] Barry considered Shaw a 'world figure' and would 'hate a refusal'. His 'views and those of the book would hardly coincide, he would certainly condemn the military mind and what he'd write of its literary merits, I'd shudder to think!'[32] Connie Neenan tried to persuade Barry to allow Devin Adair Publishing, New York to publish, but in the final analysis Barry said he was 'never keen that this book should be first published by a non-Irish firm'.[33] He had four offers in one week, one British publisher 'suggested cutting out some of the more anti-British parts when they would be pleased to publish, but', Barry told Connie Neenan, 'I will not alter a word or a comma to suit them. The book will be published as written, or not at all'.[34] He was happy therefore, with M. J. Costello's *Irish Press* arrangement 'much happier that the book will not have to be published in Britain.'[35] By 25 August 1949 Tom told Mr Dempsey of the *Irish Press* that he wanted them to go ahead, as 'no American publication should be attempted until the book is first published here'.[36] He confirmed the publication of his book to the *Irish Press* on 14 March 1949, and received 'two sets of proofs of the first fifteen galleys' on 24 May and the complete set by 8 June, 1949.[37]

Guerilla Days in Ireland was published in hardback by the Irish Press Ltd, Dublin, in 1949 and was shortly co-published in several countries.

His hatred for the Essex Regiment and Major Percival, is openly expressed in the book and he details the night he went into Bandon to shoot him, but failed because Percival did not come his way:

> Disappointed we trudged out of Bandon back to our headquarters, little thinking that Major Percival, who was to fail so dismally against West Cork IRA was later to become commander of the pathetic surrender of 1941 at Singapore. We could not foresee that our target of that night would, as Lieut General Percival, Commander-in-Chief of ninety thousand British troops, surrender himself, his army, and many month's supplies, after a skirmish and without a real fight to a much smaller force of Japanese.[38]

Obviously Lieut-Gen. Arthur Ernest Percival did not like Tom Barry's biting remarks about him and threatened a libel suit against the publishers for defamation of character. The director upon receipt of the letter, sent for Barry. Barry read it. 'That's all right. I'll take care of it, ' he said and walked out of the room.

Barry wrote to a journalist friend with the *Irish Press* whom he had known through writing articles for the paper and who was now in London. He asked his friend to call on Percival and tell 'the bastard' that if the case was brought on it would have to be tried in Ireland. He had escaped before, 'but by God, he won't get away the next time!'

At a later date the director was talking to Barry and questioned him about Percival. 'You won't hear any more from that brute!'

Percival is said to have replied to his visitor, 'I have my cottage and my pension. I'll keep away from Barry.'[39]

Despite this altercation, Percival in the early 1960s wrote to Liam Deasy and said he would like to meet himself and Tom Barry. It was meant to be a friendly gesture. Deasy was agreeable, but Barry would only meet him at the point of a gun. The meeting between Deasy and Percival never took place as Percival became ill and died on 31 January 1966.[40]

Ewan Butler interviewed Barry for his book *Barry's Flying Column* in the late 1960s and informed him that Major Percival had been awarded the OBE for his part in the 1920–1922 action in Ireland. His retort shows that the passage of fifty years had done nothing to assuage his hatred of Percival: 'Good old OBE! Percival should have got a bar to it for his valiant defence of Singapore!'[41] Barry's book sold so well it became a world bestseller. It eventually became required reading at military academies including Sandhurst and West Point. Leaders like Mao, Fidel Castro and guerrilla commanders in Middle Eastern countries all studied his method of guerrilla warfare.[42]

American Tour to End Partition of Ireland

Barry, always conscious of injustice in one part of the country, continued to keep the question of the partition of Ireland to the fore. In August 1949 he wrote to his friend Connie Neenan, in America, about 'the new League of Nations' which had begun its sitting in Strasbourg. 'This body will show to the Irish people that it does not give three dams (sic) about "Partition" or any other aspect of Irish freedom,' he wrote. 'Perhaps then the Irish people will realise this bluff which politicians have been shouting for the last eighteen months. I have often wondered that when the bluff is exposed, would the Irish people care sufficiently to make our rulers take realistic action.'[1] A few days later he informed his friend Richard Dalton in America that he was pleased that the issue of 'the British made partition of Ireland' was raised in Strasbourg 'giving it world wide prominence'. However 'what is required is a plan of action,' he wrote. But he doubted if any Irish political party would 'tell the British "Get our or we will make it as costly for you in the Six Counties as we did in the Twenty-Six!" and then go ahead to formulate and implement a plan to do so if the British refuse to leave … Heaven knows, I do not want to see any more armed action if it can be avoided, but I am convinced that unless the British are of [the] opinion that such action will eventually be taken they will not leave go their hold.'[2]

The next month he wrote again to Connie: 'One may well ask why people like me do not force the issue with political parties, but how in the name of Heavens could we get a hearing *now* when the whole of our people are dam (sic) well mesmerised with the political dictum, "Be quiet, trust us and propaganda will finish partition very soon" … that is what the people believe now.' It will be 'the beginning of the year' at least, he wrote, 'until the population' realises that they are being 'gulled … but until then one dares not to doubt the political saviour of the Nation.'[3]

By November he was 'unanimously selected by the joint committee' in the United States to be the invited speaker in New York on behalf of the '26 County Area'. He agreed to join 'a Public Demonstration against Partition' in New York on 15 November 1949.[4] At the invitation of the American League for An Undivided Ireland, 'General Tom Barry as a proven military leader in the south' addressed a public meeting of over 6,000 in 'Manhattan Center' on 17 November, 1949. 'Thousands were unable to gain admission and stood on Thirty-fifth Street, listening attentively through the PA system.' He called for 'Dáil Éireann, the Parliament of the Republic of Ireland, on behalf of all the people within the shores of Ireland to declare that Britain withdraw from Northern Ireland.' If this was not done then there should be a recruitment of '100,000 for the Local Defence

Force' as well as the purchase of '£20 million of arms and ammunition.' Furthermore, he asked for 'the replanning of our economy now so that the people will be able to maintain life and health … when the guns begin to bark.'[5]

The Boston Globe reported the 'deafening applause' that 'greeted' the speaker's 'frank and fearless' statements. 'The issue was not between people in the 26 and those of the 6 counties,' Barry said, 'nor is it one between Catholic and Protestant, and still one between different classes resident in our land. It is only an issue that rests and will rest for all time while it exists, between Ireland and Britain.'[6]

The League for an Undivided Ireland, founded in the spring of 1947, held an Irish Race Convention in November in New York. Numerous Irish and American organisations were enlisted to 'campaign in America to abolish partition'. They took as their motto, *Ireland, One and Indivisible, Though the Heavens Fall.*[7]

The Ancient Order of Hibernians extended 'a hearty welcome' to Barry and hoped that his 'mission' in America would 'prove as successful' as his 'unequalled feats of daring when Ireland needed men'. With Barry 'as leader of the movement' for 'the abolition of the infamous border' the Order knew 'the cause' was in 'capable' hands. 'No one man in Ireland has a better right to speak for Ireland,' and 'the great hope is that Emmet's epitaph would be written by men like General Tom Barry'.[8]

Tom accompanied by Senator James G. (Jeremiah) Lennon of Armagh and Malachy Conlon, MP, went on a gruelling tour, travelling by air transport, rail, and car.[9] In Pittsburgh on 20 November 1949, he told his 'enthusiastic' audience: 'We had to take the 26 Counties of Southern Ireland by force. We will probably have to use the same methods in Ulster'.[10] To the thousands who had gathered he emphasised that 'the word Partition in Irish ears means the occupation of the Six Counties of Ulster by the British'. *The Pittsburgh Post Gazette* reported on 'the mild-mannered man whose soft-spoken sound served as a strange contrast to the fury of his words'. General Barry made it clear that he was not in America to raise funds, 'the Irish government has set aside $100,000,000 to purchase arms,' and would engage the 'Irish army' to end partition. He told his audience that 'the British would either yield Ulster or have it taken from them.' Ireland is 'getting back into character after a lull of impatient peace and awkward neutrality', he said, and he would like 'to settle the issue peaceably' but doubted 'that such a result would be reached.'[11]

Over the next few days he was engaged in League meetings; then he flew to Chicago and told 'the assembled thousands' that 'America never enslaved another race.' He was 'here' he said 'as a guest of the United Irish Societies' and was not representing any political party, 'the fact is I have never in my life been a member of any political party'. His voice rang clear. 'My one aim is to unite the Irish people – one race … it is futile to say that partition will end if we are patient, and if we stay quiet that the Border will fade away, or melt away like ice-cream in the summer time. The Border will not fade away, or the partition will not be ended until such time as the united strength is used in a supreme effort to get rid of it.'[12] In Baltimore, 26 November, in Philadelphia 28 November, in Boston 29 November he continued to speak to large gatherings, and got front page newspaper headlines, with an editorial in The New York *Irish Echo*.[13]

The Boston Herald reported that Tom Barry's speech brought cheers from the audience when he called for Ireland to go to war against England unless all British armed forces and administrative personnel were withdrawn from 'the British imposed puppet state' of Northern Ireland within a year, 'or else the Irish nation will use all of the forces at its disposal to drive out the occupying invaders.

'We must be prepared to pay the price if we are to redeem our Northern brothers from British bondage and unite our ancient nation ... No sane man, particularly those who have experienced war, will want to see it again, with its attendant death and miseries. But what alternative for a conquered people, when the only language their conquerors can understand is that of war?'[14]

Barry proposed that all parties in the Irish parliament be forced to drop party politics, during this last phase of Ireland's struggle for freedom 'and declare the dissolution of the Northern Ireland Parliament.' The Irish fight for freedom was 'spiritual as well as material', he said. 'When a nation fights for its freedom it is fighting also for the dignity of mankind.'[15] His final meeting was in Providence, Rhode Island, 30 November. Departing from his prepared script on the last day of his ten day tour *The Advocate* reported that 'the slim, grey-haired military veteran' declared that 'the keys to peace are right and justice and not strength, economic and military.'[16] Before leaving the Commodore Hotel, he told the waiting press and other dignitaries that he was returning to Ireland 'with the hope that our people at home have now realised that the nation and all its resources must be swung into an action program by a united people in Ireland, backed by the united American-Irish actionists.'[17]

On 10 December, 1949, the front page headline in the *New York Irish Echo* was, 'IRISH PROTESTANTS OPPOSE PRAYERS FOR BRITISH KING – FAVOR IRISH REPUBLIC'. A joint Diocesan Synod in Dublin 'pledged loyalty to Ireland'. Capt. T. McKeever said their church 'had not recognised Partition of any sort, and they were proud of this fact', but this should not stop them from praying for the welfare of the head of 'the Anglo Communion and of the Commonwealth ... we do not ask to pray for him as the king of this part of the country, nor do we translate any of the prayers into a political petition', said Mr Maude. The members of the synod did not want to drive a wedge between the people in the two parts of the island. The archbishop said there were members of the Church of Ireland with Republican ideals. A. W. Cotton, a Dublin delegate stated, 'we in the Church of Ireland are not under the Church of England, we were in existence before the Church of England was heard of, and we will exist probably when there is no king of England.'[18] Tom commented favourably on the synod's 'loyalty to Ireland'.[19]

While Tom Barry, Malachy Conlon and Jeremiah Lennon were in America, degrading leaflets were issued by a group of men who were described later as 'England's agents in this [US] country'. And the question was asked, 'Is there British money behind all this?'[20] The men were critical of Barry on his American tour and all the 'groups trying to unify the race' and Irish American organisations. The leaflet stated that 'Tom Barry, James Lennon or Malachy Conlon do not speak for or represent the Irish Republic or the Irish people. All three speak and represent corruption, hypocrisy and treachery.' They claimed that Barry and his companions travelled on British passports. However, this was refuted when the numbers and details of their Irish Republican passports were published. 'The IRA Veterans of the Cork First, Second and Third Brigades – all soldiers of the pre-Truce period' issued a pamphlet with passport details. This had the endorsement of the veterans of the above brigades from New York, New Jersey, California, Boston and Chicago.

The veterans called the group who had issued the leaflet 'loud-mouthed in their acts of vilification of true and tried Irish patriots, and at a time when every effort is being pushed or should be pushed for the restoration of the six northern counties and make Ireland a united and independent republic.' The pamphlet lists the 15 successful ambushes that Barry participated in, together with his leadership on barracks' attacks. 'In addition, Barry made West Cork untenable for British law, British spies and British government. Barry's successful attack on Rosscarbery barracks cleared for him 270 square miles of territory without a British armed post. A masterly stroke of strategy and genius!'

The pamphlet gives many of his military actions during the War of Independence – feats 'unequalled in the Black-and-Tan fight!' It lists many of Barry's other actions and asks (in bold print) 'Where were the members of the smear-gang during the above periods?' And where were they 'when the blood of young Irishmen was being shed on the roadsides in Ireland during the Tan war?'

The IRA veterans' pamphlet is full of bite as it lists the background and activities of the 'smaer' group – 'Any further attempt by British hirelings to libel or slander … will be met with all the resources at our command.'

The attitude of this protesting group was hurtful and saddened Barry greatly. However, it only helped to enhance his reputation.[21]

The Ancient Order of Hibernians, New York apologised to Tom on behalf of all Hibernians. The action of such a group 'to discredit' Tom's 'unblemished character' who 'were ashamed to put their names' to such leaflets and have them distributed 'cannot be considered anything less than revolting to the men and women of our race at home and abroad who are today working side by side in the cause of Irish freedom.

'Be assured … in the not too distant future when Ireland takes her place amongst the free nations of the world, Emmet's epitaph may be written by men like General Tom Barry.'[22]

In 1951, Tom's friend Connie Neenan with Ernie O'Malley's help tried to get a film made on Barry's activities and those of his West Cork comrades in the fight for Irish freedom. Con became friendly with some movie 'big shots', he told Tom. Jim Feeney 'the ONLY director with guts enough to make a film, extreme action, plus the fact he has been sympathetic all down the line, brings a combination which ought to be fruitful.' Then Ernie O'Malley met John Wayne the 'most popular of all movie actors today,' according to Neenan. It was O'Malley's hope that because 'his rating' was 'the highest … mostly on action pictures', plus the influence of John Ford, 'America's greatest director', this would become a success. The Ernie O'Malley/Connie Neenan project materialised.

One day, some time later, with a twinkle in his eye, Barry said to his friend Christy Barrett, 'Can you imagine me up there on the screen, in and out of bed with all the coleens of West Cork!' He told Christy he would not stand for that. There was enough action; such a film 'wouldn't need that distraction.'[23]

Barry declined an invitation to unveil a 1916 memorial in Limerick, because he felt unworthy as he had not participated in the Rising. Seán T. O'Kelly told him that 'no man living is more worthy to unveil such a memorial than yourself. The fact that you were not out in the Easter Rising has to my mind no bearing on the question. You did much more in the cause of the independence in Ireland later on than most of those who were in 1916 ever did.' Still he declined. Leslie, who was in the GPO during the 1916 Rising, was then asked and agreed to do the honour.[24] Whenever the president was in Cork he sought out Barry's company. They went to festivals and exhibitions, such as an informal private visit to the Seamus Murphy exhibition at the [Cork City] library.[25] Barry was an avid reader, mainly non-fiction, correspondence shows he shared his views with Seán T., Connie Neenan in America and the writer and social revolutionary, Peadar O'Donnell. (A collection of his books are held in Cork City Library.) He also loved the races and enjoyed his trips to Cheltenham. It was the only time, he said, that he could look down on the queen! These trips also gave him an opportunity to visit his relatives in England.[26]

When President Seán T. O'Kelly was due to resign, the Clones Branch of The Old IRA and National ex-Servicemen's Association 'unanimously passed a resolution' that 'Comdt General Tom Barry be invited to stand as an independent non-political candidate at the forthcoming Presidential election.' They wanted members of the Old IRA countrywide and unity of all political parties 'to rally' in support of 'this eminent Irishman'. They stated that the Americans 'have brought back that famous war-time General Eisenhower', therefore they saw it fit 'to invite General Barry to offer his services to the nation once more.' Though Barry felt honoured that he should be considered, he was not interested, and does not appear to have given it a second thought.[27] The Knights of St Finbarr, Corkmen's Association in Massachusetts honoured him as 'a noble man' and 'famous son of Cork,' and added his name to most distinguished guests.

They sent him wishes of 'health and happiness in pursuance of your civic duties to your illustrious city.'[28]

In 1956 Tom helped organise a project with Muintir na Tire for 'the afforestation plantation at the scene of the Kilmichael Ambush'. On behalf of Old IRA members he wrote that 'the only stipulation' he sought was 'that the plantation would not encroach the battle position where the blood of our dying comrades soaked the earth and rocks.'[29]

As the 1950s progressed, secret IRA drilling continued throughout the country. The men in County Cork were again preparing. Barry was now completely out of the IRA movement; yet when called on to train the men, he did so willingly. 'I'd be always for men who'd try and finish the job that we didn't finish', he told Nollaig Ó Gadhra. 'Perhaps in my own way I did all I could to help them.'[30]

In the 1956–1957 campaign, some of the IRA 'lads met Barry in a house in Cork' on a few occasions. He always started with a spirited talk. 'He made it quite clear that they [Old IRA] didn't fight for a 26 county Ireland but for a 32 county. He emphasised that, a number of times', Bob Kehoe, Wexford, recalls. In advising them, he said that attacking barracks, putting a bomb at the door and having covering fire as had been done in the War of Independence would not work 'forty years later.' Modern 'heavy machine-guns used by the RUC and British army' would make such an attempt by the IRA 'suicidal'. He gave them advice on armaments, told them that 'the secret of guerilla warfare was never to create a pattern', he advised them to enlist the support of the local people and always wished them the best of luck. 'What was evident was his loyalty to his own men. He spoke of team work – that a chain is only as good as its weakest link.'[31]

In the 1956–1962 period there were sporadic attacks in the six counties. In Coalisland an RUC man was killed in a booby trap in August 1957. After renewed sweeps, Kevin Mallon and Francie Talbot were arrested and charged in November. The case hinged on a statement they were alleged to have made. However, they claimed that they had been beaten and tortured. Barry was made aware that they were not involved in the incident, so, with others, he organised the collection of signatures and money for their defence. The case 'became a cause célèbre.' Barry brought over a solicitor from Wales, named Elwin Jones. The jury threw out the case, and the men were released.[32]

In June 1956 Barry informally presented Thomas F. O'Higgins with a tricolour 'in memory' of his uncle, Kevin O'Higgins (pro-Treaty whom Barry greatly respected, and who was assassinated in 1927). This was the flag that Barry had raised in 1949 over the City Hall, Cork. Being 'deeply touched' by Barry's 'kind thought', T. F. O'Higgins suggested that 'because of the national significance' of the flag, and also, because he believed that the symbol would encourage 'younger people' to 'regard loyalty to the Republic reproclaimed in 1949, to its flag and its legacy, as not only a duty but a pleasure. The presentation of this flag underlines in many respects this fact,' O'Higgins wrote, therefore, 'the occasion should not be left go unnoticed'.[33]

Described as 'a man made for turbulence, Tom had 'heroic qualities that were best suited for heroic situations'. Even at this late stage of his life when the raids and border campaign began, he would have gone up and fought in the north if he had been pressed to do so.[34] His attitude to the British in Ireland was like that of Dan Breen: 'If there is a man in my house and I ask him to leave and he doesn't leave, then I'm entitled to force him to go.'[35]

'A True Humanitarian'

In the early 1950s an old IRA comrade of Barry was being pressed by the bank to pay off a debt of £30,000 which would mean selling his farm. He went to Tom, who immediately came to his aid.

The pair walked in one morning to the bank manager. In the back conference room they were asked to take a seat. Barry took out his colt, placed it on the table and sat down, his friend sat beside him and the bank manager opposite. Within a short space of time Barry, periodically fingering the gun, succeeded in getting the debt reduced to £10,000.

'We've another call to make,' Barry said to his friend as they came out the door. Down they went to the solicitor; the performance, complete with gun, was repeated. And, of course, the solicitor agreed that he would send no more letters on behalf of the bank.

This was typical of Barry. Though he lived within the state, accepted the laws of the state, yet when the welfare of his friends was threatened, he used a cavalier attitude in helping them achieve their objective. As the years progressed he helped many of his friends in difficult circumstances with such actions. On another occasion there was a question of right-of-way, where, with the aid of a solicitor, one wealthy landowner was in the process of taking a section of land from a small not-so-well-off farmer, an old IRA veteran. On request, Barry came to the man's assistance, wrote a strong letter, which he had signed by other Old IRA veterans mentioning the power of the gun and that he still had an accurate shot. The problem was settled without any further interference.

Another IRA veteran was not, for personal reasons, on very friendly terms with Barry. They had fallen out some years previously over a commemoration ceremony. However, when the veteran found that a new wall replacing the fence boundary had been moved in on his property and when other avenues did not seem to work, he went to Tom Barry. Though the two men had not spoken to one another for years, Barry got into action in his own flamboyant fashion and said that the wall had better be built 'where it should be bloody well built or if not …' Of course the wall was built, as it should have been in the first place!

The foregoing stories were all given to me first hand by the people concerned, but because of such daring actions and the unflinching aura which seemed to exude from the man, other apocryphal legends seem to have built up around him.

A typical Cork story tells of his effort to try to get a car during the Black and Tan years. He went into the Ford Motor Company in Cork and demanded a car.

'Why should we give you a car? You're not at war with the Americans!'

'Hold on,' said Barry. 'Have you a piece of paper?'

He wrote down, 'In the name of the Irish Republic I declare war on America.'

'Now give me a car!'[1]

As there does not appear to have been such a car, the story belongs to the mythology of the man who became 'larger than life'. It shows how people expected Barry to behave.

This man, who could be so ruthless, was extremely kind, especially to those whom he felt, life had not treated too kindly. Den Carey was out of work for a period and Tom took him one day to buy a new suit of clothes. 'That was his form; he'd do anything for you. I never saw a mean trick out of him. Because he was so straight, so outspoken in what he thought, people didn't always agree with him, and even though he knew a falling-out might ensue, nevertheless he voiced his opinion.'

Upon hearing that any of his old comrades were in hospital he would call to see them, and after he had left, invariably they would find an envelope with money in it under the pillow. One man told me that he had been in difficult circumstances and had been involved in an accident. Barry paid him a visit and brought a book, which he pulled out of his pocket upon leaving. 'Maybe you'd read that some time,' he said, throwing it on the bed as he left. Opening the book later the man found £20 inside a sealed envelope. There are several such related incidents of kindness.

Most visits to his Old IRA comrades in hospital meant at least a £10 note in a sealed envelope. He was noted for his generosity and compassion. Visits to schools of special care children often meant that Barry, on departure, left an envelope for the teacher or director to buy something for the children. Though earning good wages as superintendent in the Harbour Board, he kept little for himself, as he 'believed it was his duty to help those in need'.[2]

A woman whose husband wasn't well, wrote to 'Mr Barry' – 'This will seem an impertinent request … I wish to trespass on your goodness to ask you for the loan of £10 until Wednesday … If I have not returned it to your home address by that afternoon ... keep this as an IOU against me … Don't ask me what put you into my head – a friend of my own whom I could ask is out of town.' She missed Tom when she called at his place of work, but would, she said, call to his home 'about 3.15 p.m. for an answer.'[3] This is one of many such letters from people who had no connection with Barry. Even a son of an RIC man who left the force during the 'troubles' asked Tom to do something for his father, perhaps organise a pension.[4]

Many people wrote to him asking for his assistance in obtaining a pension for them, and several acknowledged his intervention. He was involved with Liam Deasy in 'pleading' for pensions for 'well deserved' men. Liam would ask Tom to 'outline a few incidents' of which 'you have the personal knowledge.' The men themselves lacked the ability to write-up their own claims.[5] But he would be outraged when men not entitled to an IRA pension tried to obtain one. 'He'd get angry that they would dare try'. If they were not in any way involved in the war he wouldn't sign the form. Sometimes 'this coloured their motives' and their thinking of Barry changed later. John Browne, said he 'never knew of any man with such high principles'.[6]

When Mick O'Herlihy, one of 'the boys of Kilmichael' was burned to death in an accidental fire in Dublin in 1949, Tom and Liam Deasy organised a collection for funeral expenses and had the body brought back and buried in his home churchyard of Skibbereen. Both Tom and Liam paid off the balance in the final 'account'.[7]

Dr Ned Barrett felt he could always write to Barry about a problem which one of his compatriots had. 'He was sure to show a tremendous concern. He was extremely loyal to his comrades. As an example, an old IRA man, a patient of mine, had broken his leg and was on a miserly pension of £15 a year, and when I wrote to Barry about him, he went to work and succeeded in getting it brought up to £80, which shows his compassion. He was a true humanitarian.'

He also felt that it was his duty as well as an honour to attend the funerals of all his comrades. 'Though they may have played a small part in a fight, yet he always tried to show them the respect they deserved by attending their funerals.' When relatives of IRA veterans who had been 'down on their luck' were left with funeral expenses, 'it is known that Tom helped'.[8] Because IRA veterans gave so much 'to the country' in their early years many were left in poor circumstances. Towards the end of 1949 and 1950 Tom tried to organise a fund to assist families and relatives with payment for IRA veterans' funerals. With Seán MacCárthaigh's encouragement, he decided to approach the Cork GAA County Board. However, this did not appear to bear fruit.[9] Republicans, regardless of the decade of action, who were unable to acquire legal representation, for IRA activities, could rely on Tom for reassurance and defraying of costs.[10]

He was 'always helping, helping – particularly men who had fought with him, he loved to hear of their success, and was the first and always to their side if any of them met hard times. The good turns he did for so many will never be known because [many] were never prepared to admit it', Denis Conroy recalls. 'The words of the song will be true of Tom, *we may have good men, but we'll never have better.*'[11]

Barry loved to help the young and was always conscious of those unable to fund further education, so from time to time he discreetly and confidentially sponsored 'a few lads in university'.[12]

The Co-operative philosophy appealed to him, so when Fr James McDyer, in Donegal, sought his help he willingly agreed. However, when some members of the community decided to sell their produce outside the Co-op, he said, 'The Irish people are not worth fighting for.'[13]

'Barry was an intelligent man, there were very few subjects, whether commerce, economics, the industry of the country, all phases of history or whatever, that he could not discuss. He wasn't a man that just went out and got a gun to free Ireland, he knew the kind of Ireland he wanted.'[14]

He was not 'a Socialist' as 'some would describe it', he told Brian Farrell on a television programme. 'But I have a social conscience. I believe the poor and the less well-off should always be helped … I'm an individualist – that's all!' He insisted that those who had worked hard yet had financial problems or 'fell on hard times', should be assisted by those who could afford it. Share the wealth, and relieve hardships for fellow Irish, was his motto.[15]

But it was for his military achievements, he was most noted worldwide. Even thirty years after his guerilla activities, Tom was in demand for training young men. Ché Guevara of Cuba wrote to him, acknowledging his achievements as a guerilla commander and asked if he would train and advise his men, but Barry turned down a lucrative offer. He also gave a negative response to a similar offer from Menachen Begin, Israel. He had fought in Ireland for the freedom of his own country and could never be a mercenary soldier.[16]

Jim Wall found he was the only man of the IRA executive who returned to the houses at the Knockmealdown slopes where meetings were held to consider the ending of Civil War. His visits to these places, including where Liam Lynch was shot, was his method of recalling how history was made; also he wanted to thank the people for their kindness.[17]

Though he had disagreed with De Valera's stance against the IRA throughout the decades from the 1930s on, was angry with him at the suffering of many families and had strong words with him in the 1950s, he decided to visit Dev during the later stage of his life in Áras an Uachtaráin and 'make his peace with him'. Despite spending some hours in discussion, Barry never disclosed to anybody what occurred.[18]

UNVEILING MICHAEL COLLINS MONUMENT – HEALING WAR WOUNDS

'Here at this monument to commemorate for all time the greatness of the contribution made by Michael Collins in our struggle for freedom, let us bury the dead past of dissensions', said General Tom Barry, on a mild Easter Sunday in April 1966 when he stood beside the birthplace of Michael Collins before an estimated 15,000 people.

Dr Ned Barrett was one of those responsible for inviting the general to unveil a monument at Sam's Cross on 18 April to Michael Collins. 'I knew Seán Collins, Michael's brother, and discovered that the family had a great affection for Tom Barry. Seán said that Michael spoke highly of Tom's achievements and his acts of bravery. So when everything was weighed up, though they fought on opposite sides in the Civil War, it was suggested that we would ask Tom.'

It was a memorable ceremony. Men, who had bitterly opposed each other in the Civil War, now came together in an impressive tribute. In his address Tom Barry expressed his honour at having been asked: 'honoured firstly because of the greatness of the man being remembered, one of the chief architects of the fight for Irish freedom. Without Michael Collins' great patriotism, courage, capacity, realism and his untiring work against the British forces of occupation, none of us who lived through Ireland's fight for freedom believed, or now believes, that Ireland could have successfully withheld the enemy terrorism during those long dark days after 1916. Secondly, I readily accepted the invitation because I realised that this splendid committee of West Cork men have endeavoured by every means in their power to avoid giving any tinge of party politics to this ceremony.

'They have, in this case, tried successfully to honour the memory of one of the great men, not alone of this generation, but of Ireland's long history of armed resistance to foreign rule back through the ages.

'And thirdly, I have realised that this committee has studiously avoided raking up the embers of our tragic civil strife. "Micheál Ó Coileán 1890–1922" is evidence of that ... I intend to follow that example here today.'

Tom Barry went on to outline the life of General Michael Collins and demonstrated a touch of sadness as he spoke about the burning of Michael's home the day after his own successful Rosscarbery ambush. For the benefit of the younger generation he detailed the power of the 'mighty British force against a small army of Volunteers'. While saying that Michael Collins contributed more than any other man to the fight for Irish Independence he said he realised that 'this struggle was one of team work and that other leaders of that period played their part in the victory.'

Having been presented with a replica of the memorial, this erect military figure, standing in silence while the tricolour fluttered in the gentle breeze, 'did more on that day to heal the wounds of the Civil War than any man before or since'.

After the war was over – the battle of brothers – he stretched across his hand in friendship, just as Michael Collins would have done had the positions been reversed. 'Let us leave it that each of us, like I did myself, believed in the correctness of our choice. I concede that those who were on the opposite side believed that their decision was the right one too. But let us end futile recriminations of an event which happened over forty-three years ago. . .'

The men who had participated in both sides of the Civil War sat together for a few pints in Sam's Cross pub that evening, as they reminisced on West Cork actions together and apart.[1]

Barry demonstrated publicly how he was prepared to accept and understand that those who took the Treaty side were entitled to their opinion. John L. O'Sullivan, who with Seán Hales, captured many of the towns in West Cork with a section of the pro-Treaty forces during the Civil War, became a great friend of Tom Barry's in later years.

'Any meeting I was at, even though there may have been a majority present who were anti-Treaty, Tom Barry always made sure I was well treated. We often discussed the Civil War, but this is as it should be – agree to differ.'[2]

Tom Barry was 'a highly principled man', according to John Browne, a former detective in the garda siochána. He was invited as a special guest to attend the 1916 commemoration ceremonies in Dublin in 1966 to honour the 1916 Rising. Not being a veteran of the Rising he felt 'unworthy and not entitled' to attend the ceremonies, so he turned down the invitation. ' "I was fighting with the British at that time," he said. 'But Leslie was entitled to be there. With Tom there were no grey areas'.[3]

A few months after the Michael Collins ceremony, on 10 July 1966 with the surviving members of 'The Boys of Kilmichael' Tom marched to that historic spot to unveil a memorial. This time there were no guns only pipe-bands and a 'heroes' welcome. 'It was a moving moment,' reported the *Cork Examiner*, 'when guerrilla General Tom Barry led ten of the survivors who were present up the slight incline to the base of the memorial.

'They marched in step, heads high and bare, medals testifying to other days, and the thousands who lined the memorial cheered and applauded. For these were the men who knew greatness in tragic times and their contributions were not forgotten.'[4]

Tom Barry and 10 of the men who fought beside him on 28 November 1920 were the guests on that day 46 years later. Fr C. O'Brien, PP, unveiled the memorial and delivered the address.

Four months later on 18 November the veteran members of the flying column assembled once again, this time in Crossbarry to commemorate another historic event.

'The risen people of West Cork could not be bribed or terrorised; they rose against the tyranny of a foreign nation and threw off the shackles which bound them,' Barry said as he looked proudly at the men who stood before him and paid tribute to them as the flying column 'which thrashed the British at Crossbarry on 19 March 1921.'

Paying a tribute to the heroes of that historic engagement, and especially those who gave their lives, Commandant General Tom Barry unveiled a monument to mark the area where the largest battle against the British forces in Ireland was fought. On that historic day in 1966 thousands from all parts of the country attended and 30 of the 104 survivors were present. They marched to the memorial sited at the spot where the first shots of the ambush were fired.

In his address General Barry outlined the epic battle for his listeners and, the *Southern Star* records, 'There was remembrance in all their eyes, of how they had fought and how they had seen the Tans run away from them. As Tom Barry said, "The people will be freed, they will know what they are freed from, but will they know what they are freed for?"'

On that day, as on several other occasions, he was highly critical of those of Irish origin outside the country who were unprepared to lend a hand. 'People of that time had learned that what you wanted you must get for yourself. Even their great allies, the Americans, had not sent over a single officer, even an Irish-American, to help the Irish in their fight for what they (and the British) said they had fought the First World War for, the freedom of small nations.'

For Tom Barry, as well as the old IRA present, there were memories of ambushes fought in various parts of Ireland. 'I hope that all who pass by here will remember those valiant soldiers and sincere patriots who fought so bravely and gave their lives generously so that Ireland would break the chains of her slavery.'

He remembered his early days and paid tribute to one family in particular, the Hales family, who were responsible for involving him in the fight for Irish freedom: 'While Tom, the first commander of the Third West Cork Brigade lay in a British prison after torture by the enemy, three of his brothers, Seán, Bob and Bill were fighting in the brigade flying column.' It is perhaps a record that the three brothers took part in the Crossbarry ambush, and the fourth would have been there 'if he hadn't been in jail', Tom Barry recalled.[5]

During this period (mid-1960s) Tom, with a group of dedicated people in Cork city, became involved in *Sceim na gCeard Cumann* – an organisation concerned with the teaching of Irish for workers. An off-shoot of this organisation under the title of *Lorg na Laoch* – The Path of the Heroes – set out mainly to educate young people on historical facts. At a meeting one evening, it was suggested that General Tom Barry should be asked to speak to groups about each ambush at the ambush sites. 'He was reluctant at first. Then he said, "Give me one good reason why I should do this". So I had to think carefully as it was easy to antagonise Tom', said Jerh Cronin. 'Then I said, "If we take out a group of young people and they hear you speak at Kilmichael, Crossbarry, Rosscarbery and so on, they will be able to tell their grandchildren who in turn will tell their grandchildren – look how far ahead it will go – that they were present to hear the man who actually commanded the Volunteers who took part in these ambushes."

'He thought a moment. "That's reason enough for me," he said. He had great respect for youth.'

During the summer these groups went on tours. Criostóir de Baróid, one of the organisers, found it a most educational experience. 'He described every battle from Kilmichael to Crossbarry to Rosscarbery and Toureen; and he could call out where each man stood on the particular day. Watching the vigour of this man as he spoke, silhouetted against the sky, has left a lasting memory.'[6]

On constant demand to speak to historical societies, to army personnel or visiting tour groups, Tom never refused to travel to ambush locations and give his personal recollections. His companion was very often the young Detective Sergeant, John Browne who helped field questions. 'It was always such an invigorating experience to see the agile Tom with a mind still so sharp that he drew his audience towards him.'[7]

Following the three important unveilings in 1966, Tom resolved to withdraw from public life and not make any more public statements, yet as Criostóir de Baróid said, 'There is a prayer which you could apply to Barry ... Never was it known that anyone who implored his help or sought his intercession was left unaided.'[8]

Such was the case when, toward the end of 1967, a 1,000 acres estate in Lisselane, Ballinscarthy, near Clonakilty, was offered for sale by the owner Mr C. O. Stanley. The sale of 462 acres of this land in one lot aroused the indignation of the people of the area. Public meetings were held and the land commission was called on to acquire the portion offered for sale. It was discovered that Mr Stanley had previously offered the entire estate to be sold to one buyer, with the exception of Lisselane House and grounds. The West Cork Land League was pressing for what was originally put on the market to be offered to neighbouring small farmers.

In the the *Southern Star* a correspondent under the name of J. J. took up the issue on the side of Stanley selling his estate to whomsoever he wished, which would take the workers on the estate into account. A spate of correspondence to the paper began. Then a Cork group, Dóchas Chorcaí, whose principal aim was the halting of rural depopulation, came into the picture. They discovered that because of the various opinions highlighted in the paper – some without full investigation – that the West Cork people were split; opinions divided. So it was decided to call on Tom Barry, 'a man whose courage in war is only surpassed by his oral courage in upholding the right of the underman'.[9]

On Thursday night, 30 November 1967, in the packed Patrician Hall, Ballinscarthy, Tom Barry with some local public representatives addressed an eager audience. The meeting was held under the auspices of the West Cork Land

League, whose objectives embraced resistance to ranching, thus aiding equitable land distribution. The meeting, on the division by the land commission of the 1,000 acre Lisselane Estate, had an atmosphere of tension. With force in his voice Commandant General Tom Barry spoke. Despite his former resolution to retire from public life, he said, he had come to West Cork because he was struck by the justice of the cause and the dedication of a committee, none of whom stood to gain one acre from any land division in the area:

> I come here tonight to repay a debt of gratitude to the landless people and the small farmers of West Cork. When times were hard and we had few friends among the mighty, forty-five years ago, they protected me and the men who fought with me; they gave me their beds, their homes, and their scanty stores of food.

He had come, he said, because he, like others, believed that if the Lisselane thousand-acre estate was to be sold, it should be vested in the uneconomic smallholders and land-less men of West Cork.

From the outset he emphasised the good qualities of the owners and hoped that a solution to the problem could be achieved which would be satisfactory to the owners. He particularly stressed that there was no antagonism or hostility to the present owners, but he believed it was utterly wrong that in any area where young men had to flee the land to get their daily bread, that an estate of a thousand acres should be in the possession of one man. 'He spoke in measured tones, and argued his points logically'.

He suggested a deputation of seven Dáil deputies, and others if required, should meet the minister for lands and the taoiseach to discuss the problem. Following his suggestion of the deputation he said, 'I want everyone in this hall to stand NOW and be counted. If they have anything to say why this should not go ahead, let them speak NOW!' A total stillness followed.

Diarmaid Ó hUallaigh proposed that the meeting request Commandant General Tom Barry to lead a deputation of TDs and committee members to the minister for lands. There followed a unanimous display of hands and a general emotional applause to conclude the meeting.[10]

The media took up the issue. A crew from RTÉ spent some days in the area filming and researching a programme for television, but because Mr Stanley was not available to appear it was felt that the story might seem one-sided and the programme was never shown.

Peadar O'Donnell who, since the 1930s, had been involved in protecting the rights of small landowners, threw himself behind the cause.

Once again the *Southern Star* correspondent J. J. took up the issue:

> Commandant General Barry enjoys a reputation as a soldier and a man of principle, second to none. We accept that he firmly believes that it is wrong for one man to own one thousand acres of land. This is an honest statement of opinion. One of the hazards famous men have to bear is the efforts of people who would like to use them for ignoble ends ... agitation about the Lisselane Estate was punctuated by a burst of oratory which was redolent of the bigotry and the sectarianism of Paisleyism ... [11]

Week followed week and letters flowed into the *Southern Star*. Letters appeared in other papers, very often in response to Tom Barry's name. In fact there seemed to be two controversies: (1) the estate versus the small holder and (2) for and against Tom Barry.

Dr Lucey, Bishop of Cork and Ross, said to Tom, 'I don't know how to sort out this business. I think,' he said,' we'll have to have another revolution!'

'By God I think we should,' said Tom, and paused. 'But I wouldn't be too sure of your support when it comes!'[12]

As Barry predicted, the bishop then went on and spoke against the principle suggested by the West Cork Land League and Tom Barry. He had an idea of gathering local workers together to grow vegetables on the land; but his concept had already been tried in the area, according to Leo Meade, secretary of the West Cork Land League, and was unsuccessful. So the controversy continued and the 'letters to the editor' spread over many months. Barry does not appear to have replied to any of the letters. He didn't have to; others seemed to express what he would have said. Action was more important to him.

'Barry's intervention put the issue on a higher plane. He generated a fire, gave us new life, got us all working together, and he insisted in keeping religion and politics out of it', explained Leo Meade.

He worked with determination for the delegation and with Fr Denis Houten, the West Cork Land League and Dóchas Chorcaí. The issue covered a period of almost two years but, according to Leo Meade, the final result was 'exceptionally satisfactory'.

Fifteen local farmers who had less than thirty acres of land each had their holdings brought up to over 60 acres through the land commission. The remaining land, divided into six farms of 70 acres, was sold to outside farmers who had only about 25 acres. Their 25 acres were sold in their localities to make other farms viable.

Leo Meade says it has meant that there are now about 40 children where once there was none. 'It is a perfect example of a settled area where local organisations and a community has now built up. So the end result was success.'[13]

All those involved have no doubt that the event would not have such a satisfactory conclusion were it not for the intervention of Tom Barry. Most of all, his persuasive powers and his diplomacy cemented friends and neighbours who were in danger of division.

The following year, 1969, a RTÉ television documentary remembered Kilmichael and Crossbarry, drawing on some of the participants in these ambushes and the views of the commander of the Third West Cork Flying Column. On this occasion Barry remembered 'all the people of West Cork – without them there would have been no fight. We lost 64 men altogether and they are in our thoughts tonight,' he told Brian Farrell.[14] Tom Barry had 'retained a certain glorified integrity' because of his 'personal bravery' and 'of the very real achievements, in which he was a participant in the extraordinary military struggle with the odds so unequal – which brought out qualities of personal valour and of loyalty – these do indeed stand the test of time,' according to Professor Gearóid Ó Tuathaigh, in an RTÉ radio programme. Furthermore he 'never shirked in giving his views' and made 'statements that were often seen to be abrasive. The granite-like integrity of the man and the personal bravery ... retained for him this romantic glow, this heroic mould.'[15]

At 72, he was in constant demand to deliver lectures at army centres, colleges, universities, historical societies, and could speak for hours without notes. At UCG, he spoke for one a half-hours and spent almost another hour and a half answering questions. 'Isn't it a good job I'm not a professor, my lectures would last all day!' he quipped. A few weeks later he spoke to students and priests in Maynooth. Monsignor Tomás Ó Fiaich got them to learn 'The Boys of Kilmichael'. As Barry entered the hall they almost 'lifted the roof'. When Tomás Ó Fiaich introduced him as the man who was once excommunicated from the Catholic Church, he responded as he took the rostrum, 'Not once, but five times!'[16]

Tom was asked in 1969 by Nollaig Ó Gadhra if he was happy and if he had his life to live again would he take the same road? He responded: 'I think I'm the happiest man in Cork. I would say, in Ireland! I have no property. I have no money. I have enough to live on. And I'm glad I've lived the life I did.'[17]

In the heather-covered countryside of Kilmichael, 50 years after the ambush, over 3,000 people turned up to hear the commander who planned, fought and helped to win the ambush. The other survivors were also there.

'They wore their Sunday suits and in their eyes shone the stars of old memories. It was not difficult to picture them in the breeches and gaiters and trench coats they once had worn. There was vigour in their years and the spiritual toughness, which had seen them through turbulent days, was evident in the mould of their faces.'[1]

It was 9 August 1970. The commemoration date was brought forward from 28 November, the actual anniversary date, so that these now elderly men could take part under better weather conditions than they experienced on 28 November 1920. Old IRA men and members of Cumann na mBan came in their hundreds, from many parts of the country to celebrate the event and hear the veteran guerrilla leader speak. Having recounted the details including the false surrender, it was inevitable that General Barry would refer to the troubles in the north of Ireland – troubles, which had erupted the previous year.

'We are living in strange times and from some utterances by certain people, we should not be here at all to remember with pride those men who died with guns in their hands. Rather would it seem that we should apologise for them.'[2]

He made it quite clear that the objective of a 32 county Republic was the same as 50 years ago when the Republic was proclaimed and IRA men fell in battle. It was confirmed he said by three-quarters of the adult population of Ireland at the British general election of 1918 and defended in arms afterwards by the Irish Republican army.

'The ending of partition is the responsibility of not alone the people of Ireland, but of every Irishman wherever he may be.'

He said it was not alone the right, but 'the bounden' duty of all who seek to end the foreign armed occupation of the north-east to use every means to do so. 'One hopes that it can be done peacefully, but it will be only effected from the strength of a united Republican movement.'

Concluding, he stated that the chequered history of Ireland 'showed a mixture of victories and defeats and they had much to learn from it, particularly the need for unity and cold hard planning.'[3]

A report of his speech appeared in all the national dailies on 10 August, and on 14 August a letter to the *Irish Times* signed by Noel Browne, TD, under the heading of 'Fighting Cocks' suggested a 'Joxer Daly-style fighting … Taking that well-known pair of bellicose right-wing political doctrinaires, Republican General Tom Barry from the south, and Unionist Mr William Craig from the north, put them into a big wind-filled thin brown-paper bag and defy them to fight their way out of it … militants on both sides who favour arming preferably other Irishmen to kill one another ... '

Letters of reply began to appear in the *Irish Times,* the last on 14 September, during which time Tom Barry's 'right-wing' stance, a utopian Irish state and the merits and demerits of what government, Churches and Tom Barry had or had not done were all debated.

On 19 August Margaret Duffy took up Dr Browne's argument; 'Dr Noel Browne's comparison of General Barry and William Craig is as preposterous as ever I heard ... Dr Browne should remember that he would not be sitting in Dáil Éireann today were it not for men like General Barry and his comrades ...'

An interesting long letter appeared on 22 August from Críostóir de Baróid, Corcaigh, in which he outlined many of the deeds performed by Tom Barry, telling of a man 'in the hungry 1930s who was unemployed and seriously ill in hospital, without hope or resource for his wife and young family.' A visitor called and unobtrusively laid an envelope on his bed. 'The envelope contained £10. The visitor was Tom Barry! Hundreds of such stories can be told of such instances, independent man with a heart of truth; and of the worthy causes of the down-and-outs, of the homeless, of the victims of privilege or of arrogant authority, who have found in him an outspoken, fearless champion ...

'Nobody will be naïve enough to say that Tom Barry or any other man can do no wrong. But I fail to see how anyone can say that he is right-wing. By what contortions of reasoning can he be put on the same wing as Mr Craig ... a man who has proved to precipitate civil strife rather than grant the minority the rights guaranteed by the very constitution which Mr Craig himself accepts? ...'

Noel Browne continued to defend his attitude. Tom Barry writing on 24 August thanked those who had written on his behalf; and of Noel Browne, he said, 'Down the years he has rampaged within Fianna Fáil, then Clann na Poblachta, and now rests, temporarily I am sure, with Labour ... pity this politician of delusions and confusions.'

Eventually the controversy ended, but Críostóir de Baróid said that Tom was extremely upset that there had to be such 'washing in public of dirty linen'.[4]

In an *Irish Independent* series by Raymond Smith, 8 December 1970, under the heading 'What is Republicanism?' Barry expressed his opinion that, in the main, the young Volunteers of 1919–1921 were satisfied:

> that they were following in the footsteps of the greatest men in all our history – the men of 1916 – that one day they would drive out the foreign army, and end the subjection of the Irish nation.
> That was the main plank of the Irish Republicanism of over 50 years ago. The young men were growing up and as a Flying Column moved extensively around the countryside, they could not help but be affected by the disparity in the lives of the people.
> They saw the lords of the ascendancy in their castles and manors, surrounded by servants and wealth, owning large stretches of land, holding fishing and shoot-

ing rights, living as masters of a population where the large majority of the people were poor and a section of them lived in misery and dire distress.

Young men had their minds and their feelings disturbed, of course, and many must have vowed that when the armed battle was won, there would be changes in the lives of their people.

According to Barry, the IRA billeted in the manors, levied subscriptions to the brigade arms fund, prevented evictions, confiscated the lands, produce and farm stocks of executed spies and informers and tried to feed the hungry poor. 'It was then that it dawned on some that the slogan "Undo the conquest with all its evils" was a more fitting one than "Up the Republic". Yet the first objective was to remain – that of driving out the British occupying forces ... Today ... [1970] the chief objective remains as it was over half a century ago, but we see no reason why the undoing of the conquest cannot go on simultaneously with the driving out of the occupying forces. But, alas, we see no signs of an intelligent attempt at effecting either objective.'[5]

Barry, in this interview in the *Irish Independent*, talked about splinter groups not aiding Republicanism, and he also spoke of unity among all politicians in the Dáil. 'It surely can be said that every member of the Dáil would prefer to sit in a parliament of an All-Ireland Republic but they inherited a truncated Twenty-Six/Six County Ireland because their predecessors were not strong enough to force the Republic of the Proclamation in 1921 from the grip of the British occupying forces.'

He maintained that organisations and individuals outside the Dáil who wished to end partition should take a searching look at their policies and tactics. He concluded his interview: 'Foolish talk about not recognising the Parliament we have here in the Twenty-Six counties must be ended, too, as every one living in the area does recognise the state. Every time one travels in a bus or train, buys a postage stamp, avails of the health services, or accepts a wages' packet from which income tax has been deducted, one recognises the state.'[6]

In June 1971, when there was a suggestion of celebrating the Truce of 1921, Barry described it as 'spitting on the Irish nation'. He was speaking at the unveiling of a memorial at Carrowkennedy, Westport, commemorating an ambush of crown forces there 50 years previously, by members of the West Mayo Flying Column.

He claimed, in his talk, that what the Truce finally brought 'was deaths, executions and counter-executions in a Civil War that brought this country to the verge of destruction'. He criticised the newspaper advertisement by the department of defence, which specified that the Truce commemoration reception would only be for the relatives of those who died before 11 July 1921.

'What they are trying to say is that anyone who died after that date did not die for Ireland. The relatives of men such as Cathal Brugha, Liam Mellows, Michael Collins, Seán Hales, Dick Barrett of Cork and Seán Sabhat did not qualify and could not be invited. It would be a gross lie to say that these men and those who died in the Civil War – regardless of which side they were on – or that the men who died in the streets of Belfast at the hands of the British troops did not die for Ireland.'[7]

'But what man can state the principles for which men gave their lives for Ireland without referring to the reign of terror in our six northern counties over the past two years?' he asked.

As to the suggestion made two years previously to send the Irish army into the six counties, he termed it the 'talk of unthinking fools'. He said the army could not have invaded 'even the Aran Islands' at that particular time; they weren't prepared 'in mind or equipment for such an action, having been kept short of men, arms and ammunition', over the years. He added that this part of the country was 'torn asunder with political splits and counter-splits and we were a nation without a unity of purpose'.

On this sunny June day in the rugged Mayo countryside he referred to the Arms Trial and complained of attempts to smear the name of his own wife by associating her with the arms plot.

In conclusion he urged that people should remember that 'our six counties were conquered and are being occupied by force. If we had the power, the will and the army, we had a perfect right to take them back by force at the opportune time.'[8]

A month later, on 11 July 1971, he spoke in Crossbarry at the fiftieth anniversary commemoration of that famous engagement. He said it was the last time he would speak at a commemoration and went on to suggest that Easter Sunday should be a memorial day for the honour of dead Irish patriots. Again he referred to the six counties saying that 'No Irishman can stand on a Republican platform without mentioning the scandalous state of affairs which exists there …' John Whelton who laid a wreath for the men who gave their lives for the freedom of Ireland said a few words on behalf of all his comrades 'living and dead'.[9]

In July 1971 Martin O'Leary, a 20 year old Cork Republican died following an explosion at Mogul Mines, Co. Tipperary. A force of 200 gardaí walked with the hearse and 'an estimated 500 gardaí ringed' St Finbarr's cemetery during the ceremonies. This was at the height of 'the troubles' in Northern Ireland and there was fear of conflict. He was buried in the Republican Plot. The grave had been opened during the night 'without the permission of the corporation'. Official IRA chief-of-staff, Cathal Goulding gave the oration. Barry, who was not present, disliked the Official IRA's move away from traditional Republicanism and because of this 'invasion' he felt the Republican plot 'was dishonoured by the inclusion of a modern [Official] Republican alongside veterans' of the War of Independence. The incident copper-fastened his decision that the Republican plot would not be his final resting place.[10]

In the summer of 1972 when Tom was unveiling a memorial in Kilkelly, to the memory of the men who were killed in East Mayo, during the War of Independence, John Snee in introducing him spoke of the bravery and resoluteness of all those who fought for Ireland, 'but' he said, 'there was only one Tom Barry!'[11]

A group of about 24 Provisional IRA came down from Northern Ireland to meet with him and get his views. They met in the old Connolly Hall in Cork where Barry gave them a 'good talk' on tactics.

Joe Cahill, IRA activist and chief-of-staff over a number of years, found Tom Barry very supportive of the northern 'struggle for freedom'. Barry 'believed in the justice of the cause, right throughout the 1950s, 1960s and 1970s,' Joe Cahill recalls. 'Whenever we took active men to meet him, he advised and encouraged them to complete the job that he and his men started. He'd get very angry at the way Nationalists in Northern Ireland were treated as second-class citizens.'

Many men engaged in the struggle in South Armagh and other parts of Northern Ireland sought his advice. 'His active interest in the IRA was beneficial to the men', said Cahill, who admits that Barry gave him many tips, 'whenever' the two men spent worthwhile hours in discussion. 'He always maintained that the objective was the same – the fight for freedom – though the means of achieving it had altered.'

'Barry has to be admired,' said Joe Cahill. 'He wasn't an armchair general. He was a military genius. In the conflict he led by example. Throughout the decades, the goal of a United Ireland in his lifetime, was his greatest wish. Not all that long before he died, I met him. He had one desire, he said. If he had the energy, he would love to get some men together and have one other go at the British establishment, to see could he achieve his aim – bring them into discussions.'[12]

A few nights after Bloody Sunday (30 January 1972) Brendan O'Neill, Dave O'Sullivan and group of Cork men organised a mass meeting in the City Hall with Barry as the principal speaker. Thousands packed in and the overflow lined over the Lee Bridge as Republican men from each decade, the 1920s, 1930s, 1940s up to the 1970s stood on the stage. 'The atmosphere was electric'.[13]

As time passed Tom, concerned about the ongoing conflict in the north, had no time for stone-throwing or petrol-bombing civilian targets. In fact this 'made him angry'.[14] 'I won't be associated with the putting of bombs in pubs.'[15]

He told Sighle Humphreys how he had tried 'to get a united effort in the Six Counties ... but to no avail ... A certain man came to me and I knew they would not attend any meeting with the others who have accepted [a united effort]. Of course that is the basic cause of our 800 years subjection – no unity, discipline and the continuation of some leaders of their determination to be top dogs. If I were ten years younger,' he wrote, 'I'd try and write a book giving the real cause of our continuous failures. Anything that you [Sighle], Con or the others or St Peter [could do] could not get unity nowadays, so your meeting will be futile and I will not attend ... I would go up to your meeting but I abhor meetings that I believe are futile'. Three weeks previously he had organised Cork signatures, he said, sent them to Dublin for political consideration, but this 'was blocked somewhere on the line'.[16]

Early in 1973 he had surgery in the back of his neck and his eyes as a result of a slight accident. He feared he would lose his sight. When Leslie came to the hospital after the operation he had 'his eyes covered'. Stoically he said, 'well, we will take this in the same way as we took life's ups and downs since we married in 1921!'[17] Tom often described their marriage 'as a perfect marriage'. The secret is 'that two people understood one another and didn't step in one another's paths'. Each allowed the other to lead their separate lives. 'We were individuals, but we were always there for one another', Leslie commented.[18]

Then another obstacle was thrown in his path. In 1973 Liam Deasy (commanding officer, West Cork Brigade, later adjutant, First Southern Division) ... published a book on the West Cork Brigade activities in the War of Independence – *Towards Ireland Free*. Fr Chisholm stated in his Editorial Note that he got the closest co-operation from Liam Deasy and that the facts 'derive directly from him or meet with his approval'. However, 'I am conscious', he wrote, 'that all too often it is my own style which prevails.'[19]

When the Deasy book was published, the contents incensed Barry so much that he wrote a letter to all daily and some weekly newspapers '... frankly, when I first glanced through the book, I was puzzled at some of Deasy's statements, but later I was angered at his presentation of events and his alleged informants. The omissions, of great importance, were so vital to a true picture of what occurred that it was hard to understand.

'Individuals are all praised fulsomely and excessively, but coupled with that, a picture is given which denigrates the Flying Column, and if true, must show the Column Commander as a moron, incapable of commanding a single sniper, not to mention a flying column ... '

He went on to ask why Deasy, whom he says had the book partly written 30 years previously, did not publish it until 52 years after the events when many of those who participated were already dead. He mentions his own book, which had been published 25 years before this date in several countries, had been serialised in the *Irish Press* and the *Southern Star* and was not challenged by Deasy or any of the brigade men. He noted that the contents of the two books varied greatly. Furthermore, the major ambushes had been written by participants and published in the 1950s in *Rebel Cork's Fighting Story*. 'Their versions differ greatly from Deasy's, yet neither he nor anyone else made one refutation or correction. Why?' he asked.[20] Immediately he set about writing a booklet called *The Reality of the Anglo-Irish War 1920–1921 in West Cork*, subtitled *Refutations, Corrections and Comments on Liam Deasy's Towards Ireland Free*. This was published the following year.[21]

In his booklet he stated that 'the onerous' task placed on him 'could have been avoided had the Rev. John Chisholm' written to him and asked for his 'comments or any statement at distinct variance with Deasy's version.'[22]

Dr Chisholm told me he met Tom Barry by appointment in the Imperial Hotel, Cork, with the edited manuscript of Deasy's book which he asked Barry to read. Barry's reply was abrupt: 'whatever has to be said about the Third West Cork Brigade is in *Guerilla Days*'. Barry told me that he did not feel like reading a whole manuscript and that it was up to the editor to establish the facts. He said in his booklet that he would have clarified points if Deasy had written to him. However, Barry could have been annoyed that Liam Deasy did not approach, or contact, him personally.

Taking the ambushes and incidents in which he was involved and which he felt were not accurately portrayed in the Deasy book, Barry analysed these and gave what he saw as the facts.

As an example he takes an incident when Deasy says that he, Deasy, with another unarmed Volunteer, on hearing the column was in trouble, went to 'the Dunmanway area to muster a couple of men and dig out a couple of shot-guns – before going on to decimate the British, no doubt! Even every Fianna boy of that period knew that the effective range of a shotgun was not more than fifty yards. How in the name of common sense would even a rookie lance-corporal consider sending in a couple of shotgun-men to attack the British forces with their high-powered modern weapons having twenty times the shotgun range? ... if anyone can contemplate its ever having occurred, he can place any man who thought of it and attempted to carry it out higher in gallantry and idiotic behaviour than Lord Raglan who led the charge of the Light Brigade at Balaclava.'

The booklet is full of bite, using such phrases as: 'This disposes of one part of Deasy's fairy tale', 'Deasy continued his garbled account', 'Deasy's other hysterical statements', 'Deasy had the impertinence', 'Deasy's final chapter is equally incorrect'.

Barry stated that, of all the accounts, that of Kilmichael 'angered me most'. The incorrect sectional divisions, incorrect description of the ambush, but most of all the omission of the false surrender (as already dealt with) was, he emphasised, a gross distortion of the facts. It depicted him as 'a blood-thirsty' commander. The omission of the false surrender was questioned by reviewers. As it had never previously been queried, Barry felt hurt, angered and compelled to respond. In his booklet he dealt 'only with matters' which he considered 'to be controversial'. So, he wrote, 'I am jumping from one incident to another.' And he wondered if some of the material of 'Deasy's or Father Chisholm's alleged history' derived from the source given to the Military History Bureau, because if so, this source 'must have included some very tall tales.'[23]

He found his 'head reeling' as he read Deasy's account of Crossbarry which 'compares our position with that of the Wild Geese before Fontenoy, and ... actually quotes Davis' lines ... one really grows tired of the numerous contradictions apparent from page to page,' he wrote. There is the story of Deasy with

Barry and John Lordan in Cronin's pub toasting a glass to the day ahead, when they didn't even know what was ahead (Crossbarry ambush). Barry states that members of the flying column were not allowed to drink on active service. His 'mind' as they 'awaited the approaching military gunfire' was far from observing 'daybreak followed by a beautiful sunrise that ushered the finest day we [the column] had in a long time.'[24]

In the last page of the booklet Barry stated: 'As for those accounts of suggestions, which he [Deasy] claims he made to me, as commander of the column, it is of interest to note a comment by one reviewer of *Towards Ireland Free*. That reviewer observed that he counted five times when Deasy stated: "I suggested and Tom Barry agreed" and the reviewer further remarked: "This does not sound like Tom Barry". That Deasy never made one of those suggestions has, I think, been clearly proved by me in dealing with his version of the events of Crossbarry. Survivors of the column will know that, had he done so, he would have been told to get out of the column quickly.'[25] When Barry was appointed column commander in 1920, he undertook the ultimate responsibility of deciding what members fought in the column.

Historian, Pádraig Ó Maidín in a review, disagreed with the Deasy 'consultations' and 'council meetings'; furthermore, he listed ambushes and actions 'which were won not by council meetings or staff consultations but by a commander who had sole and absolute command, who planned every detail in every action and won battle after battle fighting and thinking on his feet'.[26] In deciding to write the booklet Barry believed he had no option as he 'could not allow gross inaccuracies to go unchallenged … the facts were often far less glamourous' than the Deasy book portrayed.[27] 'In the telling of the victories, the details matter, matter very much, just as much as they mattered in the fight itself', Pádraig Ó Maidín wrote. 'Out of Barry's pain and anger that moved him he has given us a deeper insight into the reality of the war in West Cork and into the men who fought it … we have, in these few pages, a major work of military history' of the 'qualities that made Barry a fighter, unique perhaps in our history.'[28]

Barry's booklet upon publication created an immediate controversy. The *Southern Star* took up the issue, which resulted in a series of letters to that paper. Facts were again at stake. The old IRA men were forced to take sides.

After the publication of Barry's book and before Liam Deasy's book was published in paperback, a group of old IRA veterans were asked to disassociate themselves from Barry's booklet and to endorse the Deasy book. J. M. Feehan wrote to the *Sunday Independent* that 'The original letter with signatures is in possession of Mr Flor Begley' (a signatory). Begley had been the piper at Crossbarry and in earlier years had praised Tom Barry, but in the intervening period had disagreed with him over a matter unrelated to their military activities. Dr Nudge Callanan, a reluctant signatory, did not know who initiated the suggestion.[29]

A letter 'to disassociate' themselves from 'the contents' of Barry's booklet and agreeing that 'Liam Deasy's book was a complete account of the organisation and activities of the Third West Cork Brigade' with fourteen signatures appeared in all Irish newspapers on 11 December 1974. On 23 December, Barry wrote to all the papers pointing out that in many cases some signatories 'were never even in the vicinity of a single one of the fights dealt with' in the booklet, nor did they participate in an ambush about which they disagreed with Barry's account. He listed locations where signatories were at the time of specified ambushes; therefore he suggested that 'perhaps the signatories would like to agree to set up a small board of outside historians to decide:

(a) Whether they were qualified to give an opinion of the Brigade history covered by my booklet and
(b) Whether Deasy's version or mine is the correct one.
I will gladly co-operate in any such project.

In his letter he made it clear that he was not 'disparaging the records of some' of 'the signatories who gave splendid military service'.

Although the controversy blew over after the letters, especially to the *Southern Star*, petered out, some bitterness remained. Seeds of doubt had been sown because of the Deasy–Barry controversy. Though I must say that Nudge Callanan was later 'so sorry' he agreed to sign. In fact Tom Barry was 'and would always be' his hero. A photo of Barry dressed in trench coat, hair blowing in the wind, hung on the wall of his study. He had not, at the time of signing, read the Deasy book – neither had John Fitzgerald, nor had Denis Lordan, and Paddy O'Brien who was not well at the time, believed that all he was doing was agreeing with the competence of Liam Deasy.[30]

Tom Barry in his critique stated at the outset that he was not in any way accusing Paddy O'Brien who, he wrote, 'has been a life-long friend of mine and I still have a high regard for his long service in the Irish Republican army.' He hoped that 'Paddy and his family ... whose life-work I admire so much, will understand I have no alternative but to tear asunder Deasy's published account' of the training camp and the Kilmichael 'fight'. He hadn't met O'Brien prior to his Deasy challenge, but had earlier visited O'Brien in hospital, as he (O'Brien) had been ill for some years. However, he was annoyed with the errors in the Kilmichael account and the omission of the false surrender.[31]

Delivering, on location, lectures on Crossbarry and Kilmichael to the Irish army in the 1960s Barry told the men to be as critical as necessary of the commander (himself), and to point out any mistakes he had made. Criticism of his actions and decisions whether correct or incorrect was his to respond to and to accept.[32] But, as he was a stickler for facts – any difference of facts annoyed him; hence his anger with the Deasy book.

The degree of bitterness that surfaced and the sequence of events during these exchanges, tell their own sad story. Deasy who had been ill for some time, died in August 1974. Tom Barry's booklet delivered to the publisher in January 1974, 'long before Mr Deasy's illness was known to either the author or publisher', was not published until November due to 'printing industry' difficulties. And the signatures against Barry did not appear until December 1974, almost four months after Deasy's death.[33]

Barry stated that, 'it has not been an easy booklet to write' because 'one does not like to take apart the writings of one who was once an associate, even though our ways diverged sharply after he wrote this book'. He felt that he owed it to the brigade and the flying column, however, to set the record straight for future writers. There is no doubt but that this book drove a wedge between the two men. Some members of Liam Deasy's family in West Cork felt it should not have happened, and believed that Liam Deasy would not have instigated the signatures. 'We [the extended family] did not like the book'. They were 'most unhappy' about the Kilmichael ambush controversy. 'Liam thought a lot of Barry.'[34]

It was a sad split after an era of togetherness. Tom Barry's batman and friend, Christy Barrett, said that 'the general was very upset. Liam Deasy had been his friend all his life.' They had met at funerals, commemorations and had got together on occasions, so 'he couldn't understand' why the accounts of so many of the engagements in *Towards Ireland Free* differed from other published accounts.[35]

The hero who lives long loses his aura; his moment passes and he is seen as an ordinary man. Only the hero who dies young remains, in memory and writing, forever young. Tom Barry, the hero, though still youthful in appearance, was growing old.

During the latter part of his life he became difficult, especially at commemoration committee meetings, often portraying a stubborn almost intolerant attitude. There was one particular night in Dunmanway where the committee met to discuss events for the forthcoming Kilmichael ceremonies. For some reason an argument arose as to whether the horse and side car with the Bantry Volunteers came up the road or down the road towards the ambuscade (they could have come from either the Dunmanway or Macroom direction from Bantry). Several of those present mention that night as the night Barry got into a tantrum and in fact appeared to be contradicting himself. It almost created pandemonium, and indeed it was not easy to call Barry to order and ask him to wait until the meeting was over.

He also developed a habit of trying to insist on doing everything the way he wanted it done. 'By God, he had aggression; even in his later life he was overflowing with it. He must have been some man to meet at the wrong side of a gun during those early days', was how one observer described him.

He attended the meetings in Cork for the organisation of a commemoration ceremony in Cobh, and everything was arranged for two o'clock. However, Barry arrived at one o'clock on the Sunday with a number of men, went to the grave and carried out the ceremony. The local men assembled at two o'clock with all other Old IRA men; when they marched to the island they discovered that a ceremony with the laying of a wreath had already been performed. 'It was disappointing,' said an IRA veteran.[36]

Barry had said, when he spoke at the dedication of the monuments at Kilmichael and Crossbarry, that he would not speak again on a public platform (although he later did), but each year out of courtesy the commemoration committee would write and invite all survivors. Invariably Barry would write back, thanking them and stating that he did not attend these events any more and enclosing a subscription for the wreath.

In 1979 the committee decided that, as his wife was not well, they would not trouble him by writing because he would have to write back with the usual explanation. When the group, assembled for the anniversary commemoration at Kilmichael, they found a wreath had already been placed. Barry with a few friends had come down the previous day, Saturday, and placed a wreath 'just because he wasn't asked, and we had been asking him over the past years and he wouldn't come!'[37]

Usually when he went to West Cork to attend funerals and meet old friends he would have an enjoyable day. Sometimes, though, he might take a drop 'over and above' and could be a little troublesome, but usually he only allowed himself to become merry. Though without the gift of a singing voice, he would, after a few drinks, start:

> *Down by the Glenside I met an old woman. . .*
> *I listened a while to the song she was singing,*
> *Glory oh, Glory oh, to the Bold Fenian men.*

And he would finish in a raised voice:

> *Sure I went on my way thanking God that I met her…*
> *We may have good men today, but we'll never have better,*
> *Glory oh, Glory oh, to the Bold Fenian men.*[38]

While in West Cork usually he'd call into Kathy Hayes' pub if in the Rosscarbery area, and with former comrades talk about old times and historical events, including actions and ambushes.

One night, returning with a friend from Rosscarbery, some argument arose between them; Barry, who could be troublesome when he had drink taken, said, 'Get out and I'll fight you!'

The driver stopped. Barry got out and began to peel off his coat and the car drove off.

'I knew all these roads,' he said. 'I walked every one of them.' He was out near Coppeen and went to someone's house and asked to be driven back to Cork.

He was taken to the Grocer's club where he knew his companion would be. Barry went in and tapped his companion on the shoulder. When he stood up, Barry drew back his fist, floored him, and walked out. Barry, still fit and dapper, was over seventy years old at the time.

In a pub one night a group was chatting and a slight argument arose; one of the company said to Barry, 'What would you know about it anyway, you're only a Kerry man!

'Stand up, a Kerryman I'm not!' said Barry raising his fist and hitting his companion full force.

Another night he was coming out of a pub in Cork with a companion from the First World War and the two had an argument. 'As one British soldier to another ... ' his comrade began. Barry stood for a moment, drew his fist on the plate glass window and smashed it.

Those who knew him well accepted his faults and spoke of him as a true and dear friend.[39]

In the 1970s he attended a big rally in Cork where he spoke on the Price sisters who were on hunger strike in Britain. In 1980 at Crossbarry, before allowing the IRA veterans to disperse, he concluded, 'and in addition today, I don't want you to fall out until the same prayers are said for the men who are being crucified in H-Block, Long Kesh. I want you to say the prayers for them, too, to show our unity with these men, many of whom are completely innocent and are rail-roaded by the same British that killed these men whom we are commemorating.'[40]

Despite all his aggression, he maintained courtesy when the occasion called for it. When Sighle Humphreys sent him a document for approval and apologised for inconvenience, he wrote, 'Don't worry about tormenting me ... I like you too much for that'. Unable to go to a meeting in Dublin as Leslie was ill, he told Sighle, 'I hate to refuse you anything Sighle, but now being in my eightieth year I dislike even seeing my name in print. When I was young and active in the Republican movement, I always felt that anyone over fifty years of age should have stepped down and leave it to the younger people. I have not changed my mind since.' He told her to tell the others that he was unable to attend the meeting 'for domestic and personal reasons.'

'All attempts in the past – and they have been legion – to the course of action' for a United Ireland 'have failed. I cannot see any hope either for this one,' he wrote. 'I have my own opinion as to how this struggle will end and my own views as to the strategy and tactics being adopted by Republicans, but I will not write them down. However I wish you well in your efforts ...'[41]

When 'the troubles' were at their height in the north of Ireland and prisoners went on hunger-strike to seek political status, Sighle Humphreys sent a communication to Barry asking that his name be added to a support group. 'A very long – 25 minutes phone call' to Tom elicited a negative response, Sighle wrote. 'He said that the men who were carrying out the recent killing – especially that last shooting of [there is a blank] could not be called IRA they were just independent groups working on their own. He said that he had recently been invited to Derry and Belfast but had refused both invitations. Since the hunger-strike began he had been approached to use his influence in certain quarters but had also refused and told whoever had approached him that he should realise that the organisation was losing support from all quarters and that they had only themselves to blame.'[42]

A severe blow came to Leslie in the mid 1970s. When the coalition government was in power she was telephoned and told, without ceremony, that she was not being re-appointed to the chairmanship of the Red Cross. Tom was hurt because neither of them ever became involved in party politics. Leslie had been decorated by 'the German, Italian and Netherlands governments for her outstanding service to the Red Cross Society, and in 1978 received the international committee's highest award, the Henri Dunant Medal.'[43]

In the autumn of his life he and his wife Leslie would take long walks down the quays and all along the Mardyke, and would often sit on a bench beside the flowers and trees, pleasantly chatting to one another. Then one day fate intervened and divided the couple. On 20 August 1975 – following the announcement of the death of De Valera – Leslie, while on the telephone, collapsed with a stroke and was taken to St Finbarr's Hospital. Though she was extremely low for some time, she gradually regained her senses but remained paralysed from the waist down.

He was positively bitter 'with God for being so cruel', his friends recall. It took him some time to accept the fact that she would never completely recover.

Each day found him visiting her, morning and evening, and as she grew a little better, her senses being restored somewhat, their meetings gave him more pleasure; the two would chat about old times, discussing past events. Christy Barrett, who often travelled by bus with him, recalls him reading passages from the newspaper to her.

'You could set your watch at eleven o' clock every morning as he passed the City Hall on his way to the hospital. And like a perfect gentlemen he would always raise his hat in greeting if there was a woman present.'[44]

Mick McCarthy believes that his attention to his wife during the last years of his life 'showed his humanity as a dedicated husband; visiting her twice and sometimes three times a day, often under adverse conditions, is a great credit to him. They were happy together.'[45]

In a sad touching letter to his friend Sighle Humphreys he wrote:

Well Sighle, I told a priest friend of ours that I had become a Roman Catholic Atheist. For the first 3$\frac{1}{2}$ months of her illness I went to daily Mass and Communion for her. But her pain and suffering increased and all the Mass cards and prayers of others did not seem to matter a damn. If God was the merciful and just God I thought he was in my youth and if he had any interest in us mortals, Leslie has seen none of it.

Everybody dies and I would have accepted her death without bitterness if she had been spared all the pain and suffering of the past 9$\frac{1}{2}$ months. But why was she singled out when I know hundreds of ruffians, who broke every commandment and rule of decency, pass away peacefully in their sleep or after a few days illness. Leslie will never know I feel like this; so I go into Mass every Sunday.

Your friend,

Tom.[46]

In another heart-rending letter, over a year later to Donncha Ó Dulaing he wrote:

The Barrys have struck a very bad patch, hence delay in reply. Leslie Mary lies paralysed for almost two and half years in St Finbarr's Hospital. During that period I also have had a spell in the cardiac unit ... an operation ... left me weak, I seem to be pulling back again. I visit Leslie Mary daily, by bus. and hope to return to twice daily visits. I'm not complaining, as this is life and to hell with death![47]

Christy Barrett, his helper-friend of many years, remained in Barry's flat, cooking the meals, cleaning, washing, and generally fulfilling the role of companion.

At times Tom sat on a bench in the Mardyke, where often he had sat with Leslie Mary; or he would tend to the flowerbed that surrounded the bust of Michael Collins – his former comrade and later adversary in war.

As the evening shadows were about to descend on Cork city he could often be seen sitting on a bench on the quay, alone, gazing across the River Lee with the spires of St Mary's church beyond and the Shandon Bells in the distance.

From Mardyke Bench to Final Curtain

Against the background of what became known as 'The Troubles' in Northern Ireland, especially in the 1970s, Tom Barry in a frank interview elucidated his personal views:

'Basically I'm a physical force man. If violent methods are used, you can only counter them with violence. What's the use in turning the other bloody cheek? Yes I discovered that long ago. But, I would only agree with bombing military targets, and military targets only. The fight to get the British out of Ireland forever is the right of every Irish person, but the killing of non-military personnel in the northern part of our country is something I abhor. The IRA have every right to attack the occupying forces, but nobody, and I emphasise the word *nobody* has the right to bomb civilian targets. The lives of the ordinary citizens must be protected, and I have always made that quite clear.'

It was a warm mid-April day in 1979. We sat on a bench in the Mardyke, Cork. Tom looked out over the mown lawn, past the shrubs towards the blue sky beyond. His words were measured, as always. He admitted he had gone to the north of Ireland during the early 1970s on the invitation of the IRA but said he found too many opposing forces of opinion on policy, and too many splinter groups, thus making difficult a united effort of tactics against British domination. Therefore he felt he couldn't be of much help.

He also admitted that many IRA leaders called on him from time to time, but he said he 'told them to their face' he disagreed with any 'ruthless bombing which sapped the lives of innocent people.'

When the column occupied Lord Tom Kingston's house before the Burgatia engagement he felt sorry, mainly for the man's wife and family. 'My family were gone to Liverpool; it was their decision. And when Lord Tom pleaded with me to let him go to England I consented. Mind you if it was proved that he had been responsible for getting even one of my men killed, I'd have shot him. He went off and didn't trouble us again. I always believed in abiding by the code of war except when those Essex savages committed barbaric deeds, then I ordered that they be shot at sight.'

He laughed when he thought of the soldiers in Skibbereen to whom he gave a good time, but anger rose when mention was made of the deaths of Galvin, Begley and O'Donoghue. 'The marks on their bodies showed treatment conducted by savages who called themselves soldiers of the British king.' Torture or ill-treatment was not war but savagery to him, and he referred again to incidents in the north. Torturing anybody, no matter whom, or killing civilians, was wrong. 'I fell out with the IRA because of the bombing campaign of Birmingham, and I do not agree with using places like restaurants, bars or any other public buildings as a target, or such incidents as a means of gaining a United Ireland.'

He went back over the pains taken in his guerrilla days to protect innocent civilians. Before the Toureen ambush he had ordered the Roberts family to be taken, under guard, to a neighbour's house and kept there until after the ambush. At Crossbarry, before occupying Beasleys' and Harolds' farmhouses on the roadside near the area, he had ordered the occupants to be removed and held under guard at neighbours' houses. The guard was necessary in case of informants. Drimoleague Barracks' attack was a risky venture, as it meant removing several families who lived across the road from the quarters; this had to be done piece-meal for fear of detection.

'It had to be done. I would never, if I could help it, put the ordinary people at risk. The men of the column who volunteered were taking a chance, but they knew they were gambling with their lives. This was always made quite clear to them. They had volunteered – though I was aware of this, my heart bled at the loss of one of them.

'Yes, I put them at risk. We were all at risk, but that's what war is about – the necessary war for a nation's freedom ... I agree there is perhaps a conflict here. You push them forward to do a job, to kill and perhaps be killed. You can't think too deeply about them then. Afterwards, when they get killed, one cannot but feel the loss.'

Did he see a link between the fight in the north today and the fight in his day?

'Well! They are fighting for the same objectives as the men of 1916 did and as we did. They want the British out. It's an ongoing fight, but the means to gain it have changed, not for the better, I might add, because the Provos have polarised the people against them. That was where we gained, we had the majority of the people behind us – not at first of course, but we won their confidence. They are not doing that. They are putting their own people, even down here south, against their aims.'

He regretted not being able to experience a United Ireland in his lifetime. 'Thinking back on it, we would have been better off, the country would have been, if we had no Truce, though I was all for it then; but I only wanted a temporary break, a tester, but the negotiations messed things up – that dastardly Civil War and everything ... Even in the 1930s if I had my way then, the climate was right to go up north and get the people behind us; we might have a different Ireland today. Each generation now has its own fight to fight and no matter what people say, it will go on until Ireland is united.'

The failures of past generations he claimed were due to lack of unity. 'Take Owen Roe, left alone after his victory at Benburb; Sarsfield left surrounded at Limerick until he surrendered; the men of Wexford and Wicklow left unaided in the 1798 Rising; and those brave 1916 men left to their military defeat while the rest of Ireland kept quiet. Also we have to remember that the achievement of unity is coupled with planning and leadership, and this required discipline and organised effort. If the Irish could remember this, forget their squabbles, co-operate and unite, then perhaps they could make a fresh start with a reasonable hope of success.'

Had he any suggestions as to how the problem in the north could be solved?

'It's up to the commanders to make their own decisions. It's not for me to say what the Provos should do. I only know I would handle it differently, but each commander has his own way of doing things. I back the Provos right to get the British out, but they need better planning, and the targets should be military targets only ... Yes, negotiations should be more progressive now in this generation ... I don't know why they're not successful. . . I cannot see why the northern Protestants would not be happy in a United Ireland. Surely we have reached a point in civilisation when people should work together. Why shouldn't Protestants and Catholics work together in a united effort, in a United Ireland? We have a great bloody country if we'd only pull together and work it properly ... '

As he turned a softness crept across his face.

'It's strange, you know, there's always money for war and defence. Yet when money is wanted for houses or education there is none. Human beings are peculiar, there's no doubt about it. Look at England, and what it is costing them to hold on to the six counties – those things seem to be taken for granted.

'Yes, all wars are foul,' he said, 'but the war of freedom has to be fought. If the mighty power will not release its grip otherwise, then the release has to come around by war.'

He dismissed the insinuation in some books that the War of Independence was a 'glorious war'. 'There is no such thing. You fight because you have to and you do the best you can – that's what we did. All you have to do is kill more of them than they kill of you.'

'People said you had no fear,' I said.

'Of course I was afraid sometimes. I don't think the man is born who has no fear. I conquered it I suppose. I needed bravery to command. I would never send a man to do any task which I wouldn't do myself because of fear. But let history be my judge!'

There was such gentleness about this man one wondered how he could kill a spy. But it was all part of the war: 'You did what had to be done.' After a thoughtful pause the next sentence came like a bullet from his colt: 'We didn't kill half enough of the British bastards!'

Suddenly he leaned close and whispered into my ear, 'I'll take some secrets to the grave with me.'

Some stories he told were shocking; one could almost feel the blood rising. Some were strange and sad, and others were funny – all based on a myriad of experiences from the man who said he was happy and contented with himself.

The man who fought in three wars before his twenty-fifth birthday – the

First World War, the Anglo-Irish War and the Civil War – was a little dissatisfied with the Ireland, which had emerged. Another IRA Kilmichael veteran put it thus: 'We fought for Ireland, we died for Ireland and now we won't work for Ireland.'[1]

In an *Irish Press* interview Barry said, 'nowadays people tend to be money-mad; everybody seems to be concerned with money, money, money. We all like to have a few bob in our pockets to spend, but it is gone to ridiculous lengths now.'[2]

The man who who told me that he wouldn't place a wreath on the grave of a famine victim, because they didn't mobilise to stick a pike in a few landlords despite the fact that they would have had the backing of the majority of the Irish people, took the filter tip of his smoked cigarette from its holder, put it into his match box which went into his left pocket and put the holder into the top pocket. Everything he did was exact. He rubbed the flecks of ash from his trousers, and as he got up and turned, his well-polished shoes shone beneath the rays of the sun.

He lifted his soft, grey hat in a polite gesture before we parted on the understanding of another meeting.

The May flowers were in bloom as Tom Barry walked with me down the narrow path in the grounds of Fitzgerald Park in the Mardyke, Cork. It was a sunny Saturday morning.

The cane with a silver top – a general's cane – was placed across his legs as he sat. Was he a proud man?

'How do you describe pride? If you mean proud of what I have achieved in life, the answer is yes; but if you mean vain, I don't think so. I hope not. Most of us try to do the best we can with our lives. Some don't do a damn thing of course. When I think of my wife and all that she has done for people, and she's left lying there.'

He paused, getting lost in his thoughts for a moment.

In a *Sunday Independent* interview he had said, 'I see goddamn rapists and exploiters and robbers and murderers go out in their sleep. Why does she have to get it like this?'[3]

A sadness crept across his face, so we changed the subject.

There was a touch of sadness, not to be lingered upon, at the fact that his family was not around him – that his parents were buried in England, that his father was buried without his being present. His older brother was killed when struck by a train in America, a sister went to Australia and married there, another sister followed, other members of the family were now dead ...

Tom and his wife Leslie had no children, but 'the good Irish people' were their family. 'This pair had given their time, energy and money to the people of Ireland'.[4] They really held no worldly possessions, never owned their own house, but lived for most of the latter part of their lives in a rented flat over

Woodford Bournes at the corner of Patrick Street, Cork.[5]

Tom had admiration for many of the great men who fought for Irish freedom down through the ages. He liked to talk about them: the men of Wexford, the Fenians and 'Tom Clarke, a man who had to eat his food in the filth of an English dungeon with his hands tied behind his back. The spirit of that man, whom one would say had had enough, came back a middle-aged man and fought in 1916. And after all that he faced the execution squad bravely. All for Ireland!'

Eamon de Valera was a man he admired, even though he was jailed by him many times. 'Sometimes he was right and sometimes he was wrong.'

Michael Collins should have lived, but then it was that horrible 'fight between brothers that brought it about. He wanted peace, just as De Valera did, as some more of us did ... Collins did so much for Ireland ... '

He showed me a copy of a letter to his solicitor in which he said he wanted a strictly private funeral. His plot for himself and his wife would be close to the Republican one but not in it. As he carefully folded it he grinned, then laughed, "Twill be all over before anybody knows about it.'

The sun had shifted high in the sky when suddenly a dark cloud obscured the golden rays. He rose, looked around, 'Light and shade,' he said. 'A mirror of the facts of life!'

We walked in silence towards the bustle of city traffic, towards his flat over Woodford Bournes.

He put his hand gently on my shoulder, bent towards me and whispered, 'If you write something about me and I'm still around I'd like to see it. If I'm gone, it doesn't matter a damn!'

A warm shake-hands was followed by the raising of his hat, and we parted. (The flat was gutted to make way for a fast-food outlet. Tom and Leslie's papers and letters were mixed up in the rubble. But a concerned builder salvaged some, contacted a friend, and bundled everything into black plastic bags.)

He was not feeling well during an informal celebration held on 1 July 1980 to mark his eighty-third birthday. That night he became ill and was taken to the Regional Hospital, Cork, where he died in the early hours of 2 July. His life had run a complete cycle; it was as if he had timed it. In life he was exact, and it seems almost as if he had ordered his death so that his precise age could be quoted without the addition of even an extra week.

His body lay in an oak coffin, draped with the tricolour, before the altar of the church of SS Peter & Paul in Cork city. His 'loving wife, Leslie' whom he had hoped would go before him, had a wreath of yellow and white chrysanthemums sent. Unable to attend the funeral, she lay in her hospital bed where she would remain until she died over three and three-quarter years later (April 1984). Only a group of friends, relatives and a contingent of the special branch were present, while a police helicopter hovered overhead. His wife's nephew, Fr Cathal Price, who said that the general had asked for a simple funeral without fuss, celebrated the Mass. 'Let us do that and give thanks for the man whose life touched our lives, and that of our country. Let us give thanks to God that the tremendous qualities that he had were used for us, and through us, and together let us give thanks.'[6]

On 4 July, without the presence of a firing party, without the pomp or ceremony usually accorded to great men, one of Ireland's most famous sons was quietly laid to rest in St Finbarr's Cemetery, Cork.

Kilmichael – the Aftermath

British forces, converging on Kilmichael, carried out largescale reprisals around the ambush area. Shops and homes, haybarns and outhouses were destroyed at Kilmichael, Johnstown and Inchageela. Proclamations were posted up in public places and printed in the daily press:

NEW POLICE ORDER IN MACROOM

December 1, 1920

Whereas foul murders of servants of the crown have been carried out by disaffected persons, and whereas such persons immediately before the murders appeared to be peaceful and loyal people, but have produced pistols from their pockets, therefore it is ordered that all male inhabitants of Macroom and all males passing through Macroom shall not appear in public with their hands in their pockets. Any male infringing this order is liable to be shot at sight.

By Order
AUXILIARY DIVISION, R.I.C.
Macroom Castle

NOTICE

December 2, 1920

The General Officer Commanding the 17th Infantry Brigade, Cork, requests that all business premises and shops be closed between the hours of 11 a.m. and 2 p.m., Thursday, December 2, 1920, as a mark of respect for the officers, Cadets and Constable of the Auxiliary division, RIC, killed in ambush near Kilmichael, 28, November, 1920, and whose Funeral Procession will be passing through the City on December 2nd.

F. R. EASTWOOD, MAJOR
BRIGADE MAJOR, 17th INF. BDE.

BRITISH DEAD AT KILMICHAEL

(Regimental Museum of the Royal Corps of Transport, Bullen Barracks, Aldershot, Hampshire.)

Killed
Captain F. W. Craik, MC, late Bedford Regiment.
Captain P. N. Graham, late Northumberland Fusiliers.
Major F. Hugo, OBE, MC, late Indian army.
Captain W. Pallester, late Royal Air Force.
Captain W. Wainwright, late Dublin Fusiliers.
Cadet W. T. Barnes, DFC, late Royal Air Force.
Cadet L. D. Bradshaw, late Royal Air Force.
Cadet J. C. Gleave, late Royal Air Force.
Cadet A. G. Jones, late Suffolk Regiment.
Cadet W. Hooper-Jones, late Northumberland Fusiliers.
Cadet E. W. H. Lucas, late Royal Sussex Regiment.
Cadet H. O. Pearson, late Green Howards Regiment.
Cadet F. Taylor, late Royal Air Force.
Cadet B. Webster, late Black Watch.
Cadet C. D. W. Bayley, late Royal Air Force.
Temporary Constable A. F. Poole, late West Kent Regiment.

Wounded:
Cadet H. F. Forde, MC, late Royal Air Force.
Missing:
Cadet C. J. Guthrie, late Royal Air Force.

PROCLAMATION BY GENERAL NEVILLE MACREADY,
Commander-in-Chief of the British Forces in Ireland
December 10, 1920

Extracts:
NOTE WELL:
That a state of armed insurrection exists. The forces of the crown in Ireland are hereby declared on active service.

Any unauthorised person found in possession of arms, ammunition or explosives will be liable on conviction by a Military Court to suffer Death.

Harbouring any person who has taken part ... is guilty of levying war against His Majesty the King, and is liable on conviction by a Military Court to suffer Death.

No person may stand or loiter in the streets except in pursuit of his lawful occupation.

All meetings of assemblies in public places are forbidden and for the purpose of this Order six adults will be considered a meeting.

All occupiers of houses must keep affixed to the inner side of the outer door a list of the occupants setting forth their names, sex, age and occupation.

The Decree of his Lordship, Most Reverend Dr Daniel
Coholan, Bishop of Cork.
Published in a letter to the *Cork Examiner*:

Dear Sir – Kindly give me space to publish and thus promulgate the following decree:

DECREE OF BISHOP OF CORK IN REFERENCE TO AMBUSHES, KIDNAPPING AND MURDER

Beside the guilt involved in these acts by reason of their opposition to the law of God, anyone who shall within these spaces of Cork, organise or take part in an ambush or kidnapping or otherwise be guilty of murder or attempted murder shall incur by the very fact the censure of excommunication.

(Signed)
Daniel Coholan, Bishop of Cork.
(Witness)
Patrick Canon Sexton, Farranferris, Cork.
18 December 1920

BRITISH MISTAKES AT CROSSBARRY

No action has ever been won in any war except for mistakes or omissions by the losing side – *General Tom Barry.*

1. The OC of the Essex made the stupid error of having his lorries travel in advance of his ground forces, thus allowing three or four lorries to be attacked by the IRA. Had his ground forces met O'Connell's flankers before the lorries were attacked, a very serious situation would have arisen; several hundred British could have been deployed on our right flank to attack while the Kinsale, Cork and Ballincollig troops, close by, were closing in from the south, east and north-east.
2. Whoever was in charge of the Essex cannot have made any attempt to rally or control his troops. I, and many others, saw them race away from at least seven or eight lorries beyond those attacked and outside our range of fire, and make off cross-country to the south. The Essex were no problem after the first five minutes; perhaps, too, they had memories of a few hammerings and of our contempt for them as fighters.
3. The efforts of the British from the south, east and north-east appeared to have been completely unco-ordinated. Their north-eastern units, estimated at 200, made an attempt to narrowly encircle Kelleher and Spud, which was quickly countered. Instead of this, any OC worthy of the rank would have sent half his troops northward, direct from their positions, for a quarter of a mile, with instructions to turn west there, and extend westward to cut off any escape to the north.
4. All the British seemed to have been mesmerised by the IRA going over to the offensive, thus destroying the plans they had for a complete encirclement of the Brigade Flying Column and its destruction when one of our lines was smashed.

MISTAKES OF THE FLYING COLUMN AT CROSSBARRY

1. The man who exposed our presence lost us at least three more lorries.

2. Our hardest-hit section commanded by Denis Lordan was in a bad position. The cover was bad, but when I first saw it at daybreak, it was too late to seek another to command the road from Crossbarry Cross, as the British from the west were already on us.

OUR ADVANTAGES

1. The far superior qualities of our troops as fighting men and the excellence of the officers and their section commanders who could out-think and out-fight any of the enemy commanders. I did not see one man over-excited during the day.
2. Our sections were properly deployed to counter encirclement, as events proved.
3. Our luck in getting in the first half dozen blows.
4. When the IRA commenced its retirement in column of sections in extended order, they moved as if on a parade ground.

The following order reproduced by courtesy of the Cork Public Museum, is typical of the written communications which were circulated by headquarters of Cork No. 3 Brigade to its battalions:

ÓGLAIGH NA hÉIREANN
HEADQUARTERS
CORK NO. 3 BRIGADE

15/6/21
Dept. of Intelligence
Divisional Intelligence Memo No. 2.
To:

OC ....

1. Cases have occurred recently of spies, generally of the ex-soldier type, moving freely round the country on the pretence of looking for work but in reality getting information for the enemy. It is clear that many Volunteers have lost their lives as the result of the activities of these persons.

All officers must take steps to ensure that a strict watch is kept for strangers in every Company area, that unknown persons coming into any district will be arrested and detained pending inquiries if the local officer is not satisfied as to their identity and business, and all Volunteers must be constantly on the alert regarding strangers and report the presence of such to their superior officers.

APPENDIX II

The meeting to end the Civil War continued through 24, 25, and 26 March. Being interrupted by hostile raiding forces on 25 March the members were obliged to move into the Nire Valley, where the session was continued and concluded at John Wall's of Glenanore. No minutes of these meetings are available. The written record came from captured documents published in the *Irish Independent* of 9 April, 1923.

Three points of view emerged in the long conferences:

1. Liam Lynch's view, which was simply to fight on, notwithstanding any losses or disasters, until their opponents were forced to negotiate. He believed they were still quite capable of offering serious resistance to the imposition of the Treaty and that they were in duty bound to do so. There was little unqualified support for that view.
2. The point of view which believed that a continuation of the armed struggle was no longer the best means of advancing the cause of the Republic, and that by negotiation the Free State authorities could be got to agree to certain principles in the sphere of government which would leave the Irish people uncommitted to the Treaty and Republicans free to advocate and advance their cause without restriction. Specifically, this meant finding some way of making it possible for Republicans to participate in the political and parliamentary life of the nation without taking an oath of allegiance to a foreign monarch.
3. The point of view which recognised that the Free State authorities were not willing to negotiate at all, that the maximum military effort had been made and had failed, and that the war should be ended, because further sacrifices of life would not advance the cause of the Republic. From this point of view a dumping of arms was the most acceptable way of ending armed resistance.

Three significant aspects of the situation were considered in relation to these points of view. First, the heavy losses by death or capture of officers and men; second, the policy of executions which had been suspended by the Free State authorities in February, but resumed again in March; and third, the lack of weapons which would enable attacks on posts to be made successfully.

The total strength of the army was then about 8,000 all ranks. Jails and internment camps held an estimated 13,000 prisoners. Against the 8,000 still in the field the Free State government could muster 38,000 combat troops. There was no effective answer to the executions' policy short of retaliation equally lawless and cruel, and Liam had forbidden any such action. Michael Cremin was negotiating the purchase of mountain artillery on the Continent, but there was no indication that he would be successful.

Two resolutions were considered. Frank Aiken proposed and Seán MacSwiney seconded:

That Government be empowered to enter into negotiations roughly on the basis of principles 1, 2 and 3 of President's memo. Dated 9/2/23. Report to be laid before executive at next meeting.

DÁIL ÉIREANN
(Government of the Republic of Ireland)

Proclamation

The government of the Republic anxious to contribute its share to the movement for peace, and to found it on principles that will give governmental stability and otherwise prove of value to the nation, hereby proclaims its readiness to negotiate an immediate cessation of hostilities on the basis of the following:

1. That the sovereign rights of this nation are indefeasible and inalienable.
2. That all legitimate governmental authority in Ireland, legislative, executive, and judicial, is derived exclusively from the people of Ireland.
3. That the ultimate court of appeal for deciding disputed questions of national expediency and policy is the people of Ireland – the judgement being by majority vote of the adult citizenry and the decision to be submitted to, and resistance by violence excluded, not because the decision is necessarily right or just or permanent, but because acceptance of this rule makes for peace, order and unity in national action, and is the democratic alternative to arbitrament by force. Adequate opportunities and facilities must of course be afforded for a full and proper presentation to the Court of all facts and issues involved, and it must be understood that 1 and 2 are fundamental and non-judicable.
4. That no individual, or class of individual, who subscribe to these principles, of national right, order and good citizenship can be justly excluded by any political oath test or other device, from their proper share and influence in determining national policy, or from the councils and parliament of the nation.
5. That freedom to express political or economic opinions, or advocate political or economic programmes, freedom to assemble in public meetings, and freedom of all press, are rights of citizenship and of the community which must not be abrogated.
6. That the military forces of the nation are the servants of the nation and, subject to the foregoing, amenable to the national assembly when freely elected by the people.

We are informed that many in the ranks of our opponents will accept these principle, as we accept them. If that be so, peace can be arranged forthwith.

We hope that this advance will be met in the spirit in which we make it, and that it will be supported by all who love our country and who desire a speedy and just ending to the present national troubles.

As evidence of our good-will, the Army Council is issuing an Order to all Units to suspend aggressive action – the Order to take effect as soon as may be, but not later than noon, Monday, 30 April.

EAMON DE VALERA
President
Dublin
27 April 1923

APPENDIX IV

Tom Barry's opinion on 'The Revolution'
correspondence with Rev. Father Henry, OFM, *The Capuchin Annual*
(16/9/1963 [from Tom Barry's papers])

1. In all fairness to the British Empire in 1916 there were no disabilities for Catholics in Ireland, instead they were perfectly free to practice their Faith. It was different altogether in the Penal Days, in 1798 and up to Catholic Emancipation when all disabilities for Catholics were removed.

2. Leadership down through the ages since the Penal Days, i.e. 1798. 1867, even Land Fights was essentially by Protestants.

3. The Vatican (I know their difficulties) had never lent a helping hand since the Bull issued by Pope Adrian IV, gave the British the Right of conquest in Ireland. In fact, you will find that even in 1921, Mr. De Valera had to publicly correct a message sent by the Pope on the signing of the Treaty. The Vatican has always been concerned for the status quo and has never taken a stand against revolution. Indeed, when Catholic Nuns and Priests during the Penal Days were being hunted, caught and executed, the then Powers of the Vatican gave them no help whatever.

4. In the plantation did the Bench of Bishops of Ireland back any other attempt at freeing this country. You will remember Bishop Moriarty's statement that 'Hell is not hot enough nor eternity strong enough to punish the Fenians'. There has never been from any Bishop a proclamation in support of any armed attempt to give Ireland freedom.

5. In my own days, with a few honourable exceptions like Archbishop Walsh, Bishop O'Dwyer and Bishop Fogarty, there was no support for the men of 1916. Although the Hierarchy backed the Anti-Conscription movement in 1918. I do not have to remind you of Bishop Daniel Coholan's excommunication against the I.R.A. when he had to look at Volunteers dying without the benefit of Confession. At that period, I myself, was on several occasions refused Absolution. Most of the Clergy of the Country backed the ban on the fighting men. There were, however, many who supported us and gave us the benefit of the Sacraments.

Despite this, I am not confusing members of the Vatican, Bishops and Priests with the Catholic Church, because I know quite well that the Catholic Church can not be wrong, whereas its members, from the Vatican down, can and have been throughout the ages on Ireland's armed efforts for freedom. In the years of the 1920–23 struggle we continued saying our prayers, attending Mass and receiving the Sacraments when and where possible.

... the Irish Revolution had been going on spasmodically for over seven hundred years before the Rising of 1916. It had manifested itself many times throughout the centuries against confiscation of lands and properties of the Gael; the destruction of the Catholic religion; the maintaining of the ascendancy; the keeping in check and subjection the peasant and the worker – even the strike of the Dublin workers or rather lock out of those men in 1913 was part and parcel of the Revolution. The Irish Revolution did not start in 1916. The Rising of Easter of that year was but a continuation of previous struggles deep rooted in the minds of those great leaders who decreed it and saw to the resurrection of a subject people at the cost of their own lives.

How does one judge the success or failure of a revolution? There has never in all the histories of all the Nations been a completely successful revolution. Each mind within the revolutionary forces has its own set of values of the degrees of importance of the results achieved. I had never the honour of knowing the dead leaders who made 1916 but I have read enough about them and spoken with those who knew them well to venture the assertion that if they had lived through the Anglo-Irish fight, and the Treaty aftermath they quite possibly would have divided into two or more parties. Clarke, the man of steel, Connolly, the social Revolutionary, Pearse the Gael, the dreamer and the romantic who had written 'The Sovereign People', Plunkett the religious mystic and all the others can only have been agreed on the dominant aim of the 1916 Rising – To drive the British occupation forces from the land; to establish a Republic and to undo the Conquest, and it is necessary to re-mark here that the armed struggle was only one phase of the Revolution. Had the I.R.A. on the 11th July, 1921, driven the invader from our shores (and it certainly had not been strong enough militarily to do so) the Republic would not have been established nor the conquest undone. It would take many years more of planning and working before one could decide whether the revolution has succeeded or in-deed failed ...

Those of us who lived through the period of struggle and were engaged in armed action were a rather immature twenty-two or twenty-three years of age, with no training in philosophy or economics ... the I.R.A. were not fighting for material and spiritual conditions ... There could be men within the movement imbued with those high motives but I never met one of them. The truth is that the issue was knit again because of 1916 and the General Election of 1918 and those men of the I.R.A. trained and armed to fight the British to force their evacuation. Those who were acti-vely engaged were fully occupied in defending their own lives and the institutions set up by the Republic, attacking the British Forces and attempting to destroy the machinery of the British dominion over Ireland. There was little time to think of anything else.

Letter from Tom Crofts to Pension Board in relation to Tom Barry's pension

Grattan Hill,
Cork.
23rd, April, 1940.

Oscar Traynor Esq T.D.
Minister of Defence.

A Chara,

Tom Barry was called before the Service Pensions Board in January 1939 for examination on his claim to a service pension. In January 1940 – one year afterwards – he received the scandalous award of $5^{163}/_{183}$ years Rank B.

He appealed and submitted statements in support of Rank and Service from the following: – An Taoiseach, P. J. Rutledge, Gearóid O'Sullivan, Pa Murray, Bill Quirke, Seán Moylan, Florrie O'Donoghue, Tom Hales, Seán Buckley, Dan Holland, Con Crowley, Michael O'Herlihy and myself.

About a month ago, Tom was called before the Board for oral examination on oath. On the same day Bill Quirke, Gearóid O'Sullivan, and myself were also examined on oath. Since then Ernie O'Malley, Florrie O'Donoghue and Seán Buckley have also given evidence on oath. ALL this evidence was given on oath and in the hundreds of cases which I previously verified, I was never even once put on my oath. Neither I am informed were any of the others. This in itself is an extraordinary feature of the case especially coming on top of Tom's peculiar award.

I have seen all the written evidence submitted on behalf of Tom Barry's appeal and there is no doubt that it is conclusive, but moreover I have met the men who also testified on oath in Tom's case after they had been to the Board and from what they told me of the evidence they had to give I am satisfied that the evidence on oath was equally conclusive. Strange to say that despite all this Barry is again to go before the Board and bring more witnesses and furthermore, the Board themselves have called witnesses to testify as to (A) Barry's pre-Truce Service; (B) Barry's Rank 1st Critical Date: (C) Barry's Rank 2nd Critical Date and (D) Barry's Civil war service. The extraordinary fact about this is that the latest two men to be called by the Board – Maurice Donegan and Florence Begley – can have very little or no knowledge on the four points they have been called to give evidence on. Maurice Donegan was a member of the Bantry battalion staff in the early part of Tan War and was arrested early on. 'He was not released until after the Treaty'. Barry's activities were around the Bandon battalion area which was about thirty-five miles from Donegan's area so he could give no information about Barry's activity during that period and he could hardly swear what Barry's rank was in July 1921 considering that he (Donegan) was in jail about nine months at that time and for about six months afterwards. Again, Flor Begley was a very minor officer attached to the Brigade Quartermasters and Adjutants staff and he cannot have any idea of Barry's Rank and very little of his Service.

Why has Barry been treated like this? That is the question that every officer who is aware of Barry's humiliation is asking. There is the further humiliation to all of us senior officers who testified in writing and on oath as to Barry's Rank and Service. We now see the Board calling very junior officers, who could not possibly testify in such a manner as we were able to do, as witnesses as to whether Barry and all of us were swearing falsely or not.

You will I am sure be the first to admit that Barry's case has been handled in a totally different manner to that of any other prominent officer. I would like to know if there is any truth in the suggestion that because Frank Aiken and Tom Barry are and have been bad friends in the recent past, certain members of the Board have taken up a hostile and unfair attitude in Barry's case.

We know that you personally are anxious that Tom like all others should get his due and a square deal. I recall your statement in a conversation with me in Cork last Easter Sunday twelve months, when you told me that you were extremely anxious to see Tom fairly treated regarding his pension. Therefore you will understand that there is nothing personal meant when I state that Barry and all of us who knew him are determined to see his case to the bitter end if certain members of the Board persist in their hostile attitude and do not give him the award he is entitled to on this appeal.

He has had a rotten deal and his claim is open and above Board if there was ever was one. Will you please examine his file and if you do I am sure that you will at once take the proper steps to see he gets a fair deal.

I shall be glad to hear from you as soon as possible. I hope that you are keeping quite well.

Mise le meas,

_____

Tom Crofts

(The following appears to be a letter from Mrs O'Driscoll to Mr Cornelius O'Driscoll, who forwarded it to Tom Barry. It is handwritten, with Number 34.S.P./55115 scribbled across it.)

c/o D Keohane
Gurtacrue
Midleton
August 25th [1943]

Dear Mr Barry,

I am in West Cork at present, but expect to see you when I return to the City.

The above address is permanent while in Ireland. This is a copy of the letter which was forwarded to [me] early January 14th 1943.

I am directed to inform you that in accordance with the terms of the Military Service Pensions Act, 1934, the Minister for Defence has granted you a Pension of £15, Fifteen Pounds – Per annum, which is Payable as from the 1st October 1934 and which will be subject to deduction under section 20 (1) of the Act in respect of receipts by you from Public Moneys.

I have also to state that it is your duty to inform the Minister at once of any receipts by you of any Public Moneys as defined by sections 2000 of the act.

To Mr Cornelius O'Driscoll
43.09 – 53 Street,
Woodside,
New York

Sincerely
Mrs O'Driscoll

THE BOYS OF KILMICHAEL
(Original words written by John F. Hourihane)

While we honour in song and in story
The memory of Pearse and MacBride;
Whose names are illumined in glory
With martyrs who long since have died.
But forget – not the boys at Kilmichael
Those brave lads so firm and true,
Who fought 'neath the green flag of Erin
And conquered the red white and blue.

The cold winter's morning was dawning
O'er mountain and valley and hill;
And the winds of November were wailing
Through woodland and fast rippling rill.
With a sharp ringing blast of the whistle
That rang out in the clear morning air;
The column rose up from their slumber
As quite as a fox from his layer.

With Barry their gallant commander
Through a country side slumbering still;
By Kenneigh's round tower famed in story
They marched over moorland and hill.
The rugged cliffs now rose before them
And onward they moved very light;
Then into their ambush crept slowly
Awaiting their glorious fight.

The sun o'er Mount Owen was descending
'Twas the eve of a cold winter's day;
When the Tans we were wearily waiting
Drove into the spot where we lay.
Then over the hills rang the echo
Of the peal of the rifle and gun;
And the fire of their lorries gave tidings
That Barry's famed column had won.

As the storm of battle was raging
And the bullets sprayed rapidly round;
Three shots from the enemy's muzzles
Dropped our brave gallant three to the ground.
They died as they lived for their country
No cowards were they for her cause;
Their blood they were willing to shed
'Gainst England's cruel hellish laws.

When the smoke of the battle had ended

And the enemy's guns were secure;
We set out o'er the hills and the valleys
To the far distant camp at Granure.
The men in their triumph marched onward
And a prayer for their heroes they said;
A line in that march was now vacant
O'Sullivan, McCarthy and Deasy were dead.

Three Volleys at Castletown-Kenneigh
Gave a last proud salute to the dead;
As three heroes were buried at midnight
By the light of the stars over-head.
O'Sullivan, Deasy, McCarthy,
Their glorious names will live on;
'Till the goal of their triumph is reached
And the ultimate victory is won.

Their banners were ours before sunset
And high over Dunmanway town;
Our battle-soaked colours were waving
O'er the foes of our land that were down.

The cool winter's evening was casting
Its shadows o'er bogland and moor;
As our men marched wearily southwards
Through a countryside rough and obscure.
Then onward by Manch and Kilkaskin
Around by O'Hurley's great hold;
The Third Brigade Column kept moving
Through a night wet and bitterly cold.

Then we gave three long cheers for old Ireland
And prayed for our comrades now dead;
Picked up our guns and our sabres
And started our long march ahead.

But now that the battle is over
And the smoke of the bombshell is passed;
Again we march forward to victory
And fight down the foe to the last.
For we'll in the end be triumphant
With our tricoloured banner, unrolled;
With the names of Tom Barry's Flying Column
Inscribed in bright letters of gold.

John F Hourihane wrote the above ballad, which originally contained three verses, after the famous battle of Kilmichael in November 1920. Hourihane of Grilough, Ballinacarriga, Ballineen, a member of C Company, Third Bat., Third. Cork Brigade, who later emigrated to Boston Massachusetts, USA. In order to perpetuate and preserve the above event, Mr Hourihane has lately completed the full version as it appears here. In doing so he has made it that generations yet unborn, will have a more vivid understanding and better knowledge of the famous episode and its participants – Tom Barry

THE MEN OF BARRY'S COLUMN

When British Terror failed to win
Allegiance from our people then,
The Black and Tans they were brought in,
They thought they'd teach us manners;
But instead of teaching they were taught
A lesson which they dearly bought,
For when Kilmichael's day was fought,
Low was their bloody banner.

They sought to wipe the column out,
From east to west, from north to south,
'Till at Crossbarry's bloody rout
They woke from their day dreaming.
Though ten to one they were that day
Our boys were victors in the fray,
And over the hills we marched away
With bagpipes merrily screaming.

The Essex brutes who tortured Hales,
They scoured the land to fill the jails,
They thought their foul deeds would pale
The cheeks of Irish mothers.
Paid dearly for their deeds were they
When passing by Toureen one day,
We dearly made the Essex pay
And well avenged our brothers.

When Barry saw the Tans efface,
The spirit of his fighting race,
Right through his soul did madly chase
His blood went boiling over.
He marched his men to Rossa's town
And burned that famous fortress down,
And never again will Britain's crown
Her foothold there recover.

Chorus:

So piper pay a martial air
For the gallant boys who conquered there,
No merry tune to banish care,
Or mournful or solemn.
The grander tune of all is played
By the fighting squad of the Third Brigade,
Whose glorious deeds will never fade,
The men of Barry's Column.

THE THIRD WEST CORK BRIGADE

We'll raise our voice in Ireland's praise
Glad are our hearts today,
For Ireland's sons have proved their worth
In the good old IRA
All parts fought well for Roisin Dubh
But we a record made.
In good old Cork, in famed West Cork
The Third West Cork Brigade

At Newcestown we struck a blow
For Ireland and Sinn Féin.
At Ballinhassig next we proved
Our right we would maintain
The English foe we twice laid low,
We faced them undismayed
In good old Cork, in famed West Cork,
The Third West Cork Brigade.

The Black and Tans to Ireland came
To send us to our doom.
Their toughest warriors sallied forth
In lorries from Macroom.
But at Kilmichael's bloody fight
Their conquering course was stayed,
By good old Cork, by famed West Cork,
The Third West Cork Brigade.

Then at Crossbarry's battlefield
Tom Barry's boys saw red.
For ten to one the Saxon host
Before our onslaught fled.
And o'er the hills we made our way
Whilst our gallant piper played.
In good old Cork, in famed West Cork
The Third West Cork Brigade.

Rosscarbery's barrack strong and grim
Next fell before our fire
For Black and Tans and RIC
Had gone down to the mire.
The echo of our fierce attack
Was heard through glen and glade,
In good old Cork, in famed West Cork
The Third West Cork Brigade.

BIBLIOGRAPHY

Primary Sources

Manuscript Sources

University College, Dublin, Archives
Frank Aiken Papers
Ernest Blythe Papers
Desmond Fitzgerald Papers
Sighle Humphreys Papers
Seán MacEntee Papers
Mary MacSwiney Papers
Richard Mulcahy Papers
Ernie O'Malley Papers & Notebooks
Moss Twomey Papers

Trinity College, Dublin, Records Office
Erskine Childers Papers

National Library of Ireland, Archives
Michael Collins Papers
John Devoy Papers
Joseph McGarrity Papers
Kathleen MacKenna Napoli Papers
Leon O'Broin Papers
Florence O'Donoghue Papers
Annie O'Farrelly Papers
Dr Dorothy Price Papers
Irish Republican Army & Sinn Féin Comhairle Ceanntair Papers

Irish Military Archives
Coppeen Captured Papers
Michael Collins/IRA Papers
Brigadier G. O'Connor Notebook
Gougane Barra Captured Papers
A Series – Captured Documents
CW Series – Captured Documents
G2/X Series – IRA activities

National Archives, Dublin
Records of the Ministry and Cabinet of Dáil Éireann in the State Paper Office.
Department of Justice Records
Sinn Féin Papers

Cork Archives Institute
Seamus Fitzgerald Papers
Donal Hales Papers
Siobhán (Creedon) Lankford Papers
Riobárd Langford Papers
Terence MacSwiney Papers

Liam de Róiste Papers
Madge Twomey Papers

Cork County Museum
Michael Leahy Papers
Terence MacSwiney Papers
Tomás MacCurtain Papers
Miscellaneous Papers relative to Tom Barry

Cork County Library
Pádraig Ó Maidín Papers

RTÉ Radio Archives
Tapes – Titles:
AA1947; AA1996; AA2782; AA3472; BB2063; D00738; Kerry Radio (1998 Tape)

RTÉ TV Archives
Kilmichael Ambush, 1966
Documentary with Tom Barry – not transmitted, 1966
Seven Days, 1969
Documentary Kilmichael Ambush 2000
Ballyseedy Ambush

Public Record Office, London
Colonial Office files

RIC Weekly Summaries, 1920-21
RIC Inspector General and County Inspectors' Monthly Reports
Irish Office Press Statements

War Office, London
Military Courts of Inquiry Reports

Imperial War Museum, London
Sir Hugh Jeudwine Papers
A. E. Percival Papers
Sir Peter Strickland Papers

Private Recordings
John Browne, UCG Lecture Recording
Jean Crowley, Cork Talk Recording
Eamonn Moriarty, army officers' Location Lecture Recording
Dave O'Sullivan, Video Recording

Private Manuscripts
Dr Gerard Ahern Papers
Tom Barry Papers
Sheila Barry Irlam Papers
Dan Cahalane Papers and Notebooks
Michael Collins (Waterford) notebooks/diary.
Liam Deasy Papers
Jim Kearney Papers (Letters)
Liam Lynch Papers (Letters)

Edward (Ned) O'Sullivan Statement
Dr Ned Barret Papers
Bill Hales Papers
Donal Hales Papers
D. V. Horgan Papers
Jim Hurley Statement & Notes
Liam O'Regan Collection
John Pierce – Mary Collins Pierce Letters
John Young Papers
Yvonne Purcell Papers

Newspapers, Periodicals and Journals

Irish Times; Irish Independent; Freeman's Journal; Cork Examiner; Cork Co. Eagle; Cork Weekly Examiner; Cork Constitution; Cork Free Press; The Times; Sunday Express; Daily Sketch; Daily Mail; Daily News; Sunday Review; Sunday Independent; Sunday Press; Clare Champion; Limerick Leader; Southern Star; Kerryman; An tÓglach; An Phoblacht; Boston Globe; Boston Herald; Irish Echo (New York); Irish World and American Industrial Liberator; Gaelic American; Detroit News; Pittsburgh Post Gazette; Irish World; The Advocate (American).

Bandon Historical Journal; Church of Ireland Gazette; Mungret Annual; Irish Historical Studies; Capuchin Annual; Irish Sword; Kerryman Supplements; The Month; Southern Star Centenary Supplement; Northern Star: Irish Political Review.

Oral Testimony

My reliance has been on the many people who gave unselfishly of their time, some of whom allowed themselves to be quizzed rather vigorously on their observations of, and participation in, events; their contribution has been essential. (Dates of interviews given in footnotes.)

Interviews
Flying column Participants

Third Cork Brigade: Ned Barrett, (Kilbrittain), Tom Barry, Pat Buttimer, Nudge Callanan, Danny Canty, Dan Collins, Liam Deasy, Miah Deasy, Jim Doyle, Jerh Fehilly, John (Jack) Fitzgerald, Nelius Flynn, Ned Galvin, Bill Hales, Dan Hourihane, Tom Kelleher, Jim Kearney, Denis Lordan, Minie Manning, Paddy O'Brien, Tadgh Ó Cáthasaigh, Dan O'Callaghan, Denis O'Callaghan, Tim O'Connell, Charlie O'Donoghue, Pat O'Donovan, Jack O'Driscoll, Charlie O'Keeffe, James O'Mahony, Denis O'Neill, Jack O'Sullivan, John L. O'Sullivan, Ned O'Sullivan, Patrick O'Sullivan, Dan Cahalane, Sonny O'Sullivan, John Whelton, Ned Young.

Second Cork Brigade: Matt Flood, Paddy O'Brien (Liscarrol), Diarmuid Mullins, Moss Connors, John Fanning.

First Cork Brigade: Billy Barry, Seán Hyde, Dan Sandow O'Donovan, Patrick O'Sullivan (Kilnamartra), Bill Powell.

Other Areas: Frank Aiken, Todd (C. S.) Andrews, Ernest Blythe, Vinny Byrne, M. J. Costello, Emmet Dalton, Seán MacBride, Dave Neligan.

Cumann na mBan & Women Activists: Peg Barrett, Leslie Bean de Barra, Máire Comerford, Ciss Crowley, Hannah (O'Leary) Deasy, Kathy Hayes, Kathleen (Lane) Lordan, Bridie (Crowley) Manning, Madge (Hales) Murphy, Mary (O'Donovan) Caverley, Lily (O'Donovan) Coughlan, Annie O'Leary, Kitty O'Leary, Brigid O'Mahony, Hannah (O'Donovan) O'Mahony, Eileen (Lynch) O'Neill, Molly (O'Neill) Walsh, May Twomey.

Republican Activists – 1920 onwards: Ned Barrett, (Clonakilty), Den Carey, Jerh (Jerry) Cronin, Bob Keogh, Jack Dohney Lynch, Joe Cahill, Mick McCarthy, Ruairí Ó Brádaigh, John O'Donovan, Brendan O'Neill, Dave O'Sullivan.

Other Relevant Interviews: Criostóir de Baróid, Pádraig Ó Cuanacháin, Michael Barry, Stephen (AJS) Brady, Christy Barrett, John Browne, Paddy Casey, Nellie Casey, Fr John Chisholm, Richie Coughlan, Jean Crowley, Joan Dineen, Seán (John) Feehan, Julia Nolan O'Flynn, Liam French, William (Billy) (Senior) Good, Eamonn Moriarty, Liam (Bill) O'Donoghue, Dan Joe O'Mahony, Denis O'Mahony, Pádraig Ó Maidín, Seamus O'Quigley, Michael O'Sullivan, Nora O'Sullivan, Cully Lawton, Eily (Hales) McCarthy, Tom McCarthy, Dómhnall MacGiolla Phoil, Seán (John) O'Riordan, Margaret White, Bernie Whyte, Louis Whyte, Seán Kelleher and Kieran Wyse.

Secondary Sources

Anderson, Brendan, *Joe Cahill: A Life in the IRA* (Dublin 2002)

Andrews, C. S., *Dublin Made Me* (Cork & Dublin 1979)

Aubane Historical Society and Jack Lane, *Seán Moylan: in his own words* (Cork 2003)

Augusteijn, Joost, *From Public Defiance to Guerrilla Warfare: the Experience of Ordinary Volunteers in the War of Independence, 1916–921* (Dublin 1996)

— (ed.) *The Irish Revolution 1913–923* (Dublin 2002)

Ballineen/Enniskeane, Heritage Group, *Dick Barrett (1889–1922) His Life and Death* (Cork 1997)

Barry, Tom, *Guerilla Days in Ireland* (Dublin1949)

— *The Reality of the Anglo-Irish War, 1920–21, in West Cork: Refutations, Corrections and Comment on Liam Deasy's' 'Towards Ireland Free'* (Tralee 1974).

Béaslaí, Piaras, *Michael Collins and the Making of a New Ireland*, Vol. 1 & 2 (Dublin 1926).

Begley, Diarmuid, *The Road to Crossbarry: The Decisive battle in the War of Independence* (Cork 1999).

Bell, J. Bowyer, *The Secret Army* (Dublin 1989)

Bennett, George, *The History of Bandon* (Cork 1869)

Bennett, Richard, *The Black and Tans* (London 1959)

Boyce, D. G. *Nationalism in Ireland* (London1982)

Bew, Paul, *Ideology and the Irish Question: Ulster Unionism and Irish Nationalism 1912–1921* (Oxford 1994)

Bowman, John, *De Valera and the Ulster Question, 1917–73* (Oxford 1982)

Brady, Ciaran (ed.), *Interpreting Irish History* (Dublin 1994)

Brady, Conor, *Guardians of the Peace* (Dublin 1974)

Breen, Dan, *My Fight For Irish Freedom* (Tralee 1964)

Brennan, Michael, *The War In Clare 1911–1921: Personal Memoirs of the War of Independence* (Dublin 1980)

Brennan, Robert, *Allegiance* (London 1950)

Butler, Ewan, *Barry's Flying Column* (London 1971)

Browne, Charlie, *The Story of the Seventh* (Macroom n.d.)

Brinton, Crane, *The Anatomy of Revolution* (London 1953)

Carroll Joseph T., *Ireland in the War Years 1939–1945* (Devon 1975)

Clarke, Kathleen, *Revolutionary Women: Kathleen Clarke, 1878–1972: An Autobiography* (Dublin 1991)

Clifford, Brendan (ed.), *A Selection from the Writings of General F. P. Crozier* (Belfast 2002)

— (ed.) and (Walsh, Pat, intro.) C. J. C. Street, *The Administration of Ireland, 1920: With Review of his other writings* (Belfast 2001)

Comerford, Máire, *The First Dáil* (Dublin 1969)

Collins, Michael, *The Path to Freedom* (Dublin 1922)

Coogan, Tim Pat, *The IRA* (London 1971)

— *Michael Collins: A Biography* (London 1990)

— *De Valera: Long Fellow, Long Shadow* (London 1993)

Cooney, James, *Macroom People & Places* (Macroom 1976)

Cronin, Seán, *The McGarrity Papers* (Tralee 1972)
— *Frank Ryan: The Search for The Republic* (Dublin 1980)
Crowley, Flor, *In West Cork Long Ago* (Cork 1979)
Crozier, Brigadier General F. P., *Ireland Forever* (London 1932)
— *The Men I Killed* (London 1930)
Curran, J. M. *The Birth of the Irish Free State, 1921–1923* (Alabama 1980)
Dalton, Charles, *With the Dublin Brigade (1917–1921)* (London 1929)
Deasy, Liam, *Towards Ireland Free* (Cork 1973)
— *Brother Against Brother* (Cork 1982)
Doherty, Gabriel and Dermot Keogh, *Michael Collins and the Making of the Irish State* (Cork 1998)
Duggan, John P., *A History of the Irish Army* (Dublin 1991)
Dwyer, T. Ryle, *Eamon de Valera* (Dublin 1980)
— *Michael Collins and The Treaty: His Difference with De Valera* (Cork 1981).
— *Tans, Terror and Troubles: Kerry's Real Fighting Story, 1913-23* (Cork 2001)
— *Guests of the State* (Kerry 1994)
— *De Valera: The Man & The Myths* (Dublin 1991)
Elliot, Marianne, *The Catholics of Ulster: A History* (London 2000)
English, Richard, *Ernie O'Malley, IRA Intellectual* (Oxford 1998)
— *Armed Struggle: A History of the IRA* (Dublin 2003)
— and Graham Walker, (eds.) *Unionism in Modern Ireland: New Perspectives on Politics and Culture* (London 1996)
Everett, Katherine, *Bricks and Flowers* (London 1949)
Farrell, Brian, *The Founding of Dáil Éireann: Parliament and Nation-Building* (Dublin 1971)
— (ed.), *The Creation of the First Dáil* (Dublin 1974)
Farrell, Michael. *Northern Ireland, The Orange State* (London 1975)
Feeney, Brian, *Sinn Féin: A Hundred Turbulent Years* (Dublin 2002)
Figgis, Darrell, *Recollections of the Irish War* (London 1927)
Fitzpatrick, David, *Politics and Irish Life, 1913–21: Provincial Experience of War and Revolution* (Dublin 1977)
— (ed.), *Revolution? Ireland, 1917–1923* (Dublin 1990)
Foster, R. F., *Modern Ireland 1600–1972* (London 1988)
Forester, Margery, *Michael Collins: The Lost Leader* (London 1971)
Galvin, Michael, *The Kilmurry Volunteers* (Cork 1994)
Garvin, Tom, *Nationalist Revolutionaries in Ireland, 1858–1928* (Oxford 1927)
— *1922: The Birth of Irish Democracy* (Dublin 1996)
Gaughan, J. A., *Austin Stack: Portrait of a Separatist* (Dublin 1977)
Gleeson, J., *Bloody Sunday* (London 1962)
Griffith, Kenneth and O'Grady, Timothy E., *Curious Journey: An Oral History of Ireland's Unfinished Revolution* (Cork 1998)
Greaves, C. D., *Liam Mellows and the Irish Revolution* (London 1971)
Hanley, Brian, *The IRA 1926–1936* (Dublin 2002)
Hart, Peter, *The IRA & Its Enemies: Violence and Community in Cork, 1916–1923* (Oxford 1998)
— (ed.), *Narratives: British Intelligence in Ireland 1920–21* (Cork 2002)
Hartnett, Mossie, *Victory and Woe*, (ed.) James H. Joy (Dublin 2002)
Hogan, David, *Four Glorious Years* (Dublin 1953)
Hopkinson, Michael, *Green Against Green: The Irish Civil War* (Dublin 1988)
— (ed.), *The Last Days of Dublin Castle: The Diaries of Mark Sturgis* (Dublin 1999)
— *The Irish War of Independence* (Dublin 2002)
Hull, Mark M., *Irish Secrets: German Espionage in Wartime Ireland 1939–1945* (Dublin 2002)
Jordan, Anthony J., *Seán MacBride* (Dublin 1993)

Jones, Thomas, *Whitehall Diary, Volume 111, Ireland 1918–1925*, (ed.) Keith Middlemas (Oxford 1971)

Kee, Robert, *Ourselves Alone; The Green Flag*, vol. 3 (London 1976)

Keogh, Dermot, *Twentieth-Century Ireland: Nation and State* (Dublin 1994)

Kerry's Fighting Story, 1916–1921 (Tralee 1949)

Kilmichael/Crossbarry Commemoration Committee and the Ballineen/Enniskeane Heritage Group, *The Wild Heather Glen: the Kilmichael Story of Grief and Glory* (Cork 1995)

Kotsonouris, Mary, *Retreat from Revolution: The Dáil Courts, 1920–25* (Dublin 1994)

Laffin, Michael, *The Partition of Ireland, 1911–1925* (Dublin 1983)

Lane, Jack and Brendan Clifford, *The Cork Free Press* (Cork 1997)

— *Kilmichael: The False Surrender: a discussion. Why the Ballot was Followed by the Bullet* (Cork 1999)

— *A North Cork Anthology* (Cork 1993)

Lankford, Siobhán, *The Hope and the Sadness* (Cork 1980)

Lawlor, Sheila, *Britain and Ireland, 1914–23* (Dublin 1983)

Lee, J. J., *Ireland 1912–985: Politics and Society* (Cambridge 1989)

Lee, Joseph, & Ó Tuathaigh, Gearóid, *The Age of de Valera* (Dublin 1982)

Limerick's Fighting Story, 1916–1921 (Tralee 1998)

Longford, Earl of, and O'Neill, Thomas P., *Eamon de Valera* (Dublin 1970)

Lyons, F. S. L., *Ireland Since the Famine* (London 1971)

Macardle, Dorothy, *The Irish Republic 1911–1925* (London 1937)

— *Tragedies of Kerry*, (Dublin 1924)

McDonnell, Kathleen Keyes, *There is a Bridge at Bandon* (Cork & Dublin 1972)

MacEoin, Uinseann (ed.), *Survivors* (Dublin 1980)

— *The IRA in the Twilight Years 1923–1948* (Dublin 1997)

MacEvilly, Michael, *Andy Cooney* (forthcoming)

Macready, General Sir Neville, *Annals of an Active Life*, 2 vols (London 1924)

Manning, Maurice, *The Blueshirts* (Dublin 1987)

McCann, John, *War By The Irish* (Tralee 1946)

McGarry, Ferghal, *Frank Ryan* (Dublin 2002)

— (ed.), *Republicanism in Modern Ireland* (forthcoming)

Memories of Dromleigh, A Country School: 1840–1900, compiled by past pupils (Cork 1990)

Mulcahy, Risteárd, *Richard Mulcahy (1886–1971) – A Family Memoir* (Dublin 1999)

Murphy, Brian P., *Patrick Pearse and the Lost Republican Ideal* (Dublin 1991)

— *John Chartres: Mystery Man of the Treaty* (Dublin 1995)

Murphy, John A., *Ireland in the Twentieth Century* (Dublin 1942)

Murphy, Ned, *Newcestown: Echoes of The Past* (Cork 1994)

Neeson, Eoin, *The Civil War 1922–1923* (Dublin 1989)

Neligan, Dave, *The Spy in the Castle* (London 1968)

Ó Brádaigh, Ruairí, *Dílseacht: The story of Comdt General Tom Maguire and the Second (All-Ireland) Dáil* (Dublin 1997)

Ó Broin, Leon, *Revolutionary Underground: The Story of the Irish Republican Brotherhood, 1858–1924* (Dublin 1976)

— *Protestant Nationalists In Revolutionary Ireland: The Stopford Connection* (Dublin 1985)

O'Callaghan, Seán, *Execution* (London 1974)

Ó Ceallaigh, Daltún, *Reconsiderations of Irish History and Culture* (Dublin 1994)

O'Connor, Ulick, *A Terrible Beauty is Born* (London 1975)

— *Oliver St John Gogarty* (London 1981)

O'Donnell, Peadar, *The Gates Flew Open* (Cork 1966)

O'Donoghue, Denis J., *History of Bandon* (Cork 1970)

O'Donoghue, Florence, *No Other Law* (Dublin 1956)

— *Tomás MacCurtain: Soldier and Patriot* (Tralee 1971)

Ó Dúlaing, Donncha, *Voices of Ireland* (Dublin 1984)

O'Farrell, Patrick, *Ireland's English Question* (London 1971)

O'Halpin, Eunan, *The Decline of the Union: British Government in Ireland 1892–1920* (Dublin 1987)

— *Defending Ireland, The Irish State & Its Enemies* (Oxford 1999)

O'Halloran, Clare, *Partition and the Limits of Irish Nationalism* (Dublin 1987)

O'Hegarty, P. S., *The Victory of Sinn Féin* (Dublin 1924)

O'Mahony, Seán, *Frongoch: University of Revolution* (Dublin 1987)

O'Malley, Ernie, *On Another Man's Wound* (Tralee 1972)

— *The Singing Flame* (Tralee 1979)

O'Neill, Joseph, *Blood-Dark Track: a family history* (London 2001)

O'Riordan, Manus, *Forget Not the Boys of Kilmichael* (Ballingeary 2002)

— *The Voice of a Thinking Intelligent Movement* (Dublin 2001)

Ó Súilleabháin, Micheál, *Where mountainy men have sown*, (Tralee 1965)

Pakenham, Frank, *Peace by Ordeal* (London 1972)

Phillips, W. A., *The Revolution in Ireland 1906–1923* (London 1923)

Rebel Cork's Fighting Story (Tralee 1947)

Regan, John M., *The Irish Counter Revolution, 1921–1936* (Dublin 1999)

Ryan, Desmond, *Seán Treacy and the Third Tipperary Brigade, IRA* (Tralee 1945)

Ryan, Meda, *The Tom Barry Story* (Cork 1982)

— *The Real Chief – The Story of Liam Lynch* (Cork 1986)

— *The Day Michael Collins was Shot* (Dublin 1989)

— *Michael Collins and the Women in his Life*, (Cork 1996)

— *The Tom Barry Story* (Cork 1982)

Street, C. J. C., *The Administration of Ireland, 1920* (London 1921)

Taylor, Rex, *Michael Collins–The Big Fellow* (London 1961)

Townshend, Charles, *The British Campaign in Ireland 1919–1921* (Oxford 1975)

— *Political Violence in Ireland: Government and Resistance since 1848* (Oxford 1983)

Walsh, Joe, *The Story of Dick Barrett*,(Cork 1972)

Walsh, Margaret, *Sam Maguire* (Cork 2003)

Ward, Margaret, *Unmanageable Revolutionaries: Women and Irish Nationalism* (Dingle 1983)

Winter, Ormonde, *Winter's Tale: An Autobiography* (London 1955)

With the IRA in the Fight for Freedom (Tralee 1955)

Younger, Calton, *Ireland's Civil War* (London 1972)

NOTES

Abbreviations

Adj.	Adjutant
A/G	Adjutant General
Bde.	Brigade
CI	County Inspector
Cork 1	First Cork Brigade (Mid-Cork)
Cork 2	Second Cork Brigade (North Cork)
Cork 3	Third Cork Brigade (West Cork)
Coy.	Company
CS	Chief of Staff
DI	District Inspector
DIV.	Division
GHQ	General Headquarters
IG	Inspector General
IO	Intelligence Officer
IRA	Irish Republican Army
IRB	Irish Republican Brotherhood
n.d.	Not dated
n.t.	Not transmitted
OC	Officer in Command
Org.	Organiser
RIC	Royal Irish Constabulary
RTÉ	Radio Telefís Éireann
TV	Television

Archives/Records

CCL	Cork County Library
CCM	Cork City Museum
CAI	Cork Archives Institute
CO	Colonel Office
IWM	Imperial War Museum
MA	Military Archives, Dublin
NLI	National Library of Ireland
PRO	Public Records Office
TCDA	Trinity College Dublin Archives
UCDA	University College Dublin Archives

INTRODUCTION

1 Tom Barry, *Guerilla Days In Ireland*, p. 3–5; The 1916 Proclamation.
2 Liam Deasy's notes, Liam Deasy private papers.
3 For details see, Máire Comerford, *The First Dáil*; *The Creation of the Dáil*, ed. Brian Farrell.
4 Lionel Curtis, *Ireland (1921)*, p. 55, Pat Walsh, *Introduction – The Anglo-Irish Treaty and the 'Lost World' of Imperial Ireland* – courtesy of Jack Lane.
5 J. J. Lee, 'The Challenge Of A Collins Biography', p. 29, in *Michael Collins and the Making of the Irish State*, eds, Gabriel Doherty and Dermot Keogh.
6 Curtis, *Ireland (1921)*, pp. 55, 56, Pat Walsh, *Introduction – The Anglo–Irish Treaty*.
7 *Ibid.*, pp. 55, 56.
8 Tom Barry, a talk to group in Cork including people from Northern Ireland, early 1970, recording

courtesy of Jean Crowley.

9 Jack Hennessy and Tom Barry – Documentary, presenter Brian Farrell, *RTÉ TV Archives*, 1969.

10 J. J. Lee, 'The Challenge of a Collins Biography', in Doherty and Keogh, p. 23.

11 Tom Barry, talk given to a group in Cork, recording courtesy of Jean Crowley.

12 Tim O'Donoghue, *The Fall of Rosscarbery Barracks*, December 1937, A/0618, Irish Military Archives.

13 Ronan Fanning, *Michael Collins an Overview*, pp. 204, 206, in Doherty and Keogh.

EARLY LIFE

1 Eddie (Edward), Tom (Bernie – Bernadine), Margery (Margaret), Eileen (Ellen), Kitty (Catherine Mary), Mick (Michael), Maria Mary, Elizabeth Mary Gertrude, Jack (John), Eva, Gerald, Joanna, Maureen, Ann. Details from Sheila Barry Irlam (Tom Barry's niece) and from Gerald Barry (Tom's cousin) who is assembling 'a family tree'. I am indebted to Con O'Callaghan for putting me in touch with Sheila and Gerald. The Barry's homestead in Killorglin was at Chubs Corner. It was demolished for road-widening, by Kerry County Council, in the 1990s. The Barry home was beside Timothy Chub O'Connor's timber yard – hence the name Chubs Corner, Frank McGillycuddy to author, 26/2/2003, courtesy of Maurice O'Keeffe.

2 Family details from Gerald Barry; Tom Barry, author interview. Interviews with Tom Barry stretch over a period – 4/9/1974, 18/9/1974, 25/10/1974, 2/12/1974, 29/12/1974, 18/1/1975, 25/1/1975, 17/4/1976, 28/4/1977 – due to overlapping of topics, herein after known as, 'author interview', special interview on Northern Ireland 18/4/1979; also Jerh Fehily, interview 7/9/1978.

3 Jerh Fehily, author interview 7/9/1978.

4 Kathy Hayes, author interview 14/9/1979.

5 Tom Barry, author interview.

6 Kathy Hayes, author interview 14/9/1979; Tom Barry, author interview.

7 *Mungret Annual* – He started in Mungret in 1911, Mike McGuire, Limerick City Library details.

8 George Bennett, *History of Bandon*, 345. Bennett believed that 'some Jacobite wag' wrote the latter two lines.

9 Denis J. O'Donoghue, *History of Bandon*, p. 22.

10 WO35/206, Sir Peter Strickland Papers, Imperial War Museum (IWM).

11 Barry, *Guerilla Days In Ireland*, p. 2.

12 Tom Barry, author interview. He said that members of the family were 'all allowed' make their own decisions. His father had a great belief in the army and military matters. Tom spoke with pride of his parents who reared a large family. I could find no evidence for Peter Hart's suggestion that he 'did not get along' with his father and that this was partially 'the reason he ran away to join the army'. Peter Hart, *The IRA & Its Enemies*, p. 32, footnote, 48. Contemporaries in Bandon, where I grew up, neither saw nor heard anything to confirm conflict between Tom and his father. Later communication shows a good relationship.

13 *Cork Examiner*, 10/11/1915.

14 *Cork County Eagle*, 22/1/1916.

15 Ewan Butler, *Barry's Flying Column*, p. 21.

16 Tom Barry author interview; Tom Barry to Kenneth Griffith and Timothy O'Grady, *Curious Journey*, pp. 86, 87; also *RTÉ Sound Archives*, AA2782/, n.d.

CAUGHT UP IN THE MOVEMENT

1 Dr Thomas Dillon Memoir, 3738, TCAD. At the Volunteer and Sinn Féin conventions held in October 1917, structures were changed with the decided aim towards self-government.

2 See Brian Murphy, *Patrick Pearse and the Lost Republican Ideal*, pp. 88–110; John A. Murphy, *Ireland in the Twentieth Century*, pp. 11, 12.

3 Barry *Guerilla Days* 1; Tom Barry, personal records, TB (Tom Barry) private papers

4 Charlie O'Keeffe author interview 14/9/1974: Tom Barry interview; Sir Peter Strickland Papers, WO35/206, IWM.

5 Charlie O'Keeffe author interview 14/9/1974.

6 Barry, *The Reality of the Anglo-Irish War 1920–21 In West Cork*, p. 8; Charlie O'Keeffe, author interview 6/11/1978; Kathy Hayes, author interview 16/4/1976.

7 Bill Hales, author interview 14/9/1974 ; Tom Barry, author interviews; also Tom Barry to Kate O'Callaghan, RTÉ Sound Archives, n.d.; Tom Barry – in wide-ranging interview with Nollaig Ó Gadhra, RTÉ Sound Archives, 1969.

8 So called because of the colour of their uniform.

9 *Irish Bulletin,* 20 July 1920.

10 Kathleen Keyes McDonnell, *There is a Bridge at Bandon,* p. 147. Percival was on 'a man hunt' for William Keyes McDonnell. He and his men raided and wrecked their home and their Corn Mills at Castlelack on numerous occasions.

11 Charlie O'Keeffe, author interview 7/12/1975; Tom Barry to Kate O'Callaghan, RTÉ Sound Archives, n.d.

12 Barry, *The Reality,* p. 8;Seán Buckley, Third Brigade I/O 25/1/1940, Tom Hales, Third Brigade O/C, n.d. Con Crowley, Brigade Staff Captain, 20/1/1940 and Mick Herlihy, Company Captain, 23/1/1940 in Sworn Statements to the Military Service Registration, Board, Dept. of Defence, Sheila Barry Irlam Papers.

13 Butler, p. 39.

14 Charlie O'Keeffe, author interview 6/11/1978.

15 Tom Kelleher, author interview 13/6/1974.

16 Tom Barry to Raymond Smith, *Irish Independent,* 8 December 1970.

17 Tom Barry to Kate O'Callaghan, n.d. *RTÉ Sound Archives.*

18 Florence O'Donoghue Papers, , MS 31,320, NLI; Tom Barry's manuscript, TB private papers; Tom Barry to Griffith and O'Grady, *Curious Journey,* p. 143; See also Barry, *The Reality,* p. 8. Officers: Seán Buckley, Charlie Hurley, Liam Deasy.

19 Liam Deasy, note to author 9/1/1972; also Liam Deasy, *Towards Ireland Free,* p. 141.

20 Tom Barry, Kenneth Griffith interview, RTÉ Sound Archives, n.d.

21 Danny Canty, author interview 6/8/1979; also notebook, Florence O'Donoghue Papers, MS 31,320, NLI; Kate O'Callaghan RTÉ Radio interview, n.d. RTÉ Sound Archives.

22 Seán MacCárthaigh in 'Personal Recollections' to Tom Barry 16/8/1948, TB private papers.

23 Tom Kelleher, author interview 17/3/1974.

24 *Ibid.,* 17/3/1974; Barry 'put it up to' Seán MacCárthaigh one night 'that I should give a lecture, but I did not feel competent, and I had much more pleasure and benefit in listening to yours.' MacCárthaigh to Barry 16/7/1948; see also Florence O'Donoghue Papers, 'We were thinking of a long campaign'. MS 31,320, NLI.

25 Brigid O'Mahony, author interview 14/5/1980.

26 Tom Barry's notes – TB private papers.

27 Tom Barry, author interviews; Seán O'Driscoll, FO'D Papers, MS 31,301 (8), NLI; Tom Barry, UCG Lecture to History Students, 1969, Recording, courtesy of John Browne, ex-detective sergeant; see also Barry *Guerilla Days,* pp. 20–22.

28 John Fitzgerald, author interview 16/8/1974; Barry, *The Reality,* p. 22.

29 Danny Canty, author interview 7/12/1974.

30 Butler, p. 46.

31 Jerh Cronin, author interview 10/1/1981.

TRAINING, AMBUSHES, ACTION, AUXILIARY CONFRONTATION

1 Lieut-General Arthur Ernest Percival, b. 26/12/1887, d. 31/1/1966. Received several honours, including OBE for his service in Ireland 1920–21 and twice mentioned in dispatches – *Who Was Who 1961–1970.*

2 Barry, *Guerilla Days,* p. 27.

3 Florence O'Donoghue Papers, MS. 31,320, NLI; Barry, *Guerilla Days,* pp. 27, 28.

4 Tom Barry manuscript, TB private papers. The townland/district is sometimes spelled Tureen, but the more acceptable local spelling is Toureen.

5 Butler, pp. 54, 55.

6 Con Crowley, *Rebel Cork's Fighting Story,* pp. 102, 103; Tom Barry manuscript, TB private papers, also Barry, *Guerilla Days,* p. 31.

7 Barry, TB private papers.

8 Strickland Papers, *Report by 6th Division,* IWM.

9 Butler, pp. 53, 54.

10 Keyes McDonnell, pp. 183, 184 – catalogue of the devastation; Michael Lyons, list of further premises destroyed, p. 16, *Bandon Historical Journal,* No. 12.

11 Co. Inspector Monthly Reports, October – November 1920, CO904/112.

12 Tom Barry manuscript, TB private papers; see also Butler, p. 39.

13 *Ibid.,* also Barry *Guerilla Days,* p. 34.

14 Deasy p. 159; Tom Barry TB private papers.

15 *Ibid.*, p. 159.

16 Barry, *Guerilla Days*, p. 38.

17 Ned O'Sullivan to author, 28/1/1978; see also Meda Ryan, the *Southern Star*, 17 August, 1985.

18 Tom Barry, *RTÉ/TV Documentary*, 1966.

19 Deasy, pp. 163–165; Tom Barry, TB private papers.

20 Liam Deasy to author 5/12/1972.

21 Paddy O'Sullivan, author interview 3/1/1974.

22 Barry, *Guerilla Days*, p. 37.

23 Brigid O'Mahony and Babe Crowley Personal Papers; Barry, *Guerilla Days*, p. 38

24 Richard Coughlan, author interview, 26/5/1975. They fired on him on two different occasions while working in a field, also aimed at a neighbour and damaged his two legs, leaving him crippled for life. Also Danny Canty, author interview 7/12/1974 – Danny Canty knew a neighbour who was badly disabled in one of these 'pot shot' games.

25 Keyes McDonnell, pp. 143, 144.

26 Micheál Ó Súilleabháin, *Where Mountainy Men Have Sown*, pp. 90–91.

27 Mick Sullivan to Ernie O'Malley, E.O'M, N. P17b/111, UCDA.

28 Florrie O'Donoghue Papers, Captured Document, MS. 31393, NLI.

29 Paddy O'Sullivan, author interview 3/1/1974; Ó Súilleabháin, *Where Mountainy*, p. 159, 160; Pádraig Ó Cuanacháin, *The Irish Times*, An Irishman's Diary, 28/11/2000; Manus O'Riordan, *Irish Times*, Letter to Editor, December 2000; O'Riordan, *Ballingeary*, pp. 11,12.

30 Liam Deasy, Personal Narrative, P7A/D/45, MP, UCDA.

31 Katherine Everett, *Bricks and Flowers*, p. 154.

32 General Crozier, *Ireland Forever*, p. 99; Butler, p. 61; Tom Barry notes, TB private papers.

33 Sir Peter Strickland Papers, typewritten report, IWM; Sir H. Jeudwine, *Record of Rebellion*, Vol. 1, IWM.

34 From the outset of the formation of the flying column 'column officers and section commanders were appointed by the column commander, irrespective of the ranks held by the men previous to their enrolment in the column', Barry, *Guerilla Days*, pp. 24, 25.

35 Deasy, p. 168; also Liam Deasy, author interview 5/12/1972.

36 Tom Barry, notes, TB private papers; Barry, *Guerilla Days*, p. 135. The occasion specifically mentioned (in notes) is the column's retirement to Guarranreigh after the Crossbarry ambush. 'We had dived for food and security so often into this area that my friend, Seán O'Hegarty, the OC Cork No. 1, had often acidly asked if we had any food or houses in West Cork instead of trespassing all over his brigade. Seán's Volunteers at Guarranreigh gave us a great welcome.' On an occasion in May 1921 'we gave Seán's lads plenty to eat' in Crookstown area. In a letter to Liam McGowan, *Irish Press*, Tom wrote, 'whenever West Cork officers' entered other Cork Brigade areas 'during hostilities they were always received with the greatest kindness' with the addition of 'special precautions' and 'protection'. 4/6/1948, TB private papers; Deasy, p. 294; Michael Galvin records, 'Crossbarry and Kilmurry Company co-operated closely with Third Brigade through 1920–21' – Michael Galvin, *The Kilmurry Volunteers*, p. 130.

37 Florrie O'Donoghue's handwritten report, n.d. A/0629, Military Archives, Dublin; Galvin, p. 130; see also Deasy, p. 294, regarding the close co-operation of brigades.

38 Seán MacCárthaigh in 'Personal Recollections' to Tom Barry 16/7/1948, TB private papers; Criostóir de Baróid, author interview 12/1/1981; see Meda Ryan, *Michael Collins and the women in his life*, pp. 47, 48.

39 Tom Barry manuscript, TB Private papers; Barry, *The Reality*, p. 14; Tom Barry to Nollaig Ó Gadhra, RTÉ Sound Archives, 1969.

40 Tom Barry, manuscript TB private papers; also Tom Barry, *Rebel Cork's Fighting Story*, p. 106; Barry, *The Reality*, p. 14; also Tom Barry to Nollaig Ó Gadhra, RTÉ Sound Archives, November 1969.

41 Pat O'Donovan, author interview 12/4/1975. Paddy O'Brien's uniform is now in Collins Barracks. I am indebted to Gerry White for this information.

42 The Kilmichael/Crossbarry Commemoration Committee, *The Wild Heather Glen*, pp. 71, 121. Barry was to reflect later in life that no shot should have been fired 'until 1920, until they were properly trained. The few shots that were fired only prepared the British for what was to come', Tom Barry to Griffith and O'Grady in*Curious Journey*, p. 144.

43 *Wild Heather*, p. 77.

44 Dan Canty, author interview 6/8/1972.

45 Charlie O'Keeffe, author interview 6/11/1976.

46 Tom Barry, author interview; Pat O'Donovan, author interview 18/9/1978.

47 Tom Barry to Nollaig Ó Gadhra, RTÉ Sound Archives, 1969; Tom Barry to Donncha Ó Dulaing, RTÉ Sound Archives, n. d. c. early 1970s; Tom Barry to Brian Farrell, RTÉ/TV, 1969; Tom Barry manuscript, TB private papers; Percival Papers, 4/1, IWM.

48 Tom Barry to Brian Farrell, 1969, RTÉ TV Archives; Ann (Kelly) Hegarty to author 23/7/1999; The basin, out of which they drank, was passed around – Tom Barry, lecture to history students of University College, Galway (UCG) 1969, recording, courtesy of John Browne, ex detective sergeant, Tom Barry's friend.

49 Pat O'Donovan to Brian Farrell presenter, 1969, RTÉ/TV Archives.

50 Tom Barry, UCG 1969, recording, courtesy of John Browne.

51 Donncha Ó Dulaing, early 1970's, RTÉ Sound Archives.

52 Jim Kearney, author interview 10/3/1974.

53 Tom Barry manuscript, TB private papers; Ned Sullivan (Schull Coy. Capt.) author interview 28/1/1974; Tom Barry to Donncha Ó Dulaing, early 1970s, RTÉ Sound Archives; Ned O'Sullivan to Tom Barry 13/9/1949, TB private papers; Edward (Ned) O'Sullivan, statement. The men on the side-car were: Michael McLean, Con Sheehan, Tom McCarthy, John Collins, Tom O'Driscoll – Edward (Ned) O'Sullivan private papers. McLean, a short time afterwards, was captured by the Auxiliaries, dragged after a lorry and tortured to death.

54 Barry, *Guerilla Days*, pp. 43, 44.

55 Tom Barry, author interview; Tom Barry to Donncha Ó Dulaing, early 1970s, RTÉ Sound Archives; 'Kilmichael Ambush' on ambush site, Seamus Kelly presentation, RTÉ/TV Archives, Documentary transmitted in November 1966; Tom Barry to Nollaig Ó Gadhra, 'I gave the order and take full responsibility for it', 1969, RTÉ Sound Archives; Tom Barry, RTÉ/TV Archives, transmitted November, 1969; Tom Barry, *Lecture* on location to Irish army officers, late 1950s, courtesy of Eamonn Moriarty. After Kilmichael, Barry warned his men before each ambush to be aware of a false surrender.

56 Barry, *Guerilla Days*, pp. 45, 46. Pat Deasy's gun is now in the Cork Public Museum.

57 Tom Barry to Donncha Ó Dulaing, RTÉ Radio Recording; Tom Barry, RTÉ/TV Archives, Documentary, 1966; the record of the brandy flasks is stated in proofs to *An Cosantóir*, 1941, but omitted by censor in publication, written by eyewitness (Tom Barry), TB private papers.

58 Crozier, pp. 198,199. For biographical details of General Crozier see Brendan Clifford, *The Men I Killed*, pp. 4–19. F. P. Crozier, commander of the Auxiliaries in Ireland, 1919–1920 wrote: 'The average consumption of liquor in the Auxiliary division totalled £5 per head per week or £30,000 a month in canteens alone when it is considered that the police often demanded free drinks from publicans as the price of "protection".'

59 Tom Barry, RTÉ TV Documentary, 1966; Tom Barry to Kenneth Griffith, 1968, RTÉ Sound Archives; Tom Barry to Donncha Ó Dulaing, early 1970s, RTÉ Sound Archives.

60 John Whelton, author interview 15/10/1980.

61 'We got a local carpenter to put make-shift coffins together, and we buried the bodies in a bog that first night,' said Pat Buttimer. 'We had no sleep for a whole week.' They kept shifting the bodies sometimes hiding them with furze bushes, moving them on, at times 'in a common car with bags around the wheels.' Pat Buttimer, Gleann Company, author interview 15/10/1980.

62 Deasy, pp. 170–174.

63 Barry, *The Reality*, p. 11; Stephen O'Neill, *The Kerryman*, December 1937.

64 Barry, *The Reality*, p. 17.

65 Crozier, p. 128.

66 Meda Ryan research 1970s to early 1980s for *The Tom Barry Story;* see also James Gleeson *Bloody Sunday*, p. 81; Butler, p. 70.

67 Tim O'Connell author interview 17/3/1975 and Pat O'Donovan author interview 12/4/1975.

68 Barry, *Guerilla Days*, p. 44; Tom Barry to Nollaig Ó Gadhra, 1969, 'We were about sixty yards up from the first lorry when we heard these fellows shouting, "We surrender! We surrender!" They knew by then that the first lorry was wiped out. I saw some of them myself throwing their rifles away. And three of our chaps stood up then, three Volunteers, and the next thing was they opened fire with revolvers and they killed two of them standing up', RTÉ Radio Archives; also Tom Barry, *Lecture* to Irish army officers, 1966, recording, courtesy of Lieut Col Eamonn Moriarty.

69 Tim O'Connell, author interview 17/3/1975; Pat O'Donovan, author interview 12/4/1975;

James O'Mahony, author interview 1/12/1974. In January 1921 the twenty-three year-old Tim O'Connell, while 'on the run' was captured by the Auxiliaries. He was wearing the coat with a bullet hole – one of the bullets that had hit Pat Deasy, he said. He was beaten so severely in Dunmanway workhouse, that he became unconscious, had facial injuries, nose problems and deafness for the remainder of his life. See also, *Wild Heather,* pp. 91, 92.

70 Jack O'Sullivan, author interview 20/4/1976. He was definite that there were shouts of surrender and the Auxiliaries began firing again.

71 Tom Barry, author interview.

72 See Stephen O'Neill, *The Kerryman,* December 1937; Barry, *Guerilla Days,* pp. 36–49; Barry, *The Reality,* pp. 17, 18; Eyewitness, *An Cosantóir, Kilmichael,* 9 and 16 May, 1941.

73 Deasy, pp. 170–172.

74 Barry, *The Reality,* p. 14.

75 Deasy, Editor's Note, November 1972.

76 Flor Crowley, book review, *Southern Star,* 4 January 1975.

77 Deasy, p. 171.

78 Deasy, pp. 170–172; Fr Chisholm, author interview 23/9/1998. Fr Chisholm spoke of Liam Deasy's inability to describe people. Fr Chisholm said that he visited places to get a feel of locations, as for instance the training camp at Glandore. This, he said, enabled him to stand there and 'imagine' the training camp and the view overlooking the sea.

79 Barry, *The Reality,* p. 13.

80 *Ibid.,* p. 14.

81 Stephen O'Neill, *The Kerryman,* December 1937, Barry's account, *An Cosantóir,* May 1941, *Irish Press,* 17 and 18 May, 1948; *Guerilla Days,* pp. 36 – 51.

82 Barry, *The Reality,* p. 17.

83 *Ibid.,* p. 58

84 Deasy, pp. 170–172.

85 Jack Lane and Brendan Clifford, *Kilmichael: The False Surrender,* p. 31.

86 'Publisher's Notice' at the beginning of *The Reality of the Anglo-Irish War.*

87 Paddy O'Brien, author interview 21/5/1975.

88 Liam O'Brien to author, 17/3/2002.

89 J. M. Feehan to *Independent Newspapers,* 11/12/1974, P. Ó Maidín Papers, Cork County Library.

90 Paddy O'Brien, author interview 21/5/1975, 17/1/1976; Pat O'Donovan, author interview 12/4/1975, 18/9/1978; Dan Hourihane, author interview 28/1/1973; Tim O'Connell, author interview 17/3/1975; James O'Mahony, author interview 1/12/1974; Jack O'Sullivan, author interview 14/4/1975, 18/2/1975; Ned Young, author interview 6/3/1974, 12/4/1975, 17/1/1976; Denis Lordan author interview 7/7/1974. Denis Lordan was not there, but his brother John (d. 1930) was there. The Kilmichael false surrender came up in interview on Crossbarry. He dealt with his brother's recollections.

91 Paddy O'Brien, author interview 17/1/1976.

92 Den Carey, author interview 10/1/1975.

93 Tom Barry to Nollaig Ó Gadhra, 1969, RTÉ Sound Archives – this was before the Deasy book or any questioning of the false surrender.

94 Barry, *The Reality,* p. 17.

95 Tom Barry to Brian Farrell, November 1969, RTÉ/TV Archives; Barry in a letter to Miah McGrath dealing with another episode (see below re Dunmanway Road killing) said, 'I have met Liam Deasy and Seán Buckley since the instalments appeared of which you complain [Dunmanway Road killing] and they made no comment on them'. (This was after the Kilmichael instalments. If they had a complaint on the treatment of the Kilmichael engagement, it would surely have been aired in correspondence.) Tom Barry to Miah McGrath, 26/5/1948, TB private papers.

96 Deasy, pp. 166–167. Sometimes spelled Craik in Br. records.

97 Deasy, pp. 167; Barry, *The Reality,* p. 18.

98 Fr Chisholm to author, 23/10/1978.

99 Deasy, p. 167.

100 Major Percival Papers, 4/1 IWM.

101 Raymond [Flor Crowley] the *Southern Star,* 6 November 1971. Flor's brother was only 12 years of age, and his father kept repeating to Col Craik that he was at school.

102 For list of casualties, see Appendix 1. In the 'Malicious Injury Application' a few weeks later Col Buxton swore 'Cadet Forde was in a terribly serious condition, and Lieut Guthrie was

missing', *Cork Examiner*, 12 January 1921.

103 Charlie Browne, *The Story of the 7th*, p. 34; Paddy O'Sullivan author interview 3/1/1974; Manus O'Riordan, *The Irish Times*, Letter to Editor, 26 December 2000; O'Riordan, *Kilmichael Schizophrenia, Ballingeary Historical Journal 2002*; Padráig Ó Cuanacháin, letter to author, 4/3/2002; Micheál Ó Súilleabháin describes Lehane's murder on 1 November 1920, and that of unarmed Christy Lucey nine days later. 'These marauding Auxiliaries were trapped at Kilmichael', *Where mountainy men*, pp. 158–160.

104 A man named Shambo Callaghan dug up the body; see also *Wild Heather Glen*, p. 153.

105 A. J. S. Brady, author interview 9/11/1974. – 'He did not get the compensation until after the Truce.' Forde's father in the Macroom Quarter Session claim, sought £15,000, *Cork Examiner*, 18 January 1921.

106 Bill Munroe in Gleeson, *Bloody Sunday*, pp. 74, 75.

107 *Irish Press*, 18 May, 1948; Tom Barry, *An Cosantóir*, 9 May 1941; Barry, *Guerilla Days*, pp. 43–45; author interviews with participants, Pat O'Donovan, 12/4/1975; Tim O'Connell, 4/3/1975 and 24/4/1976; Dan Hourihane, 28/1/1973 and 26/4/1973; Tom Barry in manuscript, TB private papers.

108 Brigadier-General Crozier, *The Kerryman*, 12 March 1938; 'All mention that he was an Auxiliary commander being avoided at the inquest', Crozier, p. 196; Gleeson, pp. 74, 75; *Southern Star*, 11 February 1922: also A. J. S. Brady, author interview, 9/11/1974.

KILMICHAEL – THE FALSE SURRENDER QUESTION

1 Peter Hart, *The IRA & Its Enemies*, p. 36; In an RTÉ/TV Documentary, Pat Butler production, November 2000. Peter Hart expressed similar views in a *Radio Kerry* programme in 1998, presented by Sinéad Spain.

2 General staff 6th Division, *The Irish Rebellion*, Sir Peter Strickland Papers, IWM.

3 Peter Hart letter to Irish Times, 10/12/1998; also Hart, 26.

4 Pat Butler, Presenter, RTÉ/TV Documentary on Kilmichael, November 2000.

5 RTÉ Sound Archives – several recordings with different interviewees; RTÉ/TV Archives; *An Cosantóir 1941*; *Irish Press 1948*; Tom Barry, *Lecture t*o Irish army officers, 1966, courtesy of Lieut Col Eamonn Moriarty; Griffith and O'Grady interview in *Curious Journey*, p. 182; Barry, *Guerilla Days*, pp. 44, 45.

6 Tom Barry to Kenneth Griffith – he describes the ambush, the Auxiliaries shouting, and the subsequent events. 1968, not transmitted, RTÉ Sound Archives.

7 Presenter, Seamus Kelly, transmitted November 1966, RTÉ/TV Archives.

8 Tom Barry, *UCG Lecture*, 1969, recording courtesy of John Browne.

9 Hart, pp. 27, 36. Kevin Myers, *Irish Times – Irishman's Diary*, 29 May 1998.

10 'Official Report', *The Times*, 2 December 1920.

11 'Official Report', compiled by the General Staff 6th Division, typewritten after Truce, Strickland Papers, IWM.

12 IO (Major C. J. C. Street), *The Administration of Ireland, 1920*, originally published in early 1921 – new edition by Brendan Clifford and Pat Walsh, Athol Books, pp. 63, 64.

13 Hart, p. 36.

14 *Ibid.*, p. 24.

15 'Official Report', *The Times*, 2 December 1920.

16 *Irish Press*, 18 May, 1948; Tom Barry, *An Cosantóir*, 9 May 1941; Barry, *Guerilla Days*, pp. 43–45; author interviews with participants, Pat O'Donovan, 12/4/1975; Tim O'Connell, 4/3/1975 and 24/4/1976; Dan Hourihane, 28/1/1973 and 26/4/1973; Tom Barry in manuscript, TB private papers.

17 Hart, text p. 34, footnote 58.

18 Dan Hourihane, author interviews, 28/1/1973 and 26/4/1973; see also *Wild Heather*, p. 73.

19 Dan Hourihane, author interview 26/4/1973; *Wild Heather Glen*, p. 71.

20 Hart, p. 35, footnote 61, 62; see p. 33, footnote 56, AF interview 19 November 1989.

21 *Ibid.*, p. 131.

22 Carbon copy, letter, T. O'Neill to Tom Barry 5/6/48 in relation to Crois na Leanbh and scouts and rifle-men who were shot when taken unawares, TB private papers; Barry, *Guerilla Days*, p. 64.

23 Hart, p. 131. Tom Barry, in a lecture in UCG, spoke of how this first scout signalled from a distance – recording, courtesy of John Browne.

24 See biographical notes, *Wild Heather*, pp. 53–124.

25 Hart, p. 33, footnote 56. In this footnote reference is also made to interviews conducted by Fr Cisholm and the Ballineen/Enniskeane Area Heritage Group.

26 *Ibid.*, p. 330, also footnotes in pp. 24 to 33.

27 Sinéad Spain presented a radio discussion with Nollaig Ó Gadhra, Brian Murphy, Pádraig Ó Cuanacháin and Peter Hart, Radio Kerry, September 1998.

28 Hart, p. 33, footnote 56.

29 *Ibid.*, p. 34, footnote 58.

30 After Kilmichael all three participated in other activities with Barry's flying column engagements, which included scouting, *Wild Heather,* pp. 68, 69, 100, 101, 121, 122.

31 Hart, p. 35 footnotes 61, 62 and p. 33, footnote 56 – 'AF, 19 November 1989'.

32 Jack Lane, *The Northern Star – Irish Political Review,* Vol. 17, No. 5, May 2002.

33 See *Wild Heather* for details of the men's pride in having taken part in the Kilmichael ambush. See also *Southern Star* and the *Cork Examiner* for the annual commemoration November/December – held on a Sunday close to 28 November. Gerry Adams, Sinn Féin president and MP for West Belfast gave the oration at the 1983 commemoration. Due to the 'Northern troubles' at the time there was opposition. Newspapers reported on the two survivors, Jack O'Sullivan and Ned Young, as being 'full of enthusiasm'. *An Phoblacht*, 1 December 1983, recorded that due to actions of certain people, 'Jack O'Sullivan confirmed that he had come under pressure … to avoid Kilmichael this year, as did Ned Young.' Dómhnall MacGiolla Phoil and Seán Kelleher organisers of the commemoration that year confirmed that these men and other Kilmichael veterans' relatives, were under considerable pressure to deny association with the ambush.

34 Fr John Chisholm, author interview 21/9/1998.

35 Joan (Collins) Dineen and Margaret (Collins) White, to author, 6/12/1998. Their mother was Jim O'Sullivan's sister.

36 Louis Whyte, PRO Kilmichael commemoration committee, to author 26/11/1998 & 10/3/2002.

37 Dómhnall MacGiolla Phoil (initially involved with the Kilmichael commemoration committee in 1965) to author 3/12/1998.

38 Seán Kelleher, secretary, Kilmichael commemoration committee, to author 26/11/1998.

39 Pádraig Long, letter to editor, *Cork Examiner,* July 1998. Johannah Hallahan (who lived near Kilmichael) and Kathryn Duggan to author 4/9/2003.

40 Tom Barry, to Brian Farrell, presenter, *Seven Days*, transmitted November 1969, RTÉ/TV Archives.

41 With Seamus Kelly – 'Kilmichael Ambush' transmitted 1966, RTÉ/TV Archives.

42 Jack Lane, *The Northern Star – Irish Political Review,* p. 18, May 2002.

43 Tom Barry interview RTÉ Sound Archives, also RTÉ/TV Archives, 1966, transmitted – also 1968 not transmitted; Barry, *Guerilla Days*, 47; Tom Barry, talk to Cork group, recording, courtesy of Jean Crowley.

44 Dómhnall MacGiolla Phoil, author interview 3/12/1998. In the 1930s after the Pension Board was set up many men came to Flor Crowley, a teacher, to help them fill out claim forms. 'He said if all the men who said they were in Kilmichael were actually there, it would have amounted to over a hundred.'

45 Tom Barry to Brian Farrell, presenter, *Seven Days,* transmitted November 1969, RTÉ/TV Archives.

46 Tom Barry Papers, also Eyewitness, *An Cosantóir,* 9 May 1941.

47 Tom Barry, Documentary, unedited – not transmitted, RTÉ/TV Archives.

48 Tom Barry to Kenneth Griffith, 1968, not transmitted, RTÉ Sound Archives; also Tom Barry to Griffith and O'Grady, p. 182.

49 Tom Barry, 1969, RTÉ, Sound Archives.

50 This video, with the O'Sullivan family, was not made for public viewing. Dave was Barry's friend. Barry's directness comes through (1970s), courtesy of Dave O'Sullivan.

51 *Irish Press*, 23 December 1974; in 1945, Seán MacBride, legal advisor, responded to Barry's wish to take a case due to a 'defamatory' statement in a book not named, published 1923, saying the ambush OC was 'cutting up dead bodies with an axe'. By the time Barry heard of the book, 1945, it was 'statute barred'. Seán MacBride to Barry, 12/10/1945 and 18/10/1945,TB private papers.

52 Tom Barry to Dan Nolan 9/4/1979, from *Anvil Press*, courtesy of Rena Dardis. Hart, p. 32, has written that Barry 'gave an order to fix bayonets and posted men to prevent any Auxiliaries escaping.' Note, only two of his men had bayonets. In setting up the ambush he posted part

of No. 3 section across the road to prevent the Auxiliaries from taking up firing positions in the rocks there. His ambush strategy worked.

53 The first account appears after the ambush; another is a filed typewritten report, and another is in a printed internal document. In the first account the man in uniform and wearing a steel helmet has a lorry pulled across the road and 'shooting began'. In the later two the Auxiliaries are 'confronted' by 'a man in a steel helmet' and 'British uniform' whose 'lorry has broken down and he required assistance' – *The Times*, 2 December 1920. In the Strickland Papers under the title, *The Irish Rebellion in the 6th Divisional Area from after 1916 Rebellion*, the report tells of 'the patrol' being 'caught by three fires, i.e.: from the three sections described in the Rebel Commandant's report.' It goes on to tell that 'the dead and wounded were indiscriminately hacked with axes and bayonets; shot-guns were fired into their bodies, and many were savagely mutilated after death.' This report together with what they call the 'Rebel Commandant's report on the affair' were typed and bound, and there was also a limited printing to December 1921'. In the printed version they number the soldiers as sixteen travelling in two lorries, Strickland Papers, IWM; Jeudwine Papers, Vol. 1, IWM.

54 Hart, p. 25.

55 *Ibid.*, p. 34.

56 Tom Barry's notes, TB private papers; also the *Irish Press*, 18 May, 1948; Barry, *Guerilla Days*, p. 48.

57 Deasy, p. 173.

58 Curtis, *Ireland (1921)*, reprinted 2002, in Pat Walsh, *Introduction: The Anglo-Irish Treaty*, pp. 61, 62. I am indebted to Jack Lane for this reference. This work contains an interesting analysis of the 'Round Table'.

59 Piaras Béaslaí, *Michael Collins*, Vol. 11, p. 97; Ernie O'Malley, *On Another Man's Wound*, p. 217.

60 My interviews with participants throughout the 1970s and early 1980s, already listed, also in bibliography.

61 General Staff 6th Division, *The Irish Rebellion*, pp. 63, 64 – the 1st p. 64, – there are 2 page 64s, Sir Peter Strickland Papers, IWM.

62 Hart, p. 26, footnote 18; *Irish Times*, 1998, Kevin Myers, 29 May, Pádraig Ó Cuanacháin, 5 June; Peter Hart, 23 June; D. R. O'Connor Lysaght, 30 June; Pádraig Ó Cuanacháin, 7 July; Peter Hart, 22 July; Brian P. Murphy, 10 Aug.; Peter Hart, 1 Sept; Brian P. Murphy, 7 September; Peter Hart, 14 September; Meda Ryan, 10 November; Peter Hart, 10 December – all 1998. Editor's Note closed the correspondence on this date; see also *The Examiner*, 4, 19 Aug. and 2 Sept 1998.

63 Brian P. Murphy, Letter to Editor, *Irish Times*, 10 Aug. 1998; also Lane and Clifford pp. 16.

64 Tom Barry, UCG Lecture, 1969, recording, courtesy of John Browne.

65 Michael Hopkinson, *The Irish War of Independence*, p. 75.

66 Tom Barry to a group in Cork early 1970s, recording, courtesy of Jean Crowley; Brendan Ashe letter to author, 27/5/'99 stated, 'I have yet to come across a West Cork unit which was supplied with 100 rounds per man for any operation.'

67 Peter Hart, *Irish Times*, 1 September 1998. Response: Meda Ryan, 10 November 1998.

68 Liam Deasy, author interview 5/12/1972; also Deasy, p. 173; also Liam Deasy, 'Auxiliaries (all ex officers of the British army with active service experience in the 1914–18 war) approached Kilmichael where the column had taken up positions …' P7A/0/45, Mulcahy Papers, UCDA

69 Peter Hart, *Irish Times*, 14 September 1998.

70 Liam Deasy, p. 168; also Liam Deasy, author interview 5/12/1972.

71 In the Ballyvourney–Macroom district the Cork No. 1 Brigade had been planning 'the pass of Keimaneigh ambush … a big scheme' bringing in 'a lot of men'. This was called off after Kilmichael. Mick Sullivan says that Kilmichael 'spoilt a big job … afterwards we were delighted when Barry pulled off his ambush.' Bill Powell who was engaged in this operation remembers 'how happy' they were with the 'ambush on the Macroom Auxies'. It 'possibly saved the slaughter of so many of our men'. Dan 'Sandow' O'Donovan expressed similar sentiments, Mick Sullivan, O'Malley Papers, P17b/111, UCDA. Bill Powell, author interview 10/7/1974; Dan 'Sandow' O'Donovan, author interview 24/11/1973; see also Browne, *The Story of the 7th*, pp. 32, 33.

72 Liam Deasy, author interview 5/12/1972. Not related to this incident. But Barry was a perfect timekeeper– I can verify it personally: 'You're on time!' he would say.

73 Tom Barry to Nollaig Ó Gadhra, 1969, RTÉ Sound Archives.

74 Typewritten report, *The Irish Rebellion*, Strickland Papers, IWM. In press report mention is made

of the 'searches' on that day – 4 December, 1920, *Cork County Eagle*.

75 Printed booklet, *6th Division Report*, Strickland Papers; Printed booklet, *Rebellion, Vol 1*, p. 27, Jeudwine Papers, IWM; Major C. J.C. Street (IO), *The Administration of Ireland, 1920* – Introduction and Review by Brendan Clifford and Pat Walsh, p. 62.

76 Barry, *The Reality*, p. 16; Author interviews with section 2 Volunteers – Dan Hourihane, 26/4/1973, Pat O'Donovan, 18/9/1978, James O'Mahony, 1/12/1974; Tom Barry's account of their shock, will be dealt with later, Tom Barry to Dan Nolan, 9/4/1979, Anvil Press, courtesy of Rena Dardis; account in Strickland Papers, IWM; Barry, *Guerilla Days*, pp. 44–49; *Rebel Cork's Fighting Story*, pp. 109–111; Tom Barry to Nollaig Ó Gadhra, 1969, RTÉ Radio Archives; Tom Barry to Donncha Ó Dulaing, early 1970s, RTÉ Radio Archives; *Seven Days*, Brian Farrell, presenter, 1969, RTÉ/TV Archives; Tom Barry, *Lecture* to Irish army officers, recording, courtesy of Eamonn Moriarty.

77 Hart, p. 26, footnote 18.

78 Report, *The Irish Rebellion*, Strickland Papers, IWM; Hart, p. 25.

79 There is one other feature in the typewritten (Rebel Commandant's and Official) report as it is presented. It may or may not be a typographical error. Strangely there are two page 64s with the allegedly Barry's report which is at the end of 63 and part of 64. The military report follows at the end of 64 and continues to another page 64. If the 'Rebel Commandant's report' was omitted from the typewritten report, there would be no page errors. It could be deduced that the extra page was later inserted. Out of a total of 133 pages of text and 46 pages of appendices this appears to be the only page with numbering duplication – *The Irish Rebellion* 'compiled by General Staff 6th Division', Strickland Papers, IWM; Report Vol 11, p. 15, Jeudwine Papers, IWM.

80 Barry, *The Reality*, p. 58.

81 Thomas Jones, *Whitehall Diary*, Vol. 111, p. 41.

82 Brigadier General Crozier, 'Unpublished Memoirs' *The Kerryman*, March 1938.

83 *Ibid.*

84 Report of *The Irish Rebellion*, Sir Peter Strickland Papers, IWM; Hart, p. 24.

85 Tom Barry notes, TB private papers; also Barry, *Guerilla Days*, p. 51.

86 Tom Barry, UCG Lecture, 1969, recording, courtesy of John Browne.

87 Stephen (A. J. S.) Brady, author interview 14/11/1974.

88 *Cork Examiner*, 12 January 1921.

89 Stephen (A. J. S.) Brady, author interview 9/11/80. Stephen Brady's father was Rev. A. J. Brady who officiated at the removal of the bodies from Macroom Castle; *Wild Heather*, p. 152.

90 Stephen (A. J. S.) Brady author interview 9/11/80. Mr Brady said he knew some of 'the boys' in the castle. One day he asked one senior official why the British don't get out of Ireland and 'let us rule ourselves'. His response was that 'that's what should be done. But the British will always fight first and talk later if they have to!' For report on ambush from British viewpoint see *The Irish Rebellion*, Strickland Papers, IWM.

91 Bill Munroe, *The Auxiliary's Story* in Gleeson, pp. 70–76.

92 Major A. E. Percival, Percival Papers, 4/1, IWM.

93 Peter Hart, *Irish Times*, 10 December 1998.

94 Dómhnall MacGiolla Phoil to author 17/9/2000; O'Riordan, pp. 1–6.

95 Military Court of Inquiry, report, W.O.35/152; *The County Eagle*, 4 December 1920.

96 Lieut Col Eamonn Moriarty to author, 23/11/ 2002 – details of arms and ammunition; shrapnel is described as 'a shell which bursts in the air and scatters bullets or pieces of metal. 'The British Webley revolver of the period fired a ·455 inch round-nosed, soft lead bullet (12 lead/1 tin or 1% antimony) weighing 17 gram. It was a low velocity round of approx. 600 fps. Muzzle velocity, and did not have great penetrative power. On impact it would flatten and it's cross-section area would increase significantly, thus causing gaping wounds with great internal damage', Lieut Col Eamonn Moriarty to author; Military Authority, *Textbook of Small Arms*, p. 211; Barry *Guerilla Days*, p. 39.

97 Tom Barry, *Guerilla Days*, pp. 43, 44; In *The Irish Rebellion*, there is an account of an intelligence officer who left ammunition in accessible locations around the house as a ruse for a girl who worked for him, and known to him to be a republican sympathiser. When she stole the ammunition, she was not dismissed. Then faulty ammunition was left 'lying around' on a few occasions. She was on leave for a few days, and when she returned she said her brother 'met with an accident'. It was discovered that this was due to the 'explosives of his revolver'. The 'ruse worked on other occasions' also, according to the report, Strickland Papers, IWM.

98 Bill Munro in Gleeson, p. 74.

99 *Cork Examiner*, 12 January 1921. It noted that 'claims for compensation amounting to a huge sums [sought] by the relatives of the victims of the Kilmichael ambush'.

100 *Cork Examiner*, 18 January 1921; *Cork Examiner*, 12 January 1921; Military Court of Inquiry, War Office 35/152.

101 John A. Murphy, *Léargas* Programme on Kilmichael ambush, Pat Butler presenter, November 2000, RTÉ/TV Documentary.

102 *Cork County Eagle*, 4 December 1920.

103 Crozier, p. 117. According to Piaras Béaslaí, 'The evidence before the military enquiry, which enquired into these deaths was faked from beginning to end', Béaslaí, Vol. 2, p. 87.

104 Tom Barry, carbon copy of letter to *Irish Press*, 28 November 1932, TB private papers. A response to this does not seem to be among his papers. This does not mean that he did not get one, as there are gaps in the correspondence.

105 Quotes here: Tom Barry to Liam Sweetnam, 4/6/1948, TB private papers. The number of letters in May and June 1948 will be dealt with in later footnotes.

106 Proofs in Tom Barry private papers. There is an acknowledgement of the omission in *An Cosantóir*, 9 May and 16 May 1941.

107 Hart, p. 34.

108 Peter Hart, letter to editor, *Irish Times*, 10 December 1998. The letter has a footnote: 'This correspondence is now closed, Ed. I.T.'

109 Military Court of Inquiry WO 35/152;.see also *Irish Times* 12 January 1921; also Charles Townshend, *The British Campaign in Ireland*, p. 125–131.

110 *Constabulary Gazette*, July 1920. General Tudor, inspector general of the RIC recommended the recruiting of the Auxiliaries for service in Ireland.

111 *Cork County Eagle*, 4 December 1920.

112 Lane and Clifford, p. 23

113 Hart, p. 36.

From Lashing November Rain to Hospital Bed

1 Eyewitness, *An Cosantóir*, 16 May 1941.

2 Pat O'Donovan author interview 16/7/1979.

3 Barry, *With the IRA in the Fight for Freedom*, p. 126.

4 Barry *Guerilla Days*, p. 47.

5 Tom Barry interview. Over 50 years later tears welled up in his eyes as he spoke of that night.

6 Barry's notes also letter to Miah McGrath, 26/5/1948; also Barry *Guerilla Days*, p. 48.

7 Tom Barry to Miah McGrath 26 May 1948, TB private papers, also Barry *Guerilla Days*, pp. 53, 54.

8 Details in letter (carbon copy) Tom to Miah (McGrath), 26 May 1948, also Tom Barry's notes, TB private papers; see also Barry, *Guerilla Days*, pp. 53, 54.

9 Jerh Cronin, author interview 10/1/1981.

10 Florrie O'Donoghue, MS 300,301, FO'D Papers, NLI.

11 Flor Crowley, *In West Cork Long Ago*, p. 15.

12 C. S. Andrews, *Dublin Made Me*, p. 155.

13 Letter with full text of *The Boys of Kilmichael* from John F. Hourihane, Boston to Tom Barry, 28 July 1948, TB private papers. This song has been recorded by Seán O'Shea and by Jimmy Crowley who added his own verse.

14 Seán (John) O'Riordan, author interview 28/7/1984. The O'Riordan sisters called Fr Gould who administered the last rites. Men buried Denny at night as they could 'not dare to return by day'. Mary Hourihane and Kate Murphy, neighbours, in McSweeney, pp. 73, 74.

15 London, WO35/66, PRO; see also Joost Augusteijn, *From Public Defiance to Guerilla Warfare*, pp. 212 –214.

16 General Strickland Papers, IWM, London. See reports *The Times* 1, 2, 3 December, 1920. There appears to be a conflict with 15 dead recorded in some British reports and 16 in others. In August 1920, the British government had formed a Publicity Bureau in Dublin Castle to 'explain and defend the government's Irish policy'. As there was often conflict between what was called troops and police it was suggested in September that there should be the 'framing and issuing communiqués' from the chief secretary's office. After martial law was proclaimed in the 6th Divisional area communiqués had to concur with GHQ as 'the Military governors controlled both Troops and Police'. By the end of 1920 after the *Freeman's Journal* personnel were court-martialled, the *Cork Examiner* which had hitherto 'supported Sinn Féin and

attacked the crown forces on every occasion, became so moderate in tone' an official communiqué records, 'that its staff were eventually threatened by the IRA'. (Jeudwine Papers, Volume 2. IWM). Consequently, newspapers reported the statements, doctors' reports and propaganda on the Kilmichael ambush, as it had been given by the publicity bureau. Papers such as the *Southern Star* 'had to be submitted for censorship' weekly (Seán Buckley, *Southern Star*, 12 December, 1936. Col Hudson, commanding officer in Skibbereen paid his weekly visit to Dick Connolly, *Southern Star*).

17 Butler, p. 77.

18 Strickland Papers, 363, IWM.

19 Butler, p. 78.

20 Strickland Papers, 363; also Jeudwine Papers, IMW.

21 County Inspector Monthly Report, CO904/110.

22 Tom Barry, author interview.

23 Keyes McDonnell, pp. 193–195; Johannah Hallahan (12 years old at the time) and Kathryn Duggan to author 4/9/2003.

24 *Sunday Independent*, 6 July, 1980; Jim McSweeney, *Memories of Dromleigh – A Country School*, p. 73.

25 Browne, pp. 26, 27, 32–34; Hart, p. 36; McSweeney, eyewitnesses, Mary O'Mahony and Kate Murphy, p. 73.

26 Author interviews, Lily O'Donovan Coughlan, Pat O'Donovan's sister 3/7/1978; Dan Hourihane, 26/4/1973; Jack O'Sullivan, 20/4/1976; Ned Young, 12/4/1975; Seán O'Riordan, 28/7/1984. There are many horrific stories.

27 Pat O'Mahony in a letter to Tom reminisced on the ordeal, and the anxiety that he and his carers felt. 14/6/1948, TB private papers; see also Barry *Guerilla Days*, p. 56.

28 Letter and personal recollections to Tom Barry from Seán MacCárthaigh, 16/8/1948, TB private papers; see also Barry, *Guerilla Days*, p. 56.

29 Barry, *Guerilla Days*, p. 55.

30 Correspondence between Tom Barry and Miah McCrath, 15 May, 24 May, 26 May, 14 June, 15 June, 24 June, 1948. TB private papers; see also *Irish Press*, 20 May 1948; Tom Barry, *Guerilla Days*, p. 55.

31 Letters Miah Galvin to Tom Barry, 25/5/1948 &11/6/1948; Tom Barry to Miah Galvin, 26/5/1948 and 14/6/1948. He wished he 'could have written more happily about those three lads', TB private papers.

32 Strickland – *History of the 6th Division in Ireland November 1919 – March 1922*, Strickland Papers, IWM.

33 Details of Essex men in Barry's notes; also correspondence to and from Tom Barry, Seán MacCárthaigh, intelligence officer, 1948; Tom Barry's notes; Barry to Miah McGrath, 26 May 1948, TB private papers.

34 *The Times*, 13 December 1920.

35 *The Times*, 13 and15 December 1920; see also *The Burning of Cork City – A Tale of Arson, Loot and Murder* for depositions and statements.

36 Charlie to his mother, hand written letter, 16/12/1920, FO'D Papers, Ms. 31,226, NLI.

37 Charles to Edith, n.d. K Company Aux. Div. Dunmanway, FO'D Papers, Ms. 31,226, NLI..

38 Crozier, *Ireland Forever*, pp. 115, 116.

39 Jones, Vol. 111, pp. 50–52.

40 Report of the 'Trial of Cadet Sergeant Hart' *Cork Weekly Examiner*, 15 January 1921.

41 Flor Crowley 'Raymond' *Southern Star*, 23 October 1971.

42 British Cabinet conclusion 81/20 (3) dated 30/12/1920.

43 Mark Sturgis Diary, 19 December 1920, CSO, 1920–1921, 39 59/3, PRO.

44 Peadar O'Donovan, *Southern Star Centenary, 1889–989*, p. 45.

45 British Cabinet conclusion 81/20 (3) dated 30/12/1920.

46 'Trial of Cadet Sergeant Hart', *Cork Weekly Examiner*, 15 January 1921; Strickland wrote in his diary: 'R. C. Canon shot in Dunmanway. I fear by K. Coy. RIC. It's a devil – written to Dublin tonight.' Strickland Papers, P363, Diary, IWM; Canon Magner had been a curate in Bandon prior to his transfer to Dunmanway – Michael Lyons, *After Kilmichael*, p. 12, *Bandon Historical Journal* 1996.

47 *Cork Weekly Examiner*, 15 January 1921.

48 Brendan Clifford, introduction to Crozier, *The Men I Killed*, p. 18; *The Times*, 18 February, 1921. I am indebted to Jack Lane and Brendan Clifford for this reference.

49 Charlie to his mother, hand-written letter, 16/12/20, FO'D Papers, Ms 31,226, NLI.

50 Crozier, p. 197.

51 Hand-written order, dated 12/12/1920 with names of Daniel Coholan, Bishop of Cork, Patrick Canon Sexton, publication date 18/12/1920, TB private papers; see Appendix I; see *Cork Examiner*, 18 December 1920.

52 Ned O'Sullivan to Tom Barry, 13/9/49. section commander Mick O'Donovan confirmed background details for Barry. TB private papers.

53 Seán MacCárthaigh, 'Personal Recollections' to Tom Barry, 16/8/1948, TB private papers.

54 Liam Deasy, author interview, 5/12/1972; see also Deasy, p. 181.

55 Tom Barry to Liam MacGowan, 1 May 1948. The carbon copy of the letter is torn – part of it is missing, TB private papers.

56 Strickland Papers, p. 363 – Diary, IWM.

57 Tom Barry's manuscript, TB private papers.

58 Denis O'Mahony, author interview 24/8/1974; also Tom Barry manuscript, TB private papers.

59 Barry, *Guerilla Days*, p. 59.

LORD TOM, BURGATIA, ROSSCARBERY, MICHAEL COLLINS

1 *The Times*, 6 to 9 December 1920. Michael Collins is titled 'Commander-in-Chief of Sinn Féin'. Archbishop Clune was uncle of Conor Clune who was shot and tortured while in custody on the eve of 'Bloody Sunday'.

2 See *Southern Star*, December and January 1920 and 1921; see also *Cork Examiner* for a number of attacks.

3 Tom Barry interview, he spoke of the difficulty of that period and 'what seemed an insurmountable task ahead'.

4 Jim Kearney, author interview 12/9/1974.

5 Tom Barry to Mr Dempsey, editor, *Irish Press*, 23/7/1949, TB private papers.

6 Tom Barry manuscript, TB private papers.

7 Leslie Price, author interview 22/4/1973; see Ryan, *Michael Collins and the Women*, pp. 78–80; Leslie Price Papers; Major General Strickland interview, *The Irish Times*, 22 January, 1921.

8 Tom Barry manuscript, TB private papers; Tom Barry to Nollaig Ó Gadhra, 1969, RTÉ Sound Archives; Tom Barry, author interview.

9 Tom Barry's notes, TB private papers; see also Barry, *Guerilla Days*, pp. 70–73.

10 Tom Barry manuscript, TB private papers; Tom Barry to UCG students 1969, recording courtesy of John Browne; see also Barry, *Guerilla Days*, p. 75.

11 Tom Barry, author interview.

12 John L. O'Sullivan, author interview 31/7/1974.

13 Tom Barry, manuscript TB private papers; Barry, *Guerilla Days*, p. 81; radio recording, not transmitted, RTÉ Sound Archives; Tom Barry, UCG Lecture, 1969, recording courtesy of John Browne; see also *Cork Examiner*, 4 February 1921.

14 F. Begley to Tom Barry 12/5/47; Mick Deasy to Tom Barry 21/5/48, TB private papers; Tom Barry manuscript, TB private papers; John Whelton, author interview 15/10/1980; Pat Buttimer, author interview 15/10/1980; Barry, *Guerilla Days*, pp. 78–86; Butler, pp. 102–3.

15 Jim Kearney, author interview 31/3/1975.

16 Jack O'Sullivan, author interview 18/2/1975; Jim Kearney, author interview 31/3/1975; John Whelton, author interview 15/10/1980; Pat Buttimer, author interview 15/10/1980; Tom Barry, UCG Lecture, recording, courtesy of John Browne.

17 Michael Collins to Helena, 5/3/1921, John Pierce private papers; see Ryan *Michael Collins and the Women*, p. 81; also *Cork Examiner*, 4 February 1921.

18 *An t-Óglach*, 13 May, 1921; *Irish Times*, 4 February 1921; Daily newspapers, 25 April 1921.

19 Tom Barry, Notes and manuscript, TB private papers.

20 Liam O'Regan, editor, *Southern Star*, son of Joe O'Regan, document in his possession. Joe O'Regan, Aughadown was a member of the Lisheen IRA Cumann, and Barney O'Driscoll, Union Hall, was 'also a member of Skibbereen Urban Council'.

21 Tom Barry, manuscript, TB private papers; also Barry, *Guerilla Days*, pp. 91, 92.

22 Kathy Hayes, author interview 14/9/1974; also Tom Barry manuscript, TB private papers.

23 Tom Barry, Lecture to UCG students, 1969, recording, courtesy of John Browne.

24 The IRA men killed were: Lieut John (Seán) Phelan, Lieut Patrick O'Sullivan, section commander, Bart Falvey. Wounded IRA men were: Seán Hartnett, Dan O'Mahony (Belrose) and Charlie Hurley. See Tom Kelleher, *The Kerryman*, 7 October 1967; Nollaig Ó Gadhra, 1969, RTÉ

Sound Archives; see Michael Lyons, *Bandon Historical Journal*, 16, No. 12 (1996).

25 Tom Barry to Joe O'Regan, 2/4/1968, this was a response to Joe O'Regan's 'tribute to Dan O'Brien', Private Collection, Liam O'Regan, editor, *Southern Star*.

26 Jim Kearney, author interview 31/3/1975; Tom Kelleher, author interview 9/4/1979.

27 Flor Begley, P17b/111, O'M. Papers, UCDA; Tom Barry, author interview.

28 Correspondence between T. [Tom] O'Neill and Tom Barry, 3/5/48, 5/5/48, 29/5/48, TB private papers. O'Neill states that there were 10 Volunteers inside the ditch and these escaped.

29 Tom Barry's manuscript, TB private papers.

30 Captured document, Florence O'D Papers, MS.321,460, NLI.

31 Percival Papers, 'stool pigeons', IWM; Tom Barry manuscript, TB private papers; correspondence and questionnaire between Jim O'Mahony and Tom Barry 15/2/1947 & 24/2/47, TB private papers; also Barry, *Guerilla Days*, p. 98.

32 Percival Papers, 4/1–8, IWM.

33 . Crozier, pp. 168, 287; see also Crozier, Appendix C, D, E, F.

34 Barry, *Guerilla Days*, pp. 98, 99.

35 Tom Barry's notes, TB private papers; see also Barry, *Guerilla Days*, p. 99.

36 Tom Barry manuscript, TB private papers. British official communique, 24 February 1921, named the dead as Constable Perrier, Constable Kerins, Corporal Stubbs and Private Knight of the Essex Regiment.

37 Tom Kelleher, author interview 9/4/1979; also Tom Barry's manuscript, TB private papers; see also Barry, *Guerilla Days*, p. 102.

38 Jim Kearney, author interview 18/10/1980.

PERCIVAL'S SPIES AND INFORMERS

1 Tom Barry's manuscript: Tom Barry letter to Miah Galvin, 26 May 1948, TB private papers; Barry, *Guerilla Days*, pp. 103, 104; Denis Lordan, author interview 7/7/1974; Jim Kearney, author interview 18/10/1980.

2 Jones, Vol. 11, pp. 45, 46; Pat Walsh, pp. 6–10, introduction to Street, *The Administration*. Tom Barry had typed passages from C. J. Street's writings. Street wrote under IO in earlier works.

3 Lord Russell, King's Liverpool Regiment, Skibbereen, to Butler, p. 86.

4 Tom Barry, author interview; Dan Cahalane, author interview 30/1/1977.

5 Barry, *Guerilla Days*, p. 116; Tom Barry, author interview.

6 Bill Hales, author interview, 14/9/1974; Donal Hales and Madge Hales, Hales Family Papers.

7 Béaslaí, Vol. 11, 173–185.

8 May Twomey, author interview 30/11/1974; Tom Barry, author interview; Tom Barry, n. d. RTÉ Sound Archives; see also Barry, *Guerilla Days*, p. 112.

9 Tom Barry's manuscript, TB private papers; also Tom Barry, *Guerilla Days*, pp. 105, 106; Tom Barry, RTÉ recording, not dated, RTÉ Sound Archives.

10 Percival Papers, 4/1, IWM.

11 Jeudwine Papers, 72/82/2, IWM.

12 Percival Papers 4/1, IWM.

13 Flor Begley, 15/3/60, FO'D Papers, MS. 31,301(5) NLI. The name is not given in this instance, but is given in Seán MacCárthaigh to Tom Barry 16/8/1948, TB private papers; Flor Begley, E. O'Malley Papers, P17b/108, UCDA;.see also details in Percival Papers, 4/1, IWM; Strickland Papers, typewritten report 25, 26, IWM.

14 Percival Papers 4/1, IWM.

15 Strickland, *Irish Rebellion*, p. 70 and App. V., IWM.

16 Jeudwine Papers, *Record Rebellion in Ireland*, Vol. 11, 25–34, IWM.

17 Strickland Papers, draft document, IWM.

18 Percival Papers 4/1, IWM.

19 Liam Deasy, author interview 5/12/1972; see also, General Order No. 20, 'a convicted spy shall not be executed until his conviction and sentence have been ratified by the brigade commandant concerned'. Prior to this the suspect would be arrested 'and placed before a Court of Inquiry' – the conviction should be absolute.

20 Tom Barry, author interview; Tom Barry manuscript and notes, TB private papers; see also *Irish Press*, 1 and 2 June 1948.

21 Tom Barry author interview, Tom Kelleher, author interview 9/4/1979; see also *Irish Press*, 1 and 2 June 1948; Barry, *Guerilla Days*, 109, 110

22 Tom Barry, author interview; also Donal Corvin, *Sunday Independent*, 7 March 1976.

23 Deasy, pp. 200, 201.

24 Jim Kearney, author interview 18/10/1980.

25 Tom Barry to editor *Irish Press*, 1 May 1948, torn copy of letter. *Irish Press* editor William Sweet-nam, to Tom Barry, 12 May 1948. Barry lists all of them, and their addresses on a separate sheet. TB private papers; see also *Irish Press* 1 and 2 June 1948; Barry, *Guerilla Days*, pp. 105–114.

26 Danny Canty, author interview 6/8/1972; Jim Kearney, author interview 18/10/1980.

27 Montgomery to Percival, 12/10/1923, Percival Papers, IWM.

28 Barry, *Guerilla Days*, p. 112.

29 Tom Barry, manuscript, TB private papers.

CROSSBARRY'S LANDMARK SUCCESS

1 Denis O'Mahony, author interview 5/4/1974.

2 Tom Barry, author interviews; Flor Begley, brigade acting adj.; also Barry, *Guerilla Days*, p. 12; Mc-Carthy, the engineer, did not join until after 23 March 1921.

3 Flor Begley Report, Florence O'Donoghue Papers. MS 31,301, NLI; see also Dick Russell to Flor-rie O'Donoghue [no month] 27 Tues. 1962, FO'D Papers, MS. 31,300, NLI; *Crossbarry Remem-bered*, AA1947, 30/3/1980, RTÉ Sound Archives, several participants in the ambush con-tributed to the discussion.

4 Dr Nudge Callanan, author interview 14/10/1980.

5 Section commanders: Seán Hales, John Lordan, Mick Crowley, Denis Lordan, Tom Kelleher, Peter Kearney and Christy O'Connell.

6 Tom Barry to Nollaig Ó Gadhra, RTÉ Sound Archives; Barry, *Guerilla Days*, p. 123; Barry had sent scouts to Kinsale and they returned with the news the Cumann na mBan girls also conveyed personally. In the Deasy, p. 293, there is mention of the enemy observing a 'peace day'. Barry in *The Reality*, p. 28, writes: 'Good Lord, why did we not go in to meet them half-way, and have a real St Patrick's Day celebration!'

7 The foregoing is compiled from Tom Barry to Kate O'Callaghan, RTÉ Sound Archives. (In this re-cording Barry put in a stipulation that the recording would be transmitted on its own, as he did not want any distortion); Tom Barry to Donncha Ó Dulaing, early 1970s, RTÉ Sound Ar-chives; 'Crossbarry Remembered', participants contributed to discussion, RTÉ Sound Archives; Tom Barry, *Lecture* to Irish army officers, Eamonn Moriarty tape recording; Seán MacCár-thaigh, 'Recollections' to Tom Barry, 16/8/1948, TB private papers; Flor Begley, Florence O'Donoghue Papers, Ms 31, 301 (5), NLI; Seán MacCárthaigh to Liam Deasy 18/7/63, quoted Diarmuid Begley, *The Road to Crossbarry*, 78; Percival Papers, 4/1 typewritten report 25,26, IWM. The incident of lorries 'setting out', etc., is described as 'an exciting episode' in the Per-cival records; see WO 35 161 Private British army inquiries into the death of Charlie Hurley and three 'unidentified' deceased, Public Records Office, Surrey.

8 Tom Kelleher, *The Kerryman*, December 1937; Kelleher, *Rebel Cork's Fighting Story*, p. 158.

9 Barry, *The Reality of the Anglo-Irish War*, p. 30.

10 Kate O'Callaghan, n.d. RTÉ Sound Archives; Barry, *The Reality*, p. 29; Barry is critical of Deasy ac-count, pp. 232–249, which does not tally with Tom Kelleher's account *The Kerryman*, Decem-ber 1937, nor Kelleher, *Rebel Cork's Fighting Story*, p. 157–160; see also Eyewitness, *An Cosan-tóir* 3/1/41 and 10/1/41; *Looking West, Memories of Crossbarry*, earlier recording – compilation transmitted 28/5/1986, Jim Fahy presenter – many contributors, RTÉ Sound Archives.

11 Typewritten document, pp. 25, 26, Percival Papers 4/1, IWM; also Report on battle of Cross Barry, 19 March in *The Irish Rebellion*, Strickland Papers IWM.

12 The 'informant's' name is given in a letter from Seán MacCárthaigh to Tom Barry, 16/8/1948, TB private papers. Later, following an IRA court-martial, Barry allowed this man's death sen-tence to be 'commuted to exile for life it being Truce times', Flor Begley, 15/3/60, FO'D Papers, Ms 31, 301, NLI.

13 Flor Begley, 'They held up and made prisoners of 6 or 7 lads', P17b/111 O'Malley Papers, UCDA; Flor Begley, MS 31,301 (5) FO'D Papers NLI.

14 Butler, p. 127.

15 Tom Barry's notes, T. B. private papers; Barry, *Guerilla Days*, pp. 126, 127; Eyewitness, *An Cosan-tóir*, 1/10/1941; Tom Kelleher, *The Kerryman*, December 1937; Kelleher in *Rebel Cork's Fighting Story*, p. 159; Nollaig Ó Gadhra, 1969, RTÉ Sound Recording; Compilation, *Looking West*, inter-views by Jim Fahy, RTÉ Sound Archives.

16 Tom Barry to Nollaig Ó Gadhra, RTÉ Sound Archives, 1969; Tom said later: 'Somehow one knew that it was his fate to die in such a way.' Tom Barry, 'Charlie Hurley Remembered',

Rebel Cork's Fighting Story, pp. 161, 162.

17 Tom Kelleher, *The Kerryman*, December, 1937; Liam Deasy states that the bagpipes 'must have caused as much bewilderment to the enemy as stimulation to us', P7A/D/45, Mulcahy Papers, UCDA.

18 Tom Kelleher, *The Kerryman*, December 1937, Kelleher, *Rebel Cork's Fighting Story*, pp. 158,159; Flor Begley Report 15/3/60, FO'D Papers, MS 31,301 (5) NLI; Diarmuid Begley, *The Road to Crossbarry*, pp. 86–92.

19 Barry, *Guerilla Warfare*, unpublished document, TB private papers. 'In the course of a study of guerilla operations extending over 20 years no other fight broke through a cordon which affords a more inspiring example' than that action at Crossbarry ambush.

20 *Report 6th Division*, Strickland Papers, V11, 70, IWM. The report states: 'How far it [carrying hostages] prevented ambushes it is difficult to say – as a matter of fact, there were hardly any cases of convoys accompanied by a "mascot" being attacked'.

21 Bill Powell, author interview 15/3/1975; Dómhnall MacGiolla Phoil to author 20/11/2001.

22 Tom Kelleher, *The Kerryman*, December 1937; also Kelleher, *Rebel Cork's Fighting Story*, p. 160.

23 The foregoing is obtained from Tom Kelleher author interview 6/4/1974; Tom Barry manuscript, TB private papers; Tom Barry, *Irish Press*, 7, 8, 9 June, 1949; Tom Kelleher, *The Kerryman*, December 1937, Kelleher, *Rebel Cork's Fighting Story*, pp. 159,160; Eyewitness, *An Cosantóir*, 3 and 10/1/41; Begley, pp. 79–92; Flor Begley Report, Florence O'Donoghue Papers Ms 31,301; Barry *Guerilla Days*, pp. 128–131; Tom Barry told Nollaig Ó Gadhra, 'I put my hand on Kelleher's shoulder, and told him he had done enough …' 1969, RTÉ Sound Archives; *Looking West*, Jim Fahy interviews, RTÉ Sound Archives; *Crossbarry Remembered*, Kate O'Callaghan interview, n.d. RTÉ Sound Archives; Barry *The Reality*, pp. 31–38.

24 Eyewitness, *An Cosantóir*, 10/1/1941.

25 Seán Feehan to author April 1981.

26 Pax O'Faolain in in Uinseann MacEoin, *Survivors*, p. 149.

27 Butler, p. 134.

28 Tom Barry to Donncha Ó Dulaing, early 1970s, RTÉ Sound Archives.

29 Strickland Papers, IWM. Report on battle of Cross Barry, 19 March 1921.

30 Eyewitness, *An Cosantóir*, 10 January, 1941.

31 Tom Barry to Kate O'Callaghan, n.d. RTÉ Sound Archives.

32 *Crossbarry Remembered*, n.d. RTÉ Sound Archives.

33 Lieut Col Eamonn Moriarty, to Irish army officers, *Recording on Location – Crossbarry*, courtesy of Eamonn Moriarty.

34 This, it is believed is Jack Hourihane's composition (see Appendix VI). In the Tom Barry Papers there is another song entitled, 'Crossbarry Abu' written by Pat O'Mahony, of the Third West Cork Brigade.

35 Tom Barry, unpublished document, TB private papers.

36 Participants in *Crossbarry Remembered*, recording some time earlier, transmitted 28/5/1986, RTÉ Sound Recording; *Looking West*, Jim Fahy interviewed participants, RTÉ Sound Recording; Irish Army Officers' Recording, 1966, courtesy of Eamonn Moriarty; Tom Barry to Kate O'Callaghan, n.d. RTÉ Sound Recording.

37 Dr Nudge Callanan, author interview 14/10/1980.

38 Tom Barry, manuscript, TB private papers.

39 Criostóir de Baróid, author interview 11/1/1981.

40 Liam Deasy, notes to author, 5/12/1972; see also Deasy, p. 249.

41 Tom Barry, *Irish Press*, 10 June 1949; also Tom Barry's notes, TB private papers.

42 Denis Lordan, author interview 7/7/1974.

43 Tom Barry's notes, TB private papers; see also Tom Barry, *Irish Press*, 10 June 1949; Barry, *Guerilla Days*, p. 134.

44 Denis Conroy to Donncha Ó Dulaing, – occasion of his death, 2/7/ 1980, RTÉ Sound Archives.

45 Barry, *Guerilla Days*, p. 36; Liam Deasy, Personal Narrative, P7A/D/45, MP, UCDA.

46 Flor Begley, E. O'Malley N. P176/107, UCDA.

47 Barry, *Rebel Cork's Fighting Story*, p. 162; Seán MacCárthaigh to Tom Barry, 16/8/1948, TB private papers; Tom Barry, author interview; Leslie Price, author interview 22/4/1973; Brdie Crowley (Manning), author interview 24/7/1974; Bridget O'Mahony, author interview 3/2/1979; Liam Deasy, author interview 5/12/1972; Denis Lordan, author interview 7/7/1974; Mick McCarthy, in Uinseann MacEoin, *The IRA*, p. 638.

FORMATION OF THE FIRST SOUTHERN DIVISION

1 Tony Woods in MacEoin, *Survivors*, p. 329.

2 *Cork Examiner*, 20 March 1921.

3 The homes of Volunteers, Jack Hartnett and Paddy O'Leary were burned. O'Leary was in Spike Island prison at the time, having been captured after Upton ambush.

4 *Cork Examiner*, 30 April 1921.

5 *Daily Mail*, 21 March 1921.

6 *Cork Examiner*, 21 March 1921.

7 Charlie O'Keeffe, author interview, 7/12/1975.

8 Tom Kelleher, author interview 6/4/1974.

9 Tom Barry, author interview; Tim O'Donoghue, *The Fall of Rosscarbery Barracks*, A/0618, Military Archives, Dublin.

10 Tom Barry, author interview. It was while speaking of Rosscarbery that he reminisced on his youth there. Tom Kelleher, author interview 9/4/1979; Jack O'Sullivan, author interview 25/4/1976; O'Donoghue, A/0618, Military Archives, Dublin.

11 Tom Kelleher, author interview 9/4/1979. Initially Barry called for volunteers to execute this dangerous task.

12 Tom Kelleher, author interview 9/4/1979; Jack O'Sullivan, author interview 25/4/1976; Denis Lordan, author interview 7/7/1974; Tom Barry, author interview; Tom Barry notes, TB private papers, Tom Barry, *The Irish Press*, 25/5/1948; O'Donoghue, A/0618, Military Archives, Dublin.

13 Tim O'Donoghue, A/0618, 1X, Military Archives, Dublin; Tim O'Donoghue, *Rebel Cork's Fighting Story*, pp. 163–66; Butler, pp. 140–142; *Irish Press*, 25/5/1948; Tom Barry's manuscript, TB private papers, Tom Barry, author interview; Denis Lordan, author interview 7/7/1974; Tom Kelleher, author interview 9/4/1979'; Jack O'Sullivan, author interview 20/4/1976.

14 *Cork Examiner*, 1 April, 1921.

15 Béaslaí, Vol. 11, p. 182.

16 Butler, pp. 145, 146; Hales Family Papers, held by Ann Hales, courtesy of Maura Murphy and Eily Hales McCarthy.

17 Tom Barry, manuscript, TB private papers; Barry, *Guerilla Days*, p. 155.

18 Tom Barry, author interview; Seán Buckley, *Southern Star*, 12/12/1936; Tom Barry, *Guerilla Days*, p. 156; Tom Barry, to Griffith and O'Grady, *Curious Journey*, pp. 220, 221; Tom Barry in conversation with Dave O'Sullivan. He told of the dinner with Col Hudson, home video (early 1970s) courtesy of Dave O'Sullivan.

19 Tom Barry to Donncha Ó Dulaing, early 1970s, RTÉ Sound Archives.

20 Madge Hales Murphy, author interview 6/3/1973. Madge was bound to secrecy. Michael Collins had sent Madge on this responsible mission.

21 Barry to Raymond Smith, *The Irish Independent*, 7 July 1971.

22 Tom Barry, manuscript, TB private papers.

23 Ernie O'Malley, *On Another Man's Wound*, p. 306.

24 Tom Barry, *Guerilla Days*, p. 159; Seán Hegarty, FO'D Papers, MS 31,206, NLI.

25 Tom Barry, notes, TB Papers, Butler, pp. 148–150; Barry, *Guerilla Days*, p. 159, O'Malley *On Another Man's Wound*, p. 307; Deasy, p. 266–268; Meda Ryan, *The Real Chief – The Story of Liam Lynch*, pp. 66–68; Ernie O'Malley, *On Another Man's Wound*, p. 154–158.

26 Tom Barry manuscript, TB private papers; Barry, *Guerilla Days*, p. 159.

27 Tom Barry manuscript, TB private papers; also Barry, *Guerilla Days*, p. 161.

28 Ryan, *The Real Chief*, pp. 29–32.

29 O'Malley, *On Another Man's Wound*, p. 308; Florence O'Donoghue, *No Other Law*, pp. 154–158; Barry, *Guerilla, Days*, pp. 161, 162; Tom Barry's notes and manuscript, TB private papers.

30 See Deasy, pp. 272, 273; Barry, *Guerilla Days*, p. 164; *Cork Examiner*, 10, 11, 12 May 1921.

31 Barry, *Guerilla Days*, p. 166.

32 Report of Activities, 20/5/1921, FO'D Papers, MS. 31,206, NLI; Tom Barry manuscript, TB private papers; Barry, *Guerilla Days*, pp. 179–170.

33 Tom Barry, unpublished piece, TB private papers.

To Michael Collins and GHQ

1 Butler, pp. 153, 154; Jeudwine Papers, IWM; see also John P. Duggan, *A History of the Irish Army*, pp. 57–66.
2 Barry, *Guerilla Days*, p. 175.
3 Brigid O'Mahony, author interview 3/2/1977; Barry, *Guerilla Days*, p. 176.
4 Tom Barry in conversation with Dave O'Sullivan, *Home video* held by Dave O'Sullivan.
5 Tom Barry, author interview; Tom Barry's notes and manuscript, TB private papers; Tom Barry, *Irish Press*, 23 June 1948; Barry, *Guerilla Days*, pp. 176–178; Butler, pp. 155–157.
6 Tom Barry, notes, TB private papers; Tom Barry, *Irish Press*, 24 June 1948.
7 Bob [Robert Barton] to Tom Barry, n.d. c. 1948 – first page missing. TB Papers.
8 Tom Barry to Kenneth Griffith, RTÉ Sound Archives
9 Tom Barry, author interview; Tom Barry, manuscript, TB private papers; Tom Barry, *Irish Press*, 24, 25 June 1948; *Guerilla Days*, pp. 179–183; Butler, pp. 157–160.
10 Tom Barry to Kenneth Griffith, RTÉ Sound Archives.
11 Patrick Jung, *The Thompson submachine-gun during and after the Anglo-Irish war*, in, *The Irish Sword*, Vol. XX1, p. 191. I am indebted to Michael Mac Evilly for this reference.
12 Tom Barry, notes and manuscript, TB private papers.
13 Tom Barry, author interview; Tom Barry, manuscript, TB private papers; Barry, *Guerilla Days*; Butler, pp. 160–162.

Through Boggy Slopes to Deep Valley Desmond

1 Pat O'Donovan, author interview 18/9/1978; Lily (O'Donovan) Coughlan, author interview 12/8/1978; Dan Cahalane, author interview 29/11/1976; Liam Deasy, author interview 5/12/1972;Tom Barry, author interview; Barry, *Guerilla Days*, p. 199, Deasy, pp. 283–286.
2 Lily (O'Donovan) Coughlan, author interview 12/8/1978. Lily and Mary's brother Pat had fought in Kilmichael. Their home, being some distance from the main road regarded as a 'safe house', was a place of assembly.
3 Barry, *The Reality*, p. 48.
4 Tom Barry, manuscript, TB private papers; Tom Barry, *The Irish Press*, 28 June 1948.
5 Tom Barry manuscript, TB private papers; Tom Barry, *The Irish Press*, 28 June 1948; *Frustrating a Round Up*, 1/5/21, A/0618, XV111, Military Archives, Dublin.
6 Tom Barry to Raymond Smith, the *Irish Independent*, 7 July 1971.
7 Captured Document, TB private papers; see also Tom Barry, *The Irish Press*, 29 June 1948; FO'D Papers, Ms. 31,393, NLI.
8 Barry, *Guerilla Days*, p. 211.
9 Leon Ó Broin, *Protestant Nationalists in Revolutionary Ireland: The Stopford Connection*, p. 176.
10 Denis O'Mahony, author interview 5/4/1974.
11 Danny Canty, author interview 5/4/1973.
12 Tom Barry manuscript, TB private papers; Barry, *Guerilla Days*, p. 214.
13 Jeudwine Papers, *Rebellion* Vol 1. 24, IWM.
14 Tom Barry, *Irish Press*, 1 July 1948.

Appointed IRA Deputy Divisional Commander

1 Leslie Price, Sighle Humphreys Papers, P106/1412(1), UCDA; Tom Barry, TB private papers.
2 Tom Barry to Kenneth Griffith, unedited and not transmitted, RTÉ Sound Archives.
3 Jim O'Mahony's 'recollections' to Tom Barry 15/2/1949; Denis Lordan, author interview 7/7/1974; Charlie O'Keeffe, author interview 6/11/1976; see also Deasy, p. 296.
4 Tom Barry, *Irish Press*, 1 July, 1948; Leslie Price de Barra, Sighle Humphreys Papers, P106/1412 (1) and (2), UCDA; O'Broin, Dorothy Stopford recollections, p. 179. The earl was held at Murphy's of Scaife, at John L. O'Sullivan's and a number of other houses, as the IRA kept moving him to frustrate any informers.
5 Tom Barry notes, TB private papers; *Irish Press* 1 July 1948.
6 Tom Barry manuscript, TB private papers; *Irish Press* 1 July 1948; Barry, *Guerilla Days*, p. 217.
7 Tom Barry, manuscript, TB private papers; Barry, *Guerilla Days*, pp. 211, 212.
8 Tom Barry, *Reality*, p. 49.
9 Field Marshal Sir Henry Wilson's Diary, 18 and 23 May 1921, C. E. Callwell, *Field Marshal Sir Henry Wilson, His Life and Diaries*.
10 Liam Deasy, author interview 5/12/1970; The men were Jim O'Mahony, Jerh McCarthy, Liam and Tom. The meeting had been held at White's Rathrout; see also Deasy, pp. 306, 307: Jerh

Cronin to author on his courage, 10/1/1981.

11 *Daily Mail*, 28 June 1921; *Irish Press*, 1 July 1948. Dan O'Mahony, seriously wounded in the leg was the IRA's only casualty.

12 FO'Donoghue Papers, MS 31421 (12), NLI; Military Registration Board File.

13 Tom Barry to Raymond Smith, *Irish Independent*, 7 July 1971.

14 *Ibid*.

15 Strickland Diary, 17 May 1922, Strickland Papers, IWM.

16 Tom Barry manuscript, TB private papers; Tom Barry, author interview.

17 Tom Barry to Raymond Smith, *Irish Independent*, 7 July 1971.

18 Tom Barry to Nollaig Ó Gadhra, 1969, RTÉ Sound Archives.

19 Callwell, 18/5/1921.

20 Montgomery to Percival 14/10/23, Percival Papers 4/1, IWM.

21 Tom Barry to Raymond Smith, *Irish Independent*, 7 July 1971.

22 Leslie Price, Statement, Sighle Humphreys Papers, P106/1412 (1) and (2), UCDA; Leslie Price de Barra, author interview 22/4/1973.

23 Percival Papers, 4/1, 18, IWM.

24 Tom Barry manuscript, TB private papers; Deasy, p. 297.

25 Tom Barry to Raymond Smith, *Irish Independent*, 7 July 1971.

26 Denis O'Callaghan, author interview 20/2/1974; Tom Barry in response to an audience question following a lecture to history students, UCG, recording, courtesy of John Browne.

27 Tom Barry to Raymond Smith, *Irish Independent*, 7 July 1971.

28 Flor O'Donoghue, P176/96, O'Malley Notebooks, UCDA.

29 Eyewitness, *An Cosantóir*, 3 January 1941.

30 Tom Barry manuscript, TB private papers.

31 Tom Barry and Professor John A. Murphy, in conversation, RTÉ Sound Archives.

32 Tom Barry manuscript, TB private papers; Barry, *Guerilla Days*, pp. 212, 213 and pp. 63, 64.

33 Hart, p. 133; Barry, *The Reality*, p. 14.

34 Paddy O'Brien's son, Liam O'Brien confirms the camaraderie of the men; see P17b series, Liam Deasy, Barney O'Driscoll, Stephen O'Neill, Billy O'Sullivan, Flor Begley, Jack Fitzgerald, Ralph Keys, Seán Lehane – all of Barry's flying column, O'Malley Notebooks, UCDA.

35 Flor Begley, O'Malley Notebooks, P17b/111, UCDA.

36 Comdt Christy O'Sullivan to Irish army officers, on location Kilmichael, recording, courtesy of Eamonn Moriarty.

37 Tom Barry to Nollaig Ó Gadhra, 1969, RTÉ Sound Archives.

38 Col M. J. (later Major General) Costello, *An Cosantóir*, 10/3/1941.

39 Another song *The Third West Cork Brigade*, 'In good old Cork, by famed West Cork,The Third West Cork Brigade.'

40 Tom Barry in a document – first two pages missing, TB private papers.

TRUCE AND MARRIAGE TO LESLIE MARY PRICE

1 Leslie's story, Leslie Price de Barra, Sighle Humphreys Papers, P106/1412 (1), UCDA.

2 John Browne to author 16/10/2002.

3 *An tÓglách*, 19 August, 1921;Tom Barry, author interview; Tom Barry, n.d. RTÉ Sound Archives; Tom Barry, to Griffith and O'Grady, *Curious Journey*, pp. 240, 241.

4 Tom Barry, Documentary, n.d. not transmitted, RTÉ Sound Archives; Tom Barry to Griffith and O'Grady, *Curious Journey*, pp. 243, 244.

5 Tom Barry to C/S, 19 October 1921 & C/S to O/C, S.D. 27 Oct 1921, MP, P7A/26 also C/S to Collins 21 October 1921, P7A/72, MP, UCDA.

6 Emmet Dalton, author interview 4/4/1974. Collins was one of the five-man delegation negotiating a settlement with the British government.

7 Tom Barry to Nollaig Ó Gadhra, 1969, RTÉ Sound Archives.

8 Emmet Dalton, author interview 4/4/1974.

9 John Browne, to author 22/10/2002; see Ryan, *Michael Collins and the Women*, p. 114, Collins told Sir John Lavery, 'There's a gun in the pocket!' when asked to remove his coat.

10 Jenny W. Power to Sighle H., Sighle Humphreys Papers, 15/11/1921, P106/728, UCDA. Referes to as Jenny in Sighle Humphreys Papers and Jennie in Máire O'Neill's biography.

11 *Ibid*., Sighle Humphreys Papers, 21/11/1921, P106/732, UCDA.

12 Ryan, *The Real Chief*, p. 76.

13 Tom Barry, unpublished document, TB private papers.

14 Tom Barry to Nollaig Ó Gadhra, 1969, RTÉ Sound Archives; In houses countrywide IRA members assembled. In Daniel McSweeney's (son Michael McSweeney) in Ballyvourney, Seán Hegarty Cork No. 1 Brigade (Tom Barry's friend), with 13 others gathered on that day, to decide on the course of action they would take because of the signing of the Treaty. Donal McSweeney to author, 20/4/2003.

15 Tom Barry to Griffith and O'Grady, *Curious Journey*, p. 270. Documentary, n.d. not transmitted, RTÉ Sound Archives.

16 Liam Lynch to his brother, Fr Tom 12/12/1921, in Meda Ryan, *The Real Chief*, p. 87.

17 Tom Barry, unpublished document, TB private papers.

18 Meda Ryan, *The Day Michael Collins was Shot*, p. 31.

19 M. Twomey Papers, P69/179 (140), UCDA army council: Liam Lynch, Liam Mellows, Seán Moylan, Rory O'Connor, Tom Barry; Tom Barry Report, Military Service Registration Board, Dept of Defence.

20 Erskine Childers Diary, 11 March 1922, Childers Papers, Trinity College Archives Department; Oscar Traynor, O'Malley Papers, P17B/95, UCDA.

21 Michael Hopkinson, *Green Against Green*, pp. 64, 65.

22 F. M. Carroll, 'The American Committee for Relief in Ireland, 1920–922', *Irish Historical Studies*, Vol. XX111, No. 89, May 1982, p. 47.

THE DUNMANWAY FIND OF INFORMERS' DOSSIER

1 Flor Crowley 'Raymond' – Black and Tan Diary, *Southern Star*, 23 October, 30 October, 6 November, 13 November, 20 November, 1971.

2 Flor Crowley, *Southern Star*, 23 October 1971.

3 *6th Divisional Report*, Strickland Papers, Typescript, IWM.

4 Ormonde Winter, *Report on Intelligence Branch of the Chief of Police, Dublin Castle*, WO 35/214, Public Records Office, London.

5 *Record of the Rebellion In Ireland*, Jeudwine Papers, IWM.

6 *The Irish Times*, 22 January 1921. It should be noted that the journalist in a query to Strickland used the term 'murder gang' when referring to the IRA; *The Evening Standard*, 25 January 1921.

7 Keyes McDonnell, p. 196; *The Cork Examiner*, 15 February, 1921; RIC Div. commissioner confirmed to Mark Sturges the existence of the 'Anti-Sinn Féin League', Mark Sturges Diary, 14 December 1920, 30/59, PRO; Jim Kearney, author interview 15/2/1976; Sonny Sullivan, author interview 14/8/1974.

8 Hannah O'Mahony, author interview 28/4/1978; Nelius Flynn, author interview, 24/6/1973; see Percival Papers, IWM.

9 *The Cork Constitution*, 6 May 1922.

10 Dan Canty, author interview 5/4/1973; *Southern Star*, 29/4/1922.

11 Mary Leyland, *Cork Examiner*, 25/7/2000.

12 CO 762/133, Statement by Matilda Woods to the Irish Grants committee for £5,000 compensation, 31/1/1927. As there is no record that the bodies of Capt. Woods, Thomas and Samuel Hornibrook were located, Matilda Woods' statement on the manner of death has to read with caution. Public Record Office, Surrey; Danny Canty, author interview 5/4/1973.

13 *Southern Star*, 29 April 1922. Charlie O'Donoghue and Stephen O'Neill, both of whom were with Michael O'Neill on the night of the fatal killing, attended the inquest.

14 *The Morning Post*, 1 June 1922. 'The shooting on both sides was maintained until 8 o'clock, when the three persons surrendered owing to lack of ammunition …; in Matilda Woods' statement, she says that Herbert Woods was 'hung drawn and quartered in the presence of my father and brother', then her father and brother 'had to make their own graves.' But as she was not present nor in Ireland, her statement has to be disregarded. CO 762/133, Public Record Office.

15 *The Cork Constitution*, 29 April 1922; *Cork County Eagle*, 6 May 1922; *Irish Times*, 2 May 1922. *The Cork Constitution* 2 May 1922; *Irish Times* 2 May 1922, James Bradfield's name incorrectly given as Shorten.

16 Hart, pp. 286–292.

17 *Ibid.*, p. 314.

18 Dan Cahalane, author interview 25/2/1981. He had the diary and documents and studied them carefully. Flor Crowley studied and worked on this 'find'. Though many of the names are in the Tom Barry private papers, in letters, arising out of his investigation, there is not an exact copy of lists.

19 Eileen Lynch O'Neill, author interview 28/11/2002; *The Cork Constitution*, 28 April 1922; *Irish*

Times, 28 April 1922; see Sorcha Crowley, 'Saving Sam Maguire's homestead' in *Irish Times* 5/2/2003; also Margaret Walsh, *Sam Maguire.*

20 Brendan O'Neill, author interview 24/11/2002.

21 *Irish Times*, 2/5/1922.

22 Criostóir de Baróid in 'Archon' *Southern Star* 1/12/2001; Cork County Council Report, *Irish Times*, 5/5/1922.

23 *Cork County Eagle*, 6 May, 1922.

24 Brian Murphy, *The Month*, p. 383, September–October 1998; *The Cork Constitution*, 29 April, 1922; *Irish Times* 28 April, 1922.

25 *The Cork Constitution*, 10 May 1922. The newspapers at this period also reflect the pogroms experienced by Catholics in the north of Ireland, and the condemnation by the Protestant community in the 26 counties.

26 Criostóir de Baróid in 'Archon' *Southern Star*, 1/12/2001, the convention was held in the Mansion House, Dublin on 12 May 1922, Protestant Bishop of Killaloe presided, and 31 representative dignitaries of the Protestant churches including the high-sheriff of Dublin and the president of the Dublin Chamber of Commerce signed a resolution.

27 Hart, p. 284.

28 Jim Kearney, letter to author 20/1/1994 – also unpublished letter to *Irish Times*; Denis Lordan, author interview 7/7/1974; Charlie O'Keeffe, author interview 7/12/1975.

29 Jim Kearney, author interview 24/2/1974.

30 Billy Good, author interview 24/4/1974; *Southern Star*, 'Archon' 1/12/2001, Criostóir de Baróid to author, 9/3/2002.

31 Flor Begley to Florence O'Donoghue, 15/3/60, MS 31,301, FO'D Papers, NLI; Tom Barry, TB private papers.

32 *Cork Constitution*, 5 May 1922.

33 Report on Bandon District council meeting, *Cork Constitution*, 9 May 1922. Seán Buckley listed among 'the greatest patriots, Wolfe Tone, Lord Edward, Mitchel, Martin and hundred of others were all Protestant.' It was Seán Buckley who first introduced Tom Barry to the officers of the Third Cork Brigade.

34 *County Eagle and Munster Advertiser*, 6 May 1922.

35 *Irish Times*, 5/5/1922.

36 Denis Lordan, author interview 7/7/1974.

37 *Southern Star*, 'Archon' 1/12/2001.

38 Captured Document, Florrie O'D Papers, FO'D intelligence officer 26/9/1920, MS 31,202, NLI.

39 Florrie O'Donoghue IO, to Ernie O'Malley, O'MN. P176/96, UCDA.

40 Ryan, *Michael Collins and the Women*, pp. 47, 48; Criostóir de Baróid, author interview 12/1/1981.

41 FO'D Papers, captured document HQ 1 6th Infantry Brigade, 17/6/1921, MS 31,223 (3) NLI.

42 Peter Hart, 'The Protestant Experience of Revolution in Southern Ireland', in *Unionism in Modern Ireland*, ed. Richard English, pp. 89–90.

43 *Ibid.*, pp. 90, 92, 93, 94.

44 Tom Barry's notes, no. 75; Mick Costello to Tom Barry, 6/4/1948, TB private papers; Mary Kotsonouris, 'The Courts of Dáil Éireann', in *The Creation of The Dáil*, ed. Brian Farrell, pp. 93–95. See also Mary Kotsonouris, *Retreat from Revolution: The Dáil Courts, 1920–24*; Deasy, p. 201; Some West Cork judges: Tadhg Ó Séaghdha, Jack Hurley and Freddy Murray, Tadhg Ó Séaghdha, statement, Yvonne Purcell Papers.

45 Tom Barry to Nollaig Ó Gadhra, 1969, RTÉ Sound Archives; Tom Barry in discussion with Dave O'Sullivan, home video, early 1970s, courtesy of Dave O'Sullivan; see also Duggan, pp. 55, 56.

46 Tom Barry to Nollaig Ó Gadhra, 1969, RTÉ Sound Archives; Tom Barry in discussion with Dave O'Sullivan, home video, early 1970s, courtesy of Dave O'Sullivan.

47 Tom Barry in home video, early 1970s, courtesy of Dave O'Sullivan.

48 Hart, in English, pp. 89–94.

49 Tom Barry to Donncha Ó Dulaing, n.d. c. early 1970s, RTÉ Sound Archives.

50 Tom Barry to Liam Mac Gowan, *Irish Press*, 1 May 1948, TB private papers.

51 Hart, p. 288.

52 *Ibid.*

53 *Ibid*; O'Broin, *Protestant Nationalists*, p. 177; Brian Murphy, September–October 1998, *The Month*, p. 383.

54 Murphy, *The Month*, p. 383; Hart, pp. 288–292.

55 Hart, pp. 282, 283.

56 Here Hart makes reference to Seán Moylan's (North Cork TD not West Cork) derogatory remark on 'Unionists' (Union with Britain and against an Irish Republic) being the 'domestic enemy.' Seán Moylan did not use the word Protestant – not all Unionist were Protestants. Hart, pp. 291, 288.

57 Hart, p. 290.

58 *Ibid.*, p. 288.

59 Hart in English, Initials given: (e.g., C. R. 25 October 1993; R. G. and G. D. – 17, 18 April 1993; W. M. 17 April 1993; G.H. 17 April 1993; K.O. 20 April 1993; G.D. 19 April 1993; D.J. 21 April 1993; F.B. 6 December 1993; B.T. 9 November 1994; T.N. 17 November 1994), in Hart, The IRA (Bibliography, p. 330). Hart states that sources for 'Protestant men and women begin with a "B"' (e.g., BB, 17 April 1993; BF, 17 April 1993; BG, 18 and 19 April 1993; BO, 21 April 1993; BM, 20 April 1993; BP, 21 April 1993; BP and BH, 20 April 1993 (275); BW and BX, 15 November 1994; BY, 17 November 1994).

60 Dan Cahalane, author interview 21/2/1994. In conversation with Dan Cahalane it was obvious that the IRA 'did not really know much' about the pogroms of Catholics in the north of Ireland. 'We had our own concerns'.

61 Jack Fitzgerald, Ernie O'MN, P17b/112, UCDA.

62 Hart in English, p. 94.

63 Begley, pp. 42–44, Flor Begley (Diarmuid Begley's father) IRA intelligence officer, on an occasion had severe influenza and was being cared for in a house in Bandon when 'a sympathetic' RIC sergeant sent word 'that his presence there had been reported to the police.' Though weak, he made his way through the fields and was eventually nursed back to health by Mrs Bishop, a Protestant; Tom Barry, n.d. c. early 1970s, RTÉ Sound Archives.

64 Flor Begley, O'M,N, P17b/111, UCDA; Flor Begley, IO, had several names on his lists, both Catholic and Protestants are listed as 'spies' and 'informers'.

65 Murphy, *The Month*, p. 382; Erskine Childers *The Irish Revolution*, quoted by Brian Murphy, p. 382. During the Civil War Erskine Childers ran his 'Republican Press' office for a time in Woods' house north of Bandon – both were Protestants; British official *Record of the Rebellion,* Vol. 11, Jeudwine Papers, IWM.

66 Jack Lane, *An Atonement for Bandon?* pp. 6, 7, in *The Northern Star*, May 1999; Murphy, *The Month*, pp. 382, 383; Hart, pp. 305, 306; British official, *Record of the Rebellion,* Vol. 11, p. 26, Jeudwine Papers, IWM.

67 *British Intelligence In Ireland 1920–21: The Final Reports*, pp. 16, 49, 102, ed. Peter Hart; Jack Lane, in *Irish Political Review*, December 2002.

68 Jack Lane, *Irish Political Review*, December 2002; *Record of the Rebellion in Ireland*, Vol. 11, Jeudwine Papers, IWM.

69 *Record of the Rebellion*, Vol. 11, Jeudwine Papers, IWM; Montgomery to Percival, 14/10/23, Percival Papers, 4/1, IWM; Smith's Diary, Strickland Papers, IWM.

70 *Record of the Rebellion*, Jeudwine Papers, IWM.

71 Murphy, *The Month*, pp. 382, 383. Dorothy Stopford in a letter to her mother mentioned 'the slavery' and 'the brutal rule' and 'what to expect from England … The brigade staff sent out battalion special orders that they were to look after me and see that I got no abuse from anyone'. She told her mother not to worry about her safety in the Kilbrittain/Bandon area. 'It is a great life – I love all the boys – girls like brothers and sisters, they are all Christian names.' Dorothy to her mother, 17 July (no year, c.1 922). Dr Dorothy Price Papers, MS 31,341(4), NLI; see also correspondence to the *Irish Times*, October and November 1994.

72 Risteárd Ó Glaisne to Tom Barry, 5/8/1949, TB private papers.

73 *Ibid.* Other odd pages are undated as earlier and later pages are missing. The correspondence is hand written. Some pages, because of the condition of the collection, are missing from Ó Glaisne's lengthy correspondence to Barry.

74 Risteárd Ó Glaisne to Tom, August 26/8/1949, TB private papers.

75 Tom Barry to Rev. Father Henry, 16/9/1963 and Tom Barry's 'Comment', unpublished, TB private papers.

76 Tom Barry's manuscript, TB private papers; see also Barry, *Guerilla Days*, p. 114.

77 Monica Sullivan to Tom Barry – First page missing, hence no date or address, TB private papers.

78 Curtis, *Ireland* (1921), pp. 59, 60, in Pat Walsh, *Introduction: The Anglo-Irish Treaty*.

79 Barry, *Guerilla Days*, pp. 113, 114.

80 Tom Barry to Griffith and O'Grady, *Curious Journey*, p. 143.

CIVIL WAR AND JAIL BEGINS

1 Florence O'Donoghue, FO'D Papers, MS 31,261 (1), NLI; Michael Farrell, *Irish Times*, 14 December 1982.

2 O'Malley, *The Singing Flame*, p. 82.

3 *Ibid.*

4 O'Donoghue, *No Other Law*, 245.

5 J. Bowyer Bell, *The Secret Army*, 49; FO'D Papers, MS31,396, NLI.

6 Neenan in MacEoin, *Survivors*, p. 243. Connie Neenan who later became a true friend of Tom Barry's, was adj. First Southern Division, went to the US in 1926 and was appointed IRA representative in America in 1927, resigned in 1929 and became involved in Clan na Gael ; see J. McGarrity Papers, MS 17534 (3), NLI.

7 MacBride in *Survivors*, p. 128.

8 Florence O'Donoghue, Eyewitness, FO'D Papers, MS.31,396, NLI. Cathal Brugha sat in front seat; see also Ryan, *The Real Chief*, pp. 113–115.

9 MacBride in MacEoin, *Survivors*, p. 128.

10 Ryan, *The Real Chief*, pp. 114, 115; MacBride in MacEoin, *Survivors*, p. 128; O'Malley, *The Singing Flame*, pp. 82, 83; see also O'Donoghue, *No Other Law*, p. 246.

11 Florence O'Donoghue, FO'D Papers, MS 31,396, NLI; Tom Barry, unpublished document, TB private papers; O'Malley, *The Singing Flame*, p. 83.

12 Seán MacBride, author interview 6/2/1977; Florence O'Donoghue, MS 31,396, FO'D Papers, NLI.

13 Ryan, *The Day Michael Collins Was Shot*, p. 17.

14 *Ibid.*, pp. 17–21; Lloyd George to Michael Collins 22/6/1922, MP, P7/B/244 1 and 2, UCDA; Mick O'Sullivan, O'MN P17b/111, UCDA; see also Hopkinson, *Green*, pp. 112–114; Bowyer Bell, *The Secret Army*, pp. 49, 50; O'Donoghue, *No Other Law*, pp. 251, 252.

15 Lloyd George to Michael Collins, 22/6/1922, MP, P7/B/244/1 & 2, UCDA.

16 Ryan, *The Real Chief*, pp. 107–109; Tom Barry, Military Registration Board, Dept of Defence.

17 Order: 26/6/22. A/0943/1 – 15, Military Archives, Dublin.

18 Tom Barry, unpublished document, TB private papers.

19 Tom Barry, author interview; Tom Barry, Military Registration Board, Dept of Defence.

20 Dave Neligan, *Curious Journey*, ed. Griffith and O'Grady, p. 284.

21 Peadar O'Donnell in MacEoin, *Survivors*, p. 26; Peadar O'Donnell, *The Gates Flew Open*, p. 13.

22 Pádraig Ó Cronin for governor, 15/7/1922, TB private papers.

23 O'Donnell in MacEoin, *Survivors*, p. 26; Gleeson in MacEoin, *Survivors*, p. 273.

24 Tom Barry to OC Dublin Brigade, 1/7/'22, P7a/80 MP, UCDA; also Lot 177/N.12, Military Archives, Dublin.

25 Dave Neligan, author interview 27/8/1974; also Neligan, *Curious Journey*, ed. Griffith and O'Grady, pp. 284, 285.

26 Ignatius O'Rourke to Tom Barry, 2 October 1963 – it appears from this correspondence that Tom Barry had given his side of the story 'after the passing of 41 years'.

27 Ernest Blythe, author interview 8/1/1974.

28 O'Donnell in MacEoin, *Survivors*, p. 26.

29 Ignatius O'Rourke to Tom Barry, 2/10/1963, Tom Barry notes, TB private papers; O'Donnell, *The Gates*, pp. 13, 14.

30 O'Donnell in MacEoin, *Survivors*, pp. 26, 27.

31 The story of this episode of Tom Barry's life is taken from Tom Barry's own notes and a long memoir from Ignatius O'Rourke, the jail official, to Tom Barry 2 October 1963, who had not at that stage been 'in receipt of a service pension'. O'Rourke left the army 'with the mutineers in April 1924'; also O'Donnell, *Survivors*, p. 27.

32 Tom Barry notes, TB private papers.

33 Tom Barry, *Irish Press*, 23 June, 1948.

34 Tomás Ó Maoileóin in MacEoin, *Survivors*, p. 99.

35 Tom Barry gives the names of participants in his own notes. TB private papers; Tom Barry, *Irish Press*, 23 June 1948; for details, see Ryan, *The Day Michael Collins was Shot*, pp. 92–105 and 130–145.

36 Ryan, *The Real Chief*, pp. 134, 135; Letters by Capt. T. C. Courtney to S. P. Cahalane – one of the intermediaries, Lynch family papers; Mulcahy Papers, P7/D/65/22/20, UCDA; O'Kelly to

Hagan, 26 August 1922, Hagan Papers, quoted in Dermot Keogh, *Twentieth Century Ireland*, pp. 11,12.

37 Ernest Blythe, author interview 25/11/1973.

38 O'Donnell, *The Gates*, p. 14.

39 Brendan O'Neill, author interview 9/1/1981.

40 Ernest Blythe, author interview 25/11/1973. For life of Dick Barrett, see, Joe Walsh, *The Story of Dick Barrett* also Ballineen and Ennikeane Heritage Group, *Dick Barrett (1889–1922) His Life & Death.*

FROM JAIL ESCAPE TO LEADER OF MEN

1 Tom Barry author interviews.

2 Gleeson in MacEoin, *Survivors*, p. 273.

3 Pat Buttimer, author interview 15/10/1980.

4 Eoin Neeson, *The Civil War in Ireland 1921–1923*, p. 168.

5 Dan Cahalane, author interview 30/1/1977.

6 Captured document, 3/10/1922, A/099/4, L3, Military Archives, Dublin.

7 Handwritten unnamed, 26/9/1922, A/0991/4, Military Archives, Dublin.

8 Tom Barry author interview.

9 Andrews, *Dublin Made Me*, p. 279.

10 Executive meeting, 28 October, 1922, Moss Twomey Papers, P69/39 (134), (136), (137), UCDA.

11 Liam Lynch to all divisions, 26/11/1922, MT Papers, P/39 (135), UCDA.

12 Ernie O'Malley Papers, P17a/58. Ernie O'Malley wrote to the D/P on 20 October saying he did not know what title Barry held at that stage. On the 27 October he reported on the officers' titles, including Barry's (from previous day's meeting). List in No. 79. *Phoblacht na hÉireann*, 27 October 1922.; Military Registration Board, Dept of Defence.

13 Bill Powell, author interview 2/5/1976.

14 Liam Lynch to all divisions, 26/11/1922 (there is a typographical error in the report which dates the meeting 16/9/23 instead of 16/11/23), P69/39 (134), MT Papers, UCDA.

15 Billy Barry, author interview 17/3/1974; see Ryan, *The Day Michael Collins was Shot*, Appendix 1 – The Story of John McPeak and the Slieve na mBan – the stealing of the armoured car, pp. 151–161.

16 Connie Neenan to Tom, 30/7/1948, reminding Tom of the incident. TB private papers.

17 Bill Powell, author interview 2/5/1976.

18 Div. adj. to C/S, GHQ, 30/12/1922, P69/25 (59), MT Papers, UCDA.

19 C/S to O/C First Southern Division, 10/10/1922, MT Papers, P69/25(166) UCDA.

20 Jerh Cronin, author interview 10/1/1981.

21 Dorothy Macardle, *Tragedies in Kerry*, pp. 14–17; Pat Butler, RTÉ Documentary *Ballyseedy*, 12/11/1997, RTÉ/TV Archives; T. Ryle Dwyer, *Tans, Terror and Troubles*, pp. 366–371.

22 Bill (Liam) O'Donoghue, author interview 24/2/1980.

23 Bill Powell, author interview 2/5/1976.

24 Jennie W. P. to Sighle Humphreys, 22 December 1922, Sighle Humphreys Papers, P106/736, UCDA.

25 Jack Fitzgerald to Ernie O'M. and Stephen O'Neill to Ernie O'M. O'MN, P17b/112, UCDA; Jack Fitzgerald, author interview 16/8/1974.

26 Seán Hales, TD, pro-Treaty was shot dead on 7 December, then anti-Treaty prisoners Rory O'Connor, Joe McKelvey, Liam Mellows and Dick Barrett were executed by pro-Treatyites in retaliation.

27 Tom Barry to adj. general, 15/12/1922, MT Papers, P69/25 (84), also P69/25 (86) & P69/25 (27), UCDA.

28 Tom Barry, MT Papers, P69/25 (27), UCDA.

29 Tom Barry to O/C's 19/12/1922, MT Papers, P69/25 (71), (72), (73), UCDA.

30 Jack Hennessy, RTÉ Sound Archives, n.d. not transmitted.

31 Dan Cahalane, author interview 25/8/1980.

32 Charlie O'Keeffe, author interview 6/11/1976.

33 Tom Barry to Griffith and O'Grady, *Curious Journey*, pp. 299, 300.

34 Ernest Blythe gave the official number as 84 or 85, see MacEoin, *Survivors*, p. 8.

35 Ernest Blythe, author interview 25/11/1973.

36 Tom Barry from Cappa, 26/1/23, MT Papers, P69/25 (7) UCDA.

37 De Valera to McGarrity, 5 February 1923, McGarrity Papers, 17440, NLI.

38 Deasy to O'Malley, O'MNB, P17b/86; Deasy's statement, O'MP, P17a/22; also 30 January 1922, O'MP, P17a/99, UCDA; Statement/Proposal, FO'D, MS 31,260, NLI; Copy of statement Liam Deasy's personal documents – to author– see Ryan, *The Real Chief*, p. 145.

39 Liam Lynch to his brother Tom, Lynch private papers; Ryan, *The Real Chief*, pp. 108–118.

40 C/S to Fr T. Ó Dubagháin, 1 February 1923, Pádraig Ó Maidín Papers, CCL.

41 Bill Quirke, O'MP, P17b/86; Ernie O'Malley to C.S. 10 February 1923, O'M P., P17a/40, UCDA.

42 Tom Barry to Pádraig Ó Maidín, 21/7/1976. Barry was handed Deasy's 'apologia' by 'a senior brigade officer's widow' after he had 'attacked Liam Deasy's "history" of the West Cork Brigade', Pádraig Ó M Papers, CCL.

43 Ryan, *The Real Chief*, p. 149, 150; see also Longford and O'Neill, *Eamon De Valera*, 215; Hopkinson, *Green*, pp. 232, 233.

44 Charlie Browne, O'MN. P17b/112, UCDA.

45 Jack Fitzgerald to Ernie O'Malley, E. O'MN. P17b/112, UCDA.

REPUBLICANS 'DUMP ARMS AND CEASE FIRE'

1 Todd Andrews, author interview 16/3/1980.

2 Pat Butler, Documentary, *Ballyseedy*, transmitted, 12/11/1997, RTÉ/TV Archives; Dorothy Macardle, *The Tragedies of Kerry*, pp. 14–17; Ryle Dwyer, pp. 367–369.

3 FO'D Papers, 11, 12, 25, 26 February1923, MS 31, 186, NLI.

4 Connie (Neenan) to Tom Barry, 30 July 1948, reminding Tom of the incident, TB private papers.

5 Captured documents, P7a/199, MP, UCDA; see also *Irish Independent*, 9 April 1923.

6 Council meeting document, MP, P7a/199, UCDA.

7 Ryan, *The Real Chief*, pp. 153, 154.

8 FO'D Papers, 28 March 1923, MS 31,186. NLI.

9 O'Donoghue, *No Other Law*, pp. 298, 299.

10 Irish Daily Papers, 8 March, 1923; *Irish Press*, 3 June, 1935; *Irish Independent*, 4 June, 1935; Frank Aiken Papers, P104/1283(4)(6) UCDA.

11 Andrews, *Dublin ...*, p. 280.

12 *Ibid.*, p. 282.

13 *Ibid.*, p. 283.

14 Members present were: Eamon de Valera, Liam Lynch, Tom Barry, Frank Aiken, Tom Crofts, Tom Derrig, Seán Dowling, Austin Stack, Seán McSwiney, Humphrey Murphy, Bill Quirke and Seán Hyde.

15 Tom Barry's notes, TB Papers.

16 Longford and O'Neill, *Eamon De Valera*, pp. 217, 218; T. Ryle Dwyer, *De Valera's Darkest Hour*, p. 139; O'Donoghue, *No Other Law*, pp. 300, 301; Ryan, *The Real Chief*, pp. 158–60. At the time De Valera was sporting a beard, *Sunday Independent*, 2/7/1970.

17 Tom Crofts Military Service Board, Dept of Defence; Meda Ryan, *The Real Chief*, pp. 162–72; see also Maurice Twomey, *Evening Herald*, 2 February 1972; also Ned Murphy, *Evening Herald*, 31 January 1 & 2 February 1972.

18 FO'D. Papers, MS 31,425; Frank Aiken Papers, Barry was one of the three members 'unanimously' elected to the council. Tom Barry, *Irish Press*, 3 June, 1935, *Irish Independent*, 4 June, 1935; F. Aiken Papers, P104/1283 (4), (5), (6), (7), UCDA. The three members representing the Republican government: Eamon de Valera, P. J. Ruttledge, M. Colivet. Army council: Liam Pilkington, Frank Aiken, Tom Barry.

19 Document, A/0628, Military Archives, Dublin.

20 Tom Barry to Mary MacSwiney, 9 May 1923, Terence MacSwiney Papers, U329, Cork Archives Institute; see also M. Twomey Papers, P69/39 (137), UCDA.

21 Florrie O'Donoghue notes, FO'D Papers, MS 31,186 UCDA.

22 Frank Aiken Papers, P104/1283 (4,) (5), (6), (7), UCDA.

23 Frank Aiken Papers, 'Appeal to Mr de Valera – Gravity of Situation Recognised'. There is blank space in the memorandum for the person, place or body to whom arms should be handed in, P104/1256, UCDA.

24 Tom Barry to Nollaig Ó Gadhra, 1969, RTÉ Sound Archives.

25 Republican government and army council meeting 20–27 April 1923, O'Malley Papers, P17a/12; 'To all Battalion O/Cs', 24 April 1923, O'Malley Papers, P17a/25; Aiken's message 28 May, 1923, MP, P17b/90, UCDA.

26 CW/OPS/14/J, Military Archives, Dublin.

27 Letter to Chairman, Supreme Council IRB, 21/5/1923, MS. 31,421 (3) F. O'Donoghue Papers,

NLI. F. Aiken Papers, minutes of government and army council meeting, 30/6/1923, P104/1267 (4) and minutes of army executive meeting, 11 and 12 July, 1923, P104/ 1264 (2), (3), and P/104/1266 (6), UCDA. T. Crofts was O/C First S. Div., T. O'Sullivan, O/C Third E. Div.; see also Moss Twomey Papers, 10 August 1924, P69/179 (126) UCDA.

28 Frank Aiken Papers, government and army council minutes of meeting, held 30/6/1923, P104/1267 (4), UCDA; Moss Twomey Papers, P69/179 (126), UCDA.

29 *Irish Independent*, 7 June, 1935; *Irish Press*, 7 June 1935; Frank Aiken Papers, P104/1285 (1), (2), (3), (4), UCDA.) P104/1256, UCDA.

30 Tom Barry, 4 June 1935, Frank Aiken Papers, P104/1283 (5) and (7), UCDA. Barry regretted that this 'confidential' army executive discussion was made public because of a controversy initiated by Frank Aiken in 1935.

31 Frank Aiken Papers, P104/1283 (4), (5), (6), (7), UCDA.

32 To Chairman, Army Executive Council, IRA – Executive meeting 11/7/1923. Signed, Tom Barry (Comdt General) F. Aiken Papers, P104/1264 (1), UCDA.

33 Minutes of Army Executive Meeting, 11 and 12 July 1923, Frank Aiken Papers, P104/1264 (2), (3) MT Papers, UCDA.

34 Frank Aiken Papers, P104/1264 (4) and (8), UCDA.

35 Minutes of Army Council Meeting, 11 July – Barry present, discussion on general election, MT Papers, P69/179 (64), UCDA.)

36 Peg Barrett, author interview 18/6/1973; see also Longford and O'Neill, pp. 226, 227.

37 C/S Report to executive meeting held 10 August 1924, Moss Twomey Papers, P69/179 (126) – (129), UCDA.

38 F. Aiken Papers, P104/1264 (2) & (3) & P104/1266 (6), UCDA.

39 19 October, 1923 – hand written letter, M. Twomey Papers, P69/43 (167), UCDA.

40 Frank Aiken to Tom Barry, 2 November 1923, MT Papers, P69/43 (166), UCDA; Seamus Robinson and a numbers of others offered help, MT Papers, P69/43 (174), (175), UCDA.

41 Quoted, John M. Regan, *The Irish Counter-Revolution 1921–936*, p. 175, Note 37 – Dept. C/S Parkgate M/D – Two other West Cork men listed with Barry are 'Spud' Murphy and 'Flyer' Hogan (perhaps that should read 'Flyer' Nyhan, as 'Flyer' Nyhan was engaged in 'anti-Blueshirt' activity. He had been at the command post with Tom Barry, in the Kilmichael ambush, November 1920.)

42 Tom Barry to Frank Aiken, 21/11/1923, MT Papers, P69/43 (153), (154), (155), UCDA.

43 Jim Kearney, author interview 18/10/1980; MT. Papers, P69/179 (126), (127), UCDA.

44 Tomás de Barra to C/S GHQ, 24 November, 1924, MT Papers, P69/27 (58), UCDA; Tadg O'Sullivan, O'M N, P7b/108, UCDA.

45 Chief-of-staff to O/C First Southern Division 9/12/1924, P69/27 (50), MT Papers, UCDA.

46 *Cork Examiner*, 21/12/1923; Tom Crofts, *Cork Examiner*, 30/12/1923. Tom Crofts 'deemed it necessary to respond' to a report on 29 December 1923 re Barry's arrest. Tom Crofts wrote to C/S because of negative talk re Tom Barry. 'It even went outside the country where it was freely stated that men in Cork were obtaining their freedom at the expense of others.'

47 Tom Barry to Frank Aiken, MT Papers, P69/141 (4), UCDA.

48 Details from Seán Hyde to author interview 6/7/1974; Tom Barry to Pádraig Ó Maidín, 21/7/1976, P. Ó Maidín Papers, Cork County Library; E.O'Malley N. P17b/86, UCDA.

49 Tom Barry to Nollaig Ó Gadhra, 1969, RTÉ Sound Archives.

'GOAL FOR THE DECLARATION OF A REPUBLIC'

1 Jennie Wyse Power to Sighle Humphreys, 7 February 1922, SH Papers, P106/743, UCDA.

2 Draft Agenda for Convention. MT Papers P69/46, UCDA.

3 *Ibid.*

4 Army council to Fianna Fáil, 28 April, 1927, MT Papers, P69/48 (34), UCDA.

5 Army council to E. de Valera, 17/5/1927, MT Papers, P69/48 (128), UCDA.

6 Army council to E. de Valera 1/5/1927, P69/48 (30) MT Papers, UCDA.

7 Correspondence between P69/48 (29) (30) (31) (32), MT Papers, UCDA.

8 Danny Canty, author interview 7/12/1974.

9 Pat Buttimer, author interview 18/10/1980; Criostóir de Baróid, author interview 11/1/1981; *Cork Examiner*, January 1931.

10 John O'Donovan, author interview 28/10/1976.

11 Dan Cahalane, author interview 25/8/1980. This was Pat O'Donovan's house; he had fought in the Kilmichael ambush. Many of Barry's Column and Third Cork Brigade men were there.

12 Seán Cronin, *Frank Ryan – The Search for the Republic*, p. 44.

13 See Maurice Manning, *The Blueshirts*, pp. 17–27.

14 Tom Barry to Moss Twomey, 13 May 1932, MT Papers, P69/52 (63) & (64), UCDA.

15 Correspondance between Tom Barry and Moss Twomey, MT Papers, P69/52 (62) & P69/52 (58) – May, June, July 1932, UCDA.

16 Tom Barry to Moss Twomey, 13 May 1932, P69/52 (63), (64), Tom Barry to Moss Twomey, 3 June, 1932 and 11 July, 1932, P69/52 (60) & (61), UCDA; Moss Twomey to Tom Barry, 6 June 1932, P69/52 (59); Report P69/52 (45), MT Papers, UCDA. Barry had resigned his executive position.

17 Moss T., C/S to O/C Cork No. 1 Brigade, meeting with Fianna Fáil, 19 July 1932, MT Papers, P69/52 (54) (55) (56) (57), UCDA.

18 Long confidential report – 15, 16, 17 July 1932, MT Papers, P69/52 (55), (56), (57), UCDA.

19 C/S to Tom Barry 19 July 1932, MT Papers, P69/52 (53), UCDA.

20 Tom Barry to Moss Twomey C/S, (handwritten) 20 July 1932, P69/52 (48) & (49) & (50) & (51) & (52), MT Papers, UCDA.

21 *The Sunday Express*, 24 July, 1932.

22 Tom Barry to Moss Twomey, 25 July 1932, MT Papers, P69/52 (47), UCDA.

23 Memo August 1932, P69/53 (374), MT Papers, UDCA.

24 Barry in a letter to Moss Twomey, 'I would have been at the station to see you off only I had to get back to work.' 28/11/1932, P69/54 (53) (54), MT Papers, UCDA.

25 Letter to Seán Martin – sender not given, 6/12/1932, P69/54 (52), MT Papers, UCDA.

26 Tom Barry to Moss Twomey, 28/11/32, MT Papers, P69/54 (53) (54), UCDA.

27 Report on general army convention, 17, 18, 19 March 1933, MT Papers, P69/187 (90) – (118), UCDA.

28 Tom Barry to Moss Twomey, 23/3/1933, (handwritten) MT Papers, 69/53 (259), (260), (261), (262), UCDA.

29 Moss Twomey to Tom Barry, 27/3/1933, MT Papers, P69/53 (257), UCDA.

30 Tom Barry handwritten note, 27/3/1933, P69/53 (258), MT Papers, UCDA.

31 Tom Barry to C/S, 3/4/1933, MT Papers, 69/53 (212), UCDA.

32 Tom Barry to Moss Twomey, 10/4/1933, P69/53 (161), P69/51 (33), (34), (35), MT Papers, UCDA.

33 Tom Barry to C/S, 10/4/1933, 69/53 (161), MT Papers, UCDA.

34 Moss Twomey to Joe McGarrity, 26 October 1933, Joe McGarrity Papers, MS 17,490, NLI.

35 Tom Barry 16/5/1933, MT Papers, P69/53 (8), UCDA.

36 C/S to O/C, West Cork, 23 May 1933, P69/53 (2) MT Papers, UCDA.

37 Tom Barry to C/S, 8/5/1933, P69/53(9), MT Papers, UCDA.

38 Barry, O/C West Cork to C/S, 19/5/1933, P69/53 (6), O/C West Cork to C/S, 18/5/1933, P69/53 (7); unsigned letter to C/S, 20/5/1933, P69/53 (3), MT Papers, UCDA.

39 Tom Barry, memo, n.d., P69/53 (327), MT Papers, UCDA.

40 'Programme for Training Camp', his is a detailed document under headings, and though it does not have Barry's name or signature attached, it has all the hallmarks of his work structure, and even spelling such as, 'picquets', and corresponds with his views in a document in his papers, P69/51 (33) (34) (35), MT Papers, UCDA.

41 Minutes of army convention, 17,18,19 March 1933, MT Papers, P69/187 (86 – 118), UCDA. I am indebted to Michael MacEvilly for this reference; see forthcoming publication, Michael Mac-Evilly, *Andy Cooney*.

42 Minutes of convention, March 1933, MT Papers, P69/187 (86 – 118), UCDA; see also Keogh, *Twentieth*, pp. 81–87; For details on tensions between the IRA and the Catholic Church, see Brian Hanley, *The IRA 1926–1936*, pp. 63 – 70.

43 Tim Pat Coogan, *The IRA*, p. 103.

44 Tom Kelleher, author interview 9/4/1979; Jerh Cronin, author interview 10/1/1981.

45 Jim Kearney, author interview 18/10/1980; Speakers were O'Duffy, MacDermot, Dillon and Blythe; see also MacEoin, *The IRA*, p. 257.

46 Kathy Hayes, author interview 19/10/1980.

47 Jack Doheny Lynch, author interview 10/1/1981.

48 Handwritten notebook record of March 1934, IRA Convention, P67/525, Seán MacEntee Papers, UCDA.

49 Frank Edwards in MacEoin, *Survivors*, p. 11.

50 Tom to Leslie, 12.20 p.m. (exact, as always) 24 April 1935, TB private papers.

51 J. Bowyer Bell, *The Secret Army*, pp. 149–151, Uinseann MacEoin, *The IRA In The Twilight Years*, p. 12; Tom to Leslie, 24 April 1935, TB private papers.

52 Frank Aiken Papers, P104/1285 (2), UCDA.

53 *Cork Examiner*, 14 May 1935; *Irish Press*, 14 May 1935; *Irish Independent*, 14 May 1935.

54 *Cork Examiner, Irish Press, Irish Independent*, 3 June 1935; Frank Aiken Papers, P104/1283 (4), (5), (6), UCDA.

55 *Cork Examiner*, 3 June 1935.

56 *Irish Press, Irish Independent*, 6 June 1935; *Cork Examiner*, 5 June 1935; Frank Aiken Papers, P104/1284 (3), UCDA.

57 *Irish Independent*, 7 June and 8 June 1935.

58 *Irish Independent, Irish Press, Cork Examiner*, 7 June 1935.

59 Frank Aiken Papers, P104/1286 (1), (2), (3), (4), UCDA.

60 *Irish Independent, Irish Press, Cork Examiner*, 8 June 1935.

61 *Irish Independent, Irish Press, Cork Examiner*, 14 June 1935; Frank Aiken Papers, P104/1288 (1) (2) (3) (4), UCDA.

62 *Cork Examiner, Irish Independent, Irish Press*, 12 June 1935.

63 *Cork Examiner, Irish Independent, Irish Press*, 12 June 1935; Frank Aiken Papers, P104/1287 (1) (2), UCDA.

64 *Cork Examiner*, 28 June 1935 – it is dated 12 June, 1935. Charles Russell in a letter to the *Irish Independent* (17 June 1935) writes of a peace conference he was at in Cork where Tom Barry, Fr Duggan and Liam Deasy were present, and he drove them through Cork sentries. As Liam Deasy was in jail since January 1923, this information does not appear correct. The meeting referred to may have taken place prior to the outbreak of the Civil War, *Irish Independent*, 17 June 1935.

65 Uinseann MacEoin, *The IRA in the Twilight Years*, p. 12.

66 Hanley, p. 157.

67 *Ibid.*, p. 158.

68 Jack Doheny Lynch, author interview 10/1/1981; Sheila Barry Irlam (Tom's niece) to author, March 2002.

69 Jerh Cronin, author interview 10/1/1981.

70 Den Carey, author interview 11/1/1981.

FROM IRA CHIEF-OF-STAFF TO IRA PENSION HUMILIATION

1 Tom Barry, author interview. There is no truth or justification in the suggestion that Admiral Somerville was shot because he was a Protestant, as in, Joseph O'Neill, *Blood-Dark Track*. For an account of Ireland's difficulties at this period, see Hanley.

2 MacEoin, *The IRA*, p. 13; see also Bowyer Bell, pp. 155, 156.

3 Tim Pat Coogan, *The IRA*, p. 155.

4 Bowyer Bell, p. 161.

5 Tim Pat Coogan, *The IRA*, p. 150.

6 Den Carey, author interview 11/1/1981; also Tim Pat Coogan, *The IRA* 151.

7 Bowyer Bell, pp. 164–166; see also MacEoin, *The IRA*, pp. 16, 17.

8 Tom Barry, author interview; Bowyer Bell, *p.* 164, 165. For the life of Frank Ryan see, Seán Cronin, *Frank Ryan: The Search for the Republic*; Fearghal McGarry, *Frank Ryan*.

9 Tom Barry to Joe McGarrity, 15 March 1937, McGarrity Papers, NLI.

10 Peadar O'Donnell to Cumann na mBan executive, 20 April 1934, Sighle Humphreys Papers, P106/1154, UCDA.

11 Hanley, pp.1 56–160.

12 Den Carey author interview 11/1/1981; Jerh Cronin author interview 10/1/1981.

13 Jack Doheny Lynch, author interview 10/1/1981; Den Carey, author interview 14/1/1981.

14 Dr Ned Barrett, author interview 9/12/1980.

15 Den Carey, author interview 11/1/1981.

16 *Ibid*; Jack Dohney Lynch, author interview 10/1/1981; Dr Ned Barrett, author interview 9/12/1980; see also Bowyer Bell, p. 165, 166; MacEoin, *The IRA*, p. 66.

17 Tom Barry, author interview; Den Carey, author interview 11/1/1981.

18 Brendan O'Neill, (Jim O'Neill's son) to author, 10/4/2003; Jimmy Wynne, Dundalk, in MacEoin, *The IRA*, p. 521.

19 Eunan O'Halpin, *Defending Ireland*, p. 127; Bowyer Bell, pp. 166, 167.

20 Hanley, pp. 157–160; J. Bowyer Bell, pp. 163–167.

21 MacEoin, *The IRA*, p. 66.

22 Jack Doheny Lynch, author interview 12/1/1980.

23 Seán Cronin, *The McGarrity Papers*, pp. 161–163.

24 Tom Barry letter to Seán Cronin, 13/2/1975, quoted, Cronin, *Frank Ryan*, p. 106.

25 Seán Cronin, *Frank Ryan*, p. 106.

26 Sheila Humphreys to Seán Cronin, in Cronin, *Frank Ryan*, p. 109.

27 FO'D Papers, document notes, MS 31,490, NLI.

28 *An Phoblacht*, 15/5/1937.

29 Tom Barry to Seán Cronin, 13/2/1975, quoted in Cronin, *Frank Ryan*, p. 110.

30 *An Phoblacht*, 15/5/1937.

31 *Ibid.*

32 Tom Barry, *An Phoblacht*, 15 May 1937.

33 Tom Barry to Nollaig Ó Gadhra, 1969, RTÉ Sound Archives.

34 Tom Barry, author interview; Tom Barry to Nollaig Ó Gadhra, 1969, RTÉ Sound Archives.

35 *An Phoblacht*, 26/6/1937.

36 Ned Barrett, author interview 19/7/1979. Wedding date of Tom Kelleher to Síle Crowley, 24 July 1937; Seán Kelleher to author, 28/11/2002.

37 Den Carey, author interview 11/1/1981.

38 Tom Barry to Dr T. Ryle Dwyer, a letter in response to a query, 25/5/1975. I am grateful to T. Ryle Dwyer for this personal correspondence.

39 Eunan O'Halpin, 'British Intelligence, the Republican Movement and the IRA's German links, 1935–1945', in McGarry. I am grateful to Eunan O'Halpin for manuscript. Irish government intelligence kept a close eye on Tom Barry's activities, though some of government suspicions on Barry were unfounded.

40 Seán Mac Bride, author interview 6/2/1977.

41 MacEoin, *The IRA in the Twilight Years*, p. 67.

42 Seán O'Neill to Uinseann MacEoin, in MacEoin, *The IRA*, p. 740. ??

43 Bowyer Bell, p. 168.

44 Jack Doheny Lynch, author interview 10/1/1981; Tom Barry to Nollaig Ó Gadhra, 1969, RTÉ Sound Archives.

45 Tom Barry to Seán Cronin, 29/6/1978, quoted Cronin, *Frank Ryan*, pp. 178, 179; MacEoin, *The IRA*, p. 67.

46 Tom Barry to Sighle Humphreys, 12 June 1936, Sighle Humphreys Papers, P106/839, UCDA.

47 Tom to Nollaig Ó Gadhra, 1969, RTÉ Sound Archives.

48 Cronin, *Frank Ryan*, p. 179.

49 Agreement between Eamon de Valera and Neville Chamberlain, April 25 – Act of An Dáil gave effect to the agreement 16 May 1938.

50 Coogan, *The IRA*, p. 127; see also Barry, *The Reality*, p. 48.

51 Jerh Cronin, author interview 10/1/1981.

52 Tom Barry to Seán T. (O'Kelly) 11 October 1938, TB private papers.

53 Tom Barry to Donal Corvin in *Sunday Independent*, 7 March 1976.

54 Tom Barry to Dr T. Ryle Dwyer, 25/5/1975. I am grateful to T. Ryle Dwyer for this personal letter.

55 FO'D Papers, MS 31 490, NLI; Jerh. Cronin, author interview10/1/1981; Criostóir de Baróid, author interview 11/1/1981. In June 1949, Downing Street got 'a request from an Irish committee' for their repatriation, *Cork Examiner*, 22/1/1983.

56 Copy of letter, Tom Crofts to Oscar Traynor, TD, 23 April 1940, TB private papers.

57 Mrs O'Driscoll to Mr Barry 25 August [1943] TB private papers. Cornelius O'Driscoll must have been on the pension board. I have been unable to get further clarification on this.

58 Tom Crofts to Oscar Traynor, TD, 23 April 1940, TB private papers.

59 Jack Doheny Lynch, author interview 10/1/1981 – 'They'd be delighted to lock him up.'

SECOND WORLD WAR

1 Longford and P. O'Neill, pp. 313 – 317.

2 Tom Barry to The Commandant, The Military College, The Curragh, 8 July 1940, TB private papers. M. J. Costello (afterwards Major General), had taken the pro-Treaty side during the Civil War, organised the Irish Military College in 1926, commander of the First Southern Division during the 1939–1945 period.

3 Pat Buttimer, author interview 15/10/1980.

4 Tom Barry to The Commandant, The Military College, The Curragh, 8 July 1940 and Tom Barry to An Taoiseach, 12 July 1940, TB private papers.

5 Military Records, 'A' Series, Military Barracks, Dublin.

6 Liam French, author interview 12/10/1980.

7 Tom Barry to Nollaig Ó Gadhra, 1969, RTÉ Sound Archives.

8 Eamon de Valera to Tom Barry 25 August 1941, TB private papers.

9 Tom Barry in a long document gives his opinion, TB private papers.

10 Major Gen. M. J. Costello, author interview 2/2/1980.

11 Notes on memo Seventh Brigade on 'Sniping'. Portion of letter copy to Mick (Costello), first and last part missing – hence date missing, TB private papers. He suggested that 'every marksman in a platoon should be trained in sniping duties … I would put before the essentials given in the memo, those of marksmanship, determination and patience as first essentials for a good sniper.' Furthermore, he pointed out the disadvantage of giving 'platoons' a 'roving commission'.

12 John Browne to author, 3/10/2002.

13 T. Ryle Dwyer, *Guests of the State*, pp. 108–112.

14 Tom Barry to Dr T. Ryle Dwyer, 25/5/1975. I am grateful to T. Ryle Dwyer for this personal letter; see further details, Ryle Dwyer, *Guests*, pp. 108–119.

15 Eunan O'Halpin, 'British Intelligence, the republican movement and the IRA's German links, 1935–45', in Ferghal McGarry, I am grateful to Eunan O'Halpin for manuscript.

16 Lieut Gen. M. J. Costello, author interview 2/2/1980.

17 *Ibid.*, Lieut G. Costello was 'grateful' to Tom Barry and praised him highly; Series of *An Cosantóir*, January to June 1941, Tom Barry's proofs and correspondence, TB private papers.

18 Tom Barry in detailed typewritten paper – It is not dated, and could perhaps have been written after the war. TB private papers.

19 Correspondence in TB private papers, November 1943. Both of his parents are buried in Allerton Cemetery, Liverpool , Sheila Barry Irlam, Tom Barry's niece, to author, April 2002. Gerald Barry to author. Gerald, Tom's cousin, is compiling 'a family tree' of the Barrys.

20 Leslie to Tom, 28 September 1965, TB private papers. There is very little personal correspondence in the collection – as some of the papers got destroyed.

21 Tom Barry, author interview; Leslie, author interview.

22 Mick McCarthy (former IRA comrade and a Harbour Board employee), author interview 13/10/1980.

23 Jack Doheny Lynch, author interview 12/1/1980.

24 Tom Barry, author interview.

25 *Cork Examiner*, 8 June 1946.

26 Keesing's Contemporary Archives, (1946) Cork County Library.

27 Jack Doheny Lynch, author interview 12/1/1981; Cristóir de Baróid, author interview 11/1/1981.

28 Tom Barry to Nollaig Ó Gadhra, 1969, RTÉ Sound Archives.

29 Tom Barry, in response to an audience question after a lecture to UCG history students, 1969, courtesy of John Browne.

30 Dept of Local Government, 6 July 1945, TB private papers.

No 'Distortion of History' Call

1 Mr McDumphy, bureau director, to Tom Barry, 16 July 1948, TB private papers.

2 Tom Barry to Mr McDumphy, n.d. as it is part of carbon copy of letter – earlier part missing, TB private papers.

3 Tom Barry to Mr McDumphy, 4/7/1948, TB private papers.

4 Tom Barry to Mr McDumphey, bureau director – second page of carbon copy of letter, first part with date missing, TB private papers.

5 Tom Barry to Mr McDumphy, bureau director, 4/7/1948, TB private papers.

6 Tom Barry to Dr T. O'Higgins, 5/7/1948, TB private papers.

7 Tom Barry to history students, 1969, University College, Galway, recording courtesy of John Browne.

8 Liam O'Donoghue, teacher and historian, author interview 24/2/1980.

9 Barry, *The Reality*, p. 9. He wrote. 'Locked unopened for fifty years they would remain until 'a group of historians who would from that material, write a military history of the period'; Pádraig Ó Maidín, *Cork Examiner*, 22/11/1975. Tom Barry author interview – Barry couldn't

abide facts being distorted. History should be written in as honest a manner as was humanly possible. I experienced his annoyance and his firmness on this point.

10 Críostóir de Baróid, author interview 11/1/1980; Den Carey, author interview 11/1/1981; Part of copy of lecture, TB private papers.

11 Seamus Murphy to Tom Barry, 7/4/1947; Seán T. O'Kelly, President of Ireland to Tom 24/5/1947; Other correspondence related to the monument, n.d. TB private papers. Committee members: Tom Barry, Liam Deasy, Tom Hales, Maurice Donegan, Dan Holland and John Buckley – other friends including many former Cumann na mBan members also helped in the organisation.

12 Mick McCarthy, author interview 13/10/1980.

13 P. C. O'Mahony, Sec. to Tom Barry, 8/4/1949 & 23/4/1949, TB private papers.

14 Con Spain to Jack, 28 March 1949. The 'jack' appears to have passed on the original letter to Tom, TB private papers.

15 Ted O'Sullivan, TD, Dáil Éireann, Third West Cork Brigade to Tom Barry 24/2/1947; Mick Costello to Tom Barry with words of encouragement, 21/4/1948, TB Papers.

16 Jack Young collected statements from Joe Keane, Jimmy Crowley, Denis MacCarthy, Seán Murphy, 'absolutely correct statement' – Jack Young. There are acknowledgments to Pete Kearney, Flor Begley, Tom Kelleher and many, many more. Because of the condition of the collection, pages of the manuscript are severed from the original binding and are scattered – out of sequence. Most of the statements were returned; however he kept some questionnaires and responses. Jack Young to Tom 8/7/47; others n.d. TB private papers.

17 Leslie Price de Barra, author interview, 22/4/1973.

18 Tom Barry to Miah Galvin, 26/5/1948, TB private papers.

19 Tom Barry to Con [Connie Neenan] 13 June 1948, TB private papers. (Connie Neenan had emigrated to America after the Civil War.)

20 Con to Tom, 20/6/1948, TB private papers.

21 Tom Barry to editor *Irish Press*, 7 April 1948, TB private papers.

22 Tom to Liam Mac Gowan, *Irish Press*, 1/5/1948; Tom Barry to William Sweetnam, *Irish Press* editor, 1/5/1948.

23 W. Sweetnam to Tom Barry, 12/5/1948, TB private papers.

24 Ack. W. Sweetnam, editor *Irish Press*, to Tom Barry, 12 May 1948; Tom Barry to Mr Nolan, *The Kerryman*, 20 April 1948, TB private papers.

25 Tom to Liam, *Irish Press* 4/6/1948, TB private papers.

26 Tom to Connie Neenan, 13 June 1948, TB private papers.

27 Tom Barry to Liam Mac Gowan, 1 May 1948, TB private papers.

28 Tom Barry to Mick Costello, 2 May, 1948, Mick Costello to Tom Barry, 21 April, 1948, TB private papers.

29 W. Sweetnam, *Irish Press* to Tom Barry 25/6/1948, TB private papers. The carbon copy of Barry's letter of complaint is missing from the collection – either lost or destroyed.

30 Tom Barry to W. Sweetnam, editor, *Irish Press* 11 May 1948 and W. Sweetnam to Tom Barry, 12 May 1948. TB private papers.

31 J. C. Dempsey to Tom Barry, 13 April 1949 & Tom Barry to J. C. Dempsey, manager *Irish Press*, 21 April 1949, TB Personal Papers.

32 Tom Barry to W. Sweetnam, *Irish Press*, 30 June 1948, TB private papers.

33 Tom Barry to Liam Mac Gowan, 4 June 1948, TB private papers. Joe McGrath, friend and colleague of Michael Collins, went pro-Treaty, later became a great friend of Tom Barry.

THE REPUBLIC OF IRELAND BILL

1 Pat O'Mahony to Tom, 14/6/1948, TB private papers.

2 Pat O'Callaghan to Tom 1/11/1955, TB private papers.

3 Ita Ní Rossa, to Tom, n.d.; P. Loughran, Last page of letter – remainder missing, TB private papers.

4 Ita Ní Rossa to A Chara, n.d. TB private papers.

5 Pete Kearney to Tom, July 1948; Seán Moylan to Tom, 20/5/1948, TB private papers.

6 Seán Moylan to Tom 7/7/1948; Dan Breen to Tom 11/5/1948; Tom Condon to Jim Hurley, 26/6/1948 and Jim Hurley to Tom Barry, 30/6/1948 – with enclosure of Tom Condon's letter, TB private papers.

7 Seán Ó hÓgáin, Dublin to Tom Barry, 4/6/1948, TB private papers.

8 Tom Barry, Letter to Editor, *Irish Press*, 25 June 1948, TB private papers. Tom, himself, was never

a member of the IRB.

9 Robert Barton to Tom Barry, n.d. as first part of letter missing, c. June 1948, TB private papers.

10 Eamonn Dore to Tom, n.d. c. June 1948, TB private papers.

11 Laurence McVerry, Newry, to editor, *Irish Press*, July 1948, copy forwarded to Barry, TB private papers.

12 C. Mac Aonghusa to Comdt Gen. Tom Barry 31/5/1948, TB private papers.

13 Tom Barry to C. Mac Aonghusa, 2/6/1948, TB private papers.

14 Tom in second page of letter to Corrigan Park Reconstruction committee, n.d. as first page missing, TB private papers.

15 Tom Barry to President of Ireland, Seán T. Ó Ceallaigh, 24/6/1948, TB private papers.

16 Runaí on behalf of the President of Ireland to Tom Barry, 27 June 1948, TB private papers.

17 Tom Barry to Seán T. Ó Callaigh, Uasal, 1/9/1948, TB private papers. It is not known if the dinner ever took place.

18 *Cork Examiner*, 9/9/1948. Dr Noel Browne & Dr T. F. O'Higgins were present.

19 Programme and Special Guests seating, TB private papers, *Cork Examiner*, 9 September 1948.

20 T. Ryle Dwyer, *De Valera The Man & The Myths*, pp. 298–302; *The Detroit News*, 22 March 1948; Statements by *Representative of American League for An Undivided Ireland*, 5 February 1948; Pat McCavery to Tom Barry 12/4/1949, TB private papers.

21 Letter to Tom 10 April 1948 – Malachi Quinn, Hon. Chairman, Seosamh Heuston, hon. treas., Desmond Crean, hon. secretary.

22 Tom to councillor J. Breen, Lord Mayor of Dublin, 23 November 1948. Apparently there was 'dissension' between members and Tom made suggestions as to how the 1798 committee could settle this. The copy of letter is torn. TB private papers.

23 Peadar O'Donnell to Tom 13/2/1949; Tom Barry notes, TB private papers.

24 *Ibid.*, Tim Pat Coogan, *The IRA*, 322.

25 *Cork Examiner*, 18 April 1949.

26 Barry, *Guerilla Days*, p. 5.

27 *Cork Examiner*, 18 April 1949; Ref. SC/6717 Southern Headquarters, Collins Barracks, Cork; Col J. O'Hanrahan to Tom Barry 15 April 1949 – Details of ceremonies and time table, TB private papers.

28 Tom Barry to Col J. O'Hanrahan, 11 April 1949. A dance in the City Hall terminated at midnight.

29 Sec. Officers' Mess to Tom 10 April 1949; Tom to Sec. Officers' Mess, 11 April 1949; Invitation to Tom and Leslie, TB private papers.

30 Jack Doheny Lynch, author interview 10/1/1981.

31 Mick Costello to Tom Barry, 25 July 1948; Peadar O'Donnell to Tom Barry, n.d. TB private papers.

32 Tom to Mick [Costello] 27 July 1948, TB private papers.

33 Connie Neenan to Tom Barry 1/4/1949, TB private papers.

34 Tom to Connie Neenan 9/2/1949, TB private papers.

35 Mick Costello to Tom Barry, 29/1/1949; Tom Barry to Mick Costello, 31/1/1949 & 10/3/1949.

36 Tom Barry to J. C. Dempsey, 25/7/1949; J. C. Dempsey to Tom Barry 23/7/1949; Tom Barry to Connie Neenan 2/2/1949; Tom Barry to Connie Neenan, 14/3/1949, TB private papers. A number of letters had preceded this correspondence between Barry and *Irish Press*.

37 Tom Barry to Connie Neenan 14 March 1949; J. C. Dempsey, *Irish Press* to Comdt General Tom Barry, 24 May 1949, J. C. Dempsey to Tom Barry 8 June, 1949, TB private papers.

38 Barry, *Guerilla Days*, p. 27.

39 Jack Doheny Lynch author interview 10/1/1981; One publisher George Allen & Unwin asked Tom to 'tone down' the reference to Percival that the statements were 'libellous', also the use of phrases such as 'Essex Torture Squad' should not be used – Letter 4/3/1949, TB private papers; Barry wouldn't change a word because 'it is true!'

40 Liam Deasy, author interview 5/12/1972.

41 Butler, pp. 39–41.

42 Seán Feehan to author, 14/4/1980. When the book went out of print The Mercier Press published it again in hardback in 1955. It was published in paperback by Anvil Books in 1962 and has been reprinted many times since.

AMERICAN TOUR TO END PARTITION OF IRELAND

1 Tom to Connie, 13 August 1949, TB private papers.

2 Tom to Richard Dalton, U.S.15/8/1949, TB private papers.

3 Con to Tom, 16/9/1949, TB private papers.

4 Tom Barry to J. C. Dempsey, 15 October 1949, TB private papers.

5 He flew from Shannon to New York on 12 November 1949, Flight 171, Reservations Supervisor to Tom Barry, 25/10/1949, TB private papers; *The Gaelic American*, 26 November 1949; *The Boston Globe*, 29 November 1949.

6 *The Boston Globe*, 29 November 1949; *The Advocate*, New York, 26 November 1949.

7 *The Irish World And American Industrial Liberator*, 19 November 1949; Pamphlets and letters in TB private papers.

8 President, Ancient Order of Hibernians to Tom 24/11/1949, TB private papers.

9 *The Irish World and American Industrial Liberator*, 19 November 1949.

10 *The Gaelic American*, 3 December 1949

11 *The Pittsburgh Post Gazette*, 21 November 1949. $100,000,000 is the amount given in the newspaper, as mentioned by Barry. This must be a typographical error, as the amount of $1,000,000 or even $100,000 is more credible. There is no evidence available that the Irish government had set aside this amount for arms for the Irish army; however, in keeping with his character, it is doubtful if Barry would have mentioned funds unless he had this information and had spoken to the government prior to making the statement. He was on good terms with this inter-party government.

12 *The Irish World*, 26 November 1949.

13 *The Irish World*; *The Boston Herald*; *The Irish Echo* (New York), 19 December 1949.

14 *The Boston Herald*, 30 November 1949.

15 *Boston Daily Globe*, 29 November 1949.

16 *The Advocate*, 3 December 1949.

17 *The Irish Echo*, New York, 10 December 1949.

18 *Ibid*.

19 Tom to Con, 16/12/1949, TB private papers.

20 The men were Frank Monaghan and James Conaty of Cavan, Campbell of Tyrone, Tony Cribben of Mayo, Conlon of Kildare, Joe Stynes and Edward Morrissey of Dublin, and John McGinn of Monaghan. *A Refutation of the False Attacks on Tom Barry*, Malachy Conlon and Jeremiah Lennon.

21 *A Refutation of the False Attack on Tom Barry, Malachy Conlon and Jeremiah Lennon – a Reply*, n.d. circa November–December 1949, It states: 'This pamphlet ... is issued with the indorsement of the Veterans of the above brigades from New York, New Jersey, California, Boston and Chicago', FO'D Papers, MS.31, 490, NLA; Criostóir de Baróid, author interview 11/1/1981.

22 J. F. McGrath, President AOH Bronx, New York, to General Tom Barry, 24 November 1949, TB private papers.

23 Connie Neenan to Tom 4/12/1951, TB private papers; Christy Barrett to author 11/4/2001. Tom Cooper, Killarney, made a film *The Dawn* in the 1930s, loosely based on the Kilmichael ambush.

24 Seán T. Ó Ceallaigh, 21/5/1956, TB private papers.

25 Seán T. O'Kelly to Tom, 24/5/56, TB private papers.

26 I am indebted to Eamonn Kirwin, Librarian, Cork City Library for drawing my attention to this collection; Jean Crowley to author, 3/4/2002.

27 Notes, and newspapers cutting, n.d. TB private papers.

28 Seán F. O'Hourihane, Sec. St Finbarr, Corkmen's Association, Mass, 17/3/1956.

29 Tom Barry to Mr Kelly, Carpenter, Shangashel, 8/12/1956, TB private papers.

30 Tom to Nollaig Ó Gadhra, speaking of Seán South and the 1950s Northern campaign, RTÉ Sound Archives, 1969.

31 Bob Kehoe, author interview 28/11/1998.

32 Ruairí Ó Brádraigh to author, 10/3/2002; Bowyer Bell, p. 367.

33 Thomas F. O'Higgins, office of the minister for health, to Tom Barry, 8 June 1956, TB private papers.

34 Criostóir de Baróid, author interview 11/1/1981.

35 Jerh Cronin, author interview 10/1/1981.

'A TRUE HUMANITARIAN'

1 Thomas McCarthy to author 14/2/1981.

2 Den Carey, author interview 11/1/1981; Criostóir de Baróid, author interview 12/1/1981; Jerh Cronin, author interview 10/1/1981; Brendan O'Neill, author interview 10/1/1981.

3 Personal letter to Tom 23 May 1948, TB private papers.

4 Letter to Tom 18/5/1948; there are snippits of other such letters; because of the scattered condition of some, pages and names are missing, TB private papers.

5 For example, Liam Deasy to Tom, 5/5/1947, TB private papers.

6 John Browne to author 16/10/2002.

7 Liam Deasy to Tom, 7/4/1949 – reply to Tom's of '4th instant, TB private papers.

8 Dr Ned Barrett, author interview 9/12/1980.

9 Seán MacCárthaigh to Tom, 28/10/1949 – a water marked letter & another with date blurred responding to Tom's correspondence, TB private papers. MacCárthaigh was president of the GAA for a period and also lord mayor of Cork.

10 Pádraig Ó Cuanacháin to author, 11/4/2002.

11 Denis Conroy to Donncha Ó Dulaing, on the occasion of Tom Barry's death, 2/7/1980, RTÉ Sound Archives.

12 John Browne to author, 23/10/2002.

13 Seán Spellissy to author 5/9/2003.

14 Mick McCarthy, (comrade in arms and co-worker at the Harbour Board), author interview 12/10/1980.

15 Tom Barry, author interview; Tom Barry to Brian Farrell, 1969, RTÉ TV Archives.

16 Seán Chambers to author 10/11/1998. Tom Barry gave the June 1954 letter to Jimmy Chambers, a comrade and flying column friend. His brother Philip Chambers was captain of the local company. Barry told his friend John Browne, that money, no matter how much, would not induce him to become a mercenary; that his fight for Ireland was for 'freedom' and 'independence'.

17 *Sunday Independent*, 2/7/1970; Tom Barry, author interview.

18 Jean Crowley, author interview 12/11/2002.

UNVEILING MICHAEL COLLINS MONUMENT – HEALING WAR WOUNDS

1 The foregoing is compiled from: *Sunday Press*, 12 April, 1966; *Cork Examiner* 19 April, 1965; *Evening Echo*, 20 April, 1965. According to the report: Among those present were Liam Deasy, former West Cork Brigade OC and Frank Thornton 'the only surviving member of Collins' personal intelligence staff at GHQ in Dublin'. On Wicklow granite, Seamus Murphy designed the plaque; John L. O'Sullivan (who took the Treaty side) to author 19/10/1980, on the 'healing of divisions'.

2 John L. O'Sullivan, author interview 19/10/1980.

3 John Browne to author, 16/10/2002.

4 *Cork Examiner*, 11 July, 1966; Tom Barry, chairman, All West Cork Memorial Committee to Seán Murphy, Paddy O'Brien, Ned Young and other members of Kilmichael Memorial Committee, set up on 12 August 1963. They sought finances for the erection of the memorial from 'American friends' as well as interested friends and relatives.

5 *Southern Star*, 19 November 1966.

6 Jerh Cronin, author interview 10/1/198. Criostóir de Baróid, author interview 12/1/1981.

7 John Browne to author, 16/10/2002.

8 Criostóir de Baróid, author interview 12/1/1981.

9 Copy of letter to Peadar O'Donnell, 26 November 1967, TB private papers.

10 *Southern Star*, 2 December 1967; *Cork Examiner*, 1 December 1967; Criostóir de Baróid, author interview 12/1/1981.

11 *Southern Star*, 20 January, 1968.

12 Pádraig Ó Cuanacháin to author, 4/3/2002 & 19/3/2002.

13 Leo Meade, author interview 28/1/1981.

14 Tom Barry in presenter, Brian Farrell, RTÉ TV Archives, 1969 – material from these programmes used throughout this study.

15 Gearóid Ó Tuathaigh to Donncha Ó Dulaing, 2/7/1980, RTÉ Sound Recording.

16 Lecture of UCG history students, 1969. Recording, courtesy of John Browne. John Browne did not record the lecture in Maynooth. John Browne to author, 23/10/2002.; Fr T. J. (Tom) Hogan to author, 17/7/2003.

17 Tom Barry to Nollaig Ó Gadhra, 1969, RTÉ Sound Archives.

'HEAD-REELING' CONTROVERSY

1 *Cork Examiner*, 10 August 1970.

2 *Ibid*.

3 *Ibid.*

4 Criostóir de Baróid, author interview 12/1/1981.

5 Raymond Smith interview with Tom Barry, *Irish Independent*, 8 December 1970.

6 *Ibid.*

7 Tom Barry, *Irish Independent*, 7 June 1971.

8 *Ibid.*

9 *Cork Examiner*, 12 July 1971; Tom Barry, home video, courtesy of Dave O'Sullivan.

10 Kieran Wyse, Cork County Library, to author 16/5/2000; *Cork Examiner*, 8/7/1971, 9/7/1971.

11 Ruairí Ó Brádraigh to author 10/3/2002 – he 'recalled this speech again on his 100th birthday'.

12 Joe Cahill to author, 27/6/2003.

13 Dave O'Sullivan to author, 29/10/2002; Brendan O'Neill to author, 12/11/2002. Among the men on stage were, Joe Cahill, John Whelton, Paddy Lane, Daithí O'Connell, Mick McCarthy, Alfie Lane – and more activists from each decade.

14 Christy Barrett to author, 11/4/2002.

15 Raymond Smith, *Irish Independent*, 3/7/1980.

16 Tom to Sighle Humphreys, 12 December 1973, Sighle H. Papers, P106/837, UCDA.

17 Leslie – Tom to Sighle Humphreys, 30 June 1973, Sighle Humphreys Papers, UCDA.

18 Christy Barrett, author interview 11/4/2002; Maureen O'Sullivan to author 22/6/2002; Leslie Bean de Barra, author interview, 20/7/1975.

19 John E. Chisholm, 2 November 1972, Editor's Note, *Towards Ireland Free*.

20 Tom Barry letter, dated 1/10/1973, to all national daily newspapers, also Barry, *The Reality*, pp. 5, 6; see *Toureen* by Con Crowley, *Burgatia* by Jack Corkery, *Crossbarry* by Tom Kelleher, *Rosscarbery Barracks* by Tim O'Donoghue, *Kilmichael* by Tom Barry – *Rebel Cork's Fighting Story*; Pádraig Ó Maidín, in a review wondered why written accounts of 'ambushes and actions' by participants on each occasion, were not taken into account in the Deasy book, *Cork Examiner*, 22/1/1975.

21 Anvil Books Ltd., November 1974. Tom Barry's Letter to editor is dated 1 October 1973 – sent to all Irish dailies and *Southern Star*, pub. 4/1/1975 in conjunction with extracts from his booklet.

22 Tom Barry, letters to editors of Irish newspapers, letter dated, 1 October 1973.

23 Barry, *The Reality*, pp. 9–18.

24 *Ibid.*, pp. 28–38. Deasy, pp. 233–249.

25 *Ibid.*, pp. 58, 59; review, Raymond, *Southern Star*, September 1973

26 Pádraig Ó Maidín, *Cork Examiner*, 2/1/1975.

27 Dick Cross, *Irish Independent*, 13/12/1974.

28 Pádraig Ó Maidín, *Cork Examiner*, 2/1/1975.

29 Nudge Callanan, author interview 14/1/1980; letter J. M. Feehan, 11/12/1974, Pádraig Ó Maidín Papers, Cork County Library; *Cork Examiner*, 11/12/1974.

30 Nudge Callanan, author interview 14/1/1980; John Fitzgerald, author interview 20/4/1975; Denis Lordan, author interview 18/3/1975; Paddy O'Brien, author interview 17/1/1976.

31 Barry, *The Reality*, p. 13.

32 Recording of lectures to Irish army officers, 1966, courtesy of Lieut Col Eamonn Moriarty.

33 Dan Nolan to Tom Barry 30/8/1974, TB private papers; editors note – *The Reality*.

34 Miah Deasy, Liam's brother, to author 7/11/1980. Author's conversation with members of the Deasy family, 9/11/1980.

35 Christy Barrett, author interview 11/4/2002. Christy always called Tom Barry 'The General'.

36 Mick McCarthy, author interview 12/10/1980.

37 Dómhnall MacGiolla Phoil to author 11/3/1980.

38 Den Carey, author interview 11/1/1981.

39 *Ibid.*; Jerh Cronin, author interview 10/1/1981.

40 Brendan O'Neill, author interview 10/1/1981.

41 Tom to Sighle Humphreys 12/1/1976, P106/838, UCDA.

42 Sighle Humphreys Papers. Sighle has corrected some of her sentences in her notes. P106/1566 (6), UCDA. I am indebted to Brian Hanley, University of Dublin, Trinity College, for this reference.

43 Donncha Ó Dulaing, *Voices of Ireland*, p. 106.

44 Christy Barrett, author interview 11/4/2002; Nora and Michael O'Sullivan to author 29/5/1980.

45 Mick McCarthy, author interview 11/1/1981.

46 Tom to Sighle Humphreys, 12 June 1976, Sighle Humphreys Papers, P106/839, UCDA.

47 Tom Barry letter to Donncha Ó Dulaing, read on radio programme, 2/7/1980, RTÉ Sound Archives.

FROM MARDYKE BENCH TO FINAL CURTAIN

1 Pat O'Donovan author interview 20/2/1980. The reference was in relation to continuous strikes and workers in jobs comparing their pay with those of others.

2 *Irish Press*, 7 April 1980, interview with T. P. O'Mahony.

3 *Sunday Independent*, 7 March 1976. Interview by Donal Corvin.

4 Criostóir de Baróid, author interview 12/1/1981.

5 A plaque organised by Pádraig Ó Cuanacháin marks the building.

6 *Irish Press*, 4 July 1980. Nellie Casey was amongst the many gathered outside Tom Barry's flat as the ambulance took him away. 'We stood in silent prayer and sadness.'

INDEX

275, 278
Dwyer, T. Ryle, 227, 233

Edwards, Frank, 212
Ennis, 198
Enniskeane, 38, 157, 159-160, 183-184
Essex Regiment, 25, 27, 31-33, 39, 69, 72-74, 76,
  78-80, 85-86, 88-91, 94, 99-100, 102, 118-119,
  123, 126, 135-136, 143, 157-158, 185, 249,
  283, 291

Fanning, Ronan, 17
Feehan, Seán, 102, 276, 307
Fehilly, Dr, 73
Fehilly, Jerh, 19, 118, 306
Fennell, Desmond, 169
First Southern Division, 107, 116-117, 137, 190-
  191, 200, 274
Fitzalan, Lord, 121
Fitzgerald, Fr Ned, 98
Fitzgerald, [John] Jack, 30, 166, 186, 189, 277
Fitzmaurice, Francsi, 159
Fitzpatrick, Mick, 226
Ford, John, 255
Forde, H. F., 47, 56, 62, 65, 290
Freeman's Journal, The, 62
French, Liam, 232
French, Lord, 62, 71, 121, 151

Galvin, Joe, 74
Galvin, John, 73
Gilmore, George, 203
Gloundaw, 121, 128, 130
Good, Billy, 161
Gormanstown, 180-181
Goulding, Cathal, 272
Gray, David, 233
Greenwood, Hamar, 15, 61, 65-66, 74, 76, 132,
  157
Griffith, Arthur, 153, 160, 172
Griffith, Kenneth, 49, 54
Guerilla Days in Ireland, 18, 46, 55, 66, 88, 117,
  163-164, 242, 244-245, 248-249, 275
Guthrie, Cadet Cecil, 36, 47, 50, 59, 290

Halahan, Major, 100
Hales, Bill, 24, 91
Hales, Donal, 113
Hales, Madge, 115
Hales, Robert, 24
Hales, [John] Seán, 32, 99, 115, 133, 135-136,
  148, 172, 180, 182, 185, 263, 271
Hales, Tom, 24-27, 32, 133, 152-154, 161-162,
  165, 172, 179, 200, 208, 297
Hallahan, Johanna, 54
Halpin, Lt Col, 240
Hannon, Col J., 247
Harbord, Ralph, 158
Harbord, Rev. R. C. M., 158

Hart, Cadet Sgt, 75-76
Hart, Peter, 9, 49-52, 55, 57-58, 60, 62-63, 66-67,
  72, 143, 158-160, 163-168
Harte, Pat, 27, 32
Harty, Rev. Dr, 191, 195
Hawkes, William, 35
Hayes, James, 109
Hayes, Kathy, 19-21, 24, 85, 211, 279
Hegarty, Denis, 78
Hegarty, Diarmuid, 140
Hempel, Edouard, 233
Henderson, Leo, 174
Hennessy, Jack, 16, 38, 46, 51, 187
Henning, Thomsen, 233
Higginson, Brig. Gen., 71, 149-150
Hogan, Jer, 70
Hogan, Michael, 35
Holland, Dan, 97, 297
Hornibrook, Samuel, 157-158
Hornibrook, Thomas, 157-158
Houlihan, Bill, 193
Hourihan, Dan, 51
Hourihane, John, 70, 299-300
Hudson, Col, 85, 114-115
Humphreys, Sighle, 152, 222, 226, 273, 280-281
Hurley, Anna, 118
Hurley, Charlie, 25, 28, 30, 32-34, 37, 55, 57-58,
  60, 68, 69, 70, 78-79, 86, 92-93, 98, 100, 105-
  107, 132-133, 148, 161, 238, 244
Hurley, Frank, 118
Hurley, Jim, 83, 108
Hurley, Marcella, 130

IRA, 9-11, 15, 23-24, 26-29, 32-36, 38-40, 46, 51,
  54-55, 57, 60, 62-63, 66, 69, 72, 74, 76-96, 98-
  102, 107-109, 111, 113-121, 123, 125, 130,
  132-141, 143, 149-154, 156-173, 175, 178,
  181, 183-184, 191-192, 195-196, 198-216, 218-
  222, 224-228, 230-234, 236, 238, 240-241,
  247, 249, 254-256, 258-261, 264, 269, 271-
  273, 276, 279-280, 283, 286, 291-292, 296
IRB, 23, 37, 123-124, 196, 245
Irish Independent, 242, 270-271, 293
Irish Press, 46, 49, 54, 65-66, 73, 77-78, 95, 164,
  241-245, 249-250, 274, 286
Irish Times, 49, 57-58, 66, 160, 269-270

Jeudwine, Hugh, 92, 167-168
Kealkil, 140, 182, 185, 200, 209

Kearney, Jim, 78, 83, 86, 90, 161, 198, 211
Kearney, Peter, 110, 244
Keating, Seán, 226
Kelleher, Cornelius, 72
Kelleher, Jeremiah, 63
Kelleher, Seán, 53
Kelleher, Tom, 27, 29, 86, 90, 98, 100-102, 107-
  110, 126, 162, 208, 210, 224, 227, 240, 291
Kelly, Timothy, 13

Plunkett, Count, 14-15
Powell, Bill, 101, 183-185
Price, Cathal, 287
Price, Eamonn, 148, 245
Price, Leslie, 79, 105-106, 132, 140, 146-149,
    152, 155, 159, 175, 186, 200, 202, 212-213,
    217, 225, 229-230, 233-236, 241, 245-246,
    255, 263, 274, 280-282, 286-287
Price, Mick, 203, 206
Price, Seán, 146
Price, sisters, 280

Quirke, Bill, 180, 186, 297

Reality of the Anglo-Irish War in West Cork, The,
    42, 44-45, 274
Rebel Commandant's report, 49, 50, 55-58, 59,
    60-63
Rebel Cork's Fighting Story, 46, 241, 274
Reynolds, Col David, 215
Rice, John Joe, 116
Rigney, Paddy, 223
Robinson, Séamus, 25
Roosevelt, President, 233
Rosscarbery, 13, 18-21, 24, 78, 81-85, 108-110,
    112-113, 125, 137, 211, 262, 265, 279
Russell, Charlie, 183
Russell, Seán, 205, 218-222, 225-226
Ryan, Frank, 203, 218-219, 222-223

Sabhat, Seán, 271
Sadlier, Michael, 186
Schull, 30, 34, 140, 160
Sealy, Judge, 34
Sheehan, Michael, 186
Sheehy, John Joe, 226
Six counties [Northern Ireland], 142, 172-173,
    212, 216, 221, 223, 226, 233, 245-247, 251-
    253, 256, 271-273, 283, 285
Skibbereen, 13-14, 85, 108-109, 114, 122, 129,
    140, 162, 218, 260, 283
Skibbereen Eagle, 14
Smith, Raymond, 115, 138, 270
Smyth, Col Buxton, 36, 47-48
Smyth, Henry, 159
Smyth, S. F., 36
Southern Star, 86, 264-267, 274, 276-277
Spike island, 51, 82, 180
Stack, Austin, 192, 195, 245
Stanley, C. O., 265-266
Stophard,Dr Dorothy, 133
Street, Major Gen. C. J. C., 50, 91
Strickland, Major Gen. E. P., 37, 49-50, 55, 74,
    77, 79, 93, 103, 107, 117, 131, 132, 135-136,
    139, 141, 149-150, 157, 162
Dullivan, Danny, 70-71
Sullivan, Monica, 170
Sullivan, Tadgh, 81
Sullivan, Timmy, 198

Sullivan, Timothy, 76
Sunday Independent, 227, 247, 276, 286
Sweetnam, William, 241-243

Templemore, 130, 187
Third West Cork Brigade, 9-10, 13, 16, 24, 29,
    31, 34, 37, 45, 78, 92-93, 97, 103, 105, 107-
    108, 121, 144, 163, 188, 241, 244, 264, 267,
    275, 277
Thomastown, 186-187
Tipperary, 25, 71, 117-118, 150, 154, 181, 186-
    187, 194, 204, 213, 272
Tobin, Liam, 148, 180
Toureen, 32-33, 37-38, 64, 74, 105, 125, 265, 284
Towards Ireland Free, 42, 44-46, 274, 276, 278
Treaty, The, 24, 27, 97, 124, 143, 152-154, 160,
    171-175, 181-183, 185-189, 195-197, 202, 204,
    207, 232, 237, 244, 256, 263, 293, 295, 296,
    297
Truce, 56, 62, 82, 103, 115, 139-142, 145-146,
    148-149
Tudor, Gen., 15, 67
Twomey, May, 92, 184
Twomey, Moss, 175, 202-203, 205-210, 212, 218
Twomey, Sgt, 84

Upton, 9, 31, 86, 93, 98-101, 115, 161, 208

Wallace, Nora, 37
War of Independence, 9, 24, 26-27, 142, 162,
    180, 185-186, 204, 230, 232, 239, 241, 244,
    254, 256, 272, 274, 285
Waterford, 181, 192-193, 218
Weafer, Capt. Tom, 146
Whelan, Pax, 172
White, Edward, 101
Whooley, Timothy, 87
Whyte, Comd. J., 248
Whyte, Louis, 53
Wilson, Canon, 160
Wilson, President, 15
Wilson, Sir Henry, 136-137, 139, 173
Winter, John, 162
Winter, Ormonde, 157
Woods, Capt. Herbert, 157, 158
Woods, Matilda, 158

Young, Jack, 241
Young, Ned, 39, 46, 52